28th Italian Symposium on Advanced Database Systems (SEBD 2020)

Online
21 – 24 June 2020

Editors:

Maristella Agosti
Maurizio Atzori
Paolo Ciaccia
Letizia Tanca

ISBN: 978-1-7138-1850-2

Printed from e-media with permission by:

Curran Associates, Inc.
57 Morehouse Lane
Red Hook, NY 12571

Some format issues inherent in the e-media version may also appear in this print version.

Printed with permission by Curran Associates, Inc. (2021)

Edited by:
Maristella Agosti
Maurizio Atzori
Paolo Ciaccia
Letizia Tanca

Additional copies of this publication are available from:

Curran Associates, Inc.
57 Morehouse Lane
Red Hook, NY 12571 USA
Phone: 845-758-0400
Fax: 845-758-2633
Email: curran@proceedings.com
Web: www.proceedings.com

TABLE OF CONTENTS

15 YEARS OF KNOWLEDGE GRAPHS: LESSONS, CHALLENGES, OPPORTUNITIES (ABSTRACT) 1
Gerhard Weikum

USABILITY, PERFORMANCE AND SCALABILITY FOR EXPRESSIVE DATA LANGUAGES VIA CARDINALITY-BASED AGGREGATES (ABSTRACT) 2
Carlo Zaniolo

GETTING RID OF DATA (ABSTRACT) 3
Tova Milo

OPEN SCIENCE: A TUTORIAL FOR THE DATABASE SYSTEMS COMMUNITY (EXTENDED ABSTRACT) 4
Emma Lazzeri, Paolo Manghi

A BOOTSTRAPPING APPROACH FOR SEMI-AUTOMATED LEGAL KNOWLEDGE EXTRACTION AND ENRICHMENT 7
Silvana Castano, Mattia Falduti, Alfio Ferrara, Stefano Montanelli

SCALING UP RECORD-LEVEL MATCHING RULES 18
Luca Gagliardelli, Giovanni Simonini, Sonia Bergamaschi

SMART DATA EXCHANGE 30
Sergio Greco, Michele Ianni, Elio Masciari, Domenico Saccà, Irina Trubitsyna

LATTICE-BASED DISCOVERY OF HYBRID RELAXED FUNCTIONAL DEPENDENCIES 38
Loredana Caruccio, Vincenzo Deufemia, Giuseppe Polese

DETECTING AND EXPLAINING EXCEPTIONAL VALUES IN CATEGORICAL DATA 46
Fabrizio Angiulli, Fabio Fassetti, Luigi Palopoli, Cristina Serrao

PROBABILISTIC ANSWERS OVER INCONSISTENT KNOWLEDGE BASES 54
Marco Calautti, Nicola Fiorentino, Sergio Greco, Cristian Molinaro, Irina Trubitsyna

PARALLELIZING APPROXIMATE SEARCH ON ADAPTIVE RADIX TREES 62
Tobias Groth, Sven Groppe, Martin Koppehel, Thilo Pionteck

A DOCUMENT-BASED RDF KEYWORD SEARCH SYSTEM: QUERY-BY-QUERY ANALYSIS 74
Dennis Dosso, Gianmaria Silvello

CAPTURING POLITICAL POLARIZATION OF REDDIT SUBMISSIONS IN THE TRUMP ERA 86
Virginia Morini, Laura Pollacci, Giulio Rossetti

ACCOUNTING JOURNAL RECONSTRUCTION WITH VARIATIONAL AUTOENCODERS AND LONG SHORT-TERM MEMORY ARCHITECTURE 94
Mario Zupan, Svjetlana Letinic, Verica Budimir

EXPLAINABILITY METHODS FOR NATURAL LANGUAGE PROCESSING: APPLICATIONS TO SENTIMENT ANALYSIS 106
Francesco Bodria, André Panisson, Alan Perotti, Simone Piaggesi

SOME EXPERIMENTS ON DEEP LEARNING FOR FAKE NEWS DETECTION 114
Angelo Chianese, Elio Masciari, Vincenzo Moscato, Antonio Picariello, Giancarlo Sperlì

LIBJOTS: JSON THAT SYNCS! 122
Amos Brocco, Patrick Ceppi, Lorenzo Sinigaglia

OLAP QUERYING OF DOCUMENT STORES IN THE PRESENCE OF SCHEMA VARIETY 134
Matteo Francia, Enrico Gallinucci, Matteo Golfarelli, Stefano Rizzi

MASTER: A MULTIPLE ASPECTS VIEW ON TRAJECTORIES 142
Ronaldo Dos Santos Mello, Vania Bogorny, Luis Otavio Alvares, Luiz Henrique Zambom Santana, Carlos Andres Ferrero, Angelo Augusto Frozza, Geomar Andre Schreiner, Chiara Renso

A FRAMEWORK FOR COMPLEX INFLUENCE PROPAGATION BASED ON THE F2DLT CLASS OF DIFFUSION MODELS 150
Antonio Caliò, Andrea Tagarelli

A POST-ANALYSIS OF QUERY REFORMULATION METHODS FOR CLINICAL TRIALS RETRIEVAL 158
Maristella Agosti, Giorgio Maria Di Nunzio, Stefano Marchesin

PREDICTION OF NEW ASSOCIATIONS BETWEEN NCRNAS AND DISEASES EXPLOITING MULTI-TYPE HIERARCHICAL CLUSTERING 166
Emanuele Pio Barracchia, Gianvito Pio, Domenica D'Elia, Michelangelo Ceci

ON THE USE OF GIS FOR HEALTH AND EPIDEMIOLOGY CONTROL 174
Giuseppe Tradigo, Patrizia Vizza, Pietro Hiram Guzzi, Pierangelo Veltri

PRIVACY-AWARE DESIGN FOR E-HEALTH INFORMATION SYSTEMS 181
Flora Amato, Giovanni Cozzolino, Francesco Moscato, Vincenzo Moscato, Antonio Picariello, Giancarlo Sperlì

FORMAL VERIFICATION OF CONTEXT AWARE SYSTEMS 192
Fabio A. Schreiber, Maria Elena Valcher

WHERE PORCEDDU IS BETTER THAN PASTA 200
Paolo Ciaccia, Davide Martinenghi, Riccardo Torlone

CONTEXT AWARENESS IN THE TRAVEL COMPANION OF THE SHIFT2RAIL INITIATIVE 208
Alireza Javadian Sabet, Matteo Rossi, Fabio A. Schreiber, Letizia Tanca

IMPROVING LEARNING TO RANK BY LEVERAGING USER DYNAMICS AND CONTINUATION METHODS 216
Nicola Ferro, Claudio Lucchese, Maria Maistro, Raffaele Perego

INTERPRETING LINK PREDICTION ON KNOWLEDGE GRAPHS 224
Andrea Rossi

CO-POSTING AUTHOR ASSORTATIVITY IN REDDIT 228
Francesco Cauteruccio, Enrico Corradini, Giorgio Terracina, Domenico Ursino, Luca Virgili

HOW TO COPE WITH PERSONNEL UNAVAILABILITY? PROCESS MINING MAY HELP! 240
Andrea Chiorrini, Claudia Diamantini, Domenico Potena, Emanuele Storti

CROWDSOURCING FOR BUILDING KNOWLEDGE GRAPHS AT SCALE FROM THE VATICAN ARCHIVES 248
Donatella Firmani, Paolo Merialdo, Elena Nieddu, Andrea Rossi, Riccardo Torlone

AUTOMATIC DETECTION OF DYSPLASTIC NEVI: A MULTIPLE INSTANCE LEARNING SOLUTION 256
Eugenio Vocaturo, Ester Zumpano

SCALAR QUANTIZATION-BASED TEXT ENCODING FOR LARGE SCALE IMAGE RETRIEVAL 264
Giuseppe Amato, Fabio Carrara, Fabrizio Falchi, Claudio Gennaro, Fausto Rabitti, Lucia Vadicamo

TOWARDS AUTOMATIC CLASSIFICATION OF SHEET MUSIC 272
Giuseppe De Pasquale, Blerina Spahiu, Pietro Ducange, Andrea Maurino

EDGE-BASED VIDEO SURVEILLANCE WITH EMBEDDED DEVICES 284
Hanna Kavalionak, Claudio Gennaro, Giuseppe Amato, Claudio Vairo, Costantino Perciante, Carlo Meghini, Fabrizio Falchi, Fausto Rabitti

GATHERING MALWARE DATA THROUGH HIGH-INTERACTION HONEYPOTS 292
Angelo Furfaro, Francesco Lupia, Domenico Saccà

TOWARDS REUSABLE SMART CONTRACTS FOR TRUSTWORTHY COLLABORATIVE PROCESSES 300
Ada Bagozi, Devis Bianchini, Valeria De Antonellis, Massimiliano Garda, Michele Melchiori

KNN-GUIDED ADVERSARIAL ATTACKS 308
Fabio Valerio Massoli, Fabrizio Falchi, Giuseppe Amato

KNOWLEDGE-ENHANCED SHILLING ATTACKS FOR RECOMMENDATION 316
Vito Walter Anelli, Yashar Deldjoo, Tommaso Di Noia, Felice Antonio Merra, Giuseppe Acciani, Eugenio Di Sciascio

TENSOR CO-CLUSTERING: A PARAMETER-LESS APPROACH 324
Elena Battaglia, Ruggero G. Pensa

CLASSIFICATION-BASED CONTENT SENSITIVITY ANALYSIS 332
Elena Battaglia, Livio Bioglio, Ruggero G. Pensa

USER EMOTION DETECTION VIA TAXONOMY MANAGEMENT: AN INNOVATIVE SYSTEM 340
Alfredo Cuzzocrea, Giovanni Pilato, Edoardo Fadda

JKARMA: A HIGHLY-MODULAR FRAMEWORK FOR PATTERN-BASED CHANGE DETECTION ON EVOLVING DATA 349
Angelo Impedovo, Corrado Loglisci, Michelangelo Ceci, Donato Malerba

Author Index

Preface of the 28th Italian Symposium on Advanced Database Systems

This volume collects the papers selected for presentation at the twenty-eighth Italian Symposium on Advanced Database Systems (SEBD 2020), which took place online as a virtual conference from the 21th to the 24th of June 2020.

The SEBD Symposium represents the main annual forum for the Italian database community, where to meet, discuss and exchange experiences among all those, both in the academy and industry, who are interested in database systems and in all their broad range of applications. After 16 years from the previous edition in Sardinia, SEBD 2020 conference was planned to be held in Villasimius (in the southern part of Sardinia), Italy, at the Tanka Resort, by the crystal-clear sea of Simius beach. Unfortunately the COVID-19 emergency required exceptional containment measures for reducing the spread of the virus, and the decision of running the conference online, on the same days, had to be taken.

Thanks to the experience from EDBT 2020 virtual conference, reported by its organizers [1], we were able to make informed decisions on how to run the online organization of SEBD 2020. After a selection of a dozen of platform, Zoom was chosen because of its familiarity among the community and the ability of having face-showing meetings with up to 49 people on the same screen [2]. Given the peculiar social dimension of SEBD events, we did not use one-way communications of Zoom Webinars, opting instead for the Zoom Meeting environment, also for the 3 keynotes, tutorial and panel.

The welcome drink on the first evening was run on a different online platform called Gather [3], a fun game-like environment on a sea-side conference map background, where participants can communicate via audio-video calls by just moving their avatars close to each other. Each day has been divided into 2 Zoom meeting sessions: one in the morning and one in the afternoon. Even coffee breaks were included in the conference program, so that attendees had the chance to speak free using Zoom. We believe that these social moments and live presentations, despite being held remotely, prevented the risk of perceiving it as a prerecorded videocast and contributed to the success of the event.

Thanks to the valuable job of 49 PC members, the scientific program comprised 41 papers that have been accepted for presentation: 8 Research papers, 32 Discussion papers, 1 Student paper. With only a few exceptions, almost all submissions were reviewed by 3 anonymous reviewers from the PC, with a median score for accepted papers of 1,7 out of 3,0 (according to the EasyChair metric).

As already mentioned, the scientific program also included 3 invited talks by the internationally renowned scientists Tova Milo, Gerhard Weikum and Carlo Zaniolo, and a tutorial and panel on Open Science by Emma Lazzeri, Paolo Manghi, Shalini Kurapati and Stefano Bianco.

We gratefully acknowledge CC ICT-SUD for its sponsorship and support in the organization. We wish to thank all the authors who submitted papers and all the conference participants. We are also grateful to the members of the Program Committee and the external referees for their thorough work, the invited speaker and panelists, and all the other people involved in the organization of this "outlier" edition of SEBD.

Last, but by no means least, we wish to pay tribute to two colleagues and friends of ours who departed during the COVID emergency: Florian Daniel and Antonio Picariello. On April 28th, Florian Daniel died prematurely, at 42, after a brief illness. Florian was an associate professor at Politecnico di Milano; a brilliant, active and passionate scholar, a beloved and appreciated teacher, with his irony and acumen he had won the esteem and recognition of colleagues and students. Antonio Picariello (aka Picus) was one of the most passionate sustainers of SEBD and passed away just during the SEBD 2020 conference; for this reason this volume also contains a brief obituary on him.

June 24, 2020

Maristella Agosti
Maurizio Atzori
Paolo Ciaccia
Letizia Tanca

References

1. Angela Bonifati, Giovanna Guerrini, Carsten Lutz, Wim Martens, Lara Mazilu, Norman Paton, Marcos Antonio Vaz Salles, Marc H. Scholl, Yongluan Zhou. *Holding a Conference Online and Live, Due to COVID-19*. Communications of the ACM, April 21, 2020.
2. Zoom Video Communications, Inc. *Zoom Meeting online platform* https://zoom.us/
3. Gather Presence Inc. *Gather Town online platform*. https://gather.town/

In Memoriam of Prof. Antonio Picariello ("Picus")

Passed away at the age of 55

Picus at SEBD 2014 he organized in the Sorrento Coast.

Antonio Picariello passed away on June 23, 2020, while the SEBD 2020 conference was taking place: a real shock for all conference participants, many of them being close friends or collaborators of Antonio.

Antonio was well-known worldwide for his contributions in the area of Database and Multimedia Systems, and, more recently, of Big Data Analytics. His research activity started in the 1990s, initially focusing on Image Processing and then on Multimedia Databases. Since then, he collected many successful achievements, among which a fuzzy theory to manage complexity and uncertainty of multimedia data, a system for extracting and creating multimedia stories from heterogeneous data sources, indexing techniques for video and image databases, multimedia ontologies, an intelligent framework for detecting events in video surveillance and cybersecurity applications, and, more recently, a new model for multimedia social networks. Antonio is also credited as one of the first researchers to have introduced the concept of multimedia recommender system.

Antonio authored more than 250 papers, published in international journals and conferences. He has been General Chair and/or Program Committee member of several international Conferences and Workshops, associate editor, member of editorial boards and guest editor of numerous international journals, as well as Principal Investigator of many research projects, some of them in collaboration with the University of Maryland at College Park, USA. He was the promoter and organizer of the MIS (Multimedia Information System) workshop, around which one of the first international communities of friends of Multimedia was born.

In 2007 "Picus" joined the SEBD community, and since then he was one of the most active contributors. He organized the 2014 edition, which took place in Sorrento Coast and all of us remember it as a very successful and exciting event.

Besides being a man of great intelligence with extraordinary research skills, he was always humble and capable of transferring in a natural way his passion for the subjects he taught and studied to his students and colleagues. He was a good person like few others, of great humanity, always ready to support and help others in times of difficulty, and not only in the academic world, but also in everyday life (through the many charity works that have characterized his life). But above all, he was a person with a contagious smile that each of us would have liked to meet in her/his own life.

All the SEBD community misses you, Picus!

15 Years of Knowledge Graphs: Lessons, Challenges, Opportunities

Gerhard Weikum

Max Planck Institute for Informatics
Saarland Informatics Campus
Saarbrücken, Germany
Email: weikum@mpi-inf.mpg.de

Abstract. Machines with comprehensive knowledge of the world's entities and their relationships has been a long-standing vision and challenge of AI. Over the last 15 years, huge knowledge bases, also known as knowledge graphs, have been automatically constructed from web data and text sources, and have become a key asset for search, analytics, recommendations and data integration. This digital knowledge can be harnessed to semantically interpret textual phrases in news, social media and web tables, contributing to question answering, natural language processing and data analytics. This talk reviews these advances and discusses lessons learned. Moreover, it identifies open challenges and new research opportunities.

Usability, Performance and Scalability for Expressive Data Languages via Cardinality-Based Aggregates

Carlo Zaniolo

UCLA Computer Science Department
Los Angeles, CA
USA
Email: zaniolo@cs.ucla.edu

Abstract. In theory, the combined use of recursion and negation allows the declarative expression of very powerful algorithms in languages such as Datalog or SQL. However, the diffculty of writing such programs and proving that they satisfy formal non-monotonic semantics makes such an approach totally impractical for software developers. Thus, we propose a new general solution to the problem of developing advanced applications in logic-based languages. Our approach is based on the combined use of recursion and aggregates endowed with a unified definition of their semantics based on cardinality. In fact, we show that this entails the expression on a wide range of algorithms used in ML, data-mining and graph applications, which can be very appealing for practitioners because of (i) the compactness of their code, (ii) a simplified proof or verification for their stable-model semantics, (iii) their effcient implementations via a max-optimized semi-naive fixpoint algorithm, and (iv) their superior scalability via Stale-Synchronous Parallelism. To demonstrate and further enhance the usability of our proposed framework, including the several efficient and scalable applications we developed, we provide a Logical Algorithm Library (Llib) and a Logical Data-Frame System (LFrame). By integrating access to Llib libray with other Apache Spark libraries, and supporting the interoperability of our BigDatalog, RaSQL, and Datalog-ML systems with Scala, Java and Python, LFrame turns Datalog into a powerful and attractive tool for advanced application development in the Spark ecosystem.

Getting Rid of Data

Tova Milo

Tel Aviv University
School of Computer Science
Tel Aviv, Israel
Email: milo@cs.tau.ac.il

Abstract. We are experiencing an amazing data-centered revolution. Incredible amounts of data are collected, integrated and analyzed, leading to key breakthroughs in science and society. This well of knowledge, however, is at a great risk if we do not dispense with some of the data flood. First, the amount of generated data grows exponentially and already at 2025 is expected to be more than five times the available storage. Second, even disregarding storage constraints, uncontrolled data retention risks privacy and security, as recognized, e.g., by the recent EU Data Protection reform. Data disposal policies must be developed to benefit and protect organizations and individuals. Retaining the knowledge hidden in the data while respecting storage, processing and regulatory constraints is a great challenge. The difficulty stems from the distinct, intricate requirements entailed by each type of constraint, the scale and velocity of data and the constantly evolving needs. While multiple data sketching, summarization and deletion techniques were developed to address specific aspects of the problem, we are still very far from a comprehensive solution. Every organization has to battle the same tough challenges, with ad hoc solutions that are application specific and rarely sharable. In this talk I will discuss the logical, algorithmic, and methodological foundations required for the systematic disposal of large-scale data, for constraints enforcement and for the development of applications over the retained information. I will overview relevant related work, highlighting new research challenges and potential reuse of existing techniques, as well as the research performed in this direction in the Tel Aviv Databases group.

Open Science: a tutorial for the database systems community

Emma Lazzeri[1][0000-0003-0506-046X] and Paolo Manghi[1][0000-0001-7291-3210]

[1]Institute of Information Science and Technologies (ISTI), National Research Council of Italy (CNR), Via G. Moruzzi, 1, 56124, Pisa, Italy.
emma.lazzeri@isti.cnr.it

Abstract. This Tutorial, presented at the 28th Symposium on Advanced Database Systems (SEBD2020), aims at introducing the motivations and main features of Open Science, linking it to the research integrity and reproducibility of science, with a focus on the challenges in the ICT and database systems domains.

Keywords: Open Science, Open Access, Research Data Management, FAIR principles.

1 Motivations

The way research is conducted is currently influenced by external yet connected factors: scientific journals market and evaluation criteria. Research communication system today mainly relies on business models that allow researchers to read articles only if their institution pays subscriptions to gain access to a limited set of scientific journals. The global business of scientific communication is estimated to be as worth as US $ 10 billion per year [1], with an increasing trend.

This system is strongly linked to the current research evaluation models, mostly relying on bibliometric indexes based on citation metrics that present several limits, such as the Journal Impact Factor and the H-index [2,3]. Besides the intrinsic drawbacks in the use of these indexes to assess a researcher, this system limits the mechanism of verification and control of related results by "peers" and the whole scientific community, as well as the fertilization of new ideas by obstacolating the access to scientific papers to the broader audience. Furthermore, we currently neglect to give access to fundamental parts for the proof of what is reported in the published articles, simply because they are not involved in the research assessment: research data, software, methodologies, and other results. It is also worth noting that researchers currently act as editors, reviewers, and authors of scientific papers, without being remunerated by publishers that make profit also based on the unpaid raw material scientists produce [4].

2 The Open Alternative

There is indeed an alternative way of doing research: Open Science. Open Science is based on transparency and collaboration and aims at overcoming the barriers to the research results sharing and facilitating the dissemination of knowledge. Open Science means opening each step of the research life cycle. It means sharing research results as much as possible. Transparency, reproducibility, collaboration, inclusiveness, accessibility, accuracy, and re-use are the key principles of Open Science that steps from the concept that the research that is funded with public money has to be made immediately available to the community: every EU citizen has the right to access and benefit from knowledge produced using public funds [5].

The European Commission and a long list of International Funders made a clear choice towards Open Science, as it means enabling broader access to publicly funded research results and therefore helps to build on previous research results, encourage collaboration and avoid duplication of effort, speed up innovation, and involve citizens and society. Open science is defined as an "umbrella term", comprising different elements: from open access to research results (literature, data, software, etc.), to open peer review, open methodologies, protocols, workflows, from open education to citizen science. These elements need to be embedded in a system where research infrastructures and a new evaluation model go hands in hands with research integrity.

One important aspect of embedding open science in the everyday life of researchers is research data management, which implies a structured way of completing the research data lifecycle with the main objective of delivering re-usable research data that can be shared with others. A good research data management needs to follow the FAIR principles, a set of good practices to help making data Findable, Accessible, Interoperable and Reusable [6].

Openness and FAIRness are therefore the means to make science more transparent and reproducible, repeatable, replicable, reusable. In this view, research data is just one of the resources involved. Open Science is about each element of research: data, software, publications, services, etc. There is a general need to identify Open Science resources and how these are related, to ensure their openness and FAIRness. In this context, the definition and development of standards, tools and research infrastructure eliminating the barriers and facilitating the work of scientists by embedding open science good practices in their daily work is key. Several tools and infrastructures are already in place, other needs to be developed.

In this context, one of the latest initiatives of the European Commission is the launch of the European Open Science Cloud, that aims at creating a virtual research environment to access and interoperate research data and other research outputs in Europe across the different disciplines [7-9].

3 Opportunities and challenges for the database systems community

Open Science in the Database Systems sector deals with sharing software in a way that makes it reproducible, preservable, and citable, but also with new and challenging research opportunities linked to establishing infrastructures that can support best practices for research transparency and collaboration.

The "R* of Science" deal with actions that should be the basis of scientific method [10,11] . Repeating science deals with defending the thesis (repeat the same experiment with the same setup in the same lab). The method researchers claim should also be Replicable in order to be certified by others (same experiment and setup, independent lab). Reproducibility of science introduces variations in some of the aspects of research methods (experiment setup or lab). Finally, Reusing research results deals with the transfer of knowledge to enable different experiments, also by others.

Best practices in the ICT domains already exist, ranging from software collaborative development and publication, software and data papers drafting, preprint and postprint selfarchiving, dataset FAIR management and sharing and interlinking of results.

However, work still needs to be done on reproducibility. Research in this sector includes challenging aspects as the definitions of standards and templates for reporting methods, provenance and tracking, the workflow/script automation, design and development of tools and platforms for capturing, tracking, structuring, organising assets throughout the whole project research cycle.

The tutorial presented at SEBD2020 by the authors is available in open access in Zenodo [12].

References

1. Schimmer, R., Geschuhn, K. K., & Vogler, A. (2015). Disrupting the subscription journals' business model for the necessary large-scale transformation to open access. https://doi.org/10.17617/1.3
2. Okubo, Y. (1997), "Bibliometric Indicators and Analysis of Research Systems: Methods and Examples", OECD Science, Technology and Industry Working Papers, No. 1997/01, OECD Publishing, Paris, https://doi.org/10.1787/208277770603
3. Haustein S., Larivière V. (2015) The Use of Bibliometrics for Assessing Research: Possibilities, Limitations and Adverse Effects. In: Welpe I., Wollersheim J., Ringelhan S., Osterloh M. (eds) Incentives and Performance. Springer, Cham. https://doi.org/10.1007/978-3-319-09785-5_8
4. Stephen Buranyi, "Is the staggeringly profitable business of scientific publishing bad for science?", The Guardian, June 27, 2017, https://www.theguardian.com/science/2017/jun/27/profitable-business-scientific-publishing-bad-for-science
5. Neelie Kroes, Vice-President of the European Commission responsible for the Digital Agenda The Challenge of Open Access Launch of OpenAIRE, the European infrastructure for open access publishing of research results Ghent, 2 December 2010, https://ec.europa.eu/commission/presscorner/detail/en/SPEECH_10_716
6. Wilkinson, M., Dumontier, M., Aalbersberg, I. et al. The FAIR Guiding Principles for scientific data management and stewardship. Sci Data 3, 160018 (2016). https://doi.org/10.1038/sdata.2016.18
7. European Commission - EOSC, https://ec.europa.eu/research/openscience/index.cfm?pg=open-science-cloud
8. EOSCSecretariat, www.eoscsecretariat.eu
9. EOSC portal, https://www.eosc-portal.eu/
10. Jill P. Mesirov, Accessible Reproducible Research, Science, 22 JAN 2010 : 415-416, https://doi.org/10.1126/science.1179653
11. Benureau Fabien C. Y., Rougier Nicolas P., Re-run, Repeat, Reproduce, Reuse, Replicate: Transforming Code into Scientific Contributions, Frontiers in Neuroinformatics, v. 11, 2018, p.69, https://doi.org/10.3389/fninf.2017.00069
12. Link to the tutorial presentation, https://doi.org/10.5281/zenodo.3904168

A Bootstrapping Approach for Semi-Automated Legal Knowledge Extraction and Enrichment

Silvana Castano[1], Mattia Falduti[1], Alfio Ferrara[1], and Stefano Montanelli[1]

Università degli Studi di Milano
Department of Computer Science - Via Celoria, 18 - 20133 Milano
{silvana.castano,mattia.falduti,alfio.ferrara,stefano.montanelli}@unimi.it

Abstract. In this paper, we propose a bootstrapping approach for semi-automated legal knowledge extraction. The approach is characterized by the use of a reference legal ontology that is progressively enriched with relevant concepts and related terms extracted from a corpus of legal documents (i.e., Court Decision documents). Supervised, multi-label classification techniques and black-box model explanation techniques are the core components of the bootstrapping approach i) to associate CD documents with appropriate concepts in the ontology and ii) to choose the terms that are decisive for determining the association between a document and a certain ontology concept, respectively. The goal of the proposed approach is to reduce the manual involvement of legal experts as much as possible and to improve the accuracy of document classification, by progressively enriching the term sets associated with ontology concepts. Preliminary experimental results are finally provided to show the contribution of the proposed approach on a corpus of real Court Decision documents.

Keywords: legal ontology · legal knowledge extraction · automated Court-Decision analysis

1 Introduction

In the legal domain, Court Decisions (CDs) are documents written in natural language where judges give concrete application of rules and concepts that constitute the law, by deciding whether the law has been violated in relation to the facts. Therefore, CDs are a core component of the legal system since a clear and exhaustive understanding of the judge decisions represents a useful support for the activities of all the actors involved in the legal system. However, quantity, complexity, and articulation of CDs are constantly growing. As a result, effectively extracting the judge decisions about a given crime hypothesis from documents related to real trials is becoming increasingly difficult.

In such a context, techniques and tools for automated extraction of legal knowledge are strongly demanded, to support annotation, analysis, and understanding of legal documents [2, 10]. Semantic Web technologies are usually employed to create legal knowledge bases, namely *legal ontologies*, derived from i) the law, to formally represent the general rules that are relevant/prominent for specific crime hypothesis in the form of legal concepts, and ii) the case-law, to associate legal concepts with relevant law terminology extracted from CDs [12, 13, 16]. However, the discovery of new legal concepts as well as the annotation of legal documents to determine where and how concepts instances are used by judges, are manually performed by legal experts and it is a time-consuming activity, especially when a large corpus of documents is considered [3].

For these reasons, data science approaches are being proposed for automating - as much as possible - the extraction of legal knowledge from textual documents such as Court Decisions. Information retrieval techniques can be employed to detect the occurrence of the terms associated with a concept throughout the documents [7, 17]. In the literature, some contributions are also being proposed in the framework of legal argumentation mining, that is the capability to automatically detect and classify the role of possible argumentative units within a considered legal text [1, 9]. In [15], the authors propose to rely on Natural Language Processing (NLP) and machine learning techniques for mining relevant legal terms from documents. The LUIMA approach characterized by sentence-level annotations and reranking techniques has been also proposed to enforce retrieval over a CD dataset [4]. Moreover, a particularly relevant contribution is provided in [14] about extraction of case law sentences for argumentation of statutory terms, namely terms directly or indirectly defined by the law. However, the accuracy of the above solutions depends on the completeness of the term sets associated with concepts. Due to the variety of terminology adopted by judges in legal documents such as Court Decisions, the construction of accurate and complete term sets to associate with concepts is really hard to obtain.

In this paper, we propose a bootstrapping approach for semi-automated extraction of both terminological and conceptual knowledge in the legal domain. The approach is characterized by the use of a reference legal ontology that is progressively enriched with relevant terms extracted from a corpus of CD documents. Multi-label classification techniques and black-box model explanation techniques are the core components of the bootstrapping approach i) to associate CD documents with appropriate concepts in the ontology and ii) to choose the terms that are decisive for determining the association between a document and a certain ontology concept, respectively. The goal of the proposed approach is twofold. On the one side, the approach aims to reduce the involvement of legal experts as much as possible so that document classification can scale to manage large CD corpora. On the other side, the use of iterative bootstrapping cycles aims to improve the accuracy of document classification, by progressively enriching the term sets associated with ontology concepts.

The paper is organized as follows. In section 2, the proposed bootstrapping approach for semi-automated extraction of terminological and conceptual knowledge in the legal domain is presented. In Section 3, technical details about the adopted machine learning techniques are provided. In Section 4, we present some preliminary results on a real corpus of Court Decision documents. Finally, in Section 5, we give our concluding remarks and we outline our future research issues.

2 Semi-automated legal knowledge extraction

Our approach for semi-automated legal knowledge extraction is based on the iterative execution of a *bootstrapping cycle* articulated in a sequence of steps shown in Figure 1. The approach is based on a corpus of Court Decision (CD)

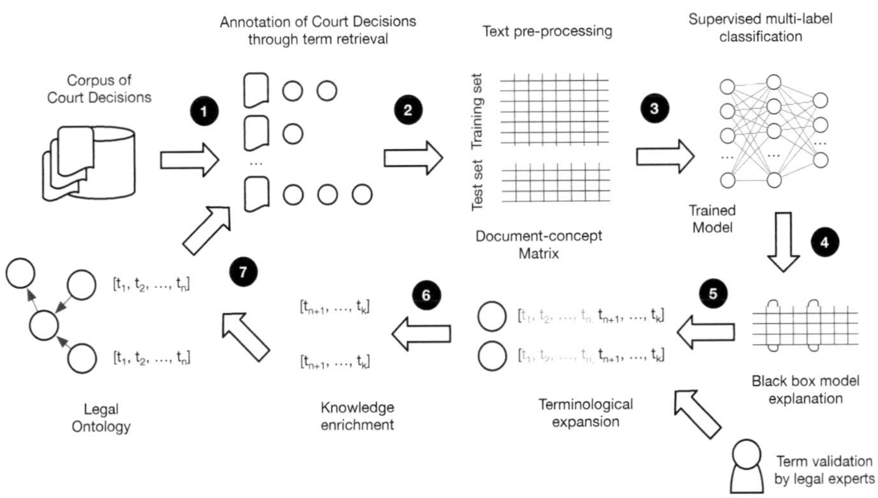

Fig. 1. A bootstrapping cycle for semi-automated extraction of terminological and conceptual knowledge

documents and on a reference legal ontology where an initial version of knowledge is provided, both conceptual knowledge and terminological knowledge. We call *conceptual knowledge* the set of *legal concepts* that is formally represented in a reference legal ontology, where concepts are interlinked by semantic relations and associated with a corresponding terminological knowledge. We call *terminological knowledge* the set of natural language terms concretely used in a considered corpus of legal documents (i.e., Court Decisions) to refer to legal concepts. The initial ontology is manually defined by domain experts and it is characterized by a set of legal concepts of interest (conceptual knowledge). A legal concept C_i in the ontology is associated with an initial *term set* T_i^0 that represents the relevant terms featuring C_i that are extracted from the corpus documents since they have been recognized by the experts to be an instance of the concept C_i (terminological knowledge).

A bootstrapping cycle k is organized as follows:

Step (1). Term retrieval technique are employed to associate document with relevant ontology concepts. For each CD document d, the set of associated legal concepts $\mathcal{C}_d$ is determined as follows:

$$\mathcal{C}_d = \left\{ C_i : \left[\sum_{t \in T_i} w(t,d) \right] \geq th \right\}$$

where $w(t,d)$ is the weight of a term t in the document d according to standard information retrieval techniques based on tokenization, tf-idf, and PMI (Pointwise Mutual Information) for compound term detection. Moreover, th is a threshold used to set the minimum cumulative weight of all the terms $t \in T_i$ that is required for associating a corresponding concept C_i with the document d.

Step (2). For each document d in the corpus, a vector-based representation $\boldsymbol{d}$ is generated to provide document embedding. In the literature, different techniques can be employed to enforce vector-based document representation, like for example bag-of-words, word2vec, and NVSM (Neural Vector Space Model). In our approach, we choose to rely on doc2vec techniques [8]. Basically, doc2vec represents an extension of the word2vec approach. The doc2vec solution has been conceived to overcome the weaknesses of the well-known bag-of-words approach by preserving both ordering and semantics of text-extracted words in the vector representation. In particular, doc2vec is based on an unsupervised algorithm that learns fixed-length feature representations from variable-length pieces of texts (e.g., documents). The algorithm represents each document by a dense vector which is trained to predict words in the document. In addition, each document vector $\boldsymbol{d}$ is associated with a *concept vector* $\boldsymbol{c}_d$, where each vector dimension denotes a concept C_i in the legal ontology whose value is set to 1 if $C_i \in \mathcal{C}_d$, or it is set to 0 otherwise.

Step (3). A multi-label classifier is employed to generate a model that is capable to predict the association of CD documents with legal concepts. In our approach, we employ a 1D Convolutional Neural Network (1D-CNN) with the goal to generalize the terminology of the documents and to enable the association of legal concepts with Court Decisions that actually contain terms other than those already included in the reference legal ontology. For each document d, the CNN receives the document vector representation $\boldsymbol{d}$ as input and it produces the corresponding concept vector representation $\boldsymbol{c}_d$ as output. As a result, a classification model M is generated to map the correspondence between corpus

The choice of CNN is due to the positive experimental results we observed in a number of considered case-studies. As a general remark, different kinds of multi-label classifier can be employed for enforcing document classification, like for example random forest and kNN.

documents and legal concepts in the ontology. In particular, by $C_i \in M(d)$ we denote that the document d is associated with the legal concept C_i through the model M.

Step (4). We exploit black-box model explanation techniques in order to select the document features (i.e., terms) that play a major role in determining the decision of the multi-label classifier about the association of concepts with the corpus documents. As a result of Step (4), for a legal concept C_i, a set T_{C_i} is generated containing terms that mainly determine the decision of the CNN classifier to associate C_i with a considered document of the corpus.

Step (5). For each concept C_i, the terms in the set $T_{C_i} \setminus T_i^k$ are candidate to be exploited for terminological expansion. Legal experts are involved in a validation activity of candidate terms. As a result, for a concept C_i, the set $R_i \subseteq (T_{C_i} - T_i^k)$ is defined containing the terms that are relevant for C_i according to the expert evaluation **Step (6)**. Finally, in **Step (7)**, the terminological knowledge T_i^{k+1} associated with each concept C_i is enriched as follows:

$$T_i^{k+1} \equiv T_i^k \cup R_i$$

At the end of Step (7), a new bootstrapping cycle can be enforced. The goal of each bootstrapping cycle is twofold. On the one side, a bootstrapping cycle aims to improve the accuracy of document classification enforced in Step (3). In the first bootstrapping cycle, the accuracy of classification can be low due to the fact that the training set is built by exploiting the terminological knowledge available in the initial version of the legal ontology. As long as the terminological knowledge of the ontology is enriched, the accuracy of the classifier is expected to increase. On the other side, a bootstrapping cycle aims to enrich the terminological knowledge of the legal ontology. The enforcement of new bootstrapping cycles is stopped when the enrichment of the terminological knowledge is terminated, namely when the expert validation (Step (5)) does not generate new terms to insert in the legal ontology.

In the following, more technical details about the black-box model explanation techniques are provided to better emphasize the original contribution of the proposed bootstrapping approach.

3 Knowledge enrichment: black-box model explanation and terminology expansion

In a given bootstrapping cycle k, the goal of black-box model explanation and terminology expansion is to exploit the current version of the legal ontology O^k and to generate a new version O^{k+1} where the term sets of THE ontology concepts are enriched with the discovered terminological knowledge. Terminology expansion is based on the multi-label classification model M^k derived from the annotation of CD documents through O^k. During the training phase, M^k learns the function that maps CD documents with terminology of O^k on the appropriate legal concepts. In addition, the model also learns to generalize such knowledge, to correctly associate legal concepts with CD documents that actually contain terms other than those included in O^k. This ability of M^k depends on two main aspects of the training process. The first one is that CD documents are encoded as vectors using doc2vec, thus documents that are semantically similar (but containing different terminology) are encoded as vectors which are "close" in the feature space (i.e., the space of terms). The consequence of this proximity is that the mapping function learned from the model M^k tends to associate neighboring vectors (i.e., documents) with the same legal concepts. The second aspect is that documents that contain O^k terms often contain further terms that are also relevant to the legal concepts in the ontology, but which were not discovered/associated in previous bootstrapping cycles. In other terms, the model M^k implicitly contains the relevant terminology required to map CD documents to legal concepts, even if this terminology is not included in O^k.

For each concept C_i, our goal is to detect the set of terms that play a crucial role in determining the classification decision of M^k, namely the terms that, if deleted from the document, more likely may produce a different classification result. Determining this set of terms is challenging due to the lack of an explicit explanation capable of describing the behavior of M^k. To this end, we exploit black-box model explanation techniques. Recently, some approaches have been proposed to provide a model explanation at least locally, which means to explain why (i.e., due to which features/terms) a model decides to assign a given class to a certain document [5]. In particular, LIME (Local Interpretable Model-agnostic Explanations) [11] allows to obtain an interpretation of any classifier, by building a local and interpretable model around a prediction. Given a document d, the idea of LIME is to train an interpretable model using new documents that are uniformly and randomly perturbed copies of d, located in the proximity of d by measuring the impact of perturbing each feature on the classification decision. For each term $t \in d$, LIME calculates a score $\eta(t, d)$ that is directly proportional to the relevance of t in determining the model decision to associate d with C_i. Given a concept C_i, we consider all the documents $D_{C_i} = \{d : C_i \in M(d)\}$ and all the terminology that is potentially relevant for C_i, that is:

$$T_{C_i} = \left\{ t : t \in \bigcup_{d \in D_{C_i}} d \right\}$$

Then, we associate each term $t \in T_{C_i}$ with a degree of relevance $\eta_{C_i}(t)$ as follows:

$$\eta_{C_i}(t) = \sum_{t \in T_{C_i}} \sum_{d \in D_{C_i}} \eta(t, d)$$

Legal experts are then involved in the validation of terms in T_{C_i}. A threshold-based mechanism based on the degree of relevance $\eta_{C_i}(t)$ can be enforced to support the validation activity of experts. In particular, terms with value of $\eta_C(t)$ higher than the threshold are proposed to the expert for insertion in the legal ontology, while terms with value of $\eta_C(t)$ lower than the threshold are proposed to be discarded. As a result of the expert validation, the set R_i is defined containing the terms that are relevant for the terminological expansion of C_i so that the new version O^{k+1} of the legal ontology can be defined.

Example. In Figure 2, we show an example of two CD documents, d_1 and d_2 associated with the concept Drug in a legal ontology O^1 about the drug criminal legislation (see Figure 3). In our example, the ontology O^1 is implemented by using the Simple Knowledge Organization System (SKOS) [6]. In particular, the legal concepts are implemented as SKOS concepts and they are interconnected through appropriate SKOS relations. For instance, the skos:related relation is used to represent a generic positive relationship between two legal concepts, like for example Drug and Criminal Procedure. For each legal concept (i.e., SKOS concept), a skos:prefLabel is defined to denote that a certain term belongs to the term set of the concept. Moreover, a number of skos:altLabel are defined to denote the possible alternative terms in the term set of the concept. For instance, a skos:prefLabel relation is defined between the Drug concept and the Narcotic Drug term, while a skos:altLabel relation is defined between the Drug concept and the Cannabis term.

> d_1: [...] *Paragraph 14 of section 1 of the same act provides:* "**Narcotic Drugs** *means coca leaves, opium,* **cannabis**, *and every substance neither chemically nor physically distinguishable from them."* [...]
>
> d_2: [...]*Defendant, who was charged by indictment with violation of 402 of the Illinois Controlled Substances Act"* [...]

Fig. 2. Example of CD document sentences associated with the legal concept Drug

The association of d_1 with the concept is due to the fact that it contains the terms Narcotic Drug and Cannabis that belong to the term set of the concept Drug in the legal ontology. The multi-label classification model M^1 trained on d_1 (and on the other documents contained in the training set) classifies d_2 as a document related to the Drug concept. This decision is due to the similarity between the documents d_1 and d_2, which implies that the two vectors obtained by doc2vec are close in the feature/term space.

Through LIME, we detect the terms of d_1 and d_2 that mainly influence the classifier decision. According to LIME, we obtain the following terms for the concept Drug: Narcotic Drug, Controlled Substances, Cannabis, Coca Leaves, Opium. In the list, Narcotic Drug and Cannabis are already present in the current ontology O^1, while the others (underlined in Figure 2) are validated by the legal experts. In Figure 3, the validated terms are included in the ontology O^1 to generate a new, enriched ontology O^2 where the term set of the concept Drug is properly extended. In the subsequent bootstrapping cycle, the ontology O^2 is exploited to automatically create the training set for the classification model M^2. Such

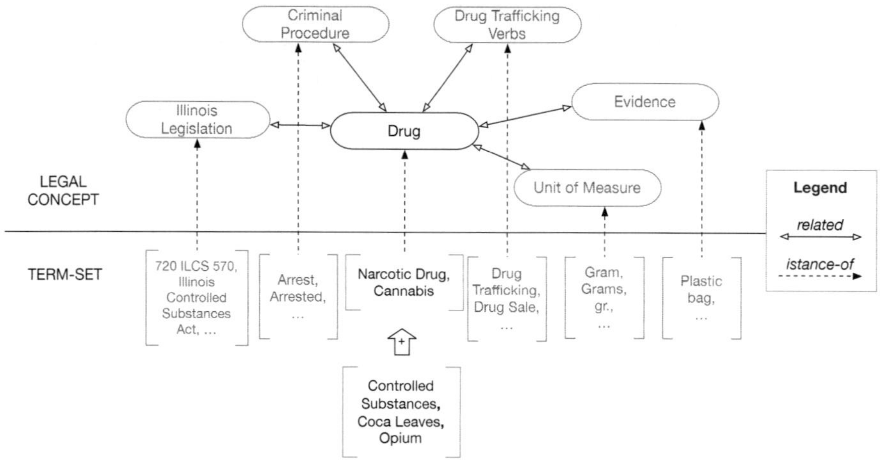

Fig. 3. Example of the concept Drug in the legal ontology

a training set will include also d_2 since the term Controlled Substances has been inserted in the term set of the concept Drug. A new round of classification and explanation can be executed to further improve the terminological expansion of ontology concepts and to generate a new ontology version O^3.

4 Preliminary experimental results

The goal of our preliminary evaluation is to assess the i) the capability of discovering new relevant terms about the concepts in the reference legal ontology and ii) the improvement in terms of accuracy of the classification process across two bootstrapping cycles. The experimentation is based on a dataset of around 180,000 Court Decisions of the State of Illinois taken from the Caselaw Access Project (CAP) providing public access to U.S. law (`https://case.law/bulk/download`) digitized from the collection of the Harvard Law Library. For the experiments, we select six concepts from our legal ontology, namely drug, drug trafficking verbs, unit of measure, illinois legislation, criminal procedure, and evidence. Document classification is enforced at the sentence level, which means that legal concepts are associated with each single sentence independently. This way, the 180,000 court decisions correspond to about 14,000,000 documents (i.e., sentences). In the first bootstrapping cycle, the initial version of the legal ontology is characterized by concepts with small term sets (see Table 1). By relying on the term sets in the ontology, we select a subset of 115,993 CD sentences that constitutes the training set of the classification step. According to our annotation techniques, a sentence is associated with a concept C_i when at least one term belonging to the term set T_i is contained in the sentence. In Table 2, for each concept considered in the experimentation, we show the number of associated sentences resulting from the annotation step.

Table 1. Term sets in the initial legal ontology of the experimentation

Legal Concept	Term Set	Size
drug	narcotic, cocaine, crack, drug, marijuana, heroin, cannabis, lsd, [...]	15
drug trafficking verbs	drug trafficking, drug sale, drug use, narcotics trafficking, [...]	18
unit of measure	gram, grams, gr., pound, kilo, [...]	10
illinois legislation	720 ILCS 570, Illinois Controlled Substances Act, Drug Abuse Control Act, [...]	6
criminal procedure	arrest, arrested, seizure, [...]	7
evidence	plastic bag, plastic bags, paraphernalia	3

Table 2. Number of sentences per concept resulting from the annotation step

drug	drug trafficking verbs	unit of measure	illinois legislation	criminal procedure	evidence
25,138	52,103	290	49,994	14,595	2,830

Each document is embedded in a 100-dimension vector using doc2vec to obtain a 115,993 × 100 corpus matrix. The model M^1 used to train the classifier is a neural network organized in three layers. Between the input and the output layer, we use a convolution filter activated by ReLU. The M^1 accuracy obtained by cross-validation is 0.77. The model M^1 is then used to perform black-box model explanation and terminology expansion using LIME. For each concept C_i, we determine a new set of terms T_{C_i}. A term $t \in \mathsf{T}_{C_i}$ is associated with the degree of relevance $\eta_{C_i}(t)$. In the experimentation, a legal expert validated the top-20 terms in the set T_{C_i} of each concept C_i. In particular, the expert associated each term t with a numerical value in $\{-1, 0, 1\}$, where T^{-1} denotes the set of terms that were not in the ontology O^1 and that are not relevant for the concept C_i; T^0 denotes the set of terms that were in O^1 (and thus have been already validated as relevant); T^1 denotes the set of terms that were not in O^1 but that are relevant for the concept C_i.

An overview of the results of terminological expansion is shown in Table 3.

The number of relevant terms retrieved in the terminological expansion (i.e., terms in T^0 or T^1) is equal to the 83% of the total number of new terms validated by the expert ($\mathsf{T}_{\mathsf{C}_i}$). The 34% of those terms was not in the term sets of the initial ontology O^1. As expected, the increment of new relevant terms is higher for the concepts that were associated with small term sets, such as illinois legislation, criminal procedure, and evidence. The number of irrelevant terms T^{-1} is limited with the exception of the concept evidence, because the criminal evidences usually consist in common objects that are used in a criminal context. These objects are thus associated with a generic terminology (e.g., garbage, suitcase) that cannot be associated per se to an evidence according to the legal expert. The new relevant terms are finally included in the new version O^2 of the ontology that is used to automatically create a new training set for a second bootstrapping cycle. The new training set consists of 158,398 CD sentences (+37% with respect to the

Table 3. Results of the black-box model explanation and terminology expansion step

	drug	drug trafficking verbs	unit of measure	illinois legislation	criminal procedure	evidence	**total**
$\mid T_i^0 \mid$	15	18	10	6	7	3	**59**
$\mid T_{C_i} \mid$	20	20	20	20	20	20	**120**
$\mid T^{-1} \mid$	1	0	3	1	6	10	**21**
$\mid T^0 \mid$	14	17	10	6	6	3	**65**
$\mid T^1 \mid$	5	3	7	13	8	7	**34**
$\frac{(\lvert T^0\rvert + \lvert T^1\rvert)}{\lvert T_{C_i}\rvert}$	0.95	1.0	0.85	0.95	0.75	0.4	**0.83**
$\frac{\lvert T^1\rvert}{(\lvert T^0\rvert + \lvert T^1\rvert)}$	0.26	0.15	0.42	0.68	0.57	0.7	**0.34**

first execution). In particular, the main increment of sentences is related to the concepts unit of measure (from 290 to 7,241 sentences) and evidence (from 2,830 to 33,417 sentences). These sentences are then used to train a new model M^2 using the same neural network architecture of M^1 and to enforce the execution of the knowledge enrichment steps. Finally, the accuracy of M^2 obtained by cross-validation is 0.81 (+5.2%).

5 Concluding remarks

In this paper, we propose a bootstrapping approach for semi-automated legal knowledge extraction. Technical details about the use of multi-label classification techniques and black-box model explanation techniques are provided to show how we associate corpus documents with appropriate concepts in a reference ontology, and how we choose the terms that are decisive for determining the association between a document and a certain ontology concept, respectively. Preliminary results on a corpus of Court Decision documents are discussed to highlight the contribution of our proposed approach in real scenarios. Future work are about the extension of preliminary experiments on a larger corpus of Court Decision documents, and the comparison of obtained results by adopting different techniques for document annotation/embedding, document classification, and black-box model explanation.

References

1. Ashley, K.D.: Artificial Intelligence and Legal Analytics: New Tools for Law Practice in the Digital Age. Cambridge University Press (2017)
2. Castano, S., Falduti, M., Ferrara, A., Montanelli, S.: Crime Knowledge Extraction: An Ontology-Driven Approach for Detecting Abstract Terms in Case Law Decisions. In: Proc. of the 17th Int. Conf. on Artificial Intelligence and Law (2019)
3. Grabmair, M., Ashley, K.D.: Facilitating Case Comparison Using Value Judgments and Intermediate Legal Concepts. In: Proc. of the 13th Int. Conference on Artificial Intelligence and Law. pp. 161–170. ACM (2011)

4. Grabmair, M., Ashley, K.D., Chen, R., Sureshkumar, P., Wang, C., Nyberg, E., Walker, V.R.: Introducing LUIMA: an Experiment in Legal Conceptual Retrieval of Vaccine Injury Decisions Using a UIMA Type System and Tools. In: Proc. of the 15th Int. Conference on Artificial Intelligence and Law. pp. 69–78. ACM (2015)
5. Guidotti, R., Monreale, A., Ruggieri, S., Turini, F., Giannotti, F., Pedreschi, D.: A Survey of Methods for Explaining Black Box Models. ACM Computing Surveys (CSUR) **51**(5), 1–42 (2018)
6. Isaac, A., Summers, E.: SKOS Simple Knowledge Organization System Primer. Tech. rep., Working Group Note, W3C (2009)
7. Lame, G.: Law and the Semantic Web: Legal Ontologies, Methodologies, Legal Information Retrieval, and Applications, chap. Using NLP Techniques to Identify Legal Ontology Components: Concepts and Relations, pp. 169–184. Springer Berlin Heidelberg (2005)
8. Le, Q., Mikolov, T.: Distributed Representations of Sentences and Documents. In: Proc. of the 31st Int. Conference on Machine Learning. Beijing, China (2014)
9. Nazarenko, A., Wyner, A.: Legal NLP Introduction. Traitement Automatique des Langues **58**(2), 7–19 (2017)
10. Palmirani, M.: Legislative XML for the Semantic Web, chap. Legislative Change Management with Akoma-Ntoso, pp. 101–130. Springer (2011)
11. Ribeiro, M.T., Singh, S., Guestrin, C.: "Why Should I Trust You?" Explaining the Predictions of Any Classifier. In: Proc. of the 22nd ACM SIGKDD Int. Conference on Knowledge Discovery and Data Mining. pp. 1135–1144 (2016)
12. Saias, J., Quaresma, P.: Law and the Semantic Web, chap. A Methodology to Create Legal Ontologies in a Logic Programming Information Retrieval System, pp. 185–200. Springer (2005)
13. Sartor, G., Casanovas, P., Biasiotti, M., Fernández-Barrera, M.: Approaches to Legal Ontologies: Theories, Domains, Methodologies, vol. 1. Springer Science & Business Media (2010)
14. Savelka, J., Ashley, K.D.: Extracting Case Law Sentences for Argumentation about the Meaning of Statutory Terms. In: Proc. of the 3rd Int. Workshop on Argument Mining. pp. 50–59 (2016)
15. Savelka, J., Grabmair, M., Ashley, K.D.: Mining Information from Statutory Texts in Multi-Jurisdictional Settings. In: Proc. of the Int. Conference on Legal Knowledge and Information Systems. pp. 133–142. IOS Press (2014)
16. Tiscornia, D.: The LOIS project: Lexical Ontologies for Legal Information Sharing. In: Proc. of the V Legislative XML Workshop. pp. 189–204 (2006)
17. Wagh, R.S.: Knowledge Discovery from Legal Documents Dataset Using Text Mining Techniques. International Journal of Computer Applications **66**(23) (2013)

Scaling Up Record-level Matching Rules

Luca Gagliardelli, Giovanni Simonini, and Sonia Bergamaschi

University of Modena and Reggio Emilia, Modena, Italy
<name.surname>@unimore.it

Abstract. Record-level matching rules are chains of similarity join predicates on multiple attributes employed to join records that refer to the same real-world object when an explicit foreign key is not available on the data sets at hand. They are widely employed by data scientists and practitioners that work with data lakes, open data, and data in the wild. In this work we present a novel technique that allows to efficiently execute record-level matching rules on parallel and distributed systems and demonstrate its efficiency on a real-wold data set.

Keywords: Data Integration · Entity Resolution · Parallel similarity join

1 Introduction

Combining data sets that bare information about the same real-world objects is an everyday task for practitioners that work with structured and semi-structured data. Frequently (e.g., when dealing with data lakes or when integrating open data with proprietary data) data sets do not have explicit keys that can be used for a traditional *equi-join* [12,13,7,9]. When that happens, a common solution is to perform a *similarity join* [10], i.e., to join records that have an attribute value similar above a certain threshold, according to a given similarity measure, as in the following example:

Example 1. (Similarity Join) *Given two product data sets, join all the record pairs with the Jaccard similarity of the product names above 0.8.*

A plethora of algorithms have been proposed in the last decades to efficiently execute the similarity join considering a single attribute, i.e., *attribute-level matching rules* (see [10] for a survey). At their core, all these algorithms try to prune the candidate pairs of records, on the basis of a single-attribute predicate—to alleviate the quadratic complexity of the problem.

Interestingly, only a few works had been focused on studying how to execute *record-level matching rules*, i.e., the combination of multiple similarity join pred-

---

icates on multiple attributes (see Section 2). Yet, this kind of rules permits to specify more flexible rules to match records, as in the following example:

Example 2. (Record-level matching rule) *Given two product data sets, join all the record pairs that have a Jaccard similarity of the product names above 0.8, or that have a Jaccard similarity of the description that is above 0.6 and the edit distance of the manufacturer lower than 3.*

Furthermore, record-level matching rules can be used to represent *decision trees* [2], hence learned with machine learning algorithms when training data is available. As a matter of fact, a decision tree for binary classification (i.e., classification of *matching/not-matching* records) can be naturally represented with DNF (disjunctive normal form) predicates—the same consideration can be done for a forest of trees.

To the best of our knowledge, no techniques have been proposed to leverage distributed and parallel computing for scaling record-level matching rules. The benefit is twofold: *(i)* distributed computation allows to scale to large data sets that cannot be handled with a single machine; *(ii)* parallel execution reduces the execution times (3 times faster in our experiments). As a matter of fact, being able to efficiently execute similarity join is crucial when time is a critical component, e.g., when users are involved in the process. For instance, in exploratory search in a data lake [11], users typically look for related data sets and low latency in performing similarity join is required for enabling the user's interactive exploration. Also, when debugging record-level matching rules, users typically try different configurations of similarity metrics, thresholds, and attributes. Hence, enabling fast execution of such rules can significantly save user's time.

Contribution. In this work we present a technique that is able to use different similarity measures to apply record-level matching rules efficiently. Moreover, we present an algorithm, *RulER*, to efficiently run record-level matching rules on MapReduce-like systems, to take full advantage of a parallel and distributed computation.

The rest of the paper is organized as follow: Section 2 provides the preliminaries. Then, in Section 3 we present our novel technique. Section 4 shows the experimental results. Finally, in Section 5 we draw the conclusions.

2 Preliminaries and Related Work

This section describes the fundamental concepts and the related work.

2.1 Matching Rule

We define a matching rule $\mathcal{R}$ as a *disjunction* (logical *OR*) of *conjunctions* (logical *AND*) of similarity join predicates on multiple attribute (i.e., at the *record level*). This design choice is driven by the fact that DNF matching rules are easy to read and thus to debug, in practice. Moreover, DNFs can be employed to represent the trained model of a decision tree (or of a random forest), hence suitable for exploiting labeled data. In this work, we focus on how to scale DNF matching rules and we do not investigate how to generate *good* DNFs (i.e., decision trees/random forests) starting from training data, which is the focus of Ardalan et al. [2]—Ardalan et al. do not investigate the parallel and distributed execution of matching rules.

2.2 Set Similarity Join

A record r_i is considered as a set of elements identified by a unique identifier. Different techniques can be employed to generate the elements from the values of a record, for example, each word can be considered as a token or it is possible to generate the n-grams, etc. Formally, given a collection of records, a similarity function sim and a similarity threshold t, the goal of set similarity join is to find all the possible pairs of records $\langle r_i, r_j \rangle$ such that $sim(r_i, r_j) \geq t$.

A naïve solution to perform the set similarity join is to enumerate and compare every pair of records, but this process is highly inefficient and not feasible in the Big Data context. To reduce the task complexity different approaches were proposed in literature [4,3,16,15]. All these approaches adopt a filter-verification approach: (1) first an index is used to obtain a set of pre-candidates; (2) the pre-candidates are filtered using a set of pre-defined filters; (3) the resulting candidate pairs are probed with the similarity function to generate the final results.

The most used filters are: prefix filter, length filter, and positional filter. All these filters can be adapted to work with different similarity measures: Dice, Cosine, Jaccard Similarity, Edit Distance and Overlap Similarity [10,15,16].

Prefix filter A key technique to perform the set similarity join efficiently is the *prefix filter* [4]. First of all, given a collection of records (i.e., sets of elements) their elements are sorted according to a global order $\mathcal{O}$, usually the document frequency of the tokens (i.e., how many documents contain that token) that is a heuristic that helps to reduce the number of comparisons [4]. Then, for each sorted set, only the first π elements are considered, i.e., the *prefixes*. A pair $\langle r_i, r_j \rangle$ can be safely pruned if their prefixes have no common elements. The prefix size depends on the similarity threshold and the similarity function. For example, the prefix filter for the overlap similarity is defined as follows: given two sets, r_i and r_j, and an overlap threshold t; if $|r_i \cap r_j| \geq t$, then there is at least one common token within the π_{r_i}-prefix of r_i and the π_{r_j}-prefix of r_j, where $r = |r_j| - t + 1$ and $s = |r_j| - t + 1$.

An example of how prefix filter works is reported in Figure 1. The prefixes for overlap threshold $t = 4$ are highlighted in grey. Since the two prefixes do not share any token, the pair $\langle r_i, r_j \rangle$ can be pruned. The intuition behind this is that the 3 remaining tokens to check can provide at most a similarity of 3, that is not enough to reach the requested threshold t.

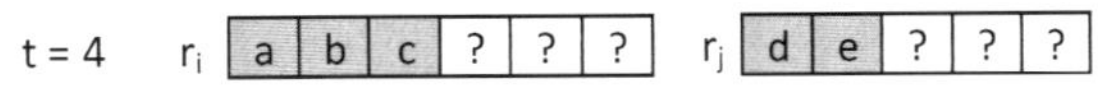

Fig. 1. Prefix filter.

Length filter A filter that is commonly used in conjunction with the prefix filter is the length filter [1]. Normalized similarity functions (e.g., Jaccard, Cosine, Dice, ED) depend on the set size, thus it is possible to exploit it to prune the pairs generated with the prefix filter. For the Jaccard Similarity the length filter is defined as: a set of elements r can reach Jaccard threshold t only with a set s of size $lb_r \leq |s| \leq ub_r$ ($lb_r = t \cdot |r|, ub_r = \frac{|r|}{|t|}$); for example, if $|r| = 10$ and $t = 0.8$, then $8 \leq |s| \leq 12$ is required.

Positional filter The positional filter [16] reasons over the matching position of tokens in the prefix. Given a pair of sets of sorted elements it checks the positions of their common tokens in the prefix, if the remain tokens to check are not enough to reach the threshold, it prunes the pair. Since it needs to scan the tokens in the prefix, this filter is more expensive than prefix and length filters, so usually it is applied only on the pairs that already passed them.

An example of how positional filter works is provided in Figure 2. The pair $\langle r_i, r_j \rangle$ passes both length and prefix filters. The first match in r_i occurs in position 1 (counting from 0), thus only 8 tokens of r_j are left to match tokens of r_i, and the pair can be filtered because it can never reach the requested threshold $t = 9$.

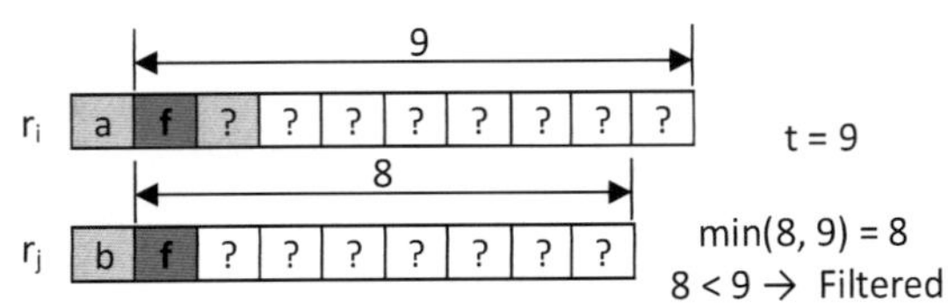

Fig. 2. Positional filter example.

Prefix filter based set similarity join An example of how a prefix filter based set similarity join works is outlined in Figure 3. Starting from a document collection, the documents are transformed in sets of elements (e.g., tokens, n-grams, etc.) and sorted according to a global order (1). Then, using the prefixes (highlighted in gray) an inverted index is built, i.e., the prefix index (2). From the prefix index, a set of pre-candidate pairs is built (3), i.e., each pair of profiles that appear together in at least one entry of the prefix index. The pre-candidate pairs are filtered using different filters (e.g., length filter, positional filter, etc.) that are fast to compute and let to discard the pairs that cannot reach the threshold (4). Finally, the pairs that pass all the filters (i.e., candidate pairs) are probed with the similarity function, and only those that have a similarity above the threshold are retained (5).

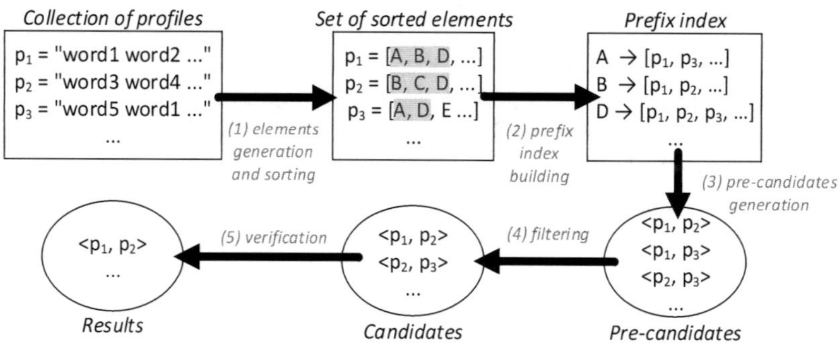

Fig. 3. Prefix filter based Similarity Join process.

3 RulER

In this section, we present our method *RulER* to efficiently scale record-level matching rules over big data sets. The presented algorithm is the self-join version for the sake of the presentation; adapting it for joining two different data sets is straightforward.

3.1 Baseline algorithm

Given a matching rule $\mathcal{R}$ a naïve solution to perform it is to process each predicate as a single similarity join and then intersect/merge the obtained results according to the requirements. In particular, we adopted two algorithms to perform the similarity joins: *PPJoin* [16] and *EDJoin* [15]. Both algorithms employ *prefix filter* (see Section 2) to find candidate pairs. *PPJoin* is considered one of the best performing similarity join algorithm [10], also its parallel implementation (i.e., Vernica Join) has demonstrated to be one of the best performing

Algorithm 1 PPJoin/EDJoin

Input: R collection of records to join
Input: $\mathcal{P}$ predicate that contains the join attribute, the threshold, and the elements pattern (i.e., tokens, n-grams, etc.)
Output: C, the pairs of records that can satisfy $\mathcal{P}$

1: $R_T \leftarrow$ *getSortedElements*$(R, \mathcal{P})$ //Transforms the records in set of sorted elements (i.e., tokens, n-grams, etc.)
2: $I \leftarrow$ *buildPrefixIndex*$(R_T, \mathcal{P})$ //Build prefix index
3: $C \leftarrow$ **flatMap** $B_i \in I$ //For each entry of the prefix index
4:     **for each** $\langle r_j, r_k\rangle \in B_i(r_j \neq r_k)$ **do**
5:         **if** *passLengthFilter*$(r_j, r_k, \mathcal{P})$ **then**
6:             **if** *passPositionalFilter*$(r_j, r_k, \mathcal{P})$ **then**
7:                 *emit*$(\langle r_j, r_k\rangle)$

for distributed computing [6]. It can work with different similarity measures like Jaccard Similarity, Dice and Cosine. *EDJoin* adapts the *PPJoin* concepts to work with the Edit Distance. We adapted both algorithms to work on Spark as proposed in [14] for *PPJoin*(i.e., Vernica Join).

The distributed algorithm to perform PPJoin/EDJoin is presented in Algorithm 1. First, the records are transformed into sets of sorted elements according to the predicate requirements (line 1). The prefix index (see Subsection 2.2) is built generating an inverted index that groups all the records that share at least one token in their prefix. Then, the algorithm iterates over each entry of the prefix index B_i, probing each pair of records $\langle r_i, r_j\rangle \in B_i$ with the appropriate filters according to the predicate $\mathcal{P}$.

Algorithm 2 outlines the baseline algorithm (i.e., *JoinChain*). A rule in DNF format is composed of different blocks P_i of predicates that are in logical *OR*, each of these blocks contains one or more predicates p_i that are in logical *AND*. First, the algorithm iterates over the P_i blocks (line 2) and for each of them initializes a set of candidates C_{P_i} (line 3). Then, each simple predicate $p_j \in P_i$ is used to apply a similarity join on the record collection R according to requirements (lines 6-9). The result of a P_i block is given by the intersection of the results provided by each similarity join applied with the predicate $p_j \in P_i$ (lines 10-13). The final candidate set is computed by merge the results of each P_i block (line 14). In the end, the candidates are verified with a verify function that ensures that all predicates are respected (line 15).

Algorithm 2 JoinChain

Input: R collection of records to join
Input: $\mathcal{M}$ matching rule in DNF form
Output: M, the pairs of records that satisfy $\mathcal{M}$
1: $C \leftarrow \{\}$
2: **for each** $P_i \in \mathcal{M}$ **do** //For each block of predicates in or
3: $C_{P_i} \leftarrow \{\}$ //Set of candidate pairs for P_i
4: **for each** $p_j \in P_i$ **do** //For each single predicate in and
5: $C_{p_j} \leftarrow \{\}$ //Set of candidate pairs for p_j
6: **if** $p_i.type = ED$ **then**
7: $C_{p_j} \leftarrow EDJoin(R, p_j)$ //Get candidate pairs with EDJoin
8: **else**
9: $C_{p_j} \leftarrow PPJoin(R, p_j)$ //Get candidate pairs with PPJoin
10: **if** $C_{P_i}.isEmpty$ **then** //Intersects candidates with previous ones
11: $C_{P_i} \leftarrow C_{p_i}$
12: **else**
13: $C_{P_i} \leftarrow C_{P_i} \cap C_{p_j}$
14: $C \leftarrow C \cup C_{P_i}$ //Merge candidates with previous ones
15: **return** $verify(C, \mathcal{M})$

3.2 The RulER Algorithm

Algorithm 2 has three main drawbacks:

(i) the *intersect* operation (line 13) is expensive in MapReduce-like systems, because it generates *shuffle*;

(ii) a predicate is independently checked by the others. For example, given a matching rule $M = (C1 \wedge C2) \vee (C3 \wedge C4)$ in which each Cx is a similarity join predicate (e.g., Jaccard Similarity $title \geq 0.8$). A pair $\langle r_i, r_j \rangle$ is probed with all predicates even if it fails/passes one of them. For example, if the pair passes the predicate $(C3 \wedge C4)$ it is not necessary to probe it with $(C1 \wedge C2)$. Or, if it fails with the predicate $C1$ it is not necessary to probe it with $C2, C3$.

(iii) Vernica Join [14], employed in the implementation of *JoinChain* algorithm (Algorithm 2 lines 7, 9), produces duplicates [6] that have to be removed. If a pair of records appears in more prefix entries, it is processed and emitted multiple times (Algorithm 1 lines 3-7).

We solved these problems in our *RulER* algorithm. The main intuition of *RulER* is to exploit the prefix indexes—one prefix index for each predicate of the matching rule—to build a graph structure, which is then employed to iterate over the records (the nodes of the graph), efficiently applying the rules and to keep only the candidates (the edges of the graph) that pass the whole rule. In other words, *RulER* adopts a record-based parallelization approach; in contrast to the existing algorithms, which adopt a prefix-based parallelization approach on a single predicate at a time.

The *RulER* matching rule execution algorithm is outlined in Algorithm 3. The algorithm takes as input a collection of records and a record-level matching rule $\mathcal{M}$ and gives as output the set of record pairs that satisfy $\mathcal{M}$. Recall that $\mathcal{M}$ is in DNF, i.e., it is composed of sets of predicates P_j in *logical or*, each set P_j contains predicates p_k in *logical and*. First of all, the values of attributes are converted into sets of elements (Line 1) according to the matching rule requirements (e.g., n-grams, trigrams, tokens, etc.); then the prefix indexes are built to find the candidate pairs (line 2)—one prefix index is needed for each predicate p_k of the matching rule. The prefix indexes are sent in broadcast to each node (line 3) to be available to each computational node (called *worker*). Then, each worker iterates over its portion of records (lines 5-6), and performs the following operations for each record r_i. First, a set of candidates for r_i is initialized as an empty set C_{r_i} (line 7). Second, for each set P_j, a set of candidates C_{P_j} is initialized as an empty set (lines 8-9) and for each $p_k \in P_j$ the candidates C_{r_i,p_k} that can match with r_i are extracted using the prefix indexes (lines 10-11). Third, the candidates C_{r_i,p_k} are pruned by removing those that already passed one of the previous P_j set of predicates (line 14), and those that did not passed previous $p_k \in P_j$ predicates (lines 15-16). Fourth, the retained candidates are probed with other filters that further improve the efficiency of the overall process (e.g., length filter, position filter, etc. [16,15]) according to the rule (line 18). Since p_k is in *logical and* with the previous predicates, only the candidates

https://spark.apache.org/docs/2.1.0/programming-guide.html#shuffle-operations

Algorithm 3 RulER

Input: R collection of records to join
Input: $\mathcal{M}$ matching rule in DNF
Output: C, the pairs of records that satisfy $\mathcal{M}$

1: $R_T \leftarrow getElements(R, \mathcal{M})$
2: $I \leftarrow buildPrefixIndexes(R_T, \mathcal{M})$
3: **broadcast**(I)
4: $C \leftarrow \{\}$ //Candidate pairs
5: **map partition** $part \in R_T$
6: **for each** $r_i \in part$ **do**
7: $C_{r_i} \leftarrow \{\}$ //Candidates for r_i
8: **for each** $P_j \in \mathcal{M}$ **do** //For each set of predicates in logical or
9: $C_{P_j} \leftarrow \{\}$ //Candidates that satisfy P_j
10: **for each** $p_k \in P_j$ **do** //For each predicate in logical and
11: $C_{r_i,p_k} \leftarrow I(p_k, r_i)$ //Gets the candidates from the prefix index
12: /*Removes candidates that already passed previous predicates in *or*
13: and those that did not pass previous predicates in *and**/
14: $C_{r_i,p_k} \leftarrow C_{r_i,p_k} - C_{r_i}$
15: **if** $C_{P_j} \neq \emptyset$ **then**
16: $C_{r_i,p_k} \leftarrow C_{r_i,p_k} \cap C_{P_j}$
17: /*Applies filters (length, positional, ...)*/
18: $C_{P_j} \leftarrow applyFilters(r_i, C_{r_i,p_k}, p_k)$
19: $C_{r_i} \leftarrow C_{r_i} \cup C_{P_j}$
20: $C.append(C_{r_i})$
21: **return** $verify(C, \mathcal{M})$

that pass the filters are kept. The resulting candidates from P_j are added to C_{r_i} (line 20). Finally, the candidates are verified (line 21).

Given a matching rule $R = (C1 \wedge C2 \wedge C3) \vee (C4 \wedge C5)$, in which each Cx is a similarity join predicate (e.g., Jaccard Similarity *title* ≥ 0.8); an example of how *RulER* executes R is outlined in Figure 4. First, a prefix index is built on the basis of the record-level matching rules expressed in the main matching rule R. Then, the index is distributed to each worker. Each worker iterates over each record in its partition extracting the possible candidates from the prefix index. The rules are applied to each candidate. If more rules are in *or* it is possible to avoid computing the other rules when one of them is verified, e.g., with $\langle r1, r2\rangle$ the rule $(C1 \wedge C2 \wedge C3)$ is not verified since the pair passes the rule $(C4 \wedge C5)$. Otherwise, if more rules are in *and*, it is possible to avoid the computation when one of them fails, for example for the pair $\langle r1, r3\rangle$, C2 fails, so C3 has not to be computed.

4 Experimental Evaluation

In this section we evaluate *RulER* with respect to *JoinChain* (see Section 3). In particular, the experimental evaluation aims to answer the following questions:

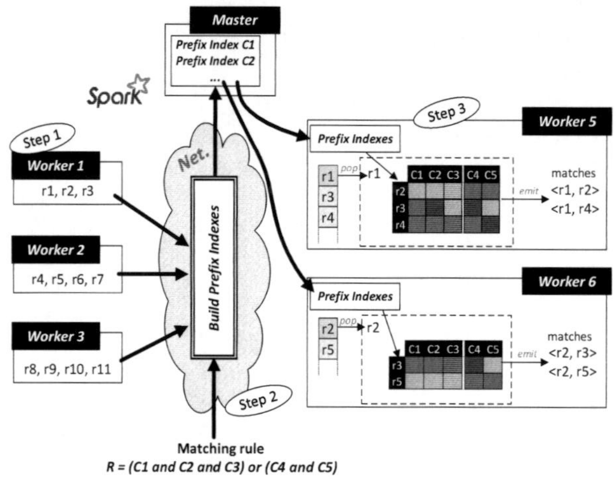

Fig. 4. *RulER* execution model: green cells represents executed and passed rules; red cells executed that do not pass the rules; grey cells not executed rules.

*Q*1: *What is the performance of RulER in terms of execution time compared to JoinChain (i.e., the naïve solution)?* (Section 4.2)

*Q*2: *How does RulER scale when varying the number of machines available for the record-level matching rule processing?* (Section 4.3)

4.1 Experimental Setup

All the experiments are performed on a ten-node cluster; each node has two Intel Xeon E5-2670v2 2.50 GHz (20 cores per node) and 128 GB of RAM, running Ubuntu 14.04. All the software is implemented in Scala 2.11.8 and available at [8]. To assess the performance of the state-of-the-art meta-blocking methods we re-implemented all of them for running on Apache Spark as well. We employ Apache Spark 2.1.0, running 3 executors on each node, reserving 30 GB of memory for

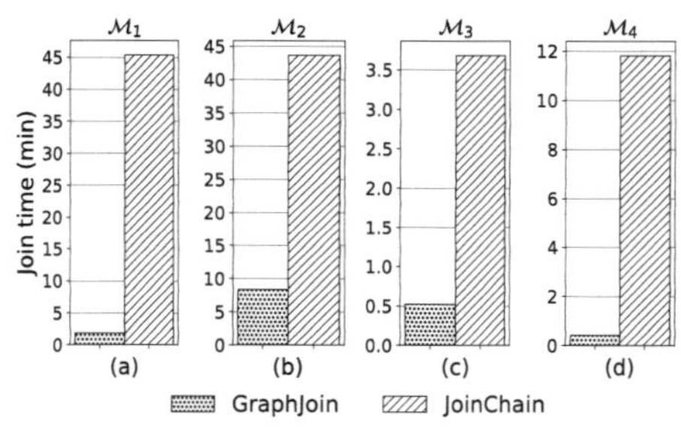

Fig. 5. Execution times of *RulER* and *JoinChain* with the rules reported in Table 1.

the master node. We set the default parallelism to twice the number of cores as suggested by best practice.

We employed the ombd data set [5] to evaluate the performance of *RulER* and *JoinChain*. It contains 2.3 millions of records about movies collected from *omdbapi.com*. This data set has a good variety of attributes (e.g., title, cast, director, writer, plot, etc.) on which it is possible to define a different kind of record-level matching rules. Moreover, it contains a sufficient number of records that make it suitable to test the performance with Spark.

The goal of our experiments is to compare the efficiency of the algorithms, not to find good matching rules. Moreover, with *RulER* it would be possible to define an order for the application of the predicates that minimize the execution time and the number of performed comparisons, but we do not explore this aspect in this work.

4.2 *RulER* vs *JoinChain*

The goal of this experiment is to compare the efficiency of *RulER* (Algorithm 3) and *JoinChain*(Algorithm 2). Both algorithms can be employed to apply a record-level matching rule $\mathcal{M}$. In this experiment we apply the rules presented in Table 1 on the omdb data set. Since both algorithms use the same functions to extract the elements from the records, to generate the prefix indexes and to verify the candidate pairs, we analyze here only the time requested to perform the *join* operation. All the experiments are performed on a single node.

Figure 5 reports the execution times of *RulER* and *JoinChain*with the rules reported in Table 1. *RulER* is always significantly faster than *JoinChain*: 24× with $\mathcal{M}_1$ (Figure 5(a)), 5× with $\mathcal{M}_2$ (Figure 5(b)), 7× with $\mathcal{M}_3$ (Figure 5(c)), 27× with $\mathcal{M}_4$ (Figure 5(d)). Moreover, Figure 6 shows the number of comparisons performed by both algorithms. Also in this case, *RulER* works better than *JoinChain* performing less comparisons: $21.6 \cdot 10^6$ less for $\mathcal{M}_1$ (Figure 6(a)), $23.0 \cdot 10^6$ less for $\mathcal{M}_2$ (Figure 6(b)), $3.8 \cdot 10^6$ less for $\mathcal{M}_3$ (Figure 6(c)), $45.1 \cdot 10^6$ less for $\mathcal{M}_3$ (Figure 6(d)).

We conclude that *RulER* is always faster than *JoinChain*.

https://spark.apache.org/docs/latest/tuning.html

	Rule	**Candidates**	**Matches**
$\mathcal{M}_1$	$(Title, 0.9, JS) \wedge (Cast, 0.8, JS)$	1725885	53023
$\mathcal{M}_2$	$(Title, 0.9, JS) \vee (Cast, 0.8, JS)$	990278774	253593213
$\mathcal{M}_3$	$((Cast, 0.9, JS) \wedge (Director, 0.9, JS) \wedge (Writer, 0.9, JS)) \vee (Title, 0.9, JS)$	61987445	34798235
$\mathcal{M}_4$	$(Director, 0.9, JS) \wedge (Title, 2, ED)$	1133134	252935

Table 1. Matching rules employed in the experiments. For each rule the number of candidate pairs obtained after the filters (i.e., prefix filter, length filter, positional filter, see Section 2) is reported, together with the number of final matching pairs.

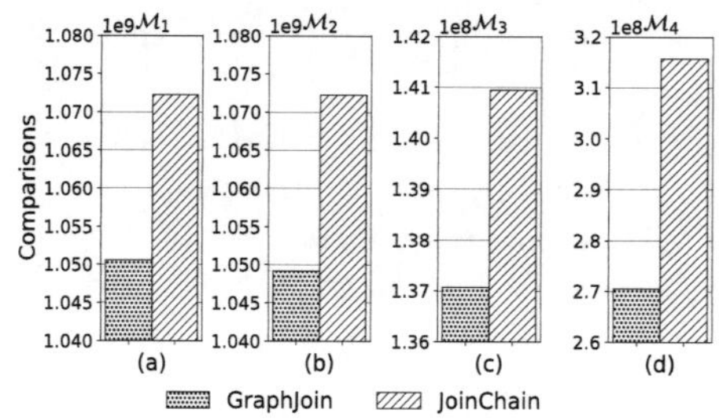

Fig. 6. Number of comparisons performed by *RulER* and *JoinChain* with the rules reported in Table 1.

4.3 *RulER* scalability

Finally, we assess the scalability of *RulER* by varying the number of nodes in the cluster (1, 3, 5, 7 and 10 nodes). For this experiment we apply the rules described in Table 1 on the `omdb` data set.

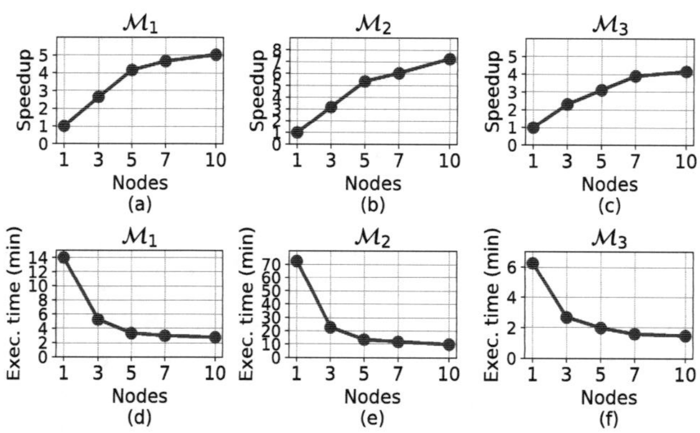

Fig. 7. Execution time and speedup of *RulER* with the rules reported in Table 1.

Figure 7 shows the scalability and the speedup of the whole process. For each step, we observe at least a 50% reduction of execution time from 1 to 3 nodes. Then, the execution times continuously decrease until reaching an overall speedup on 10 nodes of: 5.0× for $\mathcal{M}_1$, 7.3× for $\mathcal{M}_2$, and 4.16× for $\mathcal{M}_3$. $\mathcal{M}_2$ is the rule that takes more advantage in the increase of worker' nodes because it performs more comparisons than the others, as shown in Table 1.

5 Conclusion

In this work, We tackled the problem of performing record-level matching rules. We presented two solutions to perform them on parallel and distributed systems:

a baseline one (i.e. *JoinChain*) implemented by using existing solutions, and a novel approach (i.e. *RulER*) that optimizes the execution of the rules. We conducted a thorough experimental evaluation, demonstrating the efficiency of the proposed approach, which always outperforms the baseline solution in terms of execution time and number of comparisons. In the future, we plan to extend our system to automatically find the optimal execution order of the predicates that compose a rule.

References

1. Arasu, A., Ganti, V., Kaushik, R.: Efficient exact set-similarity joins. In: Proceedings of the 32nd international conference on Very large data bases. pp. 918–929. VLDB Endowment (2006)
2. Ardalan, A., Doan, A., Akella, A., et al.: Smurf: self-service string matching using random forests. PVLDB **12**(3), 278–291 (2018)
3. Bayardo, R.J., Ma, Y., Srikant, R.: Scaling up all pairs similarity search. In: Proceedings of the 16th international conference on World Wide Web. pp. 131–140. ACM (2007)
4. Chaudhuri, S., Ganti, V., Kaushik, R.: A primitive operator for similarity joins in data cleaning. In: 22nd International Conference on Data Engineering (ICDE'06). pp. 5–5. IEEE (2006)
5. Das, S., Doan, A., G. C., P.S., Gokhale, C., Konda, P.: The magellan data repository. https://sites.google.com/site/anhaidgroup/projects/data
6. Fier, F., Augsten, N., Bouros, P., Leser, U., Freytag, J.C.: Set similarity joins on mapreduce: An experimental survey. Proceedings of the VLDB Endowment **11**(10), 1110–1122 (2018)
7. Gagliardelli, L., Simonini, G., Beneventano, D., Bergamaschi, S.: Sparker: Scaling entity resolution in spark. In: EDBT 2019. pp. 602–605 (2019)
8. Gagliardelli, L., Simonini, G., Zhu, S., Bergamaschi, S.: Sparker: an entity resolution tool for apache spark (2017), `https://github.com/Gaglia88/sparker`
9. Gagliardelli, L., Zhu, S., Simonini, G., Bergamaschi, S.: Bigdedup: a big data integration toolkit for duplicate detection in industrial scenarios. In: 25th International Conference on Transdisciplinary Engineering (TE2018). vol. 7, pp. 1015–1023 (2018)
10. Mann, W., Augsten, N., Bouros, P.: An empirical evaluation of set similarity join techniques. Proceedings of the VLDB Endowment **9**(9), 636–647 (2016)
11. Nargesian, F., Zhu, E., Miller, R.J., Pu, K.Q., Arocena, P.C.: Data lake management: challenges and opportunities. PVLDB **12**(12), 1986–1989 (2019)
12. Simonini, G., Gagliardelli, L., Bergamaschi, S., Jagadish, H.V.: Scaling entity resolution: A loosely schema-aware approach. Inf. Syst. **83**, 145–165 (2019)
13. Simonini, G., Papadakis, G., Palpanas, T., Bergamaschi, S.: Schema-agnostic progressive entity resolution. IEEE TKDE **31**(6), 1208–1221 (2019)
14. Vernica, R., Carey, M.J., Li, C.: Efficient parallel set-similarity joins using mapreduce. In: Proceedings of the 2010 ACM SIGMOD International Conference on Management of data. pp. 495–506. ACM (2010)
15. Xiao, C., Wang, W., Lin, X.: Ed-join: an efficient algorithm for similarity joins with edit distance constraints. PVLDB **1**(1), 933–944 (2008)
16. Xiao, C., Wang, W., Lin, X., Yu, J.X., Wang, G.: Efficient similarity joins for near-duplicate detection. ACM TODS **36**(3), 15 (2011)

Smart Data Exchange
(DISCUSSION PAPER)

Sergio Greco[1], Michele Ianni[1], Elio Masciari[2],
Domenico Saccà[1], and Irina Trubitsyna[1]
elio.masciari@unina.it
{greco, ianni, sacca, trubitsyna}@dimes.unical.it

[1] DIMES-Università della Calabria, 87036 Rende (CS), Italy
[2] DIETI-Università degli Studi di Napoli Federico II, 80125 Napoli (NA), Italy

Abstract. The problem of exchanging data, even considering incomplete and heterogeneous data, has been deeply investigated in the last years. The approaches proposed so far are quite rigid as they refer to fixed schema and/or are based on a deductive approach consisting in the use of a fixed set of (mapping) rules. In this paper we describe a smart data exchange framework integrating deductive and inductive techniques to obtain new knowledge. The use of graph-based representation of source and target data, together with the midway relational database and the extraction of new knowledge allow us to manage dynamic databases where also features of data may change over the time.

1 Introduction

Many proposal have been made for data exchange among heterogeneous sources. However, for the best of our knowledge, no generalization of the consolidated data exchange framework, that supports both the extraction of new knowledge and flexible representation of heterogeneous data has been defined so far. In this paper we describe an extension of the data exchange framework, called *Smart Data Exchange (SDE)*, recently proposed in [13], that addresses these issues. The global scenario is showed in Fig. 1, where (i) *Source*, *Target* and *Midway* are three databases, (ii) $\Sigma_{\mathtt{SM}}$ and $\Sigma_{\mathtt{MT}}$ are extended TGDs (Tuple Generating Dependencies) mapping data from *Source* to *Midway* and standard TGDs mapping data from *Midway* to *Target*, respectively, (iii) $\Sigma_{\mathtt{M}}$ and $\Sigma_{\mathtt{T}}$ are extended TGDs defined over the *Midway* database and standard TGDs and EGDs (Equality Generating Dependencies) defined over the *Target* database, respectively.

The idea is that, by allowing an intermediate database and a richer language to derive new information, as well as information obtained by analyzing data, we may define more powerful and flexible tools for data exchange. To have a flexible and general representation of source and target databases, following the RDF approach, we decided to model them using a graph-based formalism where data are stored into ternary relations. Differently from other formalisms where data are stored into a unique relation [3, 18], we consider multiple ternary relations, but analogously to RDF our graph data consist

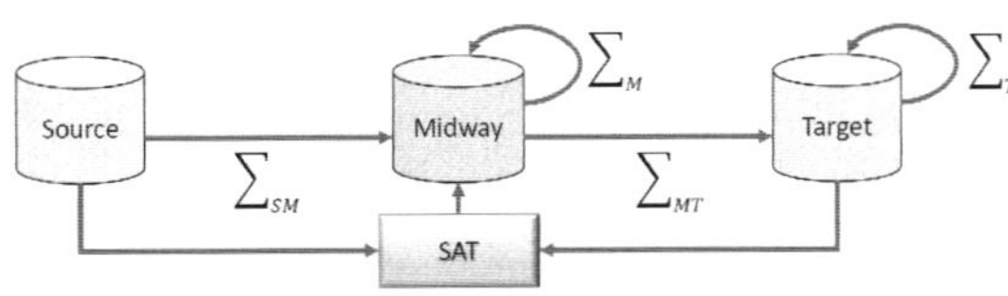

Fig. 1. Architecture

of tuples of the form (i, a, v) with i being a (resource) identifier, a an attribute name and v a value (either a constant or an identifier). The midway database is a relational database containing tuples of any arity that are either imported from the source database using the $\Sigma_{\mathtt{SM}}$ source-midway mapping rules, or are generated by the *Smart Analyzer Tool (SAT)*. Data dependencies denoted by $\Sigma_{\mathtt{M}}$ are used to generate new information useful to enrich the target database. The target database is graph-based and is built by importing data from the midway database using the mapping rules $\Sigma_{\mathtt{MT}}$. Finally, as in the standard data exchange scenario, $\Sigma_{\mathtt{T}}$ consists of a set of TGDs or EGDs.

While we assume that *SAT* is a black-box aiming to produce new data stored in the midway database (in our prototype it implements several data mining algorithms specific for the domain application), the language used to define $\Sigma_{\mathtt{M}}$ is a rich logical language that makes use of comparison predicates, *aggregate predicates* and nondeterministic *choice* constructs (well studied in the past by the community of logic databases). This language allows to obtain more realistic information that could be used in a flexible way by both data experts (for analysis purposes) and inexperienced users (for a better navigation through data). Another peculiarity of our framework is that the data exchange takes also advantages of information (under the form of facts) generated by a data analyzer module and stored into the midway database, together with the data extracted from the source database.

The idea to model data analysis during the data mapping is present in Data Posting framework [8] and its simplified version [19]. Differently from SDE, the framework proposed in [8, 19] does not use graph-based formalisms for source and target data and does not have an intermediate level for data analysis. Moreover, it does not admit the use of existentially quantified variables in the mapping rules and uncertain values in the body of mapping rules can be represented only by means of *non-deterministic* variables, whose values can be selected from specific relations, possibly restricted by target *count constraints*.

2 Background

A *Tuple Generating Dependency (TGD)* is formula of the form: $\forall \mathbf{x}\, \phi(\mathbf{x}) \rightarrow \exists \mathbf{y}\, \psi(\mathbf{x}, \mathbf{y})$, where $\phi(\mathbf{x})$ and $\psi(\mathbf{x}, \mathbf{y})$ are conjunctions of atoms, and $\mathbf{x}, \mathbf{y}$ are lists of variables. *Full TGDs* are TGDs without existentially quantified variables. An *Equality Generating Dependency (EGD)* is a formula of the form: $\forall \mathbf{x}\, \phi(\mathbf{x}) \rightarrow x_1 = x_2$, where $\phi(\mathbf{x})$ is conjunction of atoms, while x_1 and x_2 are variables in $\mathbf{x}$. In our formulae we omit the universal quantifiers, when their presence is clear from the context.

Let $S = S_1, ..., S_n$ and $T = T_1, ..., T_m$ be two disjoint schemas. We refer to S (resp. T) as the source (resp. target) schema and to the S_i's (resp. T_j's) as the source (resp.

target) relation symbols. Instances over S (resp. T) will be called source (resp. target) instances. If I is a source instance and J is a target instance, then we write $\langle I, J\rangle$ for the instance K over the schema $S \cup T$ such that $K(S_i) = I(S_i)$ and $K(T_j) = J(T_j)$, for $i \leq n$ and $j \leq m$.

The data exchange setting [11, 2] is a tuple $(S, T, \Sigma_{st}, \Sigma_t)$, where S is the source schema, T is the target schema, Σ_t are dependencies over T and Σ_{st} are source-to-target TGDs. The dependencies in Σ_{st} map data from the source to the target schema and are TGDs of the form $\forall \mathbf{x}(\, \phi_s(\mathbf{x}) \rightarrow \exists \mathbf{y}\ \psi_t(\mathbf{x}, \mathbf{y})\,)$, where $\phi_s(\mathbf{x})$ and $\psi_t(\mathbf{x}, \mathbf{y})$ are conjunctions of atomic formulas on S and T, respectively. Dependencies in Σ_{st} are also called mapping dependencies. Dependencies in Σ_t specify constraints on the target schema and can be either TGDs or EGDs.

The data exchange problem associated with this setting is the following: given a finite source instance I, find a finite target instance J such that $\langle I, J\rangle$ satisfies Σ_{st} and J satisfies Σ_t. Such a J is called a solution for I. The computation of an universal solution (the compact representation of all possible solutions) can be done by means of the fixpoint chase algorithm, when it terminates [9]. Decidable (sufficient) conditions ensuring chase termination can be found in [16, 6, 15].

Queries over relational database can be expressed using Relational Algebra, or alternative equivalent languages such safe Relational Calculus and safe, nonrecursive Datalog (with negation). To make query languages more expressive, several additional feature have been added to these languages including the possibility to manage bags (SQL), aggregates (SQL), recursion (Datalog), existential variables (Datalog$^{\pm}$) and others.

The choice constructs [20, 17] have been introduced in Datalog to get an increase in expressive power and to obtain simple declarative formulations of classical combinatorial problems, such as those which can be solved by means of greedy algorithms [20].

A *choice atom* is of the form $choice((\mathbf{x}), (\mathbf{y}))$, where $\mathbf{x}$ and $\mathbf{y}$ are lists of variables such that $\mathbf{x} \cap \mathbf{y} = \emptyset$, and can occur in the body of a rule. Its intuitive meaning is to force each initialization of $\mathbf{x}$ to be associated with a unique initialization of $\mathbf{y}$, thus making the result of executing of a corresponding rule nondeterministic. A *choice rule* is of the form: $A(\mathbf{w}) \leftarrow B(\mathbf{z}), choice((\mathbf{x}), (\mathbf{y}))$, where $A(\mathbf{w})$ is an atom, $B(\mathbf{z})$ is a conjunction of atoms, $\mathbf{x}$, $\mathbf{y}$, $\mathbf{z}$ and $\mathbf{w}$ are lists of variables such that $\mathbf{x}, \mathbf{y}, \mathbf{w} \subseteq \mathbf{z}$. The atom $choice((\mathbf{x}), (\mathbf{y}))$ is used to enforce the *functional dependency* $\mathbf{x} \rightarrow \mathbf{y}$ on the set of atoms derived by means of the rule.

The *choice-least* and *choice-most* constructs [17] specialize the choice construct so as to force greedy selections among alternative choices—these turn out to be particularly useful to express classical greedy algorithms. A *choice-least* (resp. *choice-most) atom* is of the form $choice\_least((\mathbf{x}), (c))$ (resp. $choice\_most((\mathbf{x}), (c))$), where $\mathbf{x}$ is a list of variables and c is a single variable ranging over an ordered domain. A $choice\_least((\mathbf{x}), (c))$ (resp. $choice\_most((\mathbf{x}), (c))$) atom in a rule indicates that the functional dependency defined by the atom $choice((\mathbf{x}), (c))$ is to be satisfied, and the c value assigned to a certain value of $\mathbf{x}$ has to be the minimum (resp. maximum) one among the candidate values. The body of a rule may contain even more than one choice constructs, but only one choice-least or choice-most atom. For instance, the rule $\mathtt{p(x, y, c)} \leftarrow \mathtt{q(x, y, c), choice((x), (y)), choice\_least((x), (c))}$ imposes the functional dependency $\mathtt{x} \rightarrow \mathtt{y, c}$ on the possible instances of $\mathtt{p}$. In addition, for each value of x, the minimum among the candidate values of c must be chosen. For instance, assuming that q is defined by the facts q(a, b, 1) and q(a, d, 2), from the rule above we might derive either p(a, b, 1) or p(a, d, 2). However, the choice-least atom introduces the additional requirement that the minimum value on the third attribute has to be chosen, so that only p(a, b, 1) is derived. The formal semantics is defined by rewriting rules with choice atoms into rules with negated literals and selecting (nondeterministically) one of the stable models of the rewritten program [20, 17].

3 Smart Data Exchange

In this section we present the data exchange framework informally discussed in the Introduction. We assume the existence of the following countably infinite sets: *relation names* $\mathcal{R}$, *identifiers* $\mathcal{I}$, *attribute names* $\mathcal{A}$, *constants* $\mathcal{C}$, *nulls* $\mathcal{N}$ and *variables* $\mathcal{V}$. The set of relation symbols (also called predicate symbols) is partitioned into three countable sets denoted by $\mathcal{R}_\mathtt{S}$ (source relations), $\mathcal{R}_\mathtt{T}$ (target relations) and $\mathcal{R}_\mathtt{M}$ (midway relations), whereas $\mathcal{D}_\mathtt{S} = \mathcal{I} \cup \mathcal{A} \cup \mathcal{C}$, $\mathcal{D}_\mathtt{T} = \mathcal{I} \cup \mathcal{A} \cup \mathcal{C} \cup \mathcal{N}$ and $\mathcal{D}_\mathtt{M} = \mathcal{I} \cup \mathcal{A} \cup \mathcal{C}$ denote the domains of relations $\mathcal{R}_\mathtt{S}$, $\mathcal{R}_\mathtt{T}$ and $\mathcal{R}_\mathtt{M}$, respectively. Relations in $\mathcal{R}_\mathtt{S}$ and $\mathcal{R}_\mathtt{T}$ have arity 3 and take values from $\mathcal{I} \times \mathcal{A} \times \mathcal{I} \cup \mathcal{C}$ and $\mathcal{I} \cup \mathcal{N} \times \mathcal{A} \cup \mathcal{N} \times \mathcal{I} \cup \mathcal{C} \cup \mathcal{N}$ respectively, whereas relations in $\mathcal{R}_\mathtt{M}$ may have any arity n and take values from $\mathcal{D}_\mathtt{M}^n$. The main difference between the source and the target databases is that the target database may also have nulls (corresponding to blank nodes in RDF) which are introduced to satisfy constraints. The set of source (resp. target, midway) relations define the source (resp. target, midway) database whose schema is denoted by S (resp. T, M).

The model defined above states that the source and target databases are graph-based databases stored in a relational database (using triples), whereas the midway database is a standard relational database. This choice is due to the fact that we would exchange data among heterogeneous databases and we want model data whose schema may change over the time.

Extended TGDs. An atom is of the form $p(t_1, ..., t_n)$, where $t_1, ..., t_n$ are terms (standard atom), or of the form $t_1 \theta t_2$, where θ is a comparison predicates and t_1, t_2 are terms (built-in atom). A literal is an atom A (positive literal) or its negation $\neg A$ (negative literal). A conjunction of literals is of the form $B_1 \wedge \cdots \wedge B_n$ where $B_1, ..., B_n$ are literals. A conjunction of literals is said to be *safe* if all variables occurring in built-in atoms and negated literals also appear in positive literals. From now on we assume that whenever we consider conjunctions of literals they are safe.

Definition 1. An extended TGD (ETGD) is a universally quantified implication formula of one of the following forms:

- $\varphi(x) \wedge choice(x') \rightarrow \psi(w)$,
  where $\varphi(x)$ is a safe conjunction of standard and built-in literals, $\psi(w)$ is a conjunction of atoms, $w \subseteq x$ and $choice(x')$, with $x' \subseteq x$, is a possibly empty conjunction of *choice*-atoms;
- $\varphi(x) \rightarrow q(w_0, c_1\langle w_1 \rangle, ..., c_n\langle w_n \rangle)$ (called aggregate dependency)
  where $\varphi(x)$ is a safe conjunction of standard and built-in literals, $c_1, ..., c_n$ denote aggregate functions (e.g., $min, max, sum, count$), w_0 (called "group-by" variables) and $w_1, ..., w_n$ are lists of variables such that $w_0, ..., w_n \subseteq x$ and $w_0 \cap w_i = \emptyset$ $\forall i \in [1, n]$. □

For any set Σ of data dependencies, the *dependency graph* $G_\Sigma = (V, E)$ is built as follows: V consists of the predicate symbols occurring in Σ, whereas there is an edge from p to q if there is a dependency having p in the body and q in the head. Moreover, the edge is labeled with $\neg$ (resp. ag) if p occurs negated (resp. occurs in the head atom which contains aggregate functions). A set of dependency is said to be *stratified* if the depencecy graph does not contain cycles with labeled edges. Observe that since standard dependencies are positive (that is, all body literals are positive), to check stratification it is sufficient to check stratification of ETGDs. From now on we assume that our dependencies are stratified.

The semantics of ETGDs with choice atoms can be defined as in the case of Datalog rules. To this end, in order to eliminate head conjunctions, any ETGDs $r : \varphi(x) \rightarrow p_1(y_1) \wedge \cdots \wedge p_k(y_k)$ having $k > 1$ atoms in the head is rewritten into: (i) k ETGDs $r_i : \varphi(x) \rightarrow p_i(y_i)$ $(i \in [1, k])$, if r does not contain choice atoms, and (ii) $k{+}1$ ETGDs $r_0, ..., r_k$ if r contains choice atoms, where $r_0 = \varphi(x) \rightarrow h_r(x)$ and $r_i = h_r(x) \rightarrow p_i(y_i)$ (with $i \in 1, k]$), where h_r is a fresh new predicate. Regarding the semantics of ETGDs with aggregate functions, as the set of ETGDs is stratified, we can partition it into strata so that, if a stratum contains an ETGD with aggregate functions, then it does not contain any other ETGD, and compute one stratum at time following topological order defined over the strata by the dependency graph. The computation of an ETGD with aggregate functions can be carried out in the same way of computing SQL queries with aggregates, as body predicates have been already computed and, therefore, they correspond to database relations in SQL (see also [12]).

Smart data exchange. Now we formally define the Smart Data Exchange Framework.

Definition 2. A *Smart Data Exchange (SDE)* is a tuple $(S, M, T, \Sigma_{\mathtt{SM}}, \Sigma_{\mathtt{MT}}, \Sigma_{\mathtt{M}}, \Sigma_{\mathtt{T}})$, where:

- S is the source schema containing predicates taken from $\mathcal{R}_{\mathtt{S}}$,
- M is the midway schema containing predicates taken from $\mathcal{R}_{\mathtt{M}}$,
- T is the target schema containing predicates taken from $\mathcal{R}_{\mathtt{T}}$,
- $\Sigma_{\mathtt{SM}}$ is a source-to-midway set of safe ETGDs,
- $\Sigma_{\mathtt{M}}$ is a midway-to-midway set of safe, stratified ETGDs,
- $\Sigma_{\mathtt{MT}}$ is a midway-to-target set of standard TGDs, and
- $\Sigma_{\mathtt{T}}$ is a target-to-target set of standard TGDs and standard EGDs. □

As already pointed out, we assume that the source and target relations are graph-based data and every class of objects is modeled as a named set of triples. RDF graph, microdata and JSON representations are very closed to this description [1]. The midway database is a relational database containing relations of any arity including data in the format of the source and target database.

For any SDE $E = \langle S, M, T, \Sigma_{\mathtt{SM}}, \Sigma_{\mathtt{M}}, \Sigma_{\mathtt{MT}}, \Sigma_{\mathtt{T}} \rangle$, we shall use the following notation: $\Sigma_1 = \Sigma_{\mathtt{SM}} \cup \Sigma_{\mathtt{M}}$, $\Sigma_2 = \Sigma_{\mathtt{MT}} \cup \Sigma_{\mathtt{T}}$, and $\Sigma = \Sigma_1 \cup \Sigma_2$.

Example 1. Consider a graph relation in the source database containing facts of the form $\mathtt{graph}(\mathtt{id}_1, \mathtt{edge}, \mathtt{id}_2)$ where $\mathtt{id}_1$ and $\mathtt{id}_2$ are node identifiers and edge is an attribute value denoting that there is an edge from $\mathtt{id}_1$ to $\mathtt{id}_2$. The data exchange problem consists in extracting a spanning tree to be stored in the target database. From the source database we can import edges and nodes in the midway database, as defined in the set

$\Sigma_{\texttt{SM}}$ consisting of the ETGD: $\texttt{graph}(\texttt{x}, \texttt{edge}, \texttt{y}) \rightarrow \texttt{edge}(\texttt{x}, \texttt{y}) \wedge \texttt{node}(\texttt{x}) \wedge \texttt{node}(\texttt{y})$. Assume now that the midway database also contains a fact $\texttt{root}(0)$, for instance generated by the SAT module or imported from the source database using another source-to-midway dependency. The next set of ETGDs $\Sigma_{\texttt{M}}$ shows how it is possible to generate a spanning tree rooted in the node x denoted by fact $\texttt{root}(\texttt{x})$.

$$\begin{array}{l} \texttt{root}(\texttt{x}) \rightarrow \texttt{st}(\texttt{nil}, \texttt{x}) \\ \texttt{st}(\texttt{z}, \texttt{x}) \wedge \texttt{edge}(\texttt{x}, \texttt{y}), \texttt{choice}((\texttt{y}), (\texttt{x})), \rightarrow \texttt{st}(\texttt{x}, \texttt{y}) \wedge \texttt{connected}(\texttt{y}) \\ \texttt{node}(\texttt{x}) \wedge \neg\texttt{connected}(\texttt{x}), \texttt{choice}((), (\texttt{x})) \rightarrow \texttt{nextRoot}(\texttt{x}) \end{array}$$

Here the first ETGD is used to start the computation by deriving an edge ending in the root node (the starting node is the dummy node nil), whereas the second ETGD, imposing the functional dependency $\texttt{y} \rightarrow \texttt{x}$, guarantees that the set of selected nodes is a spanning tree. The last ETGD in $\Sigma_{\texttt{M}}$ gives a node not belonging to the spanning tree if the graph is not connected; this node can be used in the future as a root to compute another spanning tree.

Spanning tree edges and nextRoot facts are then imported in the target database (as triples) using the below set of TGDs $\Sigma_{\texttt{MT}}$:

$$\begin{array}{l} \texttt{st}(\texttt{x}, \texttt{y}) \rightarrow \texttt{graph}(\texttt{x}, \texttt{st}, \texttt{y}) \\ \texttt{nextRoot}(\texttt{x}) \rightarrow \exists \texttt{y}\ \texttt{graph}(\texttt{nil}, \texttt{root}, \texttt{x}) \end{array}$$

Information stored in the target database are next analyzed to generate new information which will be stored in the midway database. For instance, from a fact $\texttt{graph}(\texttt{nil}, \texttt{root}, \texttt{x})$ the SAT module could generate a fact $\texttt{root}(\texttt{x})$ which, after been stored in the midway database, could generate the computation of another spanning tree rooted in x. □

Note that the process described in the previous example and showed in Fig. 1 is supervised, that is the activation of the module SAT is performed by the user.

The smart data exchange problem associated with this setting is the following: given a finite source instance I over a schema S and a smart data exchange $E = (S, M, T, \Sigma_{\texttt{SM}}, \Sigma_{\texttt{M}}, \Sigma_{\texttt{MT}}, \Sigma_{\texttt{T}})$, find finite instances J and K over the schemas M and T, respectively, such that $\langle I, J\rangle$ satisfies $\Sigma_{\texttt{SM}}$, J satisfies $\Sigma_{\texttt{M}}$, $\langle J, K\rangle$ satisfies $\Sigma_{\texttt{MT}}$ and K satisfies $\Sigma_{\texttt{M}}$. The pair $\langle J, K\rangle$ is called a solution (or model) for $\langle I, E\rangle$, or equivalently for $\langle I, \Sigma\rangle$, where let $\Sigma_1 = \Sigma_{\texttt{SM}} \cup \Sigma_{\texttt{M}}$ and $\Sigma_2 = \Sigma_{\texttt{MT}} \cup \Sigma_{\texttt{T}}$, $\Sigma = \Sigma_1 \cup \Sigma_2$. The set of solutions for $\langle I, E\rangle$ (or equivalently for $\langle I, \Sigma\rangle$) is denoted by $Sol(I, E)$, (resp. $Sol(I, \Sigma)$). Moreover, J is also called solution (or model) for $\langle I, \Sigma_1\rangle$ and, in cascade, K is a solution (or model) for $\langle J, \Sigma_2\rangle$. Thus, the problem of finding solutions can be split into two problems: (i) finding a solutions J for I, and (ii) finding solutions K for J. The set of solutions for $\langle I, \Sigma_1\rangle$ is denoted by $Sol(I, \Sigma_1)$, whereas the set of solutions for $\langle J, \Sigma_2\rangle$ is $Sol(J, \Sigma_2)$. Therefore, given a smart data exchange framework, starting from I with dependency Σ_1 we find solutions $J_1, ..., J_m$ and, then starting from every J_i $(1 \leq i \leq m)$ with dependency Σ_2 we find solutions $K_{i_1}, ..., K_{i_n}$. Observe that m is always finite, whereas i_n, in the general case, is not guaranteed to be finite [10].

Query answering. Since we have multiple models, we distinguish the *certain answer* derived from all models and the *nondeterministic answer*.

Definition 3. *Given a query* Q*, a database* I *and an SDE* E*, the certain answer of* Q *over* $\langle I, E\rangle$ *is* $Certain(Q, I, E) = \bigcap_{\langle J,K\rangle \in Sol(I,E)} Q(K)$. □

Since the certain answer could be equivalently defined as $Certain(Q, I, E) = \bigcap_{J \in Sol(I,\Sigma_1) \wedge K \in Sol(J,\Sigma_2)} Q(K)$, its computation can be optimized by considering the four sets of dependencies separately, that is by first computing solutions J' for $\langle I, \Sigma_{\mathtt{ST}}\rangle$, then solutions J for $\langle J', \Sigma_{\mathtt{M}}\rangle$, next solutions K' for $\langle J, \Sigma_{\mathtt{MT}}\rangle$, and, finally solutions K for $\langle K', \Sigma_{\mathtt{T}}\rangle$. Let us now introduce the concepts of homomorphism and universal model.

A *homomorphism* from a set of atoms A_1 to a set of atoms A_2 is a mapping h from the domain of A_1 (set of terms occurring in A_1) to the domain of A_2 such that: (i) $h(c) = c$, for every $c \in \mathsf{Const}(A_1)$; and (ii) for every atom $R(t_1, \ldots, t_n)$ in A_1, we have that $R(h(t_1), \ldots, h(t_n))$ is in A_2. With a slight abuse of notation, we apply h also to sets of atoms and thus, for a given set of atoms A, we define $h(A) = \{R(h(t_1), \ldots, h(t_n)) \mid R(t_1, \ldots, t_n) \in A\}$.

Definition 4. A *universal model* of (I, Σ) is a model $\langle J, K\rangle$ of (I, Σ) such that for every model $\langle J', K'\rangle$ of (I, Σ) there exists a homomorphism from K to K'. The set of all universal solutions of (I, Σ) will be denoted by $USol(I, \Sigma)$. □

Proposition 1. *For any positive query* Q*, database* I *and SDE* E*, the certain answer of* Q *over* $\langle I, E\rangle$ *is* $Certain(Q, I, E) = \bigcap_{J \in Sol(I, \Sigma_1)} Q(K_J)_\downarrow$*, where* K_J *is any universal solution of* $\langle J, \Sigma_2\rangle$ *and* $Q(K_J)_\downarrow$ *is the result of computing naively (i.e. considering nulls as constants)* $Q(K_J)$ *and deleting tuples with nulls.* □

Universal solutions for $\langle J, \Sigma_2\rangle$ can be easily computed by applying the classical fixpoint algorithm called *Chase* which computes a subset of universal solutions called *canonical* [4, 10].

As previously discussed, in several cases we are not interested in all models of $\langle I, \Sigma_1\rangle$, but only in one selected nondeterministically (e.g. the set of edges of any minimum spanning tree). Thus, we now introduce the definition of *nondeterminitic answer*.

Definition 5. The *nondeterministic answer* to a query Q over a database instance I and SDE $E = (S, M, T, \Sigma_{\mathtt{SM}}, \Sigma_{\mathtt{M}}, \Sigma_{\mathtt{MT}}, \Sigma_{\mathtt{T}})$ is $NonDet(Q, I, E) = \bigcap_{K \in Sol(J, \Sigma_2)} Q(K)$, where, J is a model for $\langle I, \Sigma_1\rangle$ selected nondeterministically. □

Observe that the nondeterministic choice of the model is applied only to dependencies in Σ_1, where users express explicitly that they want select nondeterministically a subset of tuples, whereas for $\langle J, \Sigma_2\rangle$ we consider all models. Note that, two evaluations of the nondeterministic answers could give different answers (as the choices made could be different) and that the responsibility of computing nondeterministic answers, instead of certain answers, is left to the user. Indeed, in several cases the user is not interested in specific models, but only in one model satisfying some properties (e.g. any spanning tree). Therefore, we introduce the concept of universal nondeterministc model.

Definition 6. A *universal nondeterministic model* for $\langle I, \Sigma\rangle$ is any universal model in $USol(D, \Sigma)$ selected nondeterministically. □

Proposition 2. *For any positive query* Q*, database* I *and SDE* $E = (S, M, T, \Sigma_{\mathtt{SM}}, \Sigma_{\mathtt{M}}, \Sigma_{\mathtt{MT}}, \Sigma_{\mathtt{T}})$*, the nondeterministic answer of* Q *over* $\langle I, E\rangle$ *is* $NonDet(Q, I, E) = Q(K_J)_\downarrow$*, where, let* J *be any model for* $\langle I, \Sigma_1\rangle$ *selected nondeterministically,* K_J *is a universal solution of* $\langle J, \Sigma_2\rangle$ □

4 Conclusion

In this paper we have discussed a framework supporting both analysis and flexible representation of heterogeneous data. The use of graph-based representation of source and target data, together with the extraction of new knowledge made by the SAT tool allow us to manage dynamic databases where also features of data may change over the time. The theoretical complexity of the approach is discussed in [13]. Future work should include the use of more powerful declarative languages for the midway, where limited use of function symbols is allowed [5, 7, 14].

References

1. R. Angles and C. Gutierrez. An introduction to graph data management. In *Graph Data Management, Fundamental Issues and Recent Developments.*, pages 1–32. 2018.
2. M. Arenas, P. Barceló, R. Fagin, and L. Libkin. Locally consistent transformations and query answering in data exchange. In *PODS*, 2004.
3. M. Arenas, G. Gottlob, and A. Pieris. Expressive languages for querying the semantic web. *ACM Trans. Database Syst.*, 43(3):13:1–13:45, 2018.
4. C. Beeri and M. Y. Vardi. A proof procedure for data dependencies. *J. ACM*, 31(4):718–741, 1984.
5. M. Calautti, S. Greco, C. Molinaro, and I. Trubitsyna. Logic program termination analysis using atom sizes. In *IJCAI*, pages 2833–2839. AAAI Press, 2015.
6. M. Calautti, S. Greco, C. Molinaro, and I. Trubitsyna. Exploiting equality generating dependencies in checking chase termination. *PVLDB*, 9(5):396–407, 2016.
7. M. Calautti, S. Greco, F. Spezzano, and I. Trubitsyna. Checking termination of bottom-up evaluation of logic programs with function symbols. *TPLP*, 15(6):854–889, 2015.
8. N. Cassavia, E. Masciari, C. Pulice, and D. Saccà. Discovering user behavioral features to enhance information search on big data. *TiiS*, 7(2):7:1–7:33, 2017.
9. A. Deutsch, A. Nash, and J. B. Remmel. The chase revisited. In *PODS*, 2008.
10. R. Fagin, P. G. Kolaitis, R. J. Miller, and L. Popa. Data exchange: semantics and query answering. *Theoretical Computer Science*, 336(1):89–124, 2005.
11. R. Fagin, P. G. Kolaitis, and L. Popa. Data Exchange: getting to the core. *ACM Trans. Database Syst.*, 30(1):174–210, 2005.
12. S. Greco. Dynamic programming in datalog with aggregates. *IEEE Trans. Knowl. Data Eng.*, 11(2):265–283, 1999.
13. S. Greco, E. Masciari, D. Saccà, and I. Trubitsyna. HIKE: A step beyond data exchange. In *ER Conference*, 2019.
14. S. Greco, C. Molinaro, and I. Trubitsyna. Logic programming with function symbols: Checking termination of bottom-up evaluation through program adornments. *Theory Pract. Log. Program.*, 13(4-5):737–752, 2013.
15. S. Greco, F. Spezzano, and I. Trubitsyna. Stratification criteria and rewriting techniques for checking chase termination. *PVLDB*, 4(11):1158–1168, 2011.
16. S. Greco, F. Spezzano, and I. Trubitsyna. Checking chase termination: Cyclicity analysis and rewriting techniques. *IEEE Trans. Knowl. Data Eng.*, 27(3):621–635, 2015.
17. S. Greco and C. Zaniolo. Greedy algorithms in datalog. *TPLP*, 1(4):381–407, 2001.
18. L. Libkin, J. L. Reutter, A. Soto, and D. Vrgoc. Trial: A navigational algebra for RDF triplestores. *ACM Trans. Database Syst.*, 43(1):5:1–5:46, 2018.
19. E. Masciari, I. Trubitsyna, and D. Saccà. Simplified data posting in practice. In *IDEAS*, pages 29:1–29:7, 2019.
20. D. Saccà and C. Zaniolo. Stable models and non-determinism in logic programs with negation. In *Proc. PODS Conf.*, pages 205–217, 1990.

Lattice-based Discovery of Hybrid Relaxed Functional Dependencies (Discussion Paper)

Loredana Caruccio, Vincenzo Deufemia, and Giuseppe Polese

University of Salerno, Department of Computer Science
via Giovanni Paolo II n.132, 84084 Fisciano (SA), Italy
{lcaruccio,deufemia,gpolese}@unisa.it

Abstract. Relaxed functional dependencies (RFDs) are properties expressing important relationships among data. Thanks to the introduction of approximations in data comparison and/or validity, they can capture constraints useful for several purposes, such as the identification of data inconsistencies or patterns of semantically related data. Nevertheless, RFDs can provide benefits only if they can be automatically discovered from data. In this discussion paper we present an RFD discovery algorithm relying on a lattice structured search space, and a new candidate RFD validation method. An experimental evaluation demonstrates the discovery performances of the proposed algorithm on real datasets.

Keywords: Functional Dependency · Discovery Algorithm · Approximate Match · Constraint Mining.

1 Introduction

Functional dependencies (FDs) were originally used to verify database design and assess schema quality. In the last decades, they have been used for several new purposes, such as data profiling [1], query relaxation, data cleansing, and so forth. To this end, their definition has been often extended in order to express constraints in these and other emerging application domains [7].

Recent literature refers to extended FD definitions with the term *relaxed functional dependencies* (RFDs) [3]. In particular, there exist RFDs relaxing on the data comparison, which compare tuples by using data similarity rather than equality, those relaxing on the *extent*, which admit the possibility for the RFD to hold only on a subset of data, and finally, hybrid ones, which relax on both criteria. Thresholds might be used in all categories, either to specify the similarity degree or the minimum percentage of tuples on which the RFD should hold.

In order to exploit FDs in practical domains several algorithms to discover them from data have been proposed [2,16]. However, RFDs are much more complex to specify at design time, since they also require the specification of thresholds for evaluating the similarity between attribute values and/or for deriving the minimum extent.

In this discussion paper, we describe the algorithm proposed in [6], namely DIMε, which is able to mine many different types of RFDs, relaxing on the tuple comparison and/or on the extent by using several tuple comparison methods and coverage measures [3]. The discovery technique underlying DIMε generates candidate RFDs based on Difference Matrices created from input thresholds, and on a lattice structure, also used within FD discovery algorithms [2], in order to model the search space. Moreover, DIMε provides a new validation technique.

The paper is organized as follows. Section 2 reviews the RFD discovery algorithms existing in the literature. Section 3 provides some background definitions concerning RFDs. Section 4 presents the DIMε algorithm, whereas Section 5 shows the experimental results. Concluding remarks are included in Section 6.

2 Related Work

The automatic discovery of FDs is accomplished either through column-based or row-based methods [1]. The former start generating candidate FDs based on an attribute lattice, verifying their validity, and then using holding FDs to prune the search space for candidate FDs yet to be verified [2]; the latter compare attribute values for each pair of tuples, in order to generate two different sets of attribute subsets, namely *agree-sets* and *difference-sets*, from which candidate FDs are derived [8,16]. Finally, an hybrid algorithm has been proposed in [12]. With respect to these algorithms, DIMε discovers a broader class of dependencies beyond FDs, which entails much more a complex validation phase. In fact, the validation of FDs merely requires to compute cardinalities of equivalence classes, whereas the validation of RFDs requires more complex computations on intersecting classes induced by similarity functions.

Several discovery algorithms have been proposed for *Matching dependencies*, e.g., [15], and *Differential Dependencies*, e.g., [14], two examples of RFD relaxing on attribute comparison. While these discovery algorithms are each focused on a specific RFD, DIMε is designed for a more generic class of RFDs [4], including RFDs relaxing on the tuple comparison method, those relaxing on the extent, and finally, hybrid ones relaxing on both.

3 Relaxed Functional Dependencies

Informally, an RFD is a functional dependency that relaxes on the tuple comparison, by using constraints on the distance or similarity between attribute values, and/or that relaxes on the extent, by using a coverage measure to indicate the minimum number or percentage of tuples on which the RFD must hold, and/or by using conditions restricting the applicability domain of the RFD. In what follows, we recall a formal definition of RFD from our previous survey [3].

Definition 1 (Relaxed functional dependency). *Consider a relational database schema $\mathcal{R}$, and a relation schema $R = (A_1, \ldots, A_m)$ of $\mathcal{R}$. An* RFD *φ on $\mathcal{R}$ is denoted by*

$$X_{\Phi_1} \xrightarrow{\Psi \le \varepsilon} Y_{\Phi_2} \tag{1}$$

where

- $X = X_1, \ldots, X_h$ *and* $Y = Y_1, \ldots, Y_k$, *with* $X, Y \subseteq attr(R)$ *and* $X \cap Y = \varnothing$;
- $\Phi_1 = \bigwedge_{X_i \in X} \phi_i[X_i]$ ($\Phi_2 = \bigwedge_{Y_j \in Y} \phi_j[Y_j]$, *resp.), where* ϕ_i (ϕ_j, *resp.) is a conjunction of predicates on* X_i (Y_j, *resp.) with* $i = 1, \ldots, h$ ($j = 1, \ldots, k$, *resp.). For any pair of tuples* (t_1, t_2)$\in dom(R)$, *the constraint* Φ_1 (Φ_2, *resp.) is true if* $t_1[X_i]$ *and* $t_2[X_i]$ ($t_1[Y_j]$ *and* $t_2[Y_j]$, *resp.) satisfy the constraint* ϕ_i (ϕ_j, *resp.)* $\forall\ i \in [1, h]$ ($j \in [1, k]$, *resp.).*
- Ψ *is a coverage measure defined on* $dom(R)$, *quantifying the amount of tuples violating or satisfying* φ. *Among the most commonly used coverage measures there are the confidence, the* $g3$-error, *and the probability.*
- ε *is a threshold indicating the upper bound (or lower bound in case the comparison operator is* $\geq$*) for the result of the coverage measure.*

Given $r \subseteq dom(R)$ a relation instance on R, r *satisfies* the RFD φ, denoted by $r \vDash \varphi$, if and only if: $\forall\ t_1, t_2 \in r$, if Φ_1 indicates true, then *almost always* Φ_2 indicates true. Here, *almost always* is expressed by the constraint $\Psi \leq \varepsilon$. A more general definition of RFD is provided in [3].

As an example, in a database of scientific publications it is likely to have the same address and affiliation for authors with the same name. Thus, an FD {Author} → {Address, Affiliation} might hold. However, these attributes might have been stored using different abbreviations, hence the following RFD might hold: $\mathsf{Author}_{\phi_1} \rightarrow \{\mathsf{Address}_{\phi_2}, \mathsf{Affiliation}_{\phi_3}\}$, where ϕ_1, ϕ_2, and ϕ_3 are constraints on a string similarity function. Moreover, since authors might change affiliation during their life, or there might be homonimies, the previous RFD should tolerate possible exceptions. This can be modeled by the following RFD:

$$\mathsf{Author}_{\phi_1} \xrightarrow{\psi(Author, Address, Affiliation) \leq 0.02} \{\mathsf{Address}_{\phi_2}, \mathsf{Affiliation}_{\phi_3}\}$$

4 The DiMε Discovery Algorithm

The discovery of RFDs is the problem of finding a set of *minimal* RFDs holding on a relation instance r. An RFD $X_{\Phi_1} \xrightarrow{\Psi \leq \varepsilon} Y_{\Phi_2}$ is *minimal* if there not exists a subset $Z \subset X$ such that $Z_{\Phi_1} \xrightarrow{\Psi \leq \varepsilon} Y_{\Phi_2}$ holds on r.

For sake of simplicity and w.l.o.g, in the rest of the article we assume that Y consists of a single attribute.

The *Difference Matrix and* ε*-threshold* (DiMε) discovery algorithm presented in [6] starts from user-specified thresholds, and performs a level-by-level generation of candidate dependencies to be successively validated. Candidate RFD generation is accomplished by means of an attribute lattice built by considering all the possible attribute combinations. Thus, DiMε generates attribute sets X, and then formulates all the possible RFDs $X \backslash \{A\} \rightarrow A$, with $A \in X$, to be validated. With respect to FD discovery algorithms, DiMε exploits their candidate generation strategies, and generalizes their pruning strategies, but it provides a new validation technique dealing with similarity subsets, and taking into consideration the possibility that an RFD might hold for a subset of tuples.

Tuple number	Height	Weight	Shoe size
1	175	70	40
2	175	75	39
3	175	69	40
4	176	71	40
5	178	81	41
6	169	73	37
7	170	62	39

Table 1: A sample dataset.

	1	2	3	4	5	6	7
1	0	0	0	1	3	6	5
2	0	0	0	1	3	6	5
3	0	0	0	1	3	6	5
4	1	1	1	0	2	7	6
5	3	3	3	2	0	9	8
6	6	6	6	7	9	0	1
7	5	5	5	6	8	1	0

(a) $M_{\mathsf{Height}_{\mathsf{abs}}}$

	1	2	3	4	5	6	7
1	0,0	0,5	0,1	1,1	3,11	6,3	5,8
2	0,5	0,0	0,6	1,4	3,6	6,2	5,13
3	0,1	0,6	0,0	1,2	3,12	6,4	5,7
4	1,1	1,4	1,2	0,0	2,10	7,2	6,9
5	3,11	3,6	3,12	2,10	0,0	9,8	8,19
6	6,3	6,2	6,4	7,2	9,8	0,0	1,11
7	5,8	5,13	5,7	6,9	8,19	1,11	0,0

(b) $M_{\mathsf{Height}_{\mathsf{abs}},\mathsf{Weight}_{\mathsf{abs}}}$

Fig. 1: Difference Matrices for the dataset shown in Table 1.

Candidate RFD validation The validation of candidate RFDs entails verifying that two tuples are similar on the RHS attribute, whenever they are similar on the LHS ones, and the property holds for a significant portion of the database. This is done by generating similarity subsets of tuples and using them to validate candidate RFDs. As opposed to tuple partitions built in most FD discovery algorithms, similarity subsets might also intersect. To better explicate the generation process of similarity subsets, we introduce the concept of *difference matrix.*

Definition 2 (Difference matrix of an attribute). *Let r be an instance of a relation schema R, A an attribute of R, and δ a distance function defined on the domain of A. The* difference matrix *for A is a matrix M_A whose entry (i,j) contains the value $\delta(t_i[A], t_j[A])$ of the projections of tuples t_i and t_j on A.*

As an example, let us consider the sample dataset in Table 1. Since it has all numerical attributes, we use the absolute difference, denoted with *abs*, as a distance function to construct the difference matrix $M_{\mathsf{Height}_{\mathsf{abs}}}$ (Figure 1(a)).

The definition of difference matrix can be easily generalized to attribute sets, in which an entry will contain an n-tuple of distance values, one for each attribute in the set. The difference matrix for an attribute set X can be derived from the difference matrices for the single attributes composing it, by concatenating elements with the same coordinates. An example is provided in Figure 1(b).

We exploit the notion of difference matrix to generate the *similar pattern* of a tuple t or a matrix row, which represents sets of tuples or matrix columns satisfying a given constraint wrt t. Successively, we group the tuples sharing the same similar patterns into *similar pattern subsets.*

Definition 3 (Similar pattern subsets). *Let r be an instance of a relation schema R, $X = \{A_1, \dots, A_n\}$ an attribute set of R, M_{X_Δ} a difference matrix for X, and $\phi = (\phi_1, \dots, \phi_n)$ a sequence of constraints on the values of M_{X_Δ}. A similar pattern of tuple t_i of M_{X_Δ}, denoted as $\tau_X^{t_i}$, is the sequence $(j_1, \dots, j_h)$ with $h \le |r|$ and $M[i, j_k] = (d_1, \dots, d_n)$, where d_q satisfies the constraints ϕ_q $\forall q \in [1, n]$ and $\forall k \in [1, h]$. A* similar pattern subset *S_X for X is defined as $S_X = \{j_1, \dots, j_h\}_{\{i_1, \dots, i_k\}}$ with $1 \le k \le h \le |r|$, $\tau_X^{i_p} = (j_1, \dots, j_h)$ $\forall p \in [1, k]$ and $\tau_X^{i_v} \ne (j_1, \dots, j_h)$ $\forall v \notin [1, k]$. The set of different* similar pattern subsets *for X is denoted as I_X.*

Example 1. If in the dataset of Table 1 the user specifies constraints based on the *abs* function, the $\le$ comparison operator, 1 as a threshold for both the attributes Height and Shoe Size, and 10 for the attribute Weight, then the following sets of similar pattern subsets are generated:

- $I_{\text{Height}} = \{\{1, 2, 3, 4\}_{\{1,2,3,4\}}, \{5\}_{\{5\}}, \{6, 7\}_{\{6,7\}}\}$;
- $I_{\text{Weight}} = \{\{1, 2, 3, 4, 6, 7\}_{\{1,3\}}, \{1, 2, 3, 4, 5, 6\}_{\{2,6\}}, \{1, 2, 3, 4, 5, 6, 7\}_{\{4\}}, \{2, 4, 5, 6\}_{\{5\}}, \{1, 3, 4, 7\}_{\{7\}}\}$;
- $I_{\text{Shoe Size}} = \{\{1, 2, 3, 4, 5, 7\}_{\{1,3,4\}}, \{1, 2, 3, 4, 7\}_{\{2,7\}}, \{1, 3, 4, 5\}_{\{5\}}, \{6\}_{\{6\}}\}$.

In order to validate candidate RFDs, DIMε reduces the number of similar pattern subsets for the attributes of the LHS, by eliminating singletons (since they correspond to the matrix diagonal entries that trivially compare each tuple with itself) obtaining *stripped similar pattern subsets.*

Validation of RFDs relaxing only on the tuple comparison. Stripped similar pattern subsets can be used to validate candidate RFDs based on the concept of *similar pattern subset refinement.*

Definition 4. *A set $\widehat{I}_X$ is said to* refine *another set $\widehat{I}_{X \cup A}$ if every similar pattern subset in $\widehat{I}_X$ is contained in one of the subsets in $\widehat{I}_{X \cup A}$.*

Based on the refinement notion, we derive the following lemma for RFDs.

Lemma 1. *A relaxed functional dependency $X_{\Phi_1} \to A_{\Phi_2}$ holds on an entire database instance if and only if $\widehat{I}_X$* refines *$\widehat{I}_A$.*

Example 2. Let us consider the database instance of Table 1. If we set the constraints as defined in Example 1, then according to Lemma 1 the RFD

$$\{\text{Height}_{\phi_1}, \text{Weight}_{\phi_2}\} \to \text{Shoe Size}_{\phi_3}$$

holds on the entire database. In fact, since $\widehat{I}_{\text{Height,Weight}} = \{\{1, 2, 3, 4\}_{\{1,2,3,4\}}\}$ and $\widehat{I}_{\text{Shoe\_Size}} = \{\{1, 2, 3, 4, 5, 7\}_{\{1,3,4\}}, \{1, 2, 3, 4, 7\}_{\{2,7\}}, \{1, 3, 4, 5\}_{\{5\}}\}$, each similar pattern in $\widehat{I}_{\text{Height,Weight}}$ is included in a similar pattern of $\widehat{I}_{\text{Shoe\_Size}}$.

Alternatively, the refinement property between sets of stripped similar pattern subsets can be verified by calculating $||\widehat{I}_Z||$, which is defined as:

$$||\widehat{I}_Z|| = \frac{\sum_{t_i \in r}(|s_{t_i}| - 1)}{2} \forall s_{t_i} \in \widehat{I}_Z \quad (2)$$

It represents the number of pairwise similar tuples in $\widehat{I}_Z$. Since for an attribute set $W \subset Z$, $\widehat{I}_Z$ always refines $\widehat{I}_W$, it means that $\widehat{I}_{X \cup A}$ always refines $\widehat{I}_X$. However, we know that an RFD $X_{\Phi_1} \rightarrow A_{\Phi_2}$ holds only if $\widehat{I}_X$ is a refinement of $\widehat{I}_A$. Thus, since $\widehat{I}_{X \cup A}$ cannot have similar pattern subsets of size greater than those in $\widehat{I}_X$, the RFD holds if $\widehat{I}_{X \cup A}$ and $\widehat{I}_X$ are equal, which yields the following lemma.

Lemma 2. *A relaxed functional dependency $X_{\Phi_1} \rightarrow A_{\Phi_2}$ holds on an entire database instance if and only if $||\widehat{I}_{X \cup A}|| = ||\widehat{I}_X||$.*

Validation of hybrid RFDs. In case of hybrid RFDs, DIMε should also consider as valid the RFDs holding on a subset of tuples, according to a coverage measure and a user-defined threshold. In this case, it is not possible to use the previously defined lemma to validate candidate RFDs. In particular, to accomplish the validation process it is necessary to calculate the satisfiability degree of the instance according to a coverage measure. In this paper, DIMε relies on the *g3-error* coverage measure [9], but it can also work with other coverage measures by overloading the function computing the measure from similar subsets.

The computation of the *g3-error* for RFDs with hybrid relaxation is an NP-complete problem [13], since the MINIMUM VERTEX COVER problem can be reduced to it. A solution to this problem can be found in polynomial time in case of disjoint similar pattern subsets, in which case, we can use the same strategy of AFD discovery [9]. However, since in case of intersecting similar pattern subsets each of these tuples can fall in more than one similar pattern subset of I_X, it is not possible to perform a computation local to each similar pattern subset, but more a global analysis is required. Thus, we provide an greedy solution for calculating the *g3-error* in polynomial time [10].

5 Evaluation

We implemented DIMε[1] in the Java, by using the Levenshtein distance for comparing textual attributes, the absolute difference for comparing numerical ones, and the *g3-error* as the coverage measure for extent evaluation [11]. The experiments have been performed on a machine with an Intel Xeon W 3.2GHz 8-core CPU, 64 GB RAM, with a 64-Bit Java environment. We considered six real-world datasets from the UCI Machine Learning repository[2]. During the experiment sessions we varied the similarity and the coverage measure thresholds simultaneously, in the range $[0, 4]$ with step 1, and in the range $[0, 0.4]$ with step 0.1. Only, for the Abalone dataset we considered the range $[0.0, 0.4]$.

Figure 2 shows the number of RFDs extracted by DIMε according to several tuple comparison thresholds, whereby each line represents a different extent threshold. We can observe that the highest number of RFDs is usually discovered with *g3-error* thresholds slightly above zero. Concerning the variation of tuple

[1] `https://dastlab.github.io/dime/.`

[2] `https://archive.ics.uci.edu/ml/index.php`

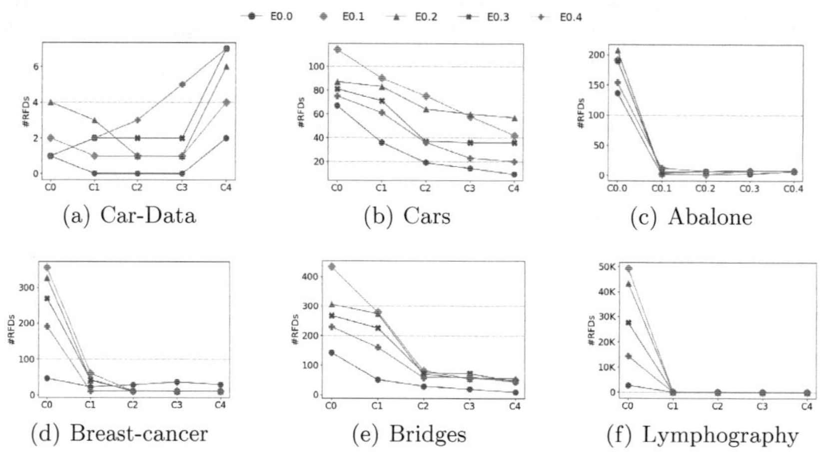

(a) Car-Data (b) Cars (c) Abalone

(d) Breast-cancer (e) Bridges (f) Lymphography

Fig. 2: Number of RFDs varying the similarity and the extent thresholds.

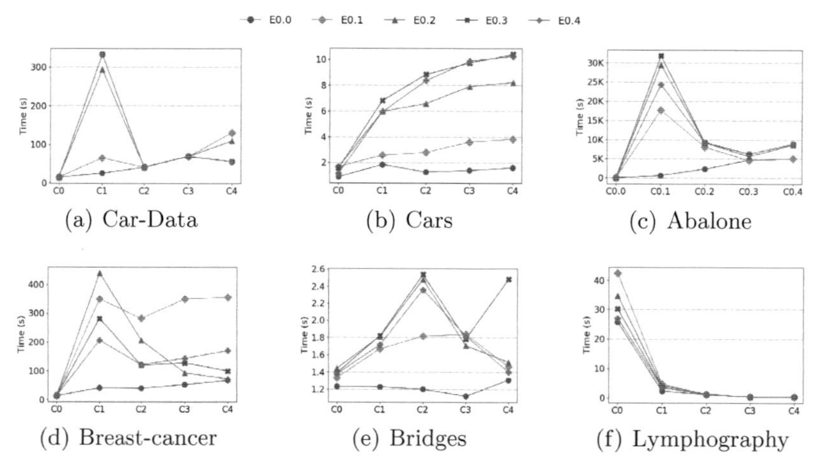

(a) Car-Data (b) Cars (c) Abalone

(d) Breast-cancer (e) Bridges (f) Lymphography

Fig. 3: Runtimes by varying the similarity and the extent thresholds.

comparison thresholds, in most cases the number of RFDs drastically drops when increasing them from 0 to 1. This is mainly due to the fact that with a zero threshold many key dependencies are obtained, which are likely to be invalidated when the tuple comparison threshold becomes greater than zero.

Figure 3 shows the execution times of DIMε. In general, although we expect higher execution times on datasets with more columns and/or rows, this is not necessarily true, because the attribute value distributions might heavily affect the computation steps to be performed, since they influence the number of tuple similarities, and hence the number of RFD candidates to be processed.

6 Conclusion and future work

The problem of discovering RFDs adds a considerable complexity to the dependency discovery process, since the relaxation criteria reduce the possibilities of pruning search paths, and prevent the possibility to exploit the properties of disjoint partitions during the validation phase. The performed evaluation highlights the effectiveness of DIMε in the discovery of RFDs relaxing on both the tuple comparison and the extent dimensions. In the future, we would like to further investigate the considered problem in order to derive an algorithm for RFD discovery capable of automatically inferring the threshold ranges of their validation, as done in [5], instead of requesting them to the user.

References

1. Abedjan, Z., Golab, L., Naumann, F.: Profiling relational data: A survey. The VLDB Journal **24**(4), 557–581 (2015)
2. Abedjan, Z., Schulze, P., Naumann, F.: DFD: Efficient functional dependency discovery. In: CIKM '14. pp. 949–958 (2014)
3. Caruccio, L., Deufemia, V., Polese, G.: Relaxed functional dependencies – A survey of approaches. IEEE TKDE **28**(1), 147–165 (2016)
4. Caruccio, L., Deufemia, V., Polese, G.: Evolutionary mining of relaxed dependencies from big data collections. In: WIMS '17. pp. 5:1–5:10 (2017)
5. Caruccio, L., Deufemia, V., Polese, G.: Discovering relaxed functional dependencies based on multi-attribute dominance. IEEE TKDE (2020), to appear
6. Caruccio, L., Deufemia, V., Polese, G.: Mining relaxed functional dependencies from data. Data Min. Knowl. Discov. **34**(2), 443–477 (2020)
7. Chang, S.K., Deufemia, V., Polese, G., Vacca, M.: A normalization framework for multimedia databases. IEEE TKDE **19**(12), 1666–1679 (2007)
8. Flach, P.A., Savnik, I.: Database dependency discovery: A machine learning approach. AI communications **12**(3), 139–160 (1999)
9. Huhtala, Y., Kärkkäinen, J., Porkka, P., Toivonen, H.: TANE: An efficient algorithm for discovering functional and approximate dependencies. The Computer Journal **42**(2), 100–111 (1999)
10. Johnson, D.S., Garey, M.R.: Computers and intractability: A guide to the theory of NP-completeness. W. H. Freeman & Co. (1979)
11. Kivinen, J., Mannila, H.: Approximate inference of functional dependencies from relations. Theoretical Computer Science **149**(1), 129–149 (1995)
12. Papenbrock, T., Naumann, F.: A hybrid approach to functional dependency discovery. In: SIGMOD '16. pp. 821–833 (2016)
13. Song, S.: Data Dependencies in the Presence of Difference. Ph.D. thesis, The Hong Kong University (2010)
14. Song, S., Chen, L.: Differential dependencies: Reasoning and discovery. ACM Transactions on Database Systems **36**, 16 (2011)
15. Song, S., Chen, L.: Efficient discovery of similarity constraints for matching dependencies. Data & Knowledge Engineering **87**, 146–166 (2013)
16. Wyss, C., Giannella, C., Robertson, E.: FastFDs: A heuristic-driven, depth-first algorithm for mining functional dependencies from relation instances extended abstract. In: DaWaK '01. pp. 101–110 (2001)

Detecting and Explaining Exceptional Values in Categorical Data
DISCUSSION PAPER

Fabrizio Angiulli, Fabio Fassetti, Luigi Palopoli, and Cristina Serrao

DIMES, University of Calabria, 87036 Rende (CS), Italy
{f.angiulli,f.fassetti,palopoli,c.serrao}@dimes.unical.it

Abstract. In this work we deal with the problem of detecting and explaining exceptional behaving values in categorical datasets by perceiving an attribute value as anomalous if its frequency occurrence is exceptionally typical or un-typical within the distribution of frequencies occurrences of any other attribute value. The notion of *frequency occurrence* is provided by specialising the Kernel Density Estimation method to the domain of frequency values and an outlierness measure is defined by leveraging the cdf of such a density. This measure is able to simultaneously identify two kinds of anomalies called *lower outliers* and *upper outliers*, namely exceptionally low or high frequent values.
Moreover, data values labeled as outliers come with an interpretable *explanations* for their abnormality, which is a desirable feature of any knowledge discovery technique.

1 Introduction

An outlying observation is one that appears to deviate markedly from other members of the sample in which it occurs. Such rare events can be even more interesting than the more regularly occurring ones as they are suspected of not being generated by the same mechanisms as the rest of the data.

We deal with categorical data and, specifically, we perceive an attribute value as anomalous if its frequency occurrence is exceptionally typical or un-typical within the distribution of frequencies occurrences of any other attribute value. To quantify such a *frequency occurrence* we specialize the classical Kernel Density Estimation technique to the domain of frequency values and get to the concept of *soft frequency occurrence*. The cumulated frequency distribution of the above density estimate is used to decide if the frequency of a certain value is anomalous when compared to the other values' frequencies. In particular, we are able to identify two kind of anomalies, namely *lower outliers* and *upper outliers*. A *lower outlier* is a value whose frequency is low while, typically, the dataset objects assume a few similar values, namely the frequencies of the other values are high. An *upper outlier* is a value whose frequency is high while, typically, the dataset objects assume almost distinct values, namely the frequencies of the other values are low. Note that the measure detects both scenarios and to automatically characterizes the target value as a lower or upper outlier.

A value can show exceptional behaviour only when we restrict our attention to a subset of the whole population. Thus, we design our technique to output the so-called *explanation-property pairs* (E, p), where E denotes a condition used to determine the target subpopulation and p represents an attribute p_a and a value p_v such that the p_v is exceptionally frequent or infrequent within the subpopulation selected by the explanation E.

The rest of the work is organised as follows. Section 2 discusses work related with the present one. Section 3 introduces the frequency occurrence function. Section 4 describes the outlierness function for ranking categorical values. Section 5 describes experimental results.

2 Related works

Categorical data has received relatively little attention as compared to quantitative data because detecting anomalies in categorical domain is a challenging problem [11].

We start by noting that there is little literature about outlier explanation [3], i.e the problem of detecting anomalous properties and/or related outlier objects equipped with features justifying their outlierness. Moreover, to the best of our knowledge, no technique is able to natively detect *upper* outliers.

Among traditional outlier detection methods explored in the context of numerical data[8] you can consider two main clusters: distance-based[6] and density-based[7]. These ideas have been properly adapted to the categorical domain.

An example of distance-based method is discussed in [6, 1]. Outliers are defined as the N observations whose average distance to the k nearest neighbors are the greatest; in order to do that an appropriate distance has to be chosen.

Detecting local anomalies, i.e. observations having outlying behavior in local areas, is another interesting discovery problem. Local anomaly detection methods for categorical data include the k-LOF [12] and the WATCH method [9].

The first one is an extension of Local Anomalies Factor (LOF) method [7] to the categorical domain while the WATCH method [9] has been designed to find out outliers in high dimensional categorical datasets using feature grouping.

Both distance and density are taken into account by the ROAD algorithm [10]. It considers the Hamming distance to compute cluster-based outliers and the density, evaluated as the mean frequency of the values, is used to identify frequency-based outliers.

With regard to the outlier explanation, [2],[3] propose a technique for categorical and numerical domains respectively that, given in input one single object known to be outlier, provides features justifying its anomaly and subpopulations where its exceptionality is evident. A generalization is proposed in [4]

3 Frequency Occurrence

In this section we give same preliminary definitions and introduce the notation employed throughout the paper.

A *dataset* $\mathcal{D}$ on a set of *categorical* attributes $\mathbf{A}$ is a set of objects o assuming values on the attributes in $\mathbf{A}$. By $o[a]$ we denote the value of o on the attribute $a \in \mathbf{A}$. $\mathcal{D}[a]$ denotes the multiset $\{o[a] \mid o \in \mathcal{D}\}$. Given a multiset V, the frequency f_v^V of the value $v \in V$ is the number of occurrences of v in V. A *condition* $\mathcal{C}$ is a set of pairs (a, v) where each a is an attribute and each $v \in \mathcal{D}[a]$. By $\mathcal{D}_\mathcal{C}$ we denote the new dataset $\{o \in \mathcal{D} \mid o[a] = v, \forall (a, v) \in \mathcal{C})\}$.

Definition 1 (Frequency distribution). *A frequency distribution $\mathcal{H}$ is a multiset of the form $\mathcal{H} = \{f_1^{(1)}, \ldots, f_1^{(w_1)}, \ldots, f_n^{(1)}, \ldots, f_n^{(w_n)}\}$ where each $f_i^{(j)} \in \mathbb{N}$ is a distinct frequency, $f_i^{(j)} = f_i^{(k)} = f_i$ for each $1 \leq j, k \leq w_i$, and w_i denotes the number of occurrences of the frequency f_i. By $N(\mathcal{H})$ (or simply N whenever $\mathcal{H}$ is clear from the context) we denote $w_1 \cdot f_1 + \ldots + w_n \cdot f_n$. For the sake of simplicity, we will refer to a frequency distribution as a set $\mathcal{H} = \{f_1, f_2, \ldots, f_n\}$ and to the number of occurrences w_i of f_i as $w(f_i)$.*

Now we define the notion of *frequency occurrence* as a tool for quantifying how frequent is a certain frequency.

Definition 2 (Hard frequency occurrence). *Given a frequency distribution $\mathcal{H}$, the frequency occurrence $\mathcal{F}_\mathcal{H}(f_i)$ of f_i, also denoted by $\mathcal{F}(f_i)$ whenever $\mathcal{H}$ is clear from the context, is the product $w_i \cdot f_i$.*

The above definition allows us to associate with each distinct value in $\mathcal{D}[a]$ a score that is related not only to its frequency in the dataset but also to how many other values have its same frequency. However, close frequency values do not interact with each other, e.g. having $f_i = 49, w_i = 1$ and $f_{i+1} = 51, w_{i+1} = 1$ is completely different from $f_i' = 50, w_i' = 2$, as in the former case $\mathcal{F}(f_i) = 49$ and $\mathcal{F}(f_{i+1}) = 51$ while in the latter we have $\mathcal{F}(f_i') = 100$ that is about twice the previous case. Intuitively, we do not desire a similar small variation in the frequency distribution to impact so largely on the *frequency occurrence* values. To force close frequency values to influence each other in order and jointly contribute to the frequency occurrence we design an ad-hoc density estimation method inspired to Kernel Density Estimation (KDE).

A *(discrete) kernel function K_{f_i} with parameter f_i* is a probability mass function having the property that $\sup_{f \geq 0} K_{f_i}(f) = K_{f_i}(f_i)$. Given an interval $I = [f_l, f_u]$ of frequencies, a frequency f_i, and a kernel function K, the *volume* of K_{f_i} in I, denoted as $V_I(K_{f_i})$, is given by $\sum_{f=f_l}^{f_u} K_{f_i}(f)$. The following expression

$$\mathcal{F}(f) = \sum_{\varphi \in I(f)} \left\{ \sum_{i=1}^{n} w_i \cdot f_i \cdot K_{f_i}(\varphi) \right\}. \tag{1}$$

where $I(f)$ represents an interval of frequencies centred in f, provides the density estimate of the *frequency occurrence* of the frequency f.

Since $K_{f_i}(\cdot)$ is a probability mass function, the frequency f_i provides a contribution to the *frequency occurrence* of f corresponding to the portion of the volume of K_{f_i} which is contained in $I(f)$, that is $V_{I(f)}(K_{f_i})$.

It is possible to eliminate the dependence from $I(f)$ by properly weighting the contribution of $K_{f_i}(\cdot)$ based on its distance from the target frequency f. Such a weight can be directly obtained from the associated kernel as the ratio between the probability of observing frequency f and the probability of observing f_i, when such frequencies are realization of a random variable distributed according to $K_{f_i}(\cdot)$. This allow us to rewrite equation 1 as follows:

$$\mathcal{F}(f) = \sum_{\varphi \geq 0} \left\{ \sum_{i=1}^{n} \left[w_i \cdot f_i \cdot K_{f_i}(\varphi) \cdot \frac{K_{f_i}(f)}{K_{f_i}(f_i)} \right] \right\}. \tag{2}$$

Note that the summation over the domain of all $K_{f_i}(\cdot)$ values is equal to 1 since it is a probability mass function. Moreover, as $\mathcal{F}$ represents a notion of density function associated with frequency occurrences, it is preferable that its volume evaluated in the frequencies $\mathcal{H} = \{f_1, \ldots, f_n\}$ evaluates to $N(\mathcal{H})$. This leads to the following final form of the *frequency occurrence* function.

Definition 3 (Soft occurrence function). *Given a frequency distribution $\mathcal{H}$, the frequency occurrence $\mathcal{F}_{\mathcal{H}}(f_i)$ of f_i, also denoted by $\mathcal{F}(f_i)$ whenever $\mathcal{H}$ is clear from the context, is given by the following expression*

$$\mathcal{F}(f) = \frac{N(\mathcal{H})}{N_{\mathcal{F}}(\mathcal{H})} \cdot \sum_{i=1}^{n} \left[w_i \cdot f_i \cdot \widehat{K}_{f_i}(f) \right], \tag{3}$$

where

$$\widehat{K}_{f_i}(f) = \frac{K_{f_i}(f)}{K_{f_i}(f_i)} \quad \text{and} \quad N_{\mathcal{F}}(\mathcal{H}) = \sum_{j=1}^{n} \left\{ \sum_{i=1}^{n} \left[w_i \cdot f_i \cdot \widehat{K}_{f_i}(f_j) \right] \right\}.$$

As for the kernel selection we exploit the binomial distribution *binopdf*$(f; n, p)$ with parameter n, denoting the number of independent trials, equal to $N(\mathcal{H})$, and parameter p, denoting the success probability, equal to $p = f_i / N(\mathcal{H})$.

4 Categorical Outlierness

The idea behind the measure we will discuss in the following is that an object in a categorical dataset can be considered an outlier with respect to an attribute if the frequency of the value assumed by this object on such an attribute is rare if compared to the frequencies associated with the other values assumed on the same attribute by the other objects of the dataset. We are interested in two relevant kinds of anomalies referring to two different scenarios.

Lower Outlier. An object o is anomalous since for a given attribute a the value that o assumes in a is rare (its frequency is low) while, typically, the dataset objects assume a few similar values, namely the frequencies of the other values are high.

Upper Outlier. An object o is anomalous since for a given attribute a the value that o assumes in a is usual (its frequency is high) while, typically, the dataset objects assume almost distinct values, namely the frequencies of the other values are low.

In order to discover outliers, we exploit the cumulated frequency distribution associated with the estimated density.

Definition 4 (Cumulated frequency distribution). *Given a frequency distribution* $\mathcal{H} = \{f_1, \ldots, f_n\}$*, the associated cumulated frequency distribution* H *is*

$$H(f) = \sum_{f_j \leq f} \mathcal{F}_{\mathcal{H}}(f_j).$$

In the following, we refer to the value $H(f_i)$ *also as to* H_i.

To quantify the degree of anomaly associated with a certain frequency, we use the area above and below the curve of the cumulated frequency distribution. Intuitively, the larger the area $A^{\uparrow}(f_i)$ above the portion of the curve included from a certain frequency f_i to the maximum frequency $f_{\max}$, and the more f_i differs from frequencies that are greater than f_i. Thus, this area is exploited to associate *lower outlier score* $out^{\downarrow}(f_i)$ to the target frequecy f_i. At the same time, the larger the area $A^{\downarrow}(f_i)$ below the portion of the curve included from the minimum frequency $f_{\min}$ and a certain frequency f_i, and the more f_i differs from frequencies that are smaller than f_i. This area can be used to associate an *uppper outlier score* $out^{\uparrow}(f_i)$ to f_i.

The outlierness associated with the frequency f_i is a combined measure of the above two normalised areas and exceptional values for an attribute a, are those associated with large values of outlierness. More details are available in[5].

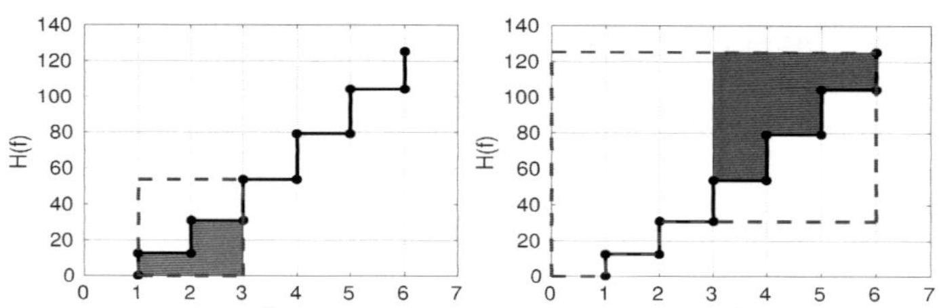

f	w
1	3
2	2
3	1
4	2
5	1
6	2

Fig. 1: Outlierness computation example. Areas involved in the computation of the score are highlighted. They are normalized properly to get the upper and lower outlierness score for the target frequency

It must be pointed out that very often a value emerges as exceptional for a certain attribute only when we restrict our attention to a subset of the whole population. This intuition leads to the definition of the notion of explanation-property pair.

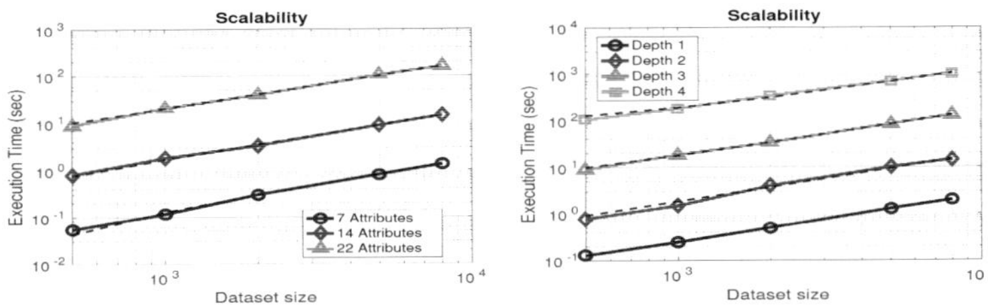

(a) (b)

Fig. 2: Scalability analysis.

Definition 5. *An explanation-property pair (E, p), consists of condition E, also called explanation, and of an atomic condition $p = \{(p_a, p_v)\}$, also called property. By p_a (p_v, resp.) we denote the attribute (value, resp.) involved in the atomic condition p.*

The *outlierness* of an explanation-property pair (E, p) is the outlierness score associated with of the value p_v with respect the attribute p_a in the dataset D_E.

We implemented an algorithm that receives in input a dataset $\mathcal{D}$ and a depth parameter $\delta \geq 1$, and returns all the pairs (E, p) among those composed of at most δ atomic conditions. The algorithm analyzes explanations of length less or equal than δ according to a depth-first strategy that allows an efficient selection of sub-populations exploiting an approach similar to the one described in [3].

5 Experimental results

First of all, to study the applicability of our method to real datasets, we have tested its scalability. Then, to clarify the different nature of our anomalies with those returned by other outlier detection methods, we compared our method with traditional distance-based and density-based outlier detection approaches and with a method tailored for categorical data. Here, the results obtained on the *Mushrooms* dataset (n = 8,124 objects and m = 22 attributes) from UCI ML Repository are reported. More experiments are discussed in [5].

Scalability. In the experiment reported in Figure 2a, we varied the number of objects n in {500, 1000, 2000, 5000, 8000} and the number of attributes m in {7, 14, 22} , while the depth parameter has been held fixed to $\delta = 3$. The dashed lines represent the trend of the linear growth estimated exploiting regression. This estimation confirms that the algorithm scales linearly with respect to the dataset size. As for the number of attributes, as expected for a given number of objects the execution time increases due to the growth of the associated search space. On the full dataset the execution time is very contained, as it amounts to about 2 minutes. In the experiment reported in Figure 2b, we varied both the number of objects n and the depth parameter δ in $\{1, 2, 3, 4\}$, while considering the full feature space. Also in this case the linear growth is represented by the dashed lines, and similar considerations can be drawn.

Comparison with outlier detection methods. We compare our method with two of the main categories of outliers: (*i*) *distance-based* approaches, that are used to discover *global* outliers; (*ii*) *density-based* approaches, which are able to single out *local* outliers. As distance-based definition, we use the average KNN score, representing the average distance from the k-nearest neighbours of the object. As density-based, we use Local Outlier Factor or LOF [7]. Both methods employ the Hamming distance. Moreover, we compare our method with the ROAD algorithm [10] that exploits both densities and distances.

We ranked the dataset objects o by assigning to each of the them the largest outlierness of a pair π such that $o \in \mathcal{D}_\pi$ and we determined our top–10 outliers as the objects associated with the largest outliernesses; then we computed their outlier scores according to the KNN, LOF and ROAD definitions. Note that all the chosen competitors require an input parameter k whose selection may be challanging, so we have computeted their scores for all the possible values of k and report the ranking positions associated with our top–10 outliers as a box-plots generated when k changes.

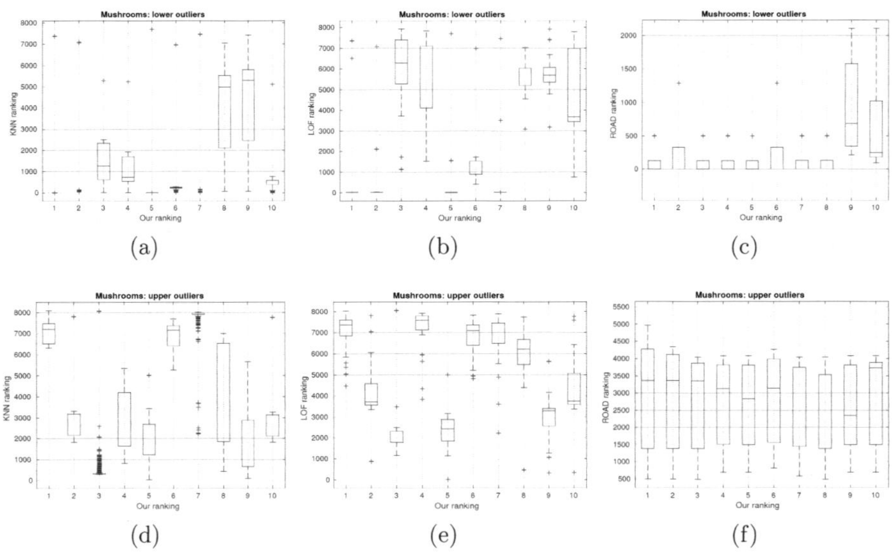

(a) (b) (c)

(d) (e) (f)

Fig. 3: Comparison with KNN, LOF and ROAD on *Mushrooms*.

The plots in fig. 3 highlight that the median ranking associated with our outliers can be far away from the top and also that, within the whole ranking distribution, the same outlier can be ranked in very different positions. In general, it seems that lower outliers are likely to be ranked better than upper outliers by our competitors, and this witnesses for the peculiar nature of upper outliers. On the *Mushrooms* dataset some of our lower outliers are, on the average, ranked very high also by the other algorithms. Some of them are almost always top outliers for all methods (see the top 1st, 2nd, 5th, and 7th outliers) thus witnessing that these outliers have both global and local nature. However, most of our outliers are not detected by these techniques.

Note that, the best rankings associated with the selected objects are obtained for very different values of the parameter k. Since, the output of the KNN, LOF and ROAD methods are determined for a selected value of k, it is very unlike that, even in presence of some agreement between our top outliers and local and global outliers, they are simultaneously ranked in high positions for the same provided value of k.

6 Conclusions

In this work we have provided a contribution to single out and explain anomalous values in categorical domains. We perceive frequencies of attribute values as samples of a distribution whose density has to be estimated. This lead to the notion of frequency occurrence we exploit to build our definition of outlier. As a second contribution, our technique is able to provide interpretable explanations for the abnormal values discovered. Thus, the outliers we provide can be seen as a product of the knowledge mined, making the approach knowledge-centric rather than object centric.

References

1. Angiulli, F., Basta, S., Pizzuti, C.: Distance-based detection and prediction of outliers. IEEE transactions on knowledge and data engineering **18**(2) (2006)
2. Angiulli, F., Fassetti, F., Manco, G., Palopoli, L.: Outlying property detection with numerical attributes. Data Min. Knowl. Discov. **31**(1) (2017)
3. Angiulli, F., Fassetti, F., Palopoli, L.: Detecting outlying properties of exceptional objects. ACM Transactions on Database Systems (TODS) **34**(1) (2009)
4. Angiulli, F., Fassetti, F., Palopoli, L.: Discovering characterizations of the behavior of anomalous subpopulations. IEEE TKDE **25**(6) (2013)
5. Angiulli, F., Fassetti, F., Palopoli, L., Serrao, C.: A density estimation approach for detecting and explaining exceptional values in categorical data. In: Discovery Science - 22nd International Conference, Proceedings. Springer (2019)
6. Angiulli, F., Pizzuti, C.: Outlier mining in large high-dimensional data sets. IEEE transactions on Knowledge and Data engineering **17**(2) (2005)
7. Breunig, M.M., Kriegel, H.P., Ng, R.T., Sander, J.: Lof: identifying density-based local outliers. In: ACM sigmod record. vol. 29. ACM (2000)
8. Chandola, V., Banerjee, A., Kumar, V.: Anomaly detection: A survey. ACM computing surveys (CSUR) **41**(3) (2009)
9. Li, J., Zhang, J., Pang, N., Qin, X.: Weighted outlier detection of high-dimensional categorical data using feature grouping. IEEE SMC (2018)
10. Suri, N.R., Murty, M.N., Athithan, G.: An algorithm for mining outliers in categorical data through ranking. In: IEEE HIS (2012)
11. Taha, A., Hadi, A.S.: Anomaly detection methods for categorical data: A review. ACM Computing Surveys (CSUR) **52**(2) (2019)
12. Yu, J.X., Qian, W., Lu, H., Zhou, A.: Finding centric local outliers in categorical/numerical spaces. Knowledge and Information Systems **9**(3), 309–338 (2006)

Probabilistic Answers over Inconsistent Knowledge Bases

(DISCUSSION PAPER)

Marco Calautti, Nicola Fiorentino, Sergio Greco, Cristian Molinaro, Irina Trubitsyna

DIMES, University of Calabria
{calautti, fiorentino, greco, cmolinaro, trubitsyna}@dimes.unical.it

Abstract. Consistent query answering is a generally accepted approach for querying inconsistent knowledge bases. A consistent answer to a query is a tuple entailed by every repair, where a repair is a consistent database that "minimally" differs from the original (possibly inconsistent) one. This is a somewhat coarse-grained classification of tuples into consistent and non-consistent does not provide much information about the non-consistent tuples (e.g., a tuple entailed by 99 out of 100 repairs might be considered "almost consistent").
To overcome this limitation, we propose a probabilistic approach to querying inconsistent knowledge bases, which provides more informative query answers by associating a degree of consistency with each query answer by associating a probability to each repair, depending on the changes needed to obtain it.

1 Introduction

There has been a great deal of work on extracting reliable information from inconsistent data, in both the AI and database communities. To deal with this problem, many semantics of query answering have been proposed. Most of them are based on the *consistent query answering* framework [2]. The idea is that a tuple should be considered a consistent answer to a query posed over an inconsistent knowledge base if the tuple is a query answer in every *repair*, where a repair is a consistent database that "minimally" differs from the original one. Different variants of the consistent query answering problem have been investigated depending on the minimality criterion—e.g., see [5]—or the employed repair primitive to restore consistency—e.g., see [3].

Regardless of the specific minimality criterion and repair primitive, all the resulting frameworks share the same drawback, which is a dichotomic classification of tuples in either consistent or non-consistent ones. This can provide very little information to users in many cases, as illustrated in the following example.

Example 1. Consider the knowledge base (D, Σ), where D contains the following facts:

employee

bob	cs	nyc
mike	cs	nyc
alice	cs	paris

and Σ is an ontology consisting of the following equality-generating dependency σ:

$$\mathsf{employee}(\mathsf{E}_1, \mathsf{D}, \mathsf{C}_1), \mathsf{employee}(\mathsf{E}_2, \mathsf{D}, \mathsf{C}_2) \to \mathsf{C}_1 = \mathsf{C}_2.$$

As an example, the fact employee(bob, cs, nyc) states that bob is an employee working in the cs department located in nyc. The dependency σ says that every department must be located in a single city. Clearly, the first two facts are conflicting with the last one. There are two repairs for this inconsistent knowledge base, which are as follows (more details on the employed notion of repair will be provided in the following):

$R_1 =$

bob	cs	nyc
mike	cs	nyc
alice	cs	nyc

$R_2 =$

bob	cs	paris
mike	cs	paris
alice	cs	paris

Repair R_1 is obtained from the original database by replacing paris with nyc, while R_2 is obtained by replacing nyc with paris. The query asking for the city of the cs department has no consistent answers. Thus, a user trying to extract this information from the knowledge base is left with no answer altogether, all she/he gets is the empty set. □

To overcome the limitation illustrated in the example above, we propose a probabilistic approach to querying inconsistent knowledge bases whose aim is to provide more informative query answers than the classical consistent query answering framework. The main idea is to give a "degree of consistency" to every repair, which is then taken into account to assign a degree of consistency to query answers.

Example 2. Consider again the scenario of Example 1. The degree of consistency of R_1 is 2/3, as nyc is supported by two facts out of three in the original knowledge base, while the degree of consistency of R_2 is 1/3, as paris is supported by only one fact out of three.

Consider again the query asking for the city of the cs department. Rather than providing no information (like classical consistent query answers do), our query answers are nyc with confidence $2/3$ (as this is entailed by R_1), and paris with confidence $1/3$ (as this is entailed by R_2), which is much more informative than returning nothing. □

The previous examples illustrate the limitation of providing only certain information and how this might be overcome by assigning a degree of consistency to query answers (notice that consistent query answers are still provided – they have degree 1).

In this paper, we consider knowledge bases where dependencies are expressed by means of *equality-generating dependencies* (EGDs). Equality-generating dependencies are one of the two major types of data dependencies—the other major type consists of *tuple-generating dependencies* (TGDs)—and can model several kinds of constraints arising in practice, such as functional dependencies and thus key dependencies.

In the presence of EGDs, the two main approaches to restore consistency are to perform fact deletions or fact updates. A drawback of the former is that entire facts are deleted to resolve inconsistency, even if they may still contain "reliable" information. Thus, in this paper we adopt a notion of repair based on fact updates (we will provide a precise definition in the following). Nonetheless, the ideas developed in this paper can be used also when a notion of repair based on fact deletions is adopted.

As we show, providing more informative query answers comes at a price: it is #P-hard. In light of this result, we discuss further developments providing polynomial time algorithms to compute approximate query answers.

Related work. Most inconsistency-tolerant approaches in the literature adopt the classical notion of repair (via fact deletions/insertions) and consistent query answer [16,19,6,18,17], while in this paper we propose a probabilistic generalization where repairs use fact updates, akin to [7,21,11,15], and query answers are probabilistic. Some works on probabilistic query answering on inconsistent knowledge bases exist [1,13,10], but [1] and [13] only consider restricted classes of dependencies, while [10] deals with the classical notion of repair.

2 Preliminaries

Basics. We assume the existence of the following pairwise disjoint (countably infinite) sets: a set Const of *constants*, a set Var of *variables*, and a set Null of *labeled nulls*. Nulls are denoted by the symbol $\perp$ subscripted with natural numbers. A *term* is a constant, variable, or null. We also assume a set of *predicates*, disjoint from the aforementioned sets, with each predicate being associated with an *arity*, which is a non-negative integer.

An *atom* is of the form $p(t_1, \ldots, t_n)$, where p is an n-ary predicate and the t_i's are terms. We write an atom also as $p(\mathbf{t})$, where $\mathbf{t}$ is a sequence of terms. An atom without variables is also called a *fact*. An *instance* is a finite multiset of facts. A *database* is a finite set of facts containing constants only. An instance containing only constants is said to be *complete*. Notice that, as opposed to databases, instances can contain duplicates—as shown in the following, instances are used in intermediate steps during repairs' computation and it is needed to keep duplicates to count the number of modifications being made. We assume the existence of a function db converting a complete instance to a database by eliminating duplicates.

A *homomorphism* is a mapping $h : \mathsf{Const} \cup \mathsf{Var} \cup \mathsf{Null} \to \mathsf{Const} \cup \mathsf{Var} \cup \mathsf{Null}$ that is the identity on Const. Homomorphisms are also applied to atoms and (multi) sets of atoms in the natural fashion, that is, $h(p(t_1, \ldots, t_n)) = p(h(t_1), \ldots, h(t_n))$, and $h(S) = \{h(A) \mid A \in S\}$ for every (multi) set S of atoms. A *valuation* is a homomorphism ν whose image is Const, that is, $\nu(t) \in \mathsf{Const}$ for every $t \in \mathsf{Const} \cup \mathsf{Var} \cup \mathsf{Null}$.

An *equality generating dependency* (EGD) σ is a first-order formula of the form $\forall \mathbf{x}\, \varphi(\mathbf{x}) \to x_i = x_j$, where $\varphi(\mathbf{x})$ is a conjunction of atoms (without labeled nulls) whose variables are exactly $\mathbf{x}$, and x_i and x_j are variables from $\mathbf{x}$. We call $\varphi(\mathbf{x})$ the *body* of σ, and call $x_i = x_j$ the *head* of σ. We will omit the universal quantification in front of dependencies and assume that all variables are universally quantified.

With a slight abuse of notation, we sometimes treat a conjunction of atoms as the *set* of its atoms. An instance J *satisfies* σ, denoted $J \models \sigma$, if whenever there exists a homomorphism h s.t. $h(\varphi(\mathbf{x})) \subseteq J$, then $h(x_i) = h(x_j)$. An instance J *satisfies* a set Σ of EGDs, denoted $J \models \Sigma$, if $I \models \sigma$ for every $\sigma \in \Sigma$. A *knowledge base* (KB) is a pair

(D, Σ), where D is a database and Σ is a finite set of EGDs. We say that the knowledge base is *consistent* if $D \models \Sigma$, otherwise it is *inconsistent*.

Acyclic EGDs. An *argument* of a set of EGDs Σ is an expression of the form $p[i]$, where p is an n-ary predicate appearing in Σ and $1 \leq i \leq n$. The *argument graph* of Σ is a directed graph $G_\Sigma = (V, E)$, where V is the set of all arguments of Σ, and E contains a directed edge from $p[i]$ to $q[j]$ labeled σ iff there is an EGD $\sigma \in \Sigma$ such that:

- the body of σ contains an atom $p(t_1, \ldots, t_n)$ such that either t_i is a constant or t_i is a variable occurring more than once in the body of σ, and
- the body of σ contains an atom $q(u_1, \ldots, u_m)$ such that u_j is a variable also appearing in the head of σ.

The *dependency graph* of Σ is a directed graph $\Gamma_\Sigma = (\Sigma, \Omega)$, where Ω is the set $\{(\sigma_1, \sigma_2) \mid G_\Sigma = (V, E) \wedge (p([i], q[j], \sigma_1), (q[j], r[k], \sigma_2) \in E\}$. We say that Σ is *acyclic* if its dependency graph is acyclic.

In the rest of the paper we consider acyclic sets of EGDs only. Thus, from now on, Σ is understood to be acyclic for every knowledge base (D, Σ). For acyclic sets of EGDs we can define a partial order $(\Sigma, <)$ where EGDs in Σ are ordered by reachability in Γ_Σ. The result of evaluating a query Q over a database D is denoted $Q(D)$.

Repairs. The notion of repair used in this paper is based on updating facts and assumes that conflicting facts denote an *attribute-level uncertainty* in the data [12,7,21,4,11,15]. Alternative approaches based on fact deletions assume that conflicting facts denote a *tuple-level uncertainty* [2,20,10]. The computation of repairs consists of a chase-like procedure that acts as follows: whenever an EGD $\varphi(\mathbf{x}) \rightarrow x_i = x_j$ is not satisfied by a database D, i.e. there exists an homomorphism h such that $D \models h(\varphi(\mathbf{x}))$ and $h(x_i) \neq h(x_j)$, we have to enforce it by making the two values equal, that is either $h(x_i)$ replaces $h(x_j)$ or vice versa. A repair is obtained through an exhaustive application of this repair step. Note that, although we follow the partial order $(\Sigma, <)$ to choose the EGD to enforce, there is a non-deterministic choice to be made when selecting an EGD and when updating values; this may lead to multiple repairs.

Example 3. Consider the set of EGDs
$\Sigma = \{\sigma_1\colon \mathsf{employee}(\mathsf{X}, \mathsf{Y}_1, \mathsf{Z}_1) \wedge \mathsf{employee}(\mathsf{X}, \mathsf{Y}_2, \mathsf{Z}_2) \rightarrow \mathsf{Y}_1 = \mathsf{Y}_2,$
$\sigma_2\colon \mathsf{employee}(\mathsf{X}_1, \mathsf{Y}, \mathsf{Z}_1) \wedge \mathsf{employee}(\mathsf{X}_2, \mathsf{Y}, \mathsf{Z}_2) \rightarrow \mathsf{Z}_1 = \mathsf{Z}_2\}$
and the database D:

bob	cs	rome
bob	math	rome
alice	math	nyc

By enforcing σ_1 into the first two facts, either cs or math can be chosen as bob's department. If the latter is chosen, then the instance D' below is obtained.

Suppose now that σ_2 is enforced into the last two facts of D'. Then, either rome or nyc can be chosen as math's city. If the former is chosen, we obtain the instance D'':

$D' =$

bob	math	rome
bob	math	rome
alice	math	nyc

$D'' =$

bob	math	rome
bob	math	rome
alice	math	rome

No further dependency enforcement is applicable at this point and thus the database derived from D'' by eliminating duplicates is a repair. □

The previous example informally illustrated the basic idea of the repair strategy we adopt. In the next section, we formally define it and show how to associate probabilities to repairs on the basis of the modifications that yielded them.

Notice that it might be possible to restore consistency in other different ways. For instance, in the first step of the example above, one may modify the employee names. However, we do not consider this option because it is unclear which (different) values should be assigned (any constant in Const is a candidate value). For instance, bob in the first fact might be replaced with rome, but this is somewhat arbitrary and indeed does not make much sense. In contrast, our repair strategy chooses candidate values that are somehow "justified" by the content of the database (e.g., in the example above, bob works for either the cs or the math department). Moreover, when EGDs are key dependencies, the aforementioned way of restoring consistency may lead to the introduction of entities that are not meaningful. Indeed, our choice has been made by different approaches relying on value updates—e.g., [7]. For special classes of EGDs, the repair strategy based on updating values coincides with the repair strategy based on fact deletions.

3 Probabilistic Repairs and Query Answers

One problem of the classical notion of consistent query answer is that query answers can provide little information in the presence of conflicting information. The alternative approach proposed in this paper is to compute probabilistic answers by taking into account in to what extent information is updated to restore consistency.

In this section, we define probabilistic repairs and probabilistic query answers. In the next section, we show how to compute a compact representation of all probabilistic repairs. In both cases, we will use *probabilistic instances*, which are used to represent a single probabilistic repair in this section and are used to compactly represent all probabilistic repairs in the next section. Probabilistic instances are instances augmented with a set of "probability assignments"—intuitively, expressions stating conditions on nulls and probabilities on the values they can take.

More formally, let $\mathcal{C}$ be the set of all expressions, called *conditions*, that can be built using the standard logical connectives $\wedge$, $\vee$, $\neg$, and expressions of the form $t_i = t_j$, true, and false, where $t_i, t_j \in \mathsf{Const} \cup \mathsf{Null}$. We will also use $t_i \neq t_j$ as a shorthand for $\neg(t_i = t_j)$. A homomorphism h *satisfies* a condition φ, denoted $h \models \varphi$, if $h(\varphi)$ is true.

A *probability assignment* is an expression of the form $P(\varphi_1 \mid \varphi_2) = p$, where φ_1, φ_2 are conditions and $p \in [0, 1]$.

A homomorphism h *satisfies* a probability assignment $P(\varphi_1 \mid \varphi_2) = p$ if the following holds true: if $h \models \varphi_2$ then $h \models \varphi_1$. Also, h *satisfies* a set Φ of probability assignments, denoted $h \models \Phi$, if h satisfies every probability assignment in Φ. For ease of presentation, a probability assignment of the form $P(\varphi_1 \mid \mathsf{true}) = p$ will be simply written as $P(\varphi_1) = p$.

A *probabilistic instance* (PI) is a pair $K = (J, \phi)$, where J is an instance and ϕ is a finite set of probability assignments. For any valuation ν, we define

$$Pr(\nu, K) = \Pi \; \{p \mid P(\varphi_1 \mid \varphi_2) = p \in \Phi \text{ and } \nu \models \varphi_2\}.$$

The semantics of K is given by the set of its *probabilistic worlds*, that is, the set of pairs (instance, probability) defined as follows:

$$pw(K) = \{(\nu(J), Pr(\nu, K)) \mid \nu \text{ is a valuation s.t. } \nu \models \Phi \wedge Pr(\nu, K) > 0\}.$$

The probabilistic repairs of an inconsistent knowledge base (D, Σ) are computed starting from the probabilistic instance $(D, \emptyset)$ and iteratively enforcing EGDs (following a topological sorting of Γ_Σ). During the repair process we keep track of which values have been updated and how many modifications have been applied using labeled nulls and probability assignments. The enforcement of an EGD, which we call probabilistic repair step, is informally shown in the next example.

Example 4. Consider the knowledge base (D, Σ), where D and Σ are from Example 3. Starting from the probabilistic instance $(D, \emptyset)$, by enforcing σ_1 into the first two facts, either cs or math can be chosen as bob's department. Therefore we obtain the following two (alternative) probabilistic instances K_1 (left) and K_2 (right):

bob	$\perp_1$	rome
bob	$\perp_1$	rome
alice	math	nyc

$P(\perp_1 = \text{cs}) = 1/2$

bob	$\perp_1$	rome
bob	$\perp_1$	rome
alice	math	nyc

$P(\perp_1 = \text{math}) = 1/2$

The only probabilistic world of K_1 is $(D_1, 1/2)$, while the only probabilistic world of K_2 is $(D_2, 1/2)$, where D_1 and D_2 are as follows (and are obtained by replacing $\perp_1$ with cs and math, respectively):

$D_1 =$

bob	cs	rome
bob	cs	rome
alice	math	nyc

$D_2 =$

bob	math	rome
bob	math	rome
alice	math	nyc

As $D_1 \models \Sigma$, $(\text{db}(D_1), 1/2)$ is a probabilistic repair. On the other hand, $D_2 \not\models \Sigma$, and thus we need to keep applying pr-steps over K_2. By enforcing σ_2 over the first and third facts of K_2 we can get the following two (alternative) probabilistic instances K_3 (left) and K_4 (right):

bob	$\perp_1$	$\perp_2$
bob	$\perp_1$	rome
alice	math	$\perp_2$

$P(\perp_1 = \text{math}) = 1/2$
$P(\perp_2 = \text{rome}) = 1/2$

bob	$\perp_1$	$\perp_2$
bob	$\perp_1$	rome
alice	math	$\perp_2$

$P(\perp_1 = \text{math}) = 1/2$
$P(\perp_2 = \text{nyc}) = 1/2$

The only probabilistic world of K_3 is $(D_3, 1/4)$, while the only probabilistic world of K_4 is $(D_4, 1/4)$, where D_3 and D_4 are as follows:

$D_3 =$

bob	math	rome
bob	math	rome
alice	math	rome

$D_4 =$

bob	math	nyc
bob	math	rome
alice	math	nyc

In the rest of the paper, for every probabilistic instances (J, ϕ), we report the probability assignments in ϕ under J.

Since $D_3 \models \Sigma$, $(\mathsf{db}(D_3), 1/4)$ is a probabilistic repair. On the other hand, $D_4 \not\models \Sigma$, and thus further pr-steps need to applied to K_4. By enforcing σ_2 over the first two facts of K_4 we can get the following two (alternative) probabilistic instances K_5 (left) and K_6 (right):

bob	$\bot_1$	$\bot_3$
bob	$\bot_1$	$\bot_3$
alice	math	$\bot_3$

$P(\bot_1 = \mathsf{math}) = 1/2$
$P(\bot_2 = \mathsf{nyc}) = 1/2$
$P(\bot_3 = \mathsf{rome}) = 1/3$

bob	$\bot_1$	$\bot_3$
bob	$\bot_1$	$\bot_3$
alice	math	$\bot_3$

$P(\bot_1 = \mathsf{math}) = 1/2$
$P(\bot_2 = \mathsf{nyc}) = 1/2$
$P(\bot_3 = \bot_2) = 2/3$

The only probabilistic world of K_5 is $(D_5, 1/12)$, while the only probabilistic world of K_6 is $(D_6, 1/6)$, where D_5 and D_6 are as follows:

$D_5 =$

bob	math	rome
bob	math	rome
alice	math	rome

$D_6 =$

bob	math	nyc
bob	math	nyc
alice	math	nyc

Since $D_5 \models \Sigma$ and $D_6 \models \Sigma$, both $(\mathsf{db}(D_5), 1/12)$ and $(\mathsf{db}(D_6), 1/6)$ are probabilistic repairs, and no further pr-step need to be applied.

Thus, the probabilistic repairs are $(\mathsf{db}(D_1), 1/2)$, $(\mathsf{db}(D_3), 1/4)$, $(\mathsf{db}(D_5), 1/12)$, and $(\mathsf{db}(D_6), 1/6)$. Notice that the sum of the probabilities of the probabilistic repairs is 1. Also, notice that D_3 and D_5 coincide. They might be replaced by a single probabilistic repair $(D', 1/4 + 1/12)$, where $D' = D_3 = D_5$. However, this does not affect query answering, that is, the probabilistic query answers are the same in both cases. □

4 Further developments

In light of previous result, in the full version of this paper we develop a polynomial time algorithm to compute approximate query answers where point probability are approximated by probability intervals. Thus, rather than providing query answers of the form (t, p), where t is a tuple and p is its probability, our approximation algorithm gives query answers of the form $(t, [\ell, u])$ guaranteeing that $p \in [\ell, u]$.

In order to do that, we define *probabilistic universal repairs*, i.e., compact representations of all repairs along with their degrees of consistency. This is one of the main tools used by our approximation algorithm, which works as follows: *(i)* it computes a universal probabilistic repair, *(ii)* it evaluates the given query over the universal probabilistic repair so as to produce a set of tuples associated with conditions (which keep track of how each tuple is derived), and *(iii)* it combines tuples' conditions with probability assignments of the universal probabilistic repair to derive the approximate intervals. Further developments should consider more general frameworks with TGDs [10] and logic rules [14,8,9].

References

1. Periklis Andritsos, Ariel Fuxman, and Renée J. Miller. Clean answers over dirty databases: A probabilistic approach. In *ICDE*, page 30, 2006.

2. Marcelo Arenas, Leopoldo E. Bertossi, and Jan Chomicki. Consistent query answers in inconsistent databases. In *PODS*, pages 68–79, 1999.
3. Leopoldo E. Bertossi. *Database Repairing and Consistent Query Answering*. Synthesis Lectures on Data Management. Morgan & Claypool Publishers, 2011.
4. Leopoldo E. Bertossi, Loreto Bravo, Enrico Franconi, and Andrei Lopatenko. The complexity and approximation of fixing numerical attributes in databases under integrity constraints. *Inf. Syst.*, 33(4-5):407–434, 2008.
5. Meghyn Bienvenu, Camille Bourgaux, and Francois Goasdoué. Querying inconsistent description logic knowledge bases under preferred repair semantics. In *AAAI*, pages 996–1002, 2014.
6. Meghyn Bienvenu and Riccardo Rosati. Tractable approximations of consistent query answering for robust ontology-based data access. In *IJCAI*, pages 775–781, 2013.
7. Philip Bohannon, Michael Flaster, Wenfei Fan, and Rajeev Rastogi. A cost-based model and effective heuristic for repairing constraints by value modification. In *SIGMOD*, pages 143–154, 2005.
8. Marco Calautti, Sergio Greco, Cristian Molinaro, and Irina Trubitsyna. Checking termination of logic programs with function symbols through linear constraints. In *RuleML*, volume 8620 of *LNCS*, pages 97–111. Springer, 2014.
9. Marco Calautti, Sergio Greco, Cristian Molinaro, and Irina Trubitsyna. Logic program termination analysis using atom sizes. In *IJCAI*, pages 2833–2839. AAAI Press, 2015.
10. Marco Calautti, Leonid Libkin, and Andreas Pieris. An operational approach to consistent query answering. In *PODS*, 2018.
11. Sergio Flesca, Filippo Furfaro, and Francesco Parisi. Querying and repairing inconsistent numerical databases. *ACM Trans. Database Syst.*, 35(2):14:1–14:50, 2010.
12. Enrico Franconi, Antonio Laureti Palma, Nicola Leone, Simona Perri, and Francesco Scarcello. Census data repair: a challenging application of disjunctive logic programming. In *LPAR*, pages 561–578, 2001.
13. Sergio Greco and Cristian Molinaro. Probabilistic query answering over inconsistent databases. *Ann. Math. Artif. Intell.*, 64(2-3):185–207, 2012.
14. Sergio Greco, Cristian Molinaro, and Irina Trubitsyna. Logic programming with function symbols: Checking termination of bottom-up evaluation through program adornments. *Theory Pract. Log. Program.*, 13(4-5):737–752, 2013.
15. Sergio Greco, Cristian Molinaro, and Irina Trubitsyna. Computing approximate query answers over inconsistent knowledge bases. In *IJCAI*, pages 1838–1846, 2018.
16. Domenico Lembo, Maurizio Lenzerini, Riccardo Rosati, Marco Ruzzi, and Domenico Fabio Savo. Inconsistency-tolerant query answering in ontology-based data access. *J. Web Sem.*, 33:3–29, 2015.
17. Thomas Lukasiewicz, Enrico Malizia, and Cristian Molinaro. Complexity of approximate query answering under inconsistency in datalog+/-. In *IJCAI*, pages 1921–1927, 2018.
18. Thomas Lukasiewicz, Maria Vanina Martinez, Andreas Pieris, and Gerardo I. Simari. From classical to consistent query answering under existential rules. In *AAAI*, pages 1546–1552, 2015.
19. Riccardo Rosati. On the complexity of dealing with inconsistency in description logic ontologies. In *IJCAI*, pages 1057–1062, 2011.
20. Dan Suciu, Dan Olteanu, Christopher Ré, and Christoph Koch. *Probabilistic Databases*. Synthesis Lectures on Data Management. Morgan & Claypool Publishers, 2011.
21. Jef Wijsen. Database repairing using updates. *ACM Trans. Database Syst.*, 30(3):722–768, 2005.

Parallelizing Approximate Search on Adaptive Radix Trees

Tobias Groth[1], Sven Groppe[1], Martin Koppehel[2], and Thilo Pionteck[2]

[1] University of Lübeck, Ratzeburger Allee 160, 23562 Lübeck, Germany
{groth, groppe}@ifis.uni-luebeck.de
[2] Otto von Guericke University Magdeburg, Universitätsplatz 2,
39106 Magdeburg, Germany
{martin.koppehel, thilo.pionteck}@ovgu.de

Abstract. Efficient searching in a number of strings is a common task in computer science and radix-trees are often used as a compact storage for string saving. One variant is the Adaptive-Radix-Tree (ART). ART has adaptive node sizes for more compact and cache-friendly memory layout. Graphical Processing Units (GPUs) can be used as hardware accelerator for massively parallel tasks and in addition they use very fast memory. We propose a parallel approximate search in the ART on CPU and GPU to optimize the throughput of queries and speed up applications that depends on these algorithms. Thereby we use the edit distance to compare two search keys in the tree and select appropriate values. We use the CPU for experimental comparison with the GPU, which have several thousand cores and modern processors typically have four to several dozens cores, but theses cores and RAM are more flexible. We propose several variations of the CPU algorithm like fixed vs. dynamic memory layouts and pointer vs. pointer-less data structures. In our experimental evaluation with OpenCL on ROCm 3.0, AMDs platform for GPU-Enabled HPC and Ultrascale Computing, the speedup and throughput of the GPU implementation for the approximate search in comparison with the best CPU variant are in the maximum up to factor 4.16 depending on the size of the tree and batch size. The speedup between the best and the worst CPU algorithm is up to factor 11.67, depending on tree and batch size.

Keywords: Adaptive-Radix-Tree(ART) · CPU acceleration · GPU acceleration · OpenCL · edit-distance · parallel · approximate search

1 Introduction

Modern multicore processors have many cores and further techniques of parallelism. Furthermore GPUs have a higher computing power and are much more optimized for parallel processing. They have up to several thousand cores, but these cores are different from the CPU ones. They are more specialized to perform a single operation on multiple data [1] (SIMD). Also a graphics card contains multiple gigabytes of very fast high-bandwidth memory, but data transfers and fixed memory hierarchies can have negative implications on the performance if not considered during algorithm design. In computer science, key-value pairs are often used, e.g. indices in database or as tags in geographic information retrieval systems [17]. These algorithms benefit from an efficient and fast access to the values by a certain key. The keys are often strings in most times. An efficient data structure for string keys is the PATRICIA-tree [15] and the more general radix tree, which is a memory-efficient storage for the keys and widely used for indexes. The memory-efficient storage is the big advantage of radix trees in comparison to other structures like the skiplist, where keys are stored independently from each other. One variant of the radix tree is the Adaptive-Radix-Tree [12] (ART), which has adaptive node sizes and a lower memory consumption than the other variants because the shared prefix of multiple keys is only stored once.

Besides searching for an exact matched key, an approximate search is interesting as well. Approximate searches are widely used to retrieve information from databases and dictionaries. Also an approximate search can be used to find an optimal sequence alignment and matching parts of DNA sequences [10]. For an approximate search in ART, we need a metric to distinguish string keys. There are several different approaches like for example the Jaccard-Coefficent [6], the Cosine-Similarity [16] and the Edit-Distance [13]. The Jaccard-Coefficent uses set operations on sets of n-grams in comparisons. This n-grams can be for example, words or characters. The Cosine-Similarity is based on the frequency of words in a text. The edit distance represents the number of insert, replace and delete operations, which are required to transform a string into another [13] and is hence very intuitive for humans. Because the edit distance is a widely used metrics for string similarity, we propose approximate search algorithms to determine edit distances between a search term and a given set of keys and we use ART in order to avoid multiple computations for shared prefixes. These algorithms are using CPU and GPU acceleration and are optimized for massively parallel execution.

Our contributions are

- highly efficient approximate search algorithms for ART on CPU and GPU,
- variants of these algorithms on the CPU, including pointer versus pointer-less data structure and using fixed versus dynamic memory allocation,
- the most efficient GPU variant with pointer-less data structure and using fixed memory allocation, and
- an extensive experimental evaluation and analysis of these algorithms.

First we look at related work in Section 2. Next the ART is explained in Section 3.1 and then the concept of the searches is described in Section 4. Finally we present a comprehensive experimental evaluation in Section 5 and conclude in Section 6.

2 Related Work

In many papers approximate searches, GPU acceleration and trees are a research topic, but the focus is different. Papers like [10] describe the basics of approximate algorithms and the calculation of the edit distance. A problem for most tree structures on GPUs is that pointers aren't optimal for GPUs. Approaches to handle pointer data structures exist in [11] and [14]. The contribution in [14] describes a tree structure for fast copying of different types of trees. A common and widely used tree is the B^+. The authors of [7] have focused on this tree and optimize their algorithms for GPGPU. It is used wherever the order of elements and parallel computing are important. Another tree structure is FAST [9], which is a binary and architecture sensitive tree. It is optimized for low latency and uses thread and data-level parallelism and explore them on CPU and GPU. Therefore the sizes for page, cache line size and SIMD width are variable. GPU LSM [4] is a data structure for dynamic dictionaries on GPU. It has support for fast insertion and deletion based on the LSM-tree. For retrieval lookup, count and range queries are supported. For the Adaptive-Radix-Tree the GPU-based radix tree (GRT) [1] variant has been developed, which is written in CUDA and supports exact and range based search. A mapping is used by the search algorithm to transfer the tree structure to the GPU memory. The authors of [3] compare the Adaptive-Radix-Tree with Judy, two variants of hashing via quadratic probing and three variants of Cuckoo hashing in an extensive experimental evaluation. The results are that hash tables perform better in OLAP and OLTP scenarios, but for range queries ART is significantly faster. In comparisons with a B^+-tree ART is slower in performing range queries. ART is two times faster than Judy, which is also an adaptive radix tree variant, but ART needs the double space of memory. Besides trees hash tables are an important data structure. Therefore [2] introduces an algorithm for building large hash tables in real time. For this purpose, they used a data-parallel approach and build the tables on GPU. They also applied their hashing methods to graphic applications. In comparison to the discussed works we consider an GPU accelerated approximate search in ART as our main contribution, which hasn't been considered for this data structure in the existing literature to the best of our knowledge. This includes the development of different parallel variants for modern CPU and GPU features.

3 Basics

3.1 The Adaptive-Radix-Tree

The Adaptive-Radix-Tree (ART) [12] is a tree designed for in-memory-databases. ART has four different node types with three different memory representations for an efficient memory layout for different node sizes. Nodes are created at the deepest possible level of the tree; this is called lazy expansions. Further path compression is used to reduce the size of the ART and to speed up the search. We present an example ART in fig. 3. The tree contains 10 keys and two node types Node4 and Node16 are used. These types contain a maximum of four and

16 children. All inner nodes except one have a shared prefix of length one. The leafs contain numbers as values.

Nodes are only created if they are required and superfluous nodes with only one child are removed. If the maximum number of children is exceeded, a bigger node is used. If the number is lower than the minimum, a smaller node is chosen. Path compression uses a hybrid approach. In every node there is space to store a fixed number of characters. If this space is exceeded, a modified approach is applied. Instead saving subsequent characters, the length of the string is saved. This length is used by the search algorithm to jump over characters in the search term and to select the next character for the branch decision. This approach leads to wrong results in some cases, because a wrong search term is marked as correct even if different characters are in the missing part of the string. This problem can be avoided if the complete key is also saved in the leaf. Hence if the search ends in a leaf node the whole key has to be compared. [12]

3.2 Edit-Distance

The edit distance can be calculated with a simple algorithm. For two keys u,v with the length m and n, a matrix M can be calculated where the initial case is $M_{0,0} = 0, M_{i,0} = i, 1 \leq i \leq m, M_{0,j} = j, 1 \leq j \leq n$. Then the further cells can be determined by applying the rules given in fig. 1a.

If $u_i = v_j$
then
$M_{i,j} = M_{i-1,j-1}$
else

$$M_{i,j} = min \begin{cases} M_{i-1,j-1} + 1 \\ M_{i,j-1} + 1 \\ M_{i-1,j} + 1 \end{cases}$$

endif
$1 \leq i \leq m, 1 \leq j \leq n$

(a) Rules for computing the edit distance

		i	n	s	t	i	t	u	t	e
	0	1	2	3	4	5	6	7	8	9
i	1	0	1	2	3	4	5	6	7	8
n	2	1	0	1	2	3	4	5	6	7
c	3	2	1	1	2	3	4	5	6	7
o	4	3	2	2	2	3	4	5	6	7
m	5	4	3	3	3	3	4	5	6	7
i	6	5	4	4	4	3	4	5	6	7
n	7	6	5	5	5	4	4	5	6	7
g	8	7	6	6	6	5	5	5	6	7

t != i
min(5+1,
6+1,
4+1)
= 5

e.g.
5 operations are needed to transform "institu" into "incom" or vice versa

(b) Edit distance example and example computation of one cell

Fig. 1. Rules and an example matrix for the edit distance

Without backtracking, the algorithm requires only the last column to compute the next. This will be used to reduce the memory consumption. We can reduce the size further and can use only one column and a variable for computation, but this takes away the possibility to revert the last computation if a branch occurs.

4 Approximate Search Algorithm

In this section we develop an approximate search for CPUs and GPUs. Furthermore, we optimize the approximate search for better throughput and to handle bigger trees.

4.1 Memory Organization

If ART is used on a GPU, a tree that is stored in a continuous memory is required because copying a big chunk of memory is faster than many small pieces of memory. Nodes are linked by offsets in order to avoid pointers, which would be invalidated by the transfer on the GPU. An example of the memory mapping is shown in fig. 2. In this example we traverse the tree with a depth-first-search algorithm. We reserve memory on the way down and insert the data on the way up. This is necessary because the offsets of all children have to be known before saving a node. The complete memory object will grow dynamically because the size of the tree is unknown. However, the memory object is continuous, so it has a fixed size and needs to be extended in case of an overflow. Therefore the overflow has to be detected and a new memory object has to be created. Then the algorithm copies all data to the new memory object, but the offset remains unchanged because it is relative to the beginning position of the memory. After the algorithm finishes, a continuous memory for the tree is created. The root node is placed at the first address of the continuous memory.

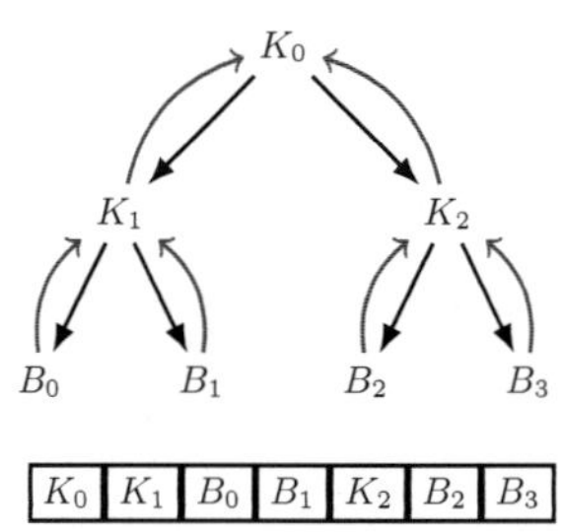

Fig. 2. Mapping of a tree in a continuous memory, red edges are back jumps. We start at K_0 and reserve memory for the node. Then we visit K_1 and reserve memory. Then we reserve memory for B_1 and we reach the end of a path. Now we store B_0 in the reserved memory and jump back. The same happens to B_1. Then all children of K_1 are stored and we store the node in the reserved memory and go to K_0. Because K_0 has another child K_2, we are processing the subtree in K_2 in an analogous way.

4.2 Approximate Search on ART utilizing CPUs

The CPU has flexible cores combined with dynamic memory and can calculate many threads in parallel. To address these advantages, we develop an algorithm (see fig. 3a), which uses these techniques to calculate the edit distance and to choose a key that is below or equal this distance. First we can use threads to run multiple searches in parallel. Furthermore, we have to find out if we can also use parallelism inside the tree. Because for calculation of the edit distance only the previous and the current columns are necessary, with dynamic memory, we can simply copy the column for each branch. Then we start a new thread with this column and the current position in the tree. We use tasks with an automatic management of threads to avoid problems with the overhead of thread start, and stop operation and with an overload if there are too many threads. If we reach a node, where all edit distance values are above the maximum edit distance, we prune the whole subtree, and use backtracking in order to visit not already visited branches of previous nodes. Note that previous columns are already determined. We only have to reset the position and remove all columns, except of the previous ones. If we reach a leaf we calculate the edit distance for the last characters and look at the last element in the column. If it is lower than or equal to the maximum edit distance, we have found a proper key and we have to save the value in a list. Because the algorithm runs in parallel, we have to lock the list and then save the value. Because we search in parallel, we need to lock the list with a write-lock. This is sufficient, because we require unique search terms in one batch and hence it does not occur that they reach the same leaf. Alternatives are that we can use multiple lists and merge them at the end. Please note that we can't allocate fixed sized memory for lock free access, because the result size in each search is different and unknown.

4.3 Approximate Search on ART utilizing GPUs

For the GPU algorithm, please see fig. 3b for an example. Because the GPU has a different architecture, our algorithm is more complex than the one on the CPU. We use parallelism for multiple search requests and for root node processing. Because we don't have dynamic memory we can't create or remove columns. Therefore, we use a static memory buffer with two columns with the maximum length of a search term and calculate the edit distance alternating the roles of two columns. First all work-items calculate the edit distance of the root node in parallel and save this value in a sequential reset buffer. Then all work-items process the deeper nodes sequentially. To save the progress and to have a proper ending condition, the maximum path length in the tree is necessary. With this length, we create a buffer, where we save the number of processed children in a node for the current path. If we reach a leaf or the maximum edit distance, we increment the counter for the processed children in the level above. Because we don't have a history of the edit distance, we have to jump to the sequential root and calculate all edit distances again. Then we reach the position again and we select the next child. To reduce this overhead for long paths we additionally reserve memory for a reset buffer in the half length of the path.

A major problem is the result buffer, because the number of results is unknown, but the buffer size has to be known before the executions starts. The result of a search can be zero to number of leafs in the tree. We limit the amount of memory and if we detect an overflow, then we abort. This leads to unfinished executions and missing results. Hence we modify the search algorithm to filter missing queries and execute them sequentially with enough memory for all results. Furthermore, we use a three level result buffer shown in fig. 4 to optimize the fill level. The size increases with the shared level. Level 1 only has space for a few results and the third level has space for millions of results. Because sharing memory between work-items require concurrent access, lock and unlock functionality is indispensable. Therefore atomics are used to increment a counter and get the old value. This value is used to exclusively access the buffer cell. For a better bandwidth and GPU usage, multiple threads can be started on the CPU and every thread gets a chunk of search queries and executes them on the GPU in parallel. Therefore every thread has separate buffers except of the tree buffer, which is always shared read-only.

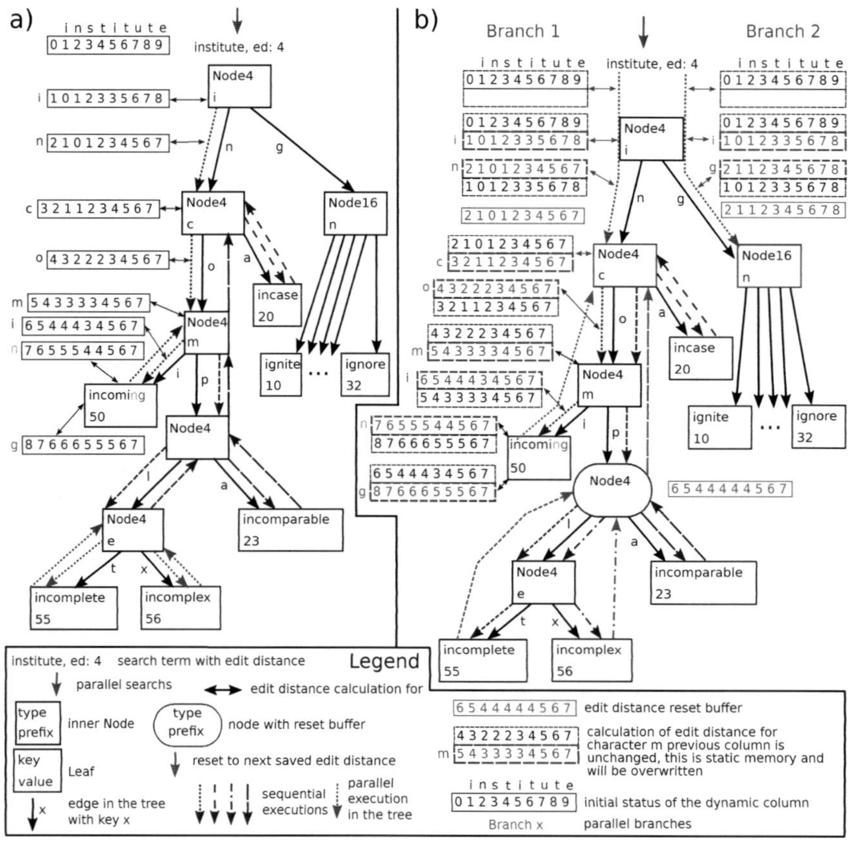

Fig. 3. Comparison of tree traversal with edit distance in a) CPU and b) GPU algorithms. We search for all keys that have a maximum edit distance of two to the search term "institute". To visualize the calculation of the edit distance, the columns for the path to the node with the key "incoming" is provided

5 Experimental Evaluation

We evaluate the proposed algorithms for CPU and GPU in this section.

5.1 Experimental Environment

The experimental evaluation runs on a Ryzen 1700X with 8 cores and 16 threads and a RX Vega 56 with 8GB HBM2-memory and 56 compute-units with 1024 processing elements each. Therefore 57344 work-items can be executed in parallel. The local memory on the GPU is 64KB large. The evaluation system is equipped with 16GB RAM and an SSD. Ubuntu 18.04 is used as software platform and we compile the code with the GCC compiler in version 8. OpenCL acceleration is provided via ROCm 3.0.

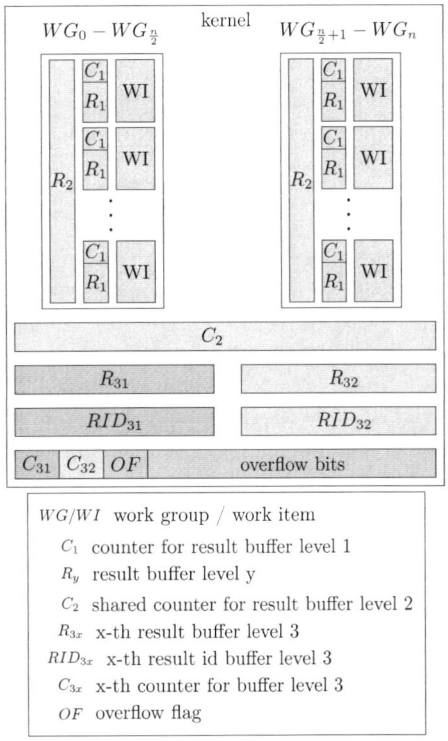

Fig. 4. A kernel work-item can store the data of unknown length using different memory levels. First it uses the level 1 buffer directly and exclusively. If this memory is full, level 2 memory is used and shared with all work-items in a work-group. If this memory is depleted, level 3 buffer is used. There are two buffers, the first half of the work groups share the first half and the second half share the second. If all buffers are depleted, the work-item tags the search with an overflow bit and the search is sequentially executed afterwards

5.2 Benchmark Data

For our experiments, a compilation of synthetic and real test data is used. The load times of a search depends on various parameters, whereby the most important ones are the number of search terms, the number of branches in a node, the depth of the tree and the length of the shared prefix. Each of these properties is examined in this evaluation. For a single experiment the other properties are fixed and then the examined property is changed. We repeat a search mostly 10 times except for single runs that take longer than one hour. These searches are only repeated three times. If a search takes longer than four hours, we used

https://www.amd.com/de/products/cpu/amd-ryzen-7-1700x
https://www.amd.com/de/products/graphics/radeon-rx-vega-56
https://www.ubuntu.com/desktop
https://gcc.gnu.org
https://www.khronos.org/opencl
https://rocm.github.io

two executions. The duration is measured and the average is calculated and displayed in graphs. If the number of search requests isn't displayed in the graph of the approximate search, 10,000 requests are made per iteration. The search terms are created by randomly choosing a key from the dataset, which is modified by a specific number of characters. Additionally to the described synthetic data and queries, and for more realistic data we use a data set from the billion triples challenge (BTC) [5]. This real-world data set contains 19,655,239 triples with 4,352,096 unique keys and the longest key has a length of 32,628. The resulting tree has a maximal path length of 34. Further the tree and the algorithms have several important parameters. The maximum edit distance describes, which max distance between a key in the result and the search term is acceptable. For the algorithm the maximum path length (MPL) and the maximum search term length (MSL) are important. The MPL describes the longest path from the root to a leaf. It is important for the stack, which describes the next child and the exit condition. The MSL describes the maximum length of a batch of search terms and is required for the length of the column. The important parameters for the performance of the CPU algorithm are the number of parallel search terms and tasks in tree. They describe how many parallel searches are made and how many parallelism is inside a tree. For the GPU there are the number of GPU threads and the kernel size. The first parameter describes how many parallel command queues will be used and the second one, how many search terms are processed in a kernel execution and will be computed in parallel.

5.3 Approximate Search on ART

For better distinction, we introduce a naming schema for the developed algorithms. Dynamic memory allocation is represented by d, fixed memory by f, pointer based ART structure by p and pointer-less offset structure by l. Hence we use the following naming schema e.g. $CPU_{p,d}$ represents the developed CPU algorithm and $GPU_{l,f}$ the GPU algorithm. Further variants are $CPU_{l,d}$, $CPU_{p,f}$ and $CPU_{l,f}$. To get proper evaluation results, we have to fine-tune the settings for all algorithms. $CPU_{p,d}$ and $CPU_{l,d}$ are much faster if we process as many queries as possible in parallel: The best configuration uses 250 parallel queries and spare on parallel computations inside the tree. Because the root node is parallelized in $GPU_{l,f}$, $CPU_{p,f}$ and $CPU_{l,f}$, the number of parallel queries depends on the root node type. For performance the optimal number of parallel queries is up to 5000 for $GPU_{l,f}$ and up to 30 for $CPU_{p,f}$ and $CPU_{l,f}$. More tasks would produce more overhead on the CPU and on the GPU the number of executions is limited by the GPU memory.

The original ART has to be modified for the approximate search, because the calculation of the maximum edit distance is only possible if all characters of the shared prefix are saved. The original ART only saves a prefix with fixed length. By replacing the fixed length prefix for correct results of the algorithm with a prefix with variable size we have to deal with a higher memory consumption. The variable size prefix is implemented by a separate buffer, whereby an offset is used to access single elements in the buffer.

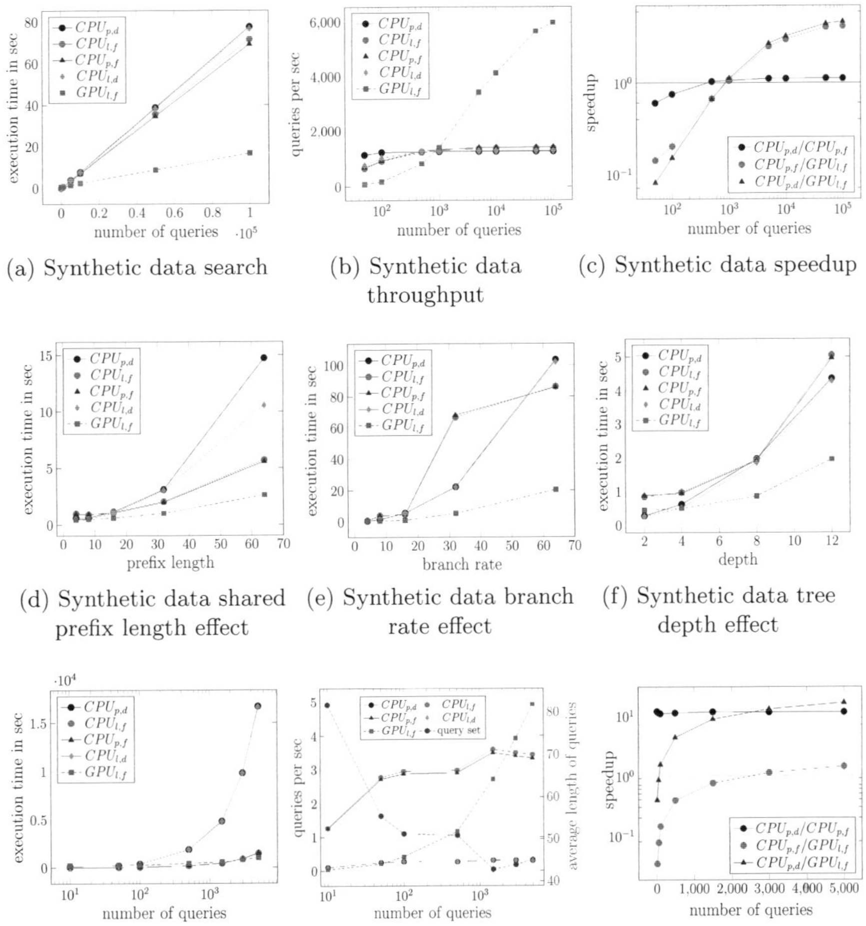

(a) Synthetic data search (b) Synthetic data throughput (c) Synthetic data speedup

(d) Synthetic data shared prefix length effect (e) Synthetic data branch rate effect (f) Synthetic data tree depth effect

(g) BTC data search (h) BTC throughput (i) BTC speedup

Fig. 5. Evaluation results of the approximate search implementations

In the experiments (see fig. 5(a-i)), the $CPU_{p,d}$ is the slowest algorithm and performs worse in comparison to the variants as more queries are processed. This is independent from the dataset and its properties. We achieve analogous results for the $CPU_{l,d}$, but the algorithm has advantages if the length of the common prefix increases. $CPU_{p,f}$ and $CPU_{l,f}$ have a better performance in all situations except of a higher branch rate. In this case, the limited parallelism is a problem and the $CPU_{p,d}$ and $CPU_{l,d}$ are initially faster, but this is changed if the number of searches is further increased. The $GPU_{l,f}$ is slower at a small number of queries because the transfer and execution overhead are higher, but if the number of queries is increased, the algorithm is faster than the other algorithms. The speedup is up to 4.16 on synthetic data and up to 1.43 on real-world BTC-data. Because the creation of queries depends on random, the average length of the used queries varies. As shown in fig. 5h (red line and axis on the right), the throughput depends on the length of search terms. If the length is increased, the edit distance calculation increases in the same way and the throughput is decreased. This effect is more significant if the parallelism is very limited. If the parallelism is higher, we can compute more long terms in parallel in the same time. Because of this effect, $CPU_{p,f}$ and $CPU_{l,f}$ are more affected than the other algorithms and have a non-linear trend.

6 Summary and Conclusions

We introduce approximate search algorithms, which run on CPU and GPU. Thereby the memory situation is observed: The CPU algorithm uses dynamic memory allocation and the GPU memory layout is adaptive but static during a run. The approximate algorithm that runs on the CPU uses tasks as an implementation of parallelism. Tasks provide a solution by splitting the workload to multiple threads. In contrast, the GPU uses a hierarchical result memory concept and processes the data in chunks. In our experiments, the approximate search on the GPU has a higher throughput and speedup compared to the CPU implementation. Inspired by the approximate search designed for the GPU, we develop and evaluate CPU variants using pointer versus pointer-less data structures and using fixed versus dynamic memory allocation. The speedup between the best CPU and the GPU variant is about 1.43, while the speedup between the worst CPU variant and the GPU is about 16.41. The current GPU implementation can only handle trees that fit into the GPU memory. It is promising for future work to extend the algorithms and enable larger trees to be processed by investigating compression for ART. Furthermore with OpenCL 2 Fine-Grained System SVM [8] the original pointer structure could be kept and the CPU and GPU can share the tree and data directly. Our future work covers also hybrid approaches with APUs, which are combinations of CPU and GPU on the same chip with shared memory.

Acknowledgements

This work is funded by the German Research Foundation (DFG) project GR 3435/15-1.

Funded by DFG Deutsche Forschungsgemeinschaft German Research Foundation

References

1. Alam, M., Yoginath, S.B., Perumalla, K.S.: Performance of point and range queries for in-memory databases using radix trees on gpus. In: 18th IEEE International Conference on High Performance Computing and Communications; 14th IEEE International Conference on Smart City; 2nd IEEE International Conference on Data Science and Systems, HPCC/SmartCity/DSS, Sydney, Australia, December 12-14. pp. 1493–1500 (2016)

2. Alcantara, D.A., Sharf, A., Abbasinejad, F., Sengupta, S., Mitzenmacher, M., Owens, J.D., Amenta, N.: Real-time parallel hashing on the GPU. ACM Trans. Graph. **28**(5), 154 (2009)
3. Alvarez, V., Richter, S., Chen, X., Dittrich, J.: A comparison of adaptive radix trees and hash tables. In: 31st IEEE International Conference on Data Engineering, ICDE, Seoul, South Korea, April 13-17. pp. 1227–1238 (2015)
4. Ashkiani, S., Li, S., Farach-Colton, M., Amenta, N., Owens, J.D.: GPU LSM: A dynamic dictionary data structure for the GPU. In: IEEE International Parallel and Distributed Processing Symposium, IPDPS, Vancouver, BC, Canada, May 21-25. pp. 430–440 (2018)
5. Harth, A.: Billion Triples Challenge data set. Downloaded from http://km.aifb.kit.edu/projects/btc-2012/ (2012)
6. Jaccard, P.: Étude comparative de la distribution florale dans une portion des alpes et des jura. Bulletin del la Société Vaudoise des Sciences Naturelles **37**, 547–579 (1901)
7. Kaczmarski, K.: B $^{+}$ -tree optimized for GPGPU. In: On the Move to Meaningful Internet Systems: OTM, Confederated International Conferences: CoopIS, DOA-SVI, and ODBASE, Rome, Italy, September 10-14. Proceedings, Part II. pp. 843–854 (2012)
8. Kaeli, D.R., Mistry, P., Schaa, D., Zhang, D.P.: Heterogeneous Computing with OpenCL 2.0. Morgan Kaufmann Publishers Inc., San Francisco, CA, USA, 1st edn. (2015)
9. Kim, C., Chhugani, J., Satish, N., Sedlar, E., Nguyen, A.D., Kaldewey, T., Lee, V.W., Brandt, S.A., Dubey, P.: FAST: fast architecture sensitive tree search on modern cpus and gpus. In: Proceedings of the ACM SIGMOD International Conference on Management of Data, SIGMOD, Indianapolis, Indiana, USA, June 6-10. pp. 339–350 (2010)
10. Krugel, J.A.: Approximate Pattern Matching with Index Structures. Phd thesis, Technical University of Munich, Munich, Germany (2016)
11. Lefohn, A.E., Sengupta, S., Kniss, J., Strzodka, R., Owens, J.D.: Glift: Generic, efficient, random-access gpu data structures. ACM Trans. Graph. **25**(1), 60–99 (Jan 2006)
12. Leis, V., Kemper, A., Neumann, T.: The adaptive radix tree: Artful indexing for main-memory databases. In: 29th IEEE International Conference on Data Engineering, ICDE, Brisbane, Australia, April 8-12. pp. 38–49 (2013)
13. Levenshtein, V.I.: Binary Codes Capable of Correcting Deletions, Insertions and Reversals. Soviet Physics Doklady **10**, 707 (Feb 1966)
14. Lu, Y., Yang, L., Bhavsar, V.C., Kumar, N.: Tree structured data processing on GPUs. In: 7th International Conference on Cloud Computing, Data Science Engineering - Confluence, Noida, India. pp. 498–505 (2017)
15. Morrison, D.R.: PATRICIA - practical algorithm to retrieve information coded in alphanumeric. J. ACM **15**(4), 514–534 (1968)
16. Salton, G., Buckley, C.: Term-weighting approaches in automatic text retrieval. Information Processing & Management **24**(5), 513 – 523 (1988)
17. Yousaf, M., Wolter, D.: How to identify appropriate key-value pairs for querying osm. In: Proceedings of the 13th Workshop on Geographic Information Retrieval. GIR '19, Association for Computing Machinery, New York, NY, USA (2019)

A Document-based RDF Keyword Search System: Query-by-Query Analysis

Dennis Dosso[1 [0000-0001-7307-4607]] and Gianmaria Silvello[1 [0000-0003-4970-4554]]

Department of Information Engineering, University of Padua
{dosso, silvello}@dei.unipd.it

Abstract. RDF datasets are today used more and more for a great variety of applications mainly due to their flexibility. However, accessing these data via the SPARQL query language can be cumbersome and frustrating for end-users accustomed to Web-based search engines. In this context, KS is becoming a key methodology to overcome access and search issues. In this paper, we further dig on our previous work on the state-of-the-art system for keyword search on RDF by giving more insights on the quality of answers produced and its behavior with different classes of queries.

Keywords: RDF · Keyword Search · Virtual Documents

1 Introduction

In the last decade, the Web of Data emerged as one of the principal means to access, share and re-use structured data on the Web [12]. RDF has become the *de facto* standard for the publication of information on the Web [14] because it eases the enrichment and discovery of data as well as their interoperability.

In the past years, we have seen a significant increase in the number of knowledge bases published as large RDF datasets, such as DBpedia , Wikidata , and OpenPHACTS . The use of RDF is growing also for the representation and management of enterprise data with heterogeneous and very large graphs, often containing millions of edges [14].

RDF datasets are typically queried through the SPARQL structured language [13], which is often difficult to use for non-expert users due to its syntax and the required knowledge of the underlying structure of the database and the utilized IRIs. This language is not intuitive for end-users and it does not allow the natural expression of their information needs based on keywords [17].

https://wiki.dbpedia.org/
https://www.wikidata.org/wiki/Wikidata:Main_Page
https://www.openphacts.org/

Keyword search is a simpler paradigm that enables users to express their information need through keywords [10]. Keyword-based methods have gained importance over time both in research and in industry as a means to facilitate access to structured data. The result of a keyword query is a *ranking* of potential answers, ordered depending on their relevance to the information need.

In this paper, we introduce the TSA+BM25 and TSA+VDP keyword search systems, first published in [6] and the new evaluation methodology presented in [5].

The new **contributions** of this paper are: (i) a study of the *quality* of the answers produced by state-of-the-art systems in keyword search on RDF: SLM, MRF-KS, SUMM, TSA+BM25, and TSA+VDP; (ii) a study of the behavior of the two most performing systems, MRF-KS and TSA+VDP, on different *classes* of queries. Each query is composed of a `CONSTRUCT` SPARQL query and a corresponding "equivalent" keyword query. These classes differ both in terms of syntax (the SPARQL pattern used to write the query) and in their semantics (the information need expressed by the query). We analyze how the syntax and the semantic impact the performances of the system at hand.

The paper is organized as follows: Section 2 summarizes the related works; Section 3 briefly describes our methods, the datasets, the evaluation metrics and the classes of queries we defined; in Section 4 we present the experiments; finally, Section 5 presents the conclusions.

2 Related Work

In recent years keyword search received a lot of attention in the research community, both in the contest of Relational Databases (RDB) and Graph DB. Good reviews about this topic are [2], [18] (for a focus on RDB) and [16] (for a focus on graph data).

Keyword Search systems may be categorized into three main classes: (i) *schema-based* (e.g. DISCOVER [1]), which uses the schema of the database to produce a structured query; (ii) *graph-based* (e.g. BANKS [3]), which explores the graph (the graph induced by the foreign keys, if we are in a relational database); (iii) *document-based* (first described in [10]), stemming from the graph-based, this class is based on the creation of textual documents, also called *virtual documents*, from the words contained in the graphs. It also uses state-of-the-art IR methods for the indexing and ranking of the answers. Thanks to this strategy, the systems belonging to this class showed to scale to real-world scenarios.

In this paper we compare our system TSA+VDP [6] to the following state-of-the-art keyword search systems:

1. *Structured Language Model* (SLM) [7] is among the few native RDF search systems. It starts the searching process from the triples that match at least one of the query keywords and then produces answers by seeking connected components in the graph. SLM is based on virtual documents and employs IR models (statistical language models) for retrieval. SLM returns a ranking of RDF subgraphs to the user and not virtual text documents as in [8, 15].

2. *Markov Random Fields-Keyword Search* (MRF-KS)[11] is based on a combination of graph and virtual-document-based approaches. This system has proven to be the most effective one on the shared benchmark in [4]. MRF-KS was originally thought to work on RDBs, even though in principle it can be used for any kind of graph data. We redesigned it to work on RDF and use it as a competing baseline.
3. SUMM [9] is a native RDF search system. The core idea behind this system is to produce a first partition of the whole graph through a BFS-based greedy algorithm. The partitions are edge-disjointed but are connected one to the other through nodes called portal nodes. Once given the keyword query, a backtracking algorithm similar to BANKS [3] is deployed to find connected subgraphs containing all the keywords. On these subgraphs, a different backtracking algorithm similar to BLINKS [8] is used to produce tree-shaped answer graphs whose leaves are nodes containing one keyword each. The systems use indexes and particular stopping conditions to speed-up the execution.

2.1 TSA+BM25 and TSA+VDP

To overcome the limitations of the previous state-of-the-art systems, in [6] we proposed two new keyword search systems, based on the virtual document approach, one the refinement of the other. These systems are composed of an off-line and an on-line phase:

Off-line phase The off-line phase is common to both systems and is called **Topological Semantical Aggregator** (TSA), a virtual document-based approach that produces documents by aggregating RDF triples containing close concepts. TSA mimics the "clustering hypothesis" defined in IR which dictates that triples characterized by similar concepts will cluster together.

The algorithm takes an RDF graph as input and creates subgraphs without considering the user query. The idea is to build a subgraph around a single "topic" which characterizes the graph semantics. To do so, the algorithm starts randomly from a node that presents an out-degree higher of an empirically-defined threshold. From that node, the algorithm starts a Breadth-First Search-like exploration that visits only nodes that present in and out-degree between certain thresholds, limiting the exploration inside a radius τ. All these parameters are also empirically-defined. In this way, a subgraph is extracted from the bigger database. Once the exploration stops, the algorithm marks the utilized nodes as visited and proceeds randomly to the next unvisited node with high out-degree. Nodes may be visited more than once if they present a high in-degree, and in this case, they are shared by many graphs. The rationale is that these nodes may contain information belonging to more topics.

The result of TSA is a collection of subgraphs covering the whole database. They are then converted to their corresponding virtual documents through the extraction and concatenation of the words contained in the IRIs and Literals in their nodes and edges. We then index these documents with Terrier.

On-line phase Given a keyword query, our first system, **TSA+BM25**, applies the ranking function BM25 to the collection of virtual documents, and obtains a ranking of graphs. This system then looks for overlapping graphs in the ranking produced. Graphs that present a percentage of shared triples beyond an empirically-found threshold are merged. BM25 is used a second time to produce a new ranking on these merged graphs, which is returned to the user. This system is rather quick, since it uses state-of-the-art implementations of BM25, but does not leverage the information contained in the topology of the graphs.

Our second system is called **TSA+VDP** (VDP stands for **Virtual Document Pruning**). The system then considers the result of the set-based union of these ranking produced by TSA+BM25, which is called *query graph* E. This graph is not necessarily connected.

TSA+VDP then starts a BFS from every subject node within E. This BFS is also limited to a radius τ', and produces subgraphs. Of these subgraphs, only the ones containing all the keywords are kept, producing a new collection, called the *best candidates* collection. The rationale is that these selected graphs will contain, with high probability, triples that are relevant to the user. Since the BFS exploration could also have introduced many non-relevant triples, the next step is a pruning algorithm over these candidate graphs. The pruning proceeds inward, removing all the triples that do not contain at least one keyword, starting from the nodes with the highest distance from the source node.

These pruned graphs are finally ranked using a Markov Random Field scoring function inspired by the one used by MRF-KS. The final ranking is the answer returned to the user.

3 Methods

3.1 Preliminaries

While SPARQL enables the user to obtain an *exact answer* to his/her information need, it is not always the most viable approach [10]. SPARQL is a structured language with a complex syntax, which also requires complete knowledge of the graph being queried. A knowledge that the standard user (one who is not familiar with the concepts of RDF graphs) may not possess.

Keyword Search is a different paradigm that can help this kind of user to retrieve her information without SPARQL. In this approach, queries are an array $< w_1, \cdots, w_n >$ of keywords. The output is a list of *answers*, ordered depending on their relevance to the information need expressed by the query. This ordering is defined by a ranking function. It is important to note that while SPARQL returns an exact answer (even an empty one is that is the case), Keyword Search is a *best effort* approach.

The nature of the answers provided by the keyword search system depends on the task. In this paper, we consider a user who has an information need that can be formulated with a SPARQL `CONSTRUCT` query, which he/she is not able to formulate. If that query existed, the answer graph can be considered as the set of all and only the triples of the database that the user wants to see. We consider this set of triples as a *ground truth* (GT). The triples of the GT are called *relevant triples.*

Our task is to produce a ranking that contains as many relevant triples as possible in answer graphs ranked as highly as possible. These graphs should also not contain too many non-relevant (noisy) triples. A good system, therefore, produces a list of (preferably not-overlapping) subgraphs extracted from the database such that the subgraphs at the top of the list contain many relevant triples.

3.2 Evaluation

If a Keyword Search System returns a list of answers, we first of all need to understand when one of these graphs is *relevant.* We follow the same approach of [6], where a *signal-to-noise ratio* is defined for each answer graph.

Definition 1. *Given a topic* $t_k \in T$*, a ranking* R_k *and the ground-truth graph* GT_{t_k}*, we define the* Signal-to-Noise Ratio *(SNR) of* $G_i \in R_k$ *as*

$$SNR(G_i) = \frac{|(G_i \cap GT_{t_k}) \setminus S|}{|G_i|} \tag{1}$$

where S *is the union set of all the relevant triples in* $G_j \in R_k, \forall j \in [1, i[$ *such that* G_j *is relevant.*

Given this definition, we say that a graph is relevant when its SNR is bigger or equal to a threshold value $\lambda \in [0, 1]$. Note how the SNR keeps into consideration the relevant triples *already seen* in the ranking, avoiding to count them twice. We can say that a *quality answer* is a graph that has a high SNR.

We call λ the *relevance parameter*, which describes the quality required for a graph to be considered relevant. In this evaluation framework, the relevance is therefore not an absolute, fixed concept, but can be varied with λ. This parameter models the preferences of a user. A user who does not want noise in its answers is modeled with a λ close to 1. A user that allows for imperfect answers is modeled with a parameter closer to 0. In what follows we study how different values of λ change the evaluation of the output of the considered systems.

As evaluation measures we use *recall* and *tb-DCG.*

Recall is the total number of relevant triples found in the ranking produced by a system – typically considering the first 1000 results – divided by $|GT|$. The recall enables to understand the extractive power of a system, the raw quantity of relevant triples extrapolated from the database. While useful, it does not convey any information about the disposition of the triples in the ranking and little information on the quantity of noise that surrounds them in the subgraphs where they are contained.

tb-DCG [5] is a more sophisticated metric, a derivation of the classic NDCG, which takes into consideration aspects such as the *relevance* of the graphs (the number of triples of the GT contained in them), their *position* (relevant graphs put early weight more) and their *uniqueness* (repeated relevant triples are not counted).

3.3 Experimental Setup

We consider two databases: LinkedMDB and IMDB. LinkedMDB is a native RDF database of circa 7M triples. IMDB is a relational database that we converted into an RDF version of about 116M triples.

For both databases, we created 100 topics, divided into 5 classes of 20 queries each. 50 were used for training the parameters of TSA+VDP, the other 50 for testing. Every topic is represented as a pair made of a `CONSTRUCT` SPARQL query and a keyword counterpart, both representing the same information need. The SPARQL query is used to extract the subgraph which works as GT for the keyword query.

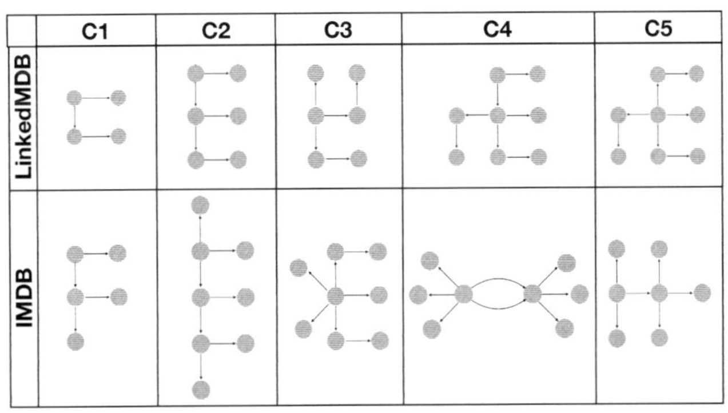

Fig. 1: The five query syntactical classes defined for LinkedMDB and IMDB.

Every class is syntactically different from the others, i.e. they differ in the shape of the pattern P, as can be seen in Figure 1. The figure presents the 10 patterns associated with each class ordered by increasing complexity. This complexity derives from the number of triples in the pattern and the shape of the connections created by these triples. Note that it is possible that two classes may differ only in the direction of one edge.

Each one of these classes is further divided into two sub-classes, differing by their semantic. For example, class `C1` of LinkedMDB is divided into `C1.1`, with queries asking for all the films of a certain director, and class `C1.2`, made of queries asking for all the films starring a certain actor.

The databases considered here, LinkedMDB 1M and IMDB 1M (of 1M triples each), are built by randomly extracting connected subsets of triples from the original datasets. The triples of the ground truths produced by the SPARQL are added to these datasets. This was necessary since only SUMM, TSA+BM25 and TSA+VDP are able to scale to the whole dimensions and we needed to be able to compare all systems.

Table 1: Performances of the algorithms on the 1M databases. † indicates the top performing systems returned by the Tukey HSD statistical test, with $\alpha < 0.01$. The best system is in bold. $\lambda = 0.1$

Dataset	Systems	tb-DCG	recall	time (sec)
LinkedMDB 1M	TSA+BM25	0.201±0.02	**0.733±0.02**†	**39.64±01.90**†
	TSA+VDP	**0.490±0.04**†	0.592±0.040†	318.78±21.60
	SLM	0.011±0.00	0.076±0.01	39.90±08.69†
	MRF-KS	0.400±0.03†	0.462±0.03	285.22±30.10
	SUMM	0.106±0.01	0.268±0.02	429.52±37.17
IMDB 1M	TSA+BM25	0.276±0.02	0.423±0.03	30.28±00.25†
	TSA+VDP	**0.583±0.04**†	**0.623±0.04**†	196.90±20.69
	SLM	0.011±0.00	0.057±0.00	**15.92±06.57**†
	MRF-KS	0.312±0.02	0.382±0.02	399.68±37.34
	SUMM	0.126±0.01	0.254±0.02	510.26±27.02

4 Experimental Performances

4.1 Average Analysis

Table 1 reports the average performances obtained by the five systems on the two databases, already presented in [6]. Considering tb-DCG, TSA+VDP is the best performing system, immediately followed by MRF-KS. The former also obtains good values of recall, only exceeded by TSA+BM25 on LinkedMDB 1M.

The two fastest algorithms are SLM and TSA+BM25. The former is very quick to produce its answers but has low effectiveness. The latter is fast thanks to its reliance on state-of-the-art implementations of BM25. On this note, TSA+VDP presents higher execution time due to its heuristics which prune and re-rank the graphs, obtaining more relevant graphs that are better ranked.

Analysis of the quality of the answers through the λ factor Note that in Table 1 we fixed λ to 0.1. This parameter was empirically chosen to show the differences in the effectiveness of the different systems. A higher λ could provoke all the values to be flattened to 0.

One may ask now what happens if we change λ. A higher λ describes a user who tolerates less noise in her answer graphs. It asks for answers that are more "tailored" around the GT. Figure 2 presents the values of recall and tb-DCG of the five systems on the two datasets as λ varies. On the x-axis we have different values for λ, from 0 to 1, with step 0.1. Every point in the plots is obtained computing the averages on the 50 queries issued on each dataset.

Let us start on LinkedMDB 1M. TSA+BM25 appears to be consistently the top-performing system in terms of recall at the varying of λ. Moreover, when $\lambda = 0$, that is when we do not count the noise in the answers, the values of average recall is around 0.9, illustrating how, on average, many relevant triples are retrieved by the system in the top 1000 positions. Immediately below TSA+BM25,

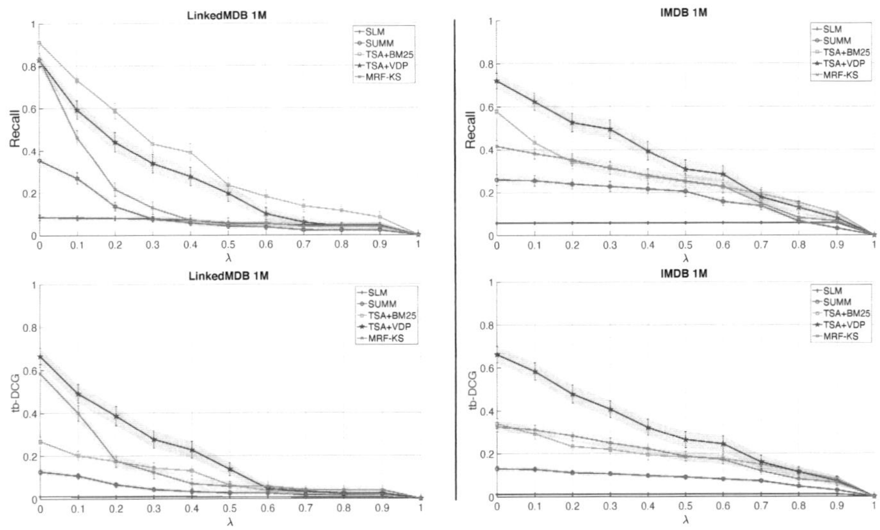

Fig. 2: Plot to confront average performances of recall and tb-DCG on the real databases LinkedMDB 1M and IMDB 1M for the different systems at the varying of λ.

we find TSA+VDP. The heuristics used by TSA+VDP eliminate some relevant triples from the ranking, thus reducing the overall recall.

For tb-DCG, it is evident how TSA+VDP sacrifices recall to obtain a better tb-DCG. In particular, TSA+VDP is consistently the top-performing system until we reach $\lambda = 0.5$. After this point, all the systems collapse on low values, due to the presence of few high-quality answers.

For IMDB 1M and the recall value, the top-performing system is now TSA+VDP, with TSA+BM25 immediately behind. This means that in the case of IMDB, BM25 is less effective in extracting relevant triples from the whole graph. The pruning heuristics of TSA+VDP improve the quality of some answers, making them relevant and therefore counted in the computation of the average recall. We also note that the trend of the SUMM method is more stable than the other systems. In fact, the system manages to get high-quality answers that satisfy many λ values. Only after a value of $\lambda = 0.5$ there is a performance decline.

Regarding tb-DCG, TSA+VDP remains the top system, with a sizeable difference from the second-placed TSA+BM25 and MRF-KS, which appear to be quite similar in performances while λ increases. SUMM maintains its stability but is still below the other systems.

This analysis clearly shows how bigger values of λ make the task harder. In comparison, however, the TSA-based systems are able to obtain consistently better results with respect to the state of the art systems.

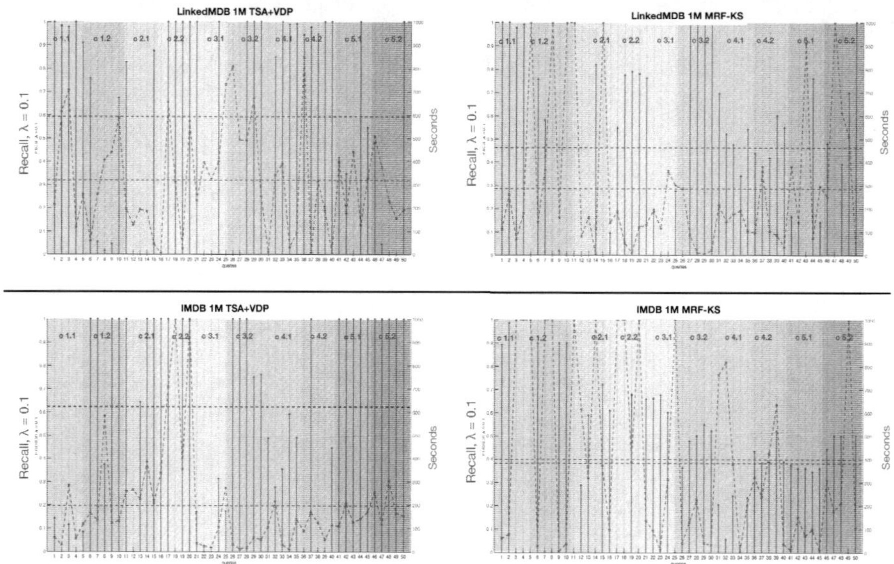

Fig. 3: Plots to compare performances of time and recall on LinkedMDB 1M and IMDB 1M for the two systems TSA+VDP and MRF-KS. The horizontal lines represent the averages for recall (blue) and time (red). A time limit of 1000s was considered for the execution of a query.

4.2 Query-by-query analysis

Recall Figure 3 shows the behavior query-by-query in terms of recall and time for the two datasets and for the two top-performing systems TSA+VDP and MRF-KS with $\lambda = 0.1$. We grouped the queries by their classes and subclasses and highlighted them with different colors.

Starting from LinkedMDB 1M, the queries of certain classes such as `C1.1` obtain good results in both systems. Others, like class `C5`, appear hard for both systems.

What is evident is that a simpler P does not necessarily imply high performances. In fact, a class such as `C1.2` presents low results in both systems, while `C4`, which has a more complex P, has higher recall with TSA+VDP. It seems that the semantic of the queries plays a critical role in determining their difficulty. Subclasses such as `C1.1` and `C1.2`, for example, show different behaviors, even if they share the same pattern structure.

For IMDB 1M, we can make the same observations. It is even more evident in this instance how a simpler syntax does not correspond to higher recall. For TSA+VDP class `C5` almost always presents a recall of 1, while many queries of class `C1` present values close to 0. This may be explained considering the fact that a simpler pattern corresponds to a ground truth with fewer relevant triples, harder to extract from the database in an effective way.

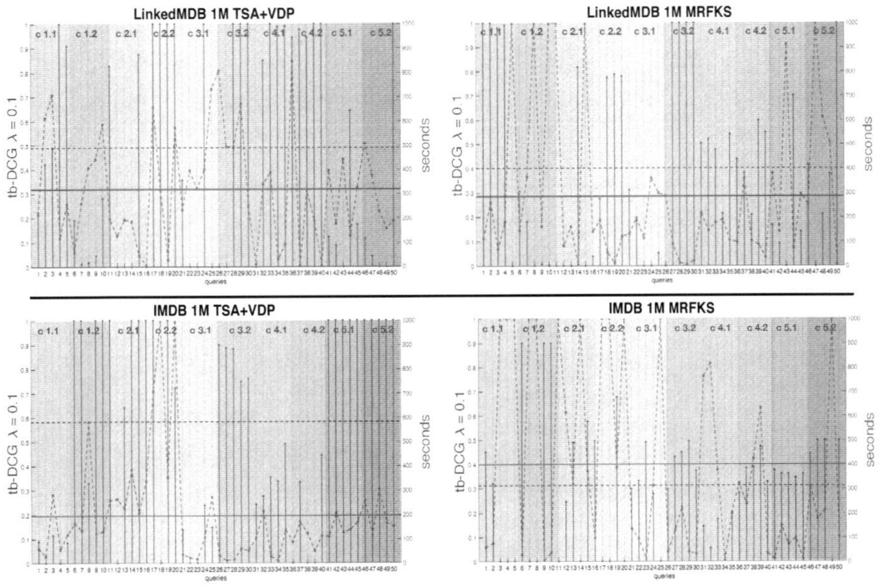

Fig. 4: Plots to compare performances of time and rb-DCG on LinkedMDB 1M and IMDB 1M for the two systems TSA+VDP and MRF-KS. The horizontal blue line represents the average precision, the red one the time.

tb-DCG Figure 4 presents similar graphics but for the tb-DCG metric.

The high variability in the behavior of the queries is immediately evident from the different performances obtained by the systems. Let us start with LinkedMDB 1M. Certain classes, such as `C4`, appear to be relatively easy for TSA+VDP. On the other hand, they are harder for MRF-KS. If we consider that `C1.2`, instead, is hard for both systems, we see how it is not necessarily true that a simpler syntax (i.e. a simpler pattern P) corresponds to an easier query to answer.

On the other hand, a class such as `C2` presents subclass `C2.1` which appears hard for both systems, while `C2.2` is easier. This suggests again how the same syntactic class can become harder or easier depending on its semantic nature, independently from the system.

For IMDB 1M, we see how similar observations can be made. Class `C5` appears simpler for TSA+VDP and harder for MRF-KS. More in general, it appears that MRF-KS struggles more in IMDB to answer the queries: its average tb-DCG is much lower than the one of TSA+VDP. This shows how it may be possible that the nature of a database (the number and structure of connections among nodes and the quantity and disposition of keywords among them) may influence the effectiveness of a system.

Time The execution times are presented in both Figure 3 and 4. Note how we used a time limit of 1000s.

Once again, queries in the same class may present different behaviors in terms of execution time. For example, MRF-KS presents relatively low values of time for subclass `C5.1` in IMDB, while subclass `C5.2` presents much higher times on average. This new evidence of the fact that the syntactical factor is not the only one that plays a role in the determination of the execution time. The choice of keywords (more or less frequent inside the database) appears to also play a role. Queries with more frequent keywords will, in fact, demand much more execution time.

5 Conclusions and Future Works

In this paper, we presented an in-depth analysis of the behavior of state-of-the-art systems with a particular focus on the quality of required answers and the behavior presented with different kinds of queries.

We used a sub-set of LinkedMDB and IMDB as databases. We defined five different classes of queries for each dataset, which differ from one another on their syntax and semantic, for a total of 100 test queries. We used recall and tb-DCG as evaluation metrics. The first one describes the simple raw power of extraction of relevant triples of a system. The latter is a more sophisticated measure that takes into consideration the relevance of the answers, their position in the ranking and the quantity of noise in them. We considered five different state-of-the-art systems: SLM, MRF-KS, SUMM, TSA+BM25, and TSA+VDP.

We performed two different classes of experiments. In the first one, we varied the minimal quantity of SNR required from an answer to be considered as relevant. We showed that the higher the required threshold, the lower the performances of the systems. TSA+BM25 and TSA+VDP consistently appeared to obtain the higher results, although we registered a progressive detriment of the performances.

The second class of experiments showed that certain classes of queries seem to be simpler than others for both systems. It resulted that not necessarily a simpler pattern P implies better results. The complexity of the query is therefore not present only in its syntax, but also in its semantic and in the keywords of choice. To corroborate this intuition, it appeared that queries belonging to the same syntactic class with different semantics presented completely different performances.

For our future works, we will keep researching, also on different databases, how different kinds of queries correspond to different behaviors, and how poor results may be mitigated with techniques as query rewriting.

References

1. Balmin, A., Hristidis, V., Koudas, N., Papakonstantinou, Y., Srivastava, D., Wang, T.: A system for keyword proximity search on XML databases. In: Proceedings of

29th International Conference on Very Large Data Bases, VLDB. pp. 1069–1072. Morgan Kaufmann (2003)
2. Bast, H., Buchhold, B., Haussmann, H.: Semantic search on text and knowledge bases. Foundations and Trends in Information Retrieval **10**(2-3), 119–271 (2016)
3. Bhalotia, G., Hulgeri, A., Nakhe, C., Chakrabarti, S., Sudarshan, S.: Keyword searching and browsing in databases using BANKS. In: Proceedings of the 18th International Conference on Data Engineering. pp. 431–440. IEEE Computer Society (2002)
4. Coffman, J., Weaver, A.C.: A framework for evaluating database keyword search strategies. In: Proc. of the 19th ACM International Conference on Information and knowledge management. pp. 729–738. ACM Press (2010)
5. Dosso, D., Silvello, G.: A scalable virtual document-based keyword search system for rdf datasets. In: Proceedings of the 42nd International ACM SIGIR conference on Research and Development in Information Retrieval, SIGIR (2019)
6. Dosso, D., Silvello, G.: Search text to retrieve graphs: A scalable RDF keyword-based search system. IEEE Access **8**, 14089–14111 (2020)
7. Elbassuoni, S., Blanco, R.: Keyword Search over RDF Graphs. In: Proc. of the 20th ACM Conference on Information and Knowledge Management, CIKM 2011,. pp. 237–242. ACM Press, New York, USA (2011)
8. He, H., Wang, H., Yang, J., Yu, P.S.: BLINKS: ranked keyword searches on graphs. In: Proceedings of the ACM SIGMOD International Conference on Management of Data. pp. 305–316. ACM (2007)
9. Le, W., Li, F., Kementsietsidis, A., Duan, S.: Scalable keyword search on large RDF data. IEEE Trans. Knowl. Data Eng. (11), 2774–2788. https://doi.org/10.1109/TKDE.2014.2302294
10. Lopez-Veyna, J.I., Sosa-Sosa, V.J., López-Arévalo, I.: A virtual document approach for keyword search in databases. In: DATA. pp. 39–48. SciTePress (2012)
11. Mass, Y., Sagiv, Y.: Virtual Documents and Answer Priors in Keyword Search over Data Graphs. In: Proc. of the Workshops of the EDBT/ICDT 2016 Joint Conference. CEUR Workshop Proceedings, vol. 1558. CEUR-WS.org (2016)
12. Pound, J., Mika, P., Zaragoza, H.: Ad-hoc object retrieval in the web of data. In: Proc. of the 19th International Conference on World Wide Web, WWW 2010. pp. 771–780. ACM Press, New York, USA (2010)
13. Prud, E., Seaborne, A., et al.: Sparql query language for rdf (2006)
14. Sahu, S., Mhedhbi, A., Salihoglu, S., Lin, J., Özsu, M.T.: The ubiquity of large graphs and surprising challenges of graph processing. PVLDB **11**(4), 420–431 (2017)
15. Su, Q., Widom, J.: Indexing Relational Database Content Offline for Efficient Keyword-Based Search. In: Proc. of the 9th International Database Engineering and Applications Symposium (IDEAS 2005). pp. 297–306. IEEE Computer Society (2005)
16. Wang, H., Aggarwal, C.C.: A survey of algorithms for keyword search on graph data. In: Managing and Mining Graph Data, pp. 249–273. Springer (2010)
17. Wu, W.: Proactive Natural Language Search Engine: Tapping into Structured Data on the Web. In: Proc. of the Joint 2013 EDBT/ICDT Conferences. pp. 143–148. ACM Press, New York, USA (2013)
18. Yu, J.X., Qin, L., Chang, L.: Keyword Search in Relational Databases: A Survey. IEEE Data Eng. Bull. **33**(1), 67–78 (2010)

Capturing Political Polarization of Reddit Submissions in the Trump Era

Virginia Morini[1] [0000-0002-7692-8134], Laura Pollacci[2] [0000-0001-9914-1943], and Giulio Rossetti[2] [0000-0003-3373-1240]

[1] University of Pisa, Italy
virginiamorini95@gmail.com
[2] ISTI-CNR, Pisa, Italy
{laura.pollacci,giulio.rossetti}@isti.cnr.it

Discussion Paper

Abstract. The American political situation of the last years, combined with the incredible growth of Social Networks, led to the diffusion of political polarization's phenomenon online. Our work presents a model that attempts to measure the political polarization of Reddit submissions during the first half of Donald Trump's presidency. To do so, we design a text classification task: political polarization of submissions is assessed by quantifying those who align themselves with pro-Trump ideologies and vice versa. We build our ground truth by picking submissions from subreddits known to be strongly polarized. Then, for model selection, we use a Neural Network with word embeddings and Long Short Time Memory layer and, finally, we analyze how model performances change trying different hyper-parameters and types of embeddings.

Keywords: Political Polarization · Classification · Text Analysis.

1 Introduction

During the last decade, the rise of social networks has drastically changed how people interact and communicate. More than 45% of world population uses Social network for an average of 3 hours per day. As these platforms grow, the number of opinions shared publicly among users increases accordingly.

In this multifaceted panorama, particular attention turned on the diffusion of political discourse online and its implications. With the significant increase of user-Generated content, research in [3] underlines that sharing political beliefs and opinions online makes people feel more active, engaged, and interested. This attitude, combined with the contemporary political situation, leads to the spreading of political polarization. This phenomenon refers to the increasing gap between two different political ideologies.

During Donald Trump's presidency, online polarization has found its fertile ground: the debate between Trump supporters and anti-Trump citizens is becoming even more complex and uncivil [1].

In this paper, we propose a model that aims at measuring the political polarization of Reddit submissions in the Trump Era. To solve the issue, we model it as a text classification task. Given new submissions, we assess their political polarization by quantifying how those align themselves with pro-Trump ideologies and vice versa.
This task is a key step of a wider study, still ongoing, that attempts to identify and analyze Echo Chambers on Social Networks. Since an Echo Chamber is a strongly polarized environment, to assess its existence, it is necessary to dispose of a tool able to measure its possible components' polarization.

For our purposes, we choose Reddit as a subject of study. Reddit, as stated by its slogan *'The front page of the internet'*, is not a traditional social network but rather a website dedicated to the social forum and discussion threads. Founded in 2005, Reddit is now the nineteenth most visited website on the internet.[1] Also, Reddit is composed of thousands of communities, each dedicated to a specific topic, called *subreddits*. Its internal structure makes it easy to find politically polarized communities to analyze. Additionally, since users can write anonymously and posts aren't limited in length, this platform is particularly active in political discussions [11].

The rest of the paper is organized as follows. In Section 2 we discuss the literature involving text classification techniques in general as well as applied to the political domain. Section 3 describes the phases of data extraction and data preparation necessary to build our final dataset. In Section 4 we explore the different stages of model selection. Finally, Section 5 concludes the paper and set future research directions.

2 Related Works

With the growth of Social Networks, researchers have focused on the study of methods to extract information from a large quantity of unstructured text data.

The first key component of this process is text preprocessing, a combination of text mining techniques that allows cleaning data for further steps. Both works of Camacho-Collados et al. [4] and Uysal et al. [16], show how a weighted usage of these methods can remarkably improve final performances of a text classifier.

Another aspect to take into account when performing classification is the type of words' representation used. Social networks textual data, as posts, are sequences of words. Capturing their semantic valence is important to represent not only single words but also the context in which they are inserted. As stated in [8], traditional types of word representations, as a bag-of-word model, encode words as discrete symbols that cannot be directly compared to one another. Consequently, this approach is not suitable for the sentences' representation.

[1] https://www.alexa.com/topsites

Table 1. For each subreddit: number of submissions collected, average number of words in submissions and political ideology.

Subreddit	# submission	mean length	Political ideology
r/The_Donald	151,395	92.02	pro-Trump
r/Fuckthealtright	78,200	82.09	anti-Trump
r/EnoughTrumpSpam	73,168	79.34	anti-Trump

Word embedding (e.g., Word2vec [10] and Glove [12]), instead, maps words to a continuously-valued low dimensional space, capturing their semantic and syntactic features.

Recently has been shown how deep learning models can be fruitfully used to address Natural Language Processing related classification tasks. The survey in [9] synthesizes powerful models for sequence learning. The authors underline how Feed Forward Neural networks do not fit well with data sequences because after each word is processed, the entire state of the network is reset. Recurrent Neural Networks (RNNs), instead, assigning more weights to previous words of a sequence are suitable for this kind of data. In particular, Long Short Time Memory network (LSTM), a type of RNN, can maintain long term dependency through a complex gates mechanism, overcoming the vanishing gradient problem of RNN [15].

Social Network textual data are widely used for various text classification applications such as information filtering [7], personality traits recognition [13] or hate speech detection [17].

Concerning political leaning classification on such type of data, literature is not so exhaustive. In [5], Chang et al. propose a model to predict the political affiliation of Facebook posts in Taiwan. They build two models, one using the K-Nearest Neighbors algorithm and the other one AdaBoost combined with Naive Bayes classifier. Rao et al. [14] use word embeddings and LSTM to predict if a Twitter post belongs to Republican or Democratic beliefs. To the best of our knowledge, researches about political classification on Reddit is sparse or nonexistent.

3 Data Description and Preparation

In this section, we describe the phases of Data Extraction and Data Preparation necessary to build our final dataset.

Data was obtained through the Pushshift API [2] that offers aggregation endpoints to analyze Reddit activity from June 2005 to nowadays. We use the submission endpoint to pick submissions posted from January 2017 to May 2019, a period covering the first two years and a half of Donald Trump's presidency.

For this text classification problem, we select submissions belonging to subreddits known to be either pro-Trump or anti-Trump. Based on subreddits descriptions and considerations explained at the end of this section, we choose `r/The_Donald` for the first group and `r/Fuckthealtright` and

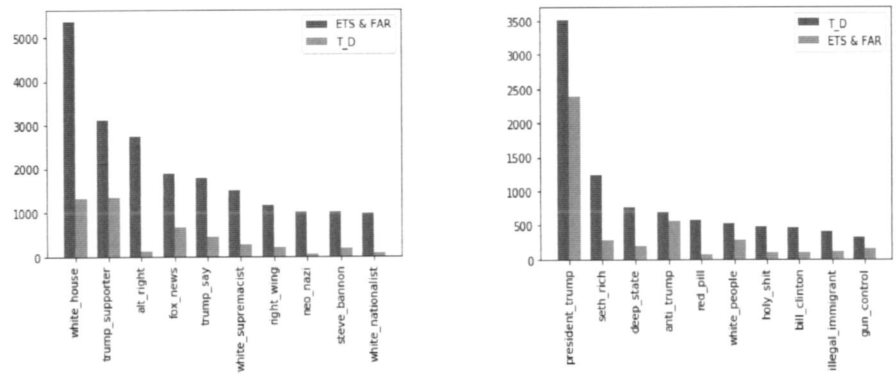

Fig. 1. Comparison between some of the 20 most frequent bigrams of each subreddit and their frequencies in the opposite one.

r/EnoughTrumpSpam for the second. To have a balanced dataset, for the anti-Trump data we merge two subreddits, strictly related both on the users and the keywords.[2] In Table 1 are illustrated some dataset statistics.

For each selected submission, we collect the fields *id*, *selftext*, and *title*, respectively, the identifier, the content, and the title of the submission. We merge the latter two fields in a unique one to give it as input for LSTM, because the *selftext* of a post may be empty or just a reference to the *title* itself. By doing so, we make sure to have a text capturing what the user is actually trying to convey. Then, we assign to each submission a label: 1 if it belongs to pro-Trump subreddit, 0 otherwise.

Due to the nature itself of the social network that promotes free speech and expression, textual data gathered from Reddit platform is dirty and noisy. For this reason, we apply a text preprocessing pipeline to give clean data to LSTM: in particular, we convert text to lowercase, then remove punctuation and number, as well as stop words.

Also, by looking at the submissions extracted, we observe that several of these are composed only by few words. This is probably because, during data extraction, we only select textual data, removing all multimedia contents related to each submission. To avoid affecting LSTM performance, we remove from our original dataset all submissions shorter than six words.

Lastly, to check the validity of our initial choice of polarized subreddits, we identify some of the most frequent bigrams of each subreddit to analyze their frequencies in the opposite one. As we can see in Fig. 1, these words are discriminant and semantically related to their belonging subreddit.

[2] https://subredditstats.com/r/EnoughTrumpSpam
https://subredditstats.com/r/Fuckthealtright

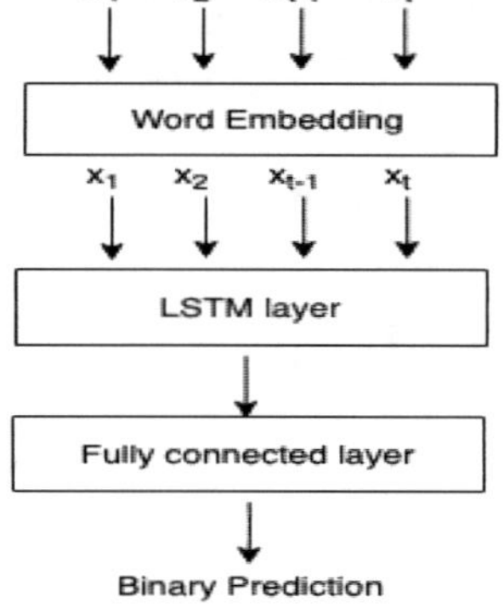

Fig. 2. High level architecture of our LSTM model.

4 Measuring Political Polarization

In this Section, we describe the model selected to measure the political polarization of Reddit submissions.

To assess the best model, we follow these subsequent steps: preprocessing of input text sequences, model selection, and testing on new instances.

Neural Network Preprocessing. To give our submissions as input for our model, we have to vectorize them, turning each one in a sequence of integers.

To do so, we create a lexicon index based on word frequency, where 0 represents padding: indexes are assigned in descending order of frequency. Each text is then transformed into a sequence of integers, replacing each word with the corresponding index of the lexicon (e.g., the sentence "president trump says" becomes [5,1,39]). We use the whole lexicon for training the model. Lastly, to optimize the matrix operations in the batch, we pad each sequence to the same length, based on the mean length of all submissions. Sequences longer than this length are truncated.

Neural Network Architecture. As stated in Section 2, since our training data consists of sequences, standard neural networks are not suitable for our task. For such a reason, we adopt a Long Short-Term Memory network [6], a type of Recurrent neural network able to model the meaning of a sentence by taking into account its paradigmatic structure. Fig. 2 shows the high level architecture of our model, composed of three layers:

1. *Embedding Layer:* This layer takes as input the sequences of integers $w_1,...,$ w_t previously created and turns them into 100-dimensional dense vectors x_t. t is the length of the sequence. During model selection, we decide to see how performance changes based on the use of Glove pre-trained word embeddings or embeddings learned directly from the text.

Table 2. Hyper-parameters tuning for models with learned embeddings and Glove ones.

Emb. type	LSTM units	Training acc.	Validation acc.
Learned	32	0.832	0.816
	64	0.837	0.816
	128	0.828	0.816
Glove	32	0.831	0.814
	64	0.839	0.819
	128	**0.846**	**0.829**

2. *LSTM Layer:* This layer consists of multiple LSTM units. Each unit maintains a memory cell. Cells encode the information of the inputs observed up to that step through the gates mechanism. The first gate is called input gate and controls whether the memory cell is updated. The second gate is the forget gate that controls if the cell is zero; lastly, the output gate controls whether the information of the cell state is visible. To avoid over-fitting, we add a dropout regularization of 0.3.
3. *Output Layer:* This layer is a fully connected layer which outputs a single neuron to perform binary predictions. We use the Sigmoid activation function to have a probability output between 0 and 1. Submissions with a probability score greater or equal than 0.5 will be labeled as pro-Trump, the others as anti-Trump. As loss function, we use Binary cross-entropy and as optimizer Adam.

Model Selection. We use a training set of 302,763 instances, perfectly balanced among the two target classes. To find the model with the highest performance, we perform a 3-fold Cross-Validation trying different values of LSTM units [32,64,128] with a fixed embedding dimension of 100. We experience such configurations, both with learned embeddings and pre-trained ones. Results are shown in Table 2. The model with higher performance is the one obtained using 100 dimensions Glove pre-trained embeddings and 128 LSTM units that reaches an accuracy score of 84,63% on the training set and 82,96% on validation.

Model Evaluation. Model performances are firstly assessed on a polarized test set built by picking unseen submissions belonging to the previously selected subreddits.[3] In detail, we extract 38,906 submissions posted from 2nd May to 1st December 2019. As shown in the first line of Table 3, model reaches an accuracy of 74%.

We further assess model performances on less polarizing topics wrt Donald Trump's persona. To do so, we choose four main topics addressing sociopolitical issues, and for each of them, we select several related subreddits via Reddit lists.[4] Three out of four are fine-grained (i.e., gun control and legalization, minority discrimination, immigration policies) while the latter is more general in the topic (i.e., political discussion). Submissions extracted are posted from January 2017

[3] r/The_Donald, r/EnoughTrumpSpam, r/Fuckthealtright

[4] http://redditlist.com/
https://www.reddit.com/r/ListOfSubreddits/wiki/listofsubreddits

Table 3. Model performances on polarized topic and on less polarized ones.

Test set	# post	Accuracy	Precision	Recall	F1-score
Polarized test set	38,906	0.741	0.691	0.812	0.746
Gun control	2,247	0.712	0.751	0.692	0.720
Minority discrimination	955	0.723	0.780	0.731	0.754
Immigration policies	400	0.722	0.776	0.725	0.749
Political discussion	**80,961**	**0.825**	**0.943**	**0.851**	**0.894**

to December 2019.
In this scenario, we do not have a ground truth to evaluate model results among the different topics. Thus, we try a different approach: validating our model through polarized users. In detail, we first compute for each user in training set his *polarization score* by averaging his posts' prediction scores. Then we select the most polarized ones (i.e., score ≤ 0.2 for anti-Trump users and score ≥ 0.8 for pro-Trump ones), obtaining 1,150 final users. So, we look for their posts among the aforementioned four topics, labeling them according to the user *polarization score* previously obtained. Finally, we assess model performances on the four new test sets.

By comparing model performances across the five differently polarized topics, we can assess model's ability to generalize. As shown by Table 3, even though test sets are not directly comparable, due to their difference in size, our model reaches quite good results with accuracy always greater than 70%. Lastly, from the sample of predictions in Table 4 we denote similar trends across different topics: submissions with an higher prediction score convey a strongly Republican view while the lower ones a definitively Democratic leaning.

5 Conclusion and Future Works

In this study, we propose a model that aims at measuring the political polarization of Reddit submissions in the Trump Era. This task is a key step of a wider study focused on the identification of Echo Chambers on Reddit. Since an Echo Chamber is a strongly polarized environment, to assess its existence it is necessary to find a way to measure its possible components' polarization.

To do so, we use a Neural Network with word embeddings and Long Short Time Memory layer to quantify how submissions align themselves with Trump's ideologies and vice versa. The best model is the one built with Glove embeddings

Table 4. For each submission: text, topic and prediction score.

Sumission	topic	score
Tropical storm Barry: Obama has transformed his hatred for America into a new type of treason	Polarized topic	0.93
Trump's re-election crisis: His internal polls show it, national polls show it, and even a poll in reliably conservative Texas shows it.	Polarized topic	0.02
Never forget: Hillary worked hard to keep wages of Haitian garment workers under 31 cents per hour	Political discussion	0.93
American soldiers aren't dying for our freedom in Syria, Iraq and Afghanistan. They're dying for nothing	Gun control	0.15
Poor Immigrants Are The Least Likely Group To Use Welfare, Despite Trump's Claims missing	Immigration	0.03
Feminist deliberately acts like a condescending asshole to men. When they react like she's being an asshole, declares that men are an issue and Buzzfeed trends it.	Discrimination	0.90

that reaches 83% of accuracy on validation and 74% on the test set. Furthermore, we assess model performances also on less polarizing topics to evaluate model's ability to generalize. We achieve quite good results across four differently polarized topics with accuracy ranging from 72% to 82%.

As future research direction, we will leverage the proposed model to discover political Echo Chambers on Reddit: more specifically, analyzing their internal structure, their size and their persistence over time.

References

1. L. M. Bartels. Partisanship in the trump era. *The Journal of Politics*, 80(4):1483–1494, 2018.
2. J. Baumgartner, S. Zannettou, B. Keegan, M. Squire, and J. Blackburn. The pushshift reddit dataset. *preprint arXiv:2001.08435*, 2020.
3. S. Boulianne. Social media use and participation: A meta-analysis of current research. *Information, communication & society*, 18(5):524–538, 2015.
4. J. Camacho-Collados and M. T. Pilehvar. On the role of text preprocessing in neural network architectures: An evaluation study on text categorization and sentiment analysis. *preprint arXiv:1707.01780*, 2017.
5. C.-C. Chang, S.-I. Chiu, and K.-W. Hsu. Predicting political affiliation of posts on facebook. In *International Conference on Ubiquitous Information Management and Communication*, pages 1–8, 2017.
6. S. Hochreiter and J. Schmidhuber. Long short-term memory. *Neural computation*, 9(8):1735–1780, 1997.
7. M. S. Jones. The reddit self-post classification task (rspct): a highly multiclass dataset for text classification (preprint). 2018.
8. K. Kowsari, K. Jafari Meimandi, M. Heidarysafa, S. Mendu, L. Barnes, and D. Brown. Text classification algorithms: A survey. *Information*, 10(4):150, 2019.
9. Z. C. Lipton, J. Berkowitz, and C. Elkan. A critical review of recurrent neural networks for sequence learning. *preprint arXiv:1506.00019*, 2015.
10. T. Mikolov, K. Chen, G. Corrado, and J. Dean. Efficient estimation of word representations in vector space. *preprint arXiv:1301.3781*, 2013.
11. R. Nithyanand, B. Schaffner, and P. Gill. Online political discourse in the trump era. *preprint arXiv:1711.05303*, 2017.
12. J. Pennington, R. Socher, and C. D. Manning. Glove: Global vectors for word representation. In *Empirical methods in natural language processing (EMNLP)*, pages 1532–1543, 2014.
13. B. Y. Pratama and R. Sarno. Personality classification based on twitter text using naive bayes, knn and svm. In *2015 International Conference on Data and Software Engineering (ICoDSE)*, pages 170–174. IEEE, 2015.
14. A. Rao and N. Spasojevic. Actionable and political text classification using word embeddings and lstm. *preprint arXiv:1607.02501*, 2016.
15. M. Sundermeyer, R. Schlüter, and H. Ney. Lstm neural networks for language modeling. In *International speech communication association*, 2012.
16. A. K. Uysal and S. Gunal. The impact of preprocessing on text classification. *Information Processing & Management*, 50(1):104–112, 2014.
17. Z. Zhang, D. Robinson, and J. Tepper. Detecting hate speech on twitter using a convolution-gru based deep neural network. In *European semantic web conference*, pages 745–760. Springer, 2018.

Accounting Journal Reconstruction with Variational Autoencoders and Long Short-term Memory Architecture

Mario Zupan[1], Svjetlana Letinic[1], and Verica Budimir[1]

Polytechnic in Pozega, Vukovarska 17, Croatia
mzupan@vup.hr

Abstract. Our tries to learn machines how to reconstruct journal entries with the aim of finding anomalies lead us to deep learning (DL) technologies. Nowadays Variational autoencoder and Long short- term memory architectures as well as other deep learning architectures solves wide range of problems, yet they are not enough implemented in a field of accounting information systems (AIS). Inside AIS, accounting data follows accounting logic and makes specific datasets constructed by different type of columns - categorical and continuous variables. Our aim is reconstruction of these variables. Development of the model capable for precise reconstruction is not an easy task. This paper describes our research for anomaly detection model architecture which will be capable to reconstruct dataset with categorical features mixed with continuous monetary value feature. We developed basic models trained on accounting journals from 2007 to 2018 and then tested in the fiscal year 2019. Still, lots of hyperparameters need to be checked if we want to improve accuracy. Deep learning research is an engineering task leaded by experience so there is no linearity in the model improvement. Consequently, this paper is our contribution to collection of experience in developing accurate, useful and intelligent accounting control system.

Keywords: general ledger · journal entry · bookkeeping · accounting · deep learning · variational autoencoder · long short-term memory · anomaly detection · accounting control system.

1 Introduction

As in every information system, human efforts, as well as interaction between modules, can cause errors. Anomalies in accounting books occur on a daily basis, and unintentional human errors, attempted fraud, and continuous legislative changes are some of the critical causes. Anomalies occur despite the fact that the most existing controls integrated into accounting modules of modern ERP systems are created in compliance with bookkeeping rules. Because small and medium enterprises (SMEs) do not have audit obligations regulated by law, manual tax inspections are the only mechanism of their accounting and tax control. In general, detection of errors, made intentionally or not, consumes a large portion of a bookkeeper's or tax inspector's time, and correction of errors is not an easy part of their job, particularly owing to the architecture and functioning of the accounting software modules. Namely, most of today's ERP systems have specialized documents (digital forms) for an every specific business event. An every digital form is connected with one or more journal entry schemes created by senior accountants. Junior accountants or non-accountant employees do not have to be familiar with journal schemes because they communicate only through forms. As long as the modern accounting modules inside ERP systems are functioning based on the described principle, a single error in the only one journal entry scheme can cause an incorrect accounting entry for the whole set of connected digital forms.

When statistic methodology had become the part of a financial audit process, life of employees involved in auditing became a lot easier. Now it is the time for improving and make more easier auditing, accounting and tax inspection processes by utilization of deep learning algorithms.

2 Related works

When the idea for this research began to form, we found a previous study dealing with the same challenge and methodology written by Schreyer, M et. al. [14], which processed two datasets extracted from an SAP ERP. The first dataset represents the *accounting document header* (e.g., document id, type, time, and currency), and the second contains *journal entry details* (e.g., general ledger account, debit, credit, and amount). Because the majority of attributes correspond to categorical variables, the authors preprocessed the journal entry attributes to obtain a one-hot encoded representation of each attribute. They obtained 401 encoded dimensions for dataset A and 576 encoded dimensions for dataset B. Each journal entry was labeled as either a synthetic global anomaly, synthetic local anomaly, or non-synthetic regular entry. Dataset A contains a total of 307,457 journal entry line items comprised of 6 categorical attributes. In total 95 (0.03%) synthetic anomalous journal entries have been injected into dataset. These entries encompass 55 (0.016%) global anomalies and 40 (0.015%) local anomalies. Dataset B contains a total of 172,990 journal entry line items comprised of 10 categorical attributes. In total 100 (0.06%) synthetic anomalous journal entries have been injected into the dataset. These entries encompass 50 (0.03%) global anomalies and 50 (0.03%) local anomalies. The described datasets became inputs in nine distinct autoencoder architectures. The training was conducted via standard back-propagation until convergence (max. 2,000 training epochs). Anomaly threshold $Beta = 0{:}01$ implying that a journal entry is labeled *anomalous* if one of its attributes was not reconstructed correctly or occurs very rarely. The best performing results are selected based on parameterizations that (1) result in a recall of 100% of the synthetic anomalies and correspond to (2) the highest area under the ROC curve (ROC-AUC). On the same accounting datasets, Schreyer, M et. al. also trained the Adversarial autoencoder to learn a semantic meaningful representation of journal entries recorded in real-world ERP system [16]. Schreyer, M. et. al. [15] also showed an adversarial attack against Computer-aided audit tools (CAAT) using deep neural networks. They first introduce a real-world thread model designed to camouflage accounting anomalies such as fraudulent journal entries. Second, they showed that adversarial autoencoder neural networks are capable of learning a human interpretable model of journal entries that disentangles the entries latent generative factors. They used AAE architecture which extends the concepts of Autoencoder Neural Networks.

Shultz, M. et. al. [17] use three-layer autoencoder, *relu* as an activation function in a step when the encoder $e(x)$ transforms the input x to a hidden representation h. The encoder (x) transforms the input x to a hidden representation h. In this step they use *leaky-relu* as an activation function. From the review of related work subsection, it can be concluded that the application of deep learning techniques in auditing is a promising research field with several open questions to be addressed. However, in the current audit practice, the full potential of such techniques is not yet realized. Mainly, less complex techniques like static rules are applied that check only a few journal entry attributes at a time.

Another study that inspired our research [3] described the use of a decision tree classification algorithm for financial journal entry fraud. This web-based application labels journal entries as either fraudulent or non-fraudulent. Classification algorithms are also tested through the Sherlock system development for identification of accounting irregularities within unlabeled accounting data extracted from general ledger [4]. Authors used Positive Nave Bayes (PNB) algorithm but they experimented with many different classification algorithms.

Anomaly detection accounting systems are developed by applying different technologies as well as inputs. Instead of accounting data, the authors of the study [10] experimented with two data mining algorithms applied on SAP R/3 security audit log data. Their results depends on different transaction threshold values.

Other available papers considered did not exploit a deep learning technology in the accountancy when solving a specific real-world problem. Still they were extremely helpful to us because they contained general thoughts regarding the application of artificial intelligence in the field of accounting [9], [5], [13]. The authors described accounting and auditing problems (bookkeeping routines, fraud detection, revenue prediction, an analysis of unstructured data, financial reporting, etc.) that might be potentially solved using machine learning technology, and described the strengths and limits of machine learning. As a common theme for related studies, *machine learning has highlighted promising results but still does not outperform the existing implementation, which is simple and deterministic* [2].

3 Methodology

Inspired by Schreyer, M. et. al. [14], [15], [16] and other related works, we conducted research into deep learning capabilities in our previous paper [18]. We trained and tested a variational autoencoder (VAE) model on a 3.731 row x 57 column dataset using journal entries for four fiscal years, namely, 2014 to 2017. The dataset was divided into a training part and a testing part at a 1:9 ratio, with a 374 x 57 testing shape and 3.359 x 57 training shape. The aim of the research was the reconstruction of all journal entries of the test dataset. The journals were audited and approved by accountants and a tax department. Our model incorrectly reconstructed 4 out of 374 journal entries of the test dataset. The entire test dataset has 183 unique rows; however, they are repeated through the years except for four years marked by the model. The model cannot reconstruct the journal entries if it sees an entry for the first time in a test part of the dataset. Consequently, the precision of the model reconstruction was 99.9893%.

Keras deep learning library has provided a significant contribution to our understanding of neural networks and artificial intelligence(AI). This high-level neural network application programming interface (API) is capable of running Google's TensorFlow, Microsoft's Cognitive Toolkit (CNTK), or the Theano deep learning library. Deep learning libraries can be used for supervised learning, in which a network is trained on labeled datasets. A supervised model can be well optimized but may be useless at the same time when new data are applied. However, neural networks can also be used for semi-supervised learning, through autoencoders and with unlabeled datasets. Semi-supervised learning is more suitable for anomaly detection problems and the nature of our particular data, namely, unlabeled and without errors or fraud entries, according to an audit by an experienced accountant.

3.1 Variational autoencoder (VAE) architecture

Semi-supervised learning can be realized through an autoencoder architecture. Autoencoders reconstruct an input given the same input, and are usually trained and tested on separate data. If they are trained and tested on the same dataset, the generalization of the model is sacrificed.

Based on the friendliness of Keras and the power of TensorFlow, a neural network model was built as a result of this research. More precisely, instead of a *classical* autoencoder, the model is a *variational* autoencoder (VAE), which was simultaneously discovered by Kingma and Welling in December 2013, and Rezende, Mohamed, and Wierstra in January 2014 [7]. According to Kingma and Welling [11], in variational auto-encoders, neural networks are used as probabilistic encoders and decoders. There are many possible choices of encoders and decoders, depending on the type of data and model. In their example they used relatively simple neural networks, multi-layered perceptrons (MLPs). For the encoder they used a MLP with Gaussian output, while for the decoder they used MLPs with either Gaussian, in case of real-valued data, or Bernoulli outputs (in case of binary data). Kingma and Welling [11] trained generative models of images from the MNIST and Frey Face datasets and compared learning algorithms in terms of the variational lower bound, and the estimated marginal likelihood. Rezende, Mohamed, and Wierstra demonstrated the ability of the model to impute missing data on MNIST, Frey Face and SVHN images datasets. They have also projected the MNIST dataset to a 2-dimensional latent space and use 2D embedding as a visualisation of the data.

In contrast to a *classical* autoencoder (AE), a VAE is capable of sampling from a latent space to create an entirely new output, which is possible because it turns the input into the parameters of a statistical distribution, namely, the mean and variance, instead of compressing its input into a fixed code in the latent space, which is how a AE operates. Our decision to use VAE was influenced by An, J. and Cho, S. [1]. They explained VAE differences from an AE based anomaly detection. First, probabilistic encoder extends the expressive power of the VAE compared to the AE in that even though normal data and anomaly data might share the same mean value, the variability can differ. Second, VAE has selective sensitivity to reconstruction according to variable variance. This is also a feature that the AE lacks in due to its deterministic nature. Third, autoencoder based anomaly detection uses reconstruction errors as anomaly scores, which are difficult to calculate if the input variables are heterogeneous. Also a 1% probability is always a 1% for any data. Thus deciding the threshold of the reconstruction error is much more objective, reasonable, and easy to understand than that of the reconstruction error.

So the main advantage of the variational autoencoder is its probabilistic manner for describing an observation in latent space. VAEs can be used to develop latent spaces of sound, music, or even text; however, in practice, the most interesting results have been obtained with pictures. Accordingly, a VAE is potentially capable of generating new journal entries from a latent space as well as reconstructing existing entries.

The VAE model (figure 2a). was trained through 1,000 epochs (figure 1a.), and our algorithm saved the best model according to the binary_cross entropy loss function. We tried to set the number of epochs as high as it is possible with the available hardware. The *model checkpoint* technique allowed us to set high number of epochs but only the best model is saved according to the binary_cross entropy metrics. Binary cross entropy measures how far away from the true value (y, which is either 0 or 1) the prediction $\hat{y}$ is for each of the features and then averages these class-wise errors to obtain the final loss according to equation 1.

$$L(y, \hat{y}) = -\frac{1}{N}\sum_{i=1}^{N}[y_i \log(\hat{y}_i) + (1 - y_i)\log(1 - \hat{y}_i)] \tag{1}$$

We used *relu* activation in all layers except the last one in decoder where we used *sigmoid* activation. Our model is compiled with *rmsprop* optimizer. According to Chollet ([7]), cross-entropy is a quantity from the field of information theory that measures the distance between the probability distributions, or in our case, between the ground-truth distribution and our reconstructed distribution.

3.2 Long short-term memory (LSTM) architecture

In addition to an autoencoder, this research exploited the capabilities of a *long short-term memory* (LSTM) architecture. LSTM is applied to a deep learning model with LSTM layers. According to Chollet [7], LSTM is a layer that saves information across numerous time steps. Whereas autoencoders are used in credit card fraud detection models, LSTM is used for price stock prediction, temperature-forecasting problems, and other time-series predictions. Owing to the fact that our VAE model inputs did not cover the monetary amount applied in our previous study[18], and was inspired by Arvaniti, V. [2], which used unsupervised data mining algorithms, *unusual financial transactions in this thesis are defined as account pairs inside journal entries containing an unusual amount of money compared to their frequent behavior*, and we expanded our research in this study by adding an LSTM model and a monetary value column to our prototype web application. The monetary values were normalized using a MinMaxScaler (default range of 0 to 1).

The LSTM model was trained through 500 epochs (figure 1b.), across 3 time steps. In a wide pallet of loss functions packed in Keras, we chose the mean_squared_error metrics. According to equation 2, the best LSTM model was saved and used to predict the amounts in the test datasets.

$$MSE = \frac{1}{n}\sum_{i=1}^{n}(Y_i - Y_i)^2 \tag{2}$$

Suppose we want to predict the fourth value in this sequence:

$$\begin{bmatrix}10\ 20\ 30\ 40\ 50\ 60\ 70\ 80\ 90\end{bmatrix}$$

Then, x_test and y_test appear as follows:

$$[10\ 20\ 30]\ [40]\ ;\ [20\ 30\ 40]\ [50]\ ;\ [30\ 40\ 50]\ [60]\ ;$$

$$[40\ 50\ 60]\ [70]\ ;\ [50\ 60\ 70]\ [80]\ ;\ [60\ 70\ 80]\ [90]$$

Suppose we have MSE = 0.02. According to equation 2, the error of the LSTM model is $\sqrt{0.02}$=0.14. Looking at our toy example target values ranging from 40 to 90, we can say that, on average, the error of the model was 0.14. This means that, when predicting a value of 40, we guessed 39.86, and when predicting a value of 50, we may have guessed 50.14, and when predicting a value of 60, we may have estimated 59.86, and so on. However, these are average values. Each individual error could have been negative or positive, making their sum zero but not their squared sum. Thus, this is simply the average of the squared difference between the predicted and actual data points.

3.3 Chart of accounts

Transactions are classified through a pre-defined chart of accounts based on a prescribed structure of the balance sheet, the income statement, and off-balance sheet items. Accounts are divided into ten classes according to the specific needs of the entrepreneur. Most enterprises use a chart of accounts from some of the most popular Croatian accounting magazine publishers and adjusted to their particular needs because the classes are not provided by law. Because the number of account digits is also not regulated by law, but based on the needs of the entrepreneur, in our research, we decided to use the first three digits.

3.4 t-Distributed Stochastic Neighbor Embedding (t-SNE) technique

In the year 2008, Laurens van der Maaten and Geoffrey Hinton presented technique t-Distributed Stochastic Neighbor Embedding (t-SNE) that visualizes high-dimensional data by giving each datapoint a location in a two or three-dimensional map [12]. In opposite to Principal Components Analysis (PCA), t-SNE handles non-linear features. In the first step, t-SNE calculates density of all points in Gaussian distribution which represents probabilities. In the second step it calculates second set of probabilities but for the Student t-distribution with one degree of freedom. In the last step t-SNE measures the difference between the probability distributions of the two-dimensional spaces using Kullback-Liebler divergence (KL) and by using gradient descent algorithm tries to minimize KL cost function.

4 Results

Both models were compiled with *rmsprop* optimizer. Layers of the both models were used *relu* and *sigmoid* activation. The model VAE was trained and saved when the loss function reached the minimum (Figure 1.). During the training, we used 10% of the dataset for testing which is presented by the orange line in the figure. It is evident that the loss function curve has some spikes. High learning-rate, batch size (number of samples processed before the model is updated) and the number of epochs (the number of complete passes through the training dataset) are the hyperparameters which demand fine tuning. Loss spikes are often encountered when training with high learning rates, high order loss functions or small batch sizes, according to the authors [8] who developed Adaptive Learning Rate Clipping Stabilizes Learning (ALRC) to stabilize the training of artificial neural networks by limiting backpropagated losses. We also knew that the hyperparameters need to be tuned because the ideal settings for one dataset will not be the same across all datasets. When tuning the hyperparameters of an estimator, Scikit Learn offers the Grid Search and Random Search functions to simplify and automate the process. We have tried both functions and convinced that both are extremely costly in computing power and time, and still depend on chosen dataset. So, between grid search and manual search we choose the second one. When we increased the batch size from 50 to 100 with the *rmsprop* optimizer (default learning rate = 0.001) and with the same number of epochs the number of spikes decreased to only one. After we changed the optimizer to *adam* (learning rate=0.001) the spikes were completely disappeared. Although we knew how to avoid the spikes, we also new that they depend on dataset what we proved by experimenting with another datasets. Bergstra, J. & Bengio, Y. [6] discussed our presumption that different hyperparameters matter on different datasets which lead us from our aim of developing accounting anomaly detection model independent from data nature. Collected knowledge about hyperparameters will be used in future researches.

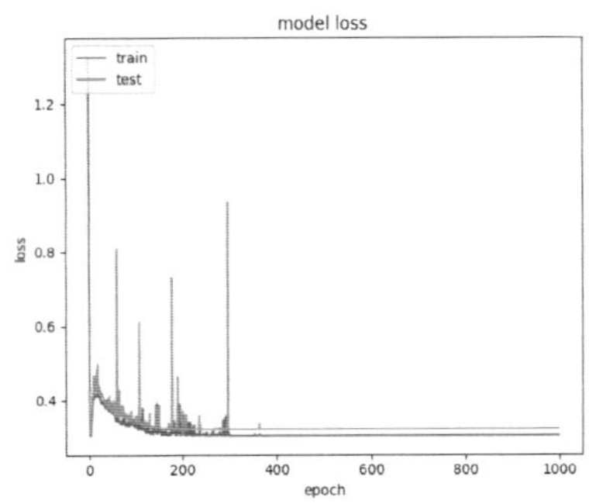

(a) VAE model

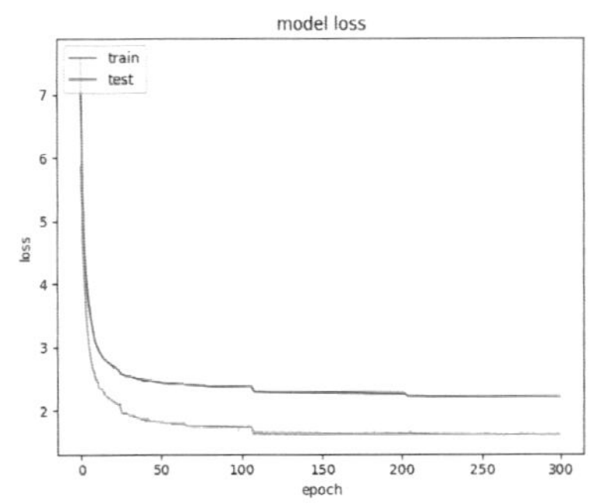

(b) LSTM-VAE model

Fig. 1: Models training: loss through the epochs

The figure 2a. shows types and connections between layers of the VAE model. First and last layer must have the same number of inputs (103) which is the same as the number of dataset columns. The model needs to learn 13,405 learnable parameters, such as weights and biases.

The models were trained on journals from 2007 to 2018 using 84,759 rows and tested on the fiscal year 2019 with 3,864 rows. The test dataset is 4.5% of the training size. Considering the document type, the account number from the chart of accounts and the debit/credit side of account, the VAE model incorrectly reconstructed 33 (table 1.) single journals entries and 7 journal entries pairs (table 2.) of 3.864 journal entries of the test dataset, that is 0.8% of the journal entries including 25 entries of the test dataset that have never happened in the trained dataset.

The LSTM-VAE model needed to learn significantly larger number of learnable parameters (162,824) with the monetary column as the extra feature in contrast to the VAE model inputs. That is 104 inputs (LSTM-VAE) in opposite to 103 inputs (VAE). As it can be seen in the Figure 2b., encoder of the model was included LSTM layer as well as the decoder, but decoder's LSTM

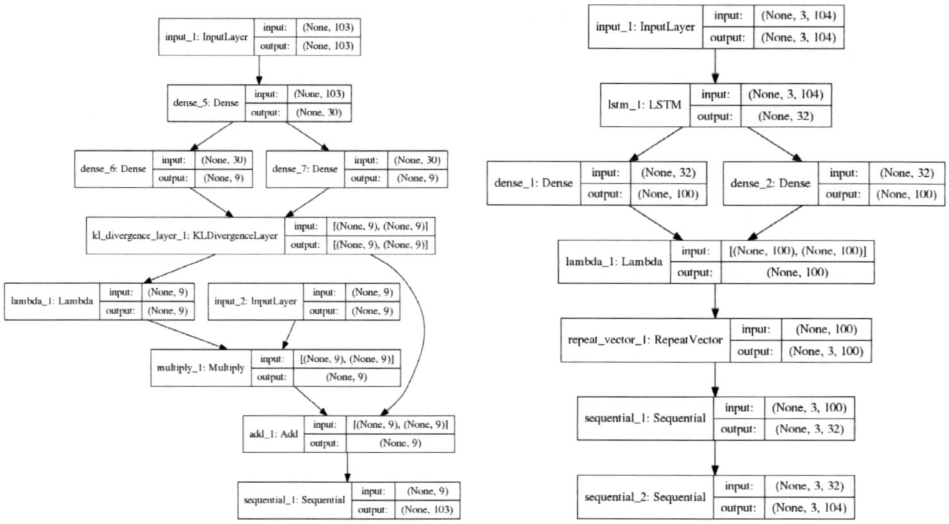

(a) VAE (b) LSTM-VAE

Fig. 2: Graphs of the models structure

Document id	Account	Debit/Credit	Repeated
FINOPENINGX	1000, 1022, 150,	Debit	16
	242, 2710, 2744,	Credit	
	27441, 298, 917, 946,	Credit	
	2608, 261,	Debit	
	275,	Debit	
	2752, 6630,	Debit	
	9301, 93011,	Debit	
	9940, 999	Debit	
PAYROLBOOK11	46161	Debit	5
ACCOUNTING	150	Credit	4
ACCOUNTING	789	Credit	2
URAEU	298	Debit	2
CASHWITHDRAW	1020	Credit	1
URAEU	6690	Debit	1
URAPE2	419	Debit	1
URAPE2	416	Debit	1

Table 1: Journal anomalies found in test dataset: single journal rows

Document id	Account	Debit/Credit	Appearing times
MATINPUT	224	Credit	3
	351	Debit	
STOCKBALANCE	6600	[Credit]	1
	7101	[Debit]	
ACCOUNTING	93011	Credit	1
	946	Debit	
CASHRECEIPT	1009	Credit	1
	1020	Debit	
URAPE3	14062	Debit	1
	221	Credit	
	24062	Credit	
	4102	Debit	

Table 2: Journal anomalies found in test dataset: journal entries pairs

layer is under Sequential layer. Although the model was trained on the same journals from 2007 to 2018 using 84,759 rows and tested on the same fiscal year 2019 with 3,864 rows, we do not have predictions for the first 4 rows due to the hyperparameter *timesteps* = 3. That gave us 3,860 predictions.

Both model needed to learn the document type, the journal account and the debit/credit side of the account. Additionally, LSTM-VAE model needed to reconstruct monetary values. We tried the model with different loss functions, number of layers and the best architecture had 138 (1.65% of the test dataset) reconstruction errors with monetary value included. It is important to mention that the LSTM-VAE model had difficulties with the very first 88 journal entries.

Despite the fact that the researched models had different inputs (monetary value included in the LSTM VAE model), decision has been led by the final aim of our research, that is development of the most accurate autoencoder. As a bonus we got the opportunity to analyze predicted versus real value.

Although the common characteristics of the journal entry clusters given by tSNE methodology and their relationship were not researched, we used tSNE to visualize dataset and the given results. tSNE reduced latent dimensions of the autoencoders to 2-dimensional space. Points in the figures 3a. and 3b. show journal entries of the tested dataset. Marked points represents entries that the VAE and the LSTM-VAE model reconstructed incorrectly. It can be seen that the both models have reconstruction errors in the same area of the 2-dimensional space. Further, the models did not have a problem to reconstruct the most obvious outliers though it was not capable to reconstruct outliers closed to the well defined clusters of the journal entries.

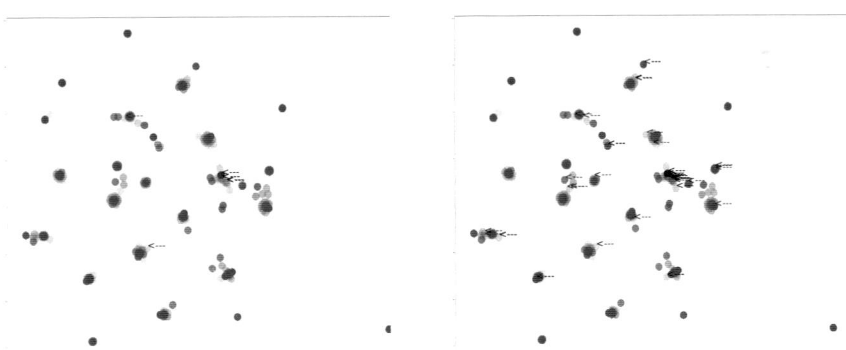

(a) VAE model (b) LSTM-VAE model

Fig. 3: tSNE visualization of the models: Real journal entries with marked anomalies

5 Conclusion and future studies

With research described within this paper we are trying to collect experience in development of an artificial intelligence models by using real datasets generated in real world accounting books and with the final aim of developing intelligence module of accounting information system capable to assist to accountants, auditors and tax officers in finding anomalies. What we were considering for anomalies are errors, intentionally made or not. Precondition for intelligent error detection task is the model which is capable to learn the whole entries in a training process and then to reconstruct every single entry from the tested dataset except these that were seen for a very first time. To reached satisfied precision as well as to help us to understand the model functioning, we used the real-world dataset which is well known to us. It does not include any kind of errors or bookkeeping rules violation, but it includes entries that were happened in the test fiscal year for a very first time.

In this research we tested two models based on autoencoder architecture. The first model is variational encoder (VAE) model and the second one is variational encoder with Long short memory layers (LSTM-VAE) model. The inputs in these models were accounting journals for 12 fiscal years of the small-sized enterprise. Journals did not include any kind of anomalies or errors.

To reach satisfied accuracy of the model, we included document types and journal accounts as unavoidable drivers of business events. Except the most necessary variables, common for every accounting system, we added the monetary value column as the input into the second model (LSTM-VAE). We will also try to add more variables as an input to our models in our future studies.

In general, we can conclude that semi-supervised methods, autoencoders, are promising technology for developing anomaly detection modules inside AIS. Our research also showed potentials of the journal entry anomalies control system development with the help of t-SNE architecture. Visualization helped us to better understand the nature of our data as well as the models functioning. We saw that both models have reconstruction errors of the journal entries in the same area of the 2-dimensional space. Errors of the LSTM-VAE model are the errors of the VAE model at same time. Maybe world of accounting could have benefits from visualization techniques as a supporting technology, so we will use t-SNE for latent dimension visualization in our future studies.

In this paper we did not analyze predicted monetary values generated with our LSTM-VAE model, because we tried to research autoencoders' learning capabilities of the bookkeeping rules and they are not dependable on monetary values. That will be researched in our future studies too.

Generally, VAE models have one more characteristic still unresearched in a field of accounting. They have capability of generating new data from the latent space. It will be interesting to see results of our model generator of fictive entries in our future researches.

Both models we developed with respect of deep learning rules are promising. Still, accuracy in an accounting, especially in anomaly detection problems is requested condition, so the hyperparameters of the models need to be tuned according to the collected knowledge. Lots of experimenting with architecture and hyperparameters are waiting for us to get the prototype for the real-world module of an account control system.

References

1. An, J., Cho, S.: Variational autoencoder based anomaly detection using reconstruction probability. Special Lecture on IE **2**(1) (2015)
2. Arvaniti, V.: Data mining journal entries: Discovering unusual financial transactions
3. Awodele, O., Akinjobi, J., Akinsola, J.: A framework for web based detection of journal entries frauds using data mining algorithm
4. Bay, S., Kumaraswamy, K., Anderle, M.G., Kumar, R., Steier, D.M.: Large scale detection of irregularities in accounting data. In: ICDM (2006)
5. Bengtsson, H., Jansson, J.: Using classification algorithms for smart suggestions in accounting systems. unpublished thesis (2015)
6. Bergstra, J., Bengio, Y.: Random search for hyper-parameter optimization. Journal of machine learning research **13**(Feb), 281–305 (2012)
7. Chollet, F.: Deep learning with python, vol. 1. Greenwich, CT: Manning Publications CO (2017)
8. Ede, J.M., Beanland, R.: Adaptive learning rate clipping stabilizes learning. Machine Learning: Science and Technology (2020)
9. ICAEW: Artificial intelligence and the future of accountancy. Tech. rep., Information Technology Faculty Chartered Accountants, Moorgate Place London EC2R 6EA, UK (09 2018)
10. Khan, R., Corney, M., Clark, A., Mohay, G.: Transaction mining for fraud detection in erp systems. Industrial engineering and management systems **9**(2), 141–156 (2010)
11. Kingma, D.P., Welling, M.: Auto-encoding variational bayes. arXiv preprint arXiv:1312.6114 (2013)
12. Maaten, L.v.d., Hinton, G.: Visualizing data using t-sne. Journal of machine learning research **9**(Nov), 2579–2605 (2008)
13. Omoteso, K.: The application of artificial intelligence in auditing: Looking back to the future. Expert Systems with Applications **39**(9), 8490–8495 (2012)
14. Schreyer, M., Sattarov, T., Borth, D., Dengel, A., Reimer, B.: Detection of anomalies in large scale accounting data using deep autoencoder networks. arXiv preprint arXiv:1709.05254 (2017)
15. Schreyer, M., Sattarov, T., Reimer, B., Borth, D.: Adversarial learning of deepfakes in accounting. arXiv preprint arXiv:1910.03810 (2019)
16. Schreyer, M., Sattarov, T., Schulze, C., Reimer, B., Borth, D.: Detection of accounting anomalies in the latent space using adversarial autoencoder neural networks (08 2019)
17. Schultz, M., Tropmann-Frick, M.: Autoencoder neural networks versus external auditors: Detecting unusual journal entries in financial statement audits. In: Proceedings of the 53rd Hawaii International Conference on System Sciences (2020)
18. Župan, M., Letinić, S., Budimir, V.: Journal entries with deep learning model. International Journal of Advance Computational Engineering and Networking (IJACEN) **6**(10), 55–58 (2018)

Explainability Methods for Natural Language Processing: Applications to Sentiment Analysis (Discussion Paper)

Francesco Bodria[1], André Panisson[2], Alan Perotti[2], and Simone Piaggesi[2,3]

[1] Scuola Normale Superiore, Pisa, Italy, francesco.bodria@sns.it,
[2] ISI Foundation, Turin, Italy, {andre.panisson,alan.perotti}@isi.it
[3] Università di Bologna, Bologna, Italy, simone.piaggesi2@unibo.it

Abstract. Sentiment analysis is the process of classifying natural language sentences as expressing positive or negative sentiments, and it is a crucial task where the explanation of a prediction might arguably be as necessary as the prediction itself. We analysed different explanation techniques, and we applied them to the classification task of Sentiment Analysis. We explored how attention-based techniques can be exploited to extract meaningful sentiment scores with a lower computational cost than existing XAI methods.

Keywords: eXplainable Artificial Intelligence, Natural Language Processing, Sentiment Analysis

1 Introduction

The World Wide Web is a great invention, as it connects everyone in the world, but simultaneously, it is a double-edged sword. In such an open-by-design architecture, everyone can express their feelings from joy to anger. In Social Networks, negative sentiments can derail into hate speech; that can be shared easily, quickly and anonymously, thus becoming a problem. To contain the generation and diffusion of such undesired content, social network companies had to deploy special teams that regularly watch the net and block this phenomenon. These monitoring and flagging tasks are mostly carried out by human employees, thus making the process inefficient: semi-automating this pipeline would allow for a significant speed-up and, consequently, better coverage of contents shared on social media. The research area that deals with this kind of tasks is Sentiment Analysis (SA): Sentiment Analysis is a sub-field of Natural Language Processing (NLP) that, combining tools and techniques from linguistics and Computer

Science, aims at systematically identifying, extracting, and studying emotional states and personal opinion in natural language. However, how can an algorithm know if a text is expressing positive or negative sentiment? This tricky question is not easy to answer, especially in the very complex and ambiguous domain of feelings in which also humans sometimes struggle. Machine Learning algorithms can be applied to Natural Language Processing. Still, the resulting models can be very complicated, becoming black-boxes that provide no information about how the sentiment classification task is performed. How can we trust the results of a black box? Trusting the model is necessary, especially if there is a need to deploy it on a large scale. eXplainable AI (XAI) is a recent research field that deals with this kind of issue.

Our Research Question is, therefore, the following: *is it possible to equip SA algorithms with XAI techniques, in such a way that sentiment labels are explained, and in a computationally feasible way?*

We start by applying state-of-the-art explainability methods to the field of Sentiment Analysis. Then we explore an attention-based method capable of extracting explanations which are both similar to the black-box predictions and computed in a small amount of time. We evaluate our methods and other XAI techniques by comparing them with the original black-box model predictions and show examples where explanations are in contrast with black-box predictions.

2 Related Work

Recently, the use of neural networks in the development of Natural Language Processing (NLP) tasks has become very popular [1]. The standard approach is to transform the input words into semantic vectors called Word Embeddings. These vectors can then be used as input for other algorithms: in our case, they will be fed into a Sentiment Analysis classifier.

Currently, the most effective techniques to create Word Embeddings are the Transformers models, which rely on the attention mechanism. The attention mechanism allows looking over all the information the original sentence holds and then create the proper word embedding according to the context. Transformers models incorporate this by encoding each word position, so it is possible to link two very distant words [2]. The Transformer model utilised in this work is BERT [3], which is one of the most popular models in NLP. The suggested approach to make Sentiment Classification is by applying Transfer Learning. As indicated by BERT authors, the learning procedure is divided into two parts: Pre-Training and Fine-Tuning. The Pre-Training phase is an unsupervised learning process. It consists of showing the model a large sentence corpus, masking a random word, and trying to predict the same word embedding of the masked input (Generative Pre-Training [4]). The second part is called the Fine-Tuning phase. It consists of stacking, after BERT, a linear layer that acts as a classifier and training the whole resulting model using a Sentiment Analysis dataset.

Explaining text classification might look like an easy task for a human, but not for a machine. The best performing models in Text Classification are deep neural networks composed of billions of parameters, and explaining such complex models is difficult or computationally expensive. Radford et a.l. [5] proposed an original approach to this problem. While training their linear model with L1 regularisation, they noticed it used surprisingly few of the learned units. Further analysis revealed a single "sentiment neuron" that was highly predictive of the sentiment value. Using the output of this neuron, they can create scores that explain each word's sentiment in a sentence. In general, there are several types of methods to explain a text classification [6]. For our case, the most suitable is the feature importance method.

Sentiment Analysis often deals with binary sentiment classification: a *negative* sentence is labelled as 0, and a *positive* one as 1. The sentiment prediction task provides a binary label to a sentence. The XAI method outputs a heatmap visualising the contribution of each word of the prediction, as shown in Figure 1.

Fig. 1: Example of a heatmap applied on text.

As a method for creating such an explanation, LIME (Local Interpretable Agnostic-Model Explanations) [7] relies on a straightforward intuition: the model may be very complex globally, but it is easier to approximate it around the vicinity of a particular instance. While treating the model as a black-box, LIME perturbs the instance and trains a local linear classifier. The weights of the linear interpretable classifier create the heatmap.

Integrated Gradients [8] is another technique that has a different approach to the problem. Formally, suppose we have a function $F : R^n \rightarrow [0, 1]$ that represents a deep network. Specifically, let x be the input at hand, and x' be the baseline input. For image networks, the baseline could be the black image, while for text models, it could be the zero embedding vector. IntGrad considers the straight-line path from the baseline x' to the input x and computes the gradients at all points along the path. Integrated gradients are obtained by cumulating these gradients. Specifically, integrated gradients are defined as the path integral of the gradients along the straight-line path from the baseline x' to the input x.

3 Methodology

In this section, we introduce our approach to extract explanation scores from a sentiment analysis classifier in a computationally feasible way. The approach used here to classify documents is based on a pre-trained BERT model. Since BERT uses attention scores, we exploit these scores for explainability purposes.

Two parts compose the BERT model: the embedding creation part and the classifier. The first one creates a vector representation of text while the latter is built on top of the first and perform classical classification. Since BERT is an attention-based model, we decide to add an attention layer between the two parts to have better insight on the model decision, as shown in Figure 2.

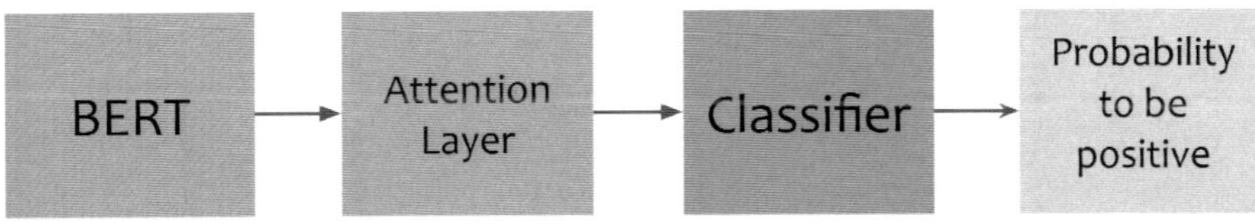

Fig. 2: Adjustment applied to the BERT model. We inserted an attention layer between BERT (encoder) and the Classifier.

Through this attention layer, the model assigns the importance of each word for the prediction task by weighing them when constructing the representation of the text. For instance, a word such as *'amazing'* is likely to be very informative of the emotional meaning of a text, and it should thus be treated accordingly. We use a simple approach inspired by Bahdanau [9] and Yang [10] with a single parameter per input channel:

$$(1) \quad a_t = \frac{exp(h_t w_a)}{\sum_{i=1}^{T} exp(h_i w_a)} \qquad (2) \quad v = \sum_{t=1}^{T} a_t h_t$$

BERT outputs an embedding vector h_t for every word t of a sentence of T words. The attention layer learns importance scores, a_t, for each word by multiplying the representations h_t with a weight vector w_a, learned during the process. The output is normalised using a softmax function to construct a probability distribution over the words. Lastly, the output representation vector for the text, v, is computed with a weighted summation over all the words using the attention importance scores as weights. This representation vector obtained from the attention layer is a high-level encoding of the entire text, and it is used as input to the classifier: a feed-forward layer with a sigmoid activation, $\sigma(W_{classifier} \cdot v)$.

The learned attention scores a_t are the output of a softmax, so they are all positive and do not incorporate the signal from the classifier. To overcome this, we multiply the attention scores obtained from the attention layer by the weights of the classifier. We take the sign and multiply it by the scores:

$$\hat{a}_t = a_t * \text{sign}(W_{classifier} \cdot (a_t h_t))$$

This is our definition of explanation scores.

For the learning phase, we freeze the BERT weights as the original pre-trained model and optimise only the attention and the classification layer.

4 Experiments

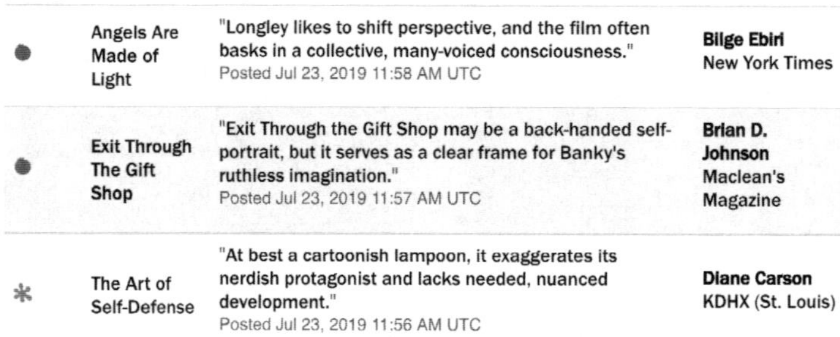

Fig. 3: Rotten Tomatoes Movie Review Dataset Examples, positive scores are expressed with a fresh tomato, while the negative with a rotten one.

Dataset. For our experiments we used, as data, movie reviews; in particular the Stanford Sentiment Treebank (SST) [11] which contains 11855 sentences in movie reviews. Movie reviews are an excellent source for our task, since users both provide text reviews and a score, thus creating a labelled dataset.

The movie reviews have initially been posted on http://rottentomatoes.com/, a popular movie fan website where users can comment and express a positive/negative sentiment, using a fresh tomato or a rotten tomato (see Figure 3). We split the original dataset of 11855 sentences in a training set (6920), a validation set (872) and a test set (1821).

Training. First, we trained our modified version of BERT as a sentiment classifier for the SST dataset mentioned before; we adopted the hyperparameters as described in the original paper [3].
Second, we used the trained BERT as a black-box classifier and labelled all reviews in the test set; we then computed the explanation scores for all labels by running LIME, IntGrad and Attention.
Third, we compared these explanation scores with the ground truth labels and the predictions on the test set of the original black-box model. To do this we have to produce a prediction from the explanation scores, so we built a simple classifier which computes the label y of a sentence j taking the sign of the sum of the score s of the words t of the sentence ($y_j = \text{sign}\left(\sum_{t=0}^{N} s_{tj}\right)$).

Validation. To compare these three explanation scores, we used the *Fidelity* [6], to capture how much each XAI technique can mimic the behaviour of the black-box model it is explaining. We also measured the similarity of our explanation scores with the ground truth labels. Both our evaluation criteria were measured using the ROC AUC scores. The results are shown in Figure 4.

IntGrad is the XAI method that best replicates the model prediction and the one that works better on the test set. This technique seems the best choice,

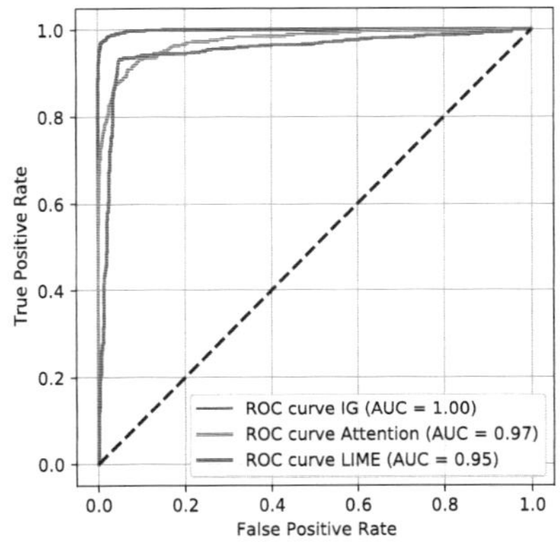

(a) Explanation scores versus black-box predictions.

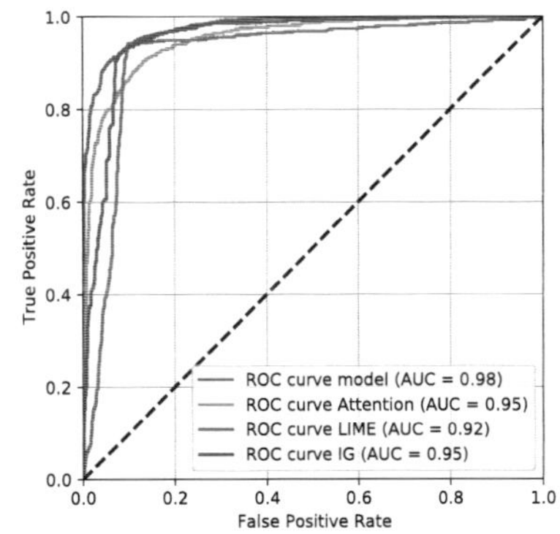

(b) Explanation scores and black-box prediction versus ground truth labels.

Fig. 4: Comparison between explainable methods.

but it still suffers from high computational costs. We evaluated the time for each method to be performed on the entirety of the test set. For the attention layer, we only needed two minutes. For IntGrad, we had to call the black-box model for every step from the baseline, so the time raises to 102 minutes. LIME is the method that performs the worst in terms of time for a total of 1440 minutes. For every sentence, we produce a synthetic neighbourhood, then call the black-box model to label it and finally learn an interpretable local classifier. Our method is less accurate but much faster, as the attention layer is part of the black-box model and does not need any additional model call.
To better appreciate the difference and similarities between the XAI methods, we show in Figure 5 an example of score assignment. The sentence is taken from the test set, and it has negative sentiment as ground truth: *"We never really feel involved with the story, as all of its ideas remain just that: abstract ideas"*.

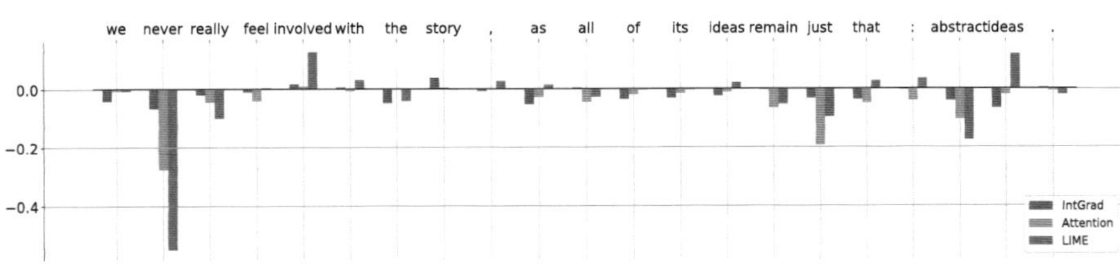

Fig. 5: Comparison between attention score $\hat{a}$ (orange), LIME Scores (blue), and Integrated Gradients scores (green) for the sentence: *"We never really feel involved with the story, as all of its ideas remain just that: abstract ideas."*

Sometimes, these XAI methods conflict with each other. In Figure 6, we show the box-plot of the distribution of correlation coefficients between all the scores along the test dataset used. We can see that overall the scores are strongly

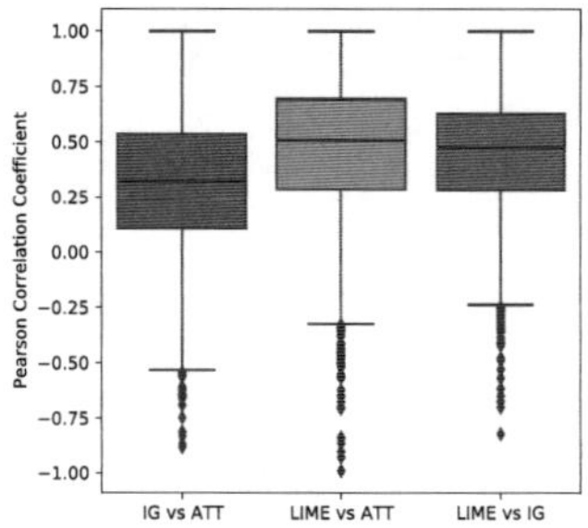

Fig. 6: BoxPlot of the Pearson Correlation Coefficients between XAI methods.

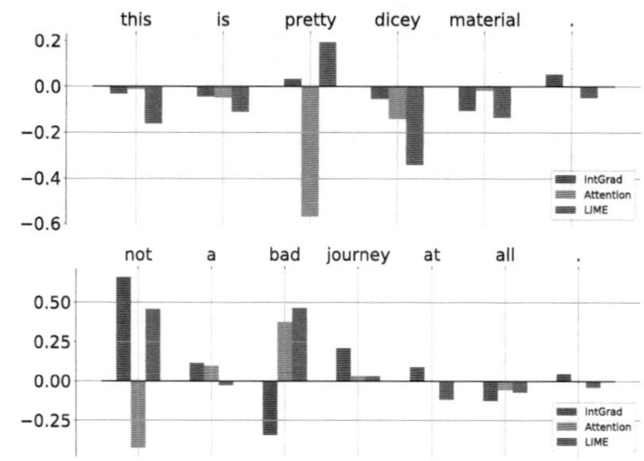

Fig. 7: Comparison between modified attention score $\hat{a}$ and LIME Scores for the sentences: *"This is pretty dicey material."* and *"Not a bad journey at all."*

correlated with each other, but we have a non-negligible number of samples that are negatively correlated. Further analyses highlight how, in some cases, LIME, IntGrad, and attention are negatively correlated in different ways. In Figure 7, we can see two different examples of this uncorrelated behaviour. The top chart shows the negative sentence *"This is pretty dicey material"*, and we can see that neither LIME nor IntGrad could capture the particular use of the word *dicey*. In contrast, the bottom one shows the positive sentence *"Not a bad journey at all"*, and in this case, IntGrad fails at capturing the use of the adjective *bad*. In these examples, explanation scores conflict with the model predictions. The model-explanation concordance is, in general, not guaranteed and has to be taken into account when developing and evaluating XAI techniques.

5 Conclusions

In this work, we show how to use attention layers to extract explanation scores about model predictions. Our method can provide explanations matching the predictions of the black-box model but requires a much lower computational time than the state-of-the-art benchmark methods of LIME and IntGrad. We found that attention scores can be used to explore the internal behaviour of deep neural network models and have XAI capabilities comparable to other approaches, requiring less computational resources. Choosing this approach is a matter of trade-off between performance and time. Different datasets, classification tasks, and black-box NLP models are to be considered in order to explore this trade-off further.

We conclude that many XAI techniques can be applied to the field of NLP to understand better the sentiment classification process (and other NLP tasks in general). However, there is much room for improvement: XAI techniques can be an enabling factor for the explanation and deployment of ML models, but the current state of the art has not yet reached the desired maturity to be applied at scale.

Acknowledgements

AP and AP acknowledge partial support from Research Project Casa Nel Parco (POR FESR 14/20 - CANP - Cod. 320 - 16 - Piattaforma Tecnologica Salute e Benessere) funded by Regione Piemonte in the context of the Regional Platform on Health and Wellbeing and from Intesa Sanpaolo Innovation Center. The funders had no role in study design, data collection and analysis, decision to publish, or preparation of the manuscript.

References

1. Richard Socher, Yoshua Bengio, and Christopher D Manning. Deep learning for NLP (without magic). In *Tutorial Abstracts of ACL 2012*, pages 5–5.
2. Ashish Vaswani, Noam Shazeer, Niki Parmar, Jakob Uszkoreit, Llion Jones, Aidan N Gomez, Łukasz Kaiser, and Illia Polosukhin. Attention is all you need. In *Advances in neural information processing systems*, pages 5998–6008, 2017.
3. Jacob Devlin, Ming-Wei Chang, Kenton Lee, and Kristina Toutanova. Bert: Pre-training of deep bidirectional transformers for language understanding. *arXiv preprint arXiv:1810.04805*, 2018.
4. Alec Radford, Karthik Narasimhan, Time Salimans, and Ilya Sutskever. Improving language understanding with unsupervised learning. *Tech.Rep., OpenAI*, 2018.
5. Alec Radford, Rafal Jozefowicz, and Ilya Sutskever. Learning to generate reviews and discovering sentiment. *arXiv preprint arXiv:1704.01444*, 2017.
6. Riccardo Guidotti, Anna Monreale, Salvatore Ruggieri, Franco Turini, Fosca Giannotti, and Dino Pedreschi. A survey of methods for explaining black box models. *ACM computing surveys (CSUR)*, 51(5):1–42, 2018.
7. Marco Tulio Ribeiro, Sameer Singh, and Carlos Guestrin. "Why should i trust you?" Explaining the predictions of any classifier. In *Proc. of the 22nd ACM SIGKDD Int.l Conf. on Knowledge Discovery and Data Mining*, pages 1135–1144, 2016.
8. Mukund Sundararajan, Ankur Taly, and Qiqi Yan. Axiomatic attribution for deep networks. In *Proc. of the 34th Int.l Conf. on Machine Learning*, volume 70, pages 3319–3328, 2017.
9. Dzmitry Bahdanau, Kyunghyun Cho, and Yoshua Bengio. Neural machine translation by jointly learning to align and translate. *arXiv preprint arXiv:1409.0473*, 2014.
10. Zichao Yang, Diyi Yang, Chris Dyer, Xiaodong He, Alex Smola, and Eduard Hovy. Hierarchical attention networks for document classification. In *Proc. of the 2016 Conf. of the North American chapter of the ACL: Human Language Technologies*, pages 1480–1489, 2016.
11. Richard Socher, Alex Perelygin, Jean Wu, Jason Chuang, Christopher D Manning, Andrew Y Ng, and Christopher Potts. Recursive deep models for semantic compositionality over a sentiment treebank. In *Proc. of the 2013 Conf. on Empirical Methods in Natural Language Processing*, pages 1631–1642, 2013.

Some experiments on Deep Learning for Fake News Detection (DISCUSSION PAPER)

Angelo Chianese, Elio Masciari, Vincenzo Moscato, Antonio Picariello, and Giancarlo Sperli

University Federico II of Naples, Italy
{name.surname}@unina.it

Abstract. The uncontrolled growth of fake news creation and dissemination we observed in recent years causes continuous threats to democracy, justice, and public trust. This problem has significantly driven the effort of both academia and industries for developing more accurate fake news detection strategies. Early detection of fake news is crucial, however the availability of information about news propagation is limited. Moreover, it has been shown that people tend to believe more fake news due to their features [13]. In this paper, we present our framework for fake news detection and we discuss in detail a solution based on deep learning methodologies we implemented by leveraging Google Bert features. Our experiments conducted on two well-known and widely used real-world datasets suggest that our method can outperform the state-of-the-art approaches and allows fake news accurate detection, even in the case of limited content information.

1 Introduction

Social media are nowadays the main medium for large-scale information sharing and communication and they can be considered the main drivers of the Big Data revolution we observed in recent years[1]. Unfortunately, due to malicious user having fraudulent goals fake news on social media are growing quickly both in volume and their potential influence thus leading to very negative social effects. In this respect, identifying and moderating fake news is a quite challenging problem[14]. Indeed, fighting fake news in order to stem their extremely negative effects on individuals and society is crucial in many real life scenarios. Therefore, fake news detection on social media has recently become an hot research topic both for academia and industry.

Fake news detection dates back long time ago[15], for a very long time journalist and scientists fought against misinformation, however, the pervasive use of internet for communication allows for a quicker spread of false information.

Indeed, the term *fake news* has grown in popularity in recent years, especially after the 2016 United States elections but there is still no standard definition of fake news [11]. Aside the definition that can be found in literature, one of the most well accepted definition of fake news is the following: *Fake news is a news article that is intentionally and verifiable false and could mislead readers* [2]. There are two key features of this definition: authenticity and intent. First, fake news includes false information that can be verified as such[8]. Second, fake news is created with dishonest intention to mislead consumers[11].

The content of fake news exhibits heterogeneous topics, styles and media platforms, it aims to mystify truth by diverse linguistic styles while insulting true news. Fake news are generally related to newly emerging, time-critical events, which may not have been properly verified by existing knowledge bases due to the lack of confirmed evidence or claims. Thus, fake news detection on social media poses peculiar challenges due to the inherent nature of social networks that requires both the analysis of their content [10, 6] and their social context[12, 3].

Our approach in a nutshell. Fake news detection problem can be formalized as a classification task thus requiring features extraction and model construction. The detection phase is a crucial task as it is devoted to guarantee users to receive authentic information. We will focus on finding clues from news contents. Our goal is to improve the existing approaches defined so far when fake news is intentionally written to mislead users by mimicking true news. More in detail, traditional approaches are based on verification by human editors and expert journalists but do not scale to the volume of news content that is generated in online social networks. As a matter of fact, the huge amount of data to be analyzed calls for the development of new computational techniques. It is worth noticing that, such computational techniques, even if the news is detected as fake, require some sort of expert verification before being blocked. In our framework, we perform an accurate pre-processing of news data and then we apply three different approaches. The first approach is based on classical classification approaches. We also implemented a deep learning approach that leverages neural network features for fake news detection. Finally, for the sake of completeness we implemented some multimedia approaches in order to take into account misleading images. Due to space limitation, we discuss in this paper the deep learning approach.

2 Our Fake News Detection Framework

Our framework is based on news flow processing and data management in a pre-processing block which performs filtering and aggregation operation over the news content. Moreover, filtered data are processed by two independent blocks: the first one performs natural language processing over data while the second one performs a multimedia analysis. The overall process we execute for fake news detection is depicted in Figure 1. In the following, we describe each module in more detail:

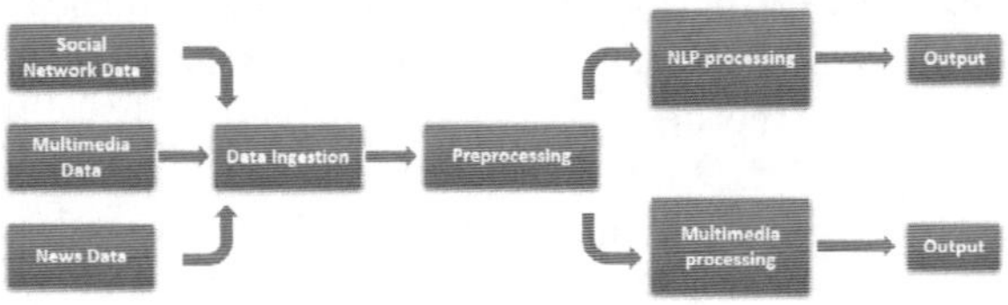

Fig. 1: The overall process at a glance

Data Ingestion Module. This module take care of data collection tasks. Data can be highly heterogeneous: social network data, multimedia data and news data. We collect the news text and eventual related contents and images.

Pre-processing Module. This component is devoted to the acquisition of the incoming data flow. It performs filtering, data aggregation, data cleaning and enrichment operations.

NLP Processing Module. It performs the crucial task of generating a binary classification of the news articles, i.e., whether they are fake or reliable news. It is split in two submodules. The *Machine Learning* module performs classification using an ad-hoc implemented Logistic Regression algorithm after an extensive process of feature extraction and selection TF-IDF based in order to reduce the number of extracted features. The *Deep Learning* module classifies data using Google Bert algorithm after a tuning phase on the vocabulary. It also performs a binary transformation and eventual text padding in order to better analyze the input data.

Multimedia Processing Module. This module is tailored for Fake Image Classification through Deep Learning algorithms, using ELA (Error Level Analysis) and CNN.

Due to space limitation, we discuss in the following only the details of the deep learning module and the obtained results.

2.1 The Deep Learning Module

The Deep Learning Module computes a binary classification on a text datasets of news that will be labelled as 0 if a news is marked as Real, and as 1 if it is marked as Fake. The Deep Learning Module classifies news content using a new language model called *B.E.R.T.* (Bidirectional Encoder Representations from Transformers) developed and released by Google. Prior to describing the algorithm features in detail, we briefly describe the auxiliary tools being used, while in Section 3 we describe the experimental evaluation that lead to our choice on BERT.

Colaboratory. Colab is intended for machine learning education and research, it requires no setup and runs entirely on the cloud. By using Colab it's possible to write and execute code, save and share analytics and it provides

https://research.google.com/colaboratory

access to expensive and powerful computing resources for free by a web interface. More in detail, Colab's hardware is powered by: Intel(R) Xeon(R) CPU @ 2.00GHz, nVidia T4 16 GB GDDR6 @ 300 GB/sec, 15GB RAM and 350GB storage.

Tensor Flow. It is devoted to train and run neural networks for image recognition, word embeddings, recurrent neural networks, and natural language processing. It is a cross-platform tool and runs on CPUs, GPUs, even on mobile and embedded platforms. TensorFlow uses dataflow graphs to represent the computation flow, i.e., these structures describe the data flow through the processing nodes. Each node in the graph represents a mathematical operation, and each connection between nodes is a multidimensional data array called tensor. The TensorFlow Distributed Execution Engine abstracts from the supported devices and provides a high performance-core implemented in C++ for the TensorFlow platform. On top there are Python and C++ frontends. The Layers API provides a simple interface for most of the layers used in deep learning models. Finally, higher-level APIs, including Keras, makes training and evaluating distributed models easier.

Keras. It is a high-level neural network API, implemented in Python and capable of running on top of TensorFlow. It allows for easy and fast prototyping through: 1) User Friendliness as it offers consistent and simple APIs that minimizes the number of user actions required for common use cases; 2) Modularity as neural layers, cost functions, optimizers, initialization schemes, activation functions and regularization schemes are all standalone modules that can be combined to create new models; 3) Extensibility as new modules are simple to add as new classes and functions.

Google BERT. This tool has been developed in order to allow an easier implementation of two crucial tasks for Natural Language Processing (NLP): Transfer Learning through unsupervised pre-training and Transformer architecture. The idea behind Transfer Learning is to train a model in a given domain on a large text corpus, and then leverage the gathered knowledge to improve the model's performance in a different domain. In this respect, BERT has been pre-trained on Wikipedia and BooksCorpus. On the opposite side, the Transformer architecture processes all elements simultaneously by linking individual elements through a process known as attention. This mechanism allows a deep parallelization and guarantee higher accuracy across a wide range of tasks. BERT outperforms previous proposed approaches as it is the first unsupervised, fully bidirectional system for NLP pre-training. Pre-trained representations can be either context-free or context based dependig on user needs. Due to space limitations we do not describe in detail the BERT's architecture and the encoder mechanism.

3 Our Benchmark

In this section we will describe the fake news detection process for the deep learing module and the datasets we used as a benchmark for our algorithms.

3.1 Dataset Description

Liar Dataset. This dataset includes 12.8K human labelled short statements from fact-checking website Politifact.com. Each statement is evaluated by a Politifact.com editor for its truthfulness. The dataset has six fine-grained labels: pants-fire, false, barely-true, half-true, mostly-true, and true. The distribution of labels is relatively well- balanced. [12] For our purposes the six fine-grained labels of the dataset have been collapsed in a binary classification, i.e., label 1 for fake news and label 0 for reliable ones. This choice has been made due to binary Fake News Dataset feature. The dataset is partitioned into three files: 1) Training Set: 5770 real news and 4497 fake news; 2) Test Set: 1382 real news and 1169 fake news; 3) Validation Set: 1382 real news and 1169 fake news. The three subsets are well balanced so there is no need to perform oversampling or undersampling.

The processed dataset has been uploaded in Google Drive and, then, loaded in Colab's Jupyter as a Pandas Dataframe. It has been added a new column with the number of words for each row article. Using the command $df.describe()$ on this column it is possible to print the following statistical information: count 15389.000000, mean 17.962311, std 8.569879, min 1.000000, 25% 12.000000, 50% 17.000000, 75% 22.000000, max 66.000000. These statistics show that there are articles with only one word in the dataset, so it has been decided to remove all rows with less than 10 words as they are considered poorly informative. The resulting dataset contains 1657 less rows than the original one. The updated statistics are reported in what follows: count 13732.000000, mean 19.228663, std 8.192268, min 10.000000, 25% 14.000000, 50% 18.000000, 75% 23.000000, max 66.000000. Finally, the average number of words per article is 19.

FakeNewsNet. This dataset has been built by gathering information from two fact-checking websites to obtain news contents for fake news and real news such as PolitiFact and GossipCop. In PolitiFact, journalists and domain experts review the political news and provide fact-checking evaluation results to claim news articles as fake or real. Instead, in GossipCop, entertainment stories, from various media outlets, are evaluated by a rating score on the scale of 0 to 10 as the degree from fake to real. The dataset contains about 900 political news and 20k gossip news and has only two labels: true and false. [14]

This dataset is publicly available by the functions provided by the FakeNewsNet team and the Twitter API. As mentioned above, FakeNewsNet can be split in two subsets: GossipCop and Politifact.com. We decided to analyse only political news as they produce worse consequences in real world than gossip ones. The dataset is well balanced and contains 434 real news and 367 fake news. Most of the news regards the US as it has already been noticed in LIAR. Fake news topics concern Obama, police, Clinton and Trump while real news topics refer to Trump, Republicans and Obama. Such as the LIAR dataset, it has been added a new column and used the command $df.describe()$ to print out the following statistical information: count 801, mean 1459.217228, std 3141.157565, min 3, 25% 114, 50% 351, 75% 893, max 17377. The average number of words per articles in Politifact dataset is 1459, which is far longer than the average sentence length in Liar Dataset that is 19 words per articles. Such a statistics suggested us to compare the model performances on datasets with such different features.

3.2 Pre-elaboration steps

The above mentioned datasets are available in CSV format and are composed of two columns: text and label. The news text need to be pre-processed for our analysis. In this respect, an ad-hoc Python function has been developed for unnecessary IP and URL addresses removal, HTML tags checking and words spell-check. Due to neural features, we decide to maintain some stop words in order to allow a proper context analysis. Thus, to ameliorate the noise problem, we created a custom list of stop words. We leverage Keras Tokenizer for preparing text documents for subsequent deep learning steps. More in detail, we create a vocabulary index based on word frequency, e.g., given the sentence *The cat sat on the mat* we create the following dictionary $word\_index[\text{the}] = 1$, $word\_index[\text{cat}] = 2$ so every word gets a unique integer value; the 0 value is reserved for padding. Lower integer means more frequent word. After this encoding step, we obtain for each text a sequence of integers. As BERT needs a more elaborated input than other neural networks wed need to produce a *tsv* file, with four columns, and no header. The columns to be added to dataset are: 1) *guid*, i.e., a row ID; 2)*label*, i.e., the label for the row (it should be an int); 3) *alpha*, a dummy column containing the same letter for all rows, it is not used for classification but it is needed for proper running of the algorithm and 4) *text*, i.e., the news content. The data needs to be converted in InputFeature object to be compatible with Transformer Architecture. The conversion process includes tokenization and converting all sentences to a given sequence length (truncating longer sequences, and padding shorter sequences). Tokenization is performed using WordPiece tokenization, where the vocabulary is initialized with all the individual characters in the language, and then the most frequent/likely combinations of the existing words in the vocabulary are iteratively added. Words that does not occur in the vocabulary are broken down into sub-words in order to search for possible matches in the collection.

4 Evaluation

In order to show that the Google BERT model we implemented outperforms the results of the current performance state of art both on Liar dataset and Polifact dataset, we report in Figure 2 and 3 the best results obtained for the other approaches commonly used in literature for those datasets. In particular, neural betworks such as CNN, BI-LSTM and C-HAN were initialized with 300-dimensional pre-trained embeddings from GloVe [9], trained on a dataset of one billion tokens (words) with a vocabulary of 400 thousand words.

We compared the performances on well-established evaluation measure like: Accuracy, Precision, Recall, F1 measure, Area Under Curve (AUC) [5] and the

Neural Network	Accuracy	Precision	Recall	F1	TP	FP	TN	FN	AUC
BERT	0.619	0.583	0.596	0.628	697	472	884	498	0.617
C-HAN	0.557	0.514	0.628	0.565	688	694	735	434	0.574
BI-LSTM	0.586	0.554	0.495	0.523	579	465	917	590	0.607
CNN	0.536	0.489	0.275	0.352	1046	847	322	336	0.539

Fig. 2: Comparison for Google BERT against state of the art approaches on LIAR datataset

Neural Network	Accuracy	Precision	Recall	F1	TP	FP	TN	FN	AUC
BERT	0.588	0.565	0.449	0.628	165	127	306	202	0.578
C-HAN	0.448	0.443	0.795	0.569	67	75	292	367	0.436
BI-LSTM	0.511	0.466	0.455	0.460	167	200	243	191	0.532
CNN	0.540	0.498	0.405	0.447	284	218	149	150	0.520

Fig. 3: Comparison for Google BERT against state of the art approaches on Polifact datataset

values reported in the obtained confusion matrices for each algorithm, i.e., True Positive (TP), False Positive (FP), True Negative (TN) and False Negative (FN).

We hypothesize that our results are quite better due to a fine hyper parameter tuning we performed, a better pre-processing step and the proper transformation.

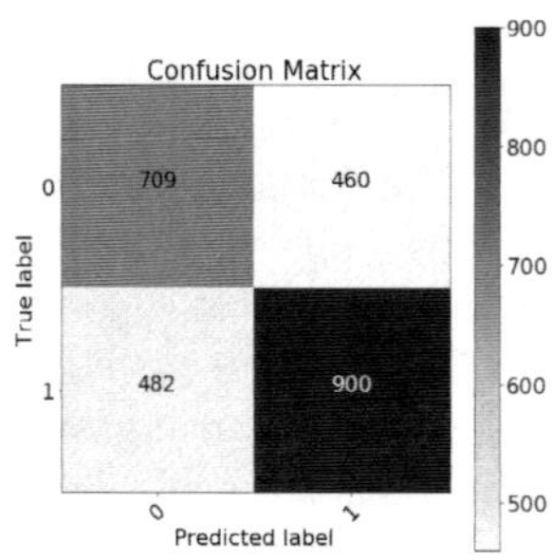

Confusion Matrix for LIAR dataset

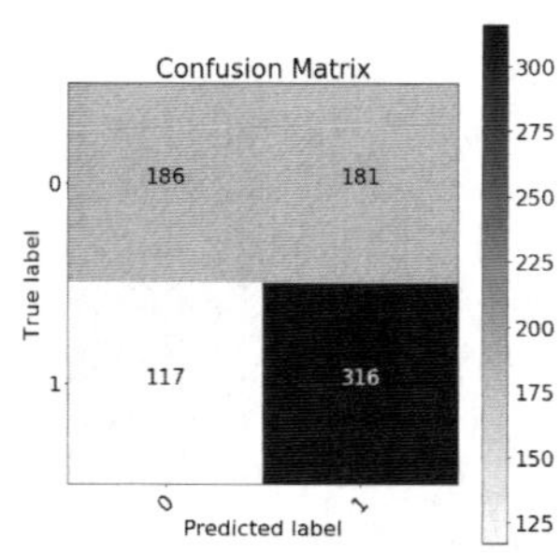

Confusion Matrix for Polifact dataset

For the sake of completeness, we report in Figure 4a and Figure 4b the detailed confusion matrices obtained for LIAR and Polifact datasets.

5 Conclusion and Future Work

In this paper, we investigated the problem of fake news detection by deep learning algorithms. We developed a framework the leverage Google BERT for analyzing real-life datasets and the results we obtained are quite encouraging. As for future work, we would like to extend our analysis by considering also user profiles' features, some kind of dynamic analysis of news diffusion mechanism[14] and geometric features[8] in our fake news detection model[7].

References

1. D. Agrawal et al. Challenges and opportunities with big data. A community white paper developed by leading researchers across the United States. Technical report, Purdue University, Mar 2012.
2. Hunt Allcott and Matthew Gentzkow. Social media and fake news in the 2016 election. Working Paper 23089, National Bureau of Economic Research, January 2017.
3. Nunziato Cassavia, Elio Masciari, Chiara Pulice, and Domenico Saccà. Discovering user behavioral features to enhance information search on big data. *TiiS*, 7(2):7:1–7:33, 2017.
4. J. Shane Culpepper, Alistair Moffat, Paul N. Bennett, and Kristina Lerman, editors. *Proceedings of the Twelfth ACM International Conference on Web Search and Data Mining, WSDM 2019, Melbourne, VIC, Australia, February 11-15, 2019*. ACM, 2019.
5. Peter A. Flach and Meelis Kull. Precision-recall-gain curves: PR analysis done right. In Corinna Cortes, Neil D. Lawrence, Daniel D. Lee, Masashi Sugiyama, and Roman Garnett, editors, *Advances in Neural Information Processing Systems 28: Annual Conference on Neural Information Processing Systems 2015, December 7-12, 2015, Montreal, Quebec, Canada*, pages 838–846, 2015.
6. Chuan Guo, Juan Cao, Xueyao Zhang, Kai Shu, and Miao Yu. Exploiting emotions for fake news detection on social media. *CoRR*, abs/1903.01728, 2019.
7. Elio Masciari. SMART: stream monitoring enterprise activities by RFID tags. *Inf. Sci.*, 195:25–44, 2012.
8. Federico Monti, Fabrizio Frasca, Davide Eynard, Damon Mannion, and Michael M Bronstein. Fake news detection on social media using geometric deep learning. *arXiv preprint arXiv:1902.06673*, 2019.
9. Jeffrey Pennington, Richard Socher, and Christopher D Manning. Glove: Global vectors for word representation. In *Proceedings of the 2014 conference on empirical methods in natural language processing (EMNLP)*, pages 1532–1543, 2014.
10. Martin Potthast, Johannes Kiesel, Kevin Reinartz, Janek Bevendorff, and Benno Stein. A stylometric inquiry into hyperpartisan and fake news. *CoRR*, abs/1702.05638, 2017.
11. Kai Shu, Amy Sliva, Suhang Wang, Jiliang Tang, and Huan Liu. Fake news detection on social media: A data mining perspective. *CoRR*, abs/1708.01967, 2017.
12. Kai Shu, Suhang Wang, and Huan Liu. Beyond news contents: The role of social context for fake news detection. In Culpepper et al. [4], pages 312–320.
13. Soroush Vosoughi, Deb Roy, and Sinan Aral. The spread of true and false news online. *Science*, 359(6380):1146–1151, 2018.
14. Shuo Yang, Kai Shu, Suhang Wang, Renjie Gu, Fan Wu, and Huan Liu. Unsupervised fake news detection on social media: A generative approach. In *Proceedings of the AAAI Conference on Artificial Intelligence*, volume 33, pages 5644–5651, 2019.
15. Xinyi Zhou, Reza Zafarani, Kai Shu, and Huan Liu. Fake news: Fundamental theories, detection strategies and challenges. In Culpepper et al. [4], pages 836–837.

libJoTS: JSON That Syncs!*

Amos Brocco[1], Patrick Ceppi[1], and Lorenzo Sinigaglia[2]

[1] Department of Innovative Technologies, SUPSI, Manno, Switzerland
{amos.brocco,patrick.ceppi}@supsi.ch
[2] Banana.ch SA, Lugano, Switzerland
lorenzo@banana.ch

Abstract. In this paper, we present *libJoTS*, a C/C++ library that provides asynchronous offline replication of arbitrary JSON data with a minimal footprint. The primary use case for this library is to easily replicate changes made to a JSON file by different users. The replication process is based on multi-version concurrency control (MVCC) to ensure non-destructive conflict management, but in contrast to other popular databases, *libJoTS* has no runtime dependencies, supports hierarchical documents with nested objects, and stores all synchronizable data into a file. The library is self-contained, and provides a simple API for C/C++ programs as well as bindings for other languages, such as Java and Python. As such it can be easily linked into any application, allowing end-users to replicate changes to data asynchronously and offline. By using files, data sharing between users does not depend on any specific technology, and can be achieved either with an online file-sharing service or offline, thus ensuring full control on data privacy.

Keywords: JSON · MVCC · Data Synchronization

1 Introduction

Nowadays, many popular applications that once ran natively (offline) on personal computers are being pushed to the cloud. At user level, one of the most significant improvements brought by cloud applications is the ability to easily share data with other people and to work online in a collaborative fashion. In this regard, replication protocols [1–3] are the cornerstone of those multi-user applications, allowing updates made to each replica to be consistently merged together. Replication can be either synchronous or asynchronous. With synchronous replication, often simply referred to as synchronization, there is a continuous flow of information that propagates changes to all replicas: as soon as new data is

* This work has been financially supported by the Swiss Innovation Agency, Project nr. 26367.1 PFES-ES.

being created or updated, data is (atomically) replicated to all remote copies. With asynchronous replication, changes are not propagated in realtime, and the system might even tolerate temporary divergence between replicas. While the synchronous approach ensures that each replica always contains the same data, the overall performance and availability is affected by network availability, reliability and speed. Concerning cloud applications, developers are currently advised to develop software that is able to work even when there is no connectivity: in this context asynchronous replication mechanisms play an important role in allowing users to work on local data, while enabling synchronization with a remote server when online. Beside technical aspects, sharing data on the cloud and storing potentially sensitive data on someone else's computer, introduce privacy, security and legal concerns [4, 5]. In this regard, the user should be able to retain as much control as possible on his/her information, either by relying on offline applications and local file storage, or by using connected applications that offer an open or generic synchronization layer that does not depend on any vendor-specific cloud API. The first approach allows for selective disclosure of information (the user decides whom to send his/her information to), but typically makes synchronization between different versions of the same data difficult. The library presented in this paper, called *libJoTS*, tackles this issue by implementing an offline asynchronous replication mechanism for arbitrary JSON data. *libJoTS* allows any native application to store data in a synchronizable format; moreover because data is always stored as a file on disk, remote sharing can also be performed using any means, like e-mail or file-hosting platforms. Finally, synchronizable files can be easily encrypted (using either symmetric or asymmetric algorithms) and/or digitally signed to prove that data was not altered.

2 Related Work

Data replication and synchronization technologies are the cornerstone of distributed storage systems and cloud-based content editing applications (for example Google Docs™). Although there exist different algorithms and protocols to keep data synchronized [8], we restrict our focus to asynchronous replication, which represents the closest concept to the proposed solution. With asynchronous replication, updates on the master (or source) storage are not copied immediately to a secondary storage (or target), but can be delayed to a later time. Such an approach gives up on strict consistency and update timeliness across the network, while supporting the development of *offline first* solutions, which can operate even without a permanent connection between clients and servers on the network. In this regard, a well-known technology is CouchDB [3], a document-oriented NoSQL database which supports multi-master asynchronous replication: each instance can be independently updated, and changes can be replicated between any instance. Unfortunately, CouchDB is not suited for deployment on mobile devices or the web, therefore similar databases that share

https://developer.chrome.com/apps/offline_apps

the same replication protocol have been developed (for example, Couchbase Lite or PouchDB). With those solutions it is possible to build applications that can operate on a local database while offline and asynchronously replicate changes to another peer when a network connection becomes available. With *libJoTS* we aim to provide transparent offline data replication, by generating a synchronizable file which can be stored and exchanged through any communication channel. Such a synchronizable file might also be signed and/or encrypted, allowing for accountability and/or confidentiality of the data being exchanged. In contrast to a diff/patch [10] solution (which also work on files), *libJoTS* is tailored for semi-structured data in JSON format and ensures that the structure is maintained in the merged document. Data is versioned and each revision is stored directly into the file, allowing for historical data retrieval. Like CouchDB, conflict management is based on MultiVersion Concurrency Control (MVCC): accordingly, replication can be performed among different synchronizable files in no specific order, without compromising the structure of the underlying data. Although there exist comparison tools expressly conceived for JSON data (see for example, RFC6902), those solutions do not maintain an historical record of all versions of the data and might still require user intervention to ensure consistency in the event of concurrent conflicting modifications. In contrast to some of the previously cited solutions, *libJoTS* does not require the source data to be decomposed into a collection of documents, and the library can be easily integrated into desktop or mobile application, being self-contained and written in C++ (with a C API and bindings for other languages, currently Java and Python, and the possibility of targeting WebAssembly in the future).

3 Use Cases

With *libJoTS* we aim at supporting the development of distributed applications that rely on synchronized data without the need for a dedicated server or a specific cloud platform, by enabling information sharing regardless of the type of communication channel (for example, shared folder, e-mail or portable storage). Each user is in control of the data and can decide when to share its own version or merge changes from other users. In the following two use cases are presented.

3.1 *Offline first* application

We consider a desktop or mobile application that lets users edit documents offline on their device and later share their work with other people. User A produces the first version of document X; this version is sent to users B and C through a cloud-based file sharing service. Both user A, B and C make their changes to the document. Subsequently, user B sends its own updated version to User A by email, who can then merge the changes made by B in its copy. At the same time

https://www.couchbase.com
https://pouchdb.com
https://tools.ietf.org/html/rfc6902

user C sends its own version to B by email. User B integrates the changes made by C, merges incoming updates from A and then forwards its final version of the document to C (Figure 1). Users can perform arbitrary editing and replication, and the process can be scaled to an even larger group of users. Moreover, each user can store copies of synchronizable files for archival or backup purposes: those file can be later processed by the library in order to restore data in the application's own format or to peform synchronization.

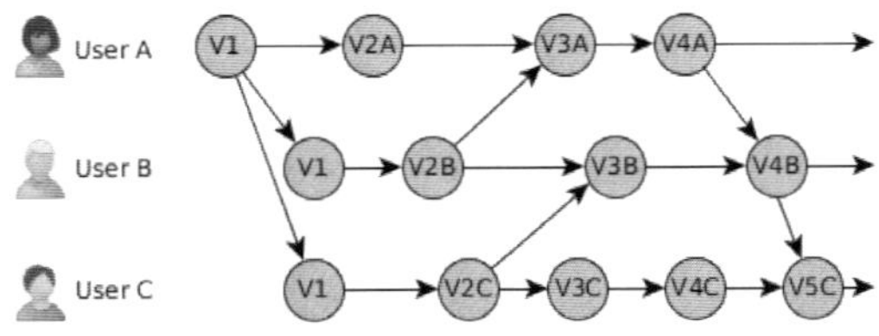

Fig. 1. *Offline first* sample workflow with multi-master replication.

3.2 Distributed configuration management

A common problem in distributed systems is configuration management. Configuration updates need to be replicated from a central server to a multitude of nodes. By means of synchronizable JSON files, *libJoTS* can be used to create mergeable configuration updates: because conflict handling is non-destructive, local changes are preserved while updates to global settings can be seamlessly integrated. Configuration updates can also be stored on disk to be merged later, and the authenticity of an update can be verified by means digital signatures.

4 libJoTS Data Model

The data model used by *libJoTS* is based on JSON documents. Similar to CouchDB the basic unit of replication is a JSON object: the replication algorithm compares two collections of JSON objects and determines the ones missing on each collection. Whereas, CouchDB and other document-oriented databases (like PouchDB) require the application to organize its data into separate JSON objects, *libJoTS* accepts either a collection of separate objects or an arbitrary JSON document (with a nested hierarchy of objects), and can seamlessly replicate their changes. Therefore, from an application's point of view, if JSON is already employed as a data interchange format, little to no change is required to make use of the synchronization capabilities of the library. The proposed approach for dealing with hierarchical JSON documents is to automatically transform an arbitrary input (for example, Listing 1.1) into a collection of objects which can be synchronized independently.

```
{"data":{"transactions":[
  {"_id":"391...32c","currency":"CHF","value":22412,"from":"13465-45566",
   "to":"34655-67554"}]},"info":{"txcount":1}}
```

Listing 1.1. Sample application JSON (*unflattened*, version *V1*)

The output of such a data transformation (Listing 1.2) is a *flattened* collection where array of objects from the input document have been replaced by a string reference, and their contents have been promoted to *first-level* objects. Optionally, nested objects can be promoted too.

```
[{"_id":"391...32c","currency":"!CHF","from":"!13465-45566","to
     ":"!34655-67554","value":22412},{"_id":"@123...8b1-u","s":["391473a1-bb89
     -4dbf-af93-7a8cc1ebc32c"]},{"_id":"root","data":{"transactions":"@123...8
     b1"},"info":{"txcount":1}}]
```

Listing 1.2. *Flattened* collection of JSON documents corresponding to Listing 1.1. Hash values (SHA-256) have been ellipsized for clarity.

We call this procedure *flattening*: each promoted object is associated with a unique identifier, which can be either created using rules specified by the user or automatically generated by the library using a hash algorithm such as SHA-256 [7], xxHash or BLAKE2. The *flattening* transformation is non-destructive and can be undone to restore the original *unflattened* hierarchical structure. To recover the order of the elements inside *flattened* arrays, we generate *ordering* documents with a list of identifiers which belong to the corresponding array in the *unflattened* JSON document. Listing 1.2 illustrates an ordering document (referenced by the *@123...8b1-u* identifier). To prevent the synchronization process from changing the relative order of the elements (as chosen by different users), ordering documents can be tied to specific user/instance identifiers: hence each user can synchronize data without losing their ordering. Moreover, strings are *escaped* using the '!' character to differentiate them from references to arrays or promoted objects.

```
{"d":{
  "391...32c":["d29...d0b"],
  "@123...8b1-u":["3fc...e82"],
  "root":["cc6...5d6"]},
 "o": {
  "3fc...e82":{"s":["391...32c"]},
  "cc6...5d6":{"data":{"transactions":"@123...8b1"},"info":{"txcount":1}},
  "d29...d0b":{"currency":"!CHF","from":"!13465-45566","to":"!34655-67554",
      "value":22412}},
 "r":"root"}
```

Listing 1.3. Synchronizable JSON document corresponding to Listing 1.1.

4.1 Synchronizable JSON

A *Synchronizable JSON* file contains a *flattened* collection of JSON objects along with versioning information. Similar to MultiVersion Concurrency Control (MVCC), concurrent updates and replication never overwrite existing data, but

https://cyan4973.github.io/xxHash
https://blake2.net

simply create a new revision for the concerned objects. The revision string is computed by *hashing* the contents of the object. All revisions but the first one have an *ancestor*: for each object, we maintain the history of revisions (also known as the *revision tree*), which is stored inside the *Synchronizable JSON*). By consulting the revision tree it is possible to determine the order of each update and thus the most recent revision (known as the *winning* revision), which coincides with the tip of the longest branch of the tree. The Synchronizable JSON data corresponding to Listing 1.1 is shown in Listing 1.3. The value associated with the key *d* (for *documents*) is a dictionary of all objects' identifiers and the corresponding revision trees, whereas the value corresponding to *o* (for *objects*) is a dictionary with the contents of each revisions. Finally, the *r* key points to the identifier of the root element (which is needed to reconstruct the original JSON document).

The replication algorithm implemented in *libJoTS* merges all changes found in a *source* document into a *target* document. Given two collections of versioned documents C_1 and C_2, the replication of C_1 to C_2 will copy all the documents and revisions of C_1 that are missing in C_2. At the same time, the revision tree for each document will be updated accordingly. If more than one revision shares the same ancestor a conflict will arise: in that case, a deterministic algorithm will choose the winning revision based on the longest revision branch and lexicographical comparison. This algorithm achieves replica convergence and eventual consistency using MVCC, as in [6].

```
{"data":{"transactions":[
  {"_id":"391...32c","currency":"EUR","value":22412,"from":"13465-45566",
   "to":"34655-67554"}]},"info":{"txcount":1}}
```

Listing 1.4. Updated JSON document (version 2a)

```
{"data":{"transactions":[
  {"_id":"391...32c","currency":"USD","value":22412,"from":"13465-45566",
   "to":"34655-67554"}]},"info":{"txcount":1}}
```

Listing 1.5. Updated JSON document (version 2b)

As an example of the whole replication process, consider the two updated documents in Listings 1.4 and 1.5. Both have been produced starting from version 1: in version *2a*, the value associated with key *currency* has been changed from *CHF* to *EUR*, in version *2b* the value has been changed to *USD*.

The corresponding synchronizable documents can be merged together to produce a new version (Listing 1.6). Both the data contained in version 2a and in version 2b are present in the resulting document, and the revision tree for *391...32c* contains a reference to both revisions. The deterministic conflict resolution algorithm will choose either one of the revisions as *winner* (in this example, the result corresponds to Listing 1.5).

```
{"d":{
  "391...32c":["d29...d0b",["151...4cf_d295e90","8be...7cb_d295e90"]],
  "@123...8b1-u":["3fc...e82"],
  "root":["cc6...5d6"]},
 "o":{
  "151...4cf":{"currency":"!EUR","from":"!13465-45566","to":"!34655-67554",
       "value":22412},
```

```
  "3fc...e82":{"s":["391...32c"]},
  "8be...7cb":{"currency":"!USD","from":"!13465-45566","to":"!34655-67554","
      value":22412},
  "cc6...5d6":{"data":{"transactions":"@123...8b1"},
      "info":{"txcount":1}},
  "d295...d0b":{"currency":"!CHF","from":"!13465-45566","to":"!34655-67554",
      "value":22412}},
"r":"root"}
```

Listing 1.6. Merged Synchronizable JSON document (2a,2b)

Because each revision is kept inside the *Synchronizable JSON* file, the more the data is updated, the bigger the size of the file becomes. This problem can be mitigated by enabling the built-in compression of the *Synchronizable JSON* file. To further limit this growth, we make use of pruning to delete the value associated with old revisions. More specifically, the *pruning* operation removes stale (i.e. non-winning) branches in each revision tree and deletes unreferenced revision objects. The client application can select the depth of the pruning operation in order to maintain an historical record of previous data values (for example, to provide an *undo* functionality).

5 API

To support the basic operations related to Synchronizable JSON files, the public API provides four core functions :

- `sync_json_update` updates or creates a *Synchronizable JSON* document from an arbitrary JSON object (in the application's own format). Since the library is stateless, the *Synchronizable JSON* object must be stored (i.e. saved to a file) by the application itself.
- `sync_json_read` reads a *Synchronizable JSON* document and converts it back into an application-compatible JSON document.
- `sync_json_replicate` replicates changes from a source *Synchronizable JSON* document to a target one.
- `sync_json_prune` removes historical information (i.e. old revisions) from a *Synchronizable JSON* document.

5.1 Offline Workflows

To better understand how the library is meant to be used by an application, in the following we present the expected workflow covering both the creation of *Synchronizable JSON* documents and offline replication of changes.

Updating a Synchronizable JSON file To generate the first version of a *Synchronizable JSON* document, the application needs to provide the input JSON file to the `sync_json_update`. The output document contains all synchronization information required for subsequent replications and can be shared with other

Additional functions for manipulating Synchronizable JSON are also available.

users. In order to update a *Synchronizable JSON* it is necessary to provide a *Synchronizable JSON* to the `sync_json_update` function, along with the updated JSON data. In a distributed scenario several *Synchronizable JSON* documents can be updated in parallel, independently from each other, without loosing the ability to later replicate their changes. In this regard, each document represents a different branch in the version tree.

Reading a Synchronizable JSON file Synchronizable JSON can be converted back to the application's own format using the `sync_json_read` function. By means of additional procedures provided by the library, specific revisions of the data can also be obtained.

Replicating a Synchronizable JSON file Using the `sync_json_replicate` function it is possible to replicate changes made to a *source* Syncronizable JSON file into a *target* file: we refer to this process as *offline replication.* Because each element of the document is versioned, the replication process does not lose any data (non-destructive conflict management). The user can also query for the differences between the new and the old version, as well as conflicting data.

5.2 Online Replication Workflows

Provided that both the source and the target peers are online at the same time (or are able to directly communicate), it is possible to optimize the replication process by sending only bits of modified data. Although not directly implemented by the library, two approaches are proposed: a *diff/patch* mechanism, and an *interactive replication protocol.*

***JSON Patch* approach** The *JSON Patch* solution requires a RFC6902 compliant *diff* and *patch* tool to produce a sequence of operations to apply to a target JSON file (at version V_M) in order to update its structure to be equal to a source version V_N. As mentioned previously, patching the application's JSON does not provide a robust solution to the replication problem, since data might be inadvertently overwritten or corrupted due to conflicting modifications; therefore we consider generating patches against Synchronizable JSON files in order to maintain the full revision history. The target peer needs to communicate its version V_M of the data to the source peer. The source peer then employs a JSON *diff* function to produce a *patch* needed to update V_M to V_N. Unfortunately, such an approach makes synchronization difficult (if not impossible) in a multi-master scenario, where multiple versions of a document with different replication histories arise from concurrent offline synchronizations made by different users: in this situation patches might not apply cleanly leading to data corruption.

Such as https://github.com/nlohmann/json

Interactive replication protocol If both the source and the target peers are online, a more efficient replication can be implemented through an interactive protocol.The source peer sends an *offer* message to the target, containing a list of document identifiers and their associated winning revision. The target replies with an array of identifiers of documents that are either unknown or whose latest revision is older than the one proposed by the source. Finally, the source provides a Synchronizable JSON document with just the missing information. Compared to the *JSON Patch* solution, an interactive replication protocol generates more traffic but does not require the source peer to keep all previous versions of a document. Moreover, it can replicate changes between different *branches* (i.e. Synchronizable JSON documents that have a different revision history). The library also provides methods to migrate data to and from CouchDB-compatible servers, hence replication through another database is also possible.

6 Benchmarks

We evaluate the performance of our library by considering a stepwise editing workflow of a JSON document. The evaluation process begins with version V_1 of a simple JSON document containing an array of objects (Listing 1.1). We subsequently create a new version by performing some changes to the data. More specifically, version V_N is modified to produce version V_{N+1} as follows: a new object is added to the `transaction` array, and the contents of an existing object (except the `_id` field) are replaced with new data. Moreover the value of the field `txcount` is updated to reflect the size (number of elements) of the `transaction` array. At each step, version V_N of the Synchronizable JSON and version V_{N+1} of the application JSON are processed by the `sync_json_update` function to produce version V_{N+1} of the Synchronizable JSON. The resulting document is *pruned* to remove all but the latest revision of the internal data. The last version of the Synchronizable JSON is subsequently replicated on the second-last version using `sync_json_replicate`, and the replication result is converted back to the application's own format using `sync_json_read`. The execution of all operations is profiled in order to measure the required time, the maximum amount of main memory used during the process (maximum RSS), and the resulting file size (for both the Synchronizable JSON and the application JSON). The library was configured to use the *SHA-256* hashing algorithm for generating revision hashes and compression was disabled (unless otherwise specified). All tests were repeated 10 times on a 64-bit Ubuntu Linux machine with an Intel© Core™ i7-6500U CPU running at 2.50GHz with 16GB or memory. The library was compiled with *gcc* version 9.2.1: the actual size of the library is less than 900 KB, with dependencies only against the standard library and the *pthreads* library. For comparison, a minimal install of CouchDB 2.3.1 takes about 40 MB, whereas version 7.1.1 of PouchDB (without JS runtime) is 123 KB.

Results also show the file size using the xxHash algorithm for comparison purposes.

6.1 Offline replication results

As shown in Figure 2, the time required to process JSON data using the library grows linearly with respect to the size of the file. In this regard, we note that the size of the final version of the file (containing a total of 1000 sub-objects) is about 133 KB, and that the total includes also the time spent loading the file from disk. As expected, reading Synchronizable JSON back into the application's own format is the least expensive operation, whereas updating or replicating data takes almost the same time. The growth in each graph is marked by a series of steps due to the allocation of memory for the internal structures of the library.

Additional testing allowed us to assess the scalability of the replication algorithm with respect to the input file size: on the same hardware, generating a Synchronizable JSON document from a 65.5 MB file with 335,389 sub-objects requires about 18 seconds (with the flattening process taking about 80% of the time), and produces a 110 MB output file. Merging two Synchronizable JSON files of such a size (where one file contains 479 updated objects with respect to the other) takes about 12 seconds, while converting the result back to the application's *unflattened* format requires about 10 seconds. With large files the total cost is clearly dominated by parsing the input JSON, which is a known problem when dealing with this format [9]. Trying to import the same amount of data into PouchDB (using the bulk docs interface) freezes the program.

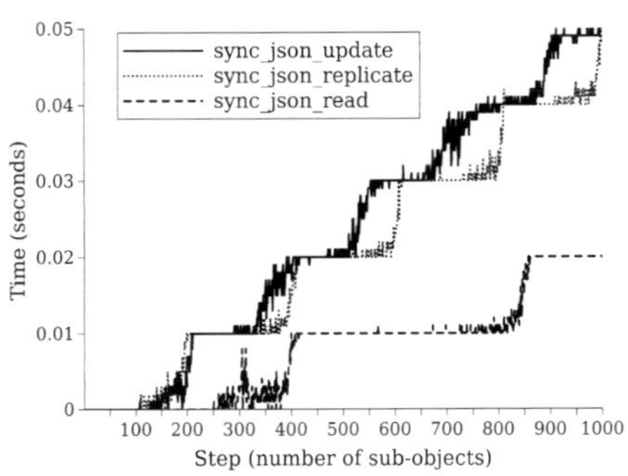

Fig. 2. Time required *vs* number of objects.

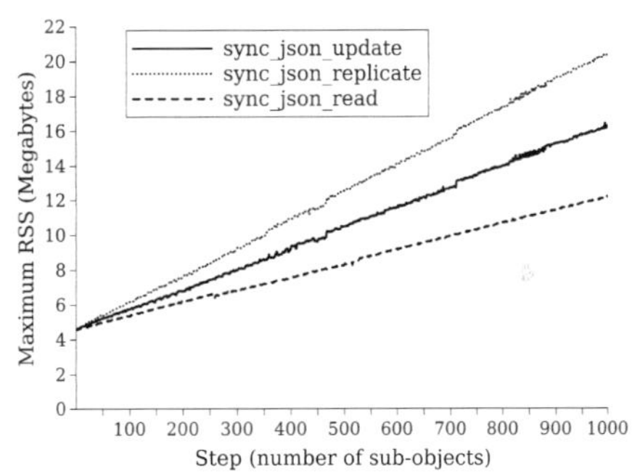

Fig. 3. Maximum Resident Set Size (RSS) *vs* number of objects.

Concerning memory allocation, Figure 3 illustrates the memory required for updating, reading and replicating data using the library. In each case the growth follows the increase in the size of the input document. Replication requires the largest amount of memory, since data from both input files need to be stored at the same time; as expected, reading takes the least memory amount. Unfortunately JSON parsing is memory intensive, and very high requirements are to be expected when dealing with large files: with the previously mentionend 110 MB Synchronizable JSON files, replication requires almost 3 GB of memory.

Figure 4 takes into consideration the cost for offline synchronization, by comparing the file size of both the original JSON file (application JSON) and Synchronizable JSON. The graph also shows the difference between two hashing algorithms (SHA-256 and xxHash) which can be used to generate object and revision identifiers. Even though pruning was used to limit the amount of historical information kept with the file, Synchronizable JSON clearly takes more space on disk compared to application JSON, because of the additional information required to support offline replication (namely, revision trees). It is interesting to note that xxHash allows for more compact synchronizable files compared to SHA-256, because it generates 64 bit hashes instead of 256 bit ones. If Synchronizable JSON files are not meant to be processed outside the library, built-in compression (based on the deflate [11] algorithm) can be enabled to further reduce the size of the file by about 40%. With respect to the workflow involving other databases with support for replication, the size of Synchronizable JSON is typically smaller: the on-disk space taken by PouchDB for the same information (stored as a structured log) is 1.3 Megabytes.

6.2 Online replication results

In order to asses the benefit of online replication (either using the *diff/patch* approach or the *interactive replication protocol*) we repeated the experiment discussed in the previous section assuming that new versions are generated on a source peer while measuring the amount of data that needs to be sent to a target peer in order to keep both replicas synchronized.

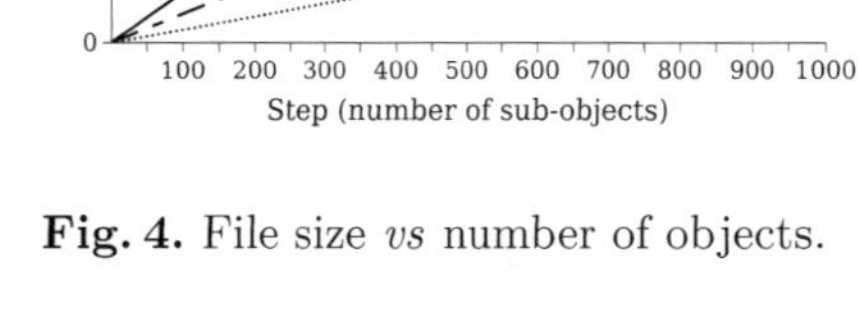

Fig. 4. File size *vs* number of objects.

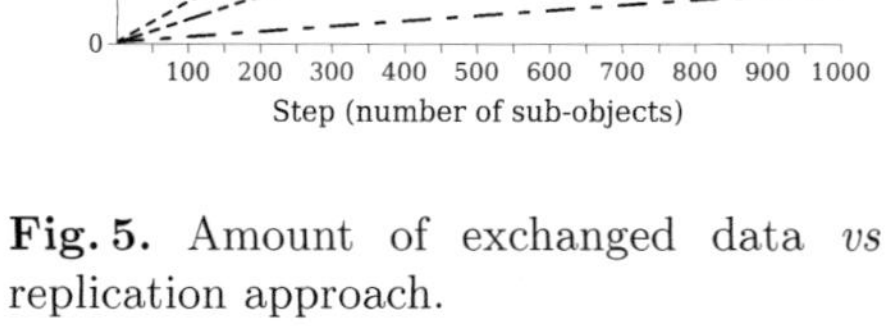

Fig. 5. Amount of exchanged data *vs* replication approach.

As shown in Figure 5, exchanging the full synchronizable JSON file consumes more bandwith than online protocols; the traffic generated using the RFC6902 approach is also significantly lower than the interactive protocol, because only a small amount of information needs to be sent to the target. However, such an approach would not work in a multi-master scenario, where multiple branches need to be synchronized. Although not shown in the graph, the resulting traffic is not meaningfully affected by the hashing algorithm, with *xxHash* producing the same amount of data as *SHA-256*.

7 Conclusions

In this paper, we presented *libJoTS*, a C/C++ library that provides asynchronous offline replication of arbitrary JSON data. The primary use case is to easily replicate changes asynchronously and independently made to a JSON document by different users. The replication process is based on multi-version concurrency control (MVCC) to ensure non-destructive conflict management. The proposed approach draws inspiration from popular document databases with built-in support for replication, but provides a standalone lightweight solution targeting offline replication of small to moderately sized JSON documents. Synchronizable JSON files can be stored on disk, digitally signed and exchanged with any type of communication technology in order to be later merged on a remote system. The API focuses on an offline-first approach, allowing for exchanging synchronizable files using any technology, but also enables online replication using a simple protocol. The library, which we plan to release in the forthcoming months, is self-contained and can be easily integrated into any desktop or mobile application. Future work will focus on implementing an on-disk storage back-end to reduce memory usage (at the expense of processing time), and abstractions to ease integration with cloud based file sharing platforms.

References

1. Souri, Alireza and Pashazadeh, Saeid and Habibizad Navin, Ahmad. Consistency of Data Replication Protocols in Database Systems: A Review. International Journal on Information Theory (IJIT). 3. 2014.
2. Vidal Martins, Esther Pacitti, Patrick Valduriez. Survey of data replication in P2P systems. RR-6083, INRIA. 2006.
3. Apache Software Foundation, CouchDB Replication Protocol, version 3, retrieved February 27. 2020.
4. Sen, Jaydip. Security and Privacy Issues in Cloud Computing. 2013.
5. Paul Voigt and Axel von dem Bussche. The EU General Data Protection Regulation (Gdpr): A Practical Guide (1st ed.). Springer Publishing Company, Incorporated. 2017.
6. CouchDB Team, CouchDB 2.0 Reference Manual, Samurai Media Limited. 2015.
7. Handschuh, Helena. SHA-0, SHA-1, SHA-2 (Secure Hash Algorithm).. In Encyclopedia of Cryptography and Security (2nd Ed.) , edited by Henk C. A. van Tilborg and Sushil Jajodia , Springer, 2011.
8. Ezéchiel, Katembo and Kant, Shri and Agarwal, Ruchi.. Analysis of database replication protocols. 2018.
9. Langdale, Geoff and Lemire, Daniel. Parsing Gigabytes of JSON per Second. 2019.
10. MacKenzie, D., Eggert, P., and Stallman, R.. Comparing and Merging Files with GNU diff and patch. Network Theory Ltd, 2002.
11. P. Deutsch. RFC1951: DEFLATE Compressed Data Format Specification version 1.3. RFC Editor, USA. 1996.

OLAP Querying of Document Stores in the Presence of Schema Variety
(DISCUSSION PAPER)

Matteo Francia, Enrico Gallinucci, Matteo Golfarelli, and Stefano Rizzi

DISI, University of Bologna, Italy

Abstract. Document stores are preferred to relational ones for storing heterogeneous data due to their schemaless nature. However, the absence of a unique schema adds complexity to analytical applications. In a previous paper we have proposed an original approach to OLAP on document stores; its basic idea was to stop fighting against schema variety and welcome it as an inherent source of information wealth in schemaless sources. In this paper we focus on the querying phase, showing how queries can be directly rewritten on a heterogeneous collection in an inclusive way, i.e., also including the concepts present in a subset of documents only.

Keywords: NoSQL · Multidimensional Modeling · OLAP

1 Introduction

Schemaless databases, in particular document stores (DSs) such as MongoDB, are preferred to relational ones for storing heterogeneous data with variable schemas and structural forms; typical schema variants within a collection consist in missing or additional fields, in different names or types for a field, and in different structures for instances. The absence of a unique schema grants flexibility to operational applications but adds complexity to analytical applications, in which a single analysis often involves large sets of data with different schemas. Dealing with this complexity while adopting a classical data warehouse design approach would require a notable effort to understand the rules that drove the use of alternative schemas, plus an integration activity to identify a common schema to be adopted for analysis.

In this paper we propose an approach to OLAP querying on DSs. The basic idea is to welcome data heterogeneity and schema variety as an inherent source of information wealth. So, instead of trying to hide this variety, we show it to users (basically, data scientists and data enthusiasts). To the best of our knowledge, this is the first approach to propose a form of approximated OLAP analyses on document stores that embraces and exploits the inherent variety of documents. OLAP querying is carried out directly on the data source, without materializing any cube or data warehouse. Remarkably, we adopt an *inclusive* solution to integration, i.e., the user can include a concept in a query even if it is present in a subset of documents only. We cover both inter-schema and intra-schema variety, specifically we cope with missing fields, different levels of detail in instances, different field naming.

2 Related Literature

The rise of NoSQL stores has captured a lot of interest from the research community, which has proposed a variety of approaches to deal with the schemaless feature. Accessing schemaless sources often requires the adoption of data integration techniques to provide a unified view of data; as this is not the primary focus of the paper, we refer the reader to a survey on the subject [6].

A distinguishing feature of our approach is the definition of a multidimensional representation of the schema to enable OLAP analyses directly on the DS. From this point of view, a work closely related to ours is [2], which proposes a schema-on-read approach for multidimensional queries over DSs. That approach differs from ours because it focuses on the multidimensional representation of JSON data and overlooks the variety issues, and because the detection of functional dependencies is activated on-demand only *after* the user has written a query. OLAP analyses on DSs are enabled also in [7], although a simpler integration approach is proposed, with no identification of functional dependencies nor multidimensional views.

On the issue of schema variety on DSs, a recent work [8] builds on a simple mapping strategy to hide the variety within a single, comprehensive query. Whereas the approach proposes a simpler querying mechanism, it only covers a limited set of schema variants and does not support OLAP.

Finally, several works have focused on bringing NoSQL back to the relational world. [11] discusses an approach to provide schema-on-read capabilities for flexible schema data stored on RDBMSs: it maps the document structure on different tables and provides a *data guide* as the union of every possible field at any level. However, no advanced schema matching mechanism is provided.

3 Approach Overview and Working Example

Figure 2 gives an overview of our approach. Although the picture suggests a sequential execution of the stages, it simply outlines the ordering for the first iteration. The user starts by analyzing the first results provided by the system, then iteratively injects additional knowledge into the different stages to refine the metadata and improve the querying effectiveness. We now provide a short description of each stage based on an example; all the details can be found in [3]. The example we use is based on a real-world collection of workout sessions, WS, obtained from a worldwide company selling fitness equipment. Figure 1 (left) shows a sample document in the collection, organized according to three nesting levels: the first level contains information about the user; the Exercises

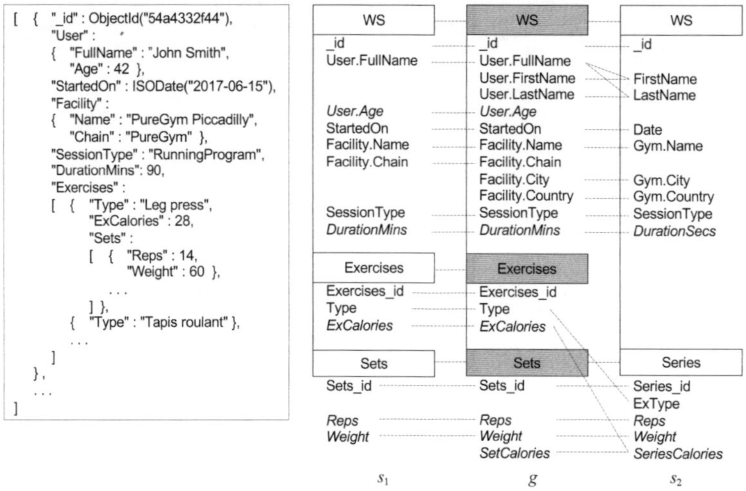

Fig. 1. A JSON document in the WS collection (left), its schema (s_1), another schema of the same collection (s_2), and the global schema (g)

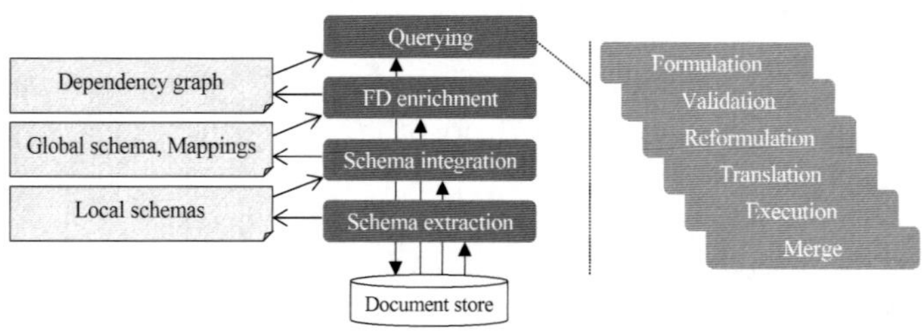

Fig. 2. Approach overview

array contains an object for every exercise carried out during the session; the Sets array contains an object for every set that the exercise was split into.

1. **Schema extraction**. The goal is to identify the set of distinct *local schemas* that occur inside a collection of documents. To this end we adopt a tree-like definition for schemas which models arrays by considering the union of the schemas of their elements, as done in [1]. This is a completely automatic stage; its implementation is loosely inspired by the free tool variety.js and consists of a routine that connects to the desired collection on MongoDB, extracts the local schemas, and writes the results on a triplestore. With reference to our example, Figure 1 shows the schema s_1 of the sample document. Each array is represented as a box, with its child primitives listed below (numeric primitives are in italics). Object fields are prefixed with the object key (e.g., Facility.Chain). The vertical lines between boxes represent nestings of arrays, with the root WS on top.

2. **Schema integration**. The goal here is to integrate the distinct, local schemas extracted from a collection to obtain a single and comprehensive view of the latter, i.e., a *global schema*, and its mappings with each local schema. To this end we rely on both *schema matching* and *schema mapping* techniques: the former allow to identify the single matches between the attributes, while the latter define the mappings between each local schema and the global one, thus enabling the rewriting of queries. A mapping between two (sets of) primitive fields P and P' requires a *transcoding function* to transform values of P into values of P'; these functions enable query reformulation in the presence of selection predicates as well as the integration of the query results obtained from all documents. The approach we adopt for schema integration includes two steps. The first step is automatic and defines a preliminary global schema as the name-based union of all local schemas [10]. In the second step, the preliminary global schema is refined by merging matching (sets of) fields in the global schema. Existing tools (e.g., Coma 3.0 [12]) can be used to automatically find a list of possible matches between arrays and primitives; then the user will browse them and possibly define additional mappings. With reference to our example, Figure 1 shows the global schema g resulting from the integration of s_1 with s_2, one more schema from WS; mappings between arrays and primitives are represented with dotted lines. The transcoding functions of mappings $\langle\{\textsf{Date}\}, \{\textsf{StartedOn}\}\rangle$ and $\langle\{\textsf{FirstName}, \textsf{LastName}\}, \{\textsf{User.FullName}\}\rangle$ are the identity function and a function that concatenates two strings, respectively.
3. **Schema enrichment**. The goal is to propose a multidimensional view of the global schema to enable OLAP analyses. The main informative gap to be filled to this end is the identification of hierarchies, which in turn relies on the identification of functional dependencies (FDs) between fields in the global schema. By assuming the presence of identifiers at every nesting level, some exact FDs can be derived from the global schema without looking at the data. However, additional FDs can exist between primitive nodes, though they cannot be inferred from the schema and can only be found by querying the data. More precisely, since DSs may contain incomplete and faulty data, we look for *approximate FDs* (AFDs) [9], i.e., FDs that "mostly" hold on data. To detect approximate FDs, we adapted the approach proposed in [4]. As a result, we determine a *dependency graph*, which provides a multidimensional view of the global schema in terms of the FDs between its primitive fields. Figure 3 shows the dependency graph for our example. Each primitive field f is represented as a circle whose color is representative of the *support* of f, i.e., of the percentage of times that f occurs in the collection (the lighter the tone, the lower the support). Identifiers (e.g., _id) are shown in bold. Directed arrows are representative of the (A)FDs detected during schema enrichment; for instance, we have _id $\rightarrow$ Facility.Name (exact FD, in black) and Facility.Name $\rightsquigarrow$ Facility.Chain (AFD, in grey). The latter FD is approximate because it only holds for a subset of documents.
4. **Querying**. The last stage enables the formulation of multidimensional queries on the dependency graph and their execution on the collection. First of

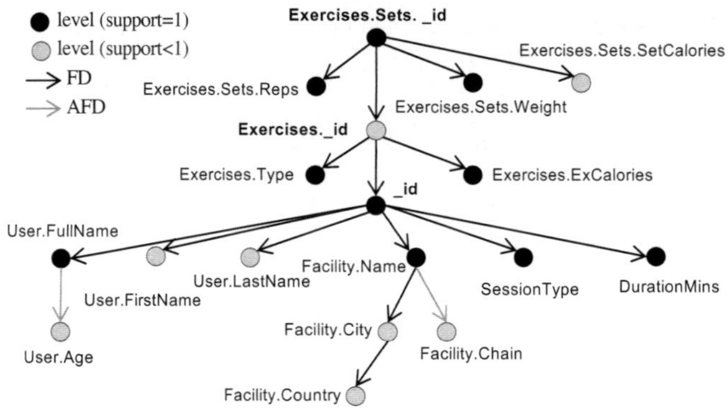

Fig. 3. Dependency graph for the global schema in Figure 1

all, each formulated query is validated against the requirements of well-formedness proposed in the literature [13]. Then, the query is reformulated into multiple queries, one for each local schema in the collection, which are translated into the query language of the DS; the results presented to the user are obtained by merging the results of the single local queries.

4 Querying

In this section we describe the final querying stage of our approach. Given a global schema g and the dependency graph $\mathcal{M}$ obtained by enriching g with (A)FDs, a *multidimensional query* (from now on, md-query) is a triple $q = \langle G, p, m, \varphi \rangle$ where: G is the query *group-by set*, i.e., a non-empty set of primitive fields in $\mathcal{M}$; p is an optional *selection predicate* defined as a conjunction of Boolean predicates on primitive fields; m is the query *measure*, i.e., the numeric primitive field to be aggregated; φ is the operator to be used for aggregation (e.g., `avg`, `sum`).

For q to be *well-formed*, there must exist in $\mathcal{M}$ one single field $\overline{f}$ such that all the other fields mentioned in q (either in G, p, or m) can be reached in $\mathcal{M}$ from $\overline{f}$. Field $\overline{f}$ is called the *fact* of q (denoted $fact(q)$) and corresponds to the coarsest granularity of $\mathcal{M}$ on which q can be formulated.

Other well-formedness constraints for md-queries are introduced in [13]: the *base integrity constraint*, stating that the fields in G must be functionally independent on each other, and the *summarization integrity constraint*. The base integrity constraint can be easily checked on the dependency graph (no arcs must exist between the fields in G). As to the summarization integrity constraint, each query undergoes a check that can possibly return some warnings to inform the user of potentially incorrect results. Specifically, summarization integrity entails *disjointness* (to avoid double counting, the measure instances to be aggregated must be partitioned by the group-by instances) and *completeness* (the union of these partitions must constitute the entire set). Disjointness is easily checked on the dependency graph by verifying if the granularity of measure m is finer than the one of all the fields in G. Completeness is obtained if all the fields in G have full support, which is easily contradicted in heterogeneous collections. To restore completeness, we adopt at query time the balancing strategies used for incomplete hierarchies in data warehouse design; basically, the `$ifNull` operator in MongoDB is used to replace a missing value in a field with a custom value.

Example 1. The following md-query on the WS collection, q_1, measures the average amount of weight lifted by elderly athletes per city and type of exercise:

$$q_1 = \langle\{\mathsf{Facility.City}, \mathsf{Exercises.Type}\}, (\mathsf{User.Age} \geq 60), \mathsf{Exercises.Sets.Weight}, \mathsf{avg}\rangle$$

We have $fact(q_1) = \mathsf{Exercises.Sets.\_id}$. Query q_1 passes the validity check with a warning, because the support of Facility.City is less than one, so balancing is used to restore completeness. On the other hand, q_1 meets the disjointness constraint because the granularity Exercises.Sets._id of the required measure, Exercises.Sets.Weight, is finer than both the granularities _id and Exercises._id of the group-by fields. □

Once a well-formed md-query q has been formulated by the user on the dependency graph, it has to be reformulated on each local schema s_i to effectively cope with inter-document variety. To this end we rely on the approach to md-query reformulation proposed in [5] for federated data warehouse architectures. This approach has been proved to be complete and to provide all certain answers to the md-query. As a result, a set of local queries $q^{(i)}$, one for each local schema s_i, are determined.

At this point, each local query $q^{(i)}$ is separately executed on the DS; specifically, $q^{(i)}$ must target only the documents that belong to local schema s_i. This is done in two steps. First, the information about which document has which schema (obtained in the schema extraction stage) is stored in a different collection (called WS-schemas in our example) in the following form: a document is created for every schema s_i, containing an array ids with the _id of every document having schema s_i. Then, query $q^{(i)}$ is executed by joining it with the list of identifiers in WS-schemas. Note that, to be executed, $q^{(i)}$ needs be translated to the MongoDB query language, which allows us to declare a multi-stage pipeline of transformations to be carried out on the documents of a collection.

Finally, a post-processing activity is required to integrate and, possibly, further aggregating the results coming from the different local queries. This operation can be performed in-memory, as OLAP queries usually produce a limited number of records and the transcoding functions provide homogeneous values.

Example 2. Consider an md-query that calculates the total amount of burnt calories by facility, excluding workout sessions that are shorter than 30 minutes:

$$q_2 = \langle\{\mathsf{Facility.Name}\}, (\mathsf{DurationMins} \geq 30), \mathsf{Exercises.ExCalories}, \mathtt{sum}\rangle$$

Consider the local schemas s_1 and s_2 in Figure 1. The reformulation of q_2 onto s_1 has no effect (i.e., $q_2^{(1)} \equiv q_2$); conversely, the reformulation onto s_2 generates the following local query:

$$q_2^{(2)} = \langle \{\mathsf{Gym.Name}\}, (\frac{\mathsf{DurationSecs}}{60} \geq 30), \mathsf{Series.SeriesCalories}, \mathtt{sum} \rangle$$

The MongoDB query obtained from q_1 of Example 1 is the following; note that the missing values of Facility.City are replaced by those of Facility.Name:

```
db.WS.aggregate(
{ { $unwind: "$Exercises" },
  { $unwind: "$Exercises.Sets" },
  { $match: { "User.Age": { $gte: 60 } } },
  { $project:
    { "Facility.City": { $ifNull: ["$FacilityCity","$FacilityName"] } },
      "Exercises.Type": 1,
      "Exercises.Sets.Weight": 1,
      "balanced": { $cond: ["$FacilityCity",false,true]} } },
  { $group:
    { "_id":
      { "FacilityCity","$FacilityCity",
        "ExercisesType","$Exercises.Type",
        "balanced","$balanced" },
      "Exercises.Sets.Weight":
      { $avg: "$Exercises.Sets.Weight" },
      "count": { $sum: 1 },
      "count-m": { $sum: { $cond: ["$Exercises.Sets.Weight",1,0] } } } } } )
```

5 Conclusions and Evaluation

In this paper we have presented an original approach to OLAP querying on DSs. Our basic claim is that the heterogeneity and schema variety intrinsic to DSs should be considered as a source of information wealth. At the core of our approach are (i) the building of a global schema that maps onto the different local schemas within a collection, (ii) the translation of this schema into multidimensional form enhanced by the detection of approximate FDs, and (iii) the reformulation of queries from the global schema onto the local schema to improve the completeness of the result.

As a proof of concept for our approach we have developed a Java prototype to support the main phases and tested it on a cluster of seven CentOS 6 machines with an 8-core i7-4790 CPU @3.60 GHz and 32 GB of RAM. Our reference real-world collection, WS, is stored on Mongo DB 3.4 and randomly sharded on the cluster; it contains 5 M workout sessions with 6 different local schemas (mostly due to missing fields), 35 M exercises, and 85 M sets.

Query formulation and translation to MongoDB are done in negligible time. Reformulation is done with polynomial complexity [5]. Thus, performances mainly depend on query execution. Consider for instance the following three md-queries:

$$q_a = \langle \{\mathsf{User.Age}, \mathsf{Facility.Chain}\}, TRUE, \mathsf{DurationMins}, \mathsf{avg} \rangle$$
$$q_b = \langle \{\mathsf{User.FullName}\}, (\mathsf{SessionType} = \text{“Advanced”}), \mathsf{Exercises.ExCalories}, \mathtt{sum} \rangle$$
$$q_c = \langle \{\mathsf{Facility.Name}, \mathsf{Exercises.Type}\}, (\mathsf{StartedOn} \geq 01/01/2018), \mathsf{User.Age}, \mathtt{max} \rangle$$

Due to the reformulation on the local schemas, 6 local md-queries are created from each of the three global ones. A simple optimization is done, when possible,

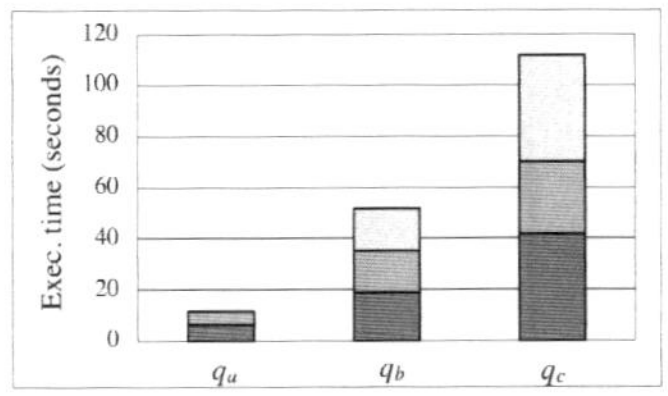

Fig. 4. Execution times of three queries (q_a, q_b, and q_c) split into the execution times of the required local queries

to merge the local queries that involve the same fields on different local schemas; for instance, with reference to Figure 1, a query counting the documents by SessionType can be translated into a single local query, as every local schema has the same representation of SessionType. Due to this optimization, q_a, q_b, and q_c are reformulated into either 2 or 3 local queries. The execution times in seconds for each query are shown in Figure 4; the times for q_b and q_c are higher due to the necessity of unwinding arrays.

References

1. Baazizi, M.A., Lahmar, H.B., Colazzo, D., Ghelli, G., Sartiani, C.: Schema inference for massive JSON datasets. In: Proc. EDBT. pp. 222–233 (2017)
2. Chouder, M.L., Rizzi, S., Chalal, R.: EXODuS: Exploratory OLAP over document stores. Inf. Syst. **79**, 44–57 (2019)
3. Gallinucci, E., Golfarelli, M., Rizzi, S.: Approximate OLAP of document-oriented databases: A variety-aware approach. Inf. Syst. **85**, 114–130 (2019)
4. Golfarelli, M., Graziani, S., Rizzi, S.: Starry vault: Automating multidimensional modeling from data vaults. In: Proc. ADBIS. pp. 137–151 (2016)
5. Golfarelli, M., Mandreoli, F., Penzo, W., Rizzi, S., Turricchia, E.: OLAP query reformulation in peer-to-peer data warehousing. Inf. Syst. **37**(5), 393–411 (2012)
6. Golshan, B., Halevy, A.Y., Mihaila, G.A., Tan, W.: Data integration: After the teenage years. In: Proc. PODS. pp. 101–106 (2017)
7. Hamadou, H.B., Gallinucci, E., Golfarelli, M.: Answering GPSJ queries in a polystore: A dataspace-based approach. In: Proc. ER. pp. 189–203 (2019)
8. Hamadou, H.B., Ghozzi, F., Péninou, A., Teste, O.: Towards schema-independent querying on document data stores. In: Proc. DOLAP (2018)
9. Ilyas, I.F., Markl, V., Haas, P., Brown, P., Aboulnaga, A.: CORDS: Automatic discovery of correlations and soft functional dependencies. In: Proc. SIGMOD. pp. 647–658 (2004)
10. Klettke, M., Störl, U., Scherzinger, S., Regensburg, O.: Schema extraction and structural outlier detection for JSON-based NoSQL data stores. In: Proc. BTW. vol. 2105, pp. 425–444 (2015)
11. Liu, Z.H., Gawlick, D.: Management of flexible schema data in RDBMSs - opportunities and limitations for NoSQL. In: Proc. CIDR. Asilomar, USA (2015)
12. Maßmann, S., Raunich, S., Aumüller, D., Arnold, P., Rahm, E.: Evolution of the COMA match system. In: Proc. OMISWC. Bonn, Germany (2011)
13. Romero, O., Abelló, A.: Multidimensional design by examples. In: Proc. DaWaK. pp. 85–94. Krakow, Poland (2006)

MASTER: A Multiple Aspects View on Trajectories

DISCUSSION PAPER

Ronaldo dos Santos Mello[1], Vania Bogorny[1], Luis Otavio Alvares[1], Luiz Henrique Zambom Santana[1], Carlos Andres Ferrero[1,2], Angelo Augusto Frozza[1,3], Geomar Andre Schreiner[1], and Chiara Renso[4]

[1] Universidade Federal de Santa Catarina - PPGCC, Florianopolis, Brazil
[2] Instituto Federal de Santa Catarina, Lages-SC, Brazil
[3] Instituto Federal Catarinense, Camboriu-SC, Brazil
[4] ISTI-CNR, Pisa, Italy

Abstract. For many years trajectory data have been treated as sequences of space-time points or stops and moves. However, with the explosion of the Internet of Things (IoT) and the flood of Big Data generated on the Internet, like weather channels and social network interactions, which can be used to enrich mobility data, trajectories become more and more complex, with multiple and heterogeneous data dimensions that can be integrated with trajectories. In this paper we introduce multiple aspect trajectories and we propose a robust conceptual and logical data model and a storage solution for efficient multiple aspect trajectory queries. The main strength of our data model is the combination of simplicity and expressive power to represent heterogeneous aspects, ranging from simple labels to complex objects. We evaluate the proposed model in a tourism scenario.

1 Introduction

With the explosion of the *Internet of Things (IoT)* and the flood of *Big Data* generated on the Internet, like weather channels and social network interactions (*e.g., Flickr, Facebook, Twitter, Foursquare*), it is now possible to collect huge volumes of movement data about people, animals, and objects like cars, buses, drones, etc. Sensors installed either indoor (*e.g., smart homes*) or outdoor allow the collection of data about the *place*, like temperature, air pollution, noise, luminosity, etc, or about the *object* that is moving around or inside this place, like the heart rate (with a smart watch), the emotional status (with a microphone that analyses the voice intonation), blood pressure, sleeping stages, etc. By collecting all these information we have a new type of movement data, *i.e.*, a trajectory enriched with different semantic aspects.

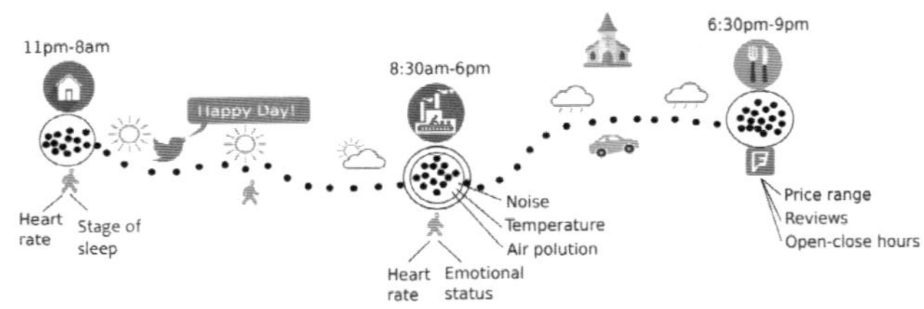

Fig. 1. An example of a multiple aspect trajectory

We can observe from Figure 1 that a trajectory became a complex object with numerous data dimensions that are contextual to the movement and heterogeneous in the form, which we define in this paper as *aspects*. The more aspects we have, the more complete is the representation of the real movement of an object, and more useful and interesting information we can infer about objects and places. The challenge is how to integrate all these heterogeneous information in a single trajectory representation, and the main questions we want to answer in this paper are: *(i) Is it possible to define a data model that is simple in structure, but generic enough to represent any aspect related to the movement, and covers a large number of applications? (ii) Is there a way to efficiently query and extract patterns from data represented in this model?*

We claim that multiple aspects represent a new view over trajectories, and a new paradigm concerning mobility data. These aspects are not only simple semantic labels, but may be complex objects and/or heterogeneous information intrinsically associated to the physical traces of the moving objects.

In this discussion paper we highlight the results of a published paper [4]. In that paper we introduced the concept of multiple aspect trajectory and propose a novel approach for modeling this kind of trajectories called *MASTER*. MASTER comprises a conceptual and a logical data model for multiple aspect trajectories, as well as a storage solution that is very appropriate for multiple aspect trajectory queries. In the full paper we also compared the MASTER model with a competitor DB called SECONDO[5]. Due to the lack of space, we omit here this comparison and we refer the reader to the full paper for details. The main novelties of MASTER compared to other state of the art works (detailed described in the full paper [4]) is that MASTER is more generic since we introduce the notion of "aspect" and how these aspects can enrich the location data. Other approaches do not support relationships between moving objects and do not propose a solutions for storing and querying huge volumes of trajectories and aspects or moving objects.

2 The MASTER Model

The main strength of our conceptual model is the combination of simplicity and expressive power for representing aspects. An aspect may be related to a moving object, to the entire trajectory or any trajectory point, and may hold any type of data, ranging from simple labels to complex objects.

For the logical model, we consider a graph-based representation (the RDF standard [6]) that is generic enough to model trajectories and aspects extracted from heterogeneous data sources, like geolocated structured record files and geolocated social media posts (*e.g.*, tweets). Finally,

we consider NoSQL databases for efficient storage and retrieval of large amounts of trajectory data. Our inspiration comes from the *polyglot persistence* approach [7], which states that a conceptual data model can be split and mapped to several database models for maximizing query performance.

We introduce a conceptual data model for multiple aspect trajectories, which is shown in Figure 2. We start the description of the model with the new concept of *aspect*.

An aspect is a real world fact that is relevant for trajectory data analysis, and it is characterized by an *aspect type*. For instance, the aspect *train* belongs to an aspect type *transportation mode*, and an aspect *rainy* belongs to an aspect type *weather condition*. An aspect type has a set of attributes and it may also be a subtype of a more general aspect type, allowing the modeling of an aspect type *subtypeOf* hierarchy, like *POI*$\leftarrow$*accommodation*$\leftarrow$*hotel*. More formally, an aspect type is defined as follows.

Definition 1. *An Aspect Type* asp_{type} = *(desc, ATT,* $asp_{supertype}$*) is a categorization of a real-world fact with a description desc, a set of attributes* $ATT = \{a_1, a_2, \ldots, a_z\}$ *that hold its properties, and a (possibly empty) supertype aspect* $asp_{supertype}$.

An aspect type and its attributes act as a metadata definition for an aspect. As a consequence, an aspect is always related to at least one aspect type and its attributes. For example, given an aspect type *weather condition*, some of its attributes could be *temperature*, *wind speed* and *climate*. In the following, we define an aspect.

Definition 2. *An Aspect asp = (desc, SAT) is a relevant real-world fact, where desc is the aspect description, and* $SAT = \{at_1, at_2, ..., at_x\}$ *is a non-empty set of aspect types, with their attributes and respective values, which the aspect may hold, being* at_i = (asp_{type_k}, ATV_k), $at_i \in SAT$*, a tuple with an aspect type* asp_{type_k} *and a non-empty set* $ATV_k = \{a_1 : v_1, a_2 : v_2, \ldots, a_n : v_n\}$ *of attribute-value pairs so that each pair* $(a_i : v_i) \in ATV_k$ *is an instantiation of a property* a_i *of* asp_{type_k} *with a (atomic or multivalued) value* v_i.

An aspect definition supports numbers, ranges, text, geometries (when an aspect describes, for example, the shape of a hurricane at a specific time instant), or any type of complex object.

Definition 3. *A Semantic Meaning SM = (asp,* asp_{type}*) is an association between an aspect asp and an aspect type* asp_{type} *that gives the context of the aspect, so that* asp_{type} *belongs to the aspect types of the aspect asp.*

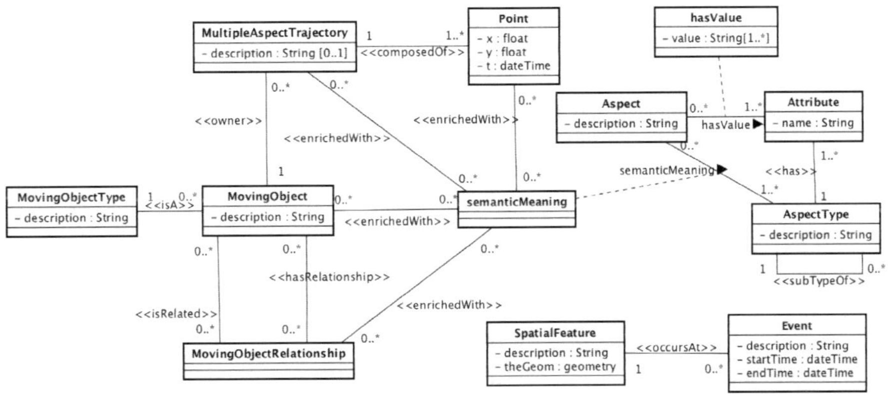

Fig. 2. The Conceptual Model for Multiple Aspect Trajectories

An aspect with a semantic meaning can be associated to a multiple aspect trajectory, a trajectory point, a moving object, or a relationship between moving objects in our conceptual model (see Figure 2). When an aspect varies frequently during the object movement, the aspect with its semantic meaning is associated to each trajectory point and it is called *volatile aspect (VA)*. Some examples are the *visited places* (or stops) and the heart rate. An aspect is also associated to a point when it represents a sparse and instant happening, like a social media post or check-in. When an aspect does not change during an entire trajectory, it is called a *long term aspect (LTA)* and is associated to the multiple aspect trajectory. Examples of this kind of aspect are the *town* on which the trajectory occurs or the person *occupation*. When an aspect holds during the entire life of an object, it is called a *permanent aspect (PA)* and is associated to the object and not to the trajectory. One example is the person *birthplace*. These aspect categories are directly related to the query performance. Queries on volatile aspects, *i.e.*, queries related to trajectory points, will be more time consuming, while long term and permanent aspects will be retrieved more quickly.

Based on these foundations, we now define a multiple aspect trajectory.

Definition 4. *A Multiple Aspect Trajectory mat = (P, S_LTA, mo, desc) is a sequence of points* $P = \langle p_1, p_2, \ldots, p_n \rangle$ *of a moving object mo, a (possible empty) set of long term aspects S_LTA, being S_LTA* $= \{sm_1, sm_2, ..., sm_p\}$ *a set of semantic meanings, and a description desc, with* $p_i = (x_i, y_i, t_i,$ *S_VA*$)$, $p_i \in P$, *being* x *and* y *the spatial position of mo at the time instant* t, *and S_VA the set of volatile aspects related to* p_i, *where S_VA* $= \{sm_1, sm_2, ..., sm_q\}$ *is a set of (possible empty) semantic meanings.*

A multiple aspect trajectory belongs to a moving object. A *moving object* is any entity that moves along space and time. This object is always associated to a type, which can be a person, a drone, an animal, a car, or even a natural phenomenon, like a hurricane. We formally define it in the following.

Definition 5. *A Moving Object* $mo = (mo_{type}, desc, S\_PA)$ *is an entity that can physically move in space and time, having a description desc, a set of (possible empty) permanent aspects S_PA, being* $S\_PA = \{sm_1, sm_2, ..., sm_r\}$ *a set of semantic meanings, and a type* mo_{type} *that categorizes it.*

A new feature in MASTER when compared to the state-of-the-art data models for trajectories is the *moving object relationship*. A moving object may hold any type of relationship with other objects, and these relationships may also be characterized by different aspects such as the type of relationship (*e.g.*, *friendship*, *professional*, *family*). We define a moving object relationship in Definition 6.

Definition 6. *A Moving Object Relationship* $mor = (mo_1, mo_2, S\_RA)$ *is a relevant association between two moving objects mo1 and mo2 that holds a (possible empty) set of relationship aspects S_RA, being* $S\_RA = \{sm_1, sm_2, ..., sm_s\}$ *a set of semantic meanings.*

Finally, we model *spatial features* and *events*. The first one denotes any relevant POI that is not spatially related to trajectory points, so it is not an aspect. Instead, it means any POI located in the trajectory neighborhood, like a nearby restaurant. In Figure 1, an example of spatial feature is the church located between the POIs *work* and *restaurant*. So, when a trajectory point intersects a relevant POI, it is modeled as an aspect. Otherwise, it is a spatial feature. Spatial features are useful for answering spatial queries like *which are the restaurants located at a distance less than* α *from the trajectory of object A?* or *which trajectories have an envelope whose area is higher than avenue B?* Similarly, an event denotes a happening that does not have a relationship with trajectories, but it is relevant for queries that investigate events in the trajectory neighborhood. An event occurs at a spatial feature and is valid for the period that it happened.

For defining the MASTER logical model we adopt the *Resource Description Framework (RDF)* [9] as our logical data model because RDF data can be modeled as a graph, which is a flexible data structure to represent the high heterogeneity of possible aspects, as well as the great number of aspect relationships with trajectories, points and moving objects. Besides, on using RDF we are consonant with the *Semantic Web* standards of *WWW Consortium (W3C)* for publishing and manipulating data on the Web [10].

Figure 3 shows the proposed logical model, where dotted arrows represent an entity-attribute relationship, continuous arrows represent relationships between entities, and the ellipsis represent entities or attributes. A predicate label followed by a cardinality pair denotes a multivalued relationship. One example is a *point* that may be enriched with zero to several *semantic meanings*. An RDF triple schema in such a modeling is represented by two ellipsis connected by an arrow. One example is a *moving object* (subject) that is the *owner* (predicate) of a *multiple aspect trajectory* (object).

The conversion of the conceptual model to a logical schema in RDF was inspired by several related approaches [2, 1, 3], which propose the following mapping rules:

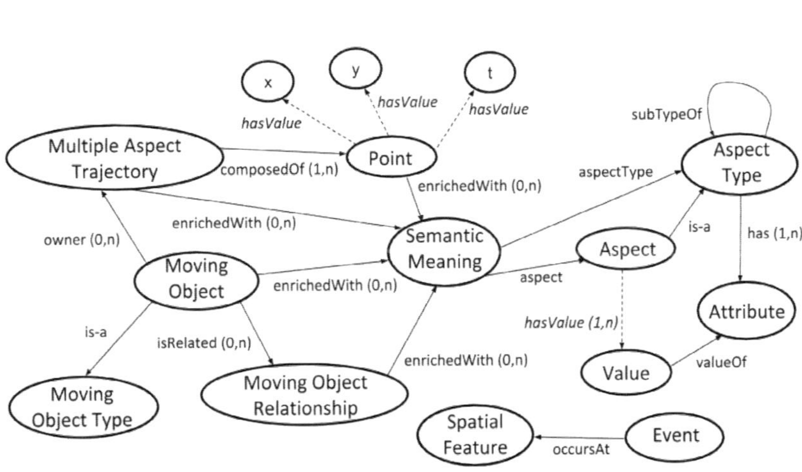

Fig. 3. The Logical Model for Multiple Aspect Trajectories

- an *entity* is converted to a *node*;
- an *attribute* of an entity (or relationship) er_m is converted to a *node* n_t, and an *edge* is defined from er_m to n_t in order to connect them;
- a *relationship* between entities is converted to an *edge* that connects the entities, or an *intermediate node* between the entities.

There is only one rule for the mapping of entities and attributes, so their conversion is straightforward. Even entities without attributes, like *MovingObjectRelationship* (see Figure 2), became nodes in the logical model because they have relationships with other entities.

We decided to consider the conversion to an edge if the relationship has no properties related to it, and the conversion to a node otherwise. On doing so, we avoid the generation of too many nodes in the RDF schema, and only the relationships that hold *semantic meaning* and *hasValue* as properties (see Figure 2) were mapped to nodes, and the second one was renamed to *Value* for sake of understanding. We also decide to maintain only the connections of *Aspect* and *Attribute* with the *Value* node to avoid a redundant edge between *Aspect* and *Attribute*.

The adopted storage solution for maintaining data represented in the MASTER logical model. This solution is called *Rendezvous* [8]. *Rendezvous* is a triplestore based on NoSQL databases for querying large RDF datasets. NoSQL databases have been proposed for managing big data efficiently [7]. Therefore, as multiple aspect trajectories are highly heterogeneous and multidimensional data, NoSQL databases are a suitable storage resource for this new type of trajectory. Compared to related work, *Rendezvous* was chosen due to its multi-

We define a label *hasValue* for this predicate to identify it as an entity-attribute or relationship-attribute connection.

model NoSQL support for storing RDF data and its efficient processing of typical SPARQL queries. *Rendezvous* manages RDF data in a distributed database.

3 Discussion and future works

The MASTER model has been evaluated over two perspectives: *(i)* a qualitative analysis at the conceptual level by modeling a tourism application, as well as an evaluation at the logical level to attest that an RDF-based storage strategy is suitable to answer the main types of multiple aspect trajectory queries; and *(ii)* a quantitative evaluation at the storage level by comparing the query running time performance of our storage solution with a baseline. With this experiment we show the feasibility of MASTER as a data model that can be efficiently stored and accessed. All details are presented in the full paper [4].

We claim that three main types of queries can be posed to multiple aspect trajectories: *(i)* queries that return *moving objects* (*e.g.*, *which are the moving objects that were born in Florianopolis and are male?*); *(ii)* queries that return *trajectories* (*e.g.*, *which are the trajectories that stayed at an accommodation place?*); and *(iii)* queries that return *aspects* (*e.g.*, *which accommodations were visited in Paris by persons that were born in Florianopolis and are male?*). These three queries are examples of *star-shaped*, *chain-shaped* and *complex* queries, respectively.

Table 1 shows these queries written in SPARQL or GeoSPARQL with an arbitrary complexity depending on the number of entities that must be considered to generate the query result, which allows an efficient processing by our RDF storage solution.

Future works include a performance evaluation over larger data sets of enriched trajectories, as well as the evaluation of other Big Data storage technologies, such as NewSQL databases, for maintaining multiple aspect trajectories. We also intend to extend MASTER to model data analytics information over multiple aspect trajectories, considering, for instance, dependencies among aspects.

Although out of the scope of this paper, it is also very important to consider privacy issues that these kinds of enriched trajectories might pose. When combining the different semantic aspects to the location information, privacy breach might happen. It is therefore crucial to develop privacy preserving methods to guarantee privacy when multiple aspects are involved.

Acknowledgments

This work was supported by the Brazilian agencies CAPES and CNPq, and the MASTER Project which received funding from the European Union's Horizon 2020 research and innovation programme under the Marie Sklowdoska-Curie agreement N. 777695.

Table 1. Typical SPARQL Queries over Multiple Aspect Trajectories

SELECT mo?	SELECT t?	SELECT a?
WHERE {	WHERE {	WHERE {
mo? is-a 'Person'	t? composedOf p?	a? *rdfs:type* 'Aspect'
mo? enrichedWith sm?	p? enrichedWith sm?	a? is-a at?
sm? aspect 'Florianopolis'	sm? aspectType at?	at? subtypeOf 'Accommodation'
sm? aspectType 'birthplace'	at? subtypeOf	sm? aspectType a?
mo? enrichedWith sm2?	'Accommodation'}	p? enrichedWith sm?
sm2? aspect 'Male'		FILTER(
sm2? aspectType 'Gender'}		geof:sfIntersects(?p, Paris))
		t? composedOf p?
		mo? owner t?
		mo? is-a 'Person'
		mo? enrichedWith sm?
		sm? aspect 'Florianopolis'
		sm? aspectType 'birthplace'
		mo? enrichedWith sm2?
		sm2? aspect 'Male'
		sm2? aspectType 'Gender'}
(a) Star	(b) Chain	(c) Complex

References

1. S. Bagui and J. Bouressa. Mapping rdf and rdf-schema to the entity relationship model. *Journal of Emerging Trends in Computing and Information Sciences*, 5(12):953–961, 2014.
2. M. Choi, C. Moon, and D. Baik. Transformation of a relational database to RDF/RDFS with er^{2}idm. *IEICE Transactions*, 96-D(7):1478–1488, 2013.
3. G. Daniel, G. Sunyé, and J. Cabot. Umltographdb: Mapping conceptual schemas to graph databases. In *Conceptual Modeling - 35th International Conference, ER 2016, Gifu, Japan, November 14-17, 2016, Proceedings*, pages 430–444, 2016.
4. R. dos Santos Mello, V. Bogorny, L. O. Alvares, L. H. Z. Santana, C. A. Ferrero, A. A. Frozza, G. A. Schreiner, and C. Renso. MASTER: A Multiple Aspect View on Trajectories. *Trans. GIS*, 23(4):805–822, 2019.
5. R. H. Güting, V. T. de Almeida, D. Ansorge, T. Behr, Z. Ding, T. Höse, F. Hoffmann, M. Spiekermann, and U. Telle. SECONDO: an extensible DBMS platform for research prototyping and teaching. In *21st ICDE 2005*, pages 1115–1116, 2005.
6. J. Z. Pan. Resource description framework. In *Handbook on Ontologies*, pages 71–90. Springer, 2009.
7. P. J. Sadalage and M. Fowler. *NoSQL distilled : a brief guide to the emerging world of polyglot persistence*. Addison-Wesley, 2013.
8. L. H. Z. Santana and R. dos Santos Mello. Workload-aware rdf partitioning and sparql query caching for massive rdf graphs stored in nosql databases. In *Brazilian Symposium on Databases (SBBD), 2017*, pages 184–195. SBC, 2017.
9. W3C. RDF - Semantic Web Standards, 2018.
10. W3C. Semantic Web - W3C, 2018.

A Framework for Complex Influence Propagation based on the F^2DLT Class of Diffusion Models
(Discussion Paper)

Antonio Caliò and Andrea Tagarelli

Dept. Computer Engineering, Modeling, Electronics, and System Engineering,
University of Calabria, Rende (CS), Italy
{a.calio, tagarelli}@dimes.unical.it

Abstract. What are the key-features that enable an information diffusion model to explain the inherent complex dynamics of real-world propagation phenomena? To answer the above question, we discuss a novel class of stochastic Linear Threshold (LT) diffusion models, which are designed to capture the following aspects in influence propagation scenarios: trust/distrust in the user relationships, changes in adopting one or alternative information items, hesitation towards adopting an information item over time, latency in the propagation, time horizon for the unfolding of the diffusion process, and multiple cascades of information that might occur competitively. Around all such aspects, our defined Friend-Foe Dynamic LT (F^2DLT) class comprises a non-competitive model as well as two competitive models, which are able to represent semi-progressivity and non-progressivity, respectively, in the propagation process. The above key-constituents embedded in our models make them unique in the literature of diffusion models, including epidemic models. To validate our models through real-world networks, we also discuss different strategies for the selection of the initial influencers to mimic non-competitive and competitive diffusion scenarios, inspired by the widely-known problem of limitation of misinformation spread. Finally, we describe a web-based simulation environment for testing the proposed diffusion models.

1 Introduction

Since the early applications in viral marketing, the development of information diffusion models and related optimization methods has provided effective support to address a variety of influence propagation problems. Nowadays, due to the shrinking boundary between real and online social life [2] and the presence of multiple, competitive spreaders over the Web, which could also act towards *misinformation*, deciding whether a source of information is reliable or not has become a critical task. The difficulty in assessing the reliability and trustworthiness of the source generating or sharing a piece of information increases the likelihood of people to be deceived by a spreading information. In addition to this, the tendency to access information from like-minded sources [5] leads users to be trapped in information bubbles, eventually causing forms of network polarization [4]. Polarization can be contrasted via actions devoted to fact-checking or misinformation debunking, but time plays a crucial role in this game, as cognitive phenomena of *confirmation bias* may easily arise.

Understanding the trustworthiness of the source of an information item is often challenging, as it requires tracking the information item of its originator, which could be unfeasible in many cases. Therefore, it beomes essential to capture the effect of *trust/distrust relationships* on both the user behavior and propagation dynamics. One big question hence arises:

> *What are the key-features that make a diffusion model able to explain the inherent dynamic, and often competitive, nature of real-world propagation phenomena?*

Contributions. To answer the above question, we discuss a class of stochastic diffusion models, named *Friend-Foe Dynamic Linear Threshold Models* (for short, F^2DLT), which has been originally proposed in [3]. Our models are inspired by the classic Linear Threshold (LT) model, whereby an individual can decide to take an action as a result of the exposure to multiple sources of influence. Major key-features of our models is that the information diffusion graph is defined on top of a *trust network*, where trust is encoded into the influence probabilities, the response of a user to the influencing attempts is described by a time-varying activation threshold function, and also a quiescence function is introduced to model the latency or delay in the propagation.

Our F^2DLT models are designed to deal with *non-competitive* and *competitive* propagation scenarios. For competitive campaign scenarios, one model is *semi-progressive*, which assumes that a user, once activated, is only allowed to switch to a different campaign, and another model is *non-progressive*, i.e., it requires a user to have always the support of her/his in-neighbors to keep the activation state with a certain campaign.

To evaluate our models, we also devised four *seed selection* strategies, which mimic different, realistic scenarios of influence propagation. Experimental evaluation conducted on real-world networks, also including comparison with stochastic epidemic models, has provided interesting findings on the meaningfulness and uniqueness of our proposed models.

2 The F^2DLT class of diffusion models

2.1 Overview

Figure 1 sketches the conceptual architecture of a framework for information diffusion and influence propagation based on our proposed models. Key-constituents

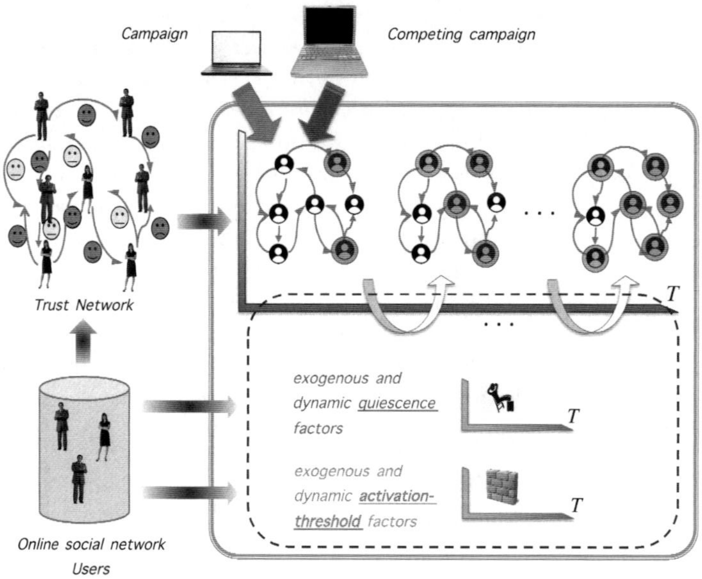

Fig. 1: Illustration of the F^2DLT framework

of this framework are the following: (i) a set of online social network users; (ii) a *trust network*, possibly inferred from a social network; (iii) user-behavior characteristics that provide information for incorporating two main aspects into the diffusion process, namely *activation-threshold* and *quiescence*; (iv) information related to one or multiple competing *campaigns*.

Also, the information diffusion process is supposed to have a certain *time horizon*, and before its expiration, users respond to the network's stimuli which may lead to being active in favor of one campaign or the opposing one. According to their own behavior, users may have the possibility of switching from the adoption of a campaign's item to that of another one.

Putting it all together, our F^2DLT based framework embeds all the above aspects that are essential to explain complex propagation phenomena, i.e., competitive diffusion, non-progressivity, time-aware activation, delayed propagation, and trust/distrust relations.

Notably, in our setting, we tend to reject as true in general, the principle "I agree with my friends' idea and disagree with my foes' idea" (which also resembles the adage "the enemy of my enemy is my friend"), since this would imply that the behavior of a user should be completely determined by the stimuli coming from her/his neighbors. In other terms, friends should be responsible for the influenceability and activation of a user, as opposed to foes, which should instead impact on delayed propagation. Therefore, in our models, the trusted connections and distrusted connections play different roles: only friends can exert a degree of (positive) influence, whereas foes can only contribute to increase the user's hesitation to commit with the propagation process.

One assumption of our framework is the availability of trust relationships between the users involved in the information diffusion context. Although this may not hold in practice, a few studies have been recently developed to infer a trust network from the time-varying interactions observed in evolving social networks, such as [6].

Activation-threshold function. Given a directed, weighted network representing an information diffusion graph built on top of a trust network, every node v is associated with an activation-threshold, $\theta_v \in (0, 1]$, which corresponds to the effort of activating the node which is needed in terms of cumulative influence. The *activation-threshold* function g, defined over the set of nodes V and the time interval of diffusion T, enhances this concept. For each node v at time $t \in T$, it is defined as:

$$g(v,t) = \theta_v + \vartheta(\theta_v, t).$$

Thus, a node v is activated when its perceived influences exceed the threshold θ_v, plus the time-evolving activation term, $\vartheta(\cdot,\cdot)$, which models the dynamic response of users at any activation attempt. Our proposed models can in principle embrace any definition for $\vartheta(\cdot,\cdot)$; here, we focus on two main scenarios.

Biased. Modeled as a non-decreasing monotone function, it captures the tendency of a user to consolidate her/his belief, according to the *confirmation-bias* principle [1]. We define this function as follows:

$$g(v,t) = \theta_v + \vartheta(\theta_v, t) = \theta_v + \delta \times \min\left\{\frac{1-\theta_v}{\delta}, t - t_v^{last}\right\} \quad (1)$$

where t_v^{last} denotes the last time v was activated and $\delta \geq 0$ denotes the increment in the value of $g(v,t)$ for consecutive time steps. Clearly, the value increases as a node keeps staying in the same active state.

Unbiased. In applications such as customer retention or churn prediction, a user could revise her/his uncertainty to activate over time. We model this in such a way that, for each v, the value of the function is maximum (i.e., 1) just after the activation, i.e., at time $t = t_v^{last} + 1$, then it starts to decrease from the following time steps:

$$g(v,t) = \theta_v + \vartheta(\theta_v, t) = \theta_v + \exp(-\delta(t - t_v^{last} - 1)) - \theta_v \mathbb{I}[t - t_v^{last} = 1] \quad (2)$$

Quiescence function. The *quiescence* value quantifies the latency in the propagation through a particular node. It is defined as a non-decreasing and monotone function $q : V, T \mapsto T$, such that for every $v \in V, t \in T$, with v activated at time t:

$$q(v,t) = \tau_v + \psi(N_-^{in}(v), t),$$

where $\tau_v \in T$ represents an exogenous term modeling the user's hesitation in being committed with the propagation process, and $\psi(N_-^{in}(v), t)$ determines an

We assume the second additive term in Eq. (1) is zero if $\delta = 0$.

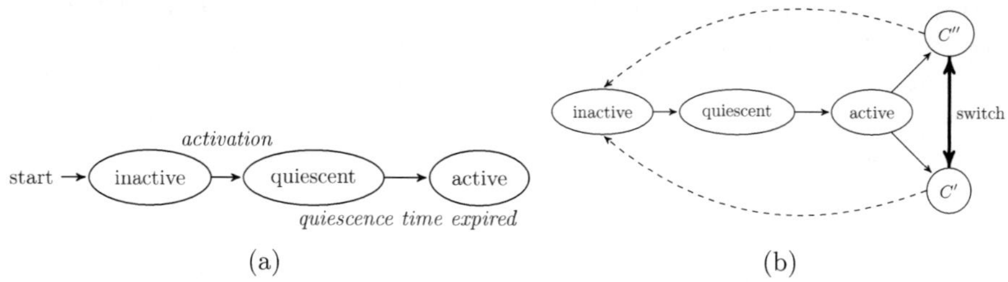

Fig. 2: Life-cycle of a node for the non-competitive model (a) and the competitive models (b). Straight lines in (b) represent the transitions common to both *spC-F^2DLT* and *npC-F^2DLT*, while dashed lines refer to *npC-F^2DLT* only.

additional delay proportional to the amount of v's neighbors that are distrusted and active, when the activation attempt is performed by the v's trusted neighbors. Here we focus on the following function:

$$q(v,t) = \tau_v + \psi(N_{-}^{in}(v),t) = \tau_v + \exp\left(\lambda \times \sum_{u \in S_{t-1}} |w_{uv}|\right) \tag{3}$$

where $\lambda \geq 0$ quantifies the user sensitivity towards negative influence.

2.2 Diffusion Models

The F^2DLT class includes three diffusion models [3], which are now briefly and informally described. The first one refers to a single-item propagation scenario, while the other two models can dela with competitive scenarios, i.e., two or multiple campaigns spreading informative items over the network in a competitive fashion. Figure 2 shows the life-cycle of a node in the non-competitive scenario and in competitive ones, respectively. It should be noted that all the models share a similar two-phase activation process. In fact, when a node is activated by its neighbors, it always becomes quiescent. Its permanence in this state depends on Eq. 3. After the quiescent time is expired, a node can be regarded as active, regardless of its activation campaign, and is considered fully committed to the propagation process. While the non-competitive model, dubbed *nC-F^2DLT*, is a progressive model (i.e., once a node becomes active cannot be deactivated in subsequent times), the semi-progressive competitive model, *spC-F^2DLT*, allows a node to switch from a campaign to another, even multiple times. Finally, the fully non-progressive competitive model, *npC-F^2DLT*, additionally allows for node deactivation.

Theoretical properties of the models. The non-competitive, progressive model *nC-F^2DLT* is proven to be equivalent to LT with Quiescence Time i.e., the activation function in *nC-F^2DLT* is monotone and submodular. On the other hand, the competitive *spC-F^2DLT* and *npC-F^2DLT* can be reduced, via graph serialization, to a progressive Homogeneous Competitive LT, with monotone, non-submodular activation function i.e., the activation function in *spC-F^2DLT* and *npC-F^2DLT* is monotone but not submodular [3].

3 Evaluation methodology

Data. We used four real-world, publicly available networks, namely: *Epinions*, *Slashdot*, *Wiki-Conflict*, and *Wiki-Vote* — please refer to [3] for details about the datasets. All networks are originally directed and signed; in addition, the two Wikipedia-based networks also have timestamped edges. The influence probability are derived so that to a network having a higher fraction of positive edges will correspond to an equivalent network where users are more willing to be involved in the propagation process.

Seed selection strategies. We defined four seed selection strategies, each of which mimics a different, realistic scenario of influence propagation.

Exogenous and malicious sources of information. This method, hereinafter referred to as M-Sources, aims at simulating the presence of multiple sources of malicious information within the network. Here, an exogenous source is meant as a node without incoming links. Formally, given a budget k, the method selects the top-k users in a ranking solution determined as $r(v) = (\bar{W}^-/(\bar{W}^- + \bar{W}^+)) \log(|N^{out}(v)|)$ for every v such that $N^{in}(v) = \emptyset$. Here, $\bar{W}^+$, resp. $\bar{W}^-$ denote the sum of trust, resp. distrust outgoing weights.

Exogenous and influential trusted sources of information. Analogously to the previous method, this one, dubbed I-Sources, is concerned with exogenous sources with emphasis on trusted links. Hence, the ranking function is: $r(v) = (\bar{W}^+/(\bar{W}^- + \bar{W}^+)) \log(|N^{out}(v)|)$.

Stress triads. This strategy is based on the notion of *structural balance* in triads. In a typical stress-triad configuration there is a node v with two incoming connections, from a node z with negative weight and from a node u with positive weight, and such that z is connected to u via a positive link. In this case, z is regarded as a *stress-node* since it could activate v through u, despite being negatively linked to v. The Stress-Triads strategy selects seeds based on the number of stress-triads that are involved in as stress-nodes.

Newcomers. We call a node $v \in V$ as a *newcomer* if all of its incoming edges are timestamped as less recent than its oldest outgoing edge. The *start-time* of v is the oldest timestamp associated with its incoming edges. Within the set of newcomers nodes, we further define two separate strategies: Least-New and Most-New. Each one consists in the selection of the the top-k newcomers with highest out-degree among those nodes with the oldest and the newest start-time, respectively. Both strategies require temporal information upon edges.

Major Findings and Usage Recommendations. We pursued different goals of evaluations depending on the particular diffusion model. More specifically, we investigated the impact of the negative influence on the final active set in the non-competitive scenario. For the competitive setting, our main goal was to understand the effect of the confirmation-bias effect, in the context of misinformation spreading. Therefore, we will have a good and a malicious actor. Finally, we conducted a comprehensive comparative evaluation of our non-competitive model against the Independent Cascade model as well as stochastic individual-contact epidemic models SIR and SEIR [3].

Here we summarize the major findings emerged from the experiments:

F1 The setting of the dynamic activation-threshold function and quiescence function plays a crucial role in positive-influence propagation and negative-influence/misinformation limitation.

F2 The average user's sensitivity in the negative influence perceived from distrusted neighbors (λ) makes the seed identification more aware of the negative influence spread.

F3 The confirmation-bias effect (δ) may lead the "stronger" campaign to increase its spread capability.

F4 The non-progressive competitive model npC-F^2DLT appears to be less sensitive to the increase of δ and tends to favor deactivation events (for users previously activated by the weaker campaign) over switched events.

F5 If compared with classic diffusion models as IC, SIR, and SEIR, the nC-F^2DLT model tends to favor a slower diffusion, since the propagation process lasts consistently longer than IC and the epidemic models.

F6 Threshold models are more suitable when it is required to model propagation phenomena where it is important to capture the difference in behavior of each individual. On the contrary, epidemic models does not exhibit this important capability, as they are more suitable to represent single contagions.

F7 l-Sources reveals higher spread capability, followed by Stress-Triads. On the contrary, the newcomers-based strategies show a significant spread capability, coupled with a negligible effect on the negative influence.

The above results provide evidence that our class of trust-aware models offers an opportunity to better represent the complexity of real-world propagation phenomena. As a consequence, our models can pave the way for the development of sophisticated methods to solve *misinformation spread limitation* and related optimization problems. Also, our models can profitably be used in a variety of applications whereby there is an emergence *to predict the time required to debunk fake information*, or *to estimate how people are affected by the spread of competitive opposite opinions* through a social network.

4 Web-based Simulation Environment

As part of our contributions to the research project NextShop PON Grant No. F/050374/01-03/X32, we developed a web application of our diffusion models, available at `http://people.dimes.unical.it/andreatagarelli/f2dlt/` . It is a simulation environment that allows a user to execute a diffusion model in the F^2DLT class, and get an interactive view of a propagation process. As input, an influence graph can be either uploaded from a file or synthetically generated; in the latter case, the user is asked to provide the following information: (i) number of nodes, (ii) number of edges, (iii) percentage of negative edges, and (iv) graph-generator model, by choosing among the Erdős–Rényi, Watts-Strogatz, and Barabási-Albert models. Once the network is created, it is displayed with positive (trust) edges represented in black, and negative (distrust) edges represented in red. Also, after selecting a F^2DLT model, both the activation threshold function and the quiescence function can be configured by setting

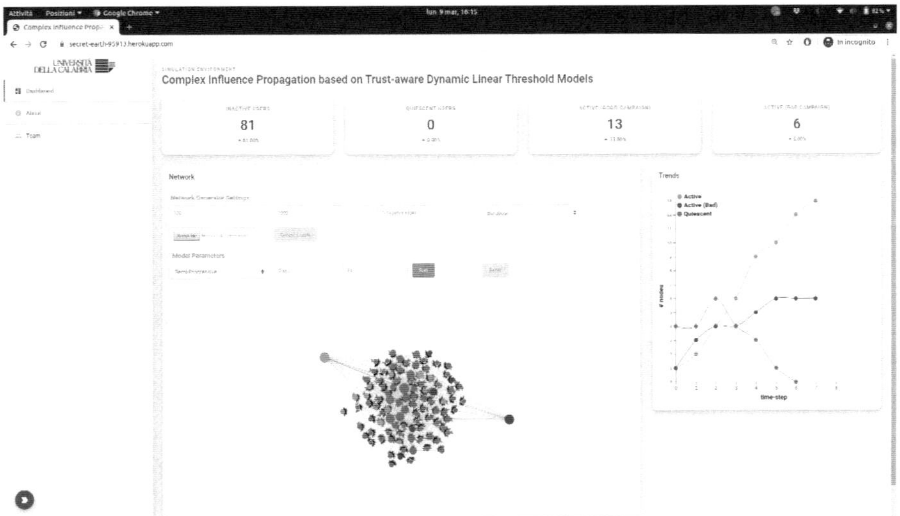

Fig. 3: Screenshot of our web-based simulation environment

$\vartheta(\cdot,\cdot)$,and $\psi(\cdot,\cdot)$. Finally, the early adopters, i.e., the seeds of the propagation process, can be selected by clicking upon specific nodes of the displayed network. While the diffusion process is running, the application updates the layout of the network, and nodes will dynamically change their color accordingly to their activation status. Moreover, the application will show a number of statistics about the propagation process, as well as the temporal evolution of the propagation process.

References

1. A. Anagnostopoulos, A. Bessi, G. Caldarelli, M. Del Vicario, F. Petroni, A. Scala, F. Zollo, and W. Quattrociocchi. Viral misinformation: The role of homophily and polarization. In *Proc. WebConf*, pp. 355–356, 2015.
2. A. Bessi, G. Caldarelli, M. Del Vicario, A. Scala, and W. Quattrociocchi. Social determinants of content selection in the age of (mis)information. In *Proc. SocInfo*, pp. 259–268, 2014.
3. Antonio Caliò and Andrea Tagarelli. Complex influence propagation based on trust-aware dynamic linear threshold models. *Applied Network Science*, 4(1):14:1–14:41, 2019.
4. K. Garimella, G. De Francisci Morales, A. Gionis, and M. Mathioudakis. The effect of collective attention on controversial debates on social media. In *Proc. ACM Web Science*, pp. 43–52, 2017.
5. D. Koutra, P. N. Bennett, and E. Horvitz. Events and controversies: Influences of a shocking news event on information seeking. In *Proc. WebConf*, pp. 614–624, 2015.
6. Domenico Mandaglio and Andrea Tagarelli. Generalized preference learning for trust network inference. *IEEE Access*, 7:174583–174596, 2019.

A Post-Analysis of Query Reformulation Methods for Clinical Trials Retrieval

DISCUSSION PAPER

Maristella Agosti[1], Giorgio Maria Di Nunzio[1,2], and Stefano Marchesin[1]

[1]Department of Information Engineering, [2]Department of Mathematics
University of Padua, Italy
{maristella.agosti, giorgiomaria.dinunzio, stefano.marchesin}@unipd.it

Abstract. The Precision Medicine (PM) track of the Text REtrieval Conference (TREC) focuses on providing useful precision medicine information to clinicians treating cancer patients. The PM track gives the unique opportunity to evaluate medical IR systems on two different collections: scientific literature and clinical trials. In this paper, we evaluate several state-of-the-art query expansion and reduction methods to see whether a particular approach can be helpful in clinical trials retrieval. We present those approaches that are consistently effective in all three TREC PM editions and we compare them to the results obtained by the research groups who participated in all three editions.

Keywords: Query reformulation · knowledge base · precision medicine

1 Introduction and Motivations

Medical Information Retrieval (IR) helps a wide variety of users to access and search medical information archives and data [6]. In [9], a classification of textual medical information is proposed: 1) Patient-specific information which applies to individual patients. This type of information can be structured, as in the case of an Electronic Health Record (EHR), or can be free narrative text. 2) Knowledge-based information that has been derived and organized from observational or experimental research. In the case of clinical research, the information is most commonly provided by books and journals, but can take a wide variety of other forms. Therefore, the design of effective tools to access and search textual medical information requires, among other things, enhancing the query through expansion and/or rewriting methods that leverage the information contained within knowledge resources. [15] identified some challenges arising from the differences between general and medical case-based retrieval. In particular, state-of-the-art retrieval methods, combined with selective query term weighing based on medical thesauri and physician feedback, improve performance significantly [16, 5]. In 2017, 2018, and 2019 the PM [11] track[1] at TREC[2] focused on an important use case in clinical decision support: providing useful precision medicine information to clinicians treating cancer patients. This track gives a unique opportunity to evaluate medical IR systems since the experimental collection is composed of a set of topics (synthetic cases created by precision oncologists) for two different collections that target two different tasks: 1) retrieving biomedical articles addressing relevant treatments for a given patient, and 2) retrieving clinical trials for which a patient – described in the information need – is eligible.

This work combines and discusses the methodology and the results originally presented at SIGIR 2019 [2] and TREC 2019 [4]. The objective is to evaluate several state-of-the-art query expansion and reduction methods to examine whether a particular approach can be helpful in clinical trials retrieval. Precisely, we compare the results obtained with our approach to the best experiments submitted to the 2017 and 2018 PM tracks [2]. Then, we select the top three query reformulations found in 2017 and 2018 PM tracks and we evaluate whether their effectiveness also holds in the 2019 PM track [4]. We conduct a systematic comparison between our approach and those proposed by the research groups that participated in all three years of TREC PM. The analysis shows the effectiveness of the proposed query reformulations in 2017 and 2018 PM tracks and confirms the trend in the 2019 PM track. The obtained runs achieve top performing results in all PM tracks [11–13]. In particular, a specific query reformulation allows the retrieval system to achieve top results in all three PM tracks.

The rest of the paper is organized as follows: Section 2 describes the approach used to evaluate different query reformulation methods. Section 3 presents the experimental setup and Section 4 compares the results obtained using our approach with those obtained by the other research groups who participated in TREC PM 2017, 2018 and 2019. Finally, Section 5 reports some final remarks.

2 Approach

The approach we propose consists of four steps: (i) indexing, (ii) query reformulation, (iii) retrieval and (iv) filtering.

Indexing. We create the following fields to index clinical trials collections: <docid>, <text>, <max_age>, <min_age> and <gender>. Fields <max_age>, <min_age> and <gender> contain information extracted from the eligibility section of clinical trials and are used in the filtering step. The <text> field contains the entire content of each clinical trial.

[1] `http://www.trec-cds.org/`
[2] `https://trec.nist.gov/`

Query Reformulation. The approach relies on two types of query reformulation methods: query expansion and query reduction.

Query expansion: We perform a knowledge-based a priori query expansion. First, we rely on MetaMap [3], a state-of-the-art medical concept extractor, to extract from each query field all the Unified Medical Language System (UMLS)[3] concepts belonging to the following semantic types:[4] `Neoplastic Process` (*neop*), `Gene or Genome` (*gngm*) and `Cell or Molecular Dysfunction` (*comd*). The *gngm* and *comd* semantic types are related to the query `<gene>` field, while *neop* is related to the `<disease>` field. For those collections where an additional `<other>` field is included – which considers other potential factors that may be relevant – MetaMap is used on `<other>` with no restriction on the semantic types, as its content does not refer to any particular semantic type. Second, for each extracted concept, we consider all its name variants contained into the following knowledge sources: National Cancer Institute (NCI), Medical Subject Headings (MeSH), SNOMED CT (SNOMEDCT) and UMLS Metathesaurus (MTH). All knowledge sources are manually curated and up-to-date. The expanded queries consist of the union of the original terms with the set of name variants. For example, consider a query only containing the word "*melanoma*" – which is mapped to the UMLS concept `C0025202`. The set of name variants for the concept "*melanoma*" contains, among many others: cutaneous melanoma, malignant melanoma, malignant melanoma (disorder). Therefore, the final expanded query is the union of the original term "*melanoma*" with all its name variants. Additionally, we expand queries that do not mention any kind of blood cancer (e.g. "lymphoma" or "leukemia") with the term *solid*. This expansion proved to be effective in [7] where the authors found that a large part of relevant clinical trials do not mention the exact disease. A more general term like *solid tumor* is preferable and more effective.

Query reduction: We reduce original queries by removing, whenever present, gene mutations from the `<gene>` field. To clarify: consider a topic where the `<gene>` field mentions "BRAF (V600E)". After reduction, the `<gene>` field becomes "BRAF". The reduction aims at mitigating the over-specificity of topics, since the information contained in a topic is too specific compared to those contained in the target documents [10]. Additionally, we remove the `<other>` field from those collections that include it – since it contains additional factors that are not necessarily relevant, thus representing a potential source of noise in retrieving precise information for patients.

Retrieval. We use BM25 [14] as retrieval model. Query terms obtained through query expansion are weighted lower than 1.0 to avoid introducing too much noise in the retrieval process [8].

Filtering. The `eligibility` section in clinical trials comprises three important demographic aspects that a patient needs to satisfy to be considered eligible for

[3] `https://www.nlm.nih.gov/research/umls/`

[4] `https://metamap.nlm.nih.gov/SemanticTypesAndGroups.shtml`

the trial, namely: `minimum age`, `maximum age` and `gender`; where `minimum age` and `maximum age` are the minimum and the maximum age, respectively, required for a patient to be considered eligible for the trial, while `gender` is the required gender. After the retrieval step, we filter out from the list of candidate trials those for which a patient is not eligible – i.e. his/her demographic data (age and gender) does not satisfy the three aforementioned eligibility criteria. In those cases where part of the demographic data is not specified, a clinical trial is kept or discarded on the basis of the remaining demographic information. For instance, if the clinical trial does not specify a required minimum age, then it is kept or discarded based on its maximum age and gender required values.

3 Experimental Setup

This section describes the experimental collections and the setup used to apply and evaluate our approach.

Experimental Collections. We report the main information related to topics and document collections below.

Topics consist of 30, 50, and 40 synthetic cases created by precision oncologists in 2017, 2018, and 2019, respectively. In 2017, each topic contained four key elements in a semi-structured format: (1) disease (e.g. a type of cancer), (2) genetic variants (primarily present in tumors), (3) demographic information (e.g. age, gender), and (4) other factors (which could impact certain treatment options). In 2018 and 2019, each topic had three of the four key elements used in 2017: (1) disease, (2) genetic variants, and (3) demographic information. Furthermore, the 2019 topics contain ten non-cancer-related topics.

Clinical Trials consist of a set of 241,006 clinical trial descriptions, for both 2017 and 2018, and of an updated version of 306,238 descriptions for 2019. The collections are derived from ClinicalTrials.gov[5] – a database of privately and publicly funded clinical studies conducted around the world. When none of the available treatments are effective on oncology patients, the common recourse is to determine if any potential treatments are undergoing evaluation in a clinical trial. Therefore, it would be helpful to automatically identify the most relevant clinical trials for an individual patient. Precision oncology trials typically use a certain treatment for a certain disease with a specific genetic variant. Such trials can have complex inclusion and/or exclusion criteria that are challenging to match with automated systems.

Experimental Procedure. We use Whoosh,[6] a Python search engine library, for indexing, retrieval, and filtering. For BM25, we keep the default values $k_1 = 1.2$ and $b = 0.75$ provided – as we found them to be a good combination [1]. For query expansion, we rely on MetaMap to extract and disambiguate concepts from UMLS. Below we report the procedure used for each experiment.

[5] `https://clinicaltrials.gov/`

[6] `https://whoosh.readthedocs.io/en/latest/intro.html`

- *Indexing*
  - Index clinical trials using the following created fields: `<docid>`, `<text>`, `<max_age>`, `<min_age>` and `<gender>`.
- *Query reformulation*
  - Use MetaMap to extract from each query field the UMLS concepts restricted to the following semantic types: *neop* for `<disease>`, *gngm/comd* for `<gene>`, and *all* for `<other>`;
  - Extract from concepts all name variants belonging to NCI, MeSH, SNOMED CT and MTH knowledge sources;
  - Expand (or not) topics that do not mention "lymphoma" or "leukemia" with the term *solid*;
  - Reduce (or not) queries by removing, whenever present, gene mutations from the `<gene>` field;
  - Remove (or not) the `<other>` field.
- *Retrieval*
  - 2017/2018 PM track: Adopt any combination of the reformulation strategies;
  - 2019 PM track: Adopt the three best reformulation strategies from 2017/2018 PM tracks;
  - Weigh expanded terms with a value $k = 0.1$;
  - Perform a search using expanded queries with BM25.
- *Filtering*
  - Filter out clinical trials for which the patient is not eligible.

Evaluation Measures. We use the measures adopted in the TREC PM tracks, that are: inferred nDCG (infNDCG), R-precision (Rprec) and P@10.

4 Experimental Results and Discussion

In Table 1, we report the results of our experiments on query reformulation (Part A) and compare them with the results obtained by the research groups that participated at TREC PM 2017, 2018 and 2019 (Part B). Given the large number of experiments we performed, we decided to only present the 5 runs with the highest P@10 for each year. Each line shows a particular combination (*yes* or *no* values) of semantic types (*neop, comd, gngm*), usage and expansion of `<other>` field (oth, oth_exp), query reduction (orig), and expansion using weighted *solid* (tumor) keyword. We use the symbol '-' to indicate that the features oth, oth_exp are not applicable for the years 2018 and 2019 due to the absence of the `<other>` field in 2018 and 2019 topics. We highlight in bold the top 3 scores for each measure, and we use the symbol ‡ to indicate the combination that performs well in all three years. For the TREC PM participants, we select those participants who submitted runs in all three years and reached the top 10 performing runs in at least one edition for each measure [11–13]. The results

A: Analysis of Query Reformulations

line	year	neop	comd	gngm	oth	oth_exp	orig	solid	P@10	infNDCG	Rprec
1	2017	n	n	y	n	n	n	0.1	**0.3931**	-	**0.3263**
2‡	2017	n	n	n	n	n	n	0.1	**0.4034**	-	**0.3361**
3	2017	y	n	n	n	n	n	0.1	0.3862	-	0.3202
4	2017	n	n	n	n	n	n	n	**0.3931**	-	0.3241
5	2017	n	n	y	n	n	y	n	0.3862	-	**0.3243**
6	2018	n	n	n	·	·	y	n	0.5680	**0.5411**	**0.4197**
7	2018	n	n	n	·	·	y	0.1	**0.5740**	**0.5403**	**0.4179**
8	2018	y	n	n	·	·	n	n	**0.5700**	0.5345	0.4134
9‡	2018	n	n	n	·	·	n	0.1	**0.5820**	**0.5446**	**0.4205**
10	2018	y	n	y	·	·	n	n	0.5680	0.5393	0.4122
11	2019	n	n	n	·	·	y	0.1	**0.5368**	**0.6239**	**0.4386**
12	2019	y	n	n	·	·	n	n	0.5237	0.5755	0.4135
13‡	2019	n	n	n	·	·	n	0.1	**0.5316**	**0.5940**	**0.4264**
14	2019	n	n	y	·	·	n	0.1	**0.5263**	**0.6070**	**0.4302**
15	2019	n	n	n	·	·	n	n	0.5105	0.5853	0.4239

B: Comparison with TREC PM other Participants

line	year	TREC PM Participant Identifier	P@10	infNDCG	Rprec
1	2017	BiTeM	0.3586	-	-
2	2017	cbnu	<	-	-
3	2017	CSIROmed	<	-	-
4	2017	ECNUica	<	-	-
5	2017	POZNAN_SEMMED	0.3690	-	-
	2017	Top 10 threshold	0.3586	-	-
	2017	Best combination of our approach	(A.2‡) 0.4034	-	0.3361
6	2018	SIBTextMining	<	<	<
7	2018	cbnu	<	<	<
8	2018	CSIROmed	<	<	<
9	2018	ECNUica	<	<	<
10	2018	Poznan	0.5580	0.4894	0.4101
	2018	Top 10 threshold	0.5240	0.4736	0.3658
	2018	Best combination of our approach	(A.9‡) 0.5820	0.5446	0.4205
11	2019	BITEM_PM	0.4711	0.4963	0.3698
12	2019	cbnu	0.4921	0.5568	0.4121
13	2019	CSIROmed	0.4921	0.4930	0.3586
14	2019	ECNU-ICA	0.5053	0.5355	0.4001
15	2019	POZNAN	0.4421	0.4810	0.3503
	2019	Top 10 threshold	0.3658	0.4320	0.3230
	2019	Best combination of our approach	(A.11) 0.5368	0.6239	0.4386

Table 1: Results for the TREC PM tasks. Part A (top) reports the results achieved using the five most effective query reformulations for each year. (‡) indicates a particular query reformulation effective in all three years. Part B (bottom) reports the results obtained by participant runs, along with the lowest score required to enter the top 10 TREC results list and the score obtained by the best combination of our approach. Further details are reported in Section 4.

reported in part B of Table 1 indicate the best score obtained by a particular run for a specific measure; the best results of a participant are often related to different runs. The symbol '–' means that the measure is not available, while '<' indicates that none of the runs submitted by the participant achieved the top 10 performing runs. For the sake of comparison, we add for each measure the lowest score required to enter the top 10 TREC results list, and the score obtained by the best combination of our approach – indicated by the line number – as if we were participants of these tracks.

Analysis of Query Reformulations. The results from Table 1 (Part A) highlight that the use of *solid* expansions with weight 0.1 as well as query gene reductions ($orig = n$) seems to improve performance consistently in 2017 – two of the three best runs in terms of P@10 (lines 1 and 2) applying both techniques. Regarding knowledge-based expansions, the semantic type *gngm* (lines 1 and 5) seems more effective than *neop* (line 3), while *comd* does not seem to have any positive effect at all. All five runs do not consider the other field ($oth = n$) nor its expansion ($oth\_exp = n$) – confirming our intuition that it might represent a potential source of noise in retrieving precise information for patients. Similarly to 2017, two of the best three runs of 2018 use no knowledge-based expansions and rely on the *solid* (tumor) expansion with weight 0.1 (lines 7 and 9). In particular, the runs combining query gene reductions and *solid* expansions (marked as ‡) provide the best performances for all the measures considered, both in 2017 and 2018. This suggests that removing highly specialized information (i.e. the gene mutation) or adding general terms (e.g. solid) benefits the retrieval. A possible reason is related to the nature of the document collections, since clinical trials often contain general requirements to allow patients to enroll. The results obtained in 2019 with the top three query reformulations from 2017 and 2018 confirm this trend. The run combining query gene reductions and *solid* expansions (line 13‡) is one of the top three runs of 2019, however two query reformulations from 2017 (line 14) and 2018 (line 11) provide better performance. This result shows how difficult the task is. In fact, even though we found a particular query reformulation approach (marked as ‡) to be highly effective in all three years – especially in 2017 and 2018 – it was not the best approach for 2019. Therefore, this analysis helps researchers to select an effective subset of query reformulations to build strong baselines for clinical trials retrieval.

Comparison with TREC PM Participants. The results from Table 1 (Part B) mark a clear division between the 2017 and 2018 tracks and the 2019 track. In 2017 and 2018, most of the participant runs did not reach the top 10 threshold in any of the considered measures – the only exception is the research group from Poznan University of Technology, whose best runs always belong to the top 10 performing runs for the track. Conversely, in 2019 all the participant groups submitted runs that achieved results higher than the top 10 threshold.

Compared with the results obtained using the query reformulations from Table 1 (Part A), we can see that all runs employing the best query reformulations obtain results higher than the top 10 threshold for all the considered measures in all three years. Furthermore, the runs using the top five query reformulations achieved consistently better results than participant runs for each measure in all three years. This is an indication of the robustness of our approach across the different collections and also of the effectiveness of the proposed query reformulations for the clinical trials retrieval. In particular, it is worth to mention that the runs using the (‡) query reformulation achieve performances that belong to the top three best performing systems of each year PM track [11–13]. Therefore, the analysis of query reformulations made on the 2017 and 2018 PM tracks confirmed its trend in the 2019 PM track and allowed us to identify a specific set of query reformulations beneficial for the retrieval of clinical trials.

5 Conclusions and Final Remarks

In this paper, we further elaborate the results originally presented at SIGIR 2019 [2] and TREC 2019 [4] to evaluate several query expansion and reduction methods and to see whether a particular approach can be helpful in clinical trials retrieval. The experimental analysis showed the effectiveness of the proposed query reformulations in 2017 and 2018 PM tracks, and we confirmed this positive trend in the 2019 PM track. The obtained runs achieve top performing results in all PM tracks [11–13]. In particular, the run marked as ‡ in Table 1 can be considered as a valid baseline to build stronger multi-stage systems in the future.

Acknowledgements. This work is partially supported by the ExaMode project, as part of the European Union H2020 research and innovation program under grant agreement no. 825292.

References

1. Agosti, M., Di Nunzio, G.M., Marchesin, S.: The University of Padua IMS Research Group at TREC 2018 PM Track. In: Proc. TREC (2018)
2. Agosti, M., Di Nunzio, G.M., Marchesin, S.: An Analysis of Query Reformulation Techniques for Precision Medicine. In: Proc. ACM SIGIR Conf. pp. 973–976 (2019)
3. Aronson, A.R.: Effective mapping of biomedical text to the UMLS Metathesaurus: the MetaMap program. In: Proc. AMIA Symposium. pp. 17–21 (2001)
4. Di Nunzio, G.M., Marchesin, S., Agosti, M.: Exploring how to combine query reformulations for precision medicine. In: Proc. TREC (2019)
5. Diao, L., et alii: The Research of Query Expansion Based on Medical Terms Reweighting in Medical IR. EURASIP J. Wireless Comm.&Networ. (1), 105 (2018)
6. Goeuriot, L., Jones, G., Kelly, L., Müller, H., Zobel, J.: Medical Information Retrieval: Introduction to the Special Issue. Inform Retrieval J. **19**(1), 1–5 (2016)
7. Goodwin, T.R., Skinner, M.A., Harabagiu, S.M.: UTD HLTRI at TREC 2017: Precision medicine track. In: Proc. TREC (2017)
8. Gurulingappa, H., Toldo, L., Schepers, C., Bauer, A., Megaro, G.: Semi-supervised information retrieval system for clinical decision support. In: Proc. TREC (2016)
9. Hersh, W.: Information Retrieval: A Health and Biomedical Perspective. Health and Informatics Series, Springer-Verlag, New York, NY, USA (2009)
10. Oleynik, M., et alii: HPI-DHC at TREC 2018: PM Track. In: Proc. TREC (2018)
11. Roberts, K., et alii: Overview of PM Track. In: Proc. TREC (2017)
12. Roberts, K., et alii: Overview of PM Track. In: Proc. TREC (2018)
13. Roberts, K., et alii: Overview of PM Track. In: Proc. TREC (2019)
14. Robertson, S., Zaragoza, H.: The probabilistic relevance framework: BM25 and beyond. Foundations and Trends® in Information Retrieval **3**(4), 333–389 (2009)
15. Sondhi, P., et alii: Leveraging Medical Thesauri and Physician FB for Improving Medical Literature Retrieval for Case Queries. JAMIA **19**(5), 851–858 (2012)
16. Zhu, D., Wu, S., Carterette, B., Liu, H.: Using Large Clinical Corpora for QE in Text-Based Cohort Identification. J. of Biomedical Informatics **49**, 275–281 (2014)

Prediction of New Associations between ncRNAs and Diseases Exploiting Multi-Type Hierarchical Clustering (Discussion Paper)

Emanuele Pio Barracchia[1,3], Gianvito Pio[1,3], Domenica D'Elia[2], and Michelangelo Ceci[1,3,4]

[1] Dept. of Computer Science - University of Bari Aldo Moro, Bari (Italy)
{emanuele.barracchia, gianvito.pio, michelangelo.ceci}@uniba.it
[2] CNR, Institute for Biomedical Technologies - Bari (Italy)
domenica.delia@ba.itb.cnr.it
[3] Big Data Laboratory, CINI Consortium - Rome (Italy)
[4] Dept. of Knowledge Technologies, Jožef Stefan Institute, Ljubljana (Slovenia)

Abstract. The study of functional associations between ncRNAs and human diseases is a pivotal task of modern research to develop new and more effective therapeutic approaches. Nevertheless, it is not a trivial task since it involves entities of different types, such as microRNAs, lncRNAs or target genes. Such a complexity can be faced by representing the involved biological entities and their relationships as a network and by exploiting network-based computational approaches able to identify new associations. However, existing methods are limited to homogeneous networks or can exploit only a limited set of the features of biological entities. To overcome the limitations of existing approaches, we proposed the system LP-HCLUS, which analyzes heterogeneous networks consisting of several types of objects and relationships, each possibly described by a set of features, and extracts hierarchically organized, possibly overlapping, multi-type clusters that are subsequently exploited to predict new ncRNA-disease associations. Our experimental evaluation shows that, according to both quantitative (i.e., TPR@k, ROC and PR curves) and qualitative criteria, LP-HCLUS produces better results.

Keywords: non-coding RNA (ncRNAs) · diseases · cancer · heterogeneous network · clustering · link prediction

1 Introduction

High-throughput sequencing technologies and recent, more efficient computational approaches, have been fundamental for the rapid advances in functional genomics. Among the most relevant results, there is the discovery of thousands of non-coding RNAs (ncRNAs) with a regulatory function on gene expression.

In parallel, the number of studies reporting the involvement of ncRNAs in the development of many different human diseases has grown exponentially. The first type of ncRNAs that has been discovered and largely studied is that of microRNAs (miRNAs), classified as small non-coding RNAs in contrast with long non-coding RNAs (lncRNAs), that are ncRNAs longer than 200nt. While miRNAs primarily act as post-transcriptional regulators, lncRNAs have a plethora of regulatory functions [10]. However, the number of lncRNAs for which the functional and molecular mechanisms are completely elucidated is still quite poor and experimental investigations are still too much expensive for being carried out without any computational pre-analysis. In the last few years, there have been several attempts to computationally predict the relationships among biological entities, such as genes, miRNAs, lncRNAs, diseases [1,11,13,15]. Such methods are based on a network representation of the entities under study and on the identification of new links among nodes in the network. However, most of them are able to work only on homogeneous networks (where nodes and links are of one single type) [5], are strongly limited by the number of different node types or are constrained by pre-defined network structures.

In this discussion paper, we describe the method LP-HCLUS [2], that is able to overcome these limitations. In particular, it can discover new ncRNA-disease relationships from heterogeneous attributed networks (i.e., consisting of different biological entities related by different types of relationships) with arbitrary structure. This ability allows LP-HCLUS to investigate the interactions among different types of entities, possibly leading to increased prediction accuracy.

LP-HCLUS exploits a combined approach based on hierarchical, multi-type clustering and link prediction. As we will detail in the next section, a multi-type cluster is actually a heterogeneous sub-network. Therefore, the adoption of a clustering-based approach allows LP-HCLUS to base its predictions on relevant, highly-cohesive heterogeneous sub-networks. Moreover, the hierarchical organization of clusters allows it to perform predictions at different levels of granularity, taking into account either local/specific or global/general relationships.

2 Method

In the following, we introduce the notation and some useful definitions.

Definition 1 (Heterogeneous attributed network). *A heterogeneous attributed network is a network $G = (V, E)$, where V is the set of nodes and E is the set of edges, and both nodes and edges can be of different types. Moreover:*

- $\mathcal{T} = \mathcal{T}_t \cup \mathcal{T}_{tr}$ *is the set of node types, where* $\mathcal{T}_t$ *is the set of target types, i.e. considered as target of the clustering/prediction task, and* $\mathcal{T}_{tr}$ *is the set of task-relevant types. Only nodes of target types are clustered and considered in the identification of new relationships.*
- *Each node type* $T_v \in \mathcal{T}$ *defines a subset of nodes in the network, i.e.,* $V_v \subseteq V$.
- *Each node type* $T_v \in \mathcal{T}$ *is associated with a set of attributes* $\mathcal{A}_v = \{A_{v,1}, A_{v,2}, ..., A_{v,m_v}\}$, *i.e., nodes of the type* T_v *are described by the attributes* $\mathcal{A}_v$.
- $\mathcal{R}$ *is the set of all the possible edge types.*
- *Each edge type* $R_l \in \mathcal{R}$ *defines a subset of edges* $E_l \subseteq E$.

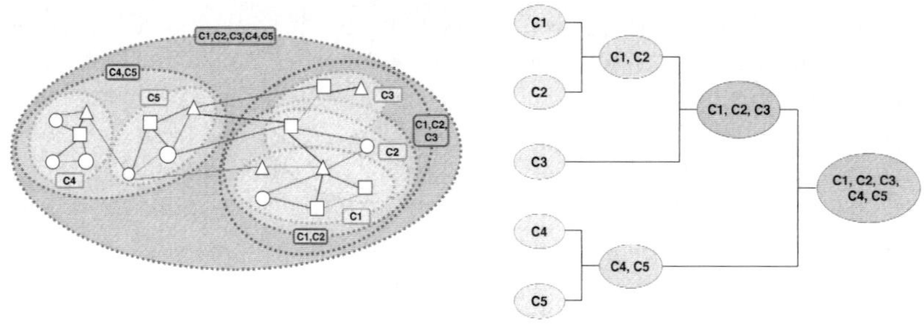

(a) (b)

Fig. 1. A hierarchy of overlapping multi-type clusters: (a) emphasizes the overlapping among multi-type clusters; (b) shows their hierarchical organization.

Definition 2 (Hierarchical multi-type clustering). *A hierarchy of multi-type clusters is defined as a list of hierarchy levels* $[L_1, L_2, \ldots, L_k]$, *where each* L_i *consists of a set of overlapping multi-type clusters. For each level* $L_i, i = 2, 3, \ldots. k$, $\forall\, G' \in L_i\ \exists\, G'' \in L_{i-1}$, *such that* G'' *is a subnetwork of* G' *(Fig. 1).*

According to these definitions, we define the task considered in this work.

Definition 3 (Predictive hierarchical clustering for link prediction). *Given a heterogeneous attributed network* $G = (V, E)$ *and the set of target types* $\mathcal{T}_t$, *the goal is to find:*

- *A hierarchy of overlapping multi-type clusters* $[L_1, L_2, \ldots, L_k]$.
- *A function* $\psi^{(w)} : V_{i_1} \times V_{i_2} \rightarrow [0, 1]$ *for each hierarchical level* L_w $(w \in 1, 2, ..., k)$, *where nodes in* V_{i_1} *are of type* $T_{i_1} \in \mathcal{T}_t$ *and nodes in* V_{i_2} *are of type* $T_{i_2} \in \mathcal{T}_t$. *Each function* $\psi^{(w)}$ *maps each possible pair of nodes (of types* T_{i_1} *and* T_{i_2}*) to a score representing the degree of certainty of their relationship.*

In this paper LP-HCLUS has been used to solve the task formalized in Definition 3, by considering ncRNAs and diseases as target types. Hence, we determine two distinct set of nodes denoted by T_n and T_d, representing the set of ncRNAs and the set of diseases, respectively. In the following subsections, we will describe the main steps executed by LP-HCLUS (see Fig. 2 for a general overview).

2.1 Estimation of the strength of the relationship

In the first phase, we estimate the strength of the relationship among all the possible ncRNA-disease pairs in the network G. In particular, we aim to compute a score $s(n_i, d_j)$ for each possible pair n_i, d_j, by exploiting the concept of *meta-path*. According to [14], a *meta-path* is a set of sequences of nodes (involving both target and task-relevant types) which follow the same sequence of edge types, and can be used to fruitfully represent conceptual (possibly indirect) relationships between two entities in a heterogeneous network. Given the ncRNA n_i and the disease d_j, the relationship between them can be considered "certain" if there is at least one meta-path which confirms its certainty.

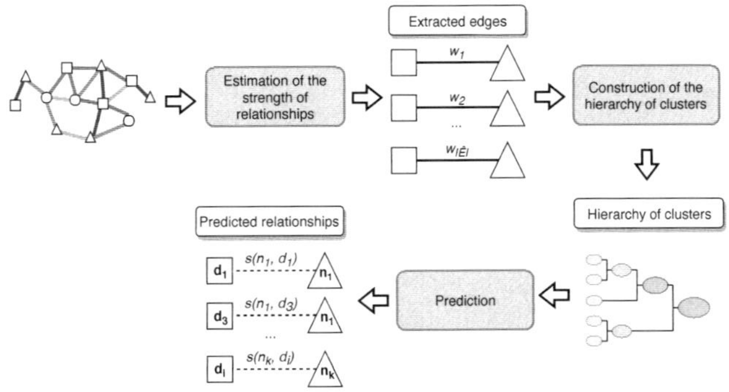

Fig. 2. General workflow of the method LP-HCLUS.

Therefore, by assimilating the score associated with an interaction to its degree of certainty, we compute $s(n_i, d_j)$ as the maximum value observed over all the possible meta-paths between n_i and d_j. Formally:

$$s(n_i, d_j) = \max_{P \in metapaths(n_i, d_j)} pathscore(P, n_i, d_j) \quad (1)$$

where $metapaths(n_i, d_j)$ is the set of meta-paths connecting n_i and d_j, and $pathscore(P, n_i, d_j)$ is the degree of certainty of the relationship between n_i and d_j according to the meta-path P. In order to compute $pathscore(P, n_i, d_j)$, we represent each meta-path P as a finite set of sequences of nodes. If a sequence in P connects n_i and d_j, then $pathscore(P, n_i, d_j) = 1$. Otherwise, following the same strategy introduced before, it is computed as the maximum similarity between the sequences which start with n_i and the sequences which end with d_j (see Fig. 3). The intuition behind this formula is that if n_i and d_j are not directly connected, their score represents the similarity of the nodes and edges they are connected to. The similarity between two sequences seq' and seq'' is computed according to the the attributes of all nodes involved in the two sequences: following [6], if x is numeric, then $s_x(seq', seq'') = 1 - \frac{|val_x(seq') - val_x(seq'')|}{max_x - min_x}$, where min_x (resp. max_x) is the minimum (resp. maximum) value, for the attribute x; if x is not a numeric attribute, $s_x(seq', seq'') = 1$ if $val_x(seq') = val_x(seq'')$, 0 otherwise. In this solution there could be some node types that are not involved in any meta-path. In order to exploit the information conveyed by these nodes, we add an aggregation of their attribute values (the *arithmetic mean* for numerical attributes, the *mode* for non-numerical attributes) to the nodes that are connected to them and that appear in at least one meta-path.

2.2 Construction of a hierarchy of overlapping multi-type clusters

We construct the first level of the hierarchy by identifying a set of overlapping multi-type clusters in the form of bicliques. To this aim, we perform three steps: *i)* **Filtering**, which keeps only the ncRNA-disease pairs with a score greater than (or equal to) β. The result of this step is the subset $\{(n_i, d_j) | s(n_i, d_j) \geq \beta\}$

	ncRNA Attributes		Attributes of other entities in the path			Disease Attributes		
Seq n.	N_id	N_att1	O_id	O_att1	O_att2	D_id	D_att1	D_att2
1	h19	lncrna	...	...	...	adrenocortical carcinomas	Neoplasms	17
2	hsa-miR-765	mirna	...	...	...	anxiety disorder	Mental Disorders	34
3	cdkn2b-as1	lncrna	...	...	...	aortic aneurysm	Cardiovascular Diseases	5
4	hsa-miR-126	mirna	...	...	...	asthma	Respiratory Tract Disease	75
5	hsa-miR-148a	mirna	...	...	...	asthma	Respiratory Tract Disease	75
6	hsa-miR-148b	mirna	...	...	...	asthma	Respiratory Tract Disease	75
7	hsa-miR-152	mirna	...	...	...	asthma	Respiratory Tract Disease	75
8	anril	lncrna	...	...	...	atherosclerosis	Cardiovascular Diseases	54
9	h19	lncrna	...	...	...	atherosclerosis	Cardiovascular Diseases	54

Fig. 3. Sequences between the ncRNA "h19" and the disease "asthma" according to a meta-path. Sequences emphasized in yellow (1 and 9) are those starting with "h19", while sequences emphasized in blue (4, 5, 6 and 7) are those ending with "asthma".

ii) **Initialization**, which builds the initial set of clusters in the form of bicliques, each consisting of a ncRNA-disease pair in $\{(n_i, d_j) | s(n_i, d_j) \geq \beta\}$.
iii) **Merging**, which iteratively merges two clusters C' and C'' into a new cluster C'''. This step regards the initial set of clusters as a list sorted according to an ordering relation $<_c$ that reflects the quality of the clusters. Each cluster C' is then merged with the first cluster C'' in the list that would lead to a cluster C''' which still satisfies the biclique constraint. This step is repeated until no additional clusters that satisfy the biclique constraint can be obtained.

The ordering relation $<_c$ defines a greedy search strategy that guides the order in which pairs of clusters are analyzed. $<_c$ is based on the cluster cohesiveness $h(c)$, that corresponds to the average score in the cluster, namely: $h(C) = \frac{1}{|pairs(C)|} \cdot \sum_{(n_i,d_j) \in pairs(C)} s(n_i, d_j)$, where $pairs(C)$ is the set of all the possible ncRNA-disease pairs that can be constructed from the set of ncRNAs and diseases in the cluster. Accordingly, if C' and C'' are two different clusters, the ordering relation $<_c$ is defined as follows: $C' <_c C'' \iff h(C') > h(C'')$.

The approach adopted to build the other hierarchical levels is similar to the merging step performed to obtain L_1. The main difference is that we do not obtain bicliques, but generic multi-type clusters. Since the biclique constraint is removed, we need another stopping criterion for the iterative merging procedure. Coherently with approaches used in hierarchical co-clustering and following [12], we adopt a user-defined threshold α on the cohesiveness of the obtained clusters. In particular, two clusters C' and C'' can be merged into a new cluster C''' if $h(C''') > \alpha$, where $h(C''')$ is the cluster cohesiveness. This means that α defines the minimum cluster cohesiveness that must be satisfied by a cluster obtained after a merging. The iterative process stops when it is not possible to merge more clusters with a minimum level of cohesiveness α.

2.3 Prediction of new ncRNA-disease relationships

In the last phase, we exploit each level of the identified hierarchy of multi-type clusters as a prediction model. In particular, we compute, for each ncRNA-disease pair, a score representing its degree of certainty on the basis of the multi-type clusters containing it. Formally, let C^w_{ij} be a cluster identified in the w-th hierarchical level in which the ncRNA n_i and the disease d_j appear. We compute the degree of certainty of the relationship between n_i and d_j as:

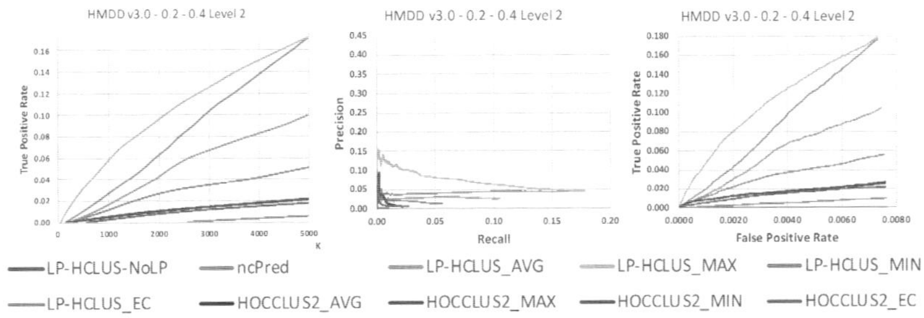

Fig. 4. TPR@k, Precision-Recall and ROC curves results for the dataset HMDD v3.0, obtained with the best configuration ($\alpha = 0.2, \beta = 0.4, level = 2$).

$\psi^{(w)}(n_i, d_j) = h\left(C_{ij}^{w}\right)$, that is, we compute the degree of certainty of the new interaction as the average degree of certainty of the known relationships in the cluster. In some cases, the same interaction may appear in multiple clusters, since the proposed algorithm is able to identify overlapping clusters. In this case, C_{ij}^{w} represents the list of multi-type clusters in which both n_i and d_j appear and we aggregate their cohesiveness values according to four different strategies: maximum, minimum, average and evidence combination [9].

3 Experiments

LP-HCLUS has been run with different values of its input parameters. In particular, following the results obtained in [12], we considered $\alpha \in \{0.1, 0.2\}$ and $\beta \in \{0.3, 0.4\}$. The considered datasets are: *i)* **HMDD v3.0** which stores 985 miRNAs, 675 diseases and 20,859 relationships between diseases and miRNAs; *ii)* **Integrated Dataset (ID)**, built by integrating multiple datasets [3,4,7,8], composed by 7,049 diseases, 70 lncRNA-miRNA relationships, 3,830 relationships between diseases and ncRNAs, 90,242 target genes, 26,522 disease-target associations and 1,055 ncRNA-target relationships.

We compared LP-HCLUS with the following competitors:
i) **HOCCLUS2** [12], a biclustering algorithm that, similarly to LP-HCLUS, identifies a hierarchy of (possibly overlapping) heterogeneous clusters. It is, however, limited to work with only two types of objects. Since its parameters have a similar meaning with respect to LP-HCLUS parameters, we evaluated its results with the same setting, i.e., $\alpha \in \{0.1, 0.2\}$ and $\beta \in \{0.3, 0.4\}$;
ii) **ncPred** [1], a system that was specifically designed to predict new ncRNA-disease associations. ncPred cannot catch information coming from other entities in the network and it is not able to exploit features associated to nodes and links.
iii) **LP-HCLUS-NoLP**, which corresponds to a baseline version of system LP-HCLUS, without the clustering and the link prediction steps. In particular, we consider the score obtained in the first phase of LP-HCLUS (see Section 2.1) as the final score associated with each interaction.

We adopted the 10-fold cross validation on the set of known ncRNA-disease relationships and, due to absence of negative samples, we evaluated the results in

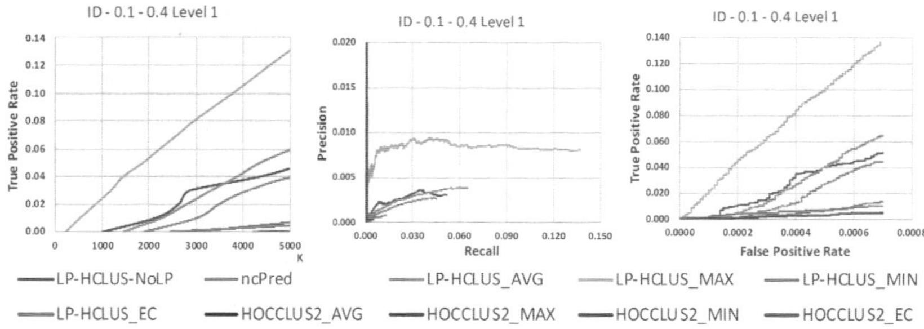

Fig. 5. TPR@k, Precision-Recall and ROC curves results for the dataset ID, obtained with the best configuration ($\alpha = 0.1, \beta = 0.4, level = 1$).

terms of TruePositiveRate@k curve. Moreover, we also report the results in terms of ROC and Precision-Recall curves by considering the unknown relationships as negative examples. We remark that ROC and PR curves can only be used for relative comparison and not as absolute evaluation measures because they are spoiled by the assumption made on unknown relationships.

In Figs. 4 and 5 we show some results obtained with the most promising configurations. From the quantitative viewpoint, we can observe that the proposed method LP-HCLUS, with the combination strategy based on the maximum, is able to obtain the best performances, for all the considered measures. From a qualitative point of view, we first performed a comparative analysis between the results obtained by LP-HCLUS against the validated interactions reported in the updated version of HMDD (i.e., v3.2 released on March 27th, 2019). We found 3,055 LP-HCLUS predictions confirmed by the new release of HMDD at the hierarchy level 1, 4,119 at level 2 and 4,797 at level 3. Next, we conducted a qualitative analysis of the top-ranked relationships predicted by LP-HCLUS using ID dataset, selecting only those with a score equal to 1.0. For this purpose, we exploited MNDR v2.0, which is a comprehensive resource including more than 260,000 experimental and predicted ncRNA-disease associations for mammalian species. Also in this case, we found some associations in both MNDR and in the list of predicted associations by LP-HCLUS. A more comprehensive analysis, reporting several additional examples, can be found in the full paper [2].

4 Conclusions

In this paper, we have tackled the problem of predicting possibly unknown ncRNA-disease relationships. The proposed approach LP-HCLUS is able to take advantage from the possible heterogeneous nature of the attributed biological network analyzed. The results confirm the initial intuitions and show competitive performances of LP-HCLUS in terms of accuracy of the predictions, also when compared with state-of-the-art competitor systems. These results are also supported by a comparison of LP-HCLUS predictions with data reported in MNDR and by a qualitative analysis that revealed that several ncRNA-disease associations predicted by LP-HCLUS have been subsequently experimentally validated and introduced in a more recent release (v3.2) of HMDD. As future work, we will evaluate the performance of LP-HCLUS in other domains.

5 Acknowledgments

We acknowledge the support of Ministry of Education, Universities and Research (MIUR) through the PON project TALIsMAn - Tecnologie di Assistenza personALizzata per il Miglioramento della quAlità della vitA (ARS01_01116). Dr. Gianvito Pio acknowledges the support of Ministry of Education, Universities and Research (MIUR) through the project AIM1852414, activity 1, line 1.

References

1. Alaimo, S., Giugno, R., Pulvirenti, A.: ncPred: ncRNA-Disease Association Prediction through Tripartite Network-Based Inference. Frontiers in Bioengineering and Biotechnology **2** (Dec 2014)
2. Barracchia, E.P., Pio, G., D'Elia, D., Ceci, M.: Prediction of new associations between ncrnas and diseases exploiting multi-type hierarchical clustering. BMC bioinformatics **21**(1), 1–24 (2020)
3. Bauer-Mehren, A., Rautschka, M., Sanz, F., Furlong, L.I.: DisGeNET: a Cytoscape plugin to visualize, integrate, search and analyze gene-disease networks. Bioinformatics (Oxford, England) **26**(22), 2924–2926 (Nov 2010)
4. Chen, G., Wang, Z., Wang, D., Qiu, C., Liu, M., Chen, X., Zhang, Q., Yan, G., Cui, Q.: LncRNADisease: a database for long-non-coding RNA-associated diseases. Nucleic Acids Research **41**(Database issue) (Jan 2013)
5. Chen, X., Yan, C.C., Luo, C., Ji, W., Zhang, Y., Dai, Q.: Constructing lncRNA functional similarity network based on lncRNA-disease associations and disease semantic similarity. Scientific Reports **5** (Jun 2015)
6. Han, J., Kamber, M.: Data mining: concepts and techniques. Elsevier/Morgan Kaufmann, Amsterdam (2006)
7. Helwak, A., Kudla, G., et al.: Mapping the human miRNA interactome by CLASH reveals frequent noncanonical binding. Cell **153**(3), 654–665 (2013)
8. Jiang, Q., Wang, Y., Hao, Y., Juan, L., Teng, M., Zhang, X., Li, M., Wang, G., Liu, Y.: miR2disease: a manually curated database for microRNA deregulation in human disease. Nucleic Acids Research **37**(Database issue), D98–104 (Jan 2009)
9. Lesmo, L., Saitta, L., Torasso, P.: Evidence combination in expert systems. International Journal of Man-Machine Studies **22**(3), 307–326 (Mar 1985)
10. Melissari, M.T., Grote, P.: Roles for long non-coding RNAs in physiology and disease. Pflügers Archiv - European Journal of Physiology **468**(6), 945–958 (2016)
11. Mignone, P., Pio, G., D'Elia, D., Ceci, M.: Exploiting transfer learning for the reconstruction of the human gene regulatory network. Bioinform. **36**(5), 1553–1561 (2020)
12. Pio, G., Ceci, M., D'Elia, D., Loglisci, C., Malerba, D.: A Novel Biclustering Algorithm for the Discovery of Meaningful Biological Correlations between microRNAs and their Target Genes. BMC Bioinformatics **14**(Suppl 7), S8 (Apr 2013)
13. Pio, G., Ceci, M., Prisciandaro, F., Malerba, D.: Exploiting causality in gene network reconstruction based on graph embedding. Machine Learning (2019)
14. Pio, G., Serafino, F., Malerba, D., Ceci, M.: Multi-type clustering and classification from heterogeneous networks. Information Sciences **425**, 107–126 (Jan 2018)
15. Wang, P., Guo, Q., et al.: Improved method for prioritization of disease associated lncRNAs based on ceRNA theory and functional genomics data. Oncotarget **8**(3), 4642–4655 (Dec 2016)

On the Use of GIS for Health and Epidemiology Control*

Giuseppe Tradigo, Patrizia Vizza, Pietro H. Guzzi, and Pierangelo Veltri

Universit degli Studi Magna Graecia di Catanzaro
Viale Europa, 88100 Catanzaro, Italy
{gtradigo,vizzap,hguzzi,veltri}@unicz.it

Abstract. Monitoring the evolution and diffusion of diseases is an important task for health monitoring. Recent phenomena, such as the spread of Coronavirus (Covid-19), highlighted the relevance of adopting Geographical Information Systems (GIS) in epidemiology modeling. GIS may offer general views and indications which domain experts and governments could use to give immediate directions to social actors and operators.
We report on the possibility of using geographic database model instruments in order to acquire, store and manage health-related data. The reported case study is about an application able to correlate TSH (Thyroid-Stimulating Hormone) with environmental data. The reported example aims to show how to acquire, analyze and integrate clinical and geographical data to evaluate possible correlations for the prevention of chronic diseases, especially neoplasms, by means of mapping disease features with environmental factors.

Keywords: Geographic Information Systems · epidemiology · Virus · TSH.

1 Introduction

In the last years, GIS tools have become more useful in the public health sector, especially in the epidemiology field [1–3]. Epidemiology models represent an important tool to manage and assess environmental risk factors, such as potential cause of illness, by quantifying their impact on human health in population at risk [4]. Therefore, they allow to carry out a number of prevention activities, and also monitoring and evaluating the effectiveness of these activities.

GIS can also be useful in associating epidemiological and health data by defining how environmental factors affect the health status of group of individuals or entire populations living in a territory, in the onset of specific diseases [5–8,

* *Discussion Paper*, a preliminary version of this paper has been published at IEEE BIBM 2019 supported by POR PIH-GIS Regional Funds.

22]. GIS systems and analysis methodologies support domain experts in studying the overlap of clinical and environmental data and can help with the identification of possible relations between clinical features and diseases. These relations can be rendered with rich epidemiological maps which represent the present and future status (prediction) of the on-set of a disease and its human-to-human transmission. Correlations between environmental risk factors and clinical data or events can then be used to evaluate or foresee the impact on human health and are usually be analyzed by using spatial analysis techniques [9–11]. These techniques allow to study disease pathogenesis and etiology, identifying any links between them and the places where they develop [12].

In literature, many contributions exist which focus on spatial epidemiology [13–15]. In [16] authors report on the use of GIS in epidemiology, focusing on methodologies involving geocoding, distance estimation, residential mobility, record linkage and data integration, spatial clustering, small area estimation, and disease mapping. Authors in [17] study the correlation between climate and geographic distribution of tuberculosis by using GIS, aiming to identify high-risk population groups and their geographic areas. Contribution in [19] investigates environmental and geographical influences on epidemiology of acromegaly in Brazil. The authors validate a method to link an acromegaly registry with a GIS mapping module aiming to represent the spatial distribution of patients and to identify disease clusters.

We present an example of GIS application to study and evaluate the correlation between geographical and clinical geographical by using TSH (Thyroid-Stimulating Hormone) data. Shapefiles of environmental layers have been used in GIS to identify specific territorial aspects and their influence on clinical outcomes. A dataset has been used containing data of patients enrolled at Magna Graecia University of Catanzaro. A preliminary version of the paper has been previously published in [18].

2 GIS in health related applications

Environmental monitoring and the analysis of clinical data aim to prevent chronic diseases, especially the neoplasms and their correlation with environmental factors. In literature there exist many definitions of both correlation (e.g. Pearson correlation) and spatial correlation (*scorr* spatial correlation function between two variables over an X-Y domain). For the purposes of the present work, we adopt a loose definition of spatial correlation as follows. Let's consider a clinical event E in the input clinical dataset and a geographical entity G; we say that E and G are spatially correlated if there exists a spatial query Q for which the location of E is *contained* in the area subtended by G. In order to investigate on spatial correlations in our dataset, different environmental layers have been used. These are available on the Geoportal of the Calabria Region in shapefile format [20]. A shapefile is a standard format for vectorial spatial data. It has been developed by the Environmental Systems Research Institute (ESRI) to extend the interoperability between ESRI systems and the other GIS [21]. The shapefile is a non topological format and it is used in Geographic Information System to store positions, shapes and attributes of geographical features. It describes primitive geometric data such as points, lines, polygons and texts, called features, and their associated information, called attributes (e.g., a data describes a river and the associated attributes could be the name or temperature of the river). In such a way, more representations of geographic data can be created, which allow to influence the power and accuracy of geospatial analyses.

The online Geoportal of Calabria Region shares a cartographic data collection containing a number of environmental layers with IODL 2.0 license. Among the available layers, we selected the ones listed below as the most useful for our investigation:

- urban area;
- extra-urban area;
- commercial and industrial settlements;
- public and private service companies;
- rural settlements;
- mining area;
- yards;
- landfill;
- scarp yards;
- local railways;
- airport areas and heliports;
- regional, provincial and district administrative range.

These layers have been used to verify and analyze possible correlations between clinical and territorial aspects. The application of shapefiles and the use of geographic layers are important to assess whether and how some pathologies or in any case clinical alterations of individuals can be directly or indirectly related to strictly territorial aspects.

Table 1. Clinical database extraction. TSH values are expressed in $\mu U/ml$.

Patient	Latitude	Longitude	Altitude	TSH
1	38.632...	16.072...	465.80	2.40
2	39.527...	15.924...	5.85	1.86
3	39.523...	15.962...	277.56	2.07
4	39.533...	15.989...	346.60	2.02
5	39.516...	15.943...	134.49	0.05
6	39.527...	15.935...	188.68	1.26
7	39.511...	15.948...	182.01	1.27
8	38.246...	16.139...	323.80	2.84
9	38.245...	16.138...	301.11	4.23
10	38.246...	16.142...	341.25	1.25
...				
2269	38.698...	15.990...	302.01	2.32

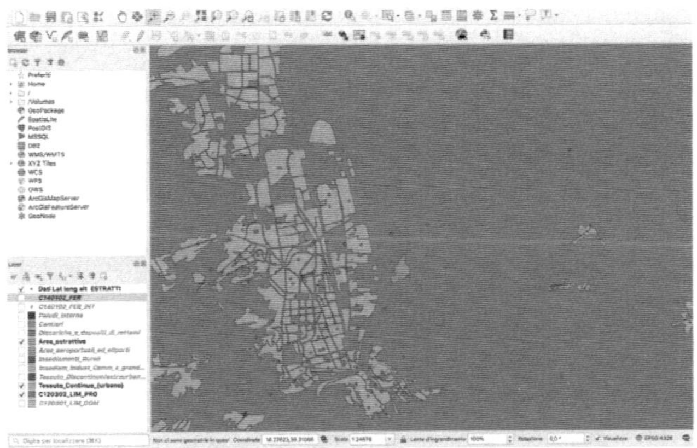

Fig. 1. Topological overlay between clinical data and extracted areas

As case study, we report the study of the correlation between the patterns of topological data with an example of thyroid's data regarding a south Italian region patients. A Health-GIS system has been implemented aiming to cross-check the TSH value with further environmental data through a topological overlay operation. The goal is to identify the geographical areas with the greatest presence of cases with specific pathology. Moreover, it is also interesting to calculate and trace the average distance covered by a patient for a specific health service.

3 Experiments

The health dataset regards single file with .xls extension in which each record represents a patient and contains:

- geo-referenced data (district, home address, latitude, longitude and altitude)
- clinical data (TSH level expressed in $\mu U/ml$)

The clinical dataset contains 2269 records and Table 1 reports an extract of the database we used for the investigation. The QGIS platform has been used to cross-check these clinical data with data relating to environmental factors. QGIS is a free and open source geographic information system to visualize and overlap vector and raster data in different formats and projections without any conversion into a common internal format. The clinical dataset has been converted in .cvs file and loaded into the QGIS system to represent spatial and clinical information together in a geographical map. Patients locations and other logistical data are geo-referenced and related with clinical data. For instance, red dots in Figure 1 refer to patients' location data extracted from the considered clinical dataset and projected on extractive areas polygons.

Starting from this representation, environmental layers listed above have been correlated with clinical dataset and some of these correlations are reported below.

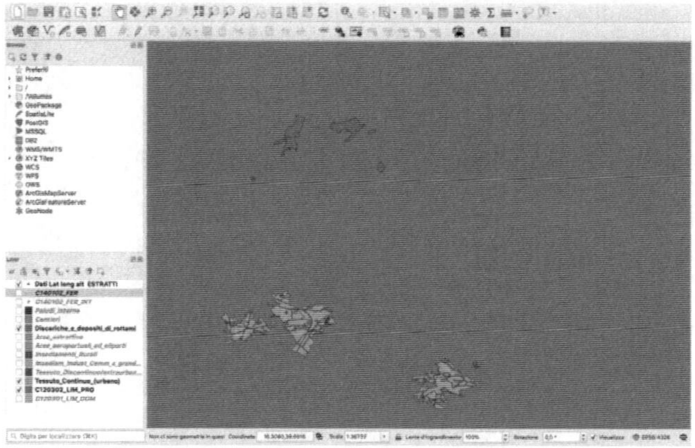

Fig. 2. Topological overlay between clinical data and landfills and scrap yards.

Since several diseases have a close link with overexposure to toxic substances, it is relevant to measure the occurrence of patients locations with potential toxic areas. Air pollution is one of the major environmental risks and in 2015 it has been recognized by the World Health Assembly (WHA) as one of the world's major public health problems. Pollutants are elements and chemical compounds deriving mostly from human activities such as, for example, industrial and commercial production. For this reason, the onset of several cancer cases in a specific geographic area has led to the urge to investigate and monitor industrial activities insisting on the same area.

Figure 1 shows the topological overlay between clinical data (points in red) and extractive areas (dark green areas) also reporting urban areas (areas in yellow). The extraction areas generate a series of pollutants whose exposure has been associated with a series of harmful effects on human health, especially for the respiratory and cardiovascular system and for neoplasms. Pollutants are mainly responsible for a substantial impoverishment of the soil (e.g., caused by deforestation and intensive agriculture), a continuous deterioration of water quality (e.g., caused especially by industrial discharges), and a growing contamination of the air (e.g., caused from the presence of fine dust and particulate in smog). Many substances such as, for example, nitrogen oxide, sulfur oxide, ozone and dust act as irritants; pollen and other agents present in the air are responsible for allergies such as asthma and seasonal colds; some toxic agents such as benzene and polycyclic aromatic hydrocarbons are carcinogenic; carbon monoxide compromises the transport of oxygen by the blood with serious effects on the brain. Other metals come into contact with various organs and tissues causing biological alterations and causing damage to the heart and the apparatus.

Figure 2 shows the topological overlay of clinical data with the level of landfills and scrap deposits (areas in brown), always bringing the urban area (areas in yellow) as reference. The economic growth of the most industrialized countries has generated a substantial increase in consumption and urbanization with a consequent increasing in waste production and in its difficult regular disposal. Waste has negative consequences on the environment and on human health. Asbestos is harmful to human health; breathing dust containing asbestos fibers can cause serious diseases, pleural tumors (pleural mesothelioma) and lung cancer.

4 Future Works

Spatial information in clinical data is crucial for prevention and monitoring evolution of global epidemiology. In this paper we analyze environmental data related with health related ones. We are working to complete a model and general purpose system able to relate clinical, environmental and epidemiology related information for real time data analysis and simulation. The aim is to support prevention in a large scale context. Our framework is general enough to support the loading and preprocessing of generic datasets in standard format (e.g. csv). We are planning to integrate user-friendly functionalities to import different datasets. We are also working on consolidating the representation of time as an analysis dimension and refining its use in the data analysis pipeline by adopting time series analysis techniques.

Acknowledgment

This research has been supported by POR CALABRIA FESR-FSE 2014-2020 PIH-GIS project CUP *J88C17000320006*. The authors thank Giuseppe Brescia for his contribution to a preliminary version of the paper.

References

1. M. Craglia and R. Maheswaran, GIS in public health practice. CRC press, 2016.
2. G. Tradigo, P. Vizza, P. Veltri, P. H. Guzzi, An Information System to Track data and processes for food quality and bacterial pathologies prevention. Italian Symposium on Advanced Database Systems (SEBD), 2019.
3. G. Tradigo, C. Pagliaro, G. Canino, P. H. Guzzi and P. Veltri, GIS for the analysis and monitoring of environmental issues related to life quality. Italian Symposium on Advanced Database Systems (SEBD). 320-326, 2015.
4. A. B. Lawson, S. Banerjee, R. P. Haining and M. D. Ugarte, Handbook of spatial epidemiology. CRC Press, 2016.
5. S. M. Fletcher-Lartey and G. Caprarelli, Application of GIS technology in public health: successes and challenges. Parasitology, 143(4): 401-415, 2016.
6. G. Tradigo, P. Veltri, O. Marasco, G. Scozzafava, G. Parlato and S. Greco, Studying neonatal TSH distribution by using GIS. In Proceedings of the First ACM SIGSPATIAL International Workshop on Use of GIS in Public Health, 36-39, 2012.
7. G. Ambrogio, R. Conte, L. De Napoli, G. Fragomeni, F. Gagliardi, Forming approaches comparison for high customised skull manufacturing. Key Engineering Materials, 651, 925-931, 2015.

8. M. V. Caruso, V. Gramigna, G. F. Serraino, A. Renzulli, G. Fragomeni, Influence of aortic outflow cannula orientation on epiaortic flow pattern during pulsed cardiopulmonary bypass. Journal of Medical and Biological Engineering, 35(4):455-463, 2015.
9. T. Olsson, L. F. Barcellos and L. Alfredsson, Interactions between genetic, lifestyle and environmental risk factors for multiple sclerosis. Nature Reviews Neurology, 13(1): 25, 2017.
10. M. Chin-Chan, J. Navarro-Yepes and B. Quintanilla-Vega, Environmental pollutants as risk factors for neurodegenerative disorders: Alzheimer and Parkinson diseases. Frontiers in cellular neuroscience, 9: 124, 2015.
11. G. Fragomeni, R. Iannelli, G. Falvo D'Urso Labate, M. Schwentenwein, G. Catapano, Validation of a novel 3D flow model for the optimization of construct perfusion in radial-flow packed-bed bioreactors (rPBBs) for long-bone tissue engineering. New Biotechnology, 52:110-120, 2019.
12. E. L. MacQuillan, A. B. Curtis, K. M. Baker, R. Paul and Y. O. Back, Using GIS mapping to target public health interventions: examining birth outcomes across GIS techniques. Journal of community health, 42(4): 633-638, 2017.
13. L. N. Carroll, A. P. Au, L. T. Detwiler, T. Fu, I. S. Painter and N. F. Abernethy, Visualization and analytics tools for infectious disease epidemiology: A systematic review. Journal of Biomedical Informatics, 51: 287-298, 2014.
14. G. Canino, P. H. Guzzi, G. Tradigo, A. Zhang and P. Veltri, A system for Geoanalysis of Clinical and Geographical Data. In Proceedings of the Third ACM SIGSPATIAL International Workshop on the Use of GIS in Public Health, 57-62, 2014.
15. G. Tradigo, C. Pagliaro, G. Canino, F. Casalinuovo, C. Graziani and P. Veltri, A model for the Geographical Analysis and monitoring of agricultural areas example and tests in south Italian regions. ACM SIGSPATIAL HealthGIS, 2014.
16. R. S. Kirby, E. Delmelle and Jan M. Eberth, Advances in spatial epidemiology and geographic information systems. Annals of Epidemiology, 27(1): 1-9, 2017.
17. R. Beiranvand, A. Karimi, A. Delpishes, K. Sayehmiri, S. Soleimani and S. Ghalavandi, Correlation Assessment of Climate and Geographic Distribution of Tuberculosis Using Geographical Information System (GIS). Iranian Journal of Public Health, 45(1): 86-93, 2016.
18. G. Tradigo, P. Vizza, G. Brescia, P. H. Guzzi, P. Veltri, A geographical patients based health information system. IEEE International Conference on Bioinformatics and Biomedicine (BIBM), 2019.
19. L. A. Naves, L. B. Porto, J. W. Corra Rosa, L. A. Casulari, J. W. Corra Rosa, Geographical information system (GIS) as a new tool to evaluate epidemiology based on spatial analysis and clinical outcomes in acromegaly. Pituitary, 18(1): 8-15, 2015.
20. Geoportale Nazionale, available online at http://www.pcn.minambiente.it/mattm/.
21. ESRI Shapefile Technical Description. An ESRI White PaperJuly, available online at https://www.esri.com/library/whitepapers/pdfs/shapefile.pdf, 1998.
22. Y. Aliakbarpoor, S. Comai, G. Pozzi, Designing a HL7 compatible personal health record for mobile devices, IEEE 3rd International Forum on Research and Technologies for Society and Industry, (RTSI), 1-6, 2017.
23. Caruso, M.V., Gramigna, V., Serraino, G.F., Renzulli, A., Fragomeni, G., Influence of aortic outflow cannula orientation on epiaortic flow pattern during pulsed cardiopulmonary bypass, Journal of Medical and Biological Engineering, 35(4): 455-463, 2015.

Privacy-aware design for E-Health Information Systems (DISCUSSION PAPER)

Flora Amato[1], Giovanni Cozzolino[1], Francesco Moscato[2], Vincenzo Moscato[1], Antonio Picariello[1], and Giancarlo Sperlì[1]

[1] University of Naples "Federico II", Dipartimento di Ingegneria Elettrica e Tecnologie dell'Informazione, via Claudio 21, 80125 Naples, Italy
<name.surname>@unina.it

[2] University of Campania "Luigi Vanvitelli" DiSciPol, Caserta, Italy
francesco.moscato@unicampania.it

Abstract. Many research works had the aim of creating frameworks able to model systems, of defining their requirements and properties, and of verifying their satisfiability. Many approaches involve the usage of the Model Driven Engineering throughout the whole system lifecycle in order to build systems that are correct by construction. Using models as primary artefacts helps to reduce costs and time of development. The possibility of having automatic code generation from model tools enact the possibility to produce (theoretically) bug-free code starting from correct models. In this work we describe the usage of a modelling and verification tool, MetaMORP(h)OSY, for performing quality control in E-Health Domain.

Keywords: Multi agent systems · E-Health · Model Driven Engineering · Formal Verification.

1 Introduction

In many applications, standards and/or regulatory processes are defined to ensure that systems are going to operate as intended. In critical systems this is very important, because an error or a failure could lead to serious damages in terms of human lives, environment and money. In these systems it is necessary to use formal methods, i.e. mathematical techniques used for the specification, development and verification of software and hardware systems.

In recent years, Model Driven Engineering (MDE) has developed a lot, laying its foundations on the massive use of models as its primary artefacts.

In literature, many research works have been devoted to exploit the abstraction resulting from the creation of models in the MDE and in the application of the modelling techniques on various kinds of systems. In particular, researchers are trying to create frameworks that allow to completely describe systems (and their requirements and properties) and to verify their correctness.

The principle is to use MDE approaches throughout the system lifecycle. The aim is to build systems that are correct by construction. Using models as primary artefacts helps to reduce costs and time of development, and since automatic code generation from model tools are already available, it is clear that is possible to produce (theoretically) bug-free code (starting from correct models). The standard use of the MDE involves the use of a Domain Specific Modelling Language (DSML) for the definition of system models. With this language, different levels of abstraction of the system under study are created. These abstraction levels must somehow contain consistent in formation about the system.

This is the reason why Model-to-Model (M2M) and Model-to-Test (M2T) translation tools are used as bridges between abstraction levels.

These transformations, besides being useful to treat models in the most convenient way, allow us to introduce automation in our process. In order to build a process that leads automatically (or semi-automatically) to the creation of a correct system, it is necessary to solve some problems of high complexity, for example:

- to guide the user in the construction of an high-level model of the system and its specific analysis properties;
- automating the definition and configuration of the analysis process (e.g. by calling the right tools at the right time)

Such approach can be used also to setup, in a very fast and flexible way, many different kind of systems, that can be applied to the analysis of complex domains, like social networks [1–4], big-data, or human-understanding interfaces [5].

Many works [5, 3] exploit Artificial Intelligence tecniques, in order to construct a model able to represent and satisfy system requirements, while other works are model-oriented [6–8]. In recent works, as [9], we propose MetaMORP(h)OSy (Meta-modeling of Mas Object-based with Real-time specification in Project Of complex Systems), a framework aiming to verify if a system model satisfies a given property. This framework is still prone to some issues related to the development of an automatic (or semi-automatic) chain of tools for the analysis and proper construction (model driven) of systems, that can be fixed with a semantic approach for the correlation of produced models [10, 11].

MetaMORP(h)OSy exploits a multi-agent modelling paradigm. A meta-formalism extending UML is used to express actors, system components and requirements. Algorithms are used in the design phase to translate Multi Agent Systems models into appropriate formal models.

2 The methodology

2.1 Methodology Description

MetaMORP(h)OSy implements a methodology for the design, validation and verification of critical systems. For this purpose, it uses techniques and approaches of MDE and MAS. In particular, MetaMORP(h)OSy exploits a multi-agent modelling paradigm. A meta-formalism extending UML is used to express actors, system components and requirements. Algorithms are used in the design phase to translate MAS models into appropriate formal models. The definition of requirements allows the choice of appropriate Observers to be performed for model analysis. After the validation of the design models, vertical transformations are implemented, which produce stubs for the generation of the system at run-time. The framework must generate monitors during the design and execution phase in order to allow the verification of the requirements. In particular, the monitors in the execution phase must compare the behavior of a system under analysis with the one predicted in design analysis.

2.2 Description Language

METAMORP(h)OSy provides the same graphic language for the system specification and its requirements formulation. This language is formally defined by a meta-model. The MetaMORP(h)OSy profile must allow the definition of:

- structural and behavioural views of the system;
- system properties and requirements to be verified;
- methods, techniques and metrics for analysing or measuring properties and requirements;
- expected and measured workloads of the systems.

Being MetaMORP(h)OSy designed to be used for critical systems, it allows the specification of temporal behaviour of agents and real-time properties[12]. The name of the modelling profile is RT-AML (Real-Time Agent Modelling Language). RT-AML describes MAS using a UML-based language. MetaMORP(h)OSy uses the BDI (Beliefs Desires Intentions) paradigm to describe agents[13].

Agents are characterized by their beliefs, the objectives they want to achieve and the plans available to achieve them. RT-AML profile uses four diagrams for MAS behaviours description: Class diagrams, RT Agent Diagrams, RT-Activity diagrams and RT-Sequence diagrams. Class diagrams are the same of UML class diagrams. They are used when it is not useful to describe objects as agents (for example in case of passive entities). The RT-Agent diagrams are the core of the RT-AML profile. They describe agents' structures, goals and beliefs. In addition, they declare the actions and the plans they can execute.

The RT-Activity diagrams allow for description of agents plans. The RT-Sequence diagrams describe agents' collaborations (and/or competitions). Their main goal is to define exchanges of messages and events (real-time stimula)

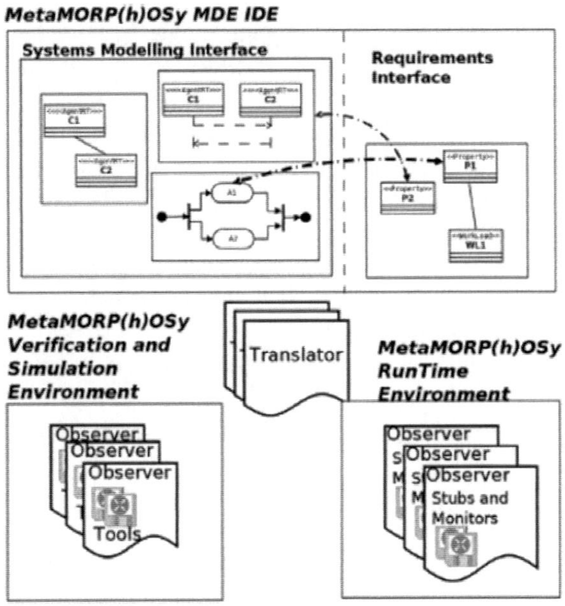

Fig. 1. Architecture of MetaMORP(h)OSy

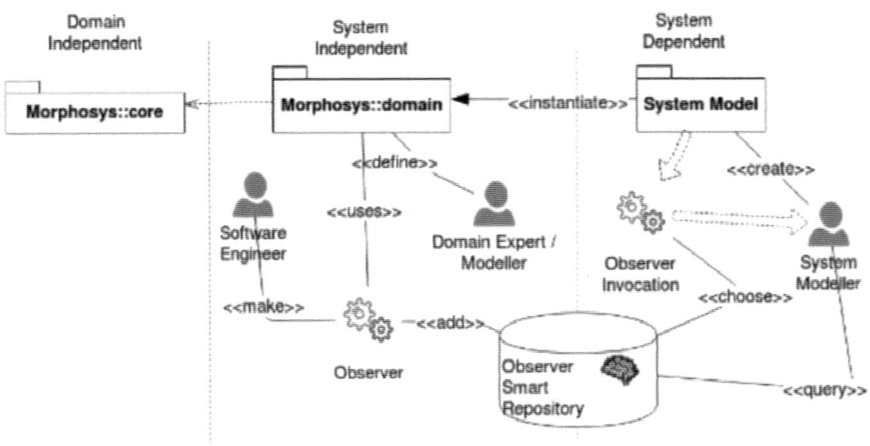

Fig. 2. MetaMORP(h)OSy component architecture

during execution of agents plans. As seen in Amato and Moscato 2015[9], main elements of RT-Agent diagram meta-model are depicted in Figure 2.

The *AgentRT* stereotype defines the structure of agents. The *PlanRT* stereotype defines the plans, which in turn define the behaviour of agents. Plans are associated with objectives, and typically these are common to multiple agents, who will work together to achieve them.

The *DgoalRT* stereotype defines decidable targets for *AgentRTs*, where a decidable target is a target whose reachability can be achieved under real-time constraints. The *BeliefRT* stereotype is used to model what the agent knows, in terms of internal status, the information about other agents and the external environment.

Stereotypes needed to model agent plans are defined in the *RT-Activity* diagram profile. *RT-Activity* Diagram inherits all these elements from the *UML Activity Diagram*, redefining states and transitions to specify real-time constraints. There are six stereotypes created ad-hoc:

ActionStateRT, *InitialState*, *FinalState*, *TransitionRT*, *SendObjectRT* and *ReceiveObjectRT*. When an agent starts a plan, he has information about his surroundings.

These Beliefs usually make up the initial state of the activity diagram, and they are specified as properties of the Initial State Stereotype. *FinalState* refers to a *DGoalRT*, and it is the final state of the activity diagram. Usually the temporal properties are relative to the final state. *ActionStateRT* derives from the classic state of the Activity Diagram UML. It is basically a state subject to real-time constraints. The stereotype in fact includes properties such as *ExecActionTime*, that is the time it takes to execute the action. In particular, to describe situations in which an agent sends or receives objects (messages or events), the stereotypes *SendObjectRT* and *ReceiveObjectRT* have been introduced. The last stereotype introduced for Activity Diagrams is TransitionRT, which is used to define time constraints on state transitions.

2.3 Model Components

Main elements of the RT-Sequence Diagram are *StimulusRT* and *MultiStimulusRT*. Before introducing the stereotype *StimulusRT* we recall the fact that a sequence diagram is basically composed by objects and lifelines. In this context, stimuli are messages that objects can send to themselves. There are five types of stimuli: *Call*, *Send*, *Return*, *Create* and *Destroy*. *StimulusRT* is used, therefore, to define stimuli subject to real-time constraints. Each *StimulusRT* element has the following properties:

- **StartTime**: when the decision to send a message during the pian is made.
- **SendTime** : when the message is sent.
- **TransmissionTime** : the time required to transmit the message.
- **StartReceiveTime** : the time the receiver starts receiving the message.
- **EndReceiveTime**: the time when the receiver has finished receiving the message.

– **Deadline** : the deadline for broadcasting.
– **MessageSync**: used to specify whether the message is synchronous or not.

MultiStimulusRT is derived from the *StimulusRT* stereotype, and it is used to define redundancy in message reception. MetaMORP(h)OSy has separate profiles for defining requirements and properties of systems. This allows to demand different requirements on the same system at different times, which is why requirement and property specifications are defined outs ide of the agent stereotypes.

A requirement is a list of properties that Observers will analyse on the models (at design-time or run-time). The properties can be functional or non-functional.

MetaMORP(h)OSy basic profile for properties defines stereo types for properties such as Availability, Reliability, Schedulability, Performances, etc. Obviously, if the properties are non-functional, it is necessary to define metrics for their definition, evaluation and monitoring. Users can add other metrics and properties to the basic MetaMORP(h)OSy profile.

Proper modules called Obervers (whose structure is defined in the modelling profile too) choose the best suitable Translator in the framework to execute proper Model Transformations and to verify requirements.

Since MetaMORP(h)OSy covers all system life cycle, it uses particular Observers at run-time for monitoring and testing purposes. So, Observers are divided by the profile into: Design Time Observers and Run Time Observers. They can be further specialized depending on translation algorithm, and analysis methods are used to analyse properties and requirements on system components.

Observers can be associated to Structural and behavioural components and obviously to the property to analyse or to monitor, as well as to the metrics used to collect and to produce results. The Observers introduce the intelligence needed to automate the system analysis. They are generated from the analysis models and they are dependent on the kind of the analysis that must be performed.

The Observers are in charge of automatically establishing and realizing the specific MDE approach to validation and verification of the system under study. They use the UML models of the system and the information contained in the analysis models in order to choose a suitable analysis process and generate the formal models needed to fulfil the analysis objectives. They enact the process, also invoking the proper analysis/solution tools. The overall MetaMORP(h)OSy component architecture is depicted in figure 2.

3 Application to e-health domain

This section describes the specialization of MetaMORP(h)OSy methodology applied in processing data[14, 15] for the E-Health domain, using results from Amato and Moscato 2015[9]. The first step is to extend the MetaMORP(h)OSy RT-AML profile for the specific application domain. For this purpose, it is necessary to extend both the AgentRT and BeliefRT stereotypes.

These new Agents specialize the *AgentRT* stereotype are:

- **Patient** represents the entity that possess Electronic Health Record and grant the authorizations for the access to records by other agents;
- **DataController**: users can use this stereotype in order to declare agents like Hospitals that implement the E-Health system ;
- DataProcessor stereotype defines providers for records management and storing;
- **DataSubProcessor** usually refers to Cloud Storage providers;
- **Physician** is the entity related to doctors that interacts with patients. In particular, Family doctors and doctors who are eventually involved in emergencies specialize this stereotype.

The *BeliefRT* is specialized introducing:

- **HealthRecord**: the electronic health record of the patient;
- **EnCryptedHR**: encrypted version of the health record;
- **HiddenRecord**: used for hiding the health record to any agent able to read the patient's data;
- **EncryptKey**: used to encrypt data;
- **DecryptKey**: used to decrypt data;
- **AccessAuth**: physicians authorizations;

Please note that access to encrypted data is achieved through the coupled use of encryption and decryption keys. In Amato and Moscato 2015[9], verification of Privacy has been traced back to a problem of state reachability of some goals with given configuration of beliefs.

The goal is to obtain the following behavior: if an agent executes a plan, whose goal is reachable. In case of access of a patient's record without having any valid authorization, the verification must fail.

In Amato and Moscato 2015[9] there are some simplifying assumptions for the requirement verification:

- communication network is considered secure;
- in the example, only one health record is considered;
- encryption exploits asymmetric algorithms;
- key sharing protocols are considered safe and they will not be explicitly considered.

The problem is the storage of the health record on a third-party storage server (DataProvider in the following).

The generic owner of the record is a patient (thePatient in the following). ThePatient can always read its Health Record (HR). In order to store the record on the storage service provider, a previous encryption of the record has to be done.

The encryption is executed directly on the patient's smart device. The doctor (theDoctor) can access the record only if it is authorized by thePatient. By the way, the doctor cannot own the description key of thePatient. For this reason, during the authorization process, theDoctor shares its encryption key with the Patient, so that it can encrypt the HR using this key.

In order to manage emergencies, thePatient stores on the DataProvider another encrypted version of its HR. This time, in the encryption process, a common key is used.

DataProvider, thePatient and theDoctor have been defined as agents, so they must be described in a structural view with appropriate Agent Diagrams. A BeliefDesire-Intention logic approach has been used in defining Agent Diagrams.

Its beliefs contain information about thePatient's, theDoctor's and emergency keys. In this diagram only three plans have been considered:

- Save: for saving the record on DataProvider;
- ReadRecord: to read the record from DataProvider;
- Authorize: to grant authorization to doctors to retrieve encrypted records from DataProvider.

Each Plan is associated to a Goal. It is reached when the final action of the plan is executed. It is important to notice that beliefs with the same name share the same information between agents.

For each agent plan, the user must define an activity diagram. In the following it will be reported activity diagrams of Save and Authorize plans. Please recall the fact that plans are used to reach a goal, and very often this is obtained thanks to the communication between agents. This concept brings the notion of synchronization, expressed in the activity diagrams through guards on control flow edges. Guards contain declarations of events that are asserted or waited during plans executions.

The activity diagram we are going to analyse is the Save plan diagram, depicted in Figure 3. The objects on the left side of an activity diagram correspond to the diagram inputs, while the objects on the right side correspond to the diagram outputs. Please notice that in the Save plan there are three parallel requests for saving the record encrypted using: its encryption key, its common encryption key for emergencies and its authorized doctor's encryption key.

The second activity diagram, depicted in Figure 4, describes the Read plan.

It shows actions that are executed by theDoctor when it requests a normal authorization to read the health record. Please notice that in this diagram there are two final states: one linked to the failure of the plan (ErrorAuth?) and one linked to the success of the plan (after receiving OkAuth!, it starts the decryption, and then theDoctor can access the record).

To finish the behavioral description of the system, proper sequence diagrams must be provided, in these diagrams, asserted events, which appear in agents' activity diagrams, are declared.

At the end of structural and behavioral description of the system, the user must prepare an Observer Diagram to declare the type of the analyses and monitoring activities it want to perform on the system.

MetaMORP(h)OSy offers many Observers which are already implemented. In some cases, it could be useful to define an ad-hoc Observer algorithm, such as it was done in Amato and Moscato 2015[9], in order to specify particular requirements on the model (like data privacy). In the following, it is reported

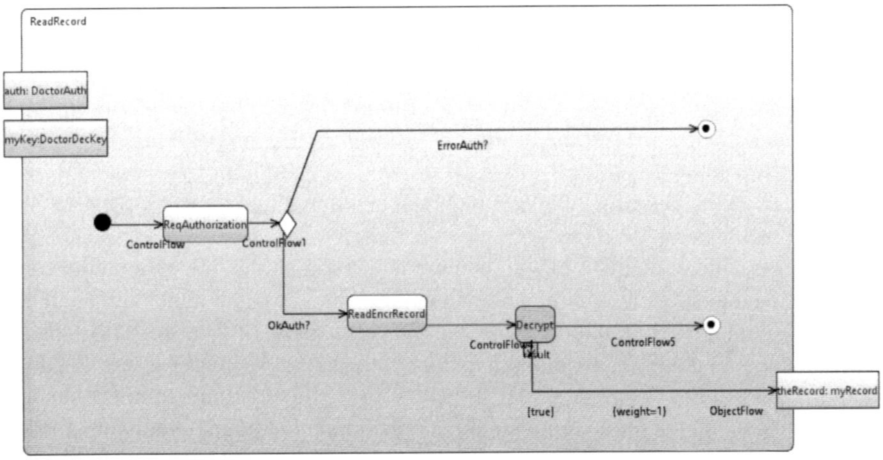

Fig. 3. Save Plan Activity Diagram

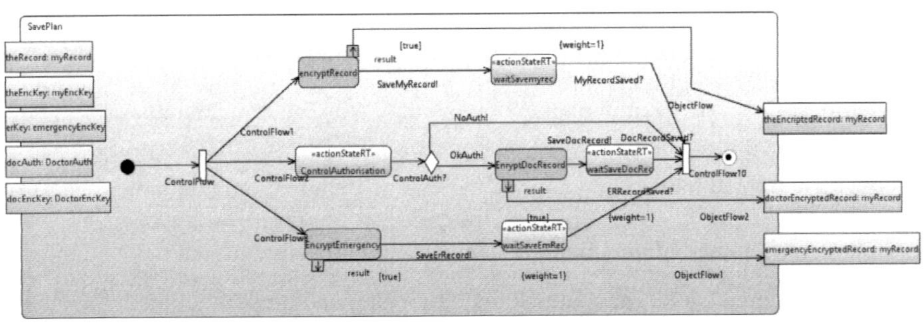

Fig. 4. Read Record Plan Activity Diagram

the solution proposed in the previously cited article. This algorithm translates the design model into Timed Automata.

A timed automaton is a finite state machine extended with a finite set of real-valued clocks. During a run of a timed automaton, clock values increase all with the same speed. Along the transitions of the automaton, clock values can be compared to integers. These comparisons are used in order to evaluate automaton transitions.

Without deepening into details, the Observer algorithm translates the RT-AML models D into a Timed Automata. This allows the use of Timed Automata analysis tools for verifying requirements. The last thing that has to be done is the translation of the data privacy requirement in an analyzable property for a Timed Automata Model Checker.

In Amato and Moscato 2015[9], the privacy requirement is expressed in terms of state reachability. The tool that the authors of the article used as model checker is Uppaal. It is a powerful tool for modelling, validation and verification of real-time systems modelled as timed automata. Uppaal supports Timed-Computational Tree Logics (CTL) for queries specification and model checking. Again, without deepening into details, it is possible to translate privacy requirements into a CTL formula. This formula become our property to be analyzed by using Uppaal. In Amato and Moscato 2015[9], two CTL formulas were defined in order to verify the privacy requirement, and the Observer has assured that the model previously described satisfies both. In the second example made in chapter 2, one of the CTL formulas used in Amato and Moscato 2015[9] was translated in a set of Prolog rules, simplifying their function.

4 Conclusions

In this work we have shown that the adoption of Multi-Agent System models, combined with the use of Model-Driven Engineering can provide significant advantages. The combination of MAS and MDE leads flexibility and intelligence in the analysis of properties and requirements of systems.

Frameworks like MetaMORP(h)OSy helps us in automating (or semi-automating) the verification and validation process. When adopting this framework, the user only needs to derive his particular modelling profile from the standard Meta MORP(h)OSy's RT-AML meta-model. As a further step, the user must produce proper diagrams and observers, in order to analyse system properties and requirements in the correct way.

In the last part of the work, an architectural description of MetaMORP(h)OSy is provided, with specific focus on its RT-AML profile specialization for particular purposes. It has been described, in addition, an example of MetaMORP(h)OSy application in E-Health domain.

Through this work, the advantages of using MetaMORP(h)OSy, in system property analysis have been highlighted for e-Health domain. We firmly believe that this kind of applications will be adopted and developed not only in the academic world, but certainly in industry world, too.

5 Acknowledge

This work was funded by "Synergy-net: Research and Digital Solutions against Cancer" Project (funded in the framework of the POR Campania FESR 2014-2020).

References

1. A. Amato, G. Cozzolino, and M. Giacalone. Opinion mining in consumers food choice and quality perception. *Lecture Notes in Networks and Systems*, pages 310–317, 2020.
2. A. Amato, W. Balzano, G. Cozzolino, and F. Moscato. Analysis of consumers perceptions of food safety risk in social networks. *Advances in Intelligent Systems and Computing*, pages 1217–1227, 2020.
3. A. Castiglione, G. Cozzolino, V. Moscato, and G. Sperli. Analysis of community in social networks based on game theory. pages 619–626. Institute of Electrical and Electronics Engineers Inc., 2019.
4. A. Amato and G. Cozzolino. Trust analysis for information concerning food-related risks. *Lecture Notes on Data Engineering and Communications Technologies*, pages 344–354, 2019.
5. R. Canonico, G. Cozzolino, A. Ferraro, V. Moscato, A. Picariello, F.R. Sorrentino, and G. Sperlì. A smart chatbot for specialist domains. *Advances in Intelligent Systems and Computing*, pages 1003–1010, 2020.
6. Madeleine Faugere, Thimothee Bourbeau, Robert De Simone, and Sebastien Gerard. Marte: Also an uml profile for modeling aadl applications. In *12th IEEE International Conference on Engineering Complex Computer Systems (ICECCS 2007)*, pages 359–364. IEEE, 2007.
7. Douglas C Schmidt. Model-driven engineering. *COMPUTER-IEEE COMPUTER SOCIETY-*, (2):25, 2006.
8. Richard Soley et al. Model driven architecture. *OMG white paper*, (308):5, 2000.
9. Flora Amato and Francesco Moscato. A model driven approach to data privacy verification in e-health systems. *Trans. Data Privacy*, (3):273–296, 2015.
10. F. Amato, G. Cozzolino, V. Moscato, and F. Moscato. Analyse digital forensic evidences through a semantic-based methodology and nlp techniques. *Future Generation Computer Systems*, pages 297–307, 2019.
11. G. Cozzolino. Using semantic tools to represent data extracted from mobile devices. pages 530–536. Institute of Electrical and Electronics Engineers Inc., 2018.
12. Hermann Kopetz. *Real-time systems: design principles for distributed embedded applications*. Springer Science & Business Media, 2011.
13. Michael Wooldridge. Agent-based software engineering. *IEE Proceedings-software*, (1):26–37, 1997.
14. A. Amato, G. Cozzolino, and V. Moscato. Big data analytics for traceability in food supply chain. *Advances in Intelligent Systems and Computing*, pages 880–884, 2019.
15. F. Amato, G. Cozzolino, F. Moscato, V. Moscato, A. Picariello, and G. Sperli. Data mining in social network. *Smart Innovation, Systems and Technologies*, pages 53–63, 2019.

Formal Verification of Context Aware Systems *

Fabio A. Schreiber[1] [0000−0002−5237−0455] and Maria Elena Valcher[2] [0000−0002−7595−3688]

[1] DEIB - Politecnico di Milano {fabio.schreiber@polimi.it}
[2] DEI - University of Padova {meme@dei.unipd.it}

Discussion Paper

Abstract. This discussion paper introduces a modeling technique, based on Boolean Control Networks, for assessing useful properties of Context Aware systems. Indeed, Context Aware systems are becoming useful components in autonomic and monitoring applications and the assessment of their properties is an important step towards reliable implementation, especially in safety-critical applications.

Keywords: Boolean Control Networks (BCN) · Context Aware Systems · Fault detection · Formal properties · Pervasive Systems · Reconstructibility · Stability assessment.

1 Introduction and Related Works

Context-aware (C-A) computing was born out of the need to master, by using a component based approach, the growing complexity of modern software systems and enforcing the separation of concerns [9]. Among the most widely used definitions of Context, and of C-A Computing, those proposed by A. Dey [7] state: *"Context is any information that can be used to characterize the situation of an entity. An entity is a person, place, or object that is considered relevant to the interaction between a user and an application, including the user and applications themselves."* and *"A system is Context-aware if it uses context to provide relevant information and/or services to the user, where relevancy depends on the users task."*

Accordingly, sophisticated and general Context models have been proposed, to support C-A applications that: (i) tailor the set of application-relevant data, (ii) increase the precision of information retrieval, (iii) discover services, (iv) build smart environments, and others [2].

In the domains of Databases and Programming Languages, the design of C-A and Self-adapting systems has been frequently based on the separation between Context and functional systems [1, 15]. The introduction of Context-awareness and Self-adaptation in safety-critical applications led to the need for specifying and assessing their properties, mainly those related to the system dependability, by means of formal methods such as Bigraphs and model-checking [6, 9].

In [13, 14] Padovitz et Al. consider a state-space approach for describing the *situation* dimension and for determining the likelihood of transitions between *situation subspaces*, all other Context dimensions remaining constant. The likelihood of the transition is evaluated by assuming notions analogous to those of velocity and acceleration in

*Fabio A. Schreiber was partially supported by INAIL, RECKON Project..

mechanical systems.
Stability is a traditional topic in control systems theory, and in [8] the authors explore "*... the extent to which control theory can provide an architectural and analytic foundation for building self-managing systems ...*". However, control systems are typically described by means of differential equations and by Matrix Algebra, while C-A systems are digital and mostly based on Logics. Inspired by biological systems, Boolean Networks (BN) and Boolean Control Networks (BCN) have been introduced, their representative equations have been converted into an equivalent algebraic form, and solutions to problems such as controllability, observability, stability and reconstructibility have been proposed [3, 10, 12].

In Section 2 the case study is outlined. In Section 3, we show how, by making use of the algebraic approach to Boolean Control Networks, it is possible to formalize, by means of a C-A system, a decision process to avoid hydrogeological disasters, as the one that happened in Abruzzo, where a hotel was hit by an avalanche [16], as well as false alarms. We can then assess the existence of globally attractive equilibrium points of the overall system, corresponding to constant inputs, and investigate some interesting structural properties such as observability and reconstructibility that formalize system features of great practical relevance. Moreover, the possibility of identifying some kinds of faults in the inputs, that could result in errors in the alarm system, is examined. Sections 4 and 5 respectively describe the results of the analysis and possible future developments.

To conclude, we think that cooperation between C-A computing and Control Systems theory can be fruitful to fill in the model gap.

2 The architecture of the monitoring system

Figure 1 shows the architecture of a C-A system [2, 7] conceived for monitoring possible snow/ground slides. Signals, coming from physical sensors on the ground, are evaluated in the context of the seismic and meteorological information provided by Web Services RSSs - which can suggest immediate danger - in order to issue alarms. The *integration* of data from the Context state with the actual physical data that are input to the functional system allows the design of a flexible and effective prevention information system which, as an example, can distinguish between the vibration caused by the detachment of a snow mass and the one caused by a skier or a deer occasionally passing near a sensor.

In the monitoring system some states produce outputs that can affect the environment, e.g. by possibly activating an alarm siren. In case of an alarm, the time to evacuate a hotel can be in the order of hours, while the seismic and meteorological conditions can change faster. The ultimate goal of this study is to be sure that, in dangerous situations, an alarm signal is issued, but at the same time that frequent changes in the Context State do not induce an oscillatory behavior of the alarm system and the resulting movement of people out and back into the hotel; the designer of the C-A system must ensure that no action is started before the preceding one is terminated. In this paper we use a simple open-loop model; however, in more complex C-A self managing applications, the system output can affect the context itself.

Our aim is therefore:

- To describe a C-A system, as in Figure 1, by means of a logic State Space model: web services provide input messages to the Context and sensors provide input signals to the Monitoring System; the Context state is a further input to the latter.
- To use BCNs and System Theory tools to asses properties of a C-A system such as: the existence of globally stable equilibrium points and the absence of oscillatory behaviors (limit cycles) under constant inputs; the reconstructibility of the system and the detection of some faults affecting the C-A system inputs.

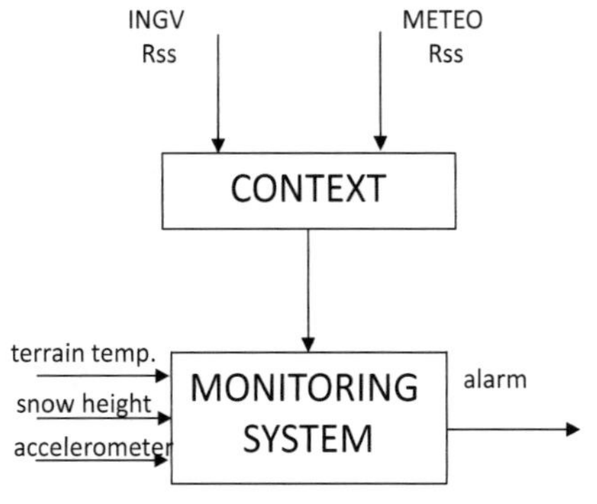

Fig. 1. Open loop Context Aware system

Although the following analysis refers to the case study, the proposed approach is quite general and can be applied whenever properties should be proved in C-A dynamic systems.

3 The BCN Model of the Hydrogeological Example

In [16] a short introduction to the algebraic representation of Boolean Control Networks can be found; in the following we introduce the BCN model of our example case.

3.1 The Context model

Context Input Variables The values of the Context Input Variables are supplied by RSS messages coming from National Web Services, such as Meteorological forecasts and the National Geophysics Institute. Even if the message frequency can be variable, for ease of modeling, we suppose that the system samples them with the same constant frequency. Moreover, we suppose that a real danger situation can be expected only when a defined number - in our example at least four - of consecutive earthquake announcements are sent together with a snow forecast.

We assume:

INGV$\{earthquake, \neg earthquake\}$:= U_1

METEO$\{snow, \neg snow\}$:=U_2

Therefore, by expressing the context input variables in terms of canonical vectors, we get:

$$\text{Context Input Vector} = \mathbf{u}(\mathrm{t}) = \begin{vmatrix} U_1 & U_2 \\ U_1 & \neg U_2 \\ \neg U_1 & U_2 \\ \neg U_1 & \neg U_2 \end{vmatrix} \in \Delta_4 := \{\delta_4^1, \delta_4^2, \delta_4^3, \delta_4^4\}$$

where δ_n^k is the canonical vector of size n whose kth entry is unitary.

Context States As previously mentioned, we assume that simultaneous snow and earthquake alerts can be regarded as reliable only if not isolated, namely if a sufficiently high number of consecutive (simultaneous) alerts are sent (and received). For this reason we introduce as Context State a counter: COUNTER$\{0, 1, 2, 3, > 3\}$ =: C
In the representation by means of canonical vectors, the counter is denoted by $\mathbf{c}$ and takes values in $\Delta_5 := \{\delta_5^1, \delta_5^2, \delta_5^3, \delta_5^4, \delta_5^5\}$, depending on how many consecutive simultaneous alerts for snow and earthquake have been received. Specifically, for $i = 1, 2, 3, 4$, we have that $\mathbf{c}(t) = \delta_5^i$ if the counter is $i-1$ at time t, while $\mathbf{c}(t) = \delta_5^5$ if the counter is at least 4 at time t. If the counter at time t has a value in $\{\delta_5^1, \delta_5^2, \delta_5^3, \delta_5^4\}$ and the context input is $\mathbf{u}(t) = \delta_4^1$ (another simultaneous snow and earthquake alert comes in), then the counter value at $t+1$ is increased by 1. If $\mathbf{c}(t) = \delta_5^5$ and $\mathbf{u}(t) = \delta_4^1$, then $\mathbf{c}(t+1) = \delta_5^5$, while in every other case the counter is reset to $\mathbf{c}(t+1) = \delta_5^1$.
Therefore, the counter updates according to the following model (BCN):
$\mathbf{c}(t+1) = \mathbf{C} \ltimes \mathbf{u}(t) \ltimes \mathbf{c}(t)$, where $\ltimes$ denotes the semi-tensor product, $C = \begin{bmatrix} C_1 & C_2 & C_3 & C_4 \end{bmatrix} \in \mathscr{L}_{5\times 20}$, the set of logic matrices of size 5×20, and
$C_1 = C \ltimes \delta_4^1 = [\delta_5^2\ \delta_5^3\ \delta_5^4\ \delta_5^5\ \delta_5^5]$
$C_2 = C \ltimes \delta_4^2 = [\delta_5^1\ \delta_5^1\ \delta_5^1\ \delta_5^1\ \delta_5^1]$
$C_3 = C \ltimes \delta_4^3 = C_2$
$C_4 = C \ltimes \delta_4^4 = C_2$
Obviously, *the number of consecutive alert situations is a design variable which allows to set stricter - if increased - or loser - if lowered - requirements on the alarm system.*

Context Output Introduce the Context model output
CONTEXT-ALERT$\{danger, quiet\}$:= U_c
Since we assume that the CONTEXT-ALERT variable U_c is *danger* (the corresponding canonical vector $\mathbf{u}_c$ takes the value δ_2^1) if and only if there have been at least four simultaneous snow and earthquake alerts, the variable $\mathbf{u}_c$ is updated following the algebraic rule:
$\mathbf{u}_c(t) = \mathbf{H_c} \ltimes \mathbf{c}(t)$ where
$\mathbf{H_c} = \begin{bmatrix} \delta_2^2\ \delta_2^2\ \delta_2^2\ \delta_2^2\ \delta_2^1 \end{bmatrix} \in \mathscr{L}_{2\times 5}$

Figure 2 shows the state diagram for the Context automaton.

This is one possible solution, but it may be regarded as somewhat dangerous: if the counter is erroneously reset, then the alert ends up being significantly delayed. An alternative solution could be that of simply decreasing the counter by one if $\mathbf{u}(t) \neq \delta_4^1$ (or if $\mathbf{u}(t) = \delta_4^i, i = 2, 3$). This solution would be more robust to possible disturbances occasionally affecting the context inputs.

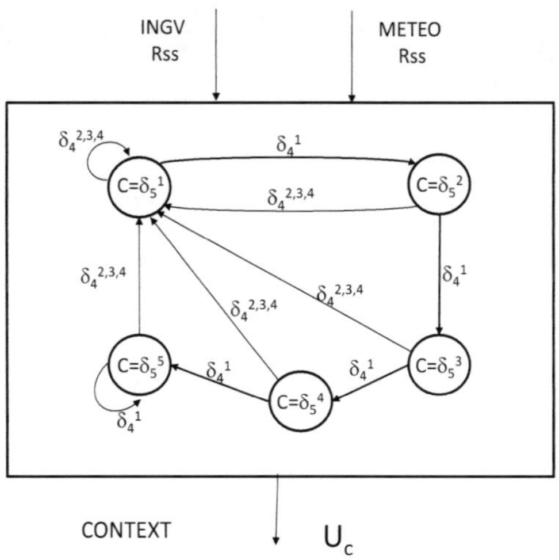

Fig. 2. Context State diagram for the hydrogeological example

3.2 The Functional System model

Functional System Input Variables We assume that, in addition to the CONTEXT-ALERT variable, the Functional System model receives three more input signals from local sensors, so that, at the end, the Input Vector $\mathbf{v}(t) \in \Delta_{16}$ is composed by the following variables determining the system dynamics:

terrain temperature $\{high, low\} := V_1$
snow height $\{high, low\} := V_2$
accelerometer $\{high, low\} := V_3$
context-alert $\{danger, quiet\} := V_4 = U_c$

Functional System State The CONTEXT-ALERT input is already the result of repeated and consecutive notifications of alert situations, so we may regard it as a variable that is hardly affected by false alarms. Also, we assume that a disturbance that can instantaneously modify the terrain temperature or the snow height, unless connected with an earthquake, is statistically not very realistic. On the other hand, the accelerometer may be a source of false alarms since it can detect a "high" signal for reasons that are not related to earthquakes: for instance, animals running close to the accelerometer. As a result, we regard as reliable only repeated alerts coming from the accelerometer. So, as in the case of simultaneous snow and earthquake warnings, we require that the accelerometer has been "high" for two consecutive time instants (before t) in order to regard the information given by the accelerometer as a real warning. Therefore, we introduce the state variable:

ACC-COUNTER$\{0, 1, > 1\}$

The canonical vector representing the accelerometer counter is denoted by $\mathbf{a}$ and takes values in $\Delta_3 = \{\delta_3^1, \delta_3^2, \delta_3^3\}$. Specifically, $\mathbf{a}(t) = \delta_3^1$ if the counter is 0 at time t; $\mathbf{a}(t) = \delta_3^2$ if the counter is 1 at time t; and $\mathbf{a}(t) = \delta_3^3$ if the counter is at least 2 at time t. If the counter at time t has a value in $\{\delta_3^1, \delta_3^2\}$ and the accelerometer vector is $\mathbf{v}_3(t) = \delta_2^1$, then the counter value at $t+1$ is increased by 1. If $\mathbf{a}(t) = \delta_3^3$ and $\mathbf{v}_3(t) = \delta_2^1$, then $\mathbf{a}(t+1) = \delta_3^3$, while when $\mathbf{v}_3(t) = \delta_2^2$ the counter is moved back to $\mathbf{a}(t+1) = \delta_3^1$. Therefore, the accelerometer counter updates according to the following BCN:

$\mathbf{a}(t+1) = \mathbf{A} \ltimes \mathbf{v_3}(t) \ltimes \mathbf{a}(t)$, where $A = \begin{bmatrix} A_1 \ A_2 \end{bmatrix} \in \mathscr{L}_{3\times 6}$, and
$A_1 = A \ltimes \delta_2^1 = [\delta_3^2\ \delta_3^3\ \delta_3^3]$
$A_2 = A \ltimes \delta_2^2 = [\delta_3^1\ \delta_3^1\ \delta_3^1]$

Functional System Output We assume that the Functional System output can take three values:
ALARM $\{temp-high, snow-high, acc-counter > 1, acc-high, ctx-danger\}$
ATTENTION $\{temp-low, snow-high, acc-counter-*, acc-*, ctx-*\ OR\ temp-high, snow-low, acc-counter-*, acc-*, ctx-*\ OR\ temp-high, snow-high, acc-counter-low, acc-*, ctx-*\ OR\ temp-high, snow-high, acc-counter-*, acc-low, ctx-*\ OR\ temp-high, snow-high, acc-counter-*, acc-*, ctx-quiet\}$
NORMAL $\{temp-low, snow-low, acc-counter-*, acc-*, ctx-*\}$
Note that the alarm is sent out only when "$acc-counter > 1$" *and* "acc-high". This means that at the time t^* the alarm signal is issued if the accelerometer has detected some movement for at least three consecutive time instants t^*, t^*-1 and t^*-2. Of course, as for the context-alert variable, *the choice of how long we want to wait before issuing the alarm signal is a design parameter that balances conflicting requirements: security on the one hand and the need to avoid false alarms on the other.*

The functional system output is denoted by $\mathbf{m}$ and takes values in Δ_3. Based on the previous description of the three possible output values, it follows that the output vector is generated based on the state $\mathbf{a}(t)$ and the input $\mathbf{v}(t)$ according to the following model:
$\mathbf{m}(t) = \mathbf{M} \ltimes \mathbf{v}(t) \ltimes \mathbf{a}(t)$, where $\mathbf{M} = \begin{bmatrix} M_1\ M_2\ \dots\ M_{16} \end{bmatrix} \in \mathscr{L}_{6\times 16}$, and
$M_1 = M \ltimes \delta_{16}^1 = [\delta_3^2\ \delta_3^2\ \delta_3^1]$
$M_2 = M \ltimes \delta_{16}^2 = [\delta_3^2\ \delta_3^2\ \delta_3^2]$
$M_i = M \ltimes \delta_{16}^i = M_2, \quad \text{for} \quad i = 3, \dots, 12$
$M_{13} = M \ltimes \delta_{16}^{13} = [\delta_3^3\ \delta_3^3\ \delta_3^3]$
$M_i = M \ltimes \delta_{16}^i = M_{13}, \quad \text{for} \quad i = 14, 15, 16$

So, overall, the system model is a BCN obtained by connecting the BCN describing the context and the BCN describing the functional model, and hence it is described by the following equations:

$$\mathbf{c}(t+1) = \mathbf{C} \ltimes \mathbf{u}(t) \ltimes \mathbf{c}(\mathbf{t}) \tag{1}$$
$$\mathbf{a}(t+1) = \mathbf{A} \ltimes \mathbf{v_3}(\mathbf{t}) \ltimes \mathbf{a}(\mathbf{t}) \tag{2}$$
$$\mathbf{v}_4(t) = \mathbf{H_c} \ltimes \mathbf{c}(t) \tag{3}$$
$$\mathbf{m}(t) = \mathbf{M} \ltimes \mathbf{v}(t) \ltimes \mathbf{a}(t). \tag{4}$$

Note that the previous system could be represented as a standard BCN having $\mathbf{u}(t) := \mathbf{u}(t) \ltimes \mathbf{v}_1(t) \ltimes \mathbf{v}_2(t) \ltimes \mathbf{v}_3(t)$ as input, $\mathbf{x}(t) := \mathbf{c}(t) \ltimes \mathbf{a}(t)$ as state vector, and $\mathbf{y}(t) = \mathbf{m}(t)$ as output. Such a representation, however, would be of larger dimension and would not contribute to a better understanding of the system properties. On the contrary, it would make the overall analysis more complicated. So, we investigate the model properties by making use of the previous description (1) - (4). This provides further evidence of the convenience of using C-A systems to model the system dynamics. Note that the current cascade structure, having two counter variables as state variables of the two connected BCNs, can be easily adapted to model a large class of C-A systems that describe a decision process, in particular, an alert system. So, even if we focus on this specific model, it is immediate to understand how the results and properties derived in the following extend to all the alert systems that can be modelled as the cascade of a Context and a Functional Systems, both of the them affected by external signals and measurements, and whose target is to generate alert/alarm notifications based on the occurrence of specific (possibly repeated) combinations of data.

4 The main results

In [16] we present a detailed description of the kind of reasoning that can be made using the model developed in the previous sections. Here we only mention the main results, referring to the original paper for a full treatment.

- We use definitions and methods as in [4, 5, 11] to find equilibrium points of BCNs corresponding to constant inputs. The analysis shows that *no limit cycles can appear in the system, and hence no contradicting alarm messages can be delivered by it.*
- Observability does not seem to be a fundamental system property for the hydrogeological model, since identifying the initial state of the system during some observation interval does not bring any practical advantage. On the other hand, reconstructibility is a more relevant property to investigate: by identifying the current system state, say $\mathbf{x}(T)$, from the observation of the input and the output in some time interval $[0,T]$, *one may anticipate whether an alert signal will lead to an alarm signal at the next time instant or not and hence be ready to run away or to provide support.* The analysis shows that *the hydrogeological system described by* (1)-(2)-(3)-(4) *is reconstructible and the definition of reconstructibility holds for* $T = 4$.
- Detection of *stuck-in faults.* We proved that *Given the hydrogeological system described by* (1)-(2)-(3)-(4), *a stuck-in fault for one of the state variables,* $\mathbf{c}(t)$ *or* $\mathbf{a}(t)$, *cannot be identified corresponding to all the input sequences, but if one of the counters gets stuck at a value that is not maximum, thus preventing the possible generation of an alarm, then the previous state estimator always allows to detect and identify the stuck-in fault at latest after* $T = 4$ *times instants from the fault occurrence.* Note, finally, that a false alarm cannot possibly be issued, because this would require not only that one of the counters is stuck to the maximum value but also that the other is at the maximum value in turn and the inputs are all high, but *this is the case when the alarm message should be issued!*

5 Conclusions and future work

In this paper we model a simple Context-aware system as a Boolean Control Network in order to use the powerful tools typical of system theory, which apply to linear analog systems, also to digital systems, whose properties are usually expressed by logical rules. The ultimate goal is to pave the way to formally assess reliability and safety properties of self adapting safety critical systems. The existence of globally attractive equilibrium points under constant input and the reconstructibility of the system have been proved, as well as the possibility of identifying some faults which could adversely affect the system output.

The main advantages of the proposed approach are on the one hand to provide a solid system theoretic framework where intuitive and practical features or goals for Context-aware systems can be properly formalised, on the other hand to offer rigorous algebraic tools to test these properties and solve those problems. The proposed solutions are easily converted into computer algorithms. We are working to apply these techniques to more complex feedback systems, where the output of the functional systems can affect in turn the state of the Context, and to enhance fault tolerance by considering possible correlations among the sensors and other system input/output devices.

References

1. Bolchini, C., Curino, C., Orsi, G., Quintarelli, E., Rossato, R., Schreiber, F.A., Tanca, L.: And what can context do for data? Commun. ACM **52**(11), 136–140 (2009). https://doi.org/10.1145/1592761.1592793, https://doi.org/10.1145/1592761.1592793
2. Bolchini, C., Curino, C., Quintarelli, E., Schreiber, F.A., Tanca, L.: A data-oriented survey of context models. ACM SIGMOD Record **36, n.4**, 19–26 (2007)
3. Cheng, D., Qi, H.: Controllability and observability of Boolean Control Networks. Automatica **45**(7), 1659 – 1667 (2009)
4. Cheng, D., Qi, H., Li, Z.: Analysis and control of Boolean networks. Springer-Verlag, London (2011)
5. Cheng, D., Qi, H., Li, Z., Liu, J.B.: Stability and stabilization of Boolean networks. Int. J. Robust Nonlin. Contr. **21**, 134–156 (2011)
6. Cherfia, T.A., Belala, F., Barkaoui, K.: Towards formal modeling and verification of context-aware systems. In: VECoS (2014)
7. Dey, A.K.: Understanding and using context. Personal Ubiquitous Computing **5**(1), 4–7 (January 2001)
8. Diao, Y., Hellerstein, J.L., Parekh, S., Griffith, R., Kaiser, G., Phung, D.: Self-managing systems: A control theory foundation. In: 12th IEEE - ECBS'05. pp. 441–448 (April 2005)
9. Djoudi, B., Bouanaka, C., Zeghib, N.: A formal framework for context-aware systems specification and verification. J. Syst. Softw. **122**(C), 445–462 (Dec 2016). https://doi.org/10.1016/j.jss.2015.11.035, https://doi.org/10.1016/j.jss.2015.11.035
10. Fornasini, E., Valcher, M.E.: Observability, reconstructibility and state observers of Boolean control networks. IEEE Tran. Aut. Contr. **58 (6)**, 1390 – 1401 (2013)
11. Fornasini, E., Valcher, M.E.: On the periodic trajectories of Boolean Control Networks. Automatica **49**, 1506–1509 (2013)
12. Fornasini, E., Valcher, M.E.: Recent developments in Boolean Control Networks. Journal of Control and Decision **3**(1), 1–18 (2016)
13. Padovitz, A., Zaslavsky, A.B., Loke, S.W., Burg, B.: Stability in context-aware pervasive systems: A state-space modeling approach. In: INSTICC. pp. 129–138 (2004)
14. Padovitz, A., Zaslavsky, A.B., Loke, S.W., Burg, B.: Maintaining continuous dependability in sensor-based context-aware pervasive computing systems. Proceedings of the 38th Hawaii International Conference on System Sciences (2005)
15. Schreiber, F.A., Panigati, E.: Context-aware self adapting systems: a ground for the cooperation of data, software, and services. IJNGC **8**(1) (2017), http://perpetualinnovation.net/ojs/index.php/ijngc/article/view/364
16. Schreiber, F.A., Valcher, M.E.: Formal assessment of some properties of context-aware systems. IJNGC **10**(3), 163–177 (2019), http://arxiv.org/abs/2005.00373

Where Porceddu is better than Pasta (DISCUSSION PAPER)

Paolo Ciaccia[1], Davide Martinenghi[2], and Riccardo Torlone[3]

[1]Università di Bologna [2]Politecnico di Milano [3]Università Roma Tre

Abstract. Preferences and contexts are fundamental aspects for deciding the best choices among possible options. We formalize the problem of *propagating preferences* from more generic to more specific contexts and study the key properties of propagation within an algebraic framework.

1 Introduction

Preferences and their influence on choices have been studied in a variety of fields, including psychology, sociology, economics, artificial intelligence, and data management. In all of the above fields, it is widely recognized that preferences highly depend on the *context*, as shown in the following example.

Example 1. We are ordering food at a restaurant in Italy: normally, then, we prefer pasta to beef. In Sardinia, though, we enjoy "porceddu" more than pasta. During summer, however, our preferred choice is just a fresh salad.

As in the example, we consider contexts as *states* (such as "Italy in summer") that can be compared via a *generalization hierarchy*, so that, say, "Sardinia" is more specific than "Italy". Preferences naturally *propagate* along the hierarchy, from the more generic to the more specific contexts (a preference defined for Italy normally holds in any Italian place). Things are not that simple, though.

Example 2. If we are in Sardinia in the summer, all the preferences given in Example 1 apply, since they refer to more generic contexts. Yet, the preferences defined in "Sardinia" and "Italy in summer" should take precedence over those given for "Italy", whereas the preference in "Sardinia" is on a par with the preference in "Italy in summer". Then, porceddu and salad are the best alternatives, since no other food is preferable to them in the given context.

Our research provides a principled approach to *context-aware preference propagation.* We develop a general framework whose only requirements are as follows:

- the contexts belong to a *poset*, i.e., a set C with a (strict) partial order relation $<_C$ on its elements: $c_1 <_C c_2$ means that the context c_1 is *more specific* than the context c_2 (and that c_2 is *more generic* than c_1);

- preferences define a strict partial order $\prec$ on the domain of objects O, where $o_1 \prec o_2$ means that the object o_2 *is preferable to* the object o_1;
- each stated preference is associated with one or more contexts.

The basic properties of the propagation process, implicitly at the basis of earlier approaches and naturally arising from the observations made for Example 2, are:

1. *coherence*: preferences only propagate from more generic contexts;
2. *fairness*: unordered contexts do not take precedence over each other;
3. *specificity*: a more specific context takes precedence over a more generic one.

Building on these properties, we focus on three main problems:

- (CFS) Determine whether there exist well-behaved (i.e., Coherent, Fair and Specific) methods for the propagation of preferences.
- (OrdRel) Efficiently determine the preference (order relation) between any two objects in a context according to a given propagation method.
- (Best) Establish the best objects in c wrt. the preferences propagated to c.

We tackle these problems through an axiomatization of the properties of propagation, and do so with an algebraic framework based on two abstract binary operators that express preference propagation by means of *Preference Composition* (PC) expressions: $+$ for unordered contexts, and $\rhd$ for ordered contexts.

Example 3. A possible PC-expression for propagating preferences to "summer in Sardinia" (c_4) is $c_4 \rhd ((c_2 + c_3) \rhd c_1)$. Here, first the preferences in "Sardinia" (c_2) and those in "summer in Italy" (c_3) are combined with $+$, since the two contexts are unordered. The result is then combined with the preferences in "Italy" (c_1) using $\rhd$, since this context is more generic than both c_2 and c_3. Finally, the result is combined with c_4 using $\rhd$, since this is the most specific context.

This paper summarizes some of the main findings reported in [3]. Here, we only focus on the axiomatization of $+$ and $\rhd$ and the study of their possible interpretations complying with the stated axioms. One of the main results is that, under mild assumptions, the well-known Pareto and Prioritized composition [1, 4] operators are the *only* possible interpretations of $+$ and $\rhd$, respectively.

Another notable achievement is a propagation method ($\mathcal{OC}$) that somehow provides the "ultimate" semantics for preference propagation. However, we refer to [3] for a full account of the solutions to Problems CFS and OrdRel. Here, we only hint at an algorithmic approach for propagating preferences according to the $\mathcal{OC}$ method, and characterize its asymptotic complexity, which, remarkably, is independent of the underlying domain size. Finally, we discuss how to determine the best objects according to the propagated preferences (Problem Best).

2 Preliminaries

We consider the well-known *binary relation model* for expressing preferences over a domain of objects O [1, 4, 8], where a *preference relation* over objects of a domain O is a strict partial order $\prec$ on O, associated with an unordered relation $\sim$. A refinement of $\sim$ allows some unordered objects to be considered as *indifferent*: an indifference relation $\approx$ is a reflexive, symmetric, and transitive subset of the unordered relation $\sim$ such that if $o_1 \approx o_2$ then, for all $o \in O$, $o_1 \prec o$ ($o \prec o_1$) entails $o_2 \prec o$ ($o \prec o_2$). If $o_1 \sim o_2$, but $o_1 \not\approx o_2$, then o_1 and o_2 are *incomparable*, denoted $o_1 \parallel o_2$.

Since $\parallel = \sim - \approx$, it suffices to consider the pair $\langle \prec, \approx \rangle$, collectively called a *preference structure*. Let θ be one of $\prec, \succ, \approx, \parallel$, where $\succ$ denotes the inverse of $\prec$; we say that the *order relation* between objects o_1 and o_2 is θ if $o_1 \theta o_2$.

Example 4. Let us consider the objects `pasta`, `beef`, `salad`, and `porceddu`. A possible preference structure over these objects is: `beef` $\prec$ `pasta`, `beef` $\prec$ `salad`, and `pasta` $\approx$ `salad`. In words, `pasta` and `salad` are both preferable to `beef`, whereas `pasta` and `salad` are indifferent. It follows that `porceddu` is incomparable with all other foods, i.e., `porceddu` $\parallel o$, for $o \in \{$`pasta`, `beef`, `salad`$\}$.

For a finite domain O, the best objects (i.e., maximal elements) in O according to $\prec$ can be selected by the *Best* operator $\beta_\prec(O) = \{o \in O \mid \nexists o' \in O, o \prec o'\}$. For instance, according to the preferences of Example 4, the best objects are $\beta_\prec(O) = \{$`pasta`, `salad`, `porceddu`$\}$. For any non-empty domain O, $\beta_\prec(O)$ is never empty [1]. In case O is infinite, $\beta_\prec$ is typically applied to a finite subset of O.

3 Preference Propagation

Throughout the paper we consider a context poset C and a domain O, and assume that each context $c \in C$ is associated with a preference structure $\langle \prec^c, \approx^c \rangle$ over O, called the *ground preference structure* in c. We also call $\langle \prec^C, \approx^C \rangle = \{\langle \prec^c, \approx^c \rangle \mid c \in C\}$ a *(preference structure) configuration* over C.

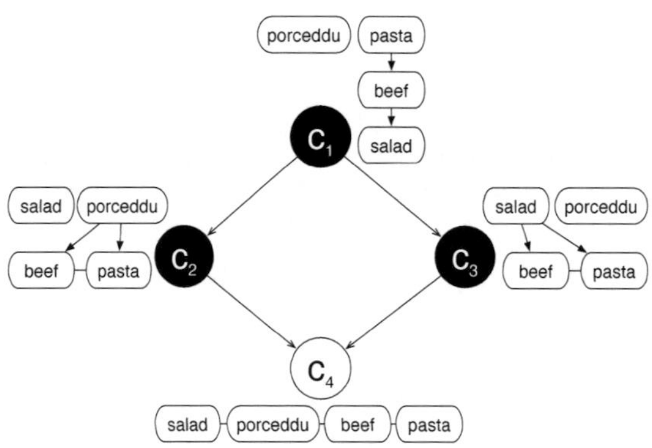

Fig. 1: A configuration for a context poset; each ground preference relation is shown next to its context (no ground preferences in c_4, shown as a white disk).

Example 5. The context poset in Figure 1 reports the ground preference structures discussed in Example 2. In context c_4 ("summer in Sardinia") all objects are indifferent. In context c_1 ("Italy"), pasta is preferable to beef and beef to salad, while, in context c_2 ("Sardinia"), porceddu is preferable to both pasta and beef, and pasta $\approx^{c_2}$ beef; similarly, pasta $\approx^{c_3}$ beef and pasta $\approx^{c_4}$ beef.

Preferences *propagate* along the poset C, and we call *complete preference relation* in c, denoted by ${}^{\mathcal{P}}{<}^{c}$, the result of combining $<^c$ with the ground preferences defined in the other contexts in C, according to a *propagation method* $\mathcal{P}$. Such a method also defines how indifference of objects is propagated to c, denoted by ${}^{\mathcal{P}}{\approx}^{c}$ (and thus also the unordered relation ${}^{\mathcal{P}}{\sim}^{c}$ and the incomparability relation ${}^{\mathcal{P}}{\|}^{c}$), thereby defining the *complete preference structure* $\langle {}^{\mathcal{P}}{<}^{c}, {}^{\mathcal{P}}{\approx}^{c} \rangle$.

In abstract terms, a propagation method $\mathcal{P}$ is a function that associates a context poset C, a configuration $\langle <^C, \approx^C \rangle$ over C, and a target context $c \in C$, with a complete preference structure $\langle {}^{\mathcal{P}}{<}^{c}, {}^{\mathcal{P}}{\approx}^{c} \rangle$. In this paper, we focus on propagation methods implemented through algebraic expressions.

We shall now capture the basic ideas underlying preference propagation.

Let us denote with $C\lfloor c \rfloor$ the *successor poset* of c, i.e., poset $C' = \{c' \in C \mid c \leqslant_C c'\}$, where $c_1 \leqslant_{C'} c_2$ iff $c_1 \leqslant_C c_2$. Context c' is *relevant* for c when a change in the ground preferences in c' may affect the propagated preferences in c.

Definition 1 (Coherence). *A propagation method $\mathcal{P}$ is* coherent wrt. C *if, for every context c in C, the relevant contexts for c according to $\mathcal{P}$ are exactly those in $C\lfloor c \rfloor$; $\mathcal{P}$ is* coherent *if it is coherent wrt. every context poset C.*

When combining preferences in unordered contexts, a cautious approach is to propagate only the preferences that hold in both contexts. The (more flexible) way we undertake just aims to avoid the propagation of conflicting preferences.

Definition 2 (Fairness). *$\mathcal{P}$ is* fair *for c in C if the following holds for all unordered contexts c_1 and c_2 in $C\lfloor c \rfloor$, all $o_1, o_2 \in O$ and all configuration $\langle <^C, \approx^C \rangle$:* ***if*** *i) $o_2 <^{c_1} o_1$, ii) $o_1 <^{c_2} o_2$, iii) $\forall c_i (c \leqslant_C c_i <_C c_1 \vee c \leqslant_C c_i <_C c_2) \Rightarrow o_1 \approx^{c_i} o_2$,* ***then*** *$o_1$ and o_2 are unordered in the complete preferences for c, i.e., $o_1 \, {}^{\mathcal{P}}{\sim}^{c} o_2$.*

A method $\mathcal{P}$ is fair *if it is fair for every context c in every poset C.*

So, if c_1 and c_2 disagree on the order of o_1 and o_2 while o_1 and o_2 are indifferent in all the more specific contexts, then o_1 and o_2 are not ordered in ${}^{\mathcal{P}}{<}^{c}$.

When combining ordered contexts, we give more importance to preferences that hold in contexts "closer" to the target context.

Definition 3 (Specificity). *$\mathcal{P}$ is* specific *for a context c in C if the following holds for every c_1 in $C\lfloor c \rfloor$, every $o_1, o_2 \in O$ and every configuration $\langle <^C, \approx^C \rangle$:* ***if*** *i) $o_1 <^{c_1} o_2$, ii) $o_1 \approx^{c_i} o_2$ for each $c \leqslant_C c_i <_C c_1$, and iii) it is either $o_1 <^{c_2} o_2$ or $o_1 \approx^{c_2} o_2$ for all $c_2 \in C\lfloor c \rfloor$ such that: 1) c_2 is unordered wrt. c_1, and 2) $o_1 \approx^{c_3} o_2$ $\forall c_3$ such that $c \leqslant_C c_3 <_C c_2$,* ***then*** *$o_1 \; {}^{\mathcal{P}}{<}^{c} \; o_2$.*

A method $\mathcal{P}$ is specific *if it is specific for every context c in every poset C.*

Thus if o_2 is preferable to o_1 in c_1 and such objects are indifferent in all the more specific contexts, then this preference does indeed propagate to context c (preferences from more generic contexts are overridden by those in more specific contexts). The preference must not propagate if this violates fairness.

Example 6. Consider Figure 1. With a fair propagation method $\mathcal{P}$, pasta and porceddu must be unordered in context c_4, since pasta $\prec^{c_2}$ porceddu whereas porceddu $\prec^{c_3}$ pasta, and similarly for beef and porceddu, i.e., pasta ${}^{\mathcal{P}}\!\sim^{c_4}$porceddu and beef ${}^{\mathcal{P}}\!\sim^{c_4}$porceddu. If $\mathcal{P}$ is specific, then pasta is preferable to beef in contexts c_2, c_3, and c_4, i.e., beef ${}^{\mathcal{P}}\!\prec^{c_2}$pasta, beef ${}^{\mathcal{P}}\!\prec^{c_3}$pasta, and beef ${}^{\mathcal{P}}\!\prec^{c_4}$pasta.

4 Preference Composition Expressions

We now characterize two binary operators, $+$ (for unordered contexts) and $\rhd$ (for ordered contexts), combining two ground preference structures $\langle \prec^{c_1}, \approx^{c_1} \rangle$ and $\langle \prec^{c_2}, \approx^{c_2} \rangle$ into a new preference structure, denoted $\langle \prec^{c_1} + \prec^{c_2}, \approx^{c_1} + \approx^{c_2} \rangle$ and, respectively, $\langle \prec^{c_1} \rhd \prec^{c_2}, \approx^{c_1} \rhd \approx^{c_2} \rangle$. Clearly, $+$ is commutative but $\rhd$ is not. Both operators are associative and idempotent and both have the *full indifference structure* $\emptyset_{\approx} = \langle \emptyset, O \times O \rangle$ as identity element, i.e., contexts in which all elements are indifferent should not influence the result. Axiomatically:

Definition 4 (+ operator). *A + operator satisfies the following axioms, for all objects $o_1, o_2 \in O$ and all preference structures $\langle \prec_1, \approx_1 \rangle, \langle \prec_2, \approx_2 \rangle, \langle \prec_3, \approx_3 \rangle$:*
i) $\langle \prec_1, \approx_1 \rangle + \langle \prec_2, \approx_2 \rangle = \langle \prec_2, \approx_2 \rangle + \langle \prec_1, \approx_1 \rangle$ *(commutativity)*
ii) $(\langle \prec_1, \approx_1 \rangle + \langle \prec_2, \approx_2 \rangle) + \langle \prec_3, \approx_3 \rangle = \langle \prec_1, \approx_1 \rangle + (\langle \prec_2, \approx_2 \rangle + \langle \prec_3, \approx_3 \rangle)$ *(ass.)*
iii) $\langle \prec_1, \approx_1 \rangle + \langle \prec_1, \approx_1 \rangle = \langle \prec_1, \approx_1 \rangle$ *(idempotence)*
iv) $\langle \prec_1, \approx_1 \rangle + \emptyset_{\approx} = \langle \prec_1, \approx_1 \rangle$ *(identity element)*
v) $o_1 \prec_1 o_2, o_2 \prec_2 o_1 \Rightarrow \neg(o_1 \prec_1 + \prec_2 o_2) \wedge \neg(o_2 \prec_1 + \prec_2 o_1)$ *(fairness)*

Definition 5 ($\rhd$ operator). *A $\rhd$ operator satisfies the following axioms, for all objects $o_1, o_2 \in O$ and all preference structures $\langle \prec_1, \approx_1 \rangle, \langle \prec_2, \approx_2 \rangle, \langle \prec_3, \approx_3 \rangle$:*
i) $(\langle \prec_1, \approx_1 \rangle \rhd \langle \prec_2, \approx_2 \rangle) \rhd \langle \prec_3, \approx_3 \rangle = \langle \prec_1, \approx_1 \rangle \rhd (\langle \prec_2, \approx_2 \rangle \rhd \langle \prec_3, \approx_3 \rangle)$ *(ass.)*
ii) $\langle \prec_1, \approx_1 \rangle \rhd \langle \prec_1, \approx_1 \rangle = \langle \prec_1, \approx_1 \rangle$ *(idempotence)*
iii) $\langle \prec_1, \approx_1 \rangle \rhd \emptyset_{\approx} = \emptyset_{\approx} \rhd \langle \prec_1, \approx_1 \rangle = \langle \prec_1, \approx_1 \rangle$ *(identity element)*
iv) $o_1 \prec_1 o_2 \Rightarrow o_1 \prec_1 \rhd \prec_2 o_2$ *(specificity)*

Preference structures can be combined with $+$ and $\rhd$ to form a *PC-expression.*

Definition 6 (PC-expression). *A* PC-expression *over C is any expression E of the form: $E ::= c \mid (E + E) \mid (E \rhd E) \mid \bot$, where c is a context in C.*

The base case is the name of some context c, denoting the preference structure $\langle \prec^c, \approx^c \rangle$; one can also compose PC-expressions (i.e., preference structures) via $+$ and $\rhd$, and denote the full indifference structure $\emptyset_{\approx}$ via the $\bot$ symbol.

PC-expressions can be used to compute complete preference structures (and thus to implement propagation methods). Fairness and specificity can be extended to PC-expressions in a straightforward way.

5 Interpreting the Propagation Operators

In this section we investigate on possible interpretations of the operators $+$ and $\rhd$. We start with a general result about *idempotent semirings.* A semiring is an algebraic structure with an associative and commutative additive operator (like $+$) and an associative multiplicative operator (like $\rhd$), which is both left- and right-distributive over addition. Let $(\mathcal{PR}_O, +, \rhd)$ be an algebraic structure, where $\mathcal{PR}_O$ denotes the set of all preference structures over a domain O. Then, with the additional hypothesis that $\rhd$ distributes over $+$, $(\mathcal{PR}_O, +, \rhd)$ would be a semiring in which both operators are idempotent, i.e., an idempotent semiring.

However, the following major result rules out the possibility of using idempotent semirings for providing an interpretation to the propagation operators, since distributivity of $\rhd$ over $+$ turns out to be incompatible with the axioms of specificity and fairness of the operators.

Theorem 1. *No $(\mathcal{PR}_O, +, \rhd)$ structure is an idempotent semiring.*

The cause of incompatibility of distributivity with the axioms of the operators lies only in assuming that $\rhd$ *right-distributes* over $+$. For this reason, here we consider the case in which $(\mathcal{PR}_O, +, \rhd)$ is an *idempotent left near-semiring*, that is, an algebraic structure satisfying all requirements of idempotent semirings except for right-distributivity of $\rhd$. We still assume that $\rhd$ left-distributes over $+$.

Consider Pareto and Prioritized composition as interpretations of $+$ and $\rhd$.

Definition 7 (Pareto and Prioritized comp.). *Let $\langle \prec_1, \approx_1 \rangle$ and $\langle \prec_2, \approx_2 \rangle$ be two preference structures over a domain O. The* Prioritized composition *of $\langle \prec_1, \approx_1 \rangle$ and $\langle \prec_2, \approx_2 \rangle$, written $\langle \prec_1, \approx_1 \rangle \circledRightarrow \langle \prec_2, \approx_2 \rangle$, is defined as*
$o_1 \prec_1 \circledRightarrow \prec_2 o_2 \Leftrightarrow (o_1 \prec_1 o_2) \vee (o_1 \prec_2 o_2 \wedge o_1 \approx_1 o_2)$
$o_1 \approx_1 \circledRightarrow \approx_2 o_2 \Leftrightarrow o_1 \approx_1 o_2 \wedge o_1 \approx_2 o_2.$
and their Pareto composition, *written $\langle \prec_1, \approx_1 \rangle \oplus \langle \prec_2, \approx_2 \rangle$, is:*
$o_1 \prec_1 \oplus \prec_2 o_2 \Leftrightarrow (o_1 \prec_1 o_2 \wedge o_1 \prec_2 o_2) \vee (o_1 \prec_1 o_2 \wedge o_1 \approx_2 o_2) \vee (o_1 \approx_1 o_2 \wedge o_1 \prec_2 o_2)$
$o_1 \approx_1 \oplus \approx_2 o_2 \Leftrightarrow o_1 \approx_1 o_2 \wedge o_1 \approx_2 o_2.$
where o_1 and o_2 are any two objects in O.

Intuitively, Prioritized composition gives precedence to preferences in $\prec_1$, while preferences in $\prec_2$ are used only if two objects are indifferent according to $\prec_1$. Conversely, Pareto considers the two preference relations equally important.

Example 7. Consider the objects: *i)* o_1: a comedy with Favino, *ii)* o_2: a comedy without Favino, *iii)* o_3: a drama with Favino, *iv)* o_4: a drama without Favino. Let $\prec_1$ be the preference relation corresponding to "I prefer comedies to all other genres" and $\prec_2$ to "I prefer movies with Favino to all other movies". If we consider $\prec_1$, then o_1 and o_2 are both preferable to o_3 and o_4; also, $o_1 \approx_1 o_2$ and $o_3 \approx_1 o_4$. With $\prec_2$, we have instead that o_1 and o_3 are both preferable to o_2 and o_4, with $o_1 \approx_2 o_3$ and $o_2 \approx_2 o_4$. Let $\prec_{\texttt{Par}} = \prec_1 \oplus \prec_2$; then $o_2 \prec_{\texttt{Par}} o_1$, $o_3 \prec_{\texttt{Par}} o_1$, $o_4 \prec_{\texttt{Par}} o_2$, $o_4 \prec_{\texttt{Par}} o_3$, with $o_2 \parallel_{\texttt{Par}} o_3$. Let now $\prec_{\texttt{Pri}} = \prec_1 \circledRightarrow \prec_2$; then $o_4 \prec_{\texttt{Pri}} o_3$, $o_3 \prec_{\texttt{Pri}} o_2$, $o_2 \prec_{\texttt{Pri}} o_1$. The intuition is that o_1 is always the best, since it satisfies both preferences, while o_4 is the worst one; o_2 and o_3 remain unordered if no priority is assumed between $\prec_1$ and $\prec_2$ (if $\oplus$ is used), whereas o_2 is preferred to o_3 when $\prec_1$ has priority over $\prec_2$ (via $\circledRightarrow$).

Both Prioritized and Pareto composition preserve strict partial orders (both yield a strict partial order when applied to two strict partial orders), whereas this is not guaranteed by replacing in their definition $\approx$ with $\sim$ [1]. It is known that both are associative and $\oplus$ is also commutative. Both operators are idempotent and have $\emptyset_{\approx}$ as the identity. Finally, we can show that $\circledtriangleright$ left-distributes over $\oplus$.

Theorem 2. *$(\mathcal{PR}_O, \oplus, \circledtriangleright)$ is an idempotent left near-semiring.*

One may wonder whether other interpretations, besides the one based on $\oplus$ and $\circledtriangleright$, exist for the $+$ and $\triangleright$ operators. Our answer is negative for an important class of operators, which we call *independent of irrelevant objects.*

Definition 8 (IIO operator). *An operator $\diamond$ is* independent of irrelevant objects *(IIO) if, for any two objects o and o' in O, the order relation between o and o' according to the combined preference structure $\langle <^1, \approx^1 \rangle \diamond \langle <^2, \approx^2 \rangle$ only depends on the order relation between o and o' according to $\langle <^1, \approx^1 \rangle$ and $\langle <^2, \approx^2 \rangle$.*

Thus, to determine the order relation between o_1 and o_2, an IIO operator does not need to consider any other objects. Both $\oplus$ and $\circledtriangleright$ are IIO. The following theorems show that $\oplus$ and $\circledtriangleright$ are the only possible IIO interpretations of $+$ and $\triangleright$: there is no other IIO interpretation of $+$ and $\triangleright$ that satisfies all the axioms.

Theorem 3. *Operator $\oplus$ is the only IIO $+$ operator.*

Theorem 4. *Operator $\circledtriangleright$ is the only IIO $\triangleright$ operator.*

6 Solutions and complexities

Problem CFS is solved by exhibiting a propagation method, called *Object-specific Cover* ($\mathcal{OC}$) propagation, based on PC-expressions using $\oplus$ and $\circledtriangleright$. It can be shown that no straightforward combination of the ground preferences in a context poset attains both fairness and specificity (each pair of objects seems to require a dedicated PC-expression). However, as a major result, $\mathcal{OC}$ implements propagation through a *single* PC-expression, denoted $\mathsf{RG}^C(c)$, for all pairs of objects; this is obtained, algebraically, by maximally "grouping on the right".

Definition 9 (PC-expression for $\mathcal{OC}$ propagation). *Let $c' \in C\lfloor c \rfloor$ and let $\{c_1, \ldots, c_k\}$ be immediately more specific than c'. The expression $\mathsf{RG}^C(c, c')$ is defined as $\mathsf{RG}^C(c, c) = c$; and $\mathsf{RG}^C(c, c') = (\mathsf{RG}^C(c, c_1) \oplus \ldots \oplus \mathsf{RG}^C(c, c_k)) \circledtriangleright c'$ if $c <_C c'$. Let $\hat{c}_1, \ldots, \hat{c}_n$ be maximal in $C\lfloor c \rfloor$. Then: $\mathsf{RG}^C(c) = \mathsf{RG}^C(c, \hat{c}_1) \oplus \ldots \oplus \mathsf{RG}^C(c, \hat{c}_n)$.*

For the poset in Figure 1, $\mathsf{RG}^C(c_4) = ((c_4 \circledtriangleright c_2) \oplus (c_4 \circledtriangleright c_3)) \circledtriangleright c_1 \equiv c_4 \circledtriangleright (c_2 \oplus c_3) \circledtriangleright c_1$.

Ultimately, $\mathcal{OC}$ is the only method guaranteeing both fairness and specificity.

Theorem 5. *For any method $\mathcal{P}$, if ${}^{\mathcal{P}}{<^c} \subset {}^{\mathcal{OC}}{<^c}$ then $\mathcal{P}$ is not specific.*

Theorem 6. *For any coherent method $\mathcal{P}$ based on $\oplus$ and $\circledtriangleright$, whose PC-expression only depends on c and C, if ${}^{\mathcal{OC}}{<^c} \subset {}^{\mathcal{P}}{<^c}$ then $\mathcal{P}$ is not both fair and specific.*

So, the $\mathcal{OC}$ semantics is "final" and therefore used to study the other problems.

For both OrdRel and Best, the exact complexity depends on the underlying context model as well as on the language used for expressing preferences. We remain parametric wrt. these aspects and assume that two context descriptions can be compared in $\mathcal{O}(\delta)$ time, and that $\mathcal{O}(\gamma)$ is the complexity of determining the order relation of any two objects according to ground preferences in a context.

Examples are the context model in [5–7], for which $\mathcal{O}(\delta) = \mathcal{O}(d)$, where d is the number of contextual dimensions and the language of [1], where, if preferences are expressed via a CNF with n conjuncts, we have $\mathcal{O}(\gamma) = \mathcal{O}(n^2)$.

Problem OrdRel can be solved by first computing the PC-expression $\mathsf{RG}^C(c)$ given by $\mathcal{OC}$ and then using it against the configuration to compute the complete preferences. However, materializing $\mathsf{RG}^C(c)$ may be inefficient due to repeated sub-expressions, leading, in the worst case, to a size of the PC-expression that is *exponential* in the number of contexts in $C\lfloor c \rfloor$. Yet, via efficient bookkeeping structures, we can solve Problem OrdRel in $\mathcal{O}(|A| \cdot (\delta + w(A) + \gamma))$ time, where A is the subset of C with only the contexts with some ground preferences, and $w(A)$ is its width. Problem Best requires at most $\mathcal{O}(N^2)$ comparisons for a set of N objects, leading to a complexity of $\mathcal{O}(|A| \cdot (\delta + N^2 \cdot (w(A) + \gamma)))$.

7 Conclusion and future work

In this paper we have discussed how preferences propagate when they depend on the context. We have proposed an algebraic model for expressing preference propagation, based on two abstract operators, and have shown that Pareto and Prioritized composition are the only natural possible interpretations satisfying all the required algebraic properties. Finally, we have studied the problem of efficiently computing the best objects according to the preferences propagated to a target context, and have shown that this can be done with polynomial complexity in all the main involved parameters.

Further research might analyze the application of the principles of preference propagation to numerical preferences. An example of the possibilities opened by this line of research is discussed in [2], where qualitative preferences expressed through constraints are imposed over numeric (quantitative) attributes.

References

1. J. Chomicki. Preference formulas in relational queries. *TODS*, 28(4):427–466, 2003.
2. P. Ciaccia, D. Martinenghi. Reconciling skyline and ranking queries. *PVLDB*, 10(11):1454–1465, 2017.
3. P. Ciaccia, D. Martinenghi, and R. Torlone. Foundations of context-aware preference propagation. *Journal of the ACM*, 67(1):4:1–4:43, 2020.
4. W. Kießling. Foundations of preferences in database systems. *VLDB*, 311–322, 2002.
5. D. Martinenghi, R. Torlone. Querying context-aware databases. *FQAS*, 76–87, 2009.
6. D. Martinenghi, R. Torlone. Querying databases with taxonomies. *ER*, 377–390, 2010.
7. D. Martinenghi, R. Torlone. Taxonomy-based relaxation of query answering in relational databases. *VLDB J.*, 23(5):747–769, 2014.
8. M. Öztürk *et al.* Preference modelling. *MCDA: State of the Art Surveys*, 27–59. 2005.

Context Awareness in the Travel Companion of the Shift2Rail Initiative*

Alireza Javadian Sabet‡, Matteo Rossi⋆,
Fabio A. Schreiber‡, and Letizia Tanca‡

‡Dipartimento di Elettronica, Informazione e Bioingegneria
⋆Dipartimento di Meccanica
Politecnico di Milano
Piazza Leonardo da Vinci 32, I-20133 Milano, Italy
{firstname.lastname@polimi.it}

Discussion Paper

Abstract. Providing personalized offers, and services in general, for the users of a system requires perceiving the context in which the users' preferences are rooted. In this work, we introduce the use of an already known model and methodology – based on the so-called Context Dimension Tree – along with a conceptual architecture to build a recommender system that offers personalized services for travelers. The research is performed in the frame of the Shift2Rail initiative as part of the Innovation Programme 4 of EU Horizon 2020.

Keywords: Context Dimension Tree · Preferences · Journey Planning · Data Tailoring · Recommender Systems.

1 Introduction

The demand for systems that provide *personalized* services increases the need to extract knowledge from different sources and appropriately reshape it. Besides, services cannot be properly adapted just by considering the static information obtained from the users' profiles: using instead a combination of such profiles with the context in which the user is going to be served is definitely more realistic. Generally speaking, *Context* can be recognized as a set of features (*i.e.* values for variables) contributing to the decisions of a user in a system [4].

This work explores and presents the essential elements vital to design a user-centered *Recommender System* (RS) for the *Travel Companion* (TC) module, currently being developed within the Shift2Rail (S2R) initiative as part of the Innovation Programme 4 (IP4). TC acts as an interface between users (typically travelers) and the other modules of the S2R IP4 ecosystem, supporting the

*This work was supported by Shift2Rail and the EU Horizon 2020 research and innovation programme under grant agreement No: 881825 (RIDE2RAIL)

users in all steps of their travel. Precisely, since supporting context-dependent data and service tailoring is paramount to ensure personalized services, we aim at extending the work carried out in [1] on the *Traveler Context-aware User Preferences*, by designing the Traveler Context Dimension Tree (TCDT) and the conceptual system architecture that identifies the essential components dealing with the creation and management of travelers' preferences. The rest of the paper is organized as follows. Section 2 discusses background; Section 3 explains the proposed methodology; Section 4 concludes the work.

2 Background and Related Work

Recommender Systems: RS are designed to recommend items to users considering their needs. The *user profiling* approaches, that emerged in the literature with the aim to determine the users' requirements and behavioral patterns [10], fall into one of the following categories: *Explicit* approaches, often referred to as *static user profiling*, predict the user preferences and activities through data mostly obtained from filling forms; *Implicit* approaches, instead, mostly disregard the users' static information and rely on the information obtained from observing their behaviors; *Hybrid* approaches are a combination of the two [12].
Context-awareness: Various models for designing context-aware systems have been described in many surveys [2][8]. The work [3] introduced the Context Dimension Tree (CDT) model – and an associated methodology – aimed at representing, and later exploiting, the information usage of *contexts*, in order to capture different situations in which the user can act, and formalize them hierarchically as a rooted labeled tree. Among the various advantages of the CDT model, its flexibility to capture the context both in the *conceptual* and *detail* level pursued us to utilize it for the sake of this work. An example of a CDT is depicted in Figure 1; the root of the tree represents the most general context, N is the set of nodes, which are either black *dimension nodes* N_D or white *concept nodes* N_C *a.k.a* dimension's values; N_D and N_C must alternate along the branches. White squares are *parameters*, shorthands to represent the nodes that have many possible values. Dashed lines specify if the N_C children of N_D are mutually exclusive. The children of r define the main analysis dimensions and are known as *top dimensions*. Each N_D should have at least one N_C.

3 Traveler Context Dimension Tree

This section explores the travelers' contexts and preferences through the CDT methodology, and introduces a conceptual system architecture that includes the main components for the ranking of the trips according to the travelers' context.

To enable context-aware recommendations for travel purposes, we identified the aspects characterizing contexts which correspond to the TC users' choice criteria that are potentially useful to score the available trips (see Figure 1).

Note that, in the application design phase, designing a CDT is performed independently of, yet in parallel with, the other routine activities involved in this phase [5]. The modeling mechanism of the TCDT intends neither to model all the available data and their structure nor how they are acquired and where they are stored; rather, it models the information that constitutes the various contexts in which the travelers may find themselves during their *reservation and travel experiences*; this information is potentially useful for supporting the system in understanding and seconding the users' preferences. The user variable *Name* is an example: the TCDT does not include it since it does not vary with the user's context; unless one might decide to use it to estimate the user gender. Note that it is common practice to employ *feature engineering* techniques to transform the dataset's feature space, improving the performance of the predictive models [11]. The ultimate purpose of using the CDT model is thus to support the analysis of such domain knowledge.

Practically, the CDT design is done iteratively, and depends on the final requirements of the application. The TCDT we propose defines the fundamental dimension and concept nodes in such a way that any further interesting features can be added by increasing or decreasing the level of granularity of the model.

3.1 Main Dimensions and Concepts

In the TCDT of Figure 1, the `Personal Data` N_D captures the socio-economic characteristics of the users through the `Profile` N_C. Different groups can be extracted according to the values of the `socio-economic factor` concept node, such as geographical origin, profession, and so on. Each group carries a set of preferences that are rather stable, thus can be associated with the notion of *user profile*. The main motivations for this dimension are to enable a warm start for the system and also to provide the chance of detecting and possibly supporting some group behaviors. As an example, consider two regions `X` and `Y` in the category of geographical groups, and suppose that, for some reason, users from `X` tend to choose eco-friendly travels much more frequently than users from `Y`. Investigating the reasons behind this tendency enables the authorities and the system to take the required actions (if applicable) for increasing the popularity of eco-friendly travels for the users living in region `Y`.

Moreover, a person can be member of some communities. The `Memberships` N_C captures the memberships of the user along with their payment methods. The `Loyalty Cards` N_D captures membership of the user in a community that potentially provides specific discounts. Moreover, we introduced N_D—`Other Memberships`—as a placeholder to capture other, less structured, communities that may follow different patterns compared to those based on `Loyalty Cards`. Tailoring the `Memberships` N_C with more levels of granularity through a combination of domain experts' knowledge and machine learning approaches like *clustering* is one of our future works.

We put a particular emphasis on supporting the needs of people with disabilities and health-related issues (HI), dedicating the `Health Issues` N_D to this purpose. The `HI_Category` N_D distinguishes the case that the issue belongs to the `PRM` category, which stands for *Person with Reduced Mobility*. The descendants of `HI_Type` N_D list some of the most critical issues. Moreover the TCDT

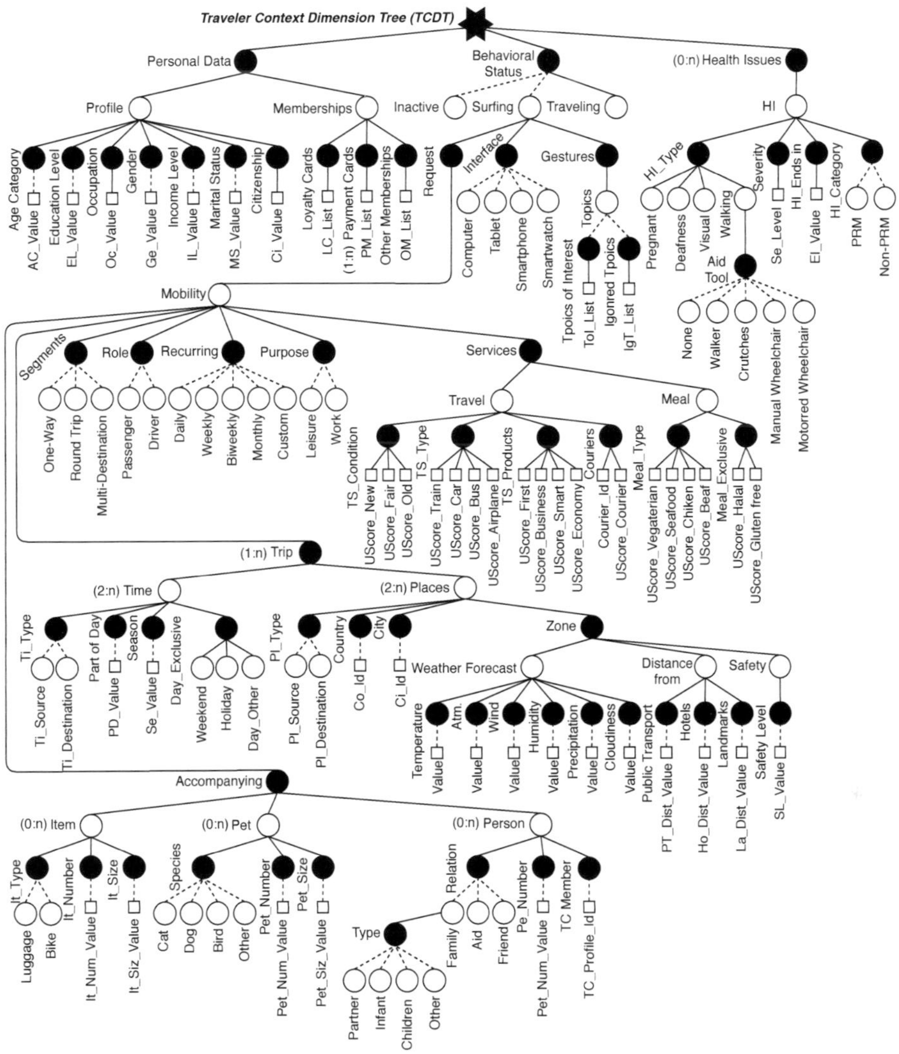

Fig. 1. Proposed Traveler Context Dimension Tree. Black circles represent dimension nodes and white circles and squares represent concept nodes. Dashed lines indicate the mutually exclusive concepts.

increases the level of granularity for the `Walking` N_C through the `Aid Tool` N_D to exemplify the concepts which should be considered during the future expansion. Knowing this concept is essential because of the particular space each of the `Aid Tools` require while recommending trips. The same importance is also applied to the *Severity* N_D, which can potentially limit the travel choices. Lastly, `HI_Ends in` N_D, enables the TC to determine if the issue is permanent or temporary.

Among the other top dimensions, `Behavioral Status` captures the current situation of the user as follows: the `Traveling` concept captures the state in which the user is traveling, or has purchased a *travel offer* and is waiting for the upcoming trip. Obviously, its two sibling N_C, drawn with dashed lines, are mutually exclusive: the `Inactive` N_C is true if the user is not interacting with the TC, while the `Surfing` N_C incorporates both implicit and explicit momentary user behaviors while interacting with the TC. More precisely, the `Interface` and `Gestures` N_D capture implicit behaviours: while users are interacting with the TC through a `Computer`, since there is extra visual space, and presumably the user has no urgent travel request, the TC proposes information regarding "eco-friendly" offers, which have lower CO_2 emissions. The users may decide to click, scroll, or ignore this information, which in turn can provide useful insights about their preferences regarding eco-friendly offers.

Explicit behaviours, instead, are captured via the `Request` N_D. Eco-friendly traveling behaviors can be promoted through so-called ride-sharing. For this reason, we foresee that when the user requests a travel offer through the TC and driving a car is a possibility, they can specify whether their `Role` is that of *Driver* or of *Passenger*, as well as, their `Purpose` and preferred `Segments`.

The user provides the locations that they are going to visit (at least source and destination). In the TCDT this value is transformed into appropriate concepts such as `Country`, `City` and `Zone`. For example, the `Zone` N_D enables the TCDT to capture the factors contributing to the user's decision through its children nodes *i.e.* `Distance from Public Transportation` services, `Hotels` and `Landmarks` (`PT`). Moreover, the `Weather Forecast` N_C is used to capture weather information according to the `Time` when the user will be in that `Zone`. The same strategy is applied to transform the actual value of the requested departure and arrival times to the `Time` N_C and its descendant nodes.

It may happen that the user has some `Accompanying Items` (e.g., a bike) and `Pets`, whose characteristics—such as their *Type*, *Species*, *Size* and *Number* —should be considered when recommending trips. Also, accompanying `Persons` not only affect travel choices from the logistic aspect but, if the `Person` is also a user of the TC, their preferences should be considered for recommending trips.

The `Services` N_D encompasses the variety of `Travel`- and `Meal`-related preferences according to the *optional* user-provided scores. Precisely, the TC, through *scores*, enables its users to provide scores between 0 and 5 representing excluded and requested respectively for the available services. Beside the preferences obtained by analyzing the history of the user's choices, the services scored as 0 allow the system to filter out such *travel offers*.

3.2 System Architecture

Figure 2 shows the conceptual architecture envisaging three main actors, namely *End Users*, *Travel Companion*, and *Third Parties*, along with their main elements to learn the users' preferences and recommending the best travel options accordingly. It provides an overall view, hiding the details of all the TC's blocks and functions; also, it does not specify the modules' physical locations (cloud, *etc.*).

Vitally, since the system deals with sensitive data, best practices concerning issues related to security and individual privacy through technical solutions [7] such as security protocols and algorithms should be taken into account.

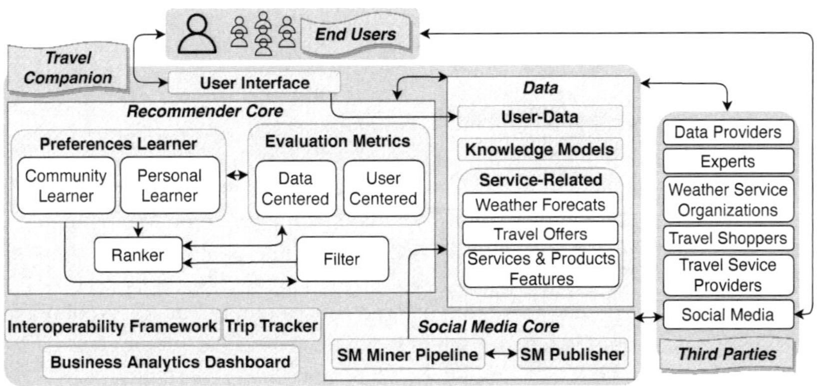

Fig. 2. Conceptual system architecture showing the main elements.

Naturally, the **Travel Companion** is, for our purposes, the most important actor, for which we provide a further breakdown into modules. The *Knowledge Models* block is useful to have a warm start for the newly-registered users, and for whose behavioral activities and specific preferences the system does not have any prior data. It also provides the opportunity to investigate the behavioral drifts that happen for the person, groups, and communities, and to acquire initial information for logistic purposes. The *Social Media (SM) Core* is composed of the two main blocks *SM Miner Pipeline* and *SM Publisher*. The *SM Miner Pipeline* employs Natural Language Processing techniques to harvest knowledge from SM platforms, seeking explicit travel-related mentions and keywords. The *SM Publisher* enables the TC to publish tailored news, promotions, and responses to specific users on SM, and allows users to share their trip information and other socializing functionalities. *Recommender Core* elements take as input user data, knowledge models, and service-related information and accordingly provide a ranked list of the trips for the user. The TC uses the S2R *Interoperability Framework* of the Sprint Project [13] and its rich domain ontology to facilitate the exchange of information between TC and other modules through the automatic concept mapping, both semantically and technologically [6,9]. After the trip plan is finalized, the *Trip Tracker* provides proper notifications about the trip (*e.g.*, disruptions), which include information explicitly required by the user or info deemed useful according to the implicitly learned preferences. Finally, the *Business Analytics Dashboard* tracks the system performance according to various KPIs and provides a platform to observe the trends and behavioral drifts.

The main **Third parties**, playing different roles about the provision of information and services to the TC, are the following: (i) *Data Providers* serve various information about the user, service, *etc.*, e.g. data about the safety of zones; (ii) *Experts* from different domains like sociology, transportation, *etc.* provide and modify the knowledge models of the TC; (iii) *Weather Service Organizations* provide weather forecasts associated with the places; (iv) *Travel Shoppers* (TS) are the organizations and services that arrange the journeys; (v) *SM* can play two primary roles: they can collect data regarding the users' attitudes and preferences, and the TC can use them to publish tailored news and promotions.

3.3 Trip Recommendations

The *travel offers* received by the TC from TS contain variables describing their characteristics (*e.g.* duration, CO_2 emissions, *etc.*). As a first step in the recommendation of *travel offers* to the user, the *Filter* block (see Figure 2) hides some of them according to the knowledge provided by the values associated with specific TCDT dimensions that are stronger preferences and act as a kind of personal constraints—*e.g.* offers that include TSPs with `Services` which users already excluded by scoring them 0. Then, the *Ranker* receives the remaining *travel offers*, plus a vector of preferences containing the *weights* capturing the importance of the TCDT values to the user and to divers communities and groups. For each received *travel offer*, the *Ranker* computes a numerical score in the interval $[0, 1]$ according to suitable evaluation metrics and uses this score to rank offers.

For example, consider a pregnant traveler, traveling with her partner for leisure; for the trip, she has excluded a specific type of meal by giving 0 score. Besides, through knowledge models, TC knows that leisure travels, have higher score for economy products (assuming that neither she has provided the optional scores for any of the products nor the TC has any history regarding her preference in leisure travels). Among the *travel offers* provided by the TS, TC filters out those that include the excluded meal. Considering her current context, the weight of her pregnancy condition potentially might be higher than that of her possible preference for economical offers, thus a *travel offer* that includes a direct flight will take over indirect flights (even though more economical), and, due to the accompanying partner, two seats next to each other might be more scored than seats with more space but in different places (even though more comfort).

4 Conclusion and Future Work

The design of an advanced learning system for travelers' preferences should not only provide the best possible rankings (and, consequently, suggestions) for travel offers, but should also adapt to changes in the behaviors and preferences of users.

The latter requirement is of great importance because preferences are highly dynamic and prone to changes according to different contexts.

In this work, we proposed a methodology to describe, at the conceptual level, the different contexts in which travelers can find themselves, with the advantage of being able to specify, for each traveler, how their preferences are affected by context changes. The methodology consists, on one side, in representing the characteristics of users, services and specific circumstances by means of a TCDT, and, on the other side, in designing a system architecture that identifies the potential sources of data and the interactions among the various system elements.

We are currently working on enriching the proposed TCDT by increasing the dimensions' level of granularity to explore the other contexts whose characteristics can contribute to the users' preferences and to their traveling decisions.

References

1. D5.2 – travel companion specifications. Technical report, IT2Rail Consortium, 2017. available from http://www.it2rail.eu.
2. Cristiana Bolchini, Carlo A. Curino, Elisa Quintarelli, Fabio A. Schreiber, and Letizia Tanca. A data-oriented survey of context models. *ACM Sigmod Record*, 36(4):19–26, 2007.
3. Cristiana Bolchini, Carlo A. Curino, Elisa Quintarelli, Fabio A. Schreiber, and Letizia Tanca. Context information for knowledge reshaping. *International Journal of Web Engineering and Technology*, 5(1):88–103, 2009.
4. Cristiana Bolchini, Carlo Aldo Curino, Giorgio Orsi, Elisa Quintarelli, Rosalba Rossato, Fabio A Schreiber, and Letizia Tanca. And what can context do for data? *Communications of the ACM*, 52(11):136–140, 2009.
5. Cristiana Bolchini, Elisa Quintarelli, and Letizia Tanca. Carve: Context-aware automatic view definition over relational databases. *IS*, 38(1):45–67, 2013.
6. Alessio Carenini, Ugo Dell'Arciprete, Stefanos Gogos, Mohammad Mehdi Pourhashem Kallehbasti, Matteo Rossi, and Riccardo Santoro. ST4RT – semantic transformations for rail transportation. In *TRA 2018*, pages 1–10, 2018.
7. George Danezis, Josep Domingo-Ferrer, Marit Hansen, Jaap-Henk Hoepman, Daniel Le Metayer, Rodica Tirtea, and Stefan Schiffner. Privacy and data protection by design-from policy to engineering. *preprint arXiv:1501.03726*, 2015.
8. Jong-yi Hong, Eui-ho Suh, and Sung-Jin Kim. Context-aware systems: A literature review and classification. *Expert Systems with applications*, 36(4):8509–8522, 2009.
9. Marjan Hosseini, Safia Kalwar, Matteo Rossi, and Mersedeh Sadeghi. Automated mapping for semantic-based conversion of transportation data formats. In *Proceedings of the International Workshop On Semantics For Transport (Sem4TRA)*, volume 2447 of *CEUR-WS*, pages 1–6, 2019.
10. Sumitkumar Kanoje, Sheetal Girase, and Debajyoti Mukhopadhyay. User profiling trends, techniques and applications. *arXiv preprint arXiv:1503.07474*, 2015.
11. F. Nargesian, H. Samulowitz, U. Khurana, Elias B Khalil, and Deepak S Turaga. Learning feature engineering for classification. In *IJCAI*, pages 2529–2535, 2017.
12. Danny Poo, Brian Chng, and Jie-Mein Goh. A hybrid approach for user profiling. In *36th Annual HICSS, 2003. Proceedings of the*, pages 9–pp. IEEE, 2003.
13. M Sadeghi, Petr Buchníček, A Carenini, O Corcho, S Gogos, M Rossi, R Santoro, et al. Sprint: Semantics for performant and scalable interoperability of multimodal transport. In *8th Transport Research Arena TRA 2020*, pages 1–10, 2020.

Improving Learning to Rank By Leveraging User Dynamics and Continuation Methods

Discussion Paper*

Nicola Ferro[1], Claudio Lucchese[2], Maria Maistro[3], and Raffaele Perego[4]

[1] University of Padua, ferro@dei.unipd.it
[2] Ca' Foscari University of Venice, Italy, claudio.lucchese@unive.it
[3] University of Copenhagen, Denmark, mm@di.ku.dk
[4] ISTI CNR Pisa, Italy, raffaele.perego@isti.cnr.it

Abstract. *Learning to Rank (LtR)* techniques leverage assessed samples of query-document relevance to learn ranking functions able to exploit the noisy signals hidden in the features used to represent queries and documents. In this paper, we explore how to enhance the state-of-the-art LambdaMart algorithm by integrating in the training process an explicit knowledge of the underlying user-interaction model and the possibility of targeting different objective functions, that can effectively drive the algorithm towards promising areas of the search space. We enrich the learning algorithm in two ways: (i) by considering complex query-based user dynamics instead than simply discounting the gain by the rank position; (ii) by designing a learning path across different loss functions that can capture different signals in the training data. Our extensive experiments, conducted on publicly available datasets, show that the proposed solution permits to improve various ranking quality measures by statistically significant margins.

Keywords: Learning to Rank · User Dynamics · Continuation Methods

1 Introduction

In [8], we explored whether the explicit knowledge of the underlying user interaction model [6] and the possibility of targeting different objective functions, by means of *Continuation Methods (CM)* [1, 5, 7], make it possible to improve the ranking models learned by *Learning to Rank (LtR)* algorithms. In particular, our investigation focused on improving the state-of-the-art LtR algorithm LambdaMart [3]. This extended abstract summarizes the main contributions discussed in [8] by relying on a extensive assessment conducted on publicly available datasets:

* Extended abstract of the paper originally published in [8]

– *modelling user dynamics into* LambdaMart: instead of proposing new features to account for user behavior and then training the LtR model on this extended set of features, we: (1) explicitly model the user dynamics in scanning a ranked result list with Markov chains trained on query log data; (2) define a novel measure which embeds this trained Markov chain (*Normalized Markov Cumulated Gain (nMCG)*), and modify the LambdaMart loss function to rely on this measure instead of the usual *Normalized Discounted Cumulated Gain (nDCG)* [9];
– *user interaction-based curriculum learning for* LambdaMart: designing a curriculum of objective functions of increasing complexity has shown to be a promising research direction. Therefore we explore if our nMCG measure provides further gain when building a curriculum based on CM techniques.

2 Methodology

An LtR algorithm exploits a *ground-truth* set of training examples in order to learn a document scoring function σ [10]. Such training set is composed of a large collection of queries $\mathcal{Q}$, where each query $q \in \mathcal{Q}$ is associated with a set of assessed documents $D = \{d_0, d_1, \ldots\}$. Each document d_i is labeled by a *relevance judgment* l_i according to its relevance to the query q. These labels induce a partial ordering over the assessed documents, thus defining an *ideal ranking* which the LtR algorithm aims at approximating. Each query-document pair (q, d_i) is represented by a vector of features x, able to describe the query (e.g., its length), the document (e.g., the in-link count) and their relationship (e.g., the number of occurrences of each query term in the document).

LambdaRank can be summarized as follows. Given a query q and two candidate documents d_i and d_j in the training set with relevance labels l_i and l_j respectively, s_i and s_j are the scores currently predicted for the documents. The lambda gradient of any given *Information Retrieval (IR)* quality function Q, as defined in [3], is:

$$\lambda_{ij} = \frac{\partial Q_{ij}}{\partial (s_i - s_j)} = \text{sgn}(y_i - y_j) \left| \Delta Q_{ij} \cdot \frac{1}{1 + e^{s_i - s_j}} \right|$$

where, the sign is determined by the document labels only, the first factor ΔQ is the quality variation when swapping scores s_i and s_j, and the second factor is the derivative of the RankNet cost [2], which minimizes the number of disordered pairs. When $l_i \geq l_j$, the quality Q increases with the score of document d_i. The larger the quality variation ΔQ, the higher the document d_i should be scored. Note that the RankNet multiplier fades ΔQ if documents are scored correctly, i.e. $s_i \geq s_j$, and boosts ΔQ otherwise. The lambda gradient for a document d_i is computed by marginalizing over all possible pairs in the result list: $\lambda_i = \sum_j \lambda_{ij}$. LambdaRank uses nDCG as Q and so ΔQ is the variation in nDCG caused by the swap of two documents.

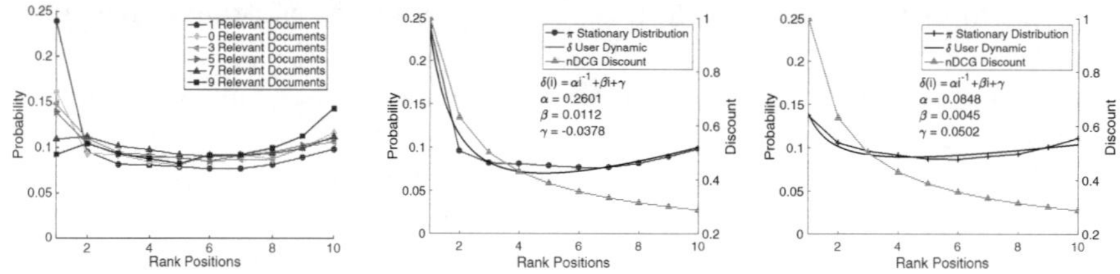

(a) Different Query Types (b) Navigational Queries (c) Informational Queries

Fig. 1. Stationary distributions for queries retrieving different numbers of relevant documents (a); and stationary distribution with its fitted curve and DCG discount for navigational (b), and informational queries (c).

2.1 User Dynamics for LtR

We summarize here our methodology [6] for including the user dynamics into the above discussed LambdaRank algorithm. We model the user dynamics with a Markovian process [11], where the user scans the ranked documents in the *Search Engine Result Page (SERP)* according to possibly complex paths, moving both forward and backward. Let us denote by $X_1, X_2, \ldots$ the sequence of random variables representing the rank positions in $\mathcal{R} = \{1, 2, \ldots, R\}$ visited by the user, where $X_n = j$ means that the nth document visited by the user is at rank j. Moreover, we assume that the probability to move from the document at rank i to the document at rank j depends on the document at rank i only and is independent of all the previously visited documents. Finally, we denote by P the transition matrix whose entries represent the transition probabilities $P = (p_{ij} : i, j \in \mathcal{R})$, where $p_{ij} = \mathbb{P}[X_{n+1} = j | X_n = i]$. The sequence of random variables $(X_n)_{n>0}$ defines a discrete-time homogeneous Markov chain.

Figure 1(a) plots the stationary distributions obtained from the Yandex query log described in Section **??**. We focus on two distinct macroscopic behavior types, and, for the sake of simplicity, we call *navigational* the queries where users concentrated on just the first item, and we consider all the other queries as *informational* since users tend to visit more documents. On the basis of the above experimental observations, we claim that the user dynamics can be described as a mixture of the navigational and informational behavior. The navigational component is represented by the inverse of the rank position $\frac{1}{i}$, while the informational component is linear with respect to the rank position i. Therefore, we model the *user dynamics* as

$$\delta(i) = \alpha i^{-1} + \beta i + \gamma$$

where the parameters α, β and γ are calibrated in order to fit the estimated stationary distributions computed on the Yandex dataset.

Figures 1(b) and 1(c) show the stationary distributions together with the fitted curves for the navigational and informational cases, respectively. In Figure 1(b) the stationary distribution is the same reported in the red line of Figure 1(a), i.e. queries with just 1 relevant document, while to compute the stationary distribution reported in Figure 1(c) we aggregate all the user dynamics corresponding to the other queries, i.e. queries without relevant documents or with more than one relevant document.

We enhance the existing LAMBDAMART algorithm by replacing the above Q with a new quality measure which integrates the proposed user dynamics δ. This new measure is called *Normalized Markov Cumulated Gain (nMCG)* and it is defined as follows:

$$\text{nMCG@k} = \frac{\sum_{i \le k} \left(2^{l_i} - 1\right) \cdot \delta^c(i)}{\sum_{h \le k, \text{ sorted by } l_h} \left(2^{l_h} - 1\right) \cdot \delta^c(h)}$$

where l_i is the relevance label of the i-th ranked document and $\delta^c(i)$ is the user dynamics function at rank i relative to the query class c, either navigational or informational. Basically, nMCG can be seen as an extension of nDCG, where the discount function is defined by the user dynamic and depends on the query class. Moreover, since δ^c depends on the query class, i.e. depends on the query q, we are optimizing two different variants of the same quality measure nMCG across the training dataset. Finally, $\Delta\text{nMCG@k}_{ij}$ can be computed efficiently as follows:

$$\Delta\text{nMCG@k}_{ij} = \frac{-\left(2^{l_i} - 2^{l_j}\right)\left(\delta^c(i) - \delta^c(j)\right)}{\sum_{h \le k, \text{ sorted by } l_h} \left(2^{l_h} - 1\right) \cdot \delta^c(h)}.$$

Hereinafter, we use nMCG-MART to refer to the described variant of LAMBDAMART aimed at maximizing nMCG.

2.2 Continuation Methods for LtR

Applying a *Continuation Methods (CM)* to a cost function C means to define a sequence of cost functions C_γ with $\gamma \in [0, 1]$, such that by increasing γ, the complexity of the function increases. Therefore, C_0 represents a highly smoothed version of the original cost function corresponding to C_1.

We implement CMs in the contest of forests of decision trees as a two steps learning process, where the initial trees are trained by minimizing a cost function C_0 and the remaining trees are trained by optimizing C_1. We did not explore in this work more complex multi-stage scenarios, which can trivially extend this work. We denote continuation methods as $C_0T_0\_C_1T_1$, meaning that the first T_0 trees of the ensemble minimize C_0, while the remaining T_1 trees minimize C_1, additively refining the prediction of the first T_0 trees.

In order to apply a CM to LAMBDAMART we need to smooth the LAMBDAMART loss function. Smoother variants of nDCG have been previously proposed, e.g. SoftNDCG [15]; however, their performance did not prove to be significantly better than the original LAMBDAMART loss function. Therefore, we look at two different smoother replacements of the nDCG measure.

The first option we consider is to use as C_0 the *Mean Square Error (MSE)* as a smooth variant of the target nDCG measure. Even if MSE is easily differentiable and an MSE equal to 0 corresponds to the maximum nDCG value, the MSE cost cannot be considered a smooth approximation of nDCG. Nevertheless, Gradient Boosted Regression Trees that minimize MSE are known to perform well, even at optimizing nDCG. The rationale of using C_0 equal to MSE is that of using a smooth function that alone exhibits good performance as a good seed for the refinement that the optimization of nDCG or nMCG may provide.

The second option we consider is to use Recall@k as C_0. Recall is not a differentiable function either, as it suffers the same issues as nDCG. Still, it is an *easier* function to be optimized because it considers binary relevance instead of graded, and it discriminates between documents above or below the cut-off k without further discounting according to document ranks. The rationale is to train the first portion of the forest in order to place the most relevant documents above the cut-off, and then to complete the training with the target metric nDCG or nMCG to adjust their relative ranking.

Since Recall is not differentiable, we devised a LambdaMart-based approach similar to nMCG-MART. We define $\Delta\text{nRecall@k}_{ij}$ as the normalized change in *Recall@k* when swapping the i-th and j-th documents in the current ranking. Given a relevance binarization thresholds ρ, $\Delta\text{nRecall@k}_{ij}$ is defined as follows:

$$\Delta\text{nRecall@k}_{ij} = \frac{-\left(\mathbb{1}_{l_i \geq \rho} - \mathbb{1}_{l_j \geq \rho}\right)\left(\mathbb{1}_{i \geq k} - \mathbb{1}_{j \geq k}\right)}{\sum_h \mathbb{1}_{l_h \geq \rho}},$$

where $\mathbb{1}_p$ is the indicator function evaluating to 1 if predicate p is true and 0 otherwise.

Finally, in addition to C_1 being equal to nDCG, we also consider the case where nMCG-MART is used as C_1. Our goal is to evaluate the added value of exploiting the user dynamics in producing the final ranking, even when the first trees of the forest where built by optimizing a different metric.

In conclusion, we compare the effectiveness of LambdaMart and nMCG-MART and we asses the benefit they can receive by a pre-training on a different metric, which allows the two algorithms to initiate their search process from a different point in the solution space, possibly leading to a better final solution.

3 Experimental Evaluation

We remark that since there is no publicly available dataset providing, at the same time, user session data, document relevance and query-document pairs features, we have to use two different datasets in our analysis. Therefore, we calibrate the user model on the click log dataset provided by Yandex [13], while the training, validation and test for the LtR model are performed on MSLR-WEB30K and MSLR-WEB10K, provided by Microsoft [12].

We used LambdaMart as the reference LtR algorithm. Specifically, we used (and modified) the open source implementation of LambdaMart provided in the LightGBM gradient boosting framework and swiped the hyper parameters

Available at https://github.com/Microsoft/LightGBM.

with cross-validation so as to maximize the average performance over the validation folds.

As significance test, we computed Fisher's randomization test with 100 000 random permutations and $\alpha = 0.05$, which is the most appropriate statistical test to evaluate whether two approaches differ significantly [14].

As name convention, all the CM approaches are referred with the name of the first objective function C_0, the corresponding number of trees used during the first training phase T_0, followed by the name of the second objective function C_1 with the corresponding number of trees T_1. Therefore, `recallT300_ndcgT200` means that the model is trained with Recall@10 for the first 300 trees and then with nDCG@10 for the following 200 trees. Moreover, we exploit as reference models for CM approaches nMCG-MART and `mseT200_ndcgT300`, which is the best performing model proposed in [7].

3.1 Experimental Results

In this section we summarize the main findings without reporting any figure or table, the complete results can be found in the original paper [8].

First, we evaluate the performance of the proposed models against the baselines on MSLR-WEB10K and MSLR-WEB30K:

- With nDCG@10, CM approaches combining Recall and nMCG, namely `recallT300_nmcgT200` and `recallT400_nmcgT100`, achieve the best performance on each fold. They are significantly different from both the baseline and the corresponding CM approaches which combine Recall followed by nDCG. This supports our hypothesis that the combination of CM and the user dynamics integrated by nMCG can boost LambdaMart performance.
- With nDCG@100, CM approaches using nMCG are less effective and `mseT200_ndcgT300` is the best performing model, significantly improving over the baseline both on each fold and on the average across folds. Moreover, CM approaches using nMCG are not significantly different from those using nDCG. However, they are still significantly improving over the baseline.
- With Recall@10, the results are somehow in between nDCG@10 and nDCG@100. `mseT200_ndcgT300` is the best performing model when the average across each fold is considered. However, if we break down the results on each fold, `recallT400_nmcgT100` is the best performing model on three folds out of five for MSLR-WEB30K. Moreover, `recallT400_nmcgT100` is significantly better than the baseline and than `recallT400_ndcgT100`.
- With Recall@100, CM approaches using nDCG, i.e. `mseT200_ndcgT300`, `recallT300_ndcgT200` and `recallT400_ndcgT100` perform better than those using nMCG. When considering the score across all the folds, `mseT200_ndcgT300` is still the best performing model. Thus, when using Recall@100 as evaluation measure, we reach conclusions similar to those inferred with nDCG@100.
- With *Expected Reciprocal Rank (ERR)*@10, `recallT300_nmcgT200` is the best performing model and it is the only approach which is significantly

better than the baseline. Moreover, CM approaches using nMCG are also significantly better than those using nDCG, with respect to both each separate fold and the average across folds.

To summarize, CM approaches exploiting the user dynamics perform better at lower rank positions, while CM approaches using nDCG, as `mseT200_ndcgT300`, are somehow better in retrieving a higher number of relevant documents in the first 100 rank positions.

Second, we repeated the previous analysis by considering the query type, i.e. we compared the proposed models on navigational and informational queries separately. On a high level the experimental results show that:

- With navigational queries, there are just a few models which are significantly better than the baselines, independently of the measure or the fold. Furthermore, none of the model performs markedly better than the others, there is instead a lot of variability depending on the measure and the fold under consideration. We argue that with navigational queries the number of relevant documents is limited and systems have little room for manoeuvre: they need to place the most relevant document at the top of the ranked list and, when doing this properly, they all perform equally well in achieving this task.
- The experimental comparison of models on informational queries provides more insights on the performance of CM approaches combined with the user dynamics. The exploitation of the user dynamics together with CM boosts the ranking of queries for which several relevant documents are available. Indeed, it helps in identifying those documents that are more relevant than others and in placing them at the beginning of the ranked list.

Finally, we analyse the tree-wise performance of the proposed models: we compare the performance of different models with a varying number of trees. All CM approaches leveraging the user dynamics results to be always better than the baselines as the number of trees increases. Moreover, each boosting of the performance corresponds exactly to the switching point T_0, showing that replacing the objective function from Recall to nMCG is beneficial for the learning algorithm at any switching point.

4 Conclusion and Future Work

This paper investigated whether integrating in LtR the knowledge of the user-interaction model and the possibility of targeting different objective functions is profitable and allows us to train more effective ranking functions. The results of the experiments, measured with different metrics and cut-offs, gave us a more clear understanding of the problem addressed and confirmed our initial intuitions. We showed, by also breaking down the analysis to different classes of queries, that the proposed continuation methods exploiting our user-aware nMCG measure consistently outperform the baselines by statistically significant margins.

As future work we will study different methods for applying click models to LtR datasets. A possibility suggested in [4] could be to exploit editorial relevance labels as a link between different datasets and use a trained click model to generate new click-based features for datasets not providing them.

Acknowledgements: This paper is partially supported by the BIGDATAGRAPES (EU H2020 RIA, grant agreement N. 780751) and the OK-INSAID (MIUR-PON 2018, grant agreement N.ARS01_009 17) projects. The work is also partially funded by the "DAta BenchmarK for Keyword-based Access and Retrieval" (DAKKAR) Starting Grants project sponsored by University of Padua and Fondazione Cassa di Risparmio di Padova e di Rovigo, and by AMAOS (Advanced Machine Learning for Automatic Omni-Channel Support), funded by Innovationsfonden, Denmark.

References

[1] Allgower, E.L., Georg, K.: Numerical Continuation Methods. An Introduction. Springer-Verlag, Heidelberg, Germany (1980)
[2] Burges, C., Shaked, T., Renshaw, E., Lazier, A., Deeds, M., Hamilton, N., Hullender, G.: Learning to Rank using Gradient Descent. In: ICML 2005. pp. 89–96. ACM Press, New York, USA (2005)
[3] Burges, C.J.C.: From RankNet to LambdaRank to LambdaMART: An Overview. Tech. rep., Microsoft Research, MSR-TR-2010-82 (2010)
[4] Chuklin, A., Markov, I., de Rijke, M.: Click Models for Web Search. Morgan & Claypool Publishers, USA (2015)
[5] Coleman, T.F., Wu, Z.: Parallel Continuation-based Global Optimization for Molecular Conformation and Protein Folding. Journal of Global Optimization **8**(1), 49–65 (1996)
[6] Ferro, N., Lucchese, C., Maistro, M., Perego, R.: On Including the User Dynamic in Learning to Rank. In: SIGIR 2017. pp. 1041–1044. ACM Press, New York, USA (2017)
[7] Ferro, N., Lucchese, C., Maistro, M., Perego, R.: Continuation Methods and Curriculum Learning for Learning to Rank. In: CIKM 2018. pp. 1523–1526. ACM Press, New York, USA (2018)
[8] Ferro, N., Lucchese, C., Maistro, M., Perego, R.: Boosting Learning to Rank with User Dynamics and Continuation Methods. Information Retrieval Journal (2019)
[9] Järvelin, K., Kekäläinen, J.: Cumulated Gain-Based Evaluation of IR Techniques. TOIS **20**(4), 422–446 (2002)
[10] Liu, T.Y.: Learning to Rank for Information Retrieval. (FnTIR **3**(3), 225–331 (2009)
[11] Norris, J.R.: Markov chains. Cambridge University Press, UK (1998)
[12] Qin, T., Liu, T.Y.: Introducing LETOR 4.0 Datasets. arXiv.org, Information Retrieval (cs.IR) **arXiv:1306.2597** (2013)
[13] Serdyukov, P., Craswell, N., Dupret, G.: WSCD2012: Workshop on Web Search Click Data 2012. In: WSDM 2012. pp. 771–772. ACM Press, New York, USA (2012)
[14] Smucker, M.D., Allan, J., Carterette, B.A.: A Comparison of Statistical Significance Tests for Information Retrieval Evaluation. In: CIKM 2007. pp. 623–632. ACM Press, New York, USA (2007)
[15] Taylor, M., Guiver, J., Robertson, S., Minka, T.: SoftRank: Optimizing Non-Smooth Rank Metrics. In: WSDM 2008. pp. 77–86. ACM Press, New York, USA (2008)

Interpreting Link Prediction on Knowledge Graphs

Andrea Rossi
Supervised by proff. Paolo Merialdo and Donatella Firmani

Roma Tre University, Rome, Italy andrea.rossi3@uniroma3.it

Abstract. Link Prediction (LP) on Knowledge Graphs (KGs) has recently become a sparkling research topic, benefiting from the explosion of machine learning techniques. Several relation-learning models are published every year, mostly relying on KG embeddings. So far, however, not much has been done to interpret the features they learn and predict, and the circumstances that allow them to achieve satisfactory performances. Our research aims at opening the black box of LP models, trying to explain their behaviors. In this work we first discuss the current limitations of LP benchmarks, showing how the use of global metrics on largely skewed datasets hinders our understanding of these models; we then report the main takeaways from our recent comparative analysis of state-of-the-art LP models [3], identifying the most influential structural features of the graph for predictive effectiveness.

Keywords: Knowledge Graphs · Knowledge Graph Embeddings · Link Prediction.

1 Introduction

Knowledge Graphs (KGs) model data as nodes linked by labeled edges. In a KG nodes represent *entities*; each edge connects a *head* entity to a *tail* entity through the *relation* specified by its label, resulting in a *fact*. KGs are employed in several domains, ranging from question answering to information retrieval and content-based recommendation. All KGs tend to suffer from incompleteness; Link Prediction (LP) tackles this issue by leveraging the known facts to infer the missing ones. LP research has been largely influenced by the recent advancements in machine learning; most LP models nowadays map the KG elements into vectors dubbed KG embeddings, learned automatically based on scoring functions that estimate the plausibility of the training facts. For instance, ⟨*Barack Obama*, *born_in*, *Honolulu*⟩ is expected to yield a better score than ⟨*Barack Obama*, *born_in*, *Beijing*⟩. In this framework, predicting the tail of an incomplete fact $\langle h, r, ?\rangle$ amounts to finding the entity that results in the best score when used as its tail. Head prediction is performed analogously. Despite the popularity of LP techniques, their strengths, weaknesses and limitations are still unknown, and the graph structural features driving predictions have been hardly investigated. Roughly speaking, we still do not really know what makes a fact easy or hard to learn and predict, and whether the corresponding predictions can be trusted or not. Our research focuses on interpreting the behavior of LP models, aiming at providing tools for explaining their predictions. As a first step towards this goal, in this paper we summarize our findings on the limitations of current benchmarks in showing how different papers in LP literature fit together. Then, we report the main results of our comparative analysis. Finally, we discuss our research plans for building interpretable methods for LP.

2 Related Works

Works related to ours are mostly *meta-analyses* focusing on specific LP methodologies. These works tend to address very specific hypotheses to interpret LP behaviours, and run experiments on a few selected models to verify them. For instance, the authors of [5] study geometrical properties of the embedding vectors, measuring their Alignment To Mean (ATM) and conicity. They show that models that operate by adding embeddings tend to learn significantly sparser vectors than the ones multiplying them; in the latter, higher conicity also seems to correlate to better performances. The work of [7] points out that the current evaluation practices just ensure that models prioritize correct answers over wrong ones on test facts. In this way, only questions that do have an answer are taken into account. The authors argue that this approach is more akin to question answering than LP, and propose a novel measure that includes questions with no correct answers (e.g. nonsensical questions, such as $\langle Apple, gender, ?\rangle$).

Finally, we acknowledge that LP is also being researched on standard graphs. In this scenario edges are usually *non-labeled*, so modeling relations is unnecessary: this makes it a related but ultimately very different task from LP on KGs.

3 Interpreting Link Prediction Results

Since the seminal work of [1], dozens of models have been developed in just a few years (see [6] for a survey). We argue that a crucial step towards interpreting these models lies in providing informative evaluation practices. We briefly highlight the most prominent limitations of current LP evaluation practices and benchmarks, and then summarize our main findings when comparing LP models.

3.1 Benchmark Limitations

All the currently most popular LP datasets have been generated by sampling facts from a KG and splitting them uniformly at random into a training, a validation and a test set. As a side effect, in such datasets the number of mentions of both entities and relations display significantly skewed distributions: less than 15% entities can be featured in more than 80% training facts. Furthermore, since the training and test set are random splits from the same original sample, the most mentioned entities in training are largely over-represented in testing too.

Since current evaluation practices rely almost solely on global metrics (e.g. *Hits@K*, *Mean Rank*, *Mean Reciprocal Rank*) over the entire test set, LP models can exhibit good performances, in proportion, by just learning to predict the most mentioned entities, while ignoring the others. In FB15k [1], one of the first LP datasets and a *de facto* standard, "United States" is both the most mentioned entity and the most common answer to relation "nationality"; in this setting, a model can obtain decent results by just learning to predict U.S. citizens only.

In our work [4] we have observed experimentally that LP models are indeed subject to this issue to some extent, as they achieve better performances when dealing with entities with more training mentions.

3.2 Comparative Analysis of Models

As mentioned above, relying exclusively on global metrics hides any variations in predictive performances across different portions of the dataset. This makes it difficult to analyze the conditions that facilitate or hinder predictions. We also acknowledge the difficulty of coming up with new datasets with different structural properties and good semantic consistency. In order to mitigate this issue, we have proposed a set of evaluation practices going beyond what is available in literature, taking into account structural properties of individual facts and entities. We have run an extensive comparative analysis [3] on a set of 16 models representative for the most successful architectures applied to LP; we have included an additional rule-based LP model as a baseline. We have trained and fine-tuned all models on the 5 most popular LP datasets, extracting fine-grained results with the predictions yielded by each model for each test fact. The full list of featured datasets and models can be found at our repository.

We have used these results to investigate the graph structural features that make facts easier to learn and predict, searching for the strongest correlations with the predictive performances of the models. The structural features we found most influential to predictive performances are the number of *peers* and the support provided by *paths*, as discussed below.

Given a prediction, its target is the entity to predict, and its *target peers* are its correct alternatives, i.e. forming a fact belonging to the dataset. When a prediction has too many target peers, LP models seem to get confused: as they try to optimize the embeddings for too many correct answers, they also let many incorrect ones in, leading to a rapid decrease in performances. In a specular way, the known entity in the prediction is called its source, and its correct alternatives are dubbed *source peers*. Source peers seem to facilitate predictions, leading to better performances; this can be explained by interpreting them as specific examples that enable analogical reasoning.

https://github.com/merialdo/research.lpca

In a graph, *paths* are chained sequences of facts. Given a fact, the paths connecting its head and tail can provide useful patterns for prediction, e.g. ⟨*Barack Obama, born_in, Honolulu* ⟩ and ⟨ *Honolulu, located_in, USA*⟩ can be useful to predict ⟨*Barack Obama, nationality, USA*⟩. In our work [3] propose a novel *RPS* measure estimating the *Relational Path Support* of any test fact. *RPS* uses TF-IDF vectors to assess the similarity between the paths co-occurring with the specific test fact and the ones usually co-occurring with the other facts that feature the same relation. We have observed that most LP models, despite just training on individual facts, are able to leverage longer-range dependencies to some extent, as higher *RPS* values always correspond to far better performances.

4 Research plan and concluding remarks

Being aware of the behaviours of current LP methods is vital to identify their weaknesses, and to ultimately build more robust, trustworthy systems.

In order to open the black box of LP systems, we aim at building a full-fledged explainability framework: given a prediction of a model, our framework would yield as an explanation the training facts that have been most influential for it. In the categorization of [2], this amounts to a *post-hoc local explanation*. The framework we aim to create should be agnostic to the architecture of the LP model to explain, thus being applicable to a set of systems as wide as possible.

As a matter of fact, explaining the predictions provided by LP models is still an open problem. To the best of our knowledge, the only technique proposed so far is [8]; this approach, however, still displays severe limitations, as it just searches for meaningful paths connecting the head and tail, without any evidence that such paths have actually been instrumental to perform the prediction.

Our research plan also includes the development of more balanced and insightful benchmarking workloads, in terms of both datasets and metrics.

References

1. Bordes, A., Usunier, N., Garcia-Duran, A., Weston, J., Yakhnenko, O.: Translating embeddings for modeling multi-relational data. In: NIPS (2013)
2. Du, M., Liu, N., Hu, X.: Techniques for interpretable machine learning. CACM (2019)
3. Rossi, A., Firmani, D., Matinata, A., Merialdo, P., Barbosa, D.: Knowledge graph embedding for link prediction: A comparative analysis (2020)
4. Rossi, A., Matinata, A.: Knowledge graph embeddings: Are relation-learning models learning relations? In: PIE (2020)
5. Sharma, A., Talukdar, P., et al.: Towards understanding the geometry of knowledge graph embeddings. In: ACL (2018)
6. Wang, Q., Mao, Z., Wang, B., Guo, L.: Knowledge graph embedding: A survey of approaches and applications. TKDE (2017)
7. Wang, Y., Ruffinelli, D., Gemulla, R., Broscheit, S., Meilicke, C.: On evaluating embedding models for knowledge base completion. In: RepL4NLP@ACL (2019)
8. Zhang, W., Paudel, B., Zhang, W., Bernstein, A., Chen, H.: Interaction embeddings for prediction and explanation in knowledge graphs. In: WSDM (2019)

Co-posting Author Assortativity in Reddit

Francesco Cauteruccio[1], Enrico Corradini[2], Giorgio Terracina[1], Domenico Ursino[2], and Luca Virgili[2]

[1] DEMACS, University of Calabria
[2] DII, Polytechnic University of Marche

Abstract. In the context of social networks, a renowned paper of Newman introduced the notion of "assortativity", also known as "assortative mixing". Strictly akin to the concept of homophily, it shows how much a node tends to associate with other nodes somewhat similar to it. Degree centrality is the most used similarity metrics for evaluating assortativity between nodes, but several more could be dealt with. Assortativity was deeply investigated in many past researches, given different social platforms. However, Reddit was not one of the social networks taken into account, even if it is a really popular social medium. In this paper, we want to find out the possible presence of a form of assortativity in Reddit; in particular, we focus our analysis on co-posters, i.e. authors posting contents on the same subreddit.

Keywords: Reddit; Co-posters; Assortativity; Social Network Analysis; Degree Centrality

1 Introduction

Assortativity and degree assortativity were introduced in a renowned paper of Newman [17]. Here, the author defines a measure of assortativity for networks showing that real social networks are often assortative, whereas technological and biological networks tend to be disassortative. He also models an assortative network and exploits it for analytic and numeric studies. At the end of this analysis, he finds that assortative networks tend to percolate more easily than disassortative ones and that they are more robust to node removal. Another important study concerning social network assortativity was proposed in [18]. In this paper, the authors confirm the results of [17] and analyze the relation between clustering and assortativity in communities inside a social network. Recently, a detailed overview of assortative mixing in complex network was presented in [19]. Here, the authors investigate assortativity, and in particular degree assortativity, in different kinds of complex network. The concept of assortativity in social networks is a specific case of homophily. It comes from the famous homophily principle "similarity breeds connection" [13] that can be applied for network ties of every type. The result is that people's personal networks are homogeneous w.r.t. many sociodemographic, behavioral, and intrapersonal characteristics.

After the famous paper of Newman, a lot of researchers started to investigate assortativity in social networks. However, in spite of this, there are several platforms (many of them famous) where assortativity has not been yet investigated. One of them is Reddit[3]. This is a heterogeneous crowd-sourced news aggregator and online social network, originally self-declared as "the front page of Internet". It was founded in 2005 and, in few years, has become an ecosystem of 430M+ average monthly active users[4]. In Reddit, users can post their contents as texts, images or links to external resources. Submitted contents (also simply called posts) can be read by other users and discussed via comments. Users can subscribe to multiple subreddits in order to receive the latests content on their front pages. An important feature of Reddit is *voting*, which represents the mechanism affecting the visibility and the ranking of both posts and comments.

This paper aims at fulfilling the gap mentioned above and presents some analyses we performed in order to evaluate assortativity in Reddit. For this purpose, we first built a dataset with all the posts published in Reddit from January 1st, 2019 to September 1st, 2019. Then, we performed several analyses on it. Starting from this dataset, we built a suitable social network representing co-posting activities in Reddit. Then, we carried out several investigations on this network and we compared the results obtained from them with the ones returned by operating on a corresponding null model. At the end of this task, we found that Reddit is assortative with respect to degree centrality, as far as the co-posting relationship is concerned and we defined a hypothesis that explains this result.

The outline of this paper is as follows: In Section 2, we describe related literature. In Section 3, we illustrate the dataset we used for our analyses. In Section 4, we perform our investigation on assortativity in Reddit. Finally, in Section 5, we draw our conclusions and have a look at future developments of our research.

2 Related work

As previously pointed out, [17] and [18] can be considered as the founding fathers of the notion of assortativity. After this papers, in [7], the authors modeled biological, technological and online social networks starting from microscopical mechanisms of growth. Exploiting this model to perform statistical evaluations, they found that the statistical properties of biological, technological and online social networks are in good agreement with those of the real-world social networks of scientists co-authoring papers in condensed matter physics. Here, assortativity plays a key role. Indeed, the authors show that online social networks are generally assortative, whereas the majority of technological and bi-

[3] `https://www.reddit.com`

[4] `https://www.redditinc.com/`

ological networks appear to be disassortative with respect to degree centrality. The investigation of [7] was expanded in [10]. Here, the authors proposed an analysis on assortativity/disassortativity for different kinds of network. Specifically, they considered the same network categories highlighted in [17, 18, 7]. They both confirmed the disassortativity of biological and technological networks and the assortativity of real social networks, analogously to what was shown in [7]. Differently from the wide-spread belief and the results of [7], they found that not all of online social networks are assortative. Almost all the results of [10] were confirmed in [9].

Online social networks simulating real life activities show an opposite behavior. The authors of [23] analyzed the assortativity and other network parameter on both standard social graphs and interaction graphs. They showed that the latter present a higher assortativity than the former. The authors of [6] present a study on degree assortativity for co-author networks. In [8], an interesting investigation on the relationship between assortativity and centrality is presented. Here, the authors study the relation between the degree-degree correlation coefficient and the BC-BC (i.e., Betweenness Centrality-Betweenness Centrality) one. In [11], a detailed study on the relation between Shannon entropy and degree assortativity was presented. Here, the authors defined a general class of degree-degree correlated networks and obtained the corresponding Shannon entropy starting from some suitable parameters. They found that the maximum entropy does not typically correspond to neutral networks but to either assortative or disassortative ones.

In [4], the authors investigated the assortativity of psychological states in real world social networks and online social networks. Specifically, they wanted to check the tendency of online social networks to be assortative, as it happens for real world social networks. The authors of [12] further analyzed assortativity on Twitter. They crawled this network and obtained 41.7 million user profiles, 1.47 billion social relations, 4,262 trending topics, and 106 million tweets. They took into consideration several network parameters, like degree distribution, diameter, reciprocity of user friendship declaration, homophily and assortativity. The authors of [3] proposed an interesting application of degree assortativity. They exploited this measure, along with several other ones, to classify YouTube users in spammers, promoters, and legitimates.

The concept of assortativity was also expanded along several directions. For instance, the authors of [22] extended and evaluated this concept on a weighted social network representing research collaborations. Another interesting extension is the concept of type assortativity that defines a way to measure if and how a social graph belonging to a single type exhibits homophily. In [2], the authors used paths, walks and random walks to define the concept of high order assortativity and showed that classical assortativity can be considered as a particular case of the new proposed notion. They also presented several examples and applications to airline networks and Enron e-mail networks.

Assortativity was also considered in several other analyses, such as node classification and network robustness measurements. The authors of [16] used assortativity to improve the prediction of node attributes, based on the fact that this measure provides information about each node, given its neighbors. This approach is particularly useful in those situations where data is inaccurate or missing. In [20], the authors measured the robustness of network community by means of a metric called "community assortativity", based on the classical notion of assortativity. Finally, in [5], the authors expanded the concept of assortativity from social networks to social internetworking systems, i.e. systems where two or more social networks interact with each other through common users called bridges.

3 Dataset description

Figure 1 reproduces how Reddit is structured. Each rounded rectangle on the left represents a subreddit. The central part depicts an example list of posts from the subreddit /r/subreddit. Here, each post is associated with a type (texts, images or link to external resources) determined by a color. In the right, we can see the structure of a post, made up of a title (the root) and comments.

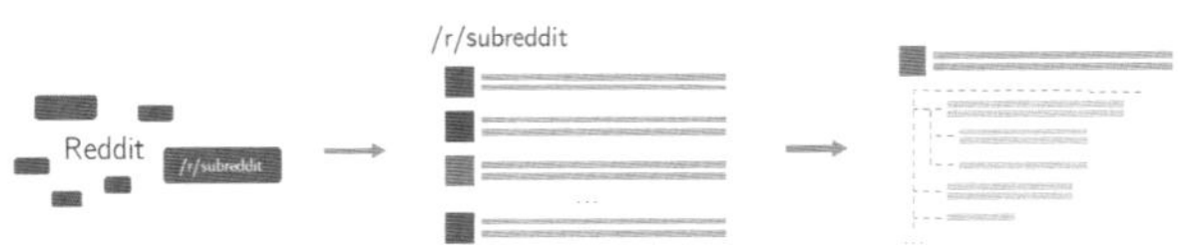

Fig. 1. A graphical overview of Reddit structure

Data used in our investigation activity was downloaded from `pushshift.io`, which is a website well-known as a Reddit data source. We obtained all the posts found on Reddit from January 1st, 2019 to September 1st, 2019. All contents posted in a month were added to the dataset at the end of the next month. We had a total of 150,795,895 posts available for our analyses. Each post had the following set of attributes provided by `pushshift.io`: `id`, `subreddit`, `title`, `author`, `created_utc`, `score`, `num_comments` and `over_18`.

The server used for our experiment was equipped with 16 Intel Xeon E5520 CPUs and 96 GB of RAM with the Ubuntu 18.04.3 operating system. Python 3.6 was the programming language used for the analyses, along with its library Pandas, for ETL operations on data, and its library NetworkX, for operations on networks. Performing ETL operations, we found that some authors who left Reddit wrote posts being in our dataset. So, we decided to delete them. After this activity, we had 122,568,630 posts in total. Beginning from this cleaned data, we figured out that the number of authors who wrote these posts was equal to 12,464,188. The number of subreddits they posted was 1,356,069.

4 Analyzing author assortativity

This section represents the core of our paper. In fact, it aims at verifying if a form of assortativity exists in Reddit. To do so, we focused on co-posters, i.e. authors who post on the same subreddit.

Co-posting network $\mathcal{P}$ is the support network we defined to perform our analyses. Formally speaking, $\mathcal{P} = \langle N, E \rangle$.

Here, N is the set of the nodes of $\mathcal{P}$; there is a node $n_i \in N$ for each author a_i who posted at least once. There is an edge $(n_i, n_j, w_{ij}) \in E$ if the authors a_i and a_j (associated with the nodes n_i and n_j, respectively) posted at least once in the same subreddit. w_{ij} indicates the number of subreddits having at least one post of a_i and, simultaneously, at least one post of a_j.

We have that the number of nodes of $\mathcal{P}$, which is 12,464,188, is exactly the same as the number of authors of our testbed. On the other hand, the arcs of $\mathcal{P}$ are about 925 billions. We computed that the density of the network is 0.00596, while the average clustering coefficient is 0.43753.

The first task done was evaluating the degree centrality of the nodes of $\mathcal{P}$. In Figure 2, we show the corresponding distribution.

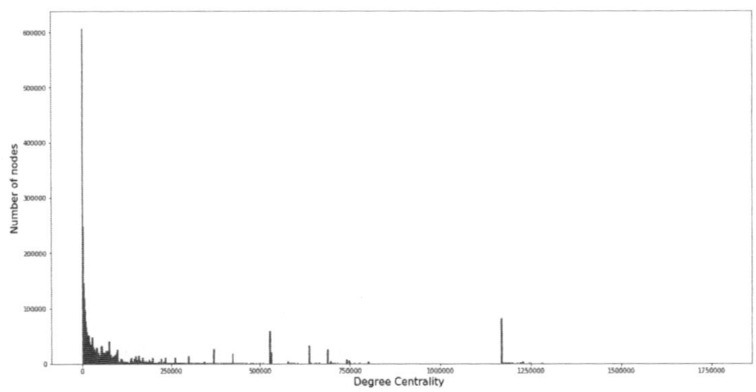

Fig. 2. Distribution of the degree centrality for the nodes of $\mathcal{P}$

As we can see from this figure, degree centrality follows a power law; this result is aligned with the theory underlying this form of centrality [21]. The maximum value of degree centrality is 1,820,412, while the minimum one is 0.

In order to check a possible existence of assortativity in Reddit, we sorted the authors according to their degree centrality, in a descending order. We then partitioned the resulting list into intervals. Specifically, we took intervals with equal width[5] $\{\mathcal{I}_1, \mathcal{I}_2, \cdots, \mathcal{I}_{40}\}$, each made up of 312,500 authors. As a consequence, $\mathcal{I}_k$, $1 \leq k \leq 39$, contained all the authors comprised in the interval $(312,500 \cdot (k-1), 312,500 \cdot k]$, open at left and closed at right of the

[5] Eventually, the last interval had a width a bit lower than the other ones.

sorted list. The interval $\mathcal{I}_{40}$ contained all the authors comprised in the interval $(12,187,500\ ,\ 12,464,188]$.

First of all, we considered the first interval, i.e. $\mathcal{I}_1$. For each interval $\mathcal{I}_k$, $1 \leq k \leq 40$, we determined how many authors of $\mathcal{I}_1$ are connected through an arc to at least one author of $\mathcal{I}_k$. The results obtained are reported in Figure 3. Then, we determined the percentage of the authors of $\mathcal{I}_k$ connected with at least one author of $\mathcal{I}_1$. The results obtained are reported in Figure 4.

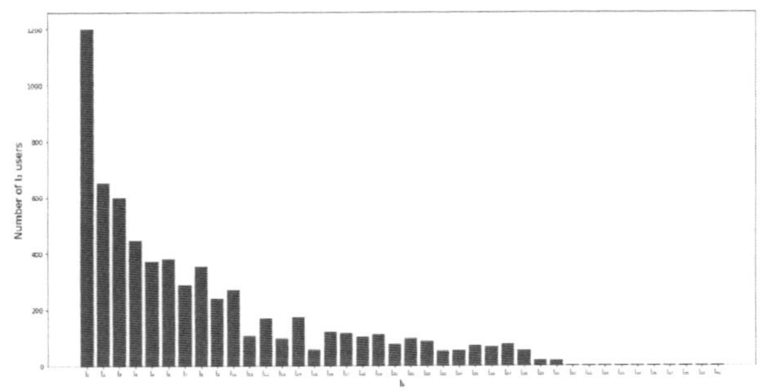

Fig. 3. Number of authors of $\mathcal{I}_1$ connected to at least one author of $\mathcal{I}_k$

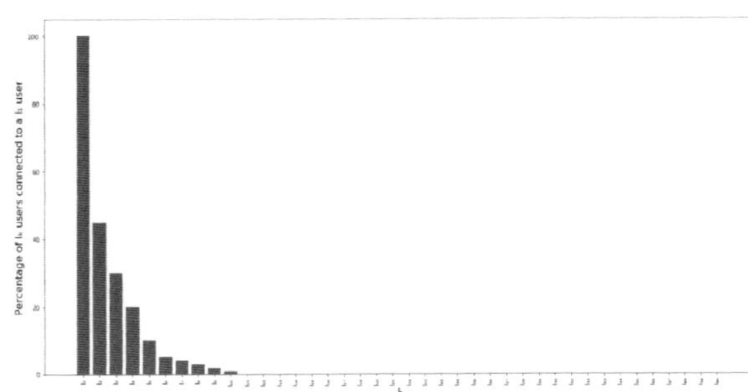

Fig. 4. Percentage of the authors of $\mathcal{I}_k$ connected to at least one author of $\mathcal{I}_1$

The analysis of Figures 3 and 4 clearly shows a strict correlation, i.e. a sort of backbone, between the authors with the highest degree centrality.

We compared our findings with the ones obtained through a null model, in order to verify the statistical significance of our results in an unbiasedly random scenario. In particular, we shuffled all the arcs between the nodes of $\mathcal{P}$ (that, in our case, represent co-postings), in order to build the null model. In this way, we left unchanged all the features of $\mathcal{P}$, excluding the distribution of co-posting relationships, which was unbiasedly random in the null model. Next, we repeated all the previous analyses on the null model. Figures 5 and 6 show the obtained results. The comparison between these two last figures and Figures 3 and 4 highlights the similarity of the distributions represented therein. Many of the intervals that obtained the highest values in Figures 3 and 4 continue to reach the highest values in Figures 5 and 6. However, in the null model, the values are much smaller. So, we can conclude that the behaviors observed are not random, but intrinsic to Reddit.

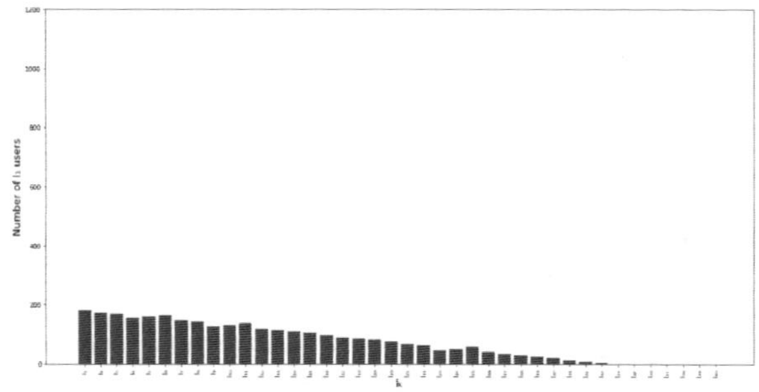

Fig. 5. Number of authors of $\mathcal{I}_1$ connected to at least one author of $\mathcal{I}_k$ in the null model

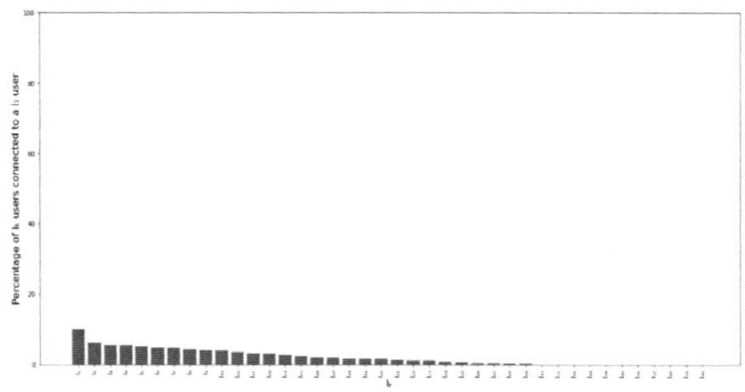

Fig. 6. Percentage of the authors of $\mathcal{I}_k$ connected to at least one author of $\mathcal{I}_1$ in the null model

However, this is not enough to prove the existence of a degree assortativity for co-posters in Reddit. Indeed, we must check if this trend is also verified for authors with an intermediate degree centrality and for ones with a low degree centrality.

For this reason, we have to redo the previous tasks done for $\mathcal{I}_1$ for all intervals. Due to space constraints, we consider only the intervals $\mathcal{I}_{20}$, as the representative of the intermediate degree centrality author intervals, and the interval $\mathcal{I}_{39}$, as the representative of the low degree centrality author intervals[6].

Figure 7 shows the number of authors of $\mathcal{I}_{20}$ connected to at least one author of $\mathcal{I}_k$. Figure 8 shows the percentage of the authors of $\mathcal{I}_k$ connected with at least one author of $\mathcal{I}_{20}$. These figures clearly highlight the existence of a correlation between the authors with an intermediate degree centrality.

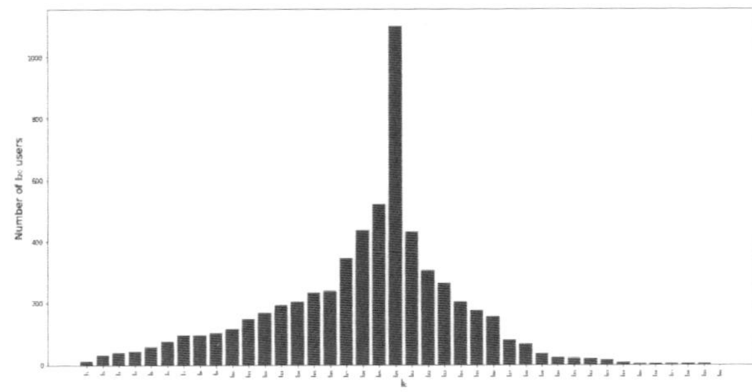

Fig. 7. Number of authors of $\mathcal{I}_{20}$ connected to at least one author of $\mathcal{I}_k$

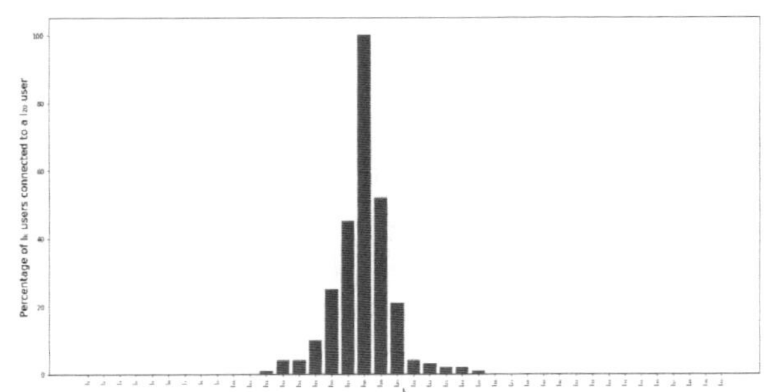

Fig. 8. Percentage of the authors of $\mathcal{I}_k$ connected to at least one author of $\mathcal{I}_{20}$

Also here, we compared the results with the null model. Figures 9 and 10 present the results obtained. Comparing them with Figures 7 and 8, we note that, again, the behaviors observed are not random, but they are a feature of Reddit.

Finally, Figure 11 reports the number of the authors of $\mathcal{I}_{39}$ connected to at least one author of $\mathcal{I}_k$, while Figure 12 shows the percentage of the authors of $\mathcal{I}_k$ connected with at least one author of $\mathcal{I}_{39}$. Here too, a strict correlation exists

[6] We did not choose $\mathcal{I}_{40}$ because the number of its authors is less than the ones of the other intervals.

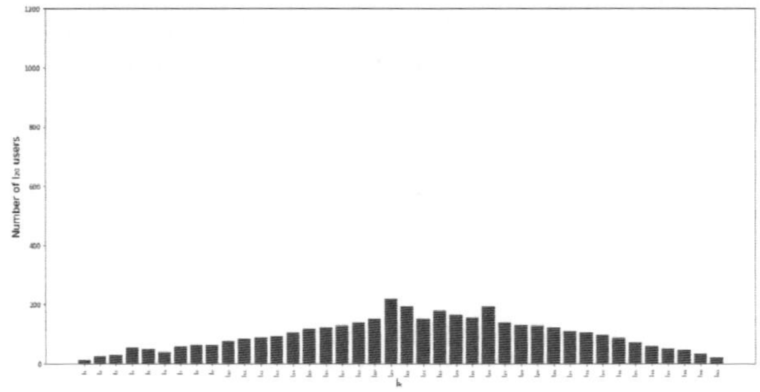

Fig. 9. Number of authors of $\mathcal{I}_{20}$ connected to at least one author of $\mathcal{I}_k$ in the null model

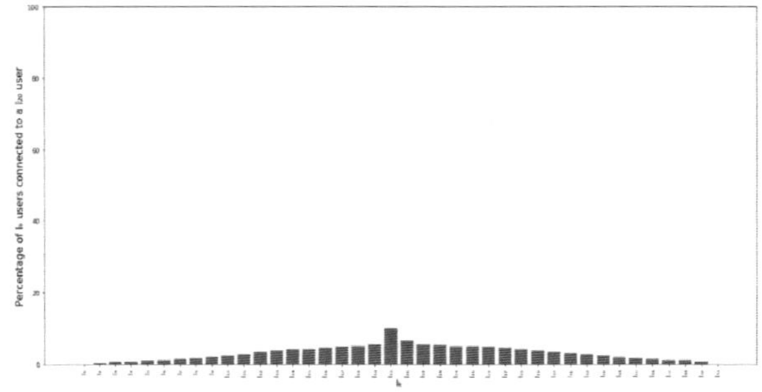

Fig. 10. Percentage of the authors of $\mathcal{I}_k$ connected to at least one author of $\mathcal{I}_{20}$ in the null model

between the authors with a low degree centrality. We compared these results with the ones obtained through the null model reported in Figures 13 and 14. Again, this comparison confirms that the behaviors observed is a property intrinsic to Reddit. The existence of a backbone among the authors with a high (resp., intermediate, low) degree centrality helps us to conclude that, actually, Reddit is assortative with respect to degree centrality, as far as the co-posting relationship is concerned.

This important finding can be explained through the concept of karma and the posting rules existing in Reddit. Indeed, each user has associated a karma, i.e. a score taking her past "reputation" into account. Users with high karma are generally very active and often submit high quality contents, appreciated by others. So, they likely have a high degree centrality. In other words, we can recognize a direct correlation between karma and degree centrality for authors. Reddit's posting rules state that each subreddit has associated a minimum threshold of karma that authors must have to post on it [14, 15, 1]. This threshold is dynamic and changes over time. When it is low, all users can post on that subreddit. When it becomes moderate, users with low karma (and maybe low degree centrality) cannot post on it. When it becomes high, only users with high karma (and maybe high degree centrality) can post on it. In this way we can segment users into groups with homogeneous degree centrality.

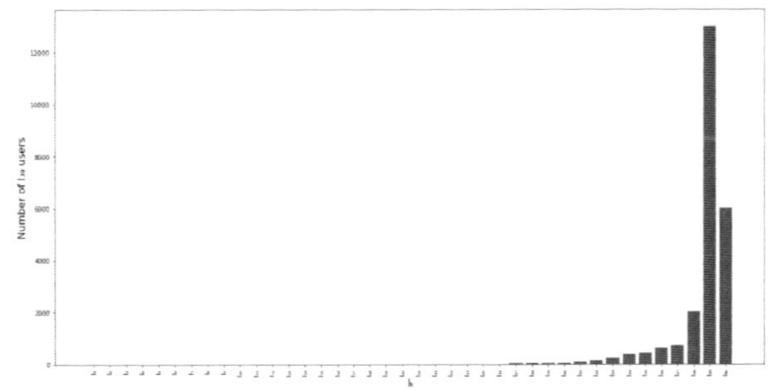

Fig. 11. Number of authors of $\mathcal{I}_{39}$ connected to at least one author of $\mathcal{I}_k$

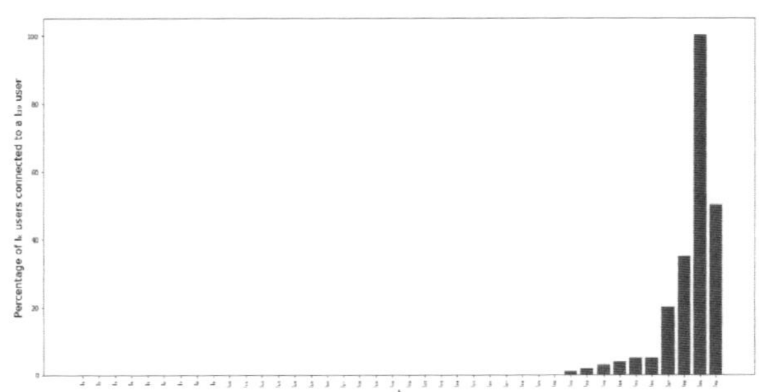

Fig. 12. Percentage of the authors of $\mathcal{I}_k$ connected to at least one author of $\mathcal{I}_{39}$

5 Conclusion

In this paper, we have presented several investigations that we performed to evaluate assortativity in Reddit. First, we have built a dataset comprising all posts found in Reddit from January 1st, 2019 to September 1st, 2019. Then, we have constructed a co-posting network that represented the reference structure on which performing our analyses. Afterwards, we have carried out several investigations on both the co-posting network and a corresponding null model. Finally, we have compared the results obtained and we have found that Reddit is assortative with respect to degree centrality, as far as the co-posting relationship is concerned.

In the future, we plan to extend this work in several directions. For example, we plan to evaluate the possible existence of other forms of assortativity or

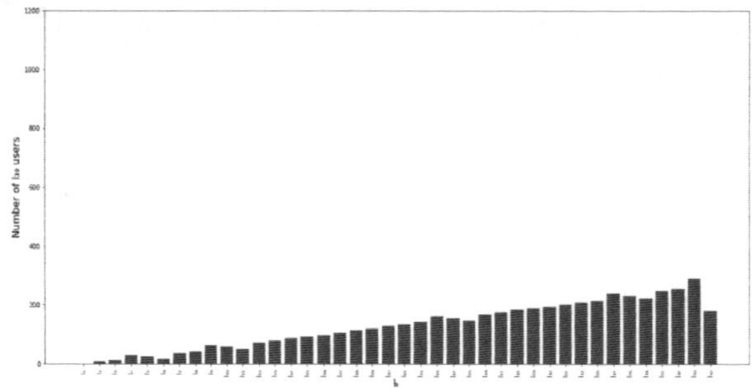

Fig. 13. Number of authors of $\mathcal{I}_{39}$ connected to at least one author of $\mathcal{I}_k$ in the null model

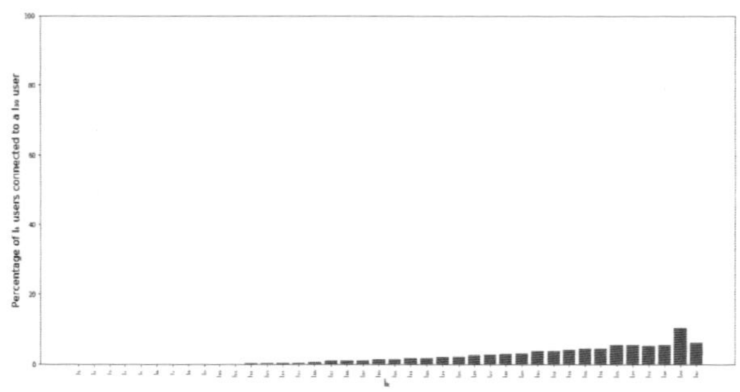

Fig. 14. Percentage of the authors of $\mathcal{I}_k$ connected to at least one author of $\mathcal{I}_{39}$ in the null model

disassortativity in Reddit. They could involve, for instance, centrality measures, other than degree centrality, or user activities, other than posting. In addition, we plan to investigate other issues analyzed in other social platforms and not yet investigated in Reddit.

References

1. K.E. Anderson. Ask me anything: what is Reddit? 2015. Emerald.
2. A. Arcagni, R. Grassi, S. Stefani, and A. Torriero. Higher order assortativity in complex networks. *European Journal of Operational Research*, 262(2):708–719, 2017. Elsevier.
3. F. Benevenuto, T. Rodrigues, V. Almeida, J. Almeida, and M. Gonçalves. Detecting spammers and content promoters in online video social networks. In *Proc. of the International Conference on Research and Development in Information Retrieval (SIGIR '09)*, pages 620–627, Boston, MA, USA, 2009. ACM.
4. J. Bollen, B. Gonçalves, G. Ruan, and H. Mao. Happiness is assortative in online social networks. *Artificial life*, 17(3):237–251, 2011. MIT Press.
5. F. Buccafurri, G. Lax, A. Nocera, and D. Ursino. Internetworking assortativity in Facebook. In *Proc. of the International Conference on Social Computing and*

its Applications (SCA 2013), pages 335–341, Karlsruhe, Germany, 2013. IEEE Computer Society.
6. M. Catanzaro, G. Caldarelli, and L. Pietronero. Assortative model for social networks. *Physical Review E - Statistical, Nonlinear, and Soft Matter Physics*, 70(3):037101–037104, 2004. The American Physical Society.
7. M. Catanzaro, G. Caldarelli, and L. Pietronero. Social network growth with assortative mixing. *Physica A: Statistical Mechanics and its Applications*, 338(1):119–124, 2004. Elsevier.
8. K.I. Goh, E. Oh, B. Kahng, and D. Kim. Betweenness centrality correlation in social networks. *Physical Review E*, 67(1):017101, 2003. APS.
9. H. B. Hu and X. F. Wang. Evolution of a large online social network. *Physics Letters A*, 373(12):1105–1110, 2009. Elsevier.
10. H.B. Hu and X.F. Wang. Disassortative mixing in online social networks. *EPL (Europhysics Letters)*, 86(1):18003, 2009. IOP Publishing.
11. S. Johnson, J.J. Torres, J. Marro, and M.A. Munoz. Entropic origin of disassortativity in complex networks. *Physical Review Letters*, 104(10):108702, 2010. APS.
12. H. Kwak, C. Lee, H. Park, and S. Moon. What is Twitter, a social network or a news media? In *Proc. of the International Conference on World Wide Web (WWW'10)*, pages 591–600, Raleigh, NC, USA, 2010. ACM.
13. M. McPherson, L. Smith-Lovin, and J.M. Cook. Birds of a feather: Homophily in social networks. *Annual Review of Sociology*, 27:415–444, 2001. JSTOR.
14. J. Meese. It belongs to the Internet: Animal images, attribution norms and the politics of amateur media production. *M/C Journal*, 17(2):1–3, 2014. M/C.
15. D. Morrison and C. Hayes. Here, have an upvote: Communication behaviour and karma on Reddit. *Informatik*, pages 2258–2268, 2013. Gesellschaft für Informatik eV.
16. D. Mulders, C. de Bodt, J. Bjelland, A. Pentland, M. Verleysen, and Y.-A. de Montjoye. Inference of node attributes from social network assortativity. *Neural Computing and Applications*, pages 1–21, 2019. Springer Nature Switzerland AG.
17. M.E.J. Newman. Assortative mixing in networks. *Physical Review Letters*, 89(20):208701, 2002. APS.
18. M.E.J. Newman and J. Park. Why social networks are different from other types of networks. *Physical Review E*, 68(3):036122, 2003. APS.
19. R. Noldus and P. Van Mieghem. Assortativity in complex networks. *Journal of Complex Networks*, 3(4):507–542, 2015. Oxford University Press.
20. D. Shizuka and D.R. Farine. Measuring the robustness of network community structure using assortativity. *Animal Behaviour*, 112:237–246, 2016. Elsevier.
21. M. Tsvetovat and A. Kouznetsov. *Social Network Analysis for Startups: Finding connections on the social web*. 2011. O'Reilly Media, Inc.
22. M. Vaanunu and C. Avin. Homophily and nationality assortativity among the most cited researchers' social network. In *Proc. of 2018 IEEE/ACM International Conference on Advances in Social Networks Analysis and Mining (ASONAM)*, pages 584–586, Barcelona, Spain, 2018. IEEE Computer Society.
23. C. Wilson, B. Boe, A. Sala, K.P.N Puttaswamy, and B.Y. Zhao. User interactions in social networks and their implications. In *Proc. of the ACM European Conference on Computer systems (EuroSys'09)*, pages 205–218, Nuremberg, Germany, 2009. ACM.

How to Cope with Personnel Unavailability? Process Mining May Help! (DISCUSSION PAPER)

Andrea Chiorrini, Claudia Diamantini, Domenico Potena and Emanuele Storti

DII, Polytechnic University of Marche, Ancona
{a.chiorrini,c.diamantini,d.potena,e.storti}@univpm.it

Abstract. Replacement planning is critical to guarantee continuity of operations in business processes in case of personnel unavailability. In this work, we propose a data-driven approach for supporting resource replacement that makes use of logs of past process executions to model a social network of resources. On this top, a similarity measure among resources is exploited to assign tasks of unavailable resource to the available ones through an Integer Linear Model.

1 Introduction

In organization management, replacement planning consists in addressing short-term lack of workforce that may be due to temporary or permanent unavailability of personnel for several reasons, including for instance vacation, resignation or illness. This issue has a larger impact on organizations when the unavailability cannot be predicted in advance, such as during strikes or emergencies. A recent example of the latter case is the COVID-19 outbreak, which is severely affecting continuity of operations in many public administrations and private companies worldwide.

Traditional approaches in the literature for resource scheduling and replacement planning address the problem typically through business rules modeled by domain experts. On the other hand, nowadays information systems (e.g., ERPs, Workflow Management Systems, CRMs) are capable to track and monitor every event occurring during a business process, such as what activities have been executed, when and by whom. This valuable information can be exploited to support more reliable kinds of data-driven analysis, e.g. through Process Mining techniques.

This paper discusses a data-driven framework for planning of resource replacement. Through the analysis of past executions of business processes the approach is aimed to model a sociogram, i.e. a social network describing how resources collaborate with each other. Several metrics have been devised in the literature to analyse different social relations among resources, including those focusing on how work moves among performers and those considering that people doing similar tasks have stronger relations than people doing completely different things [5]. Here we focus on the both aspects, using a handover of work metric (measuring how frequently work is transferred between two resources) and taking into account capabilities of resources, to evaluate the costs for assigning those activities that should have been performed by the unavailable resource(s), to others. Finally, on the basis of this information, an Integer Linear Programming (ILP) model is defined with the aim of selecting the set of candidate resources to minimize the total cost of replacement.

The work fits into the field of *organizational mining*[4], focusing on the resources (or actors) that performed events and their mutual cooperation in the fulfillment of a process. In [3] an organizational mining framework has been proposed for the discovery, rather than the enforcement, of patterns related to resource assignment using declarative process modelling languages based on rule templates. Our approach shares also the exploitation of an ILP model for task assignment with [2], although the work has a different purpose, namely proposing a recommendation system to support process participants to take a risk-informed decision in choosing the next task to execute out of a set of assigned tasks.

The novel contributions of this work are as follows: (1) we propose a sociogram modeling the handover of work relation that extends traditional models in the literature, by representing the specific type of the transferred activity; (2) on its top, a measure of similarity among resources is defined by considering the degree of collaboration between two resources, the performance and the experience of a resource to perform a given activity; (3) in order to find the best set of resources to replace the unavailable one, an Integer Linear Programming model is proposed to minimize a cost function taking into account similarity among resources.

We propose here an example related to a phone repair process for a company, that will be used throughout the paper. As shown in Figure 1, the process starts with the registration of the repair request (A) and is followed by analysis of defects (B). Then, the user is informed about the outcome (C) and in parallel the repair subprocess is performed. This is achieved by executing either a simple repair (D) or a complex one (E), and is ended by a test to verify whether the repair solved the issues (F). In the negative case, the repair subprocess is re-executed. Finally, if the test succeeds, the request is archived (G) and the process ends. Let us assume the process involves 6 users, named James, Carrie (in charge of administration activities A, C and G), Mark, Alec, Harrison and Peter (in charge of analysis, repair and test, i.e. activities B, D, E and F). Every record in the log refers to a specific case and is a sequence of events, each of which described in terms of activity, resource and duration in a certain time unit (minutes in the example), as shown in Table 1.

The example is inspired to the ProM 6 tutorial by H.M.W. (Eric) Verbeek at http://www.promtools.org/prom6/downloads/prom-6.0-tutorial.pdf

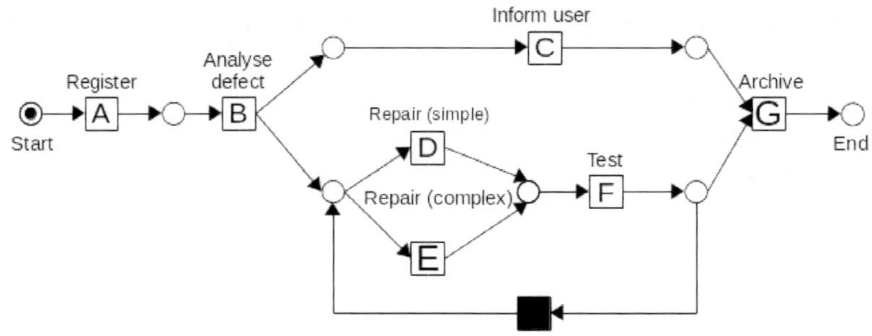

Fig. 1. The example process model.

ID	Trace
1	(A, James, 15), (B, Mark, 60), (C,James, 8), (D, Harrison, 25), (F,Alec, 18), (G, Carrie, 9)
2	(A,Carrie, 12), (B,Harrison, 74), (E,Harrison, 79), (F,Peter, 17), (C,James, 4), (G,James, 13)
3	(A,Carrie, 10), (B,Peter, 43), (D,Peter, 43), (F,Alec, 72), (C,Carrie, 7), (E,Harrison, 115), (F,Alec, 20), (G,James, 14)
4	(A,James, 20), (B,Mark, 96), (C,James, 3), (D,Mark, 31), (F,Alec, 209), (D,Alec, 53), (F,Peter, 23), (G,Carrie, 11)

Table 1. Running example: event log for the repair process. Time unit is minute.

The rest of this work is structured as follows: the next section presents a novel handover of work metric and the sociogram model. Section 3 discusses the proposed methodology for resource replacement. Finally, Section 4 reports preliminary results and draws future research extension.

2 Social network for handover of work

In this section we introduce the terminology and a model of social network for handover of work that is used in the rest of the paper.

Hereby we refer to the term *activity* as a task (or portion thereof) performed to achieve a goal, and to *resource* as any member of personnel that is capable to perform some activity.

Definition 1. *(Event, Trace & Event Log)*
Let $\mathcal{A}$ be a set of activities and $\mathcal{R}$ a set of resources. $V = \mathcal{A} \times \mathcal{R}$ is the set of possible *events*, i.e., combinations of an activity and a resource. Given a resource r, $V(r) \subseteq V$ is the set of events in which r can take part. A *trace* is a possible sequence of events, where $C = V^*$ is the set of all possible traces. An event log $\mathcal{L}$ is a subset of all bags (multi-sets) over C.

In our scenario, we assume the event log includes as attributes at least the case id, the executed activity, the resource name and the timestamp when each event has been performed. For convenience, we introduce the function $\pi_a(\sigma)$ which returns the set of activities related to events of a trace σ.

From the event log, it is possible to characterize a resource $r \in \mathcal{R}$ in terms of his/her capabilities, i.e. the set $\mathcal{A}(r)$ of activities that is able to perform. To make an example, from the log in Table 1 we derive $\mathcal{A}(Mark)$={B, D} and $\mathcal{A}(Harrison)$={B,D,E}.

Among the various relations that can be recognized in an event log between two resources, we focus here on relations of possible causality, and specifically to *handover of work*. Within a case there is a handover of work from a resource r_1 to a resource r_2 if there are two subsequent activities a_1 and a_2 where a_1 is completed by r_1 and a_2 by r_2. The metric can be defined and computed in multiple ways [5], according to the degree of causality (direct or indirect), the existence of multiple succession from a resource to itself (multiple self-transfer), and the kind of succession, i.e. arbitrary succession between two subsequent events in a trace or casual dependency. In this last case, a process model is needed to recognize which is the correct flow of activities in a trace. To make an example, with reference to the case 3, between events (A,Carrie) and (B,Peter) there is a direct and casual succession, while between (F,Alec) and (C,Carrie) there is a direct but arbitrary succession. Indeed, if we compare the log to the process model in Figure 1, there is a causal relation between activities A and B, but this does not hold between activities F and C.

In this work, we refer to the handover of work relation (1) by ignoring self-transfers, (2) by considering indirect succession and (3) casual relation, i.e. we take into consideration succession between activities, with any length, only if aligned to the process model. The reason behind (1) is that the research question of the work is related to resource replacement, for which considering handover from the same resource is not helpful. The reason of (2) and (3) is related to the need to correctly identify handover of work in real processes and avoid spurious relations. Please note that a process model, if not available, can be discovered through Process Discovery algorithms (e.g., Alpha Miner, Heuristic Miner, Inductive Miner). In the following we define the function and the formula for the calculation of the metric.

Definition 2. *(Handover of work)*
Given $r_1, r_2 \in \mathcal{R}$, $a_x \in \mathcal{A}(r_1), a_y \in \mathcal{A}(r_2)$, an event log $\mathcal{L}$, a process model $\mathcal{P}$ and a trace $\sigma \in \mathcal{L}$, the function $r_1 \otimes^{\sigma}_{a_x,a_y} r_2$ returns how many times r_1 and r_2 executed respectively activity $a_x \in \pi_a(\sigma)$ and $a_y \in \pi_a(\sigma)$ such that a causal relation between them in $\mathcal{P}$ exists. For the whole event log $\mathcal{L}$, the function is computed as:

$$q_{xy} = r_1 \otimes^{\mathcal{L}}_{a_x,a_y} r_2 = \sum_{\sigma \in \mathcal{L}} r_1 \otimes^{\sigma}_{a_x,a_y} r_2$$

Finally, the metric *handover of work* between r_1, r_2 for activities a_x, a_y in $\mathcal{L}$ is computed as:

$$h_{xy} = r_1 \odot^{\mathcal{L}}_{a_x,a_y} r_2 = r_1 \otimes^{\mathcal{L}}_{a_x,a_y} r_2 / \Big(\sum_{r_i \in R} \sum_{r_j \in R} r_i \otimes^{\mathcal{L}}_{a_x,a_y} r_j \Big)$$

The metric is computed for a couple of resources r_1, r_2 and with respect to a couple of activities a_x, a_y by dividing the total number of proper casual

	James	Marc	Carrie	Harrison	Alec	Peter
James		(A,B,0.5,2)	(C,G,0.5,2)			
Mark	(B,C,0.5,2)			(B,D,0.3,1)	(D,F,0.25,1)	
Carrie	(C,G,0.25,1)			(A,B,0.25,1)		(A,B, 0.25,1)
Harrison	(B,C,0.25,1)				(D,F,0.25,1) (E,F,0.5,1)	(E,F,0.5,1)
Alec	(F,G,0.25,1)		(F,G,0.25,1)	(F,E,1.0,1)		(D,F,0.25,1)
Peter	(F,G,0.25,1)		(B,C,0.25,1) (F,G,0.25,1)		(D,F,0.25,1)	

Table 2. Running example: handover matrix.

succession (with no self-transfer) by the total number of casual succession of a_x, a_y between any two resources r_i, r_j, with $i \neq j$.

As for the running example, given resources $James$ and $Carrie$, and activities C and G, $James \odot^{\mathcal{L}}_{C,G} Carrie{=}\frac{2}{4} = 0.5$, because the casual succession between them happens 2 times (case 1 and case 4), but the casual succession of C and G between any two resources occurs 4 times.

This information can be represented as a *handover matrix*, that is a matrix $N \times N$, where $N < |\mathcal{R}|$ is the number of active resources (i.e. resources that executed at least 1 activity in the event log). Given two resources $r_i, r_j \in \mathcal{R}$ active in $\mathcal{L}$, the cell (i, j) of the handover matrix includes a tuple $(a_x, a_y, h_{xy}, q_{xy})$, with $a_x \in \mathcal{A}(r_i)$ and $a_y \in \mathcal{A}(r_j)$, if and only if $h_{xy} > 0$. In Table 2 we report the handover matrix for the running example.

From the matrix, a *sociogram* can be defined, i.e. a graph of social relations where nodes are resources and an edge linking two resources is defined if a certain social relation is recognized between them. We refer to the following definition of a sociogram as a labeled multidigraph, i.e. a directed multigraph where two nodes may be linked by multiple labeled edges.

Definition 3. *(Sociogram)*
Given a $N \times N$ handover matrix M, a sociogram G is defined as an 8-tuple $G = (\Sigma_{R'}, \Sigma_E, R', E, s, t, \ell_{R'}, \ell_E)$ where:

- $R' \subseteq \mathcal{R}$ is the finite set of N resources in M and E is a set of arcs representing a handover of work relation;
- $\Sigma_{R'}$ and Σ_E are finite alphabets of the available vertex and arc labels, $s\colon E \to R'$ and $t\colon E \to R'$ are two maps indicating the source and target vertex of an arc;
- $\ell_{R'}: R' \to \Sigma_{R'}$ and $\ell_E\colon E \to \Sigma_E$ are two maps describing the labeling of the vertices and arcs.

In the following, for the sake of simplicity, we refer to a sociogram G as a tuple $G = (R', E)$, with E as a multi-set of arcs. Each arc $e \in E$ will be shortly represented as a tuple $e = (r_i, r_j, (a_x, a_y, h_{xy}, q_{xy}))$ linking two nodes $r_i, r_j \in R'$, being r_i the source and r_j the target of e, and $(a_x, a_y, h_{xy}, q_{xy})$ the arc label. For convenience, we introduce the operations $\pi_h(r_i, r_j, a_x) = \{h_{xy} : \exists e = (r_i, r_j, (a_x, a_y, h_{xy}, q_{xy})) \in E\}$ and $\pi_q(r_i, r_j, a_x) = \{q_{xy} : \exists e = (r_i, r_j, (a_x, a_y, h_{xy}, q_{xy})) \in E\}$ which respectively return the values of handover of work between r_i (after a_x has been completed) and r_j, and the numbers of times a_x has been executed by r_i before r_j. Furthermore, the set $G_{r_i}(a_x) = \{r' \in R' : \exists(r_i, r', (a_x, a_y, h_{xy}, q_{xy})) \in E\}$ is introduced to return the subset of resources for which an handover of work relation from r_i after completing a_x exists.

Please note that, differently from the organizational mining literature, we refer to a labeled multidigraph with multiple edges between two nodes. This enables a greater expressiveness as we can encode not only the handover of generic work between two resources, but also take into account which specific activities one resource has handed over the other.

3 Resource replacement methodology

We assume an organization relying on a Business Process Management system with monitoring capabilities of process execution. Execution traces are made available as event logs, which are then analysed and elaborated through *organizational mining* techniques to derive the sociogram as described in Section 2. This information is used to drive the *resource replacement*, that returns the set of specific resources that are selected to replace the missing ones, and their allocation to activities.

Given a sociogram $G = (R', E)$, an unavailable resource $r \in \mathcal{R}$ to replace and a multi-set $T = \{a_1, \ldots, a_h\}$ of activities assigned to r that must be performed by some other resources, the goal is to determine a set of resources $\{r_1, \ldots, r_n\} \subseteq \mathcal{R}$ that is collectively capable to replace r to perform activities in T. We take into account a *similarity* factor such that resources being more compatible to the one to replace are preferred. This takes into account handover of work relations, capabilities of resources, performance and experience.

Similarity measure. Given a resource $r \in \mathcal{R}$ to replace, a candidate resource $r_i \in \mathcal{R}$ and an activity a_j, the similarity between the r and r_j for the specific activity a_j is defined as follows:

$$sim(r, r_i, a_j) = \omega_1 \cdot coll(r, r_i, a_j) + \omega_2 \cdot perf(r, r_i, a_j) + \omega_3 \cdot exp(r, r_i, a_j)$$

The function $sim(r, r_i, a_j)$ returns the degree of affinity between the two resources on the basis of (1) the collaborations that have been established to perform the activity a_j (i.e., $coll(r, r_i, a_j)$), (2) the speed with which a_j has been performed (i.e., $perf(r, r_i, a_j)$) and (3) the experience gained by the two resources in carrying out the activity (i.e., $exp(r, r_i, a_j)$). User parameters $\omega_1, \omega_2, \omega_3 \in [0, 1]$, such that $\omega_1 + \omega_2 + \omega_3 = 1$, are introduced to weigh the three similarity factors.

In details, $G_r(a_j)$ and $G_{r_i}(a_j)$ (see Section 2) are the sets of resources to whom respectively r and r_i handed over work after performing activity a_j. Let $\hat{h}(r_x, r_y, a_j) = \frac{1}{|\pi_h(r_x, r_y, a_j)|} \cdot \sum_{h_i \in \pi_h(r_x, r_y, a_j)} h_i$ be the average handover of work

T is a multi-set because an activity may need to be performed multiple times in a process.

between r_x, executing a_j, and r_y. Finally, we introduce the function $\delta(x)$ which returns x if $x \leq 1$, and 1 otherwise. The *coll* function is defined as: $coll(r, r_i, a_j) = \frac{1}{|G_r(a_j)|} \cdot \sum_{r' \in G_r(a_j) \cap G_{r_i}(a_j)} \delta\left(\frac{\hat{h}(r_i, r', a_j)}{\hat{h}(r, r', a_j)}\right)$. It ranges in $[0, 1]$, returning 0 when the two resources do not share any collaborations, 1 if r_i interacts with all collaborators of r with the same handover of work. The *coll* function is introduced under the assumption that replacing a resource with someone acquainted to work in the same team and with similar handover relations is preferable.

The $perf(r, r_i, a_j)$ function compares the time taken by the two resources to carry out the activity a_j. Let t_r and t_{r_i} be the average time respectively taken by r and r_i to perform a_j, the $perf$ function is defined as $perf(r, r_i, a_j) = \delta\left(\frac{t_r}{t_{r_i}}\right)$. The $perf$ function ranges in $[0, 1]$, values close to 0 mean that r is much faster than r_i. When r_i is on average faster then r, assigning a_j to r_i is also better than having it performed by r, hence the value of $perf$ is set to the maximum. The average times to perform an activity, if not available in the event log, can be estimated from the model by considering the difference in time between two causally related events.

Finally, the $exp(r, r_i, a_j)$ function compares the experience of the two resources to perform a_j, computed as the number of times the resource has carried out the activity ($q_r(a_j)$ and $q_{r_i}(a_j)$ respectively). The *exp* function is defined as $exp(r, r_i, a_j) = \delta\left(\frac{q_{r_i}}{q_r}\right)$, where $q_{r'}(a_j) = \sum_{r_x \in G_{r'}(a_j)} \pi_q(r', r_x, a_j)$. This function ranges in $[0, 1]$. Values close to 0 mean that the experience of r_i is much smaller than that of r, while the function takes the maximum value when the experience of r_i is greater than or equal to that of r.

Model specification. An Integer Linear Programming (ILP) model is aimed to select the set of assignments of activities to resources in order to minimize the total cost of resource replacement.

Given a sociogram $G = (R', E)$ and a resource $r \in R'$ to replace, let $C = \{r_i \in R' : \exists a_j \in \mathcal{A}(r_i) \text{ such that } a_j \in T\}$ be the set of candidate resources having at least one capability equal to one activity in T. Finally, Let $|C|$ and $|T|$ be equal to k and h respectively.

We introduce the decision variable $x_{ij}, \forall r_i \in C$ and $\forall a_j \in T$, equal to 1 if the resource r_i is selected for replacement of r to perform activity a_j, 0 otherwise. The objective function $min\left(\sum_{i=1}^{k}\sum_{j=1}^{h} c_{ij}x_{ij}\right)$ represents the total cost of replacing the resource r, taking into account the cost factor $c_{ij} = 1 - sim(r, r_i, a_j)$. An additional constraint is set to impose that each activity in T is assigned to only one resource of C to avoid multiple assignments. Finally, a further constraint defines the binary nature of the decision variables, according to a 0-1 Integer Linear Programming model.

4 Discussion and conclusion

In this work we propose a data-driven approach to support resource replacement in organizations, based on a notion for handover of work that is capable to model collaboration among resources on the basis of causal relations between activities. Although we referred mostly to human-centric processes, the approach is general enough to be applied in cases where a mix of users and machines cooperate together, provided additional constraints on which resources cannot be selected for replacement.

We report some preliminary results of an early experimentation done on the real-world dataset published for the BPI Challenge 2012, referring to an application process for personal loan. From the log we extracted the conform subset, including 7974 traces and 47634 events, with an average number of 6 events per trace (from 3 to 41) and belonging to 8 event types (corresponding to activity names), with 62 resources. We randomly selected a resource and a day in the last 10 days of the log. The procedure is then repeated for all resources. The average number of daily activities that needs to be reassigned per resource is 6.9. On average, in our setting the replace phase took around 6 milliseconds on average per resource to achieve a solution (with an ILP model including up to 1000 variables). The most demanding phase, on the other hand, is the creation of the sociogram, which takes 285 seconds for the whole dataset. Further analysis are not reported here for lack of space and will be deepened in future work. We also plan to extend the model to take into account further social relations among resources and the case of organisations that evolve over time [1]. Furthermore, the average execution time for each activity and the current resource workload will be considered as they can be exploited to add load-balancing constraints in the replacement planning.

References

1. Annalisa Appice. Towards mining the organizational structure of a dynamic event scenario. *Journal of Intelligent Information Systems*, 50(1):165–193, 2018.
2. Raffaele Conforti, Massimiliano de Leoni, Marcello La Rosa, Wil MP van der Aalst, and Arthur HM ter Hofstede. A recommendation system for predicting risks across multiple business process instances. *Decision Support Systems*, 69:1–19, 2015.
3. Stefan Schönig, Cristina Cabanillas, Stefan Jablonski, and Jan Mendling. A framework for efficiently mining the organisational perspective of business processes. *Decision Support Systems*, 89:87 – 97, 2016.
4. Minseok Song and Wil M.P. van der Aalst. Towards comprehensive support for organizational mining. *Decision Support Systems*, 46(1):300 – 317, 2008.
5. Wil MP Van Der Aalst, Hajo A Reijers, and Minseok Song. Discovering social networks from event logs. *Computer Supported Cooperative Work (CSCW)*, 14(6):549–593, 2005.

The experiments run on a 4-core 2.2GHz processor, 16 GB RAM. IBM ILOG CPLEX API (version 12.9) was used for ILP model solving.

Crowdsourcing for Building Knowledge Graphs at Scale from the Vatican Archives (Discussion Paper)

Donatella Firmani, Paolo Merialdo, Elena Nieddu, Andrea Rossi, and Riccardo Torlone

Roma Tre University, Rome, Italy

Abstract. Project *In Codice Ratio* is developing tools to extract the knowledge contained in the ancient manuscripts of the Vatican Archives. The scarcity of datasets suitable for our setting has led us to rely on crowdsourcing in all phases of our project. In this paper we discuss our approaches for leveraging inexpensive non-expert workers to fruitfully perform labelling operations on challenging manuscripts. We describe the range of different tasks we are devising, as well as the corresponding priority and redundancy policies we are employing. We describe the datasets collected thus far and the corresponding results.

Keywords: Crowdsourcing · Knowledge Graphs · Digital Humanities

1 Introduction

Recent advancements in Knowledge Extraction from unstructured data have opened up new, exciting possibilities in digital humanities. These novel methodologies typically require large amounts of labelled data to reach satisfactory performances; nonetheless, when dealing with specific tasks in vertical domains, the lack of suitable datasets makes it unfeasible to use such approaches. As a matter of fact, in many scenarios the only available resources are raw and unlabeled. This has led several projects to rely on crowdsourcing techniques, having human operators, or *workers*, manually process and label part of the available data. By gathering the outputs yielded by the workers it is possible to build new, extensive datasets to train automatic systems on.

Our Digital Humanities project (ICR) *In Codice Ratio* [2, 6] falls within this scenario. ICR aims at extracting and harnessing the knowledge contained in the manuscripts of the Vatican Apostolic Archive (VAA). The VAA is one of the largest historical libraries in the world, with more than 85 linear kilometres of shelving. We are currently focusing on its "Vatican Registers" corpus, consisting of 43 parchment registers for a total of 18650 pages; these documents date to the XIII century, under the papacy of Honorius III, and contain the official correspondence of the Roman Curia, including legal or political letters from and to kings, sovereigns and institutions throughout Europe. The manuscripts are written in Chancery script (also called *Cancelleresca*) and they have been recently digitized in high definition images, but despite their historical relevance they have never been integrally transcribed so far.

ICR aims at *(i)* obtaining a textual transcription of the manuscripts in the Archive, and *(ii)* extracting entities, relations and facts from the obtained text to construct an extensive Knowledge Graph (KG). Performing automatic transcription from the high definition images of the document pages amounts to perform *Handwritten Text Recognition* (HTR), while extracting structured knowledge from the resulting transcription is a well known task of *Text Mining*.

Machine Learning (ML) approaches have been shown to reach state-of-the-art performances in both tasks. Since our documents are written in Medieval scripts and languages, no comprehensive datasets could be found for the adequately training ML models. In this paper we discuss how we are leveraging crowdsourcing methodologies to process, label and enrich data, in order to collect suitable datasets, we describe the crowdsourcing tasks we have devised and the assignment policies we have implemented.

Our pool of workers counts over 700 members, and it is entirely constituted by high-school students in the city of Rome, that have joined the project for free as a part of their work-related learning program. In addition to performing tasks, students also attended frontal lessons in a variety of topics, from paleography to machine learning, managed by both the engineering and humanities departments of Roma Tre University. As a consequence, they are provided with an opportunity of personal growth, and they receive guidance for their future studies and careers.

So far we have focused on the transcription phase: with the data labelled by our workers, we were able to successfully generate datasets large enough for training and developing very promising HTR models. These results allow us to start assigning to our workers the first batches of Text Mining tasks, with the goal of extracting knowledge from the transcribed text.

The rest of this paper is structured as follows. In Section 2 we report the HTR-oriented tasks we have employed so far, and we describe the obtained datasets and the corresponding transcription results. In Section 3 we discuss the typologies of tasks we have devised for text mining and knowledge extraction. We discuss related works in Section 4, and provide concluding remarks in Section 5.

2 Crowdsourcing for automatic transcription

The extraction of textual transcriptions from images is nowadays generally performed with automatic HTR models. As already mentioned in the Introduction, the lack of representative labelled datasets for the Papal Registers (i.e., similar script, abbreviations, and layout) makes it difficult to train a full-fledged HTR system without dealing with a very expensive data preparation effort.

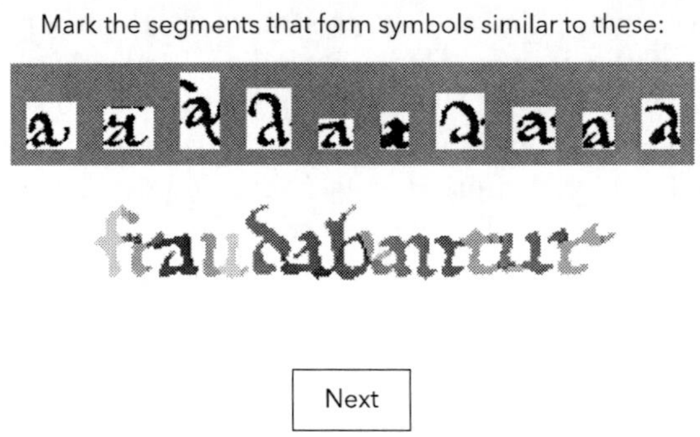

Fig. 1. Example of labeling task: given the set of segments shown in different colors, the worker is asked to select the sets of segments corresponding to the required symbol.

We have thus employed a crowd-sourcing approach to build our own dataset with workers manually identifying portions from the original images. The obtained labelled segments are then gathered into datasets large enough to enable the training of HTR models. The registers are strikingly hard to decipher, and the extensive use of abbreviations makes them even less understandable. Therefore, unlike other transcription projects [5], in our case a non-expert worker is generally unable to directly transcribe entire paragraphs, lines or even words. Therefore we ask our workers to just recognize specific symbols inside words: the resulting task is more akin to pattern matching rather than to text transcription.

In a preparatory step, we apply to the images of the manuscripts pages (i.e. written facades) a pipeline of computer vision operations. We first run a custom binarization algorithm to transform them into black and white images. We then use the alternation between black and white sections to perform line segmentation and word segmentation. In each of the obtained word images, we analyse the upper and lower profile of the writing, and cut the word wherever the stroke is absent or exceedingly thin. This is an over-segmentation, because the obtained segments are finer-grained than the actual characters in the word.

We then use this setting to generate our crowdsourcing tasks for character recognition. In each task, we use as an input the oversegmented image of a word, and we ask our workers if a specific symbol is present within the word (e.g. symbol "⁊", that is a Tironian note meaning "et"). If it is, the worker should highlight the set of consecutive segments that belong to that character. In case the symbol occurs multiple times in the word, the worker can also highlight multiple sets of segments. In order to facilitate the selection, in our UI we display each segment in a different color, as shown in Figure 1, in which the worker is asked to identify the symbols for character 'a'.

Our approach to design the task was inspired by [11], in which the authors address the problem of extracting a number of items satisfying certain properties from a larger set, and design optimal algorithms for various settings in terms of cost and time. In our tasks, if the worker has identified the character in the word,

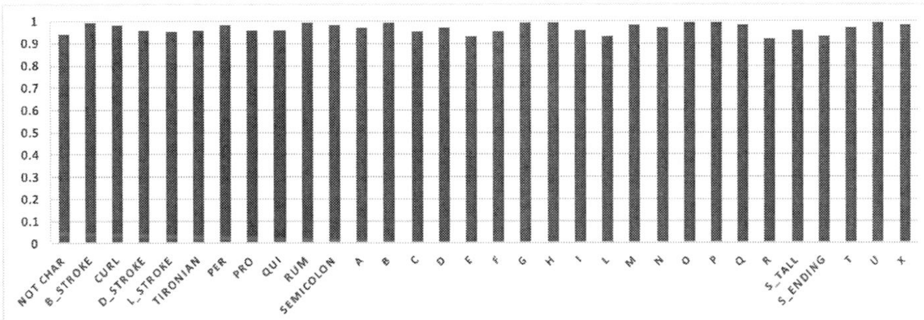

Fig. 2. Character-level predictive accuracy achieved by our HTR model on the crowd-based dataset. Class "NOT_CHAR" identifies inputs that do not correspond to any character in the alphabet. Classes from "B_STROKE" to "SEMICOLON" identify abbreviation symbols. Classes from "A" to "X" identify symbols that correspond to actual characters in the alphabet. note that there are two variants for character "S".

this correspond to a positive vote; otherwise it is a negative one. We assume that workers can make mistakes and employ redundancy to address this issue.

Specifically, we use the *rectangular* policy in [11] to aggregate votes and the *cost-optimal* paradigm in same paper to schedule tasks: for each class, we propose the same task to different workers until either positive or negative votes exceed respective thresholds N and M.[1] As soon as the crowd finds a pre-defined target amount of items for a class, we move to the next one sequentially. The same over-segmented word image can be re-used in multiple tasks, asking to recognize different symbols. At this regard, we prioritize the symbols that we lack the most in our datasets. The extracted sets of segments are used to generate labelled images, that are finally put in our transcription datasets. So far, with the contributions gathered from our workers, we were able to build various datasets, the latest - and largest - of which includes around 50k samples. We currently cover 32 classes; among these, 21 correspond to character symbols, 10 correspond to abbreviation symbols, and the remaining class identifies "not-character" elements, i.e. selections not corresponding to any valid item in the alphabet [2]. All our datasets are publicly available at our repository. [3]

We have then used the produced datasets to train our HTR model, based on Deep Convolutional Neural Networks. Our model is described in greater detail in [8]. As shown in Figure 2, character-level transcription results very promising: in each character class our prediction accuracy exceeds 90% - even in the "not-character" class. The average accuracy is 97%.

[1] We tried numerous configurations for these thresholds, and found that in our scenario using $N = M = 3$ is the best option.

[2] Labelled samples for "not-character" class are generated by combining or removing segments from samples belonging to the other classes

[3] http://www.inf.uniroma3.it/db/icr

The whole process that generates tasks, assigns them to the workers, and gathers the corresponding results, has been implemented as a Web Application hosted in the engineering department at Roma Tre University. We used a standard stack of technologies, using Java and the Spring Boot Framework, and storing data in a centralized relational DB.

3 Crowdsourcing for KG generation

After the correct transcription of a manuscript has been obtained, it is possible to extract its entities and relations, and to use them to populate a KG. In modern languages, these tasks are usually tackled by automatic classifiers based on machine learning and NLP approaches. However, similarly to the HTR step, when it comes to Medieval Latin texts the scarcity of labelled datasets makes it hard to train automatic models. Therefore, we are going to approach this phase too with crowd-based techniques. We are currently engineering two main categories of tasks for our workers: *Entity Classification* and *Relation Classification*. Each category may contain multiple types of tasks, with different requirements.

Entity Classification. We have verified that, in our manuscripts, it is possible to automatically select almost all named entities by just applying simple heuristics, e.g. searching for capitalized words. Nonetheless, human intervention is still required to classify the selected entities into semantic categories, such as "people", "locations", "organizations", "temporal data" etc.

In a basic Entity Classification task, each worker may receive the text of an entire transcribed page, with the named entities to classify already highlighted; the task would consist in labelling each entity with the corresponding class. Note that, once the correct class for an entity has been identified, it is possible to propagate it to all the other occurrences of the same entity across the manuscript. For this task, we assume that workers can make mistakes, and manage redundancy with a policy similar to the *Rectangular* strategy employed for the transcription task, extending it to the case in which multiple classes are available. The order in which tasks will be handed to the workers will depend on their priority value, that is, the number of entities it contains that have not been classified yet.

Entity Classification can be further optimized by devising automatic labeling rules. For instance, if a named entity lies in close proximity to special keywords, such as the title "episcopus" (meaning bishop), one can infer that it belongs to the "people" category. Modeling these rules requires knowledge of the specific syntactic patterns that occur most often in the manuscripts under analysis. Our workers, after they have become accustomed to the basic Entity Classification task, should ideally possess this kind of knowledge. Therefore, we plan to design advanced Entity Classification tasks based on rule building. We will provide students with the basics of rule-based logic, and divide them into groups. Each group will be receive, as an input, sets of several already labelled pages, from which they will be asked to build entity-classifying rules. We will evaluate the resulting clauses on standard metrics such as precision, recall and f-measure, and automatically select the combinations that maximize performances. We will finally apply the best performing mix of rules to pages in which the entities have not been classified yet.

Relation Classification. In order to build a KG, after extracting entities and their classes it is also necessary to identify the relations linking them. Once again, we will model basic Relation Classification tasks as tasks of manual labelling. In each task, the worker will receive as an input a single sentence containing at least two distinct entities, and will be asked to identify the relations occurring among such entities. The relation class can be chosen from a fixed vocabulary, that can be manually extended, if necessary. Once again, we will assume that workers can make mistakes, and make the crowd results more robust through redundancy, employing policies similar to those described for the basic Entity Classification task.

The *Entity Classification* and *Relation Classification* tasks will yield large amounts of labelled data that we will use to train automatic classifiers, similarly to the HTR phase. Once the KG has been populated, further facts can be inferred by leveraging recent Link Prediction techniques based on KG embedding (see [10] for a comparative analysis). In terms of general prerequisites, our workers in this phase will just require a very basic knowledge of Latin language - which is generally imparted in Italian high schools. Furthermore, in case of doubts or unclear transcriptions, they will have the possibility to interact with domain experts and paleographers. In order to assign KG extraction tasks to our workers, as well as to gather the corresponding results, we are planning to expand the web application employed for the transcription phase (see Section 2).

4 Related Works

Works related to ours can be roughly divided into Text Recognition and KG Generation works. We summarize these works in the following paragraphs, focusing on those based on crowdsourcing approaches, and refer the reader to the recent works [1, 7] for further discussion on crowdsourcing in the Text Recognition area.

Text Recognition Projects. As a matter of fact, relying on crowd-based solutions is not unusual in text recognition projects. In this area general purpose crowdsourcing platforms may not be flexible enough, therefore the most common approach involves building specialized applications following the entire lifecycle of each task. Project Transcribe Bentham [5], for instance, aims at crowdsourcing the entire transcription of Jeremy Bentham's unpublished works. The writing is in modern English and relatively easy to read, so they ask their workers to transcribe whole paragraphs or even pages. Project Read [9], on the other hand, have developed a mobile application in order to expand the set of potential volunteers; in each task the worker is asked to read aloud a handwritten text line, thus relying on speech dictation. Project Monk [14], finally, focuses on word search in handwritten manuscripts; they typically ask their workers to transcribe entire words, and use the resulting labeled images to train automatic systems for word spotting and other word-level operations.

Our work is fundamentally different from these projects as the tasks we propose to workers do not require any transcription skills: each task only requires to identify specific symbols or characters inside the image of a word and thus it can be solved by non-experts such as high-school students.

KG Generation Projects. Many open KGs nowadays are built in a collaborative fashion, meaning that they rely on contributions to add missing information or correct wrong pieces of the current contents. This collaborative effort can be seen as a very broad form of crowdsourcing, in which any user can temporarily become a volunteer worker. In this setting each task has a very loose formulation, with the worker herself choosing the entities, relations or facts to add or update. Examples of KGs built this way include FreeBase [3] and Wikidata [13].

While these approaches are viable for general purpose KGs, they do not work well when handling vertical topics that the workers may not have knowledge of, or when facts must actually be extracted from text. This has led researchers to devise more structured approaches for these scenarios.

In a completely different domain (drugs and their side effects), the work in [4] has a similar objective to ours, as they aim at building a KG from a collection of articles (from the PubMed archive) by leveraging a crowsourced dataset of annotations: in each task workers receive a sentence and a relation, and are asked whether the sentence actually conveys that relation or not. A similar approach is followed by [12], whose goal is to build a scientific KG by extracting entities, relations and facts from unstructured texts of research publications. Their approach is to perform fact extraction, integration, and analysis in a semi-superivised way. On the one hand, automatic tools are employed in each step; on the other, users are involved in all activities through visual interfaces that allow them to perform quality control, data enrichment and discovery.

5 Conclusions

In this paper we have described how crowdsourcing methodologies are allowing us to tackle the extraction of knowledge from Medieval handwritten manuscripts in our In Codice Ratio project.

We have shown that the lack of datasets suitable for our scenario affects both the transcription step and the text mining step. We have thus discussed how a pool of not expert workers can be put in condition to perform very simple tasks, yielding enough labeled data to train effective automatic systems. We have described in detail our strategies to assign tasks to specific workers, including the policies we employ to increase robustness to potential mistakes made by workers. We have reported our very promising results in character-level transcription, as well as our plans for the oncoming KG construction phase.

Among future work, we plan to inject data provenance methods in the whole process of knowledge extraction from ancient manuscripts, with the goal of improving the understanding of the results and simplifying the ability to trace errors back to the root cause.

Acknowledgments

Work funded by Regione Lazio LR 13/08 Project "In Codice Ratio" (14832).

References

1. Ammirati, S., Firmani, D., Maiorino, M., Merialdo, P., Nieddu, E.: In codice ratio: Machine transcription of medieval manuscripts. In: Digital Libraries: Supporting Open Science - 15th Italian Research Conference on Digital Libraries, IRCDL 2019, Pisa, Italy, January 31 - February 1, 2019, Proceedings. pp. 185–192 (2019)
2. Ammirati, S., Firmani, D., Maiorino, M., Merialdo, P., Nieddu, E., Rossi, A.: In codice ratio: Scalable transcription of historical handwritten documents. In: SEBD (2017)
3. Bollacker, K., Evans, C., Paritosh, P., Sturge, T., Taylor, J.: Freebase: a collaboratively created graph database for structuring human knowledge. In: Proceedings of the 2008 ACM SIGMOD international conference on Management of data (2008)
4. Bravo, À., Li, T.S., Su, A.I., Good, B.M., Furlong, L.I.: Combining machine learning, crowdsourcing and expert knowledge to detect chemical-induced diseases in text. Database (2016)
5. Causer, T., Tonra, J., Wallace, V.: Transcription maximized; expense minimized? crowdsourcing and editing the collected works of jeremy bentham. Literary and Linguistic Computing (2012)
6. Firmani, D., Maiorino, M., Merialdo, P., Nieddu, E.: Towards knowledge discovery from the vatican secret archives. in codice ratio - episode 1: Machine transcription of the manuscripts. In: Proceedings of the 24th ACM SIGKDD International Conference on Knowledge Discovery & Data Mining. KDD '18, ACM (2018)
7. Firmani, D., Merialdo, P., Maiorino, M.: In codice ratio: Scalable transcription of vatican registers. ERCIM News (111) (2017)
8. Firmani, D., Merialdo, P., Nieddu, E., Scardapane, S.: In codice ratio: Ocr of handwritten latin documents using deep convolutional networks. In: AI* CH@ AI* IA. pp. 9–16 (2017)
9. Granell, E., Martínez-Hinarejos, C.: Multimodal crowdsourcing for transcribing handwritten documents. IEEE/ACM Transactions on Audio, Speech, and Language Processing **25**(2), 409–419 (Feb 2017). https://doi.org/10.1109/TASLP.2016.2634123
10. Rossi, A., Firmani, D., Matinata, A., Merialdo, P., Barbosa, D.: Knowledge graph embedding for link prediction: A comparative analysis. CoRR (2020), https://arxiv.org/abs/2002.00819
11. Sarma, A.D., Parameswaran, A., Garcia-Molina, H., Halevy, A.: Crowd-powered find algorithms. In: 2014 IEEE 30th International Conference on Data Engineering. pp. 964–975. IEEE (2014)
12. Seifert, C., Granitzer, M., Höfler, P., Mutlu, B., Sabol, V., Schlegel, K., Bayerl, S., Stegmaier, F., Zwicklbauer, S., Kern, R.: Crowdsourcing fact extraction from scientific literature (2013)
13. Vrandečić, D., Krötzsch, M.: Wikidata: a free collaborative knowledgebase. Communications of the ACM (2014)
14. Weber, A., Ameryan, M., Wolstencroft, K., Stork, L., Heerlien, M., Schomaker, L.: Towards a digital infrastructure for illustrated handwritten archives. In: Digital Cultural Heritage, pp. 155–166. Springer (2018)

Automatic Detection of Dysplastic Nevi: a Multiple Instance Learning Solution.

(Discussion Paper)

Eugenio Vocaturo[1,2][0000-0001-7457-7118] and Ester Zumpano[1][0000-0003-1129-3737]

[1] DIMES - Department of Informatics, Modelling, Electronic and System Engineering University of Calabria, Rende, Italy
{*e.vocaturo, e.zumpano*}*@dimes.unical.it*

[2] CNR-NANOTEC National Research Council, Rende, Italy
eugenio.vocaturo@cnr.it

Abstract. Malignant melanoma is responsible for the highest number of deaths related to skin lesions. The similarities of melanoma with other skin lesions, such as dysplastic nevi, constitute a pitfall for computerized detection. The proposed algorithms and methods have had as main focus the dichotomous distinction of melanoma from benign lesions and they rarely focused on the case of melanoma against dysplastic nevi. Currently, there is a debate about *dysplastic nevi syndrome*, or rather about the number of moles present on the human body as potential melanoma risk factors. In this document, we consider the challenging task of applying a multi-instance learning (MIL) algorithm for discriminating melanoma from dysplastic nevi and outline an even more complex challenge related to the classification of dysplastic nevi from common nevi. Since the results appear promising, we conclude that a MIL technique could be at the basis of tools useful for skin lesion detection.

Keywords: Image Classification · Multiple Instance Learning · Dysplastic nevi Detection.

1 Introduction

According to the latest report of the World Health Organization (WHO), in 2018 *melanoma* has caused over 60.000 deaths and over 280.000 new cases have been diagnosed [1]. Despite the ever increasing diffusion and its aggressiveness, if melanoma is identified by an early diagnosis it is a type of curable cancer. Some clinical protocols such as the ABCDE rule [2] have been established to facilitate the task of specialists in identifying the lesion from its initial phase. These clinical protocols take into consideration features lesion such as asymmetry, irregular edges, colors, diameters greater than 6 mm and evolving stages.

The importance of an early detection of melanoma have led research communities to develop automatic frameworks called Computer Aided Diagnosis (CAD) systems, for the analysis of skin lesions. CAD include steps such as image acquisition, pre-processing, segmentation, features extraction and selection and finally classification of lesions.

This work focuses on the classification task of discriminating melanoma from dysplastic nevi. Some studies have shown that specific ethnic groups present a great number of common and dysplastic nevi on their's bodies surface [3].

Individuals with *dysplastic nevi syndrome* or dysplastic nevi with family history of melanoma face a greater risk of developing melanoma [4]. These premises justify the perception that automatic diagnosis of skin lesions must consider, besides the distinction between melanoma and common nevi, also the one between melanoma and dysplastic nevi, that is more difficult due to the similarities of the two type of lesions [5].

Nowadays, few studies are available on this specific topic, therefore this paper is a contribution to this challenging task. Our basic idea takes its cue from the work [6] in which the authors have shown how the use of simple color features, on dermatoscopic images, lets to obtain satisfactory classification performances. In the present paper, we apply a recent MIL approach [7, 8] on dermatoscopic images using only color features to verify its effectiveness in the classification steps concerning Melanomas vs Dyspastic Nevi and Dysplastic Nevi vs Common ones. The paper is organized as follows. In the next section we focus on the role that the presence of dysplastic nevi and common nevi may imply in terms of risk of melanoma onset. In Section 3 we recall the peculiarities of a MIL approach, focusing on the Lagrangian relaxation type algorithm proposed in [9]. In Section 4 some numerical results on dermoscopic images are presented and finally brief conclusions are given in Section 5.

2 Dysplastic nevi

The term "dysplastic nevus" (DN) indicates a nevus with different histological and genetic characteristics compared to common nevus. More specifically, the term derives from the Greek "dis-" (bad or malfunction) and "-plasia" (development of growth or change) [10] and indicates a potentially dangerous lesion for his guest. Several studies have attempted to correlate the degree of dysplasia of melanocytes with the risk of melanoma [11, 12].

Syndrome of dysplastic nevus (DNS) refers to subjects who have a high number of benign moles and dysplastic nevi. Dysplastic nevi are more likely to undergo malignant transformation when they occur among members of melanoma families.

In [13], the authors indicate a cumulative lifetime risk of almost 100% in individuals who have dysplastic nevi and are related to melanoma; about 30% of melanomas occur within atypical moles. In 40-50% of cases, there is a genetic

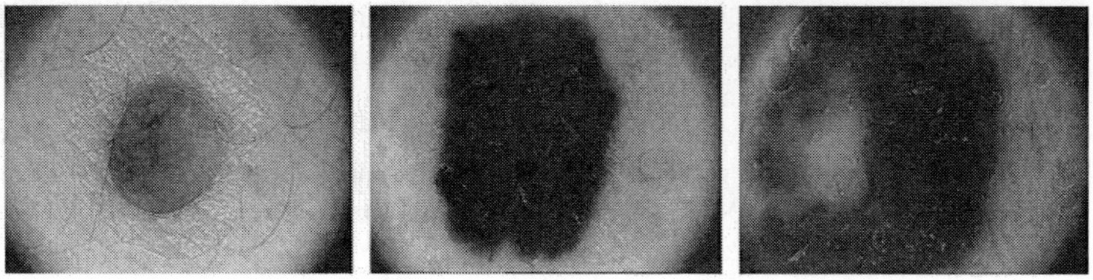

Fig. 1. Dermoscopic image of common nevus (a), dysplastic nevus (b) and melanoma (c)

predisposition for the formation of melanoma. The onset of this skin cancer has been associated with germline mutations in the CDKN2A gene, which encodes p16 (a regulator of cell division).

In [14], some studies based on histological analysis have correlated the presence of dysplastic nevi with melanoma. The caution that should be observed in correspondence with a diagnosis of a severe DNS should not be overlooked, as it could represent a miss-diagnosed in situ melanoma [15].

Basically, there are two objective criteria that have been shown to be related to the risk of melanoma:

- In [16], people with a number of nevi greater than 100 had a 7 times greater risk of melanoma than those with a count of less than 15.
- The presence of large nevi increases the relative risk of melanoma. If these nevi have a diameter less than 2.4 mm they have a relative risk of 1, while the relative risk progressively increases up to 5 if the lesion has a diameter greater than 4.4 mm [17].

Simultaneously with the definition of the exact cause-effect correlations, various solutions have been proposed over time for the automatic identification of skin lesions.

In [18] the authors, depicts a summary of many recent proposed methods by reporting the results in terms of sensitivity, specificity and dataset size. In the same work methods are categorized based on their classification scope: melanoma from benign (M vs B), melanoma from benign and dysplastic (M vs $(B + D)$) and melanoma versus only dysplastic nevi (M vs D).

The comparison among different approaches is far from being easy as each proposal has been applied on different datasets and adopts different features sets. As for the feature, an additional difference arise between global and local features. Global features are extracted taking the lesion as a whole, while local features are extracted from portions of the image. On a qualitative level, AdaBoost (AdB), artificial neural network (ANN), Support Vector Machines (SVM) appear to be the most effective methods [19]. To the best of our knowledge, nobody takes into consideration the classification task of dysplastic nevi against common nevi [20].

3 Multiple Instance learning

Machine Learning has become very important in medical image analysis. In fact, machine learning methods are currently used in the segmentation steps, in which each pixel of an image belongs to a particular tissue and in CAD systems to assign a category label to a whole image. Even, the availability of partially labeled data can be appropriately exploited using machine learning approaches [21], [22].

In particular, Multiple Instance Learning scenario is useful when disposing of local annotated labels is expensive, while global labels for whole images, such as the outcome of a diagnosis, are more readily available.

A MIL problem consists in the classification task of a set of items called *bags* and of the objects inside them called *instances*. The substantial difference compared to supervised classification consists in the fact that, in the learning phase, only the labels of the bags are known, and not those of the instances.

A natural application of the Multiple Instance Learning is in diagnostics by means of medical images, where we want to discriminate between non-healthy and healthy patients on the basis of their medical scan (bag). According to standard Mil assumption:

- if in the medical scan at least one sub-region (instance) is abnormal, then a patient is *positive*;
- if in the medical scan all the subregions (instances) are normal, then the patient is *negative*.

The classification of complex objects cannot be represented by single features vector, i.e. by single instance: this is another reason why we propose to use MIL techniques for melanoma detection.

With a MIL approach it is therefore possible to obtain global information from local one. For further details and general considerations on the MIL paradigm, we refer the reader to surveys [23]. In [24], a detailed review is given concerning Multiple Instance Learning applied for medical images and video analysis. The MIL approach, as far as we know, is still very rarely used for melanoma detection, and has never been used for the detection of dysplastic nevi.

4 Numerical experimentation

The MIL algorithm used for the classification task in this paper has been proposed in [9], and has been tested for the classification of both dermoscopic images [25, 26] taken from the PH2 database [27], and photographs datasets publicly available from two online databases https://www.dermquest.com and http://www.dermins.net [28]. The entire PH2 database contains 200 images of melanocytic lesions: 80 common nevi, 80 atypical nevi and 40 melanomas. All images were obtained using 8-bit RGB colors with a resolution of 768 $\times$ 560 pixels.

For the classification experiments we considered the 40 images of melanomas (1.a), the 80 of dysplastic nevi (1.b) and the 80 of common nevi (1.c), without taking into account the indications resulting from the manual analysis carried out by the specialists.

The only criterion is adopted at image level by considering: (i) positive the images related to melanomas and negative the ones related to dysplastic nevi and (ii) positive the images related to dysplastic nevi and negative the ones related to common nevi. Although pre-processing steps of the images allow for better performance [29, 30], the images we used were not pre-processed, i.e. they were not cleaned of the presence of noise, such as possible hair or halo left by the dermoscopic gel used to allow better illumination of the lesions.

The MIL algorithm, referred to as MIL-RL, has been re-implemented in Matlab and has been run on a Windows 10 system featuring a 2.21 GHz processor. We have duplicated all the images of melanomas, adding a Gaussian noise with zero mean with variance equal to 0.0001, as in the [6]. In this way we obtained a balanced dataset containing three classes of data, Melanomas (M), Dysplastic Nevi (DN) and Common Nevi (N) each with 80 images. The imbalance between the classes of training datasets should not be underestimated. The risk consists in undermining the classification performance of the models, which can manifest over-fitting, thus losing in generalization. For our experiments we considered the following two data set configurations:

- 160 images: 80 Melanomas vs 80 Dysplastic Nevi;
- 160 images: 80 Dysplastic Nevi vs 80 Common Nevi.

For each data set configuration, we performed two types of experiments, using a five fold and a ten fold cross-validation. The respective results are listed in Table 1 and Table 2, where we report the average of correctness, sensitivity, specificity, F-score and CPU time.

The proposed MIL optimization model is of SVM type; in order to appreciate the MIL classification paradigm, we report in the columns SVM and SVM-RBF the results obtained using a standard SVM approach [31] with linear and RBF kernels, respectively. For each data set configuration and for each experiment (5-CV and 10-CV), the best results in Table 1 and Table 2 have been underlined.

From numerical experiments it emerges that, in general, MIL-RL overcomes the SVM technique (with both linear and RBF kernels) in terms of correctness and sensitivity. Whenever accuracy is not 100%, low specificity values are a consequence of high sensitivity values. In medical fields, sensitivity plays a more important role than specificity since it is a measure of the ability to identify un-healthy patients. The F-score values show the good performance of the MIL approach in classifying melanoma from dysplastic nevi against the classic SVM technique.

We observe that the CPU times of MIL-RL algorithm are better than those recorded by linear SVM. Concerning the classification of dysplastic nevi against common nevi, the performances of all three methods appear unsatisfactory. The MIL-RL algorithm records the best values of accuracy and specificity, but overall

	5-CV			10-CV		
	MIL-RL	SVM	SVM-RBF	MIL-RL	SVM	SVM-RBF
Correctness (%)	87.50	72.50	85.63	86.25	69.38	86.25
Sensitivity (%)	92.56	77.21	87.06	91,08	69.65	87.88
Specificity (%)	81.50	67.51	85.51	82.12	69.87	85.95
F-score (%)	88.31	74.96	85.84	87.01	68.68	87.52
CPU time (secs)	0.90	1.84	0.04	1.20	2.05	0.03

Table 1. Average testing values: 80 melanomas and 80 dysplastic nevi

	5-CV			10-CV		
	MIL-RL	SVM	SVM-RBF	MIL-RL	SVM	SVM-RBF
Correctness (%)	60.63	60.00	49.38	59.38	58.13	51.88
Sensitivity (%)	35.07	54.91	53.58	31.77	43.67	58.92
Specificity (%)	84.86	67.58	46.97	87.06	73.48	46.47
F-score (%)	44.76	56.79	50.09	42.77	48.57	53.74
CPU time (secs)	1.38	1.95	0.01	1.71	2.13	0.03

Table 2. Average testing values: 80 dysplatic nevi and 80 common nevi

it is not effective to solve the proposed task. Better results could be obtained using images pre-processing steps and by using further useful features [33, 34].

5 Conclusions

In this paper we present an application of a MIL approach for the detection of melanoma by dysplastic nevi and of dysplastic nevi by common ones. These two issues are not widespread in the literature. Anyhow, pathologies such as the DNS require tools to support phisicians in diagnostic process and mobile applications useful for promoting self diagnosis. To this end, we point out that it is under implementation a module of the software Simpatico 3d that is in charge of allowing self diagnosis [35, 36, 38, 40, 41]. The obtained results show that in the first case the MIL approach is very promising, even using only color features and with no pre-processing step.

In the second case, the MIL approach as well as the SVM in the linear and Kernel RBF version, do not give satisfactory results. The excessive similarity of the lesions is not properly discriminated with approaches aimed at identifying linear separation surfaces. One way we intend to pursue is to apply MIL approaches that use spherical separation surfaces. In particular, the algorithm [32] seems to be an interesting proposal for the development of applications in which positive and negative elements have strong similar characteristics.

Future research could include the design of more sophisticated segmentation techniques in order to further improve classification results, as well as the application of the proposed method in other medical fields [39, 37] to identify other types of injuries.

References

1. http://gco.iarc.fr/today/explore.
2. R. Sanghera and P. S. Grewal, "Dermatological symptom assessment", in Patient Assessment in Clinical Pharmacy, p. 133–154, Springer, 2019.
3. Silva JH, et al., "Atypical mole syndrome and dysplastic nevi: identification of populations at risk for developing melanoma," Clinics (Sao Paulo), v.66(3):493–9, 2011.
4. A.C. Society, Melanoma skin cancer. http://www.cancer.org/acs/groups/cid/documents/webcontent/003120-pdf.pdf
5. Burroni M, et al., "Dysplastic naevus vs. in situ melanoma: digital dermoscopy analysis", Br J Dermatol, v.152(4), pp:679–84, 2005.
6. Barata C, et al. "Two systems for the detection of melanomas in dermoscopy images using texture and color features", IEEE Syst J 8(3), pp: 965–79, 2014.
7. Astorino, A., Fuduli, A., Veltri, P., and Vocaturo, E.,"On a recent algorithm for multiple instance learning. Preliminary applications in image classification". In IEEE International Conference on Bioinformatics and Biomedicine (BIBM), pp. 1615-19, 2017.
8. Astorino, A., Fuduli, A., Gaudioso, M., and Vocaturo, E., "A multiple instance learning algorithm for color images classification". Proceedings of the 22nd International Database Engineering and Applications Symposium (pp. 262-266), 2018.
9. Astorino, A., Fuduli, A., and Gaudioso, M., "A Lagrangian relaxation approach for binary multiple instance classification". IEEE transactions on neural networks and learning systems, 2019.
10. Duffy K, Grossman D., "The dysplastic nevus: from historical perspective to management in the modern era: part I. Historical, histologic, and clinical aspects". J Am Acad Dermatol., 67(1):1.e1-1.e16. quiz 17-8, 2012.
11. Greene, M. H., et al., "High risk of malignant melanoma in melanoma-prone families with dysplastic nevi". Annals of internal medicine, 102(4), pp: 458-465, 1985.
12. Jeong, D. K., et al., "A case of malignant melanoma after repeated recurrent dysplastic nevi". Archives of craniofacial surgery, 20(4), 260, 2019.
13. R. Pampena, A. Kyrgidis, "A meta-analysis of nevus-associated melanoma: Prevalence and practical implications". In: Journal of the American Academy of Dermatology. Band 77, N. 5, pp. 938–945, November 2017.
14. Arumi-Uria M, McNutt NS, Finnerty B., "Grading of atypia in nevi: correlation with melanoma risk". Mod Pathol., 16(8):764-771, 2003.
15. Reddy KK, et al., "Atypical (dysplastic) nevi: outcomes of surgical excision and association with melanoma". JAMA Dermatol.,149(8): 928-934, 2013.
16. Gandini S, Sera F, Cattaruzza MS, et al., "Meta-analysis of risk factors for cutaneous melanoma: I. Common and atypical nevi". Eur J Cancer.,41(1):28-44, 2005.
17. Xiong MY, Rabkin MS, Piepkorn MW, et al., "Diameter of dysplastic nevi is a more robust biomarker of increased melanoma risk than degree of histologic dysplasia: a case-control study". J Am Acad Dermatol.,71(6):1257-1258, 2014.
18. Rastgoo, M., et al., "Automatic differentiation of melanoma from dysplastic nevi". Computerized Medical Imaging and Graphics, 43, 44-52, 2015.
19. Vocaturo, E., Perna D., and Zumpano E., "Machine Learning Techniques for Automated Melanoma Detection", IEEE International Conference on Bioinformatics and Biomedicine, (BIBM), pp. 2310-17, 2019.
20. Vocaturo, E., and Zumpano E., "Dangerousness of dysplastic nevi: a Multiple Instance Learning Solution for Early Diagnosis", IEEE International Conference on Bioinformatics and Biomedicine, (BIBM), pp: 2318-23, 2019.

21. Litjens, G., et al., "A survey on deep learning in medical image analysis". Med. Image Anal. 42, 60–88, 2017.
22. de Bruijne, M., "Machine learning approaches in medical image analysis: from detection to diagnosis". Med. Image Anal. 33, 94–97, 2019.
23. Carbonneau MA, et al., "Multiple instance learning: a survey of problem characteristics and applications". Pattern Recogn 77:329–353, 2018.
24. Quellec G, Cazuguel G, Cochener B, Lamard M, "Multiple instance learning for medical image and video analysis", IEEE Rev Biomed Eng 10, pp: 213–234, 2017.
25. Astorino, A., Fuduli, A., Veltri, P., and Vocaturo, E. (2020). "Melanoma Detection by Means of Multiple Instance Learning". Interdisciplinary Sciences: Computational Life Sciences, 12, 24–31, 2020.
26. A. Astorino, A. Fuduli, M. Gaudioso, and E. Vocaturo, "Multiple Instance Learning Algorithm for Medical Image Classification", Proceedings of the 27th Italian Symposium on Advanced Database (SEDB), 2019.
27. Mendonça T, et al., "Ph2 —a dermoscopic image database for research and benchmarking". In: 35th annual international conference of the IEEE engineering in medicine and biology society (EMBC), pp 5437–5440, 2013.
28. A. Fuduli, P. Veltri, E. Vocaturo, E. Zumpano, "Melanoma detection using color and texture features in computer vision systems", Advances in Science, Technology and Engineering Systems Journal, vol. 4, no. 5, pp. 16-22 (2019).
29. E. Vocaturo, and E. Zumpano, and P. Veltri, "Image preprocessing in computer vision systems for melanoma detection," IEEE International Conference on Bioinformatics and Biomedicine (BIBM), pp. 2117-24, 2018.
30. E. Vocaturo, and E. Zumpano, and P. Veltri, "On the Usefulness of Pre-Processing Step in Melanoma Detection Using Multiple Instance Learning", International Conference on Flexible Query Answering Systems, Springer, pp. 374-382, 2019.
31. Vapnik V., The nature of the statistical learning theory, Springer, New York 1995.
32. Gaudioso, M., Giallombardo, G., Miglionico, G., and Vocaturo, E., "Classification in the multiple instance learning framework via spherical separation". Soft Computing, pp:1-7, 2019.
33. E. Vocaturo, E. Zumpano, and P. Veltri, "Features for Melanoma Lesions Characterization in Computer Vision Systems", 9th International Conference on Information, Intelligence, Systems and Applications, (IISA) 2018, pp. 1–8, 2018.
34. Vocaturo E., Caroprese L., Zumpano E., "Features for Melanoma Lesions: Extraction and Classification", IEEE/WIC/ACM International Conference on Web Intelligence-Companion Volume,(pp.238-243), 2019.
35. E. Zumpano, et al., "SIMPATICO 3D: A Medical Information System for Diagnostic Procedures". BIBM pp. 2125-2128, 2018.
36. E. Zumpano, et al., "SIMPATICO 3D Mobile for Diagnostic Procedures", Proceedings of the 21st International Conference on Information Integration and Web-Based Applications and Services (IIWAS), pp. 468-472, Munich, Germany 2019.
37. E. Vocaturo, E. Zumpano and P. Veltri, "On discovering relevant features for tongue colored image analysis", IDEAS 2019, (pp.1-8), ACM 2019.
38. P. Iaquinta, et al.: "eIMES 3D: An innovative medical images analysis tool to support diagnostic and surgical intervention". FNC/MobiSPC 2017: 459-464.
39. E. Vocaturo, P. Veltri: "On the use of Networks in Biomedicine". FNC/MobiSPC 2017: 498-503.
40. P. Iaquinta, et al.:. "eimes 3d mobile: A mobile application for diagnostic procedures". BIBM, 1634–1641, 2018 DOI: 10.1109/BIBM.2017.8217904.
41. L. Caroprese, et al.:. "Software Tools for Medical Imaging". ADBIS (Short Papers and Workshops) 2018: 297-304

Scalar Quantization-Based Text Encoding for Large Scale Image Retrieval

(DISCUSSION PAPER)

Giuseppe Amato, Fabio Carrara, Fabrizio Falchi, Claudio Gennaro, Fausto Rabitti, and Lucia Vadicamo

Institute of Information Science and Technologies (ISTI), CNR, Pisa
firstname.lastname@isti.cnr.it

Abstract. The great success of visual features learned from deep neural networks has led to a significant effort to develop efficient and scalable technologies for image retrieval. This paper presents an approach to transform neural network features into text codes suitable for being indexed by a standard full-text retrieval engine such as Elasticsearch. The basic idea is providing a transformation of neural network features with the twofold aim of promoting the sparsity without the need of unsupervised pre-training. We validate our approach on a recent convolutional neural network feature, namely Regional Maximum Activations of Convolutions (R-MAC), which is a state-of-art descriptor for image retrieval. An extensive experimental evaluation conducted on standard benchmarks shows the effectiveness and efficiency of the proposed approach and how it compares to state-of-the-art main-memory indexes.

Keywords: Image retrieval · Deep Features · Inverted index

1 Introduction

Full-text search engines on the Web have achieved great results in terms of efficiency thanks to the use of inverted index technology. In the last years, we experienced an increasing interest in the retrieval of other forms of expression, such as images; nevertheless, the development in those cases was not as rapid as text-based paradigms.

In the field of image retrieval, since 2014 we have witnessed a great development of learned features obtained by neural networks, in particular Convolutional Neural Networks (CNN), which have emerged as effective image descriptors. Differently from text, in which inverted indexes perfectly marry the sparse document representation in standard vector models, learned image descriptors tend to be dense and compact, thus making directly unfeasible the usage of mature text-tailored index technologies. While efficient index structures for this type of data exist [13,14], they usually come with caveats that prevent their usage in very large-scale scenarios, such as main-memory-only implementations and computationally expensive indexing or codebook-learning phases.

This paper summarizes the main contributions presented in [2], where we explored new approaches to make image retrieval as similar as possible to text retrieval so as to reuse the technologies and platforms exploited today for text retrieval without the need for dedicated access methods. In a nutshell, the idea is to use image representations extracted from a CNN (*deep features*) and to transform them into text so that they can be indexed with a standard text search engine. In particular, we propose a *Scalar Quantization* approach that transforms deep features, which are (dense) vectors of real numbers, into sparse vectors of integer numbers. The components of these integer vectors are then translated to "term frequencies" of synthetic textual documents. Sparseness is necessary for efficiency issues to achieve sufficient levels of efficiency exactly as it does for search engines for text documents.

We consider the problem of image retrieval in a large-scale context, with an eye to scalability. This aspect is often overlooked by the literature, most of the image retrieval systems are designed to work in main memory and many of these cannot be distributed across a cluster of nodes. Many techniques present in literature try to tackle this problem by heavily compressing the representation of visual features to adapt more and more data to the secondary memory. However, these approaches are not able to scale because sooner or later response times become unacceptable as the size of the data to be managed increases.

2 Related Work

In the last years, image features extracted using deep CNNs have been widely employed as effective image descriptors. *Deep features* achieved state-of-the-art results in several vision tasks, including image retrieval [6,5] and object detection [8]. As a consequence, there is an increasing interest in identifying techniques able to efficiently index and search large set of deep features.

To frame our work in the context of scientific literature, we focus on techniques that deal with emerging deep features using an inverted index. Liu et al. [13] proposed a framework that adapts the BoW model and inverted table to index deep features. However, it needs to learn a large visual dictionary when dealing with a large-scale dataset. Other works treat the features in a convolutional layer as local features by using aggregation schemes like BoW and VLAD [4,19] or try to quantize the deep features using a codebook [14]. Jegou et al. [11] proposed an approximate nearest neighbor algorithm based on product quantization (PQ), which exploits an inverted index. In PQ, the original vector is divided into M sub-vectors that are independently quantized. A codebook is learned via k-means for each of the M sub-division, and each sub-vector is compressed by storing the nearest centroid index. An implementation of PQ-compressed inverted indexes, denoted IVFPQ, is available in the FAISS library.

In our work, we propose a novel approach to generate sparse representations of deep features that can be employed to efficiently index and search the deep features by using inverted files. Without loss of generality, we use the Regional Maximum Activations of Convolutions (R-MAC) feature vector defined by Gordo et al. [9] as representative of the family of deep-learned dense real-valued representations for instance-level image retrieval. This kind of features poses challenges to the current technique of sparse encoding when dealing with non-sparse and real-valued feature vectors that this work aims to tackle. On the other hand, other types of deep features typically used in this field, such as ReLU-ed features extracted from pretrained image classifiers, have already been explored and indexed with a similar approach in a preliminary work [3].

3 Scalar Quantization

In this section, we present a novel approach to generate sparse representations for *D-dimensional vectors* originally compared with the dot product. In particular, we focus on R-MAC descriptors, which are real-valued dense vectors that are particularly powerful for applications of instance-level and content-based image retrieval. However, our method can be adapted to general euclidean vectors.

In a nutshell, we aim to define a transformation $f : \mathbb{R}^D \to \mathbb{N}^n$ that generate sparse vectors and preserves the similarities of objects as much as possible. The reason why we want to transform real-valued dense vectors into sparse vectors of natural numbers is because we want to use a full-text search engine to index the vectors so transformed. In fact, a full-text search engine based on the *vector space model* [16] generates a vector representation of a text via term frequencies, i.e. the number of occurrences of the words in it. These systems transform the texts into vector representations using the well-known TF scheme and practically use the dot product as a function of similarity between vectors. So, the abstract transformation $f(\cdot)$ represents a function that exactly generates the vectors that are internally represented by the search engine in the case of the simple term-weighting scheme. In other words, given a dictionary of n codewords we transform an object o into a synthetic text encoding t_o that is obtained as a space-separated concatenation of codewords so that the i-th codeword is repeated a number of times equal to the i-th element of the vector $f(o)$. Using this representation, the search engine indexes the text by using inverted files, i.e. each object o is stored in the posting lists associated to the codewords appearing in the text representation of o. The number of posting lists equals the number of codewords of the considered vocabulary. This approach is known in the literature as Surrogate Text Representation [1,7].

The idea behind our *Scalar Quantization* approach is to map the real-valued vector components independently into a smaller set of integer values which act as the term frequencies of a predefined set of codewords. The first step is applying a transformation to the vectors that helps preventing the presence of unbalanced posting lists in the inverted file (thus important for efficiency of inverted indices). To understand why, note that each component of the vectors is associated with a posting list storing the *id* of the vector and the value of the component itself, if nonzero. Therefore, if on average some component is nonzero for many data vectors then the corresponding posting list will be accessed many times, provided that the queries follow the same distribution of the data. The ideal case occurs when the component share exactly the same distribution (same mean and variance is sufficient). To this end, we apply a random orthogonal transformation to the entire set of data vectors, which is known to provide good balancing for high dimensional vectors without the need to search for an optimal balancing transformation [12]. An important aspect of the orthogonal transformation is that it preserves the ranking when we search using the kNN approach by ordering the vectors on the basis of their Euclidean distance to the query. Moreover, if applying the orthogonal transformation and the mean centering to all the data objects and just the orthogonal transformation to the query, we have an ordering preserving transformation with respect to the dot-product (see [2] for further details). Thus, our preprocessing step is defined as:

$$\boldsymbol{v} \rightarrow R(\boldsymbol{v} - \boldsymbol{\mu}) \tag{1}$$

$$\boldsymbol{q} \rightarrow R\boldsymbol{q} \tag{2}$$

where R is a *random* orthogonal matrix and $\boldsymbol{\mu} \in \mathbb{R}^D$ is set to center the data to zero mean. The next step is transforming the rotated vectors into term frequency vectors. We do it by quantizing the vectors so that posting entries will contain numeric values proportional to the float values of the deep feature entries. Specifically, we use the transformation $\boldsymbol{w} \rightarrow \lfloor s\boldsymbol{w} \rfloor$ where $\lfloor \cdot \rfloor$ denotes the floor function and s is a multiplication factor > 1.

The approach presented so far is intended to encode a vector of real numbers into a vector of integers preserving as much as possible the order with respect to the dot product. However, this approach does not solve the problem that in most cases these vectors are dense, which leads to low efficiency when using inverted files to index textual documents. To sparsify the term frequency vectors, that is to discard their less significant components, we must accept a further loss in precision. To achieve this, we propose to keep components above a certain threshold $1/\gamma$ and zeroing the others. The parameter $\gamma \in \mathbb{N}$ controls the sparseness of the thresholded feature. This approach is optimal when we have many components near or equal to zero; thus, we exploit the previously defined transformation (Eq. 1) to center the mean values of each dimension to zero.

To sum up, our proposed transformation is $f : \boldsymbol{v} \mapsto g_\gamma(\lfloor sR(\boldsymbol{v}-\boldsymbol{\mu}) \rfloor)$, where g_γ is a component-wise thresholding function, i.e. $g_\gamma(x) = x$ if $x > 1/\gamma$, 0 otherwise.

Dealing with negative values In order to index R-MAC features and represent them in the vector space model of text retrieval, we encode each dimension of the R-MAC features as a different codeword, and we use the TF field to represent a single value of our feature vector. However, TF must be positive (most search engine admits positive-only TFs even if this in principle would be possible), nonetheless, both negative and positive elements contribute to informativeness. In the scalar quantization approach presented above, the negative values are flatted to zero. Naive techniques such as taking the absolute value result in a degraded performance due to respectively loss or aliasing of information. In order to prevent this imbalance towards positive activations at the expense of negative ones, we use the Concatenated Rectified Linear Unit (CReLU) transformation [17]. It simply makes an identical copy of vector elements, negate it, concatenate both original vector and its negation, and then apply ReLU altogether. More precisely the CReLU of the vector $\boldsymbol{v}$ is defined as $\boldsymbol{v}^+ = ReLU([\boldsymbol{v}, -\boldsymbol{v}])$, where the $ReLU(\cdot) = max(\cdot, 0)$ is applied element-wise. After applying CReLU, we apply the transformation f to $\boldsymbol{v}^+$ as described in the previous section.

4 Experimental Evaluation

To assess the performance of our Scalar Quatization technique in content-based image retrieval task, we performed an extensive experimental evaluation on two instance-level retrieval benchmarks. A complete presentation of the results is given in [2]; here we report some of the most relevant results.

The experiments were conducted on two benchmarks. *INRIA Holidays* [10] is a collaction of 1,491 images representing a large variety of scene type and 500 queries for which result lists are provided. Usually this benchmark is extended with a distractor dataset, namely MIRFlickr1M[1], that contains 1M images. *Oxford Buildings* [15] is composed of 5,062 images of 11 Oxford landmarks downloaded from Flickr. A manually labeled groundtruth is available for five queries for each landmark, for a total of 55 queries. As for INRIA Holidays, we merged the dataset with the distraction dataset Flickr100k including 100k images[2].

We used the ResNet-101 trained model as an R-MAC feature extractor, which has been shown to achieve the best performance on standard benchmarks of instance-level image retrieval. We extracted the R-MAC features using fixed grid regions at two different scales as proposed in [18]. Then, we produced the sparse representations by using different sparsification thresholds γ.

We compared the performance of our approach with FAISS[3], which includes state-of-the-art approximate nearest neighbor algorithms based on PQ [11]. Note that PQ constitutes a suitable competitor to our approach since is a one-stage inverted-file-based index as the one used in standard textual search engines. For a fair comparison, we used the configuration for FAISS that gives the best effectiveness-efficiency trade-off for each dataset (see [2] for further details). PQ-based methods need a training set and an offline training phase to initialize the inverted index. We examined two possible scenarios dubbed IVFPQ and IVFPQ*. In the former, the index is trained on the data to be indexed, while in the latter, a set of unrelated images (the T4SA dataset[4]) is used as training set.

[1] `http://press.liacs.nl/mirflickr/`
[2] `http://www.robots.ox.ac.uk/~vgg/data/oxbuildings/`
[3] `https://github.com/facebookresearch/faiss`
[4] `http://t4sa.it`

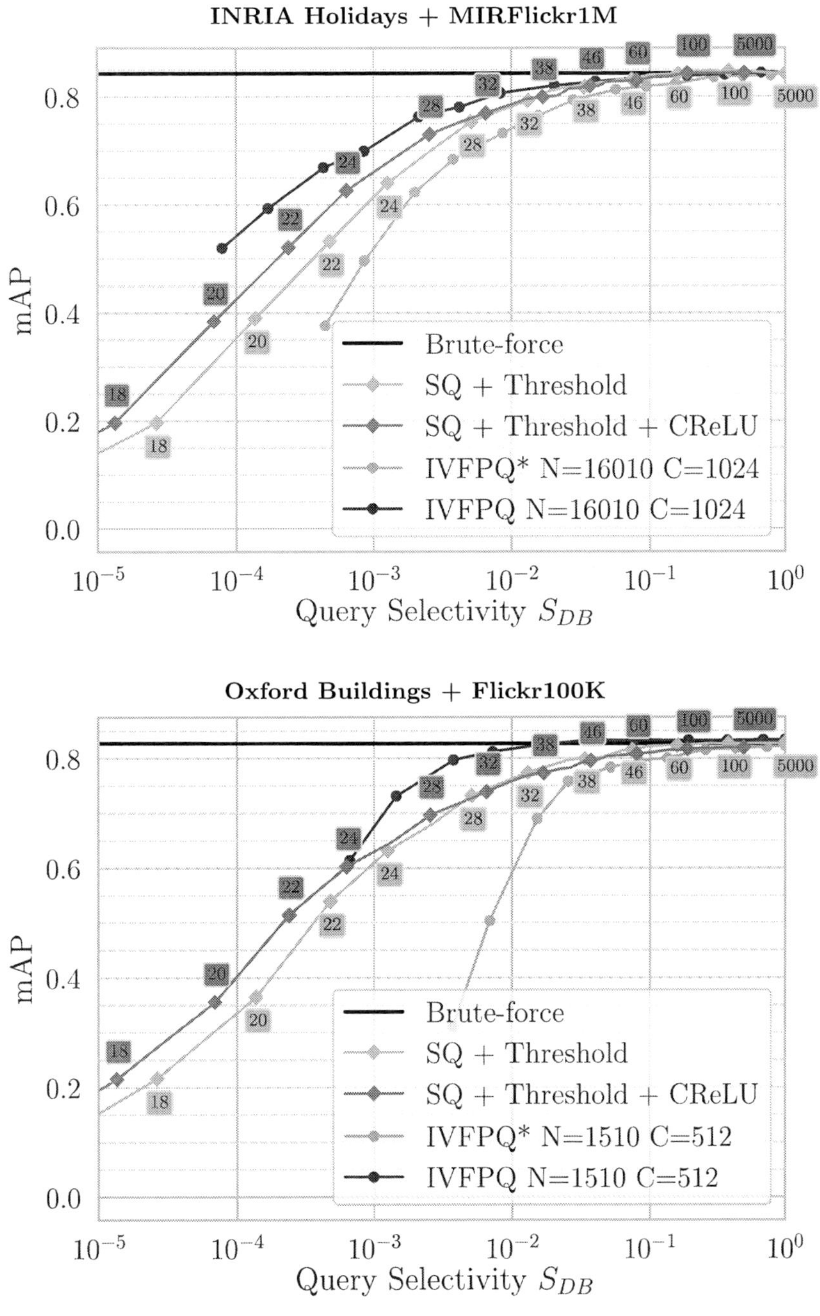

Fig. 1. Effectiveness (mAP) vs efficiency (S_{DB} — fraction of dataset accessed) trade-offs of Scalar Quantization based (SQ) and Product Quantization based (IVFPQ) methods. Curves are produced varying γ for SQ (reported near each point) and the number of accessed lists (nprobe) for IVFPQ. Brute-force represents the sequential scan baseline. IVFPQ* represents IVFPQ trained on out-of-distribution images.

To assess the quality of the results, we used the *mean Average Precision* (mAP) which is a standard evaluation measure in information retrieval. It is defined as the mean of the average precision scores for a set of queries, where the average precision equals the area under the precision-recall curve. As we put our work in the context of large scale image search, in the experiments, we report the mAP in function of the *Query Selectivity* S_{DB}, i.e. the average fraction of database accessed per query, on both the considered datasets (Figure 1). Each line is obtained varying the most effective parameter (γ for SQ, the number of accessed list *nprobe* for PQ). Well-trained PQ-based index perform best, but SQ-based methods provide a slightly degraded off-the-shelf performance without the need of any initial training set, training phase, or specialized index structure that instead highly influences IVFPQ. Moreover, the CReLU transformation consistently boost performance over plain SQ in all regimes.

5 Conclusions

This paper presented a simple and effective methodology to index and retrieve deep features without the need for a time-consuming codebook learning step. Our approach relies on transforming the deep features into text encodings, which can be subsequently indexed and searched using off-the-shelf text search engines. An important aspect is that our encoding technique is completely independent from the technology used for indexing. We can rely on the latest text search engine technologies, without having to worry about issues related to implementation problems, such as software maintenance, updates to new hardware technologies, bugs, etc. Furthermore, with our approach, it is possible to include in the image records, in addition to the visual features (which are in textual form), other information such as text metadata, geotags, etc.

Acknowledgements The work was partially supported by Smart News (CUP CIPE D58C15000270008), VISECH, ARCO-CNR (CUP B56J17001330004), ADA (CUP CIPE D55F17000290009), and the AI4EU project (funded by the EC, H2020 - Contract n. 825619). We gratefully acknowledge the support of NVIDIA Corporation with the donation of the Tesla K40 GPU used for this research.

References

1. Amato, G., Bolettieri, P., Falchi, F., Gennaro, C., Rabitti, F.: Combining local and global visual feature similarity using a text search engine. In: Proceedings of the 2011 9th International Workshop on Content-Based Multimedia Indexing (CBMI). pp. 49 –54 (june 2011)
2. Amato, G., Carrara, F., Falchi, F., Gennaro, C., Vadicamo, L.: Large-scale instance-level image retrieval. Information Processing & Management p. 102100 (2019)
3. Amato, G., Falchi, F., Gennaro, C., Vadicamo, L.: Deep Permutations: Deep convolutional neural networks and permutation-based indexing. In: Proceedings of the 9th International Conference on Similarity Search and Applications. pp. 93–106. SISAP 2016, LNCS, Springer International Publishing (2016)

4. Arandjelović, R., Gronat, P., Torii, A., Pajdla, T., Sivic, J.: NetVLAD: CNN architecture for weakly supervised place recognition. In: Proceedings of the IEEE Conference on Computer Vision and Pattern Recognition. pp. 5297–5307. CVPR 2016, IEEE (June 2016)
5. Babenko, A., Slesarev, A., Chigorin, A., Lempitsky, V.: Neural codes for image retrieval. In: Proceedings of 13th European Conference on Computer Vision. pp. 584–599. ECCV 2014, Springer (2014)
6. Donahue, J., Jia, Y., Vinyals, O., Hoffman, J., Zhang, N., Tzeng, E., Darrell, T.: DeCAF: A deep convolutional activation feature for generic visual recognition. CoRR **abs/1310.1531** (2013)
7. Gennaro, C., Amato, G., Bolettieri, P., Savino, P.: An approach to content-based image retrieval based on the lucene search engine library. In: Proceedings of the International Conference on Theory and Practice of Digital Libraries. pp. 55–66. TPDL 2010, Springer Berlin Heidelberg (2010)
8. Girshick, R., Donahue, J., Darrell, T., Malik, J.: Rich feature hierarchies for accurate object detection and semantic segmentation. In: Proceedings of the IEEE Conference on Computer Vision and Pattern Recognition. pp. 580–587. CVPR 2014, IEEE (June 2014)
9. Gordo, A., Almazán, J., Revaud, J., Larlus, D.: End-to-end learning of deep visual representations for image retrieval. International Journal of Computer Vision **124**(2), 237–254 (Sep 2017)
10. Jégou, H., Douze, M., Schmid, C.: Hamming embedding and weak geometric consistency for large scale image search. In: Proceedings of the European Conference on Computer Vision, ECCV 2008, LNCS, vol. 5302, pp. 304–317. Springer (2008)
11. Jégou, H., Douze, M., Schmid, C.: Product quantization for nearest neighbor search. IEEE Transactions on Pattern Analysis and Machine Intelligence **33**(1), 117–128 (Jan 2011)
12. Jégou, H., Douze, M., Schmid, C., Pérez, P.: Aggregating local descriptors into a compact image representation. In: IEEE Conference on Computer Vision & Pattern Recognition. pp. 3304–3311 (jun 2010)
13. Liu, R., Wei, S., Zhao, Y., Yang, Y.: Indexing of the CNN features for the large scale image search. Multimedia Tools and Applications **77**(24), 32107–32131 (Dec 2018)
14. Mohedano, E., McGuinness, K., O'Connor, N.E., Salvador, A., Marques, F., Giro-i Nieto, X.: Bags of local convolutional features for scalable instance search. In: Proceedings of the ACM International Conference on Multimedia Retrieval. pp. 327–331. ICMR 2016, ACM (2016)
15. Philbin, J., Chum, O., Isard, M., Sivic, J., Zisserman, A.: Object retrieval with large vocabularies and fast spatial matching. In: Proceeding of the IEEE Conference on Computer Vision and Pattern Recognition. pp. 1–8. CVPR 2007, IEEE (2007)
16. Salton, G., McGill, M.J.: Introduction to Modern Information Retrieval. McGraw-Hill, Inc., New York, NY, USA (1986)
17. Shang, W., Sohn, K., Almeida, D., Lee, H.: Understanding and improving convolutional neural networks via concatenated rectified linear units. In: Proceedings of the 33rd International Conference on Machine Learning. ICML 2016, vol. 48, pp. 2217–2225. JMLR.org (2016)
18. Tolias, G., Sicre, R., Jégou, H.: Particular object retrieval with integral max-pooling of CNN activations. CoRR **abs/1511.05879** (2015)
19. Yue-Hei Ng, J., Yang, F., Davis, L.S.: Exploiting local features from deep networks for image retrieval. In: Proceedings of the IEEE Conference on Computer Vision and Pattern Recognition Workshops. pp. 53–61. CVPRW 2015, IEEE (2015)

Towards Automatic Classification of Sheet Music

Giuseppe De Pasquale[1], Blerina Spahiu[2][0000-0002-6958-8215], Pietro Ducange[3][0000-0003-4510-1350], and Andrea Maurino[2][0000-0001-9803-3668]

[1]Leonardo S.p.A. Sistemi di Difesa, via Monterusciello, 75, 80078, Pozzuoli, Napoli
giuseppe.depasquale@leonardocompany.com
[2]University of Milano-Bicocca, Viale Sarca, 336 - 20126 Milan, Italy
blerina.spahiu|andrea.maurino@unimib.it
[3]University of Pisa, Largo Lucio Lazzarino, Pisa, Italy
pietro.ducange@unipi.it

Abstract. Automatic music classification has been of interest since digital data about music became available within the Web. For this task, different automatic classification approaches have been proposed but all existing approaches are based on the analysis of sounds. To the best of our knowledge, there is no automatic solution that considers only the sheet music for classification. Therefore, within the following study, we introduce a machine-learning based approach in order to assign an author to new sheet music. Different features, that best represent the style of a writer has been extracted, and are given in input for training to a kNN algorithm. In addition, the article discusses the results and cases when the classifier fails to assign the right author.

Keywords: sheet music classification · machine learning · feature extraction.

1 Introduction

Sometimes, for a trained ear, it can be easy to identify the author of an unheard music played on the piano. Often, this happens when someone tries to identifying a famous author, such as Mozart, Beethoven or Chopin, of whom many concerts, sonatas or other compositions have already been heard before. When an author has his own specific style, it is also possible to recognize him even though we are listening to a song never heard before. Of course, there are authors who have similar styles, especially those belonging to the same school as the German or Austrian school, the Russian school, the Italian school, the French school, etc. This paper aims at characterising the piano writing of three authors, namely Chopin, Beethoven and Mozart. There exists several similarities between these authors, since the German Beethoven was certainly influenced by the music of the Austrian composer Mozart. Beethoven moved to Vienna at 22 years old and trained together with Mozart and Haydn.

The scope of this paper is to investigate if the writing of Chopin, Beethoven and Mozart, their way of composing, and part of their scores can be used to classify new ones using machine learning techniques. There exist a bunch of works in classifying authors and genres, such as those discussed in [8, 13, 11, 17, 7, 9, 20], which have the aim of classifying music, classical music in particular, through the recording of a few minutes of sound, their spectral analysis and the extraction of suitable features. Such approaches are at an advanced stage in terms of sampling capacity, ability to make Fourier transforms with many points, computational skills and advanced algorithmic techniques. Moreover, such approaches can count on increasingly powerful processors with larger and larger memories capacity. The goal of these approaches is to obtain features that can characterize different song writers so that it can be easy to classify new musical scores that do not have an author. Such features convey the sequence of notes and chords, their duration and intensity, and breaks in time or frequency.

With sophisticated means it is possible to create faithfully scores starting by a piece of sound played in piano. The score of a song has all this information, thus allowing us to focus directly on the extraction of the features and their classification, leaving out the decoding phase of the sound of the musical piece.

In summary, the aim of this paper is to fill the gap and present an initial work toward an automatic classification of musical scores for classical music writers. Our contributions are two fold and can be summarized as follows: (i) to identify a set of features that best represent the style of a music composer; and (ii) to extract such features used for classification.

This paper is organized as follows: preliminaries in understanding the main concepts and definitions in music scores are given in Section 2 while the state-of-the-art is presented in Section 3. A general overview of the workflow and the analysis of the main features that better characterize the style of a composer is given in Section 4. The results of the classification approach and their analysis are presented in Section 5 while conclusions end the paper in Section 6.

2 Preliminaries

In this section we first introduce some preliminary definitions and concepts needed to understand and describe our approach.

Musical notation or semiography: is the system of signs (staff, notes, keys, etc.) used to express music graphically.

Staff: is a bundle of five horizontal and equidistant straight lines, used in musical writing to indicate, in conjunction with the clef, the height of each note.

Clef: The clef is a graphic sign that is placed at the beginning of the musical staff to indicate the position of the note to which it corresponds, thus determining the name, position and pitch of all the other marked notes of the same staff. It can also be marked inside the body itself, when the height of the notes requires a change. In a staff two types of clefs are used: Treble clef (also called G Clef because of the staff line which the clef wraps around (see first staff in Fig. 2)) and Bass clef (also called F clef because of the staff line between two dots of the clef is F (see second staff in Fig. 2)).

Notes - Rests: Musical notes mean the series of seven types of sounds: C, D, E, F, G, A and B. Graphically the notes are distinguished from the place they occupy in the staff according to the reading clef. Octaves is the distance between one note (like C#) and the next note bearing its same name (the next C# that's either higher or lower). In terms of physics, an octave is the distance between one note and another note that's double its frequency.

Beats - Measure bar - Tempo: The notes of a musical composition are divided, according to a metricorhythmic scheme, called tempo, into many distinct and consecutive groups, called *beats*, by means of vertical separation lines, called measurement bars. The bar is the set of musical values (figure and accents) between two measure bars. Tempo is the metric-rhythmic pattern of the bars, intended as a unit of duration and accentuation.

Tonality: With tonality we refer to that particular constraint that elevates the sounds of one scale, according to the place it occupies in the order of the scale itself. **Scale:** is a gradual succession of sounds contained within an octave. Scales can be distinguished by the number of sounds and, above all, by their reciprocal distance relationships. The scale is divided into: diatonic (made up of tones and semitones like the succession of the seven natural sounds) and chromatic (consists of the succession of all 12 semitones contained in the octave).

Interval: The interval is the tonal distance that passes between two sounds. Intervals can be distinguished in harmonic (those from simultaneous sounds) and melodic (those with subsequent sounds).

Melody: Melody is any rhythmic sequence of single notes, capable of expressing a musical thought.

Harmony: is the science of chords. A chord is the union of different sounds, merged into a single acoustic expression. Chords are formed, basically, by superimposing two or more sounds of the same scale.

3 Related Work

To the best of our knowledge, there is no previous work that deals with extracting features from staff for the classification of musical artists. Related published work on features extraction can be grouped into three categories: (i) through audio signals; (ii) through optical music recognition; and (iii) through musical space representation.

3.1 Features extraction through audio signals

The idea behind [19] is that a particular musical genre is characterized by statistical properties related to the instrumentation, the rhythm of its content. For this reason they propose the extraction of a set of features to represent the structure and musical instrumentation, as well as a new set of features to represent the rhythmic structure. The performance of these feature sets was assessed through the training of classifiers for the recognition of statistical models that use real-world audio collections.

Authors in [6] propose an approach for the classification of music into three major categories: rock, classical and jazz through the use of spectrograms. Humans are much better at distinguishing small pitch changes at low frequencies than at high frequencies. This scale makes the features more similar to what humans perceive. Such algorithm use the texture-of-texture models to generate feature vectors out of spectrograms. These features are capable to profile the frequency power of a sound as music progresses. Finally, an attempt is made to classify the data generated using a variety of classifiers.

The work discussed in [11] proposes a two-step methodology to classify music. First, various sources of musical instruments are identified and separated in the audio signal. Then, features are extracted from the separated signals that correspond to distinct musical instruments. Afterwards, the extracted timbre, rhythm and intonation features from the identified instruments are used to classify music clip. This procedure is similar to a human listener who is able to determine the genre of a musical signal and, at the same time, distinguish a number of different musical instruments in a complex sound music.

The goal of the contribution in [18] is to identify the most likely pianist, given a set of performances of the same piece performed by different pianists. For the classification, a set of simple features is proposed which characteristics best a musical performer: timing (variations in tempo), dynamics (variations in loudness), and articulation (the use of overlaps and pauses between successive notes). Experiments show that by using machine learning it is possible for a machine to distinguish music performers (pianists) on the basis of their performance style.

The melody extraction algorithms proposed in [16, 4] aim to produce a sequence of frequency values corresponding to the tones of the dominant melody from a musical recording. The term melody is intended as the single (monophonic) sequence of tones that a listener would reproduce if asked to whistle or sing a piece of polyphonic music. The melody extraction algorithms are commonly evaluated by humans by comparing the estimated intonation sequences with respect to the real one. For the evaluation, pieces of classical music, recordings of people singing along with the music were collected. Experiments show that there are several difficulties in extracting the melody for this particular repertoire. However, the density and the complexity of the notes were identified as the most relevant features for the classification.

3.2 Feature extraction through optical music recognition

For the classification of music genres, the work discussed in [5] proposes an approach that converts an audio signal into spectrograms. Features are then extracted from the time-frequency images which are used to model musical genres in a classification system. The features are based on a local binary pattern, a structural operator that has been successful in recent research on image classification. The experiments were performed with two well-known data sets: the Latin music database (LMD) and ISMIR 2004. The results obtained by analysing the extracted features always exceed those based on audio content only. Using the LMD data set, the accuracy of the approach is approximately 82.33%. while for the ISMIR 2004 database, the best result obtained is around 80.65%.

Authors of [9] propose an automatic system for classifying musical genres based on a strategy for selecting local features using the self-adaptive algorithm Armony Search (SAHS). Five acoustic characteristics (i.e. intensity, pitch, timbre, tonality and rhythm) are extracted. Finally, each SVM (one-to-one vector machine) classifier is fed with the corresponding local feature set and the majority voting method is used to classify each music recording.

The contribution in [14] presents a new and effective approach for the automatic recognition of the musical genre based on the fusion of different sets of features. Both acoustic and visual features are considered and merged into a final set. Evaluations show that such approach achieves an accuracy for the classification comparable or even better than other approaches of the state-of-the-art. The aim of this approach is to classify music from its representation as spectrogram and proposes a set of descriptors and classifiers to maximize the performance that could be obtained from the visual characteristics.

3.3 Feature extraction through musical space representation

This category aims to perform coherent analysis of the structure of the musical piece by representing notes in the plane that reveals affinities and structures between notes [3]. Tonnez is the classical tool that represent harmonic relationships between chords using a two-dimensional lattice [2].

4 The Proposed Approach

In the following, we describe the workflow of the proposed approach. First, we describe the general workflow starting from the input file and every step until the classification algorithm. Second, we describe in details the feature extraction process which we apply for our task in assigning the author of a composition. Third, we describe the classification algorithm.

4.1 Workflow

In Fig. 1 is given the general approach for music classification starting from music sheets. As a requirement for this research, we propose a new approach written ad hoc to extract features from scores. Since optical reading and interpretation of the scores are not subject of this research, we use piano pieces by the three authors downloaded from the Web in *midi*[1] format (step 1). Subsequently, using the MuseScore[2] notation and musical composition software, the downloaded files can be transformed into *.xml* format (step 2). Such format obtains a representation on the staff in a faithfully way for various compositions. It should be noted

[1] http://www.music.mcgill.ca/ ich/classes/mumt306/StandardMIDIfileformat.html
[2] https://musescore.org/

that the staves obtained in this way are not exactly the same as the originals, but faithfully represent the succession of notes and rests of the original compositions, keeping their duration and speed. Such transformation conserves melody, harmony, time and rhythm of a piece, which are the real content of the piece and all characteristics that distinguish one composition from the other. Next, we extract a set of features that could best represent a compositions and that could better allow to identify different music writers (step 4). This step was supported by an in-depth research of similar studies, of data sets already available and of algorithms already used for the classification of songs or musical styles. Actually, in this preliminary work, we divided each staff into *periods* composed of 8 measures and for each of them we extract a set of features. Finally, we classify each period (step 5), assigning to it a specific author (step 6).

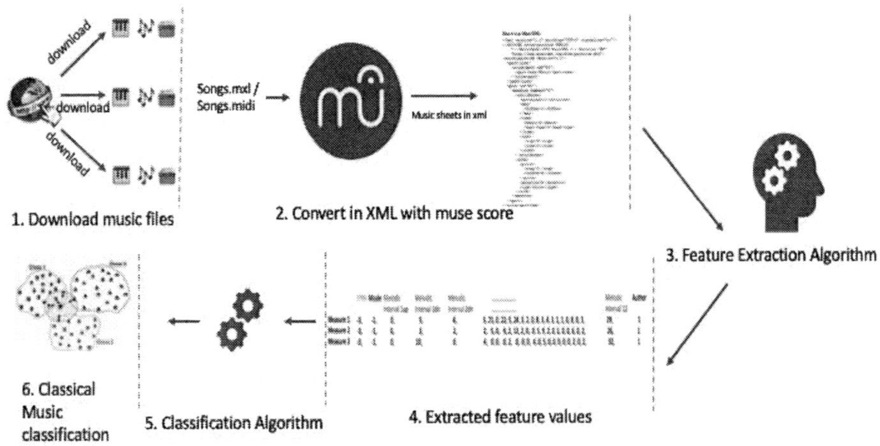

Fig. 1. General workflow for the approach

4.2 Feature Extraction

The task of identifying which are the best features, from musical sheets, that can distinguish one author from another is very difficult. A piano composition is formed by the succession of single notes and chords of different duration performed at different speeds and articulated through the synchronization of the right hand and left hand of the performer. The characteristic of a composition is the combination of melody and harmony that express the sensitivity of the authors and their inspiration supported by an excellent technique. Taking into consideration the staff of a composition, we identified several features as important for characterizing a music composition. As stated before, in this preliminary work, we divided each staff into *periods* composed of 8 measures. For each period, we extract a collection of features grouped into 4 macro-features, as shown in Fig. 2 and discussed in the following:

- **Notes:** Musical notes means the series of 7 types of sounds: C,D, E, F, G, A and B. For each note, we extract its occurrence within the period. Moreover, we extract also the occurrence of notes with accidentals (flat ♭ and sharp ♯). The number of equal notes used by the composer can be a useful feature to characterize a composition. In this study all equal notes, even belonging to different octaves are considered as the same note. Moreover, the occurrence of each note is calculated without considering its value, namely its relative duration. Thus, in total, we can extract 12 features regarding the notes macro-features.

- **Rests:** Rests represent period of silence in a music composition. For each period, we count the number of rests, without considering its relative duration.
- **Tonality:** this macro-feature includes both the *fifth* and the *mode* of the stuff. The fifth is a set of flats ♭ or sharps ♯ that are generally written immediately after the clef. It is described by an integer feature, defined in $[-7, 7]$, where the negative values regard flats and positive values regard sharps. The modulus represents the number of symbols. Given a certain number of symbols, two specific tonalities, also called keys, may be associated to the composition. Also the value zero can describe two possible keys, namely C major or A minor. Mode can have two values + 1 for major mode and - 1 for minor mode.Indeed, we recall that the *circle of fifths* is a graphic representation of the possible tonalities where the outer circle describes major mode while the inner circle describes the minor mode. It is known that generally a minor mode is more suitable for sad and melancholic music than a major mode that is more suitable for a cheerful and joyful work.
- **Interval:** An interval represents the distance in semitones between two notes. There exists two types of intervals: *Melodic* intervals (from subsequent notes) and *Harmonic* intervals (from simultaneous notes which form a chord). Regarding melodic intervals, passing from one note to another, we may identify ascending or descending intervals, if we have an increasing or a decreasing of the frequency of the note, respectively. In order to reduce the number of intervals, distances are calculated modulo 12. Since the maximum number of semitones in an octave is 12, we can identify in total 23 intervals for the melodic intervals. Indeed, we consider 11 ascending and 11 descending intervals and a neutral interval, considering that the 12th ascending interval coincides with the 12th descending interval. The melodic interval between two chords is calculated between the two highest notes of the two chords. For each interval, we calculate its frequency in the period. In the case of harmonic intervals, we calculate the distances in semitones between two notes, starting from the lowest note, thus we can extract 12 intervals. We recall that for each chord, we calculate the distances between all the possible combination of two notes that form the chord. In conclusion, we can extract 23 and 12 features for the melodic and harmonic intervals, respectively.

In the following, we show an example of how the values for a set of macro-features such as *Tonality & Melodic Intervals* are extracted for Chopin's prelude n. 20 op. 28. Each staff is divided into phrases composed of 8 measures. Each measure is represented with a row of values as in Fig. 3. The prelude under

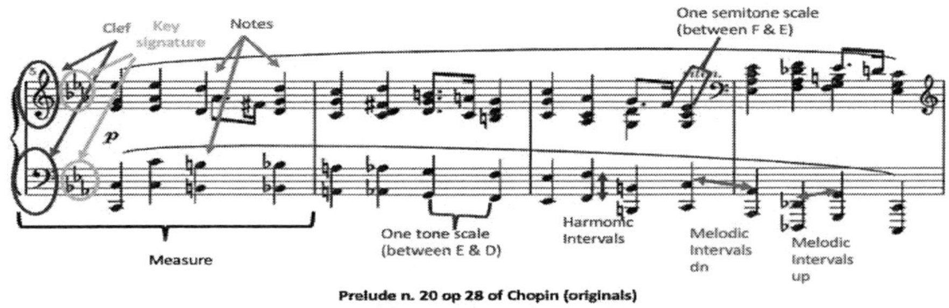

	Clef	Key Sig.	Melodic Interval 1up	Melodic Interval 1dn	Melodic Interval 2dn	...	Melodic Interval 12	Author
Measure 1	-3,	-1,	0,	5,	6,	5, 21, 0, 22, 5, 24, 3, 2, 0, 8, 3, 4, 3, 1, 1, 0, 8, 0, 3,	29,	1
Measure 2	-3,	-1,	0,	3,	2,	2, 5, 0, 9, 2,12, 2, 0, 0, 5, 9, 2, 0, 1, 0, 0, 6, 0, 2,	26,	1
Measure 3	-3,	-1,	0,	10,	0,	4, 0, 0, 0, 2, 0, 0, 0, 4, 0, 5, 0, 0, 0, 0, 0, 2, 0, 2,	32,	1

Fig. 2. Features considered for extraction from staff

examination is a prelude in C minor composed of 26 measures (13 for each hand) consisting of 13 measures in the G key (right hand) and 13 in the F key (left hand). Since we have divided the staff into periods of 8 measures, we get $\lfloor 26/8 \rfloor$ periods, i.e. 3 instances to be classified. As we are considering periods of 8 measures, the remaining two measures are not considered for the classification. In Fig. 2, we show just an extract of the prelude, containing just a portion of two periods, for the left and for the right hands, respectively. The first feature that we extract is the *Fifth*, which is the same for each period. In this case, the value of this feature is equal to -3, namely 3 flats in key, that represent the key Eb major or C minor. The value of the mode allows us to discriminate between the two possible keys. In this case, the vale of the feature *mode* is equal to -1, thus the key is C minor. Finally, for each of the 23 melodic intervals, we extract a value which represents its occurrence in the period. In the example, for the first period, we find 0 intervals where notes have ascended by one semitone ($MelodicInterval_{1up}$), while there are 5 intervals where notes have descended by 1 seminote ($MelodicInterval_{1dn}$).

	Fifth	Mode	Melodic Interval 1up	Melodic Interval 1dn	Melodic Interval 2dn	...	Melodic Interval 12	Author
Period 1	-3,	-1,	0,	5,	6,	5, 21, 0, 22, 5, 24, 3, 2, 0, 8, 3, 4, 3, 1, 1, 0, 8, 0, 3,	29,	1
Period 2	-3,	-1,	0,	3,	2,	2, 5, 0, 9, 2, 12, 2, 0, 0, 5, 9, 2, 0, 1, 0, 0, 6, 0, 2,	26,	1
Period 3	-3,	-1,	0,	10,	0,	4, 0, 0, 0, 2, 0, 0, 0, 4, 0, 5, 0, 0, 0, 0, 0, 2, 0, 2,	32,	1

Fig. 3. Feature values for Tonality & Melodic Intervals for the Prelude n. 20 op 28 of Chopin (Fig. 2)

4.3 Classification approaches

Once we have extracted a set of features for describing a period of a staff, we can classify it in order to identify its author. The classification problem has been widely studied in the database [12], data mining [15], and information retrieval communities [10]. Typically, a classification model is in charge of assign a class, among a pre-defined set of classes, to a new input pattern described as a vector in a specific multi-dimensional space. The parameters of the classifier can be learnt during a supervised learning stage adopting a labeled training set. As a preliminary experiment, we choose to test the simple kNN classification algorithm. In this case, the parameters of the model are all the instances of the training set. Given a new pattern, the kNN classifier finds the nearest k patterns (nearest neighbors) to the one to be classified [1]. The classifier then assigns to the new pattern the most frequent class, among the k nearest neighbors.

5 Experimental Analysis

In this section we describe the results of the experiments carried out for the classification of new musical sheets. Firstly, we provide a general overview of the data used for the experiment. Secondly, we describe the results of the experiment for different feature combination and finally we provide a discussion of the results.

5.1 Data Corpus

In the following experiments, we considered 131 music sheets of Chopin (61), Beethoven (29) and Mozart (41). All music sheets are converted into xml format (see Fig. 1) and after the feature extraction process, as discussed in Section 4, we obtained a complete data corpus consisting of 6063 instances (corresponding to 6063 *periods*), including 1919 from Chopin, 2010 from Beethoven and 2134 from Mozart. Actually, in this preliminary work, we classify each single instance rather than the entire music sheet.

5.2 Experimental results

In this section, we report the results for the experiments for classical music classification between three authors. In order to identify which are the features that mostly characterize a composer, we carried out a number of experiments considering different subsets of features, among the ones described in Section 4. For each experiment, we carried out a 10 fold cross-validation. We recall that in this preliminary experiments, we classify single periods extracted from music sheets, assigning to each of them a specific author.

We considered two categories of experiments. For the first category, we build models to classify periods into one of the three authors, namely Chopin, Mozart and Beethoven. As regards the second category, we consider just two authors for the classification task, namely Mozart and Beethoven. We skipped Chopin in the second category since Mozart and Beethoven share several melodic and harmonic aspects. Indeed, they acted in an overlapped period during the last years of the 18th Century. Thus, distinguishing between these two authors may be more challenging.

Table 1 shows the results of the classification task for five experiments, for each category, adopting the kNN as classification algorithm (k=5, using Euclidean distance). In the first column, we show the different combinations of macro-features that characterized a specific experiment. The second and third columns regard, respectively, the first (Complete Data Corpus) and the second category (Partial Data Corpus) of experiments. These columns summarize the accuracy on the test set, expressed in terms of the average values of the percentage of correctly classified periods. As regards the combination of macro-features, we experimentally verified that the Tonality should be always included for achieving meaningful results. For the sake of brevity, we skipped to show the results achieved without considering this macro-feature.

Table 1. Period classification accuracy for different macro-feature combinations

Combination of Macro-features	Accuracy (%) Complete Data Corpus	Accuracy (%) Partial Data Corpus
Tonality & Harmonic Intervals	75.12	79.55
Tonality & Melodic Intervals	**82.96**	**83.78**
Tonality & Notes	77.86	80.82
Tonality & Intervals	**84.18**	**84.67**
Tonality & Notes & Rests	81.25	83.11

5.3 Results discussion

We can observe that the highest accuracy is achieved if the melodic intervals are included among the features describing each phrase. Indeed, in these cases, the classifiers achieves an accuracy up to 84.18% and 84.67%, for the complete and the partial data corpus, respectively. Good accuracy levels are achieved if Tonality, Notes and Rests are considered as macro-features for classification. These results confirms that the melodic aspect is what helps to better discriminate a composition author.

In Table 2, we show the average F-measure calculated for each class, namely for each author. This indicator allows us to understand how good is the recognition of each single author by the classifier: the higher the value, the better the recognition. As expected, considering the complete data corpus, since the style of Chopin is very different from that of Beethoven and Mozart, his periods are always better recognized than the other two authors. As regards Mozart,

Table 2. Average F-measure for each author

	Complete Data Corpus			Partial Data Corpus	
Combination of Macro-features	Chopin	Beethoven	Mozart	Beethoven	Mozart
Tonality & Harmonic Intervals	0.81	0.66	0.78	0.77	0.81
Tonality & Melodic Intervals	0.87	0.78	0.83	0.83	0.84
Tonality & Notes	0.84	0.71	0.78	0.80	0.81
Tonality & Intervals	0.89	0.79	0.83	0.84	0.85
Tonality & Notes	0.87	0.75	0.80	0.82	0.83

we can see that he is always better recognized than Beethoven. Finally, as expected, considering the partial data corpus, the recognition capability of both Beethoven and Mozart increases, and the gap between the recognition between this two authors decreases.

6 Conclusions

This study has been inspired by the following statement: in some cases it is possible, for a trained ear, to recognize an author by listening to one of his/her composition that the user has never listened before. The idea is that, the information that characterizes an author, is all contained in the scores of his compositions and it is not necessary to listen to their songs to recognize them.

In this work, we have discussed a framework for the automatic classification of musical sheets. Specifically, we have adopted as inputs midi files of classical music compositions of three famous composers, namely Chopin, Mozart and Beethoven. Then, adopting an open source program, we have transformed the midi files into XML files which codify the music sheets. Each music sheet has been divided into periods of 8 measures and from each of them we have extracted a set of macro-features. Finally, we have experimented different combinations of macro-features for classifying the periods into three classes, namely the three authors, using the kNN algorithm. Preliminary results have shown that good classification accuracy can be achieved if the features which describe the tonality and the harmonic and melodic intervals are adopted.

The proposed framework may be used for recognizing the author of a musical piece, even in digital format or in forms of musical sheets, found after years for which the composer is unknown.

As future works, we plan to extract other features and to experiment additional classifiers that might help us to improve the classification accuracy. Furthermore, we plan to extend our data corpus by including more authors and more musical scores.

Acknowledgments

The contribution to this work of Pietro Ducange is founded by Italian Ministry of Education and Research (MIUR), in the framework of the CrossLab project (Departments of Excellence).

References

1. S. D. Bay. Combining Nearest Neighbor Classifiers Through Multiple Feature Subsets. In *Proceedings of the Fifteenth International Conference on Machine Learning (ICML)*, volume 98, pages 37–45. Morgan Kaufmann Publishers Inc., 1998. Citeseer, doi=10.1.1.52.455.
2. T. Bergstrom, K. Karahalios, and J. C. Hart. Isochords: visualizing structure in music. In *Proceedings of Graphics Interface 2007*, pages 297–304, 2007.

3. L. Bigo, M. Giraud, R. Groult, N. Guiomard-Kagan, and F. Levé. Sketching sonata form structure in selected classical string quartets. 2017.
4. J. Bosch and E. Gómez. Melody extraction in symphonic classical music: a comparative study of mutual agreement between humans and algorithms. In *Proc. 9th Conference on Interdisciplinary Musicology–CIM14, Berlin, Germany*, 2014.
5. Y. M. Costa, L. Oliveira, A. L. Koerich, F. Gouyon, and J. Martins. Music genre classification using lbp textural features. *Signal Processing*, 92(11):2723–2737, 2012.
6. H. Deshpande, R. Singh, and U. Nam. Classification of music signals in the visual domain. In *Proceedings of the COST-G6 Conference on Digital Audio Effects*, pages 1–4, 2001.
7. M. Genussov and I. Cohen. Musical genre classification of audio signals using geometric methods. In *2010 18th European Signal Processing Conference*, pages 497–501. IEEE, 2010.
8. T. George, E. Georg, and C. Perry. Automatic musical genre classification of audio signals. In *Proceedings of the 2nd international symposium on music information retrieval, Indiana*, 2001.
9. Y.-F. Huang, S.-M. Lin, H.-Y. Wu, and Y.-S. Li. Music genre classification based on local feature selection using a self-adaptive harmony search algorithm. *Data & Knowledge Engineering*, 92:60–76, 2014.
10. T. Joachims. *Learning to classify text using support vector machines: Methods, theory and algorithms*, volume 186. 2002. Kluwer Academic Publishers Norwell, 10.1162/089120103322753374.
11. A. Lampropoulos, P. Lampropoulou, and G. Tsihrintzis. Musical genre classification of audio data using source separation techniques. In *Proc. IEEE 5th EURASIP Conference on Speech and Image Processing, Multimedia Communications and Services*. Citeseer, 2005.
12. T.-S. Lim, W.-Y. Loh, and Y.-S. Shih. A comparison of prediction accuracy, complexity, and training time of thirty-three old and new classification algorithms. *Machine learning*, 40(3):203–228, 2000. Kluwer Academic Publishers, https://doi.org/10.1023/A:1007608224229.
13. M. McKinney and J. Breebaart. Features for audio and music classification. 2003.
14. L. Nanni, Y. M. Costa, A. Lumini, M. Y. Kim, and S. R. Baek. Combining visual and acoustic features for music genre classification. *Expert Systems with Applications*, 45:108–117, 2016.
15. T. N. Phyu. Survey of classification techniques in data mining. In *Proceedings of the International MultiConference of Engineers and Computer Scientists*, volume 1, pages 18–20, 2009. Citeseer, doi=10.1.1.148.6474.
16. J. Salamon, E. Gómez, D. P. Ellis, and G. Richard. Melody extraction from polyphonic music signals: Approaches, applications, and challenges. *IEEE Signal Processing Magazine*, 31(2):118–134, 2014.
17. J. G. sArnal Barbedo and A. Lopes. Automatic genre classification of musical signals. *EURASIP Journal on Advances in Signal Processing*, 2007(1):064960, 2006.
18. E. Stamatatos and G. Widmer. Automatic identification of music performers with learning ensembles. *Artificial Intelligence*, 165(1):37–56, 2005.
19. G. Tzanetakis and P. Cook. Musical genre classification of audio signals. *IEEE Transactions on speech and audio processing*, 10(5):293–302, 2002.
20. C. Weiß, M. Mauch, S. Dixon, and M. Müller. Investigating style evolution of western classical music: A computational approach. *Musicae Scientiae*, 23(4):486–507, 2019.

Edge-Based Video Surveillance with Embedded Devices
Discussion Paper

Hanna Kavalionak[1], Claudio Gennaro[1], Giuseppe Amato[1], Claudio Vairo[1], Costantino Perciante[2], Carlo Meghini[1], Fabrizio Falchi[1], and Fausto Rabitti[1]

[1] ISTI-CNR, via G. Moruzzi 1, 56124 Pisa, Italy name.surname@isti.cnr.it
[2] Fluidmesh Networks, via Carlo Farini 5, Milano, Italy
costantino.perciante@fluidmesh.com

Abstract. Video surveillance systems have become indispensable tools for the security and organization of public and private areas. In this work, we propose a novel distributed protocol for an edge-based face recognition system that takes advantage of the computational capabilities of the surveillance devices (i.e., cameras) to perform person recognition. The cameras fall back to a centralized server if their hardware capabilities are not enough to perform the recognition. We evaluate the proposed algorithm via extensive experiments on a freely available dataset. As a prototype of surveillance embedded devices, we have considered a Raspberry PI with the camera module. Using simulations, we show that our algorithm can reduce up to 50% of the load of the server with no negative impact on the quality of the surveillance service.

Keywords: Edge Computing · Distributed Architectures · Internet of Things · Video Surveillance · Embedded Devices.

1 Introduction

Video surveillance is of paramount importance in areas like law enforcement, military and even for a commercial environment. One of the straightforward approaches for video surveillance is to use the client-server model of communication: the surveillance devices stream the video directly to a main powerful server, where the data can be displayed to the human operators, who are responsible to analyze the video [8]. Human resources used in the field of video surveillance services are both costly and not reliable. Also, this approach presents several negative sides, like the creation of a bottleneck for the system security and reliability and the need to maintain a big and costly infrastructure of servers dedicated only to the surveillance task. Hence, with the recent advances in smart technologies, automated video surveillance, where the video streams are analyzed automatically by network edge devices, gained a lot of interest [13, 11].

The idea of exploiting the computation capabilities and the topology of a distributed network of smart cameras to reduce the amount of messaging has been proposed in [14] and [15]. In both approaches, the communication is efficiently handled using a task-oriented node clustering that partition the network in different groups according to the pathway among cameras. The former work, however, is limited to face tracking, while the second one targets collaborative person tracking with a combination of hardware acceleration and middleware. These works focus on people tracking rather than recognition and use an efficient camera clustering protocol to dynamically form groups of cameras for in-network tracking of individual persons.

This work summarizes the contribution presented in [7]. The motivating scenario that we consider for this work is that of face recognition [10, 3, 1, 4]. The surveillance system should be able to recognize faces, and track their movements in a possibly large area (e.g. an airport, a city district, a campus, etc.), using various cameras appositely installed. Real-time video surveillance requires significant storage and processing resources. This work aims to analyze the issues and solutions related to resource allocation, for executing automated edge-based video surveillance, in a fully distributed environment [2, 12]. In particular, we suppose that the (smart) camera devices themselves can cooperate to execute the needed faces detection, recognition and visual analysis tasks. In this work, we study how the image recognition algorithms can be orchestrated across several devices so that bottlenecks are reduced and resource can be managed more effectively. This work extends and enhances our previously published research work [6], where we have proposed a distributed algorithm for load balancing between Smart Sensing Units for the video surveillance task. The adaptive algorithm distributes, at run time, the recognition tasks between the resources of surveillance devices and servers. The detection and recognition tasks are executed locally by surveillance devices, which exploit both the spatial and temporal topology of the moving people, to cache and reuse locally parts of the classification features. Only when devices are not able to execute the recognition task with the cache, a recognition request is sent to the server. We extend the previously proposed adaptive algorithm considering the overhead of real classification techniques.

The rest of the paper is structured as follows. Section 2 provides the definition of the system model and problem statement, whereas Section 3 presents the algorithm for the adaptive camera-assisted person recognition. Section 4 evaluates the distributed surveillance solution through simulations. Finally, Section 5 concludes the paper.

2 System model and problem statement

In our work, we model the geographical area, where the surveillance system is deployed, as divided into sectors. A set of *Smart Sensing Units* (SSUs) are

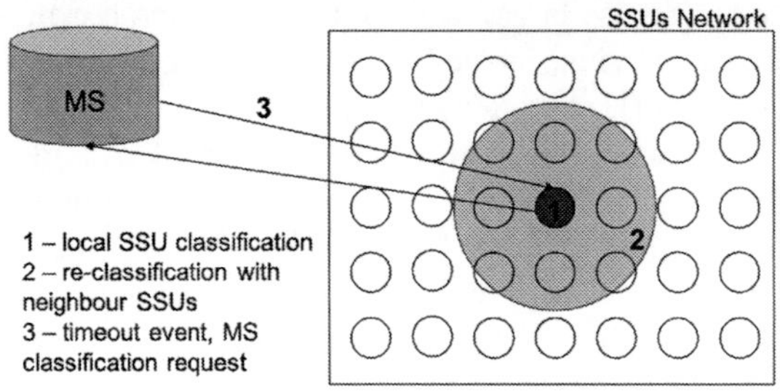

Fig. 1: System model

distributed among the sectors to execute the video surveillance task (Figure 1). Such units have various sensing, computing, storage, and communication capabilities. An SSU is a logical unit, it could be a smart camera having onboard sensing, computing, storage resources, or it could be composed of a camera connected to a computer. Moreover, we assume also the existence of a *Main Server* (MS) unit in the network. A main server is a stand-alone SSU that is characterized by (theoretically) infinite computing, storage, and communication capabilities. It also plays the role of the central server where the devices send their requests, in case of client-server modality.

In our work, we distinguish two possible scenarios: *basic* and *enhanced*. In the basic scenario, all SSUs are connected to the central MS and their functionality is limited to video observation and data streaming to the MS. In the enhanced scenario, on the other hand, all SSUs are connected in a structured peer-to-peer topology. SSUs can cooperate to execute complex tasks and build together a rich representation of the context where the infrastructure is deployed. We consider the peer-to-peer overlay connecting the SSUs to be fixed. Each SSU can contact directly the MS and its geographical neighbor SSUs. We assume the communication between SSUs is reliable, i.e., no message is ever lost or corrupted. In the enhanced scenario, each SSU has computational resources and local storage memory, where it keeps a *recognition library*, which is a collection of recognizers, each specialized to recognize a certain person. The MS's recognition library contains the recognizers for all the recognizable persons in the surveillance area, while the recognition library of an SSU is, basically, a local cache that keeps only a subset of all recognizable persons.

As an illustrative example, let us consider the following scenario, taking place in a geographical area (the surveilled area) of appropriate size, where a number of SSUs have been deployed for video surveillance purposes. Here we consider a person that is moving in the area. The system should visually recognize the person in order to evaluate the presence of this person in the area. One of the straightforward solutions for area video surveillance is to stream all the data from the SSUs to the *MS* for the following processing and storage. This approach can cause some additional system issues. At first, the interested organization needs to have a powerful server system devoted specifically to the surveillance needs.

Algorithm 1: Active thread algorithm executed by SSU

```
repeat
    recognizers.increaseAge();
    events ← getVisibleFaces();
    selection ← selectRecognizers(recognizers);
    foreach face in events do
        if alarm ←getStatus(face, selection) then
            send(FACEID, face, alarm, view);
            startAlarmActivity();
            return;
        if recognized ←getStatus(face, selection) then
            send(FACEID, face, recognized, view);
            return;
        if null ←getStatus(face, selection) then
            t_δ ←setRecognitionTimeout();
            reclBuffer.add(face, t_δ);
            send(ALARMREQUEST, face, null, view);
            return;
    wait ΔT;
until;
```

This server system needs to be powerful enough to continuously process the video streaming data that is coming from the SSUs. The second problem is connected with the delays for the person recognition, caused by possible server overloading and network bandwidth overhead in case of a high rate of requests for recognition.

In order to tackle these issues, our solution exploits a distributed architecture for face recognition, where the detection and recognition tasks are moved to SSUs when it is possible. We performed some simulations in order to move the most possible computation on the camera themselves and we used optimized strategies of distributed computation to solve the most challenging resource-demanding tasks.

3 Algorithm

In this section, we describe our enhanced algorithm for distributing the recognition processes on the SSUs. Each camera in the system keeps the list of its neighbors SSUs, which we name *view*. In order to improve the efficiency of the recognition process each camera locally keeps a recognition library that contains a subset of all recognizers for *faces*. Using these local recognizers, each camera in the network tries to recognize the face of the detected person locally and with the help of neighbor SSUs, without involving the MS, thus reducing its computational and bandwidth consumption. The size of the library is limited to *recognizersLimit* according to the available storage space of an SSU.

Three threads are executed by each of the SSUs: (1) *active thread* (Algorithm 1) is responsible for the active area monitoring, (2) *time-out thread* corresponds to the timeout event in the face recognition by neighbors and (3) *passive thread* (Algorithm 2) processes the incoming messages received by an entity.

Algorithm 2: Passive thread algorithm executed by SSU

```
on event msg(type, face, status, sender) receive do
    if type == ALARMREQUEST then
        result ← getStatus(face, selection);
        send(ALARMREPLY, face, result, sender);
    if type == ALARMREPLY then
        if sender == MS then
            if status == alarm then
                startAlarmActivity();
            integrate(recognizers, face);
            send(FACEID, face, status, view);
        else
            recBuffer.getFace(face).counter ++;
            if recBuffer.contains(face) and status == null then
                if recBuffer.getFace(face).counter ≥ view.size then
                    send(ALARMREQUEST, face, null, MS);
                    recBuffer.remove(face);
            else
                if status == alarm then
                    startAlarmActivity();
                integrate(face, recognizers);
                recBuffer.remove(face);
                send(FACEID, face, status, view);
    if type == FACEID then
        integrate(face, recognizers);
```

Every ΔT each SSU executes the active thread Algorithm 1. At first, it increases the "age" of all known recognizers in the library *recognizers*. Then, it processes the current surveillance area image and extracts the facial features for the detected persons. Finally, it selects the subset *selection* of *recognizers* with the lowest *age* parameter from the local collection.

For each *face* in *events* an SSU executes the recognition algorithm. In case *face* corresponds to the entry in *recognizers* with *alarm* status, the SSU (1) sends a notification message type FACEID with a *face* features and the *alarm* tag to the neighbor SSUs; then (2) starts predefined alarm activity, for example, video recording and live streaming to the operator displays.

In case a *face* is *recognized*, a notification FACEID is distributed between the neighbor SSUs. If there is no correspondence in *selection*, the camera establishes a recognition waiting time and adds the face features into the reclassification buffer *reclBuffer*. It also sends the recognition request ALARMREQUEST to the neighbors' SSUs. When the recognition waiting time has passed, if the object is still in the *reclBuffer*, then the camera sends the classification request ALARMREQUEST to the *MS* and removes the features from the*reclBuffer*.

When an SSU receives a message, it is processed according to the Algorithm 2. We consider three types of messages: ALARMREQUEST, ALARMREPLY and FACEID. The ALARMREQUEST message contains the request for a *face* classification. The recipient checks the status of the received *face* in the local subset of a *recognizers* list and sends an ALARMREPLY containing the results of the recognition *result* to the *sender*. The FACEID message is used for the face features broadcasting to the neighbor SSUs. Hence, whenever a camera receives this message it integrates the received face features to the local *recognizers* library.

The ALARMREPLY message corresponds to the reply to a recognition. If it comes from MS entity, the recipient integrates the recognized face and its status to the local *recognizers* and sends the face notification message FACEID to its neighbors *view*. Moreover, in case the received status is *alarm* the camera initiates some predefined alarm activity. Each SSU keeps track of the replies of all the neighbor SSUs for each $face$ in the $reclBuffer$. If no neighbor SSU is able to recognize the current $face$, then the camera sends the recognition request ALARMREQUEST to the MS and removes the $face$ from the reclassification buffer $reclBuffer$. If, on the other hand, the received status is not *null* it means the $face$ has been recognized by the sender and the camera integrates it to the local *recognizers*, removes the face from the reclassification buffer and sends the face notification message FACEID to its neighbors SSUs. In case the received status is *alarm*, the camera also initiates some predefined alarm activity.

4 Evaluation of the area surveillance algorithm

In this section, we present a simulation experiment in order to evaluate the load imposed on the MS and the performance of the distributed surveillance system.

In our simulation, we assume that the SSUs are uniformly distributed in the monitored area. Persons in the "surveillance area" move according to the mobility model described in [5] for the movements of avatars in a virtual environment. In this model, the area has a number of *hotspots* equals to n_{hs}. The hotspots are the most attractive places in the area where it is expected to find more persons there than in other places. Each person that enters the surveillance area follows the following behavior: the person chooses a random number of hotspots to visit and moves towards them, in sequence. After all the hotspots have been visited, the person leaves the surveillance area. The population of the area follows a bell-shaped curve very similar to the normal distribution in which the population starts from 0 and reaches a maximum of 800 persons. In our simulations, we considered the 10% of persons in the area to be *unknown* (i.e. associated with alarm tag).

We executed simulation of 6 hours using the *peersim* simulator [9] and the mobility model described above. We evaluate two algorithms: (1) when all the data is transmitted to the MS for the analysis (our baseline) and (2) the adaptive algorithm described in Section 3.

In the baseline model, all SSUs stream the video directly to the MS, where the MS extracts the face features and recognizes the persons. The baseline curve in Figure 2 shows the number of recognition the MS is required to process in a 60sec time interval. Other curves on the figure show the evaluation of the recognition requests to MS when the enhanced algorithm is applied and under different system parameters, such as T_{max} and ct, where T_{max} is the maximum allowed face recognition delay and ct is the time needed to compare the extracted features with one class in the recognition library. The results show that the

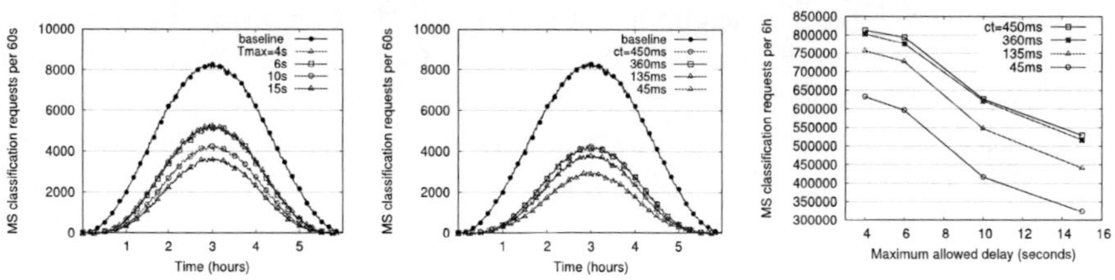

(a) $ct = 450ms$; workload A (b) $T_{max} = 10s$; workload A (c) aggregated requests to SC; 6 h experiment; workload B

Fig. 2: MS recognition requests per 60sec for different system parameters.

enhanced algorithm can reduce up to 50% of the recognition activity of the MS unit in peak hours.

Each class of the cache is a simulated sample of the face features that characterize a person. Therefore, the time needed by an SSUs to perform a single face recognition task is given by the size of the cache selection times *ct*. A higher number of the face features in the class increases the accuracy of the recognition, but at the same time increases also the *ct*.

As we can see in Figure 2a, in case of a lower T_{max} the system does not have enough time for the whole algorithm recognition cycle and it is forced to rely on the MS recognition more often. Instead, a higher T_{max} allows an SSU to perform the recognition using the cache and to receive the replies from the neighbor SSUs. Nevertheless, even in case of low T_{max}, the enhanced algorithm significantly reduces the recognition load of MS compared to the baseline solution.

Figure 2b shows the influence of *ct* time interval on the MS recognition load. Even in case of high accuracy of local recognition and relatively low T_{max}, the load of MS by recognition requests is significantly lower than the baseline solution. Moreover, lower *ct* values further decreases the load imposed on the MS by the recognition. Figure 2c shows the impact of the system parameters on the algorithm effectiveness. Lower values of *ct* and larger of T_{max} significantly reduce the MS recognition load. One of the straightforward ways to minimize *ct* time is to reduce the accuracy of the local recognition algorithm by decreasing the number of features in the sample. In case fast person recognition is not a requirement, the increment of T_{max} can also reduce the load of the MS.

5 Conclusion

In this paper, we propose a distributed edge-based protocol for area video surveillance based on image classification. In order to minimize the classification load on the main server, recognition tasks take place on the SSUs when possible. To perform person recognition, an SSU uses the local resources together with the resources of the neighbor SSUs. The surveillance devices fall back to the main server when the classification cannot be done in the desired time interval. In this extended abstract, we gave an overview of how our system works, we described the proposed algorithms and we presented simulations that show that by partially placing the recognition tasks on the local resources of surveillance devices can reduce the load on the main server up to 50%.

References

1. Amato, G., Carrara, F., Falchi, F., Gennaro, C., Vairo, C.: Facial-based intrusion detection system with deep learning in embedded devices. In: International Conference on Sensors, Signal and Image Processing (SSIP). pp. 64–68. ACM (2018)
2. Amato, G., Chessa, S., Gennaro, C., Vairo, C.: Efficient detection of composite events in wireless sensor networks: design and evaluation. In: 2011 IEEE Symposium on Computers and Communications (ISCC). pp. 821–823. IEEE (2011)
3. Amato, G., Falchi, F., Gennaro, C., Vairo, C.: A comparison of face verification with facial landmarks and deep features. In: 10th International Conference on Advances in Multimedia (MMEDIA). pp. 1–6 (2018)
4. Amato, G., Gennaro, C., Massoli, F.V., Passalis, N., Tefas, A., Trvillini, A., Vairo, C.: Face verification and recognition for digital forensics and information security. In: IEEE 7th International Symposium on Digital Forensic and Security (ISDFS). pp. 1–6. IEEE (2019)
5. Kavalionak, H., Carlini, E., Ricci, L., Montresor, A., Coppola, M.: Integrating peer-to-peer and cloud computing for massively multiuser online games. Peer-to-Peer Networking and Applications (PPNA) pp. 1–19 (2013)
6. Kavalionak, H., Gennaro, C., Amato, G., Meghini, C.: Dice: A distributed protocol for camera-aided video surveillance. In: Computer and Information Technology; Ubiquitous Computing and Communications; Dependable, Autonomic and Secure Computing; Pervasive Intelligence and Computing (CIT/IUCC/DASC/PICOM), 2015 IEEE International Conference on. pp. 477–484. IEEE (2015)
7. Kavalionak, H., Gennaro, C., Amato, G., Vairo, C., Perciante, C., Meghini, C., Falchi, F.: Distributed video surveillance using smart cameras. Journal of Grid Computing **17**(1), 59–77 (2019)
8. Mishra, R., Kumar, P., Chaudhury, S., Indu, S.: Monitoring a large surveillance space through distributed face matching. In: Computer Vision, Pattern Recognition, Image Processing and Graphics (NCVPRIPG), 2013 Fourth National Conference on. pp. 1–5. IEEE (2013)
9. Montresor, A., Jelasity, M.: PeerSim: A scalable p2p simulator. In: Proc. of P2P'09. pp. 99–100. IEEE (2009)
10. Parkhi, O.M., Vedaldi, A., Zisserman, A.: Deep face recognition (2015)
11. Song, M., Tao, D., Maybank, S.J.: Sparse camera network for visual surveillance–a comprehensive survey. arXiv preprint arXiv:1302.0446 (2013)
12. Vairo, C., Amato, G., Chessa, S., Valleri, P.: Modeling detection and tracking of complex events in wireless sensor networks. In: 2010 IEEE International Conference on Systems, Man and Cybernetics. pp. 235–242. IEEE (2010)
13. Wang, X.: Intelligent multi-camera video surveillance: A review. Pattern recognition letters **34**(1), 3–19 (2013)
14. Yoder, J., Medeiros, H., Park, J., Kak, A.C.: Cluster-based distributed face tracking in camera networks. Image Processing, IEEE Transactions on **19**(10), 2551–2563 (2010)
15. Zarezadeh, A., Bobda, C., Yonga, F., Mefenza, M.: Efficient network clustering for traffic reduction in embedded smart camera networks. Journal of Real-Time Image Processing pp. 1–14 (2015)

Gathering Malware Data through High-Interaction Honeypots

(DISCUSSION PAPER)

Angelo Furfaro[1 [0000-0003-2537-8918]], Francesco Lupia[2 [0000-0003-0775-6890]], and Domenico Saccà[1 [0000-0003-3584-5372]]

[1] University of Calabria, Rende(CS), Italy
{angelo.furfaro, domenico.sacca}@unical.it
[2] OKT srl, Rende(CS), Italy
francesco.lupia@okt-srl.com

Abstract. The widespread and ever increasing number of services and devices which expose their interfaces to the Internet make the cyberspace a fertile ground for malware activities. Hence there is a strong demand for cybersecurity solutions ensuring their safe operation. Honeypots are networked computer systems purposely designed and crafted to mimic regular services, operating systems and devices with the goal of capturing and storing information about the interactions with attacking entities and we repute them a crucial technology in the study of cyber threats and attacks. We presents the main features of EMPHAsis, a data streaming analytics system based on high-interaction honeypots, which enables the collection and analysis of relevant data about intercepted malware.

Keywords: Honeypots · Cybersecurity · Data collection · data streaming analytics.

1 Introduction

The era of Internet of Things with billions of connected devices has created an ever larger space for cyber attackers to exploit. In particular, there is a widespread amount of automated bots scanning and probing the Internet to search for vulnerable hosts. This has resulted in the need for fast and accurate detection of possible system vulnerabilities and attackers by means of the processing of the high-velocity, high-volume data from various sources to discover anomalies and/or attack patterns as fast as possible to limit the vulnerability of the systems and increase their resilience. Such data, generated in a real-time data stream, need a *big data streaming analysis* [13, 9]: the output must be generated with low-latency and any incoming data must be reflected in the newly generated output within seconds. In other words, big data streaming analytics tools must be able to identify new information, incrementally build models and access whether the new incoming data deviate from model predictions.

Even though many big data streaming analytics tools have been developed in the past few years, their usage in the field of cybersecurity is not immediate and calls for new approaches as pointed out in [5]. The main issue is how to access in real time to valuable data on possible attackers, typically log files and security alerts generated by operating systems and applications across various hosts and systems. A crucial point is to provide computer systems with software tools to identify suspicious event log activity, such as repeated failed login attempts, excessive CPU usage, large data transfers and immediate alert IT security analysts when a possible Indicator of Compromise (*IoC*) is detected.

It should be noted that the techniques and attack methods employed by malwares are typically very simple, In fact, the most used attack method is often brute-forcing login credentials of servers and, consequently, the most heavily attacked services are Telnet, FTP and SSH services. There are many tools used in computer security to catch such malicious actions and one effective solution involves the usage of honeypots. Honeypots [12] are decoy systems which aim at emulating real services on the net in order to detect and attract malicious agents. These emulated services are publicly displayed and their access is made voluntarily simple to facilitate attackers' intrusions. This is done for example by configuring accounts and services with weak credentials. After accessing the service, all the activities of the malicious agents are subject to monitoring and logging and become the object of study by specialists in the sector, in order to be able to reconstruct with extreme precision the behavior of the attacker and thus be able to prepare prevention measures to reduce the risk of future attacks. Furthermore, it is possible to obtain valuable information concerning the behavior of the attacker, the actions carried out on the target system and the types of vulnerabilities exploited to complete the malevolent activity, which can be subsequently shared with the academia and industry researchers.

Here we present the main features of EMPHAsis, a distributed system conceived to support malware detection by acting as a high-interaction honeypot [11]. The system is able to collect and disseminate information about new threats that proliferate every day on the Internet by providing researchers with fresh data that could help them to devise possible countermeasures against malicious traffic. In addition to its detection, logging and monitoring capabilities, EMPHAsis is capable to capture different malware binaries and to exploit external services for analyze them.

2 System Architecture

While malware's actions may vary depending on the targeted system, there are only few points of interest that need to be observed and analyzed: network information, the commands executed, processes created, kernel drivers loaded and the files created or modified by the malicious agent. Each attacker's action is processed by EMPHAsis according to the functional architecture depicted in Figure 1 discussed next. The system operates by constructing dynamically

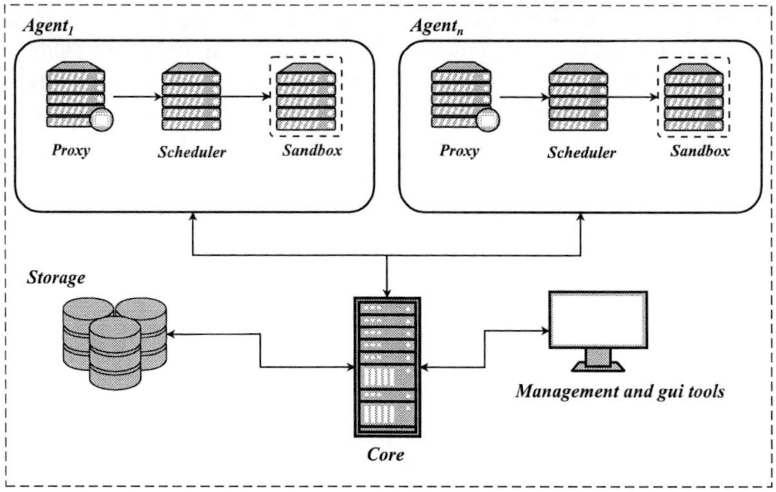

Fig. 1. *EMPHAsis architecture*

virtual environments (sandboxes) to which all traffic generated by the attacker is redirected out. Each environment is equipped with several specialized probes, whose goal is to monitor in a completely transparent way to the malicious entity, specific critical events that occur in the attack scenario at hand. All the data collected by the probes is eventually stored and indexed for subsequent use (e.g., in order to devise appropriate countermeasures) and possible disclosure.

In more details, the EMPHAsis architecture consists of several modules each of which is in charge of performing a specific task. The **core** is the most important module which plays the role of coordinating the operations between all the other modules of the system. Furthermore, it provides a graphical environment for managing the system, to help real-time monitoring and to visualize the collected data. When a connection attempt reaches the system, the **agent** module checks whether there is a configured service to handle the request. If a suitable service exists, a virtual trap environment is built and executed on the fly and all the attacker's traffic is then redirected out to it. The upper part of Figure 2 shows the main steps performed by the **agent** module in response to an attack. In more detail, as a preliminary step the *proxy* component notifies a new connection arrival to the **core** module while collecting also information about the geographical origin of the attack. Then, it continues by performing payload detection and if a suitable service is found, the request is handled and the *scheduler* component is allerted. The *scheduler* is the main responsible for the virtual trap environment setup. After receiving an alert from the *proxy*, it prepares and starts the *sandbox* and then injects one or more probes directly into the isolated environment. These probes will monitor all the actions performed by the attacker (or malware) inside the sandbox. In particular, in the lower part of Figure 2 is shown an example of a specific case where four probes are in place and used for monitoring networking events, commands executed in the system

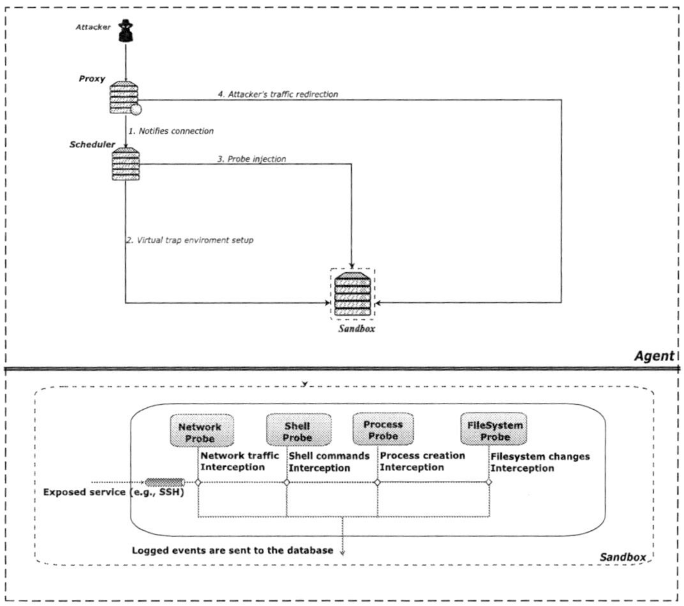

Fig. 2. *Agent module*

shell, process creations, and changes to the filesystem. It should be noted that the concrete implementation of these probes poses technical challenges. Indeed, one needs to use specific tools and instruments according to the type of operating system used by the emulated guest machine. Our probes support a custom 32-bit Linux kernel and we rely on QEMU-KVM to emulate this platform. Further implementation details can be found in [6]. It is interesting to notice that our implementation of the **agent** exploits a fake interactive session where attacker's traffic is man-in-the-middle proxied. This is achieved by using a custom shell implementation.

The **storage** module comprehends one or more nodes in a redundant configuration whose role is to offer all standard operations for storage and subsequent consultation of the collected data. An attack can produce a significant amount of information, which therefore needs to be properly cataloged and organized for subsequent consultation. To this end, our system exploits appropriate components for the storage and processing of such information, making it suitable for the production of detailed reports and in characterizing the threats detected. Additionally, the above processing can be customized by the user for the specific resources she is most interested in. In particular, an individual storage node uses both a MongoDB NoSQL database [1] and an Elasticsearch database [3]. The MongoDB holds the users' credentials required to access the control and the data analytic dashboard, stores the configuration (including custom kernel images and the probes) which will be downloaded by the **agent** module during the initialization phase of the sandboxes. and stores the captured malware sam-

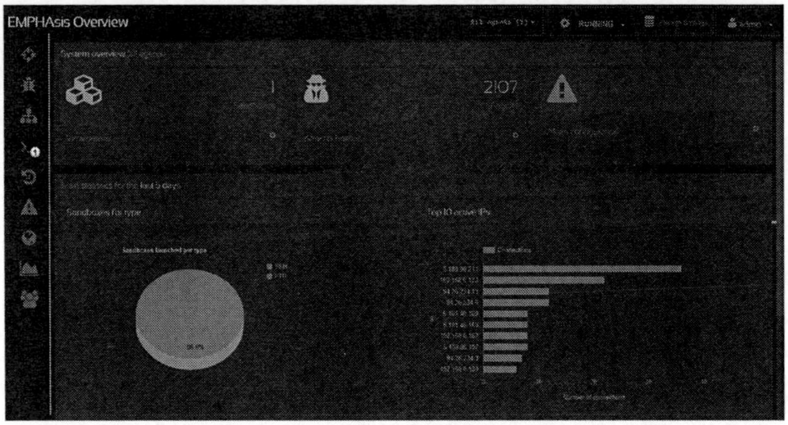

Fig. 3. Main panel of the EMPHAsis dashboard

ples. The system will then send over all the security events described above to the Elasticsearch database. Such events can be visualized by the built-in dashboard (see section 3) which exploits a Kibana instance for advanced filtering mechanisms.

A key aspect in order to achieve effective results (in terms of number of malicious actions logged and malware instances intercepted) concerns the correct positioning of the honeypots in the infrastructure to be protected. Thus, there is significant motivation for studying the best possible locations where agent modules (and honeypots in general) can be deployed in a network. Interestingly, EMPHAsis agents can be deployed both behind or outside the perimeter of the network, therefore allowing to detect also potential insider threats. In any case, deploying honeypots in a production environment can be problematic since it could expose the network to far greater risks than the threats from which it is intended to be protected. Towards this end, it is essential to study and analyze the way honeypots interact with the rest of the system before the actual deployment. This could be done by using virtual simulation environments, such as the one described in [7] which allow to reproduce multiple operating systems as well as networks in a realistic and controlled way.

3 Collected Data

All of the security events collected through the probes are sent to the storage module and stored in the Elasticsearch database allowing for fast real-time access through the dashboard. More precisely, we construct a single index which is shared by every probe of any agents running in the system. Figure 3 shows the main panel of the dashboard which displays the information about the active sandboxes, under the control of the **core** module, and the number of intercepted attacks. The lower part of the panel reports some statistics about the last five days of operation: the percentage of sandboxes launched, grouped by their type, and the top-10 IP addresses from where the majority of connections to the sandboxes have been established.

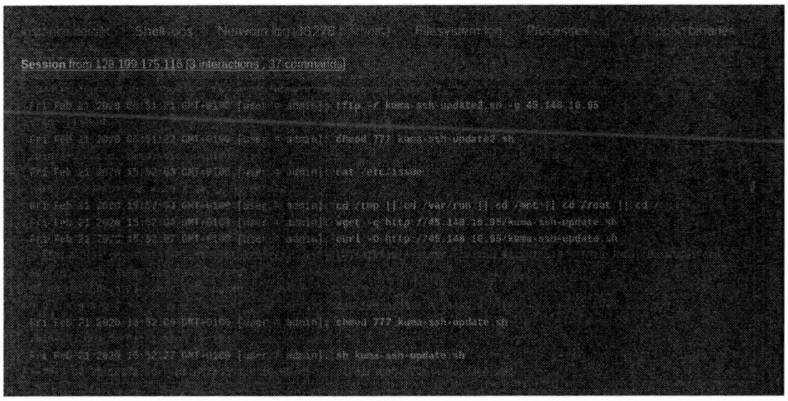

Fig. 4. Shell log tab

It is possible to inspect the details specific to each sandbox and to access the data collected by the active probes. Figure 4 shows a panel, for a given sandbox, which is organized in more tabs each of which reports specific information according to the following categories: *shell*, *network*, *filesystem* and *processes*.

For those sandboxes related to services based on interactive sessions, e.g. `ssh` or `ftp`, the flow of messages exchanged (i.e. commands executed and responses) between the attacking entity and the sandbox, is available in the *shell logs* tab (the one active in the panel of Figure 4). Figure 4 depicts a scenario where the attacker, once logged as the `admin` user, successfully attempted to download a shell script from a remote host and then executed it inside the sandbox shell environment.

Figure 5 shows the *network log* tab, which allows to visualize the information about the network events relevant to the service exposed by the sandbox. In the specific case reported in the figure, some `ssh` login attempts, part of a brute-force attack directed to gain access as the `root` user, are visible.

When a malware successfully gain access to a sandbox, from where it is possible to modify the content of the local filesystem, e.g. from a *ssh* session, such modifications are tracked and the relevant events (i.e. filesystem related system calls invocations) displayed in the *filesystem log* tab as shown in Figure 6. Such events are grouped on the basis of the specific path and ordered by the timestamp of execution.

In a similar way, the *processes log* tab displays the time intervals when processes launched by a malware from inside the sandbox are executed.

The EMPHAsis probes are able to capture and store in the system database all the files dropped by an attacker (e.g. shell scripts, binary files, source code) during a session. Before being stored, such files undergo a basic analysis by re-

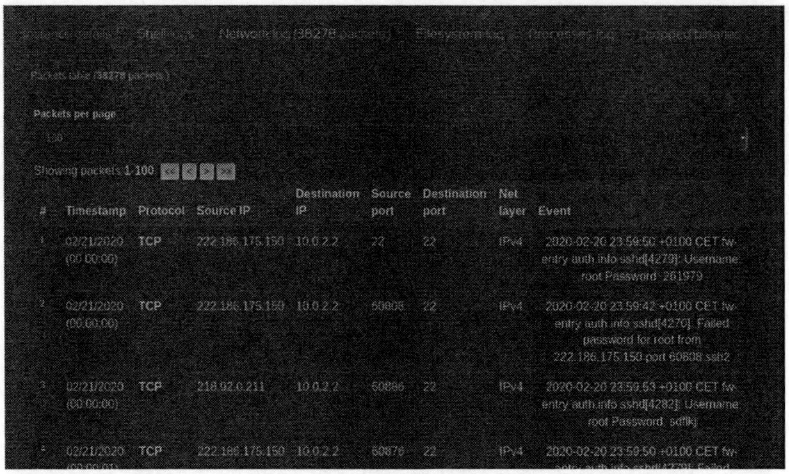

Fig. 5. Network log tab

Fig. 6. Filesystem log tab

sorting to the malware identification and classification services offered by Virustotal [14] and those developed by Cythereal [2]. In particular the Cythereal MAGIC API [2] exploits a state-of-art machine-learning based malware analysis system which is able to identify the belonging family of a malware even in presence of sophisticated code obfuscation techniques.

4 Conclusions and Future works

We presented the main functionalities of EMPHAsis and it practical applicability for malware capturing, analysis and prevention. EMPHAsis exploits high-interaction honeypots and has a modular and extensible architecture making it effective and suitable for various practical deployment scenarios. Currently EMPHAsis features the emulation of Linux based systems on top of which the great majority of Internet exposed services are based on. Moreover, it can be easily extended to support other unix-based systems. As a future work, we plan to support also computer systems based on Microsoft Windows or on Apple macOS. Another important direction of improvement is the integration of EMPHAsis with more advanced data analysis tools specifically tailored to cybersecurity events, i.e. the so called *security information and event management* systems (SIEM), like IBM QRadar [8] and ElasticSIEM [10], which has been recently developed on top of Elasticsearch. We also plan to extend the interoperability of EMPHAsis with other malware analysis tools, like for example cuckoo [4] sanbox, and to integrate in it virtual environment technologies for building more realistic and complex decoy environments [7], e.g. honeynets, and thus increasing the effectiveness in capturing more sophisticated malware.

Acknowledgments This research has been supported by the ISCOM - Italian Ministry of Economic Development under agreement EMPHAsis (CUP B51G17000300006).

References

1. Cuckoo. https://cuckoosandbox.org/.
2. Cythereal, changing the rules of cyber engagement. http://www.cythereal.com.
3. Elasticsearch. https://www.elastic.co/products/elasticsearch.
4. Mongodb. https://www.mongodb.com.
5. Pelin Angin, Bharat K. Bhargava, and Rohit Ranchal. Big data analytics for cyber security. *Security and Communication Networks*, 2019:4109836:1–4109836:2, 2019.
6. Michele Bombardieri, Salvatore Castanò, Fabrizio Curcio, Angelo Furfaro, and Helen D. Karatza. Honeypot-powered malware reverse engineering. In *2016 IEEE International Conference on Cloud Engineering Workshop, IC2E Workshops, Berlin, Germany, April 4-8, 2016*, pages 65–69, 2016.
7. Angelo Furfaro, Luciano Argento, Andrea Parise, and Antonio Piccolo. Using virtual environments for the assessment of cybersecurity issues in iot scenarios. *Simulation Modelling Practice and Theory*, 73:43–54, 2017.
8. IBM. QRadar. https://www.ibm.com/security/security-intelligence/qradar.
9. Taiwo Kolajo, Olawande Daramola, and Ayodele Adebiyi. Big data stream analysis: a systematic literature review. *J. Big Data*, 6:47, 2019.
10. Mike Paquette. Introducing Elastic SIEM. https://www.elastic.co/blog/introducing-elastic-siem, 2019.
11. Lance Spitzner. The honeynet project: Trapping the hackers. *IEEE Security & Privacy*, 1(2):15–23, 2003.
12. Lance Spitzner. Honeypots: Catching the insider threat. In *19th Annual Computer Security Applications Conference (ACSAC 2003), 8-12 December 2003, Las Vegas, NV, USA*, pages 170–179, 2003.
13. Nicoleta Tantalaki, Stavros Souravlas, Manos Roumeliotis, and Stefanos Katsavounis. Linear scheduling of big data streams on multiprocessor sets in the cloud. In Payam M. Barnaghi, Georg Gottlob, Yannis Manolopoulos, Theodoros Tzouramanis, and Athena Vakali, editors, *2019 IEEE/WIC/ACM International Conference on Web Intelligence, WI 2019, Thessaloniki, Greece, October 14-17, 2019*, pages 107–115. ACM, 2019.
14. Virustotal. How it works. https://support.virustotal.com/hc/en-us/articles/115002126889-How-it-works.

Towards Reusable Smart Contracts for Trustworthy Collaborative Processes (Discussion Paper)

Ada Bagozi[1], Devis Bianchini[1], Valeria De Antonellis[1], Massimiliano Garda[1], and Michele Melchiori[1]

University of Brescia, Dept. of Information Engineering
Via Branze 38, 25123 - Brescia (Italy)
a.bagozi@unibs.it, devis.bianchini@unibs.it,
valeria.deantonellis@unibs.it, m.garda001@unibs.it,
michele.melchiori@unibs.it

Abstract. In collaborative environments, where enterprises interact each other's without a centralised authority that ensures trust among them, the ability of providing cross-organisational services must be enabled also between mutually untrusting participants. Blockchain platforms and smart contracts have been proposed to implement trustworthy collaborative processes. However, current solutions are constrained to a specific blockchain technology and deployed on-chain the whole process, thus increasing the execution costs of smart contracts on permissionless blockchains. In this paper, we propose an approach that includes criteria to identify trust-demanding objects and activities in collaborative processes, a model to describe smart contracts in a technology-independent way and guidelines to deploy them on a blockchain. To this aim, a three-layered model is used to describe: (i) the collaborative process, represented in BPMN, where the business expert is supported to add annotations that identify trust-demanding objects and activities; (ii) Abstract Smart Contracts, based on trust-demanding objects and activities only and independent from any blockchain technology; (iii) Concrete Smart Contracts, that implement abstract ones and are deployed over a specific blockchain. Flexibility and cost reduction brought by approach are discussed in the context of a case study on remote monitoring services for the digital factory.

Keywords: blockchain, smart contract, collaborative processes

1 Introduction

In collaborative environments enterprises provide cross-organisational services to deliver integrated offerings of products and services, ensuring additional value also between mutually untrusting organisations. A real-world example is given by anomaly detection services for remote monitoring of Cyber Physical Systems in the digital factory. The Original Equipment Manufacturer (OEM) supplies the anomaly detection service, based on data streams collected from the machines of clients. In case anomalies have been identified before breakage events occur, the clients may be notified to avoid expensive repair operations, as well as costly down-times. Furthermore, insurance agencies may offer additional services to the OEM in order to limit the costs of maintenance operations under warranty, and external suppliers may know in advance scheduled maintenance interventions to prepare required spare parts. In this scenario, collected sensor data, used for monitoring and providing advanced services, must be immutable and not repudiated by clients and the implementation of anomaly detection services must be transparently shared among all participants involved in the process.

1.1 Related Work

Blockchain platforms and smart contracts have been proposed to implement collaborative processes [1, 4, 5]. In a recent research, the Caterpillar system [5] introduces an abstraction layer over the Ethereum blockchain [7] in order to support the execution of collaborative processes, represented in BPMN. Noteworthy, a process in Caterpillar is fully executed on the blockchain, coded as smart contracts, and all the states of the process instance are recorded on-chain. Moreover, the proposed solution is technology-dependent. In [3] the focus is on the benefits from the introduction of blockchain and smart contracts for the supply chain. However, the explanation about how smart contracts have been deployed is reported in a coarse-grained manner. Recent efforts also focused on the importance of conceptual modelling to demonstrate how business artefacts leverage the data-centric nature of blockchain [4] and to provide a user-centric framework to design rules deployed in smart contracts [1].

Main limitations in the current approaches are that they are technology-dependent and focus on the implementation of collaborative processes as a monolithic solution, where the whole process is deployed on-chain. This increases the execution costs on the blockchain and reduces the reuse of designed smart contracts.

1.2 Paper contribution

In [2] we proposed an approach to identify trust-demanding objects and activities in collaborative processes, a model to describe smart contracts in a technology-independent way and guidelines to deploy them in a blockchain. To this aim, a three-layered model is used to describe: (i) the collaborative process, represented using BPMN, where the business expert is supported to add annotations that identify *trust-demanding objects* and *activities*; (ii) *Abstract Smart Contracts* based on trust-demanding objects and activities only and independent from any blockchain technology; (iii) *Concrete Smart Contracts*, that implement abstract ones and are deployed over a specific blockchain, enabling the creation of a repository where a single abstract contract is associated with multiple implementations. The introduction of Abstract Smart Contracts also increases the

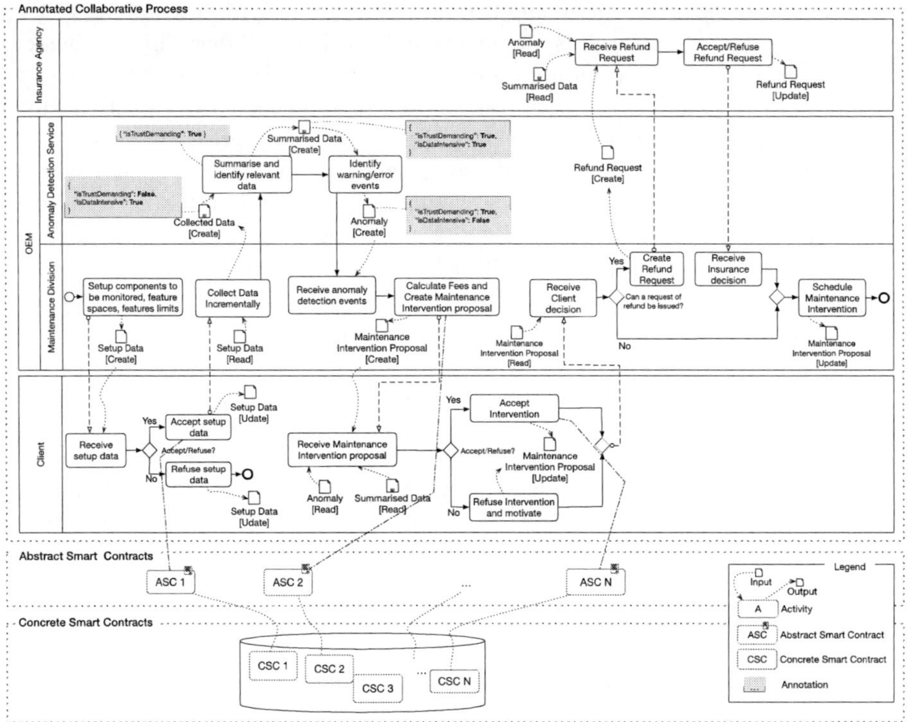

Fig. 1. Three-layered approach overview. On the top level, is reported the BPMN of the remote monitoring services case study (only a subset of annotations is reported here).

flexibility of the approach, providing a repository of reusable software components. Furthermore, only trust-demanding activities are considered to be deployed on-chain, thus saving costs and increasing process performances.

In the following, Section 2 introduces the three-layered approach; the approach architecture will be presented in Section 3; preliminary experiments will be described in Section 4; finally, Section 5 closes the paper.

2 Three-layered approach overview

Figure 1 shows the three-layered approach proposed in this paper. Specifically, a collaborative process for Remote Monitoring Services (RMS) in the digital factory is presented. Participants of the process are the OEM, one of its clients and the insurance agency, corresponding to three different BPMN pools. The OEM pool has been further organised in two sub-partitions, Maintenance Division lane and Anomaly Detection Service lane. In our model, we do not consider trust issues between participants associated with lanes within the same pool.

Annotated collaborative process layer. At the top layer, BPMN annotations are used in order to highlight *trust-demanding objects* and *trust-demanding* *activities*. The former ones are associated to data objects (e.g., activities inputs/outputs), that are shared across different participants, and therefore transactions (i.e. Create, Read, Update, Delete actions) performed on these objects should be immutable and not repudiated by any participant. In our approach, trust-demanding objects are candidates to be permanently stored within a blockchain. Trust-demanding activities correspond to automated activities whose business logic must be non-repudiated and transparently shared among all the participants of the process. In our approach, they represent the candidates to be deployed as smart contracts within a blockchain.

Abstract Smart Contracts layer. In the middle layer, annotations are used to generated *Abstract Smart Contracts* (ASC). An ASC is described by: (i) a name; (ii) a set of state variables, that can be either primitive data types or objects, on which contract functions operate; (iii) a set of participants (i.e., users registered on the blockchain or other contracts) that are allowed to interact with the *ASC* by invoking its functions; (iv) a set of functions expressed as $functionName(IN_f) : OUT_f$, where IN_f and OUT_f are the inputs and outputs of the function. Among ASC participants, also the BPMN engine is considered, since it is in charge of invoking activities implemented as smart contracts. An ASC is generated for each BPMN activity annotated as trust-demanding. In this case: (i) the ASC name is obtained from the activity name; (ii) the set of ASC variables contains the activity inputs/outputs definitions; (iii) the set of ASC participants contains the participant of the activity and the BPMN engine; (iv) the function represents the activity, its name corresponds to the activity name, its inputs (resp., outputs) correspond to the activity inputs (resp., outputs). An ASC is generated also for each trust-demanding object as follows: (i) the ASC name is obtained from the object name; (ii) the set of ASC variables contains the object definition; (iii) the set of ASC participants contains the participant of the activity that reads the object and the BPMN engine; (iv) functions are generated according to the CRUD actions on the object. Among trust-demanding objects we distinguish those characterised by high volume and acquisition speed, denoted as *data-intensive*. Transactions on such objects, if stored within a blockchain, may require increased costs. In order to strike a trade-off between costs and tamper-proofness, the full data intensive object is kept off-chain, on top of an external Distributed File System (DFS) such as the InterPlanetary File System (IPFS), while a link to it is stored on-chain. An example of ASC is given by the trust-demanding activity `Identify Warning/Error Events` in Figure 1, where: (i) $name =$ "$IdentifyWarningErrorEventsSC$"; (ii) $variables = \{summarisedDataHash, Anomaly\}$; (iii) $participants = \{AnomalyDetection-Service, BPMNengine\}$; (iv) $function = \{identifyWarningErrorEvents-Func([summarisedDataHash]) : [Anomaly]\}$. The `summarisedDataHash` input is a hash code pointing to an external DFS on which summarised data is saved. Other ASC examples are given in [2].

https://ipfs.io

Concrete Smart Contracts Layer. At the lower layer, ASC are deployed as *Concrete Smart Contracts* (CSC) over a specific blockchain. The development of CSC starting from ASC is in charge of the developer, who has the skills to deploy CSC over a specific blockchain. The developer provides the necessary code in order to implement the CSC functions. A single ASC descriptor may be associated with multiple CSC implementations, developed for different blockchain technologies. Moreover, it separates the role of business experts, who are in charge of designing the collaborative process and being supported during the identification of trust-demanding objects and activities, and the role of developers, who possess development skills for the specific blockchain technology on which CSC will be deployed.

Example. In the multi-party collaborative process of Figure 1, proper smart contracts have been identified.

Monitoring Setup Smart Contracts (MS). Setup data is created by the Maintenance Division and read by the client, who is also in charge of accepting or declining by modifying the `Setup Data` object, that therefore is identified as trust-demanding. Therefore, an ASC is generated for the `Setup Data` trust-demanding object and all activities (associated with the Maintenance Division or the Client) that create or modify such objects are recognised as trust-demanding, bringing to the generation of corresponding ASC.

Anomaly Detection Smart Contracts (AD). Anomaly Detection Service is in charge of summarising the collection of `Collected Data` objects and applying relevance evaluation in order to identify relevant data only, generating a collection of `Summarised Data` objects. Both `Collected Data` and `Summarised Data` objects are generated at high volumes, and for this reason can be considered as data-intensive. `Summarised Data` is then used by the Anomaly Detection Service to identify warning or error events, generating an `Anomaly` object. Considering that `Summarised Data` and `Anomaly` objects are read by the Client and by the Insurance Agency, both are recognised as trust-demanding. Therefore, two ASC are generated, one for `Summarised Data` object and one for `Anomaly` object. Moreover, all activities that create or modify such objects are recognised as trust-demanding, bringing to the generation of corresponding ASC.

Maintenance Intervention Preparation Smart Contract (MIP). The `Maintenance Intervention Proposal` object is created by the Maintenance Division and modified by the Client to accept/decline it. Therefore, it is identified as trust-demanding. The same considerations hold for `Refund Request` object. All activities that create and modify these objects are denoted as trust-demanding.

3 Approach Architecture

The approach architecture is shown in Figure 2. At the bottom the architecture includes the real blockchain, on which CSC are deployed. For example, on an Ethereum network, all deployed CSC can be replicated on each client node, which hosts an Ethereum Virtual Machine (EVM). A *Log Repository* is used to store the results of every CSC execution in order to implement a communication

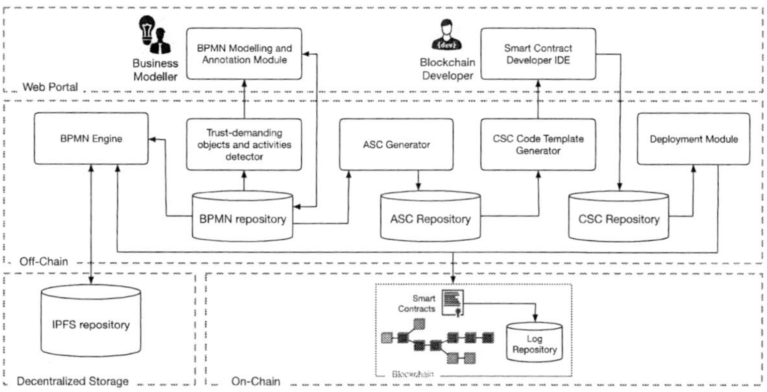

Fig. 2. Approach architecture.

channel from the smart contracts on the blockchain and external services of the collaborative process. In fact, smart contracts have no way to call external services. However, contracts can write information on a log space that is visible to external applications. A distributed storage (e.g., the above mentioned IPFS) is also considered in order to store data-intensive information without impacting on the blockchain costs.

Off-chain modules in figure implement the identification of trust-demanding objects and activities, ASC and CSC code templates generation and deployment. The BPMN is stored within the *BPMN repository*. The *ASC Generator* extracts ASC descriptors and stores them into the *ASC Repository*. The *CSC Code Template Generator* is in charge of generating templates, after choosing a specific blockchain platform. Templates are provided to the developer who completes them with code insertion. Developed CSC are stored within a *CSC Repository* and deployed on the blockchain by the *Deployment Module*. ASC/CSC repositories will contribute to increase the reuse of generated contracts. The middle layer also includes the *BPMN Engine*, that has to execute the collaborative process and must be able to invoke some activities as CSC deployed on the blockchain.

Finally, the architecture comprises a set of Web components, provided to the business modeller and the developer for editing BPMN processes, confirming or discarding suggested annotations, and editing CSC starting from the generated code templates, respectively. These, components use functionalities made available by other modules at the middle layer through RESTful APIs.

4 Preliminary Experiments

Our approach has been validated in the context of Remote Monitoring Services in the digital factory described in Section 2 and using Ethereum permissionless blockchain. However, our approach is technology-independent, and can be implemented also as a permissioned blockchain [6]. Indeed, future experiments will be focused on comparing different concrete implementations of the blockchains. Here we validated permissionless blockchain, considering that it takes more time

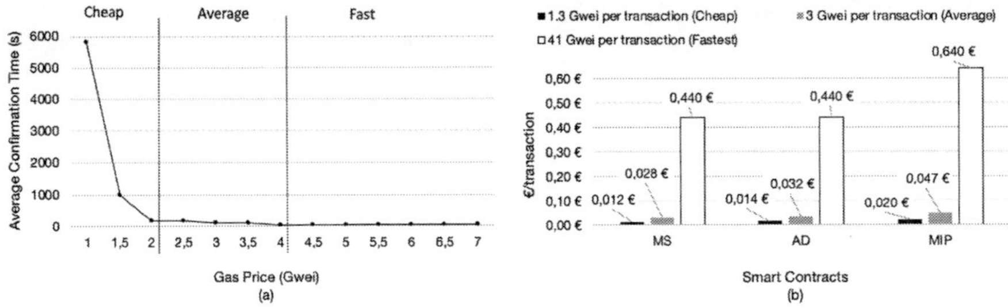

Fig. 3. Gas value required to execute all the functions of the smart contracts generated for each service in the considered case study.

to write and confirm transactions and the execution of a smart contract and the validation of a new transaction are performed by nodes that are rewarded with a fee paid by the node that initiates the transaction. Since, to the best of our knowledge, there are no collaborative processes datasets to compare our implementation with similar efforts, we performed here a cost analysis, in order to evaluate the economic effort in using a permissionless blockchain. In Ethereum-based blockchains, the cost is expressed in *gas*, which is a value established for every basic operation invoked from within the smart contract. Then, the fee paid for a transaction is expressed as the product between the gas used to process the transaction and the *gas price*, which is the amount that the node initiating the transaction is willing to pay for each gas unit.

Figure 3(a) illustrates the average time (in seconds) to confirm the transaction for each smart contract by varying the gas price, relying on the simulator provided by ETH Gas Station. As expected, the more gas price a user is willing to offer, the faster the transaction will be added to the blockchain. Figure 3(b) reports the cost per transaction required to execute each of the smart contracts implemented for the Remote Monitoring Services case study, using an Ethereum simulator. Generally, reducing the cost of the collaborative process deployment on a permissionless blockchain can be obtained by decreasing the performances of smart contract execution or limiting the elements that are deployed on the blockchain to trust-demanding objects and activity only. Indeed, our approach reduces the execution costs on the blockchain thanks to the deployment of a limited set of BPMN elements, only if necessary. In fact, only trust-demanding objects and activities will be converted in smart contracts to be deployed on the blockchain. According to the cost analysis learned by the application of our approach to the Remote Monitoring case study, as shown in Figure 3(a), from a certain amount of gas price (4.5 *Gwei*) the average confirmation time remains quite the same. Assuming that the participants have access to IPFS nodes, there is no extra cost, in terms of gas, associated with storing data-intensive objects. However, for the same application scenarios such as the anomaly detection one considered in the case study, promptness in identifying warning/error events is an

`https://ethgasstation.info/calculatorTxV.php` (accessed: July 2019)
testrpc: `https://github.com/trufflesuite/ganache-cli`

important feature of the supplied services. Therefore, this issue can be addressed by limiting the number of elements to be deployed on-chain. The proposed approach described in this paper is to meet these requirements by excluding non trust-demanding objects and activities.

5 Concluding Remarks

In this paper, we proposed a three-layered model to describe: (i) the collaborative process, represented in BPMN, where the business expert is supported to add annotations that denote trust-demanding objects and activities; (ii) Abstract Smart Contracts, based on trust-demanding objects and activities only and independent from any blockchain technology; (iii) Concrete Smart Contracts, that implement abstract ones and are deployed over a specific blockchain technology. The introduction of Abstract Smart Contracts increases the flexibility of the approach, providing a repository of reusable software components. Furthermore, only trust-demanding activities are considered to be deployed on-chain, thus saving costs and increasing process performances. Future efforts will be focused on the ASC/CSC repository. In particular, advanced matchmaking techniques (e.g. adapting Semantic Web technologies to smart contracts) will be studied to reuse existing ASC at design time or to reconciliate similar ASC. Furthemore, at runtime similar techniques will be investigated to select the proper CSC for a given ASC, depending on the cost policies implemented in different blockchains.

References

1. Astigarraga, T., Chen, X., Chen, Y., Gu, J., Hull, R., Jiao, L., Li, Y., Novotny, P.: Empowering business-level blockchain users with a rules framework for smart contracts. In: Int. Conf. on Service Oriented Computing (ICSOC 2018). pp. 111–128. Hangzhou, China (2018)
2. Bagozi, A., Bianchini, D., De Antonellis, V., Garda, M., Melchiori, M.: A three-layered approach for designing smart contracts in collaborative processes. In: 27th Int. Conf. on Cooperative Information Systems (CoopIS 2019). pp. 440–457. Rhodes, Greece (2019)
3. Casado-Vara, R., Prieto, J., De la Prieta, F., Corchado, J.M.: How blockchain improves the supply chain: case study alimentary supply chain. Procedia Computer Science 134, pp. 393–398 (2018)
4. Hull, R., Batra, V., Chee, Y., Deutsch, A., Health, F., Vianu, V.: Towards a shared ledger business collaboration language based on data-aware processes. In: Int. Conf. on Service Oriented Computing (ICSOC 2016). pp. 18–36. Banff, Canada (2016)
5. López-Pintado, O., García-Bañuelos, L., Dumas, M., Weber, I., Ponomarev, A.: Caterpillar: A business process execution engine on the ethereum blockchain. Software: Practice and Experience 49(7), pp. 1162–1193 (2019)
6. Staderini, M., Schiavone, E., Bondavalli, A.: A requirements-driven methodology for the proper selection and configuration of blockchains. In: IEEE 37th Symposium on Reliable Distributed Systems (SRDS 2018). pp. 201–206. Salvador, Bahia, Brazil (2018)
7. Wood, G.: Ethereum: A secure decentralised generalised transaction ledger. Ethereum project yellow paper 151, pp. 1–32 (2014)

kNN-guided Adversarial Attacks (DISCUSSION PAPER)

Fabio Valerio Massoli[0000-0001-6447-1301], Fabrizio Falchi[0000-0001-6258-5313], and Giuseppe Amato[0000-0003-0171-4315]

ISTI-CNR, via G. Moruzzi 1, 56124 Pisa, Italy
{fabio.massoli, fabrizio.falchi, giuseppe.amato}@isti.cnr.it

Abstract In the last decade, we have witnessed a renaissance of Deep Learning models. Nowadays, they are widely used in industrial as well as scientific fields, and noticeably, these models reached super-human performances on specific tasks such as image classification. Unfortunately, despite their great success, it has been shown that they are vulnerable to adversarial attacks - images to which a specific amount of noise imperceptible to human eyes have been added to lead the model to a wrong decision. Typically, these malicious images are forged, pursuing a misclassification goal. However, when considering the task of Face Recognition (FR), this principle might not be enough to fool the system. Indeed, in the context FR, the deep models are generally used merely as features extractors while the final task of recognition is accomplished, for example, by similarity measurements. Thus, by crafting adversarials to fool the classifier, it might not be sufficient to fool the overall FR pipeline. Starting from this observation, we proposed to use a k-Nearest Neighbour algorithm as guidance to craft adversarial attacks against an FR system. In our study, we showed how this kind of attack could be more threatening for an FR system than misclassification-based ones considering both the targeted and untargeted attack strategies.

Keywords: Adversarial Attacks · Face Recognition · Convolutional Neural Networks.

1 Introduction

Since the publication of the AlexNet [6] in 2012, Deep Learning (DL) models started to play a central role in several scientific and industrial fields. Moreover, due to the extremely high computational power reached by the modern GPUs, the use of DL techniques has become state-of-the-art for solving problems such as: vision (e.g., image classification [6], object detection [4]), natural language processing [14], and sentiment analysis [9]. Despite this rebirth, there is a severe threat that poses a strong limit to the use of Deep Neural Networks (DNNs) in real-world scenarios, especially in sensitive contexts such as surveillance systems [11] for instance. It was recently shown that DNNs are vulnerable to adversarial samples [12,1] - images to which a precise amount of noise imperceptible to human eyes is added to fool a model. As shown in the next section of the paper, it is common for the adversaries to craft malicious samples following a misclassification principle, i.e., with the goal in mind of leading a model, such as a classifier, to output a wrong prediction with very high confidence. However, if we consider the case of Face Recognition (FR) systems, the game paradigm deeply changes. Indeed, differently from the classical classification tasks, in the context of FR, a DNN is usually used merely as a features extractor [8,13] while the final task of recognition is realized by performing, for example, similarity measurements among the extracted representations. For instance, we can consider the case of Face Identification (FI) in which the features extracted from a query image has to be compared with a database of known identities to identify a person. Thus, adversarials crafted employing a misclassification principle might not succeed in fooling a similarity-based scheme. Generally speaking, we can divide the attacks against FR systems into two categories, namely: impersonation and evasion attacks. In the former case, the goal of the attacker is to lead the system to recognize two faces as belonging to the same person when that it is not true, while in the latter case he wants the system not to recognize a person. In this context, starting from the idea of deep representation attacks [10], we proposed a variant based on the use of a k-Nearest Neighbour (k-NN) algorithm as guidance, to fool an FR system that relies on similarity measurement to assess queries identity. Moreover, we showed how such an attack could give rise to a greater threat concerning misclassification-based attacks. The rest of the paper is organized as follows: in Section 2, we briefly described some known algorithms to craft adversarial samples. In Section 3 and Section 4, we described our approach and presented the results of our study, respectively. Finally, in Section 5, we reported the conclusion and future perspectives of our work.

2 Adversarial Attacks

Usually, the guiding principle followed while designing adversarial attack algorithms is to lead the model to assign a wrong label with high probability to an image. One of the first studies in this direction was proposed by [12] that designed an optimization procedure based on the L-BFGS algorithm. Specifically, the authors solved the following optimization problem:

$$\min_{\delta} \mathcal{L}(x+\delta,\ y_{gt}) + \lambda \cdot \parallel \delta \parallel_2; \quad \text{with } x+\delta \in [l,u]^m, \tag{1}$$

where $\mathcal{L}$ is the loss function, λ is a parameter found by linear search, y_{gt} is the ground truth label for the input x, δ is the adversarial perturbation, l and u represent the lower and upper bound for the pixel values respectively, and $x+\delta$

is the current adversarial sample crafted from the given input x. A faster way to produce malicious images was proposed by [5], in which the authors proposed to linearize the loss function around the current value of the parameters, thus crafting the adversarial as:

$$x_{adv} = x + \epsilon \cdot \text{sign}(\nabla_x J(\theta, x, y_{true})) \,, \tag{2}$$

The method shown in Equation 2 is known as Fast Gradient Sign Method (FGSM) and allows to craft adversarial samples by only employing a single gradient step. In Equation 2, $\nabla_x J(\theta, x, y)$ is the gradient of the loss function J evaluated around the current neural network status θ, x is the input, y_{true} is its label, and ϵ is the maximum distortion allowed on the input such that $\| x - x_{adv} \|_\infty < \epsilon$. In [7], the authors proposed a unified view on adversarial attacks and defenses. Specifically, they reformulated the adversarial training for deep models as a "saddle-point" optimization problem

$$\min_\theta \rho(\theta) = \min_\theta \mathbb{E}_{(x,y)\sim\mathcal{D}}\big[\max_{\delta\in\mathcal{S}} L(\theta, x + \delta, y)\big] \tag{3}$$

in which the inner maximization aims at finding an adversarial of a given input x while the outer minimization problem has the goal of reducing the loss after the attack. Finally, they proposed an iterative procedure named Projected Gradient Descent (PGD):

$$x_{N+1}^{adv} = \prod_{x+\mathcal{S}} (x_N^{adv} + \alpha \cdot \text{sign}(\nabla_x L(\theta, x, y)))\,. \tag{4}$$

An improved version of the iterative attacks was proposed in [3] named Momentum-Iterative FGSM (MI-FGSM). The authors integrated a momentum term that helped to escape from poor local maxima during, thus yielding stronger attacks. The main idea is first to evaluate the velocity vector in the gradient direction and then use it to craft the adversarial. The velocity vector is given by

$$g_{N+1} = \mu \cdot g_N + \frac{J(x_N^{adv}, y)}{\| \nabla_x J(x_N^{adv}, y) \|_1}\,, \tag{5}$$

where $x_0^{adv} = x$, $g_0 = 0$, μ is the decay factor of the running average, and y is the ground truth label. Finally, the adversarial example in the ϵ-vicinity measured by L_2 distance is given by

$$x_{N+1}^{adv} = x_N^{adv} + \alpha \cdot \frac{g_{N+1}}{\| g_{N+1} \|_2}\,, \tag{6}$$

where $\alpha = \epsilon/T$ with T being the total number of iterations. All the attacks we discussed hitherto focused their attention on fooling a model by letting it predict a wrong class, with high confidence, for the given input. Nevertheless, the situation changes in the context of FR systems. Indeed, in such cases, the neural network is usually not used as a classifier, but as features extractor. For each query image, the model extracts a deep representation, which in turn is compared with a database of known identities. Thus, in those cases, the previous attack techniques might not be effective as one could expect. Following this concern, interesting suggestions on how to design more suited attacks for FR systems came from [10]. In [10], the authors formulated the attack against a DNN by looking at the internal representation of a model, in other words, they focused their attack on making the deep features of an adversarial as close as possible to the one of a target query. More formally, given a doublet (I_s, I_t) where the former is the source image and the latter the target one, the goal of the crafting process is to find a new image, I_α, such that its internal representation at a specific layer l of the neural network under attack, $\phi_l(I_\alpha)$, is as close as possible to the one of the target image, $\phi_l(I_t)$. Meanwhile, I_α has to be as close as possible to the source image, I_s, in the input space. The optimization problem can be formulated as follows:

$$I_\alpha = \arg\min_I \| \phi_l(I) - \phi_l(I_t) \|_2^2, \quad \text{subject to} \quad \| I - I_s \|_\infty < \delta\,, \tag{7}$$

where δ is the maximum perturbation allowed on each pixel.

3 Proposed Approach

In our experiments, we considered adversarial samples crafted utilizing two guiding principles. On the one hand, we used a typical misclassification-based approach in which the goal of the attacks was to fool a DNN acting as a classifier. On the other hand, we proposed an attack in which we explicitly took into account a more realistic FR setup in which the DNN was used as a features extractor, and the final task of the FR was accomplished by employing similarity measurements among deep representations. In this case, we used our proposed approach where we considered a k-NN algorithm as guidance to craft adversarial samples. Finally, we compared the effectiveness of both approaches to fool an FR system. Regarding the threatened model, we considered the state-of-the-art SeNet-50 [2] from which we extracted the deep features at the penultimate layer. As source dataset, we used the test set of VGGFace2 [2], which comprises 500 identities, that we split into training and experimental sets. To be able to craft misclassification-based attacks, we attached a fully connected (FC) layer on top of the features extractor, and to train it, we used the training split cited above, the SGD optimizer with a learning rate of $1.e^{-3}$, a momentum of 0.9 and a batch size equal to 128. Then, we used the PGD [7] and the MI-FGSM [3] algorithms to craft misclassification-based adversarials.

Concerning our proposed approach, instead, we started by training the k-NN using the class centroids of the VGGFace2 [2] training split images, and then we set k=1. Subsequently, we cast the adversarial crafting procedure as an optimization problem, and we used the L-BFGS algorithm to solve it. Specifically, the main parameters to provide to the algorithm were the following: a starting point from which to begin the optimization procedure, a target, the function to minimize, and a set of parameters that were directly passed to it. The starting point was always a query image from which we wanted to craft an adversarial, while the target was the centroid of the class we wanted to move the adversarial features close to. As a minimization criterion, we used the regression loss. Specifically, the loss was evaluated among the target centroid and the current state of the adversarial sample deep features. At each step of the optimization procedure, we used the k-NN to assess if the deep representation of the adversarials were able to fool the FR system, i.e., if they were close enough to the target centroid deep representation. If so, we stopped the attack; otherwise, we continued the optimization. Moreover, to be sure that the adversarial remained closed enough to the query image so that a human eye could not distinguish between them, we empirically bounded their distance, in the pixel space, to be: $\delta <= 7$ (Equation 7). A schematic view of the overall algorithm is given in Figure 1.

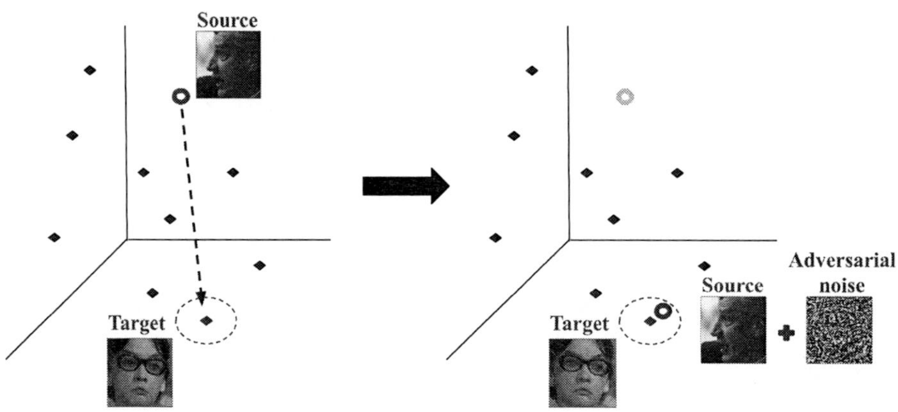

Figure 1. Schematic view of the adversarials generation process. Left: initial features representation of the source image (green circle) and target class centroid (red rhombus). Right: features of the crafted adversarial sample (red solid circle). The blue rhombus represent the centroids of other classes.

In Figure 1, we reported a face image next to the target centroid (red rhombus) only to show an example of the identity represented by the target point.

4 Experimental Results

In this section, we compared the adversarials obtained through our method with the ones obtained by misclassification ones. Specifically, we compared our k-NN guided attack against PGD [7] and MI-FGSM [3] attacks. In Figure 2, we reported a few examples of the manipulated images produced by our algorithm.

In Figure 2, we can notice how similar the images in the first and third columns appear to a human eye. Thus, even though we surfed the features space to craft the adversarials, we have been able to keep the malicious inputs very

Figure 2. Examples of adversarial attacks crafted by using a k-NN as guidance. From left to right, each column corresponds to: source image (I_s), target class image (I_t), adversarial sample (I_α), adversarial noise, respectively.

close to the original images in the pixel space. Subsequently, we compared the adversarials we generated with the k-NN with the ones crafted employing other attacks. Specifically, we considered attacks focused on fooling the classification task. Since our goal was to show that misclassification-based attacks might not be suitable to produce samples able to fool an FR system, a fundamental property to analyze was the euclidean distance among the adversarials deep features and the centroids of the respective adversarial class. Such a scenario emulates the case in with the features extracted from a query image have to be compared against a known database of known identities. The results are shown in Figure 3 for both targeted and untargeted attacks.

As we can see from Figure 3, the samples generated using the k-NN guided algorithm have an expected value of the euclidean distance from the (adversarial) class centroids lower than the ones generated with other attacks. Such a result holds for targeted as well as untargeted attacks.

As a *gedankenexperiment*, we shall suppose that the dotted-dashed black line in Figure 3 represented the threshold applied by the FR system when it had to decide on a FI task, for instance. In this case, to identify a person, the FR system evaluated the distance of the deep features of the query image from the centroids of the various available identities in the database. Thus, if

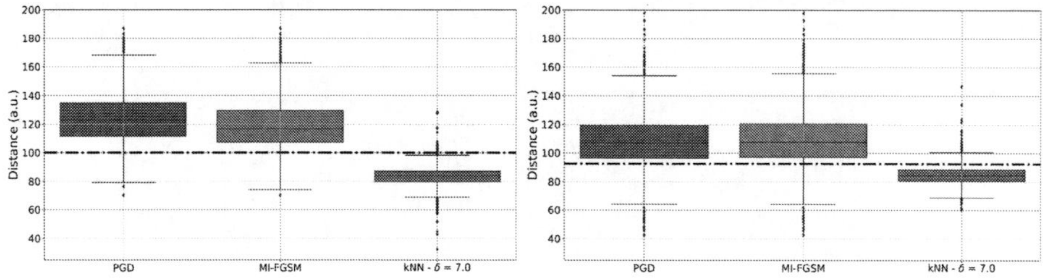

Figure 3. Euclidean distance of the adversarial features from the centroids of the adversarial class. Left: targeted attacks. Right: untargeted attacks. The dashed-dotted line represents a hypothetical threshold used by a FR system to assess the similarity of deep features.

we considered the threshold as shown in Figure 3, we observed that the attacks' success rate for misclassification-based attacks dramatically decreased compared to what happened for the k-NN guided ones. The results are reported in Table 1

Table 1. Attack success rates after applying the distance threshold as shown in Figure 3. The 100% reference value is given by the total number of crafted adversarial.

Attack Algorithm	Attack Success rate with thr (%)	
	Targeted	Untargeted
PGD	2.7	16.1
MI-FGSM	4.5	17.2
k-NN	**97.3**	**88.7**

To sum up, we can assess that, in the attempt of attacking an FR system in which a DNN is used as a backbone features extractor, the use of misclassification-based attacks might not be successful as in classification contexts to fool the recognition system. This happens because, in the FR scenario, the final output does not usually rely on the output of a deep classifier instead of a similarity measurement among deep features. Thus, it is mandatory to consider such aspects while designing attacks.

5 Conclusion and Future Perspectives

The threat of adversarial attacks poses severe limits on the use of deep learning techniques in sensitive real-world applications such as surveillance systems. Several algorithms have been proposed to fool a DNN to lead it to output a wrong prediction with high confidence. As shown, even though a classical misclassification-based attack can fool a neural network used as a classifier, the very same attack might not be strong enough to fool an FR system in which the output is based on similarity measurements carried upon deep features. Thus, different strategies have to be considered. We demonstrated that it is possible to fool an FR system through a deep features attack in which a k-NN is used as a guide in finding the proper perturbation to apply to the input image. Thus, it is possible to bring an adversarial closer to the aimed identity features compared to a misclassification-based. These results hold for the targeted and untargeted attacks. There are several potential extensions of this work. Different techniques to craft adversarials against an FR system might be considered, for example, with $k > 1$ or based on other guiding principles. On the other hand, it would be interesting trying to detect those kinds of attacks in which the adversary tries to emulate the deep representation of natural images within an attack.

References

1. Biggio, B., Corona, I., Maiorca, D., Nelson, B., Šrndić, N., Laskov, P., Giacinto, G., Roli, F.: Evasion attacks against machine learning at test time. In: Joint European conference on machine learning and knowledge discovery in databases. pp. 387–402. Springer (2013)
2. Cao, Q., Shen, L., Xie, W., Parkhi, O.M., Zisserman, A.: Vggface2: A dataset for recognising faces across pose and age. In: 2018 13th IEEE International Conference on Automatic Face & Gesture Recognition (FG 2018). pp. 67–74. IEEE (2018)
3. Dong, Y., Liao, F., Pang, T., Su, H., Zhu, J., Hu, X., Li, J.: Boosting adversarial attacks with momentum. In: Proceedings of the IEEE conference on computer vision and pattern recognition. pp. 9185–9193 (2018)
4. Girshick, R.: Fast r-cnn. In: Proceedings of the IEEE international conference on computer vision. pp. 1440–1448 (2015)
5. Goodfellow, I.J., Shlens, J., Szegedy, C.: Explaining and harnessing adversarial examples. arXiv preprint arXiv:1412.6572 (2014)
6. Krizhevsky, A., Sutskever, I., Hinton, G.E.: Imagenet classification with deep convolutional neural networks. In: Advances in neural information processing systems. pp. 1097–1105 (2012)
7. Madry, A., Makelov, A., Schmidt, L., Tsipras, D., Vladu, A.: Towards deep learning models resistant to adversarial attacks. arXiv preprint arXiv:1706.06083 (2017)
8. Massoli, F.V., Amato, G., Falchi, F.: Cross-resolution learning for face recognition. arXiv preprint arXiv:1912.02851 (2019)
9. Ortis, A., Farinella, G.M., Battiato, S.: An overview on image sentiment analysis: Methods datasets and current challenges. In: Proc. 16th Int. Joint Conf. E-Bus. Telecommun. vol. 1, pp. 290–300 (2019)
10. Sabour, S., Cao, Y., Faghri, F., Fleet, D.J.: Adversarial manipulation of deep representations. arXiv preprint arXiv:1511.05122 (2015)
11. Sreenu, G., Durai, M.S.: Intelligent video surveillance: a review through deep learning techniques for crowd analysis. Journal of Big Data **6**(1), 48 (2019)
12. Szegedy, C., Zaremba, W., Sutskever, I., Bruna, J., Erhan, D., Goodfellow, I., Fergus, R.: Intriguing properties of neural networks. arXiv preprint arXiv:1312.6199 (2013)
13. Wang, F., Cheng, J., Liu, W., Liu, H.: Additive margin softmax for face verification. IEEE Signal Processing Letters **25**(7), 926–930 (2018)
14. Young, T., Hazarika, D., Poria, S., Cambria, E.: Recent trends in deep learning based natural language processing. ieee Computational intelligenCe magazine **13**(3), 55–75 (2018)

Knowledge-enhanced Shilling Attacks for Recommendation*
(Discussion Paper)

Vito Walter Anelli, Yashar Deldjoo, Tommaso Di Noia, Felice Antonio Merra **, Giuseppe Acciani, and Eugenio Di Sciascio

Politecnico di Bari
{name.surname}@poliba.it

Abstract. Collaborative filtering (CF) recommendation models lie at the core of most industrial engines due to their state-of-the-art performance. Their leading performance owes hugely on exploiting users' past feedbacks to identify similar user or item pairs. Unfortunately this similarity computation is vulnerable to shilling profile injection attack, in which an attacker can insert fake user profiles into the system with the goal to alter the similarities and resulting recommendations in an engineered manner. In this work, we introduce *SAShA*, a new attack strategy that leverages semantic features extracted from a knowledge graph in order to strengthen the efficacy of the attack against standard CF models. Validation of the system is conducted across two publicly available datasets and various attacks, CF models and semantic information. Results underline the vulnerability of well-known CF models against the proposed semantic attacks compared with the baseline version.

Keywords: Recommender System · Knowledge Graph · Shilling attack.

1 Introduction and Context

With the increasing popularity of Internet commerce, online services, and the overwhelming volume of products, services, and multimedia content, recommender systems (RS) play a key role in mitigating the users' cognitive burden of over-choice. RS assist users' decision-making process by pointing them to a small set of items out of a large catalog (top-k recommendation list), based on users' past behaviors and preferences. The recommendation model can be broadly classified as content-based filtering (CBF), collaborative filtering (CF), and hybrid. CF models are the most popular choice in academic and industrial research (e.g.,

* Extended version [3] published at the 17th European Semantic Web Conference 2020

** Corresponding author: Felice Antonio Merra (felice.merra@poliba.it)

Amazon [19]) due to their high recommendation performance. Their key insight is that users' personal tastes correlate and then, from an algorithmic point of view, they mainly rely on the exploitation of user-user and item-item similarities. Different CF approaches can be classified into broad classes of memory-based and model-based. Memory-based approaches compute recommendations exclusively based on similarities in interaction patterns computed either across users (user-based CF) or items (item-based CF) [16]. Model-based exploits different machine learning techniques to compute a model, typically a latent representation of items and users [17], to generate recommendations. The most well-known example of a model-based approach is the matrix factorization (MF) model. Regardless of the type, both CF recommendation classes heavily rely on a sufficient amount of user preference data in order to mine reliable similarity patterns. Unfortunately, due to the open nature of many online systems, a malicious agent can add fake profiles into the platform to leverage similar values and the following recommendation outcomes in an engineered manner. Such profile injections are known as shilling attacks (or profile injection attacks) [15] whose goal are often malicious, for example for pushing or nuking a target item into a the top-k recommendation list of users for market penetration or personal gain [10].

The other alternative approach CBF (or hybrid) relies on items' descriptive attributes in conjunction with the target user's previous preference over an item in order to create a profile of the user characterizing the nature of her interest(s). While the earliest versions of CBF were purely textual using information such as metadata (tags, reviews) [21], modern versions utilize variety of other rich information sources such as social connections [6], audio and visual content [9,8] as well as users-item contextual data [2] to build more domain-dependent context-aware recommendations models. Another rich source of information and the one we exploit in this work has received increased attention from the community RS is the knowledge graph (KG). A $\mathcal{KG}$ can be viewed as a structured repository of knowledge, represented in the form of a graph, capable of encoding a diverse set of information:

- **Factual.** General statements as *Heraklion is the capital of Crete* or *Cyrus the Great was the founder of the first Persian Empire* in which an entity is described in term of a number of attributes, which are in turn connected with other entities in the $\mathcal{KG}$;
- **Categorical.** These statements bind an entity to a specific category in the $\mathcal{KG}$ (i.e., the categories related to an article in Wikipedia pages), where the categories together form a hierarchy (can be general or specific).
- **Ontological.** We can classify entities in a more formal manner by utilizing a hierarchical structure of classes. In contrast to categories, here sub-classes and super-classes are connected through an IS-A relation.

In fact, $\mathcal{KG}$ constitute the foundation of the Semantic Web and are becoming increasingly important as they can represent data exploiting a manageable and inter-operable semantic structure. They are the pillars of well-known tools like IBM Watson [7], public decision-making systems [22], and advanced machine learning techniques [4]. For what concerns recommendation based on $\mathcal{KG}$, they can be classified into: (i) path-based methods [14], which use meta-paths to evaluate the user-item similarities and, (ii) $\mathcal{KG}$ embedding-based techniques, that leverages $\mathcal{KG}$ embeddings to semantically regularize items latent representations [23,11].

The main contributions of this work are two-fold:

1. We build a novel type of shilling attacks against rating-based CF models that leverages the publicly available information resources from $\mathcal{KG}$ to build impactful shilling profile attacks against CF models.
2. To investigate the relationship between semantic data characteristics and the robustness of CF models, we carried out extensive experiments involving two popular attack strategies against three well-known CF models across two real-world datasets. In total 84 simulation attacks were conducted to verify the impact of the semantic knowledge integration.

2 Our Proposed Approach - SAShA

When an attacker successfully inserts a malicious user profile in the dataset, it needs to assign a set of rated items — besides the target item (i_t) — so that the profile can be used in CF recommendation models. Table 1 shows the composition of the explored state-of-the-art attack profiles. For instance, I_S (selected item set) is a set of items identified by the attacker to maximize the effectiveness of the attack, while I_F (filler item set) includes a random set of items whose role is to make the attack imperceptible. Details about the attack profile composition can be found in [15] and in the extended version of the current work [3].

In this work, we propose to foster the efficacy of state-of-the-art attack strategies by exploiting the semantic similarities between items using the information extracted from $\mathcal{KG}s$. The key idea is that we can compute the semantic similarity between the target item i_t and all the items in the catalog using $\mathcal{KG}$-derived features. Then, we use this information to select the filler items of each profile to generate the set I_F. A similarity value based on $\mathcal{KG}$ features leads to a more natural and coherent fake profile, thanks to the semantic nature of $\mathcal{KG}s$. Toward this goal, we propose two semantic-aware attacks by extended state-of-the art random and average attack:

- *Semantic-Aware Shilling Attack-random (SAShA-random)* is an extension of Random Attack. The baseline version is a naive attack in which each fake user is composed only of random items. We modify this attack by extract items to fill I_F from a subset of items that are most similar to i_t and use standard cosine similarity to compute item similarities by *leveraging the semantic features* [12]. Then, we build a set of most-similar items, considering the first quartile of similarity values. Finally, we extract ϕ items from this set, adopting a uniform distribution.
- *Semantic-Aware Shilling Attack-average* (*SAShA-average*) is an informed attack that extends the AverageBots attack [20]. It randomly samples the rating of each filler item from a normal distribution computed using the

Table 1: Attack strategies and their profile composition (*push* attacks).

Attack Type	I_S	I_F		I_ϕ	i_t
	Items Rating	Items	Ratings		
Random [18]	$\emptyset$	$\frac{\sum_{u \in U} \lvert I_u \rvert}{\lvert U \rvert} - 1$	$rnd(N(\mu, \sigma^2))$	$I - I_F$	max
Average [18]	$\emptyset$	$\frac{\sum_{u \in U} \lvert I_u \rvert}{\lvert U \rvert} - 1$	$rnd(N(\mu_f, \sigma_f^2))$	$I - I_F$	max

where (μ, σ) are the dataset average rating and rating variance, (μ_f, σ_f) are the filler item i_f rating average and variance, and min and max are respectively the minimum and maximum rating value.

mean and the variance of the ratings. We extend the baseline by extracting the filler items from the sub-set of most similar items. We use as candidate items the ones in the first quartile regarding their similarity with i_t.

3 Experimental Setting

In this section, we explain the experimental setting and results of the proposed attack framework (*SAShA*). We remind that full detail about the experimental procedure and evaluation can be found in [3].

Data: We conducted the proposed semantic average shilling attacks against rating-based CF models on three real-world datasets, `LibraryThing` [13] and `Yahoo!Movies`. The final statistics of the dataset used for the experiment are summarized in Table 2.
Feature Extraction and Selection. We have extracted the semantic information to build *SAShA* exploiting the public available item-entity mapping to `DBpedia`. To analyze the impact of different feature types, we have performed experiments considering categorical (CS), ontological (OS) and factual (FS) features by utilizing single-hop (1H) and double-hop (2H) strategies.

- **CS-1H/2H**, 1H includes having the property `dcterms:subject`, while 2H contains features with properties equal to either `dcterms:subject` or `skos:broader`;
- **OS-1H/2H**, 1H considers the features with the property `rdf:type`, while in 2H the properties include `rdf:type`, `rdf-schema:subClassOf` or `owl:equivalentClass`;
- **FS-1H/2H**, 1H uses all the features except ontological and categorical ones, while 2H choose features not included in the previous 2H categories.

Given the million-sized quantity of features obtained, we removed irrelevant features based on the sanity check procedure explained in [5].

Compared CF Recommendation Models: We have conducted experiments considering all the two attacks described in Section 2 against there most widely

If some domain-specific categorical/ontological features are not in the respective lists, we have considered them as factual features.

Table 2: Characteristics of the evaluation dataset: $|\mathcal{U}|$ — number of users, $|\mathcal{I}|$ — number of items, $|\mathcal{R}|$ — number of ratings.

Dataset	$\lvert\mathcal{U}\rvert$	$\lvert\mathcal{I}\rvert$	$\lvert\mathcal{R}\rvert$	$\frac{\lvert\mathcal{R}\rvert}{\lvert\mathcal{I}\rvert\times\lvert\mathcal{U}\rvert}$	#1H	#2H
`LibraryThing`	4.8K	2.2K	76.4K	0.0070	56.0K	4.2M
`Yahoo!Movies`	4.0K	2.5K	64.0K	0.0063	105.7K	6.6M

used CF models: User-kNN and Item-kNN (*Pearson Correlation*, number or neighbors: 40), and SVD (a matrix factorization model trained by considering 100 latent factors) [3].

Table 3: Experimental results for $SAShA$ at single and double hops. In **bold** we highlight the best results. (imp. %) shows the relative improvement of the best performing feature (CS, OS or FS) with respect to baseline (base) in percentage.

Prediction stability: HR@10														
		dataset	LibraryThing						Yahoo!Movies					
		Rec	User-kNN		Item-kNN		SVD		User-kNN		Item-kNN		SVD	
		feat./hop	1H	2H	1H	2H	1H	2H	1H	2H	1H	2H	1H	2H
1%	**Rnd**	base	.074		.281		.767		.189		.329		.410	
		CS	.068*	.068*	.271*	.270*	.778*	**.799***	.202	**.234***	.336	**.368***	.430*	**.473***
		OS	**.081***	**.075**	**.290***	.252	**.786***	.783*	**.217***	.172	**.345***	.304*	**.446***	.399
		FS	.072	.073	.280	.281	.786*	.787*	.213*	.208*	.338*	.341*	.442*	.440*
		imp. (%)	9.4	1.3	3.2	–	2.4	4.1	14.8	23.8	4.8	11.8	8.7	15.3
	Avg	base	.086		.313		.803		.233		.374		.489	
		CS	.081*	.081*	.301*	.301*	.814*	.815*	.220*	.204*	.357*	.338*	.467*	.408
		OS	**.093***	.084*	.313	.309	**.810**	**.816***	**.237**	**.249***	.371	**.400***	.475	**.539***
		FS	.084*	.084	.305*	.306	.811	.812*	.215*	.227	.350*	.364	.448*	.466*
		imp. (%)	8.1	-2.3	–	-1.2	1.3	1.6	1.7	6.8	-.8	6.9	-2.8	10.2
2.5%	**Rnd**	base	.157		.457		.900		.366		.508		.580	
		CS	.143*	.143*	.441*	.441*	.898	.897	.372	**.410***	.522*	**.564***	.607*	**.667***
		OS	**.170***	.157	**.467***	.455	**.902**	**.901**	**.394***	.337*	**.535***	.482*	**.635***	.560
		FS	.154	.155	.455	.455	.901	**.901**	.381*	.386*	.530*	.531*	.623*	.616*
		imp. (%)	8.2	–	2.1	-.4	.2	.1	7.6	12.0	5.3	11.0	9.4	15.0
	Avg	base	.197		**.508**		.915		**.416**		**.574**		**.685**	
		CS	.187*	.188*	.507	.507	.915	.914	.399*	.384*	.554*	.532*	.652*	.587*
		OS	**.202**	**.198**	.507	.506	.911	.914	.412	**.429***	.563*	**.593***	.656*	**.720***
		FS	.190*	.190*	.504	.503	.911	.913	.397*	.401*	.547*	.557*	.627*	.646*
		imp. (%)	2.5	0.5	-.1	-.1	–	-.1	-.9	3.1	-1.9	3.3	-4.2	5.1
5%	**Rnd**	base	.230		.557		.942		.449		.598		.702	
		CS	.213*	.213*	.558	.558	.940	.940	.455*	**.494***	.609*	**.644***	.707	**.772***
		OS	**.250***	**.231**	**.576***	**.567***	**.944**	.941	**.477***	.428*	**.622***	.577*	**.742***	.652*
		FS	.229	.229	.570*	.567*	.942	.942	.468*	.466*	.619*	.616*	.728*	.717*
		imp. (%)	8.6	0.4	3.4	1.7	.2	-	6.2	10.0	4.0	7.6	5.6	9.9
	Avg	base	.285		.605		.951		.494		.654		.788	
		CS	.269*	.269*	**.621***	**.621***	.950	.949	.479*	.466*	.639*	.621*	.744*	.688*
		OS	**.289**	.281	.610*	.614*	.948	.949	.494	.493	.646*	**.668***	.754*	**.804**
		FS	.272*	.273*	.614*	.614*	.946*	.948*	.473*	.479*	.634*	.642*	.729*	.743*
		imp. (%)	1.4	-1.4	2.6	2.6	-.1	-.2	–	-.2	-1.2	2.1	-4.3	2.0

*We mark statistically significant results ($p < 0.05$) using a paired t-test with the * symbol.*

Evaluation Metrics Let I_T be set of attacks item and U_T the users that have not rated items in I_T. We define the *Overall Hit-Ratio@k* denoted with $(HR@k)$ as the average of $hr@k$ for each attacked item according to $HR@k(I_T, U_T) = \frac{\sum_{i \subset I_T} hr@k(i, U_T)}{|I_T|}$ where $hr@k(i, U_T)$ measures the number of occurrences of the attacked item i in the top-k recommendation lists of the users in $|U_T|$ [1].

Evaluation Protocol. For each dataset, we have generated the recommendations concerning all users using the selected CF models (i.e., User-kNN, Item-kNN and MF). After computing baseline attacks, we have performed a series of *SAShA* attacks as described in Section 2 by considering different feature types (i.e., categorical, ontological and factual) extracted at 1 or 2 hops. each attack is a *push attack.* We have performed the attacks considering a different amount of added fake user profiles: 1%, 2.5% and 5% of the total number of users. We have tested the attacks considering 50 randomly sampled target items [20,10].

4 Results and Discussion

In this section, we present the results of experiments carried out. Table 3 summarizes the results of the HR@10 regarding the considered dimensions. In particular, the inner elements in the Table are related to $\mathcal{KG}$ *semantic dimension* and include: feature types in the rows (CF, OS and FS) number of hops in the columns (1H, 2H). However, the outer elements (dimensions) in Table 3, are the *attack strategies* in the rows (*SAShA*-Rnd and *SAShA*-Avg), and *CF recommendation models* in the columns (User-kNN, Item-kNN and SVD). Finally, we report the results for three levels of attack power (1%, 2.5% and 5%) reported in the three panels of the Table.

The impact of semantics. By looking at the improvement percentages, the general trend is that, for each <attack, CF> pair, one of the values for 1H or 2H is better than baseline attack performance. For instance, for <Rnd, User-kNN> on `LibraryThing`, the relative improvements for 1H and 2H are 9.4% and 1.3%, both obtained for attacks integrated with ontological features setting (OS) features. Relative improvements on `Yahoo!Movies` tend to be larger e.g., consider 14.8% and 23.8% for the same <attack, CF> pair. Regarding the impact of each feature category, in the majority of cases, ontological features setting (OS) provides the best results, followed by categorical features setting (CS). The FS seems to have a little impact on the attack effectiveness. We believe this may be due to a noise introduced by the exploitation of heterogeneous (factual) features. On the other side, ontological features make the similarity between items more evident. Finally, categorical features guarantee competing performance since CF recommendation relies on the affinity between items' categories.

Analysis of the semantic-encoded variant of attacks. The second study is devoted to comparing the impact of semantics on the different attacks (**Rnd**, **Avg**) . The **Rnd** attack provides significant (or substantially high) improvement of attack efficacy on the base version in at least one semantic-configuration.

However, regarding **Avg** attack, it is worth noticing that, even here, the injection of semantics is generally beneficial for the adversary. Nevertheless, the semantic integration, for **Avg** attack, has a lower impact than its use for **Rnd** version. We explain this behavior with the generally high performance of **Avg** attack, that leaves less room for improvements. Additionally, if we consider the different recommendation models, the semantics ensure attack performance improvement. Among all, the semantic-encoded variants of attacks are particularly effective on User-kNN in both datasets.

5 Conclusion

The goal of this work is to investigate the effect of integrating semantic information, obtained from $\mathcal{KG}s$, to foster the shilling attack efficacy. The proposed attack strategy, $SAShA$, extends *random* and *average* attacks by integrating public available semantic information. In detail, $SAShA$ takes advantage of semantics to create more effective fake profiles. Toward this goal, extensive experiments were carried out by considering different collaborative recommendation models, different attack strategies, and three categories of semantic features (categorical, ontological, and factual). Results on two real-world datasets underline the significant vulnerability of standard recommendation models when semantics are integrated into the attack strategy. We plan to investigate different sources of publicly available knowledge (e.g., `Wikidata`), to semantically extend other state-of-the-art attacks. Finally, we are interested in investigating the possibility of semantics knowledge exploitation for defensive strategies.
Acknowledgments. The authors acknowledge partial support of the following projects: Innonetwork CONTACT, Innonetwork APOLLON, ARS01_00821 FLET4.0, Fincons Smart Digital Solutions for the Creative Industry.

References

1. Aggarwal, C.C.: Attack-resistant recommender systems. In: Recommender Systems. Springer (2016)
2. Anelli, V.W., Bellini, V., Di Noia, T., Bruna, W.L., Tomeo, P., Di Sciascio, E.: An analysis on time- and session-aware diversification in recommender systems. In: UMAP. ACM (2017)
3. Anelli, V.W., Deldjoo, Y., Di Noia, T., Di Sciascio, E., Merra, F.A.: Sasha: Semantic-aware shilling attacks on recommender systems exploiting knowledge graphs. In: The Semantic Web - 17th International Conference, ESWC 2020, Heraklion, Crete, Greece, May 31- June 4, 2020, Proceedings (2020)
4. Anelli, V.W., Di Noia, T.: 2nd workshop on knowledge-aware and conversational recommender systems - kars. In: CIKM. ACM (2019)
5. Anelli, V.W., Noia, T.D., Sciascio, E.D., Ragone, A., Trotta, J.: How to make latent factors interpretable by feeding factorization machines with knowledge graphs. In: The Semantic Web - ISWC 2019 - 18th Int. Semantic Web Conf., Auckland, New Zealand, October 26-30, 2019, Proceedings, Part I. vol. 11778 (2019)

6. Backstrom, L., Leskovec, J.: Supervised random walks: predicting and recommending links in social networks. In: Proceedings of the Forth International Conference on Web Search and Web Data Mining, WSDM 2011, Hong Kong, China, February 9-12, 2011 (2011)
7. Bhatia, S., Dwivedi, P., Kaur, A.: That's interesting, tell me more! finding descriptive support passages for knowledge graph relationships. In: International Semantic Web Conference (1). Lecture Notes in Computer Science, vol. 11136. Springer (2018)
8. Deldjoo, Y., Constantin, M.G., Eghbal-Zadeh, H., Ionescu, B., Schedl, M., Cremonesi, P.: Audio-visual encoding of multimedia content for enhancing movie recommendations. In: Proceedings of the 12th ACM Conference on Recommender Systems, RecSys 2018, Vancouver, BC, Canada, October 2-7, 2018 (2018)
9. Deldjoo, Y., Dacrema, M.F., Constantin, M.G., Eghbal-zadeh, H., Cereda, S., Schedl, M., Ionescu, B., Cremonesi, P.: Movie genome: alleviating new item cold start in movie recommendation. User Model. User-Adapt. Interact. **29**(2) (2019)
10. Deldjoo, Y., Di Noia, T., Merra, F.A.: Assessing the impact of a user-item collaborative attack on class of users. In: ImpactRS@RecSys. CEUR Workshop Proceedings, vol. 2462. CEUR-WS.org (2019)
11. Di Noia, T., Magarelli, C., Maurino, A., Palmonari, M., Rula, A.: Using ontology-based data summarization to develop semantics-aware recommender systems. In: ESWC. Lecture Notes in Computer Science, vol. 10843. Springer (2018)
12. Di Noia, T., Mirizzi, R., Ostuni, V.C., Romito, D., Zanker, M.: Linked open data to support content-based recommender systems. In: Proc. of the 8th Int. Conf. on Semantic Systems. ACM (2012)
13. Di Noia, T., Ostuni, V.C., Tomeo, P., Di Sciascio, E.: Sprank: Semantic path-based ranking for top-N recommendations using linked open data. ACM TIST **8**(1) (2016)
14. Gao, L., Yang, H., Wu, J., Zhou, C., Lu, W., Hu, Y.: Recommendation with multi-source heterogeneous information. In: IJCAI. ijcai.org (2018)
15. Gunes, I., Kaleli, C., Bilge, A., Polat, H.: Shilling attacks against recommender systems: a comprehensive survey. Artif. Intell. Rev. **42**(4) (2014)
16. Koren, Y.: Factor in the neighbors: Scalable and accurate collaborative filtering. TKDD **4**(1) (2010)
17. Koren, Y., Bell, R.M., Volinsky, C.: Matrix factorization techniques for recommender systems. IEEE Computer **42**(8) (2009)
18. Lam, S.K., Riedl, J.: Shilling recommender systems for fun and profit. In: WWW. ACM (2004)
19. Linden, G., Smith, B., York, J.: Amazon.com recommendations: Item-to-item collaborative filtering. IEEE Internet Computing **7**(1) (2003)
20. Mobasher, B., Burke, R.D., Bhaumik, R., Williams, C.: Toward trustworthy recommender systems: An analysis of attack models and algorithm robustness. ACM Trans. Internet Techn. **7**(4) (2007)
21. Ning, X., Karypis, G.: Sparse linear methods with side information for top-n recommendations. In: Cunningham, P., Hurley, N.J., Guy, I., Anand, S.S. (eds.) Sixth ACM Conference on Recommender Systems, RecSys '12, Dublin, Ireland, September 9-13, 2012. ACM (2012)
22. Shadbolt, N., O'Hara, K., Berners-Lee, T., Gibbins, N., Glaser, H., Hall, W., m. c. schraefel: Linked open government data: Lessons from data.gov.uk. IEEE Intelligent Systems **27**(3) (2012)
23. Wang, H., Zhang, F., Xie, X., Guo, M.: DKN: deep knowledge-aware network for news recommendation. In: WWW. ACM (2018)

Tensor Co-clustering: a Parameter-less Approach (DISCUSSION PAPER)

Elena Battaglia and Ruggero G. Pensa

University of Turin, Dept. of Computer Science, Turin, Italy
{elena.battaglia,ruggero.pensa}@unito.it

Abstract. Tensors co-clustering has been proven useful in many applications, due to its ability of coping with high-dimensional data and sparsity. However, setting up a co-clustering algorithm properly requires the specification of the desired number of clusters for each mode as input parameters. To face this issue, we propose a tensor co-clustering algorithm that does not require the number of desired co-clusters as input, as it optimizes an objective function based on a measure of association across discrete random variables that is not affected by their cardinality. The effectiveness of our algorithm is shown on real-world datasets, also in comparison with state-of-the-art co-clustering methods.

1 Introduction

Tensors are widely used mathematical objects that well represent complex information such as gene expression data, social networks, heterogenous information networks, time-evolving data, behavioral patterns, and multi-lingual text corpora. In general, every n-ary relation can be easily represented as a tensor. From the algebraic point of view, in fact, they can be seen as multidimensional generalizations of matrices and, as such, can be processed with mathematical and computational methods that generalize those usually employed to analyze data matrices, e.g., non-negative factorization, singular value decomposition, itemset and association rule mining, clustering and co-clustering.

Clustering, in particular, is by far one of the most popular unsupervised machine learning techniques since it allows analysts to obtain an overview of the intrinsic similarity structures of the data with relatively little background knowledge about them. However, with the availability of high-dimensional heterogenous data, co-clustering has gained popularity, since it provides a simultaneous partitioning of each mode. Despite its proven usefulness the correct application of tensor co-clustering is limited by the fact that it requires the specification of a congruent number of clusters for each mode, while, in realistic analysis scenarios, the actual number of clusters is unknown. Furthermore, matrix/tensor

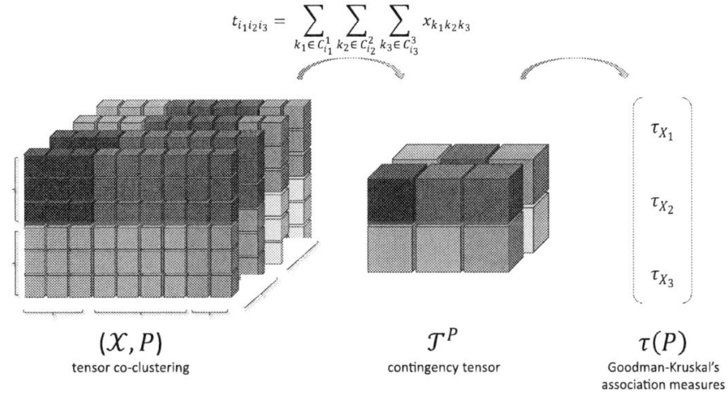

Fig. 1: An example of tensor co-clustering with the related contingency tensor and the associated Goodman-Kruskal's τ measures.

(co-)clustering is often based on a preliminary tensor factorization step or on latent block models [14, 3, 13] that, in their turn, require further input parameters (e.g., the number of latent factors/blocks within each mode). As a consequence, it is merely impossible to explore all combinations of parameter values in order to identify the best clustering results.

The main reason for this problem is that most clustering algorithms (and tensor factorization approaches) optimize objective functions that strongly depend on the number of clusters (or factors). Hence, two solutions with two different numbers of clusters can not be compared directly. Although this reduces considerably the size of the search space, it prevents the discovery of a better partitioning once a wrong number of clusters is selected. In this paper, we address this limitation by proposing a new tensor co-clustering algorithm that optimizes an objective function that can be viewed as n-mode extension of an association measure called Goodman-Kruskal's τ [5], whose local optima do not depend on the number of clusters. Compared with state-of-the-art techniques that require the desired number of clusters in each mode as input parameters, our approach achieves similar or better results on several real-world datasets.

The algorithm presented in this paper has been fist introduced in [1]. An interested reader could refer to it for further theoretical and experimental details.

2 An association measure for tensor co-clustering

The objective function optimized by our tensor co-clustering algorithm is an association measure, called Goodman and Kruskal's τ [5], that evaluates the dependence between two discrete variables and has been used to evaluate the quality of 2-way co-clustering [10]. Goodman and Kruskal's τ estimates the strength of the link between two discrete variables X and Y according to the proportional reduction of the error in predicting one of them knowing the other: $\tau_{X|Y} = \frac{e_X - \mathbb{E}[e_{X|Y}]}{e_X}$, where e_X is the error in predicting X (estimated as the probability that two different observations from the marginal distribution of X fall in different categories) and $\mathbb{E}[e_{X|Y}]$ is the expected value of the conditional error taken with respect to the distribution of Y. Conversely, the proportional reduction of the error in predicting Y while X is known is $\tau_{Y|X} = \frac{e_Y - \mathbb{E}[e_{Y|X}]}{e_Y}$.

In order to use this measure for the evaluation of a tensor co-clustering, we need to extend it so that τ can evaluate the association of n distinct discrete variables $X_1, \ldots, X_n$. Reasoning as in the two-dimensional case, we can define the reduction in the error in predicting X_i while $(X_j)_{j \neq i}$ are all known as

$$\tau_{X_i} = \tau_{X_i|(X_j)_{j \neq i}} = \frac{e_{X_i} - \mathbb{E}[e_{X_i|(X_j)_{j \neq i}}]}{e_{X_i}}$$

for all $i \leq n$. When $n = 2$, the measure coincides with Goodman-Kruskal's τ.

We will now see how to use function τ to evaluate a tensor co-clustering. Let $\mathcal{X} \in \mathbb{R}_+^{m_1 \times \cdots \times m_n}$ be a tensor with n modes and non-negative values. Let us denote with $x_{k_1 \ldots k_n}$ the generic element of $\mathcal{X}$, where $k_i = 1, \ldots, m_i$ for each mode $i = 1, \ldots, n$. A co-clustering $\mathcal{P}$ of $\mathcal{X}$ is a collection of n partitions $\{\mathcal{P}_i\}_{i=1,\ldots,n}$, where $\mathcal{P}_i = \cup_{j=1}^{c_i} C_j^i$ is a partition of the elements on the i-th mode of $\mathcal{X}$ in c_i groups, with $c_i \leq m_i$ for each $i = 1, \ldots, n$. Each co-clustering $\mathcal{P}$ can be associated to a tensor $\mathcal{T}^{\mathcal{P}} \in \mathbb{R}_+^{c_1 \times \cdots \times c_n}$, whose generic element is the sum of all entries of $\mathcal{X}$ in the same co-cluster. We can look at $\mathcal{T}^{\mathcal{P}}$ as the contingency n-modal table that empirically estimates the joint distribution of n discrete variables $X_1, \ldots, X_n$, where each X_i takes values in $\{C_1^i, \ldots C_{c_i}^i\}$. From this contingency table, we can derive the marginal probabilities of each variable X_i (i.e., the probability that a generic element of mode i falls in a particular cluster on that mode) and we can use these probabilities to compute Goodman and Kruskal's τ functions: in this way we associate to each co-clustering $\mathcal{P}$ over $\mathcal{X}$ a vector $\tau^{\mathcal{P}} = (\tau_{X_1}^{\mathcal{P}}, \ldots, \tau_{X_n}^{\mathcal{P}})$ that can be used to evaluate the quality of the co-clustering. The overall co-clustering schema is depicted in Figure 1.

3 A stochastic local search approach to co-clustering

Our co-clustering approach can be formulated as a multi-objective optimization problem: given a tensor $\mathcal{X}$ with n modes and dimension m_i on mode i, an optimal co-clustering $\mathcal{P}$ for $\mathcal{X}$ is one that is not dominated by any other co-clustering (i.e. does not exist any other co-clustering $\mathcal{Q}$ with $\tau_{X_j}^{\mathcal{Q}} >= \tau_{X_j}^{\mathcal{P}}$ for all $j = 1, \ldots, n$).

Since we do not fix the number of clusters, the space of possible solutions is huge (for example, given a very small tensor of dimension $10 \times 10 \times 10$, the number of possible partitions is 1.56×10^{16}): it is clear that a systematic exploration of all possible solutions is not feasible for a generic tensor $\mathcal{X}$. For this reason we need to find a heuristic that allows us to reach a "good" partition of $\mathcal{X}$, i.e. a partition $\mathcal{P}$ with high values of $\tau_{X_k}^{\mathcal{P}}$ for all modes k. With this aim, we propose a stochastic local search approach to solve the maximization problem.

Algorithm 1: $\tau TCC(\mathcal{X}, N_{iter})$

Input: A $m_1 \times \cdots \times m_n$ tensor $\mathcal{X}$, N_{iter}
Result: $\mathcal{P}_1, \ldots, \mathcal{P}_n$

Initialize $\mathcal{P}_1, \ldots, \mathcal{P}_n$ with discrete partitions;
$i \leftarrow 0$;
$iter\_whithout\_moves \leftarrow 0$;
while $i \leq N_{iter}$ & $iter\_whithout\_moves < max_{j=1,\ldots,n}(m_j)$ **do**
  for $k = 1$ *to* n **do**
    if $iter\_whithout\_moves < t$ **then**
      Randomly choose C_b^k in $\mathcal{P}_k$ and x in C_b^k;
    else
      $x \leftarrow next(k)$ //Select the element following the one selected at iteration $i-1$ on mode k;
      $C_b^k \leftarrow$ Cluster of x;
    end
    for C_k^j **in** $\mathcal{P}_k \cup \emptyset$ **do**
      $\mathcal{Q}_k^j \leftarrow (\mathcal{P}_k \setminus \{C_b^k, C_j^k\}) \bigcup \{C_b^k \setminus \{x\}, C_j^k \cup \{x\}\}$;
      $\mathcal{Q}^j \leftarrow (\mathcal{P}_1, \mathcal{P}_2, \ldots, \mathcal{P}_{k-1}, \mathcal{Q}_k, \mathcal{P}_{k+1}, \ldots, \mathcal{P}_n)$;
      Compute contingency tensor T^j associated to $\mathcal{Q}^j$ and $\tau^{\mathcal{Q}_j}$;
    end
    $e \leftarrow SelectBestPartition(k, b, (\tau^{\mathcal{Q}_j})_{j=1,\ldots,|\mathcal{P}_k \cup \emptyset|})$;
    $\mathcal{P}_k \leftarrow \mathcal{Q}_k^e$;
    if $e == b$ **then**
      $iter\_whithout\_moves \leftarrow iter\_whithout\_moves + 1$;
    else
      $iter\_whithout\_moves \leftarrow 0$;
    end
    $i \leftarrow i + 1$;
  end
end

Algorithm 1 provides the general sketch of our tensor co-clustering algorithm, called τTCC. It repeatedly considers modes one by one, sequentially, and it tries to improve the quality of the co-clustering by moving one single element from its original cluster C_b^k to another cluster on the same mode, C_e^k, which most improves the quality of the partition, according to a criterion chosen to measure the quality of the partition. When all the n modes have been considered, the i-th iteration of the algorithm is concluded. If all objects have been tried but no move is possible, the algorithm ends. At the end of each iteration, one of the following possible moves has been done on mode k:

- an object x has been moved from cluster C_b^k to a pre-existing cluster C_e^k: in this case the final number of clusters on mode k remains the same (let'call it c_k) if C_b^k is non-empty after the move. If C_b^k is empty after the move, it will be deleted and the final number of clusters will be $c_k - 1$;

- an object x has been moved from cluster C_b^k to a new cluster $C_e^k = \emptyset$: the final number of clusters on mode k will be $c_k + 1$ (the useless case when x is moved from $C_b^k = \{x\}$ to $C_e^k = \emptyset$ is not considered);
- no move has been performed and the number of clusters remains c_k.

Thus, during the iterative process, the updating procedure is able to increase or decrease the number of clusters at any time. This is due to the fact that, contrary to other measures, such as the loss in mutual information [4], τ measure has an upper limit which does not depend on the number of co-clusters and thus enables the comparison of co-clustering solutions of different cardinalities.

As mentioned above, the choise of the best cluster on mode k in which the selected element x should be moved depends on the way in which we decide to measure the increase in the quality of the tensor partition. We can define different measures, corresponding to different ways to implement function $SelectBestPartition$ in Algorithm 1. According to our experiments, the one with best performances in terms of speed of convergence and quality of the identified co-clusters is the following. Suppose we want to move an object on mode k: we consider only those moves that improve (or at least do not worsen) τ_{X_k} and, among them, we choose the one with the greatest value of $avg(\tau) = \frac{1}{n}\sum_{j=1}^{n} \tau_{X_j}$. It can be proven that algorithm τTCC with this selection strategy converges to a Pareto local optimum.

4 Experiments and discussion

In this section, we test the effectiveness of our co-clustering algorithm through experiments on the following three real-world datasets: the "four-area" DBLP dataset[1]; the "hetrec2011-movielens-2k" dataset[2] [2], from which we extraxt two different tensors, MovieLens1 and MovieLens2; the Yelp dataset[3], from which we extract two tensors, YelpTOR and YelpPGH. To assess the quality of the clustering performances, we consider two measures commonly used in the clustering literature: normalized mutual information (NMI) [11] and adjusted rand index (ARI) [8].

We compare our results with those of other state-of-the-art tensor co-clustering algorithms. **nnCP** is the non-negative CP decomposition [6] and can be used to co-cluster a tensor, as done by [14], by assigning each element in each mode to the cluster corresponding to the latent factor with highest value. **nnTucker** is the non-negative Tucker decomposition [12]. **nnCP+kmeans** and **nnT+kmeans** combine CP (or Tucker) decomposition with a post-processing phase in which k-means is applied on each of the latent factor matrices, similarly as what has been done by [7] and [3]. **SparseCP** consists of a CP decomposition with non-negative sparse latent factors [9]. Finally, **TBM** performs tensor co-clustering

[1] `http://web.cs.ucla.edu/~yzsun/data/DBLP_four_area.zip`

[2] `https://grouplens.org/datasets/hetrec-2011/`

[3] `https://www.yelp.com/dataset`

Table 1: Results achieved by the co-clustering algorithms on the real-world datasets (average values over 5 runs). NMI and ARI are computed for the main mode (authors in DBLP, movies in MovieLens and restaurants in Yelp).

Dataset	DBLP		MovieLens1		MovieLens2		yelpTOR		yelpPGH	
Algorithm	NMI	ARI	NMI	ARI	NMI	ARI	NMI	ARI	NMI	ARI
τTCC	0.74	0.80	**0.66**	**0.71**	**0.40**	**0.51**	0.42	**0.44**	**0.38**	**0.28**
nnTucker	**0.78**	**0.84**	0.42	0.53	0.24	0.17	**0.43**	0.39	0.28	0.19
nnCP	0.74	0.80	0.38	0.34	0.11	0.03	0.42	0.37	0.10	0.06
SparseCP	0.00	0.00	0.00	0.00	0.00	0.00	0.20	0.15	0.11	0.04
TBM	-	-	0.00	0.01	0.01	0.01	0.02	0.01	0.10	0.04
nnCP+kmeans	0.24	0.08	0.31	0.21	0.15	0.07	0.11	0.01	0.09	0.03
nnT+kmeans	0.25	0.06	0.38	0.31	0.17	0.09	0.09	0.01	0.09	0.03

via the Tensor Block Model [13]. The last four methods require as input parameters the number of clusters on each mode: we set these numbers equal to the true number of classes on the three modes of the tensor. When further parameters are needed, we follow the instructions suggested in the original papers for setting them. Algorithms **nnCP**, **nnTucker** and their variant with k-means are applied trying different ranks of the decomposition: we report the best result obtained. In this way we are giving a big advantage to our competitors: we choose the rank of the decomposition and the number of clusters by looking at the actual number of categories, which are unknown in standard unsupervised settings. Despite this, as shown in Table 1, τTCC outperforms the other algorithms on all datasets but one (DBLP) and has comparable results on another (YelpTOR). In these cases, non-negative Tucker decomposition (with the number of latent factors set to the correct number of embedded clusters) achieves the best results and non-negative CP decomposition obtains results that are comparable with those of τTCC. However, when we modify, even if slightly, the number of latent factors (see Figure2), the results get immediately worse than those of τTCC.

The number of clusters identified by τTCC is usually close to the correct number of embedded clusters: on average, 5 instead of 4 for DBLP, 5 instead of 3 for MovieLens1, the correct number 3 for MovieLens2, 5 instead of 3 for YelpPGH. Only YelpTOR presents a number of clusters (13) that is far from the correct number of classes (3). However, more than the 85% of the objects are classified in 3 large clusters, while the remaining objects form very small clusters: we consider these objects as candidate outliers. The same beahviour is even more pronounced in DBLP, where four clusters contain the 99.9% of the objects and only 2 objects stay in the "extra cluster".

Lastly, we provide some insights about the quality of the clusters identified by our algorithm. To this purpose, we choose a co-clustering of the MovieLens1 dataset. This dataset contains 181 movies and all the tags assigned by the users to each movie. We construct a $(215 \times 181 \times 142)$-dimensional tensor, where the three modes represent users, movies and tags. The movies are labelled in three categories (Animation, Horror and Documentary). Algorithm τTCC identifies five clusters of movies, instead of the three categories we consider as labels. The tag clouds in Figure 3, illustrate the 30 movies with more tags for each cluster (text size depends on the actual number of tags): it can be easily observed that

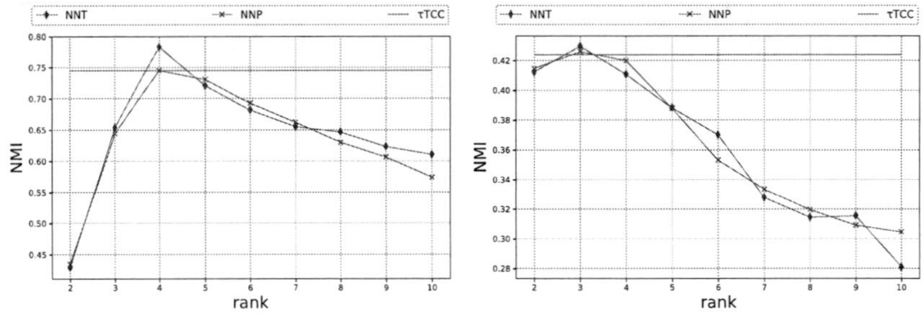

(a) DBLP (b) YelpTOR

Fig. 2: Variation of nnTucker/nnCP results w.r.t. the rank of the decomposition in DBLP and YelpTOR datasets.

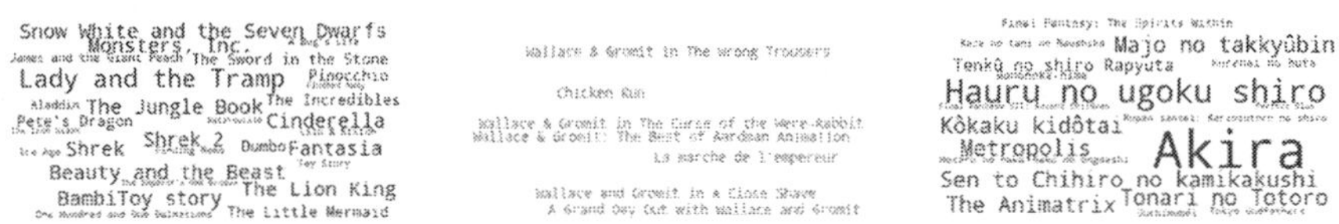

(a) Cl1 - Cartoons (b) Cl2 - Wallace&Gromit (c) Cl3 - Anime

(d) Cl4 - Horror (e) Cl5 - Documentaries

Fig. 3: First 30 movie in each cluster identified by τTCC on dataset MoveiLens1.

the first cluster concerns animated movies for children, mainly Disney and Pixar movies; the second one is a little cluster containing animated movies realized with the claymation technique (mainly Wallace and Gromit saga's movies or other films by the same director); the third cluster is still a subset of the animated movies, but it contains anime and animated films from Japan. The fourth cluster is composed mainly by horror movies and the last one contains only documentaries. On the tag mode, our algorithm finds thirteen clusters. Six of them contain more than 90% of the total tags and only 10 uninformative tags are partitioned in other 7 very small clusters, and could be considered as outliers. There is a one-to-one correspondence between four clusters of movies (Cartoons, Anime, Wallace&Gromit and Documentary) and four of the tag clusters; cluster Horror, instead, can be put in relation with two different tag clusters, the first containing names of directors, actors or characters of popular horror movies, the second composed by adjectives tipically used to describe disturbing films.

5 Conclusions

Our experimental validation has shown that our approach is able to identify meaningful clusters. Moreover, it outperforms state-of-the-art methods for most datasets. Even when our algorithm is not the best one, we have found that the competitors can not work properly without specifying a correct number of clusters for each mode of the tensor. As future work, we will design a specific algorithm for sparse tensors with the aim of reducing the overall computational complexity of the approach. Finally, we will further investigate the ability of our method to identify candidate outliers as small clusters in the data.

References

1. Battaglia, E., Pensa, R.G.: Parameter-less tensor co-clustering. In: Proceedings of DS 2019. pp. 205–219 (2019)
2. Cantador, I., Brusilovsky, P., Kuflik, T.: 2nd Workshop on Information Heterogeneity and Fusion in Recommender Systems (HetRec 2011). In: Proc. RecSys 2011 (2011)
3. Cao, X., Wei, X., Han, Y., Lin, D.: Robust face clustering via tensor decomposition. IEEE Trans. Cybernetics **45**(11), 2546–2557 (2015)
4. Dhillon, I.S., Mallela, S., Modha, D.S.: Information-theoretic co-clustering. In: Proc. ACM SIGKDD 2003. pp. 89–98 (2003)
5. Goodman, L.A., Kruskal, W.H.: Measures of association for cross classification. Journal of the American Statistical Association **49**, 732–764 (1954)
6. Harshman, R.A.: Foundation of the parafac procedure: models and conditions for an" explanatory" multimodal factor analysis. UCLA Working Papers in Phonetics **16**, 1–84 (1970)
7. Huang, H., Ding, C.H.Q., Luo, D., Li, T.: Simultaneous tensor subspace selection and clustering: the equivalence of high order svd and k-means clustering. In: Proc. ACM SIGKDD 2008. pp. 327–335 (2008)
8. Hubert, L., Arabie, P.: Comparing partitions. J. Classif. **2**(1), 193–218 (1985)
9. Papalexakis, E.E., Sidiropoulos, N.D., Bro, R.: From K-means to higher-way co-clustering: Multilinear decomposition with sparse latent factors. IEEE Trans. Signal Processing **61**(2), 493–506 (2013)
10. Robardet, C., Feschet, F.: Efficient local search in conceptual clustering. In: Proceedings of DS 2001. pp. 323–335 (2001)
11. Strehl, A., Ghosh, J.: Cluster ensembles – A knowledge reuse framework for combining multiple partitions. Journal of Machine Learning Research **3**, 583–617 (2002)
12. Tucker, L.R.: Some mathematical notes on three-mode factor analysis. Psychometrika **31**, 279–311 (1966)
13. Wang, M., Zeng, Y.: Multiway clustering via tensor block models. In: Proc. of NeurIPS 2019. pp. 713–723 (2019)
14. Zhou, Q., Xu, G., Zong, Y.: Web co-clustering of usage network using tensor decomposition. In: Proceedings of ECBS 2009. pp. 311–314 (2009)

Classification-based Content Sensitivity Analysis (DISCUSSION PAPER)

Elena Battaglia, Livio Bioglio, and Ruggero G. Pensa

University of Turin, Dept. of Computer Science, Turin, Italy
{elena.battaglia,livio.bioglio,ruggero.pensa}@unito.it

Abstract. With the availability of user-generated content in the Web, malicious users have access to huge repositories of private (and often sensitive) information regarding a large part of the world's population. In this paper, we propose a way to evaluate the harmfulness of text content by defining a new data mining task called *content sensitivity analysis*. According to our definition, a score can be assigned to any text sample according to its degree of sensitivity. Even though the task is similar to sentiment analysis, we show that it has its own peculiarities and may lead to a new branch of research. Thanks to some preliminary experiments, we show that content sensitivity analysis can not be addressed as a simple binary classification task.

1 Introduction

Internet privacy has gained much attention in the last decade due to the success of online social networks and other social media services that expose our lives to the wide public. Consequently, understanding and measuring the exposure of user privacy in the Web has become crucial [6] and many different metrics and methods have been proposed with the goal of assessing the risk of privacy leakage in posting activities [1]. Most research efforts, however, focus on measuring the overall exposure of users according to their privacy settings [12] or position within the network [11]. However, in addition to personal and behavioral data collected more or less legitimately by companies and organizations, many websites and mobile/web applications store and publish tons of user-generated content, which, very often, capture and represent private moments of our life. The availability of user-generated content is a huge source of relatively easy-to-access private (and often very sensitive) information concerning habits, preferences, families and friends, hobbies, health and philosophy of life, which expose the authors of such contents (or any other individual referenced by them) to many (cyber)criminal risks, including identity theft, stalking, burglary, frauds, cyberbullying or "simply" discrimination in workplace or in life in general. Sometimes users are not aware of the dangers due to the uncontrolled diffusion of their sensitive information and would probably avoid publishing it if only someone told them how harmful it could be.

In this discussion paper, we address this problem by proposing a way to assess the sensitivity of user-generated content. To this purpose, we define a new data mining task that we call *content sensitivity analysis* (CSA), inspired by sentiment analysis [7]. The goal of CSA is to assign a score to any text sample according to the amount of sensitive information it potentially discloses. The problem of private content analysis has already been investigated as a way to characterize anonymous vs. non anonymous content posting in specific social media [4, 9] or question-and-answer platforms [8]. However, the link between anonymity and sensitive contents is not that obvious: users may post anonymously because, for instance, they are referring to illegal matters (e.g., software/steaming piracy, black market and so on); conversely, fully identifiable persons may post very sensitive contents simply because they are underestimating the visibility of their action [12, 11]. Although CSA has some points in common with anonymous content analysis and the well-known sentiment analysis task, we show that it has its own peculiarities and may lead to a brand new branch of research, opening many intriguing challenges in several computer science and linguistics fields.

Through some preliminary but extensive experiments on a large annotated corpus of social media posts, we show that content sensitivity analysis can not be addressed straightforwardly. In particular, we design a simplified CSA task leveraging binary classification to distinguish between sensitive and non sensitive posts by testing several bag-of-words and word embedding models. According to our experiments, the classification performances achieved by the most accurate models are far from being satisfactory. This suggests that content sensitivity analysis should consider more complex linguistic and semantic aspects, as well as more sophisticated machine learning models. A more in-depth discussion on how to address these issues is reported in the full version of this paper [2].

2 Content Sensitivity Analysis

In this section, we introduce the new data mining task that we call *content sensitivity analysis* (CSA), aimed at determining the amount of privacy-sensitive content expressed in user-generated text content. We distinguish two cases, namely *binary CSA* and *continuous CSA*, according to the outcome of the analysis (binary or continuous). Before introducing the technical details of CSA, we briefly provide the intuition behind CSA by describing a motivating example.

2.1 Motivating example

To explain the main objectives of CSA and the scientific challenges associated to them, we consider the post given as an example in Figure 1. This particular post discloses information about the author and his friend Alice Green. Moreover, the

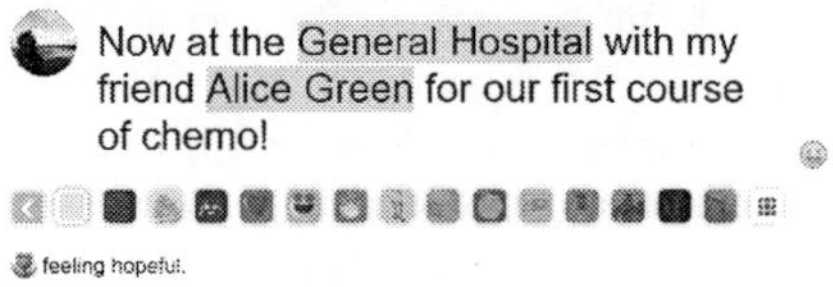

Fig. 1. An example of a potentially privacy-sensitive post.

post contains spatiotemporal references ("now" and "General Hospital"), which are generally considered intrinsically sensitive, and mentions "chemo", a potentially sensitive term. Finally, the sentence is related to "cancer", a potentially sensitive topic, and its structure suggests that the two subjects of disclosure have cancer and they are both about to start their first course of chemotherapy.

It is clear that, reducing sensitivity to anonymity, as done in previous research work [8, 4], is only one side of the coin. Instead, CSA has much more in common with the famous *sentiment analysis* (SA) task, where the objective is to measure the "polarity" or "sentiment" of a given text [7, 5]. However, while SA has already a well-established theory and may count on a set of easy-to-access and easy-to-use tools, CSA has never been defined before. Therefore, apart from the known open problems in SA (such as sarcasm detection), CSA involves three new scientific challenges.

1. **Definition of sensitivity**. A clear definition of sensitivity is required. Sensitivity is often defined in the legal systems, such as in the EU General Data Protection Regulation (GDPR), as a characteristic of some personal data (e.g., criminal or medical records), but a cognitive and perceptive explanation of what can be defined as "sensitive" is still missing [13].

2. **Sensitivity-annotated corpora**. Large text corpora need to be annotated according to sensitivity and at multiple levels: at the sentence level ("I got cancer" is more sensitive than "I got some nice volleyball shorts"), at the topic level ("health" is more sensitive than "sports") and at the term level ("cancer" is more sensitive than "shorts").

3. **Context-aware sensitivity**. Due to its subjectivity, a clear evaluation of the context is needed. The fact that a medical doctor talks about cancer is not sensitive per se, but if she talks about some of her patients having cancer, she could disclose very sensitive information.

2.2 Definitions

Here, we provide the details regarding the formal framework of *content sensitivity analysis*. We will propose a definition of "sensitivity" further in this section. The simplest way to define CSA is as follows:

Definition 1 (binary content sensitivity analysis). *Given a user-generated text object* $o_i \in \mathcal{O}$*, with* $\mathcal{O}$ *being the domain of all user-generated contents, the* binary content sensitivity analysis *task consists in designing a function* $f_s : \mathcal{O} \rightarrow \{sens, ns\}$*, such that* $f_s(o_i) = sens$ *iff* o_i *is privacy-sensitive,* $f_s(o_i) = ns$ *iff* o_i *is not sensitive.*

In some cases, sensitivity is not the same for all sensitive objects: a post dealing with health is certainly more sensitive than a post dealing with vacations, although both can be considered as sensitive. This suggests that, instead of considering sensitivity as a binary feature of a text, a more appropriate definition of CSA should take into account different degrees of sensitivity, as follows:

Definition 2 (continuous content sensitivity analysis). *Let* $o_i \in \mathcal{O}$ *be a user-generated object, with* $\mathcal{O}$ *being the domain of all user-generated contents. The* continuous content sensitivity analysis *task consists in designing a function* $f_s : \mathcal{O} \rightarrow [-1, 1]$*, such that* $f_s(o_i) = 1$ *iff* o_i *is maximally privacy-sensitive,* $f_s(o_i) = -1$ *iff* o_i *is minimally privacy-sensitive,* $f_s(o_i) = 0$ *iff* o_i *has unknown sensitivity. The value* $\sigma_i = f_s(o_i)$ *is the* ***sensitivity score*** *of object* o_i.

According to this definition, sensitive objects have $0 < \sigma \leq 1$, while non sensitive posts have $-1 \leq \sigma < 0$. In general, when $\sigma \approx 0$ the sensitivity of an object cannot be assessed confidently. Of course, by setting appropriate thresholds, a continuous CSA can be easily turned into a binary CSA task.

At this point, a congruent definition of "sensitivity" is required to set up the task correctly. Although different characterizations of privacy-sensitivity exist, there is no consistent and uniform theory [13]; so, in this work, we consider a more generic, flexible and application-driven definition of privacy-sensitive content.

Definition 3 (privacy-sensitive content). *A generic user-generated content object is privacy-sensitive if it makes* ***the majority of users*** *feel uncomfortable in writing or reading it because it may reveal some aspects of their own or others' private life to unintended people.*

Notice that "uncomfortableness" should not be guided by some moral or ethical judgement about the disclosed fact, but uniquely by its harmfulness towards privacy. Such a definition allows the adoption of the "wisdom of the crowd" principle in contexts where providing an objective definition of what is sensitive (and what is not sensitive) is particularly hard. Moreover, it has also an intuitive justification. Different social media may have different meaning of sensitivity. For instance, in a professional social networking site, revealing details about one's own job is not only tolerated, but also encouraged, while one may want to hide detailed information about her professional life in a generic photo-video sharing platform. Similarly, in a closed message board (or group), one may decide to disclose more private information than in open ones. Sensitivity towards certain topics also varies from country to country. As a consequence, function f_s can be learnt according to an annotated corpus of content objects as follows.

Definition 4 (sensitivity function learning). *Let* $O = \{(o_i, \sigma_i)\}_{i=1}^{N}$ *be a set of* N *annotated objects* $o_i \in \mathcal{O}$ *with the related sensitivity score* $\sigma_i \in [-1, 1]$*. The goal of a sensitivity function learning algorithm is to search for a function* $f_s : \mathcal{O} \rightarrow [-1, 1]$*, such that* $\sum_{i=1}^{N} (f_s(o_i) - \sigma_i)^2$ *is minimum.*

The simplest way to address this problem is by setting a regression (or classification, in the case of binary CSA) task. However, we will show in Section 3 that such an approach is unable to capture the actual manifold of sensitivity accurately.

3 Preliminary experiments

In this section, we report the results of some preliminary experiments aimed at showing the feasibility of content sensitivity analysis together with its difficulties. The experiments are conducted under the binary CSA framework (see Definition 1 in Section 2). We set up a binary classification task to distinguish whether a given input text is privacy-sensitive or not. Before presenting the results, in the following, we first introduce the data, then we provide the details of our experimental protocol.

3.1 Annotated corpus

Since all previous attempts of identifying sensitive text have leveraged user anonymity as a discriminant for sensitive content [8, 4], there is no reliable annotated corpus that we can use as benchmark. Hence, we construct our own dataset by leveraging a crowdsourcing experiment. We use one of the datasets described in [3], consisting of 9917 anonymized social media posts, mostly written in English, with a minimum length of 2 characters and a maximum length of 435 (the average length is 80). Thus, they well represent typical social media short posts. On the other hand, they are not annotated for the specific purpose of our experiment and, because of their shortness, they are also very difficult to analyze. Consequently, after discarding all useless posts (mostly uncomprehensible ones) we have set up a crowdsourcing experiment by using a Telegram bot that, for each post, asks whether it is sensitive or not. As third option, it was also possible to select "unable to decide". We collected the annotations of 829 posts from 14 distinct annotators. For each annotated post, we retain the most frequently chosen annotation. Overall, 449 posts where tagged as non sensitive, 230 as sensitive, 150 as undecidable. Thus, the final dataset consists of 679 posts of the first two categories (we discarded all 150 undecidable posts).

3.2 Datasets

We consider two distinct document representations for the dataset, a bag-of-words and four word vector models. To obtain the bag-of-word representation we perform the following steps. First, we remove all punctuation characters of terms contained in the input posts as well as short terms (less than two characters) and terms containing digits. Then, we build the bag-of-words model with all remaining 2584 terms weighted by their *tfidf* score. Differently from classic text mining approaches, we deliberately exclude lemmatization, stemming and stop word removal from text preprocessing, since those common steps would affect content sensitivity analysis negatively. Indeed, inflections (removed by lemmatization and stemming) and stop words (like "me", "myself") are important to decide whether a sentence reproduces some personal thoughts or private action/status. Hereinafter, the bag-of-words representation is referred to as *BW2584*.

The word vector representation, instead, is built using word vectors pre-trained with two billion tweets (corresponding to 42 billion tokens) using the *GloVe* (Global Vector) model [10]. In detail, we use three representation, here called *WV25*, *WV50* and *WV100* with, respectively, 25, 50 and 100 dimensions. Additionally, we build an ensemble by considering the concatenation of the three vector spaces. The latter representation is named *WVEns*. Finally, from all five datasets we removed all posts having an empty bag-of-words or word vector representation. Such preprocessing step further reduces the size of the dataset down to 611 posts (221 sensitive and 390 non sensitive), but allows for a fair performance comparison.

3.3 Experimental settings

Each dataset obtained as described beforehand is given in input to a set of six classifiers. In details, we use k-NN, decision tree (DT), Multi-layer Perceptron (MLP), SVM, Random Forest (RF), and Gradient Boosted trees (GBT). We do not execute any systematic parameter selection procedure since our main goal is not to compare the performances of classifiers, but, rather, to show the overall level of accuracy that can be achieved in a binary content sensitivity analysis task. Hence, we use the following default parameter for each classifier.

- **kNN**: we set $k = 3$ in all experiments;
- **DT**: for all datasets, we use C4.5 with Gini Index as split criterion, allowing a minimum of two records per node and minimum description length as pruning strategy;
- **MLP**: we train a shallow neural network with one hidden layer; the number of neurons of the hidden layer is 30 for the bag-of-words representation and 20 for all word vector representations;
- **SVM**: for all datasets, we use the polynomial kernel with default parameters;
- **RF**: we train 100 models with Gini index as splitting criterion in all experiments;
- **GBT**: for all datasets, we use 100 models with 0.1 as learning rate and 4 as maximum tree depth.

All experiments are conducted by performing ten-fold cross-validation, using, for each iteration, nine folds as training set and the remaining fold as test set.

3.4 Results and discussion

The summary of the results, in terms of average F1-score, are reported in Table 1. It is worth noting that the scores are, in general, very low (between 0.5826, obtained by the neural network on the bag-of-words model, and 0.6858, obtained

Table 1. Classification in terms of average F1-score for different post representations.

Dataset	Type	kNN	DT	MLP	SVM	RF	GBT
BW2584	bag-of-words	0.6579	0.6743	0.5826	0.6481	0.6776	0.6678
WV25	word vector	0.6203	0.6317	0.6497	0.6383	0.6628	0.6268
WV50	word vector	0.6121	0.6105	0.6530	0.6448	**0.6858**	0.6399
WV100	word vector	0.6367	0.6088	0.6497	0.6563	0.6694	0.6497
WVEns	word vector	0.6432	0.5859	0.6481	0.6547	0.6628	0.6416

by Random Forest on the word vector representation with 50 dimensions). Of course, these results are biased by the fact that data are moderately unbalanced (64% of posts fall in the non-sensible class). However they are not completely negative, meaning that there is space for improvement. We observe that the winning model-classifier pair (50-dimensional word vector processed with Random Forest) exhibits high recall on the non-sensitive class (0.928) and rather similar results in terms of precision for the two classes (0.671 and 0.688 for the sensitive and non-sensitive classes respectively). The real negative result is the low recall on the sensitive class (only 0.258), due to the high number of false negatives. We recall that the number of annotated sensitive posts is only 221, i.e., the number of examples is not sufficiently large for training a prediction model accurately.

These results highlight the following issues and perspectives. First, negative (or not-so-positive) results are certainly due to the lack of annotated data (especially for the sensitive class). Sparsity is certainly a problem in our settings. Hence, a larger annotated corpus is needed, although this objective is not trivial. In fact, private posts are often difficult to obtain, because social media platforms (luckily, somehow) do not allow users to get them using their API. As a consequence, all previous attempts to guess the sensitivity of text or construct privacy dictionaries strongly leverage user anonymity in public post sharing activities [8, 4], or rely on focus groups and surveys [13]. Moreover, without a sufficiently large corpus, not even the application of otherwise successful deep learning techniques would produce valid results. Second, simple classifiers, even when applied to rather complex and rich representations, can not capture the manifold of privacy sensitivity accurately. So, more complex and heterogenous models should be considered. An accurate sensitivity content analysis tool should consider lexical, semantic as well as grammatical features. Topics are certainly important, but sentence construction and lexical choices are also fundamental. Therefore, reliable solutions would consist of a combination of computational linguistic techniques, machine learning algorithms and semantic analysis. Third, the success of picture and video sharing platforms (such as Instagram and TikTok), implies that any successful sensitivity content analysis tool should be able to cope with audiovisual contents and, in general, with multimodal/multimedia objects. Finally, provided that a taxonomy of privacy categories in everyday life exists (e.g., health, location, politics, religious belief, family, relationships, and so on) a more complex CSA setting might consider, for a given content object, the privacy sensitivity degree in each category.

4 Conclusions

In this paper, we have addressed the problem of determining whether a given text object is privacy-sensitive or not by defining the generic task of content sensitivity analysis (CSA). Although the task promises to be challenging, we have shown that it is not unfeasible by presenting a simplified formulation of CSA based on binary text classification. With some preliminary but extensive experiments, we have showed that, no matter the data representation, the accuracy of such classifiers can not be considered satisfactory. Thus, it is worth investigating more complex techniques borrowed from machine learning, computational linguistics and semantic analysis. Moreover, without a strong effort in building massive and reliable annotated corpora, the performances of any CSA tool would be barely sufficient, no matter the complexity of the learning model.

Acknowledgments This work is supported by Fondazione CRT (grant number 2019-0450).

References

1. Alemany, J., del Val Noguera, E., Alberola, J.M., García-Fornes, A.: Metrics for Privacy Assessment When Sharing Information in Online Social Networks. IEEE Access **7**, 143631–143645 (2019)
2. Battaglia, E., Bioglio, L., Pensa, R.G.: Towards content sensitivity analysis. In: Proceedings of IDA 2020. pp. 67–79 (2020)
3. Celli, F., Pianesi, F., Stillwell, D., Kosinski, M.: Workshop on Computational Personality Recognition: Shared Task. In: Proceedings of ICWSM 2013 (2013)
4. Correa, D., Silva, L.A., Mondal, M., Benevenuto, F., Gummadi, K.P.: The Many Shades of Anonymity: Characterizing Anonymous Social Media Content. In: Proceedings of ICWSM 2015. pp. 71–80 (2015)
5. Liu, B., Zhang, L.: A Survey of Opinion Mining and Sentiment Analysis. In: Aggarwal, C.C., Zhai, C. (eds.) Mining Text Data, pp. 415–463. Springer (2012)
6. Oukemeni, S., Rifà-Pous, H., i Puig, J.M.M.: Privacy Analysis on Microblogging Online Social Networks: A Survey. ACM Comput. Surv. **52**(3), 60:1–60:36 (2019)
7. Pang, B., Lee, L.: Opinion Mining and Sentiment Analysis. Foundations and Trends in Information Retrieval **2**(1-2), 1–135 (2007)
8. Peddinti, S.T., Korolova, A., Bursztein, E., Sampemane, G.: Cloak and Swagger: Understanding Data Sensitivity through the Lens of User Anonymity. In: Proceedings of IEEE SP 2014. pp. 493–508 (2014)
9. Peddinti, S.T., Ross, K.W., Cappos, J.: User Anonymity on Twitter. IEEE Security & Privacy **15**(3), 84–87 (2017)
10. Pennington, J., Socher, R., Manning, C.D.: Glove: Global Vectors for Word Representation. In: Proceedings of EMNLP 2014. pp. 1532–1543 (2014)
11. Pensa, R.G., di Blasi, G., Bioglio, L.: Network-aware privacy risk estimation in online social networks. Social Netw. Analys. Mining **9**(1), 15:1–15:15 (2019)
12. Pensa, R.G., Blasi, G.D.: A privacy self-assessment framework for online social networks. Expert Syst. Appl. **86**, 18–31 (2017)
13. Vasalou, A., Gill, A.J., Mazanderani, F., Papoutsi, C., Joinson, A.N.: Privacy dictionary: A new resource for the automated content analysis of privacy. JASIST **62**(11), 2095–2105 (2011)

User Emotion Detection via Taxonomy Management: An Innovative System

Alfredo Cuzzocrea[1], Giovanni Pilato[2], and Edoardo Fadda[3]

[1] University of Calabria, Rende, Italy
alfredo.cuzzocrea@unical.it
[2] ICAR-CNR, Palermo, Italy
giovanni.pilato@cnr.it
[3] Politecnico di Torino, Torino, Italy
edoardo.fadda@polito.it

Abstract. Catching the attention of a new acquaintance and empathize with her can improve the social skills of a robot. For this reason, we illustrate here the first step towards a system which can be used by a social robot in order to "break the ice" between a robot and a new acquaintance. After a training phase, the robot acquires a sub-symbolic coding of the main concepts being expressed in tweets about the IAB Tier-1 categories. Then this knowledge is used to catch the new acquaintance interests, which let arouse in her a joyful sentiment. The analysis process is done alongside a general small talk, and once the process is finished, the robot can propose to talk about something that catches the attention of the user, hopefully letting arise in him a mix of feelings which involve surprise and joy, triggering, therefore, an engagement between the user and the social robot.

1 Introduction

Engagement is one of the most basic and important phases in interactions between human beings. In the last years there has been a growing interest about this topic throughout the human-machine-interaction (HMI) and related fields [6]. Researchers have highlighted that engagement is a very complex phenomenon, including both cognitive and affective components: it should involve attention and enjoyment [3] [15].

We refer to this term as the "starting or intention to start an interaction". In particular, we focus our attention on the fact that, in making new acquaintances, the first impression is very important, and finding as soon as possible common interests to talk about, allows starting an empathetic interaction between two persons, with all that this implies.

In order to trigger both attention and enjoyment, given these premises, it would

be useful to design a social robotic system which tries to find the topic of interest of a new acquaintance while attempting to understand what might raise a sentiment of joy attempting to catch an empathetic attention of the user.
As a matter of fact, the knowledge of the topics of interest and the "joyful" subjects for the user can lead the first stages of a conversational interaction that allows the robot to facilitate the engagement of a friendly interaction, instead of a classical trivial interaction between a robot and an human user.
To reach this goal, the robot can access the social network data of the new acquaintance trying to coarsely profile her/his interests, catching useful information to engage a possibly interesting conversation for the user.
Social networks represent a great place, maybe the best, to gather information about people's opinions, since they are generally used to express personal thoughts and to discuss with other people about specific subjects [12][30]. These opinions are really useful to understand and classify the emotion of an event, a product, a person, etc. and analyze his trend [21][22][13].

In this paper we illustrate the design of a system which can be used by a social robot in order to "break the ice" between the robot and a new acquaintance.
First of all, the robot acquires a knowledge about the construction of prototypes describing each entry of the IAB Taxonomy.

The system needs a training phase where fundamental concepts, induced by a data driven construction of a conceptual space by using the Latent Semantic Analysis (LSA) procedure and a set of topics derived by the Latent Dirichlet Allocation (LDA) methodology, representing the Tier1 categories of the IAB v2.0 taxonomy are mapped in a semantic space.
A set of tweets is therefore retrieved for each word describing each entry of the IAB Taxonomy. A set of words describing the conceptual axes of two "conceptual spaces" induced from each set of tweets associated to a single IAB entry is built. Each conceptual axis is therefore described by a specific "bag of words" which constitute the axis description. Each axis is therefore coded as a vector in a semantic space built through LSA, and it is associated to the specific IAB entry. At the end of the procedure, each entry of the IAB taxonomy is associated to set of vectors, associated to the labels of each fundamental axis of the category, in the built semantic space.

On the other hand, a system which is able to detect a pattern of basic Eckman emotions [24], given a text, is trained too.
Once the system is trained, during a general conversation with a new acquaintance, the robot asks for the user Twitter ID, and while the conversation continues, it retrieves the most recent tweets of the user.
Each tweet is then encoded as a vector in a semantic space. The semantic similarity between each tweet and each vector representing each entry of the IAB taxonomy is computed, and the highest value of similarity is retained.
The above procedure allows to associate a tweet of the user to a pattern of IAB categories; furthermore, for each tweet a vector of Eckman fundamental emotions is computed. This leads to a selection of the Tier1 categories of the IAB taxonomy which are of interest of the user and that let arise in the user a specific

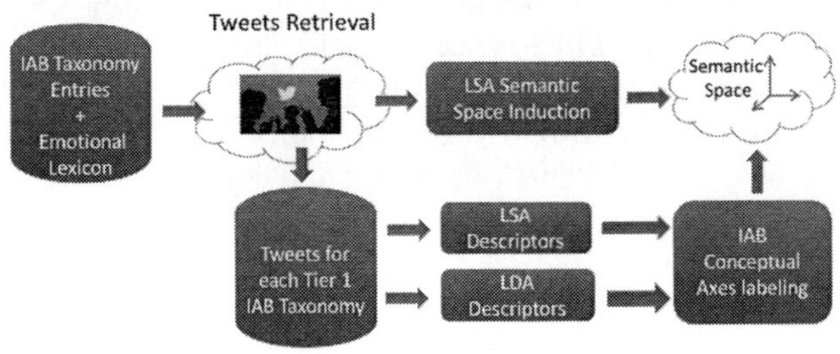

Fig. 1. *Training process*

emotion. In our case we have chosen to select the "joy" emotion, which is the most desirable when a person meets for the first time another human being.

The goal is to engage a conversation somehow polarizing it on topics that catch the attention of the user, trying to establish an empathetic relationship. Under some extensions, this approach has relationships with *adaptive metaphors*, like those developed in other scientific contexts (e.g., [5]).

2 The System

The proposed system is composed of a set of modules interacting in order to catch the attention of the user. The modularity of the proposed architecture makes it suitable to be implemented on top of Cloud infrastructure (e.g., [10]). The system has a training phase, shown in Fig.1, where a semantic space S is induced from Twitter data and a joyful-topic-detection process, illustrated in Fig. 2, which exploits the Twitter ID of the user in order to retrieve her posts and trying to catch the interests of the user that somehow let arise a "joy" emotion.

2.1 The IAB Taxonomy

The IAB (Interactive Advertising Bureau) Tech Lab Content Taxonomy is a concise taxonomy which is also an international standard to map contextual business categories [17] [18]. The latest release of the taxonomy, namely version 2.0, has been released on November 2017 and it accounts 698 entries distributed over 29 Tier-1 classes.
This taxonomy is particularly suited for being used by companies in the market, it is standardized and industry-neutral. These characteristics can be effectively exploited for profiling an user interests.

2.2 Tweets retrieval module

The dataset object of analysis is retrieved by using the Twitter APIs with the default access level. The default access level gives a random sample of the streaming

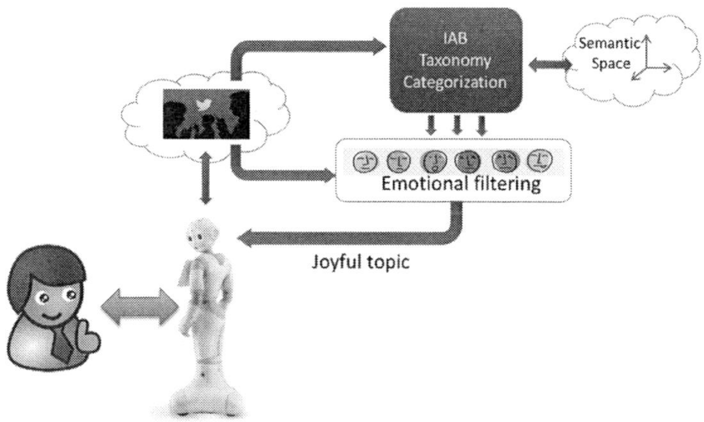

Fig. 2. *Joyful-topic-detection process*

of publicly available tweets. For our approach, we use only the tweet text content, which is preprocessed before being exploited to build a data-driven conceptual space. Stop-words are filtered out, and links are removed before processing the text since they often hide off-topic posts or even spam. Abnormal sequences of characters were discarded. The retrieval module can be used either for retrieving tweets satisfying a query composed of keywords or to download the last tweets of a given twitter user ID.

2.3 LSA-based Descriptors

The Latent Semantic Analysis (LSA) technique is a well-known methodology that is capable of giving a coarse sub-symbolic encoding of word semantics [20] and of simulating several human cognitive phenomena [19]. The LSA procedure is based on a term-document occurrence matrix $\mathbf{A}$, whose generic element represents the number of times a term is present in a document. Let K be the rank of $\mathbf{A}$. The factorization named Singular Value Decomposition (SVD) holds for the matrix $\mathbf{A}$:

$$\mathbf{A} = \mathbf{U}\Sigma\mathbf{V}^T \tag{1}$$

Let R be an integer > 0 with $R < N$, and let $\mathbf{U}_R$ be the $M \times R$ matrix obtained from $\mathbf{U}$ by suppressing the last $N - R$ columns, let $\mathbf{\Sigma}_R$ be the matrix obtained from $\mathbf{\Sigma}$ by suppressing the last $N - R$ rows and the last $N - R$ columns; let $\mathbf{V}_R$ be the $N \times R$ matrix obtained from $\mathbf{V}$ by suppressing the last $N - R$ columns. Then:

$$\mathbf{A}_R = \mathbf{U}_R\Sigma_R\mathbf{V}_R^T \tag{2}$$

$\mathbf{A}_R$ is a $M \times N$ matrix of rank R, and it is the best rank R approximation of $\mathbf{A}$ (among the $M \times N$ matrices) with respect to the Frobenius metric. The i-th row of the matrix $\mathbf{U}_R$ may be considered as representative of the i-th word.

The columns of the $\mathbf{U}_R$ matrix represent the R independent dimensions of the $\Re^{\Re}$ space S. Each j-th dimension is weighted by the corresponding value σ_j of $\mathbf{\Sigma}_R$. Furthermore, each j-th dimension can be tagged by considering the words having the highest module values of u_{ij}. This makes it possible to interpret the space S as a "conceptual" space, according to the procedure illustrated in [1][25].

2.4 LDA-based Descriptors

In the last years a Bayesian probabilistic model of text corpora, namely the Latent Dirichlet Allocation (LDA), has been proposed with the aim of finding topics in documents [2] by associating a set of words to each topic, obtaining a rough representation of a textual corpus.

One on the main advantages of LDA, like LSA, is the fact that the approach is completely unsupervisedThe only thing required by LDA to setup a priori is the number N of topics to extract. Latent topics are discovered through the identification of sets of words in the corpus that often occur together within documents. LDA is based on a generative process according to these two steps:

- For each topic $n = 1, 2, \cdots, N$, $\phi^{(n)} \sim Dirichlet(\beta)$ is a discrete probability distribution over a fixed Vocabulary constituting the $n-th$ topic distribution, and β is a hyperparameter for the symmetric Dirichlet distribution.
- For each document d_k of the document corpus, $\theta_{d_k} \sim Dirichlet(\alpha)$, which is a symmetric Dirichlet distribution for the specific document d_k over the available topics is computed. θ_{d_k} is a low dimensional coding of d_k in the topic space. For each word w_i belonging to the d_k document, $z_i \sim Discrete(\theta_{d_j})$ and $w_i \sim Discrete(\phi^{(z_i)})$ are being computed, where z_i is the topic index for w_i

The above process leads to the following distribution

$$p(\mathbf{w}, \mathbf{z}, \theta, \phi|\alpha, \beta) = p(\phi|\beta)p(\theta|\alpha)p(\mathbf{z}|\theta)p(\mathbf{w}|\phi_z) \tag{3}$$

where $\mathbf{z}, \theta, \phi$ are the latent variables of interest In LDA the posterior inference is given by:

$$p(\theta, \phi, \mathbf{z}|\mathbf{w}, \alpha, \beta) = \frac{p(\theta, \phi, \mathbf{z}|\mathbf{w}, \alpha, \beta)}{p(\mathbf{w}|\alpha, \beta)} \tag{4}$$

which represents the learning of the latent variables given the observed data. The above formula is usually computed through variational inference and Gibbs sampling, as reported in literature [14][2][29]

2.5 Emotion Detection Module

This module deals with the detection of emotions in tweets. For the emotional labeling of tweets, we have considered the six Ekman basic emotions: *anger*, *disgust*, *fear*, *joy*, *sadness* and *surprise*, exploiting an emotions lexicon obtained from the Word-Net Affect Lexicon, as described in [26] [27] and adopting a

procedure that has been illustrated in [24], which we briefly recap below.
The methodology is based on LSA and starts from the fact that any text d can be mapped into a Data Driven "conceptual" space in the sense illustrated above, by computing a vector $\mathbf{d}$ whose i-th component is the number of times the i-th word of the vocabulary, corresponding to the i-th row of $\mathbf{U}_R$, appears in d. This leads to the mapping of the text as:

$$\mathbf{d}_R = \mathbf{d}^T \mathbf{U}_R \Sigma_R^{-1} \tag{5}$$

The emotional lexicon has been split into six lists, each one associated to one of the basic Ekman emotions {*anger, disgust, fear, joy, sadness, surprise*}. Fixed an emotion e, a set of 300 artificial sentences has been built by using five randomly selected words belonging to the list related to e. This procedure has been done for each list associated with a fundamental Ekman emotion, leading to a set of 1800 artificial sentences. Furthermore, all the 1542 words of the lexicon have been considered. Each one of the 3342 (i.e. 1542+1800) b texts associated with an emotion e has been mapped into the data driven "conceptual space" induced by TSVD according to the transformation in eq.(2). The above procedure leads to a cloud of 3342 (i.e. 1542+1800) vectors that have been used to map a tweet from the conceptual space to the emotional space. In particular, we have six sets $E_{anger}, E_{disgust}, \cdots, E_{surprise}$ of vectors constituting the sub-symbolic coding of the words belonging to the lexicon for a particular emotion together with their artifact sentences. The generic vector belonging to one of the sets will be denoted in the following as $\mathbf{b}_i^{(e)}$ where $e \in \{\text{"}anger\text{"}, \text{"}disgust\text{"}, \text{"}fear\text{"}, \text{"}joy\text{"}, \text{"}sadness\text{"}, \text{"}surprise\text{"}\}$ and i is the index that identifies the i-th $\mathbf{b}_i^{(e)}$ in the e set. Specifically, $\mathbf{b}_i^{(e)}$ is computed as:

$$\mathbf{b}_i^{(e)} = \mathbf{b}^T \mathbf{U}_R \Sigma_R^{-1} \tag{6}$$

where $\mathbf{b}$ is, time by time, the vector computed starting from one of the 3342 textual artifacts b according to the procedure illustrated at the beginning of this section.
Analogously, any textual content t of a tweet can be mapped into the Data Driven "conceptual" space by computing a vector $\mathbf{t}$ whose i-th component in the number of times the i-th word of the vocabulary, corresponding to the i-th row of $\mathbf{U}_R$, appears in t. This leads to the mapping of the tweet as:

$$\mathbf{t}_R = \mathbf{t}^T \mathbf{U}_R \Sigma_R^{-1} \tag{7}$$

Once the tweet t is mapped into the "conceptual" space as a vector $\mathbf{t}_R$, it is possible to compute its emotional fingerprint by exploiting the vectors $\mathbf{b}_i^{(e)}$, which act as "beacons" for the vector $\mathbf{t}_R$, helping in finding its position inside the conceptual space.
In particular, fixed $\mathbf{t}_R$, for each set E_e it is computed the weight:

$$w_e = \max cos(\mathbf{t}_R, \mathbf{b}_i^{(e)}) \tag{8}$$

once all the six w_e weights are computed, the vector $\mathbf{f}_t$, associated to the vector $\mathbf{t}_R$, and by consequence to the tweet t, is calculated as:

$$\mathbf{f}_t = \left[\frac{w_{(anger)}}{\sqrt{\sum_e w_e^2}}, \frac{w_{(fear)}}{\sqrt{\sum_e w_e^2}}, \ldots, \frac{w_{(surprise)}}{\sqrt{\sum_e w_e^2}} \right] \quad (9)$$

The vector $\mathbf{f}_t$ finally constitutes the *emotional fingerprint* of the tweet t in the emotional space. The emotional space is therefore a six-dimensional hypersphere where all tweets can be mapped and grouped. We call the fingerprint $\mathbf{f}_t$ "emoxel", analogously as the *knoxel* in the conceptual space paradigm [4].

2.6 Conversational Engine

The conversational engine exploits a speech-recognition module which makes use of the Google speech recognition APIs; after that the speech-to-text task is performed, the recognized string is sent to a dialogue manager. A set of question-answer rules are set-up into the conversation engine in order to start a conversation that leads to the detection of the user interests by transparently invoking the most adequate procedures which analyze the social network posts of the new acquaintance.
The conversational agent engine allows for a natural human-robot interaction. The conversational module is based on a Rivescript engine, which is a a simple scripting language for realizing chatbots and other conversational entities.
We have chosen this kind of engine because of the following interesting features: it is plain text, line-based scripting language, simple to learn, quick to type, and easy to read and maintain [23]. The syntax required to build a Rivescript "knowledge base" is very simple: Question-Answers pairs are encoded in plain text; it is easy to write a set of rules that can be combined to build effective conversational agents; its core library is focused on rendering responses, and it is straightforward to make custom modules and scripts; last but not least is an Open Source tool released under the MIT license [28].
The choice of such an engine allows us to easily connect it to other kind of robots or other kind of services. As a matter of fact, the conversational engine is invoked through a REST service and the answer is delivered to the user after its processing.
A Rivescript knowledge base is made up of *Triggers/Replies* pairs. *Triggers* are identified by a "+" sign, while *Replies* are denoted by a "-" sign.
For example:

```
+ hi
- Hello there, my name is SocialRobot,
  please could you tell me your twitter ID?
```

the above pair makes it possible that whenever the user says "Hi", the conversational engine replies with "Hello there, my name is SocialRobot, please could you tell me your twitter ID? ".
At the beginning of the conversation, a specific Rivescript *Topic* is activated.

Topics are logical groupings of triggers. When the conversation is bound in a topic, what the user says can only match triggers that belong to the activated topic [23].
The topic is aimed at entertain a general conversation while the robot peeks the tweets of the user trying to roughly identify the subjects that interest the user and those that specifically trigger joyful emotions. Once the predominant subject has been identified, the robot activates another Rivescript Topic which is of particular interest for the user, trying to establish an empathetic engagement with the new acquaintance.
As an example, let us say that the system finds that, among the different higher level categories of the IAB taxonomy, the user is particularly interested in the "Automobiles" topic and that some of his tweets show the "joy" emotion for that topic, the conversation will be switched to the "Automobile" Topic and specific sentences will be said by the robot in order to catch the user attention and empathy, like "Great! with my superpowers I can see that you like automobiles. I like the *brand* automobiles! Which one do you prefer?"

3 Conclusions and future works

We have presented a preliminary work on a system that tries to catch the attention of a new acquaintance with the aim of establishing a first engagement with the user.
The system uses both LSA and LDA descriptors, as well as an emotion detection module to reach this goal. A conversational engine guides the initial process and continues with*t* the conversation.
Many issues have to be enhanced, starting from a more fine grained classification which should be also fast and reliable, the selection of specific entities that can catch in a more effective manner the attention of the user, as well as the automatic generation of conversational statements starting from the user tweets. Other lines of research shall consider privacy-preservation issues (e.g., [8, 11]), as well as complex web intelligent solutions (e.g., [7, 9]).

References

1. F. Agostaro, A. Augello, G. Pilato, G. Vassallo, and S. Gaglio, "A conversational agent based on a conceptual interpretation of a data driven semantic space.," Lecture Notes in Artificial Intelligence, vol. 3673, no. 2, pp. 381–392, 2005.
2. Blei, D., Ng, A., and Jordan, M. Latent Dirichlet allocation. Journal of Machine Learning Research,3:993–1022, January 2003.
3. Brethes L, Menezes P, Lerasle F, Hayet J (2004) Face tracking and hand gesture recognition for human–robot interaction. In: IEEE international conference on robotics and automation, vol 2. IEEE, pp 1901–1906
4. Chella, A., Frixione, M., and Gaglio, S. (2008) A cognitive architecture for robot self consciousness. Artificial intelligence in medicine, 44(2): 147–154
5. Cannataro M., Cuzzocrea A., and Pugliese A. (2001) A Probabilistic Approach to Model Adaptive Hypermedia Systems. In: 1st Int. Workshop on Web Dynamics, in conjunction on ICDT 2001
6. Corrigan Lee J., Peters C., Küster D. and Castellano G. (2016) Engagement Perception and Generation for Social Robots and Virtual Agents - Toward Robotic Socially Believable Behaving Systems - Volume I, Intelligent Systems Reference Library 105, pp 29-51, Springer

7. Cuzzocrea, A. (2006) Combining multidimensional user models and knowledge representation and management techniques for making web services knowledge-aware. Web Intell. Agent Syst. 4(3): 289-312
8. Cuzzocrea A., and Bertino, E. (2011) Privacy Preserving OLAP over Distributed XML Data: A Theoretically-Sound Secure-Multiparty-Computation Approach. J. Comput. Syst. Sci. 77(6): 965-987
9. Cuzzocrea A., De Maio C., Fenza G., Loia V., and Parente M. (2016) OLAP analysis of multidimensional tweet streams for supporting advanced analytics. In: AMC SAC 2016, pp. 992-999
10. Cuzzocrea A., Fortino G., and Rana O. (2013) Managing Data and Processes in Cloud-Enabled Large-Scale Sensor Networks: State-of-the-Art and Future Research Directions. In: 13th IEEE/ACM International Symposium on Cluster, Cloud, and Grid Computing, CCGrid 2013, pp. 583–588
11. Cuzzocrea A., and Russo V. (2009) Privacy Preserving OLAP and OLAP Security. Encyclopedia of Data Warehousing and Mining 2009, pp. 1575-1581
12. D'Avanzo E., Pilato G. (2014) Mining social network users opinions' to aid buyers' shopping decisions. Computers in Human Behavior, Elsevier, Vol.51, pp 1284-1294
13. D'Avanzo E., Pilato G., and Lytras M. D.. Using twitter sentiment and emotions analysis of google trends for decisions making. In Program, pages Vol. 51, Issue 3. 2017.
14. Darling WM. A theoretical and practical implementation tutorial on topic modeling and gibbs sampling. Proceedings of the 49th annual meeting of the association for computational linguistics: Human language technologies 2011 Dec 1 (pp. 642-647).
15. Delaherche E, Dumas G, Nadel J, Chetouani M (2014) Automatic measure of imitation during social interaction: a behavioral and hyperscanning-eeg benchmark. Pattern Recognit Lett.
16. Ekman P., Friesen W V. Constants across cultures in the face and emotion., Journal of personality and social psychology 17:124, 1971.
17. Interactive Advertising Bureau (IAB) Contextual Taxonomy, http://www.iab.net/ Retrieved December 2017
18. Kanagasabai, R., Veeramani, A., Ngan, L. D., Yap, G. E., Decraene, J., Nash, A. S. (2014). Using Semantic Technologies to Mine Customer Insights in Telecom Industry. In International Semantic Web Conference (Industry Track).
19. Landauer, T. K., and Dumais, S. T. "A solution to Plato's problem: The latent semantic analysis theory of acquisition, induction, and representation of knowledge", In Psychological review, vol. 104(2), 1990, pp. 211-223.
20. Landauer, T. K., Foltz, P. W. and Laham, D. " An introduction to latent semantic analysis", In Discourse processes, vol. 25, 1998, pp. 259-284.
21. Liu, B. (2010). Sentiment Analysis and Subjectivity. In N. Indurkhya, & F. J.Damerau, Handbook of Natural Language Processing (pp. 627-665). CRC Press.
22. Pang, B., Lee, L., and Vaithyanathan, S. (2002). Thumbs up? Sentiment Classification using Machine Learning Techniques. In Proceedings of the ACL-02 conference on Empirical methods in natural language processing - Volume 10 (pp. 79-86). Association for Computational Linguistics.
23. Petherbridge, N. "Artifical Intelligence Scripting Language - Rivescript.com," (online)
24. G. Pilato, E. D'Avanzo - Data-driven Social Mood Analysis through the Conceptualization of Emotional Fingerprints - Procedia Computer Science, 2018, (in press)
25. Santilli, S., Nota, L., Pilato, G.: The use of latent semantic analysis in the positive psychology: A comparison with twitter posts. In: Semantic Computing (ICSC), 2017 IEEE 11th International Conference on. pp. 494–498. IEEE (2017)
26. C. Strapparava and R Mihalcea. Semeval-2007 task 14: Affective text. In Proceedings of the 4th International Workshop on Semantic Evaluations, pages 70–74. Association for Computational Linguistics, 2007.
27. C. Strapparava and R Mihalcea. Learning to identify emotions in text. In SAC '08 Proceedings of the 2008 ACM symposium on Applied computing. 2008.
28. Siddharth, G., Borkar, D., De Mello, C., Patil, S. "An E-Commerce Website based Chatbot" Proc of. (IJCSIT) International Journal of Computer Science and Information Technologies, Vol. 6 (2) , 2015, 1483-1485
29. Teh, Y. W., Newman, D., Welling, M. A collapsed variational Bayesian inference algorithm for latent Dirichlet allocation. In NIPS, Vol. 6, pp. 1378-1385, 2006
30. Terrana D., Augello A., Pilato (2014). Facebook users relationships analysis based on sentiment classification. Proc. of 2014 IEEE International Conference on Seman- tic Computing (ICSC), pp. 290-296

jKarma: a Highly-Modular Framework for Pattern-Based Change Detection on Evolving Data (Discussion Paper)

Angelo Impedovo, Corrado Loglisci, Michelangelo Ceci, Donato Malerba

Dept. of Computer Science, University of Bari "Aldo Moro", Bari, Italy
{name.surname}@uniba.it

Abstract. Pattern-based change detection (PBCD) describes a class of change detection algorithms for evolving data. Contrary to conventional solutions, PBCD seeks changes exhibited by the patterns over time and therefore works on an abstract form of the data, which prevents the search for changes on the raw data. Moreover, PBCD provides arguments on the validity of the results because patterns mirror changes occurred with any form of evidence. However, the existing solutions differ on data representation, mining algorithm and change identification strategy, which we can deem as main modules of a general architecture, so that any PBCD task could be designed by accommodating custom implementations for those modules. This is what we propose in this paper through *jKarma*, a highly-modular framework for designing and performing PBCD.

Keywords: Change Detection, Evolving Data, Software Framework

1 Introduction

Pattern-based change detection (PBCD) refers to the class of change detection solutions able to find out data-points in which the data distribution changes by acting on the patterns rather than on raw data. Despite the attention it could raise, we ascertain lacking in comprehensive environments able to investigate the problem with alternative solutions or even with integrable implementations. Its main peculiarity is working in an unsupervised fashion, without relying on labeling, which often makes it preferable to the supervised approaches.

The blueprint relies on three main methodological decisions, that is, data description, pattern mining algorithm, and change identification strategy. Pattern mining algorithms are in charge of building an abstract representation of the evolving data (patterns). The change identification strategy is in charge of searching for changes expressed by the patterns by the effect of possible distribution drifts in the underlying data. In PBCDs, the changes correspond to variations that occurred on the patterns discovered over time. While the decision on which technique to use for the pattern mining and change identification components determines the algorithmic aspects of a PBCD solution, the data representation strictly concerns the formalism of the evolving data, characteristics of the original data to consider and pattern language. For instance, the PBCDs implemented in [1,2] identify the changes through a generic notion of Jaccard dissimilarity defined for three different types of patterns, that is, *frequent subnetworks*, and *δ-closed itemsets*.

Our purpose is to provide the users with a software framework that supports the study of a predictive problem (change detection) through an unsupervised data mining task (pattern mining) while disseminating existing PBCDs and promoting the development of new ones. As our best knowledge, this is the first solution that combines change detection and pattern mining, while they have been explored as separate tasks in existing frameworks. For instance, MOA [3] has been designed to work on evolving data and offers algorithms that deal with concept drift in predictive tasks. SPMF [4] presents several classes of patterns (such as, sequential patterns and periodic patterns), but no one defined for change detection. In this discussion paper, we accomplish this with jKarma, a framework written in Java and proposed in [5] which offers loosely coupled modules, does not require programming efforts and enables the use of reusable, off-the-shelf and ad-hoc implementations for algorithmic components.

2 Background and PBCD architecture

In this section we provide preliminary notions and explain the conceptual architecture under which PBCD solutions can be collocated. Given the set of items I, a transactional database is the time-ordered sequence $D = \langle T_1, T_2, \dots, T_n \rangle$. Each $T_i \subseteq I$ is a transaction observed in t_i and uniquely identified by id i. Thus, a pattern $P \subseteq I$ is a set of $|P|$ items, and, for PBCD purposes, they are discovered from transactions in time windows. A window $W = [t_i, t_j]$, with $t_i < t_j$, is the sequence of $|W| = j - i + 1$ transactions $\{T_i, \dots, T_j\} \subseteq D$. P_W denotes the set of patterns discovered on the window W.

In the blueprint of PBCD, the *Mining step* and the *Identification step* search for change-points on evolving data by using *Time-windows models*. In particular, two time-windows W and W', $W = [t_b, t_e]$ and $W' = [t'_b, t'_e]$ ($t_b \leq t'_b \leq t_{e+1}$, $t_e < t'_e$) are built (Figure 1, Step 2) and input to a pattern mining algorithm, which discovers two pattern sets P_W and $P_{W'}$ (Figure 1, Step 3). In these terms, the changes are attributed to the patterns which make P_W different from $P_{W'}$. In particular, we can determine the *i)* amount of the change through a quantification of the difference between the two pattern sets, *ii)* temporal collocation of the changes (change-points) as the time in which the difference-patterns occur (Figure 1, Step 4). For this core procedure, jKarma offers a general architecture that supports software modularity (Figure 1). It makes the decisions on the specific

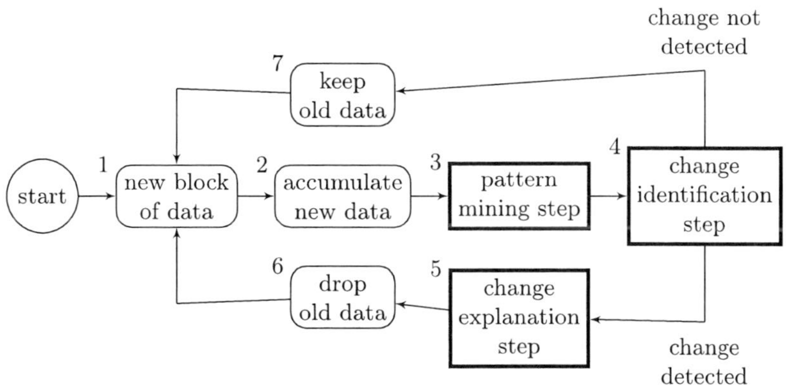

Fig. 1: Overview of the PBCD architecture

implementation for *Time-windows models*, *Mining step* and *Identification step* independent from each other. Indeed, the time-window models allow us to build sub-sequences of data regardless of their original structure (such as, itemsets, subgraphs, subtrees) and the choice of the specific model to use (such as, sliding, landmark, tilted) is not constrained neither by pattern mining nor change identification, since the time-windows are only in charge of to scan evolving data and account for new (recent) transactions and old (past) transactions (Figure 1, Steps 2, 6 and 7). The sole assumption of jKarma is the the availability of evolving data in the form of transactional databases.

The Identification step (Figure 1, Step 4) is in charge of spotting variations which the new pattern set $P_{W'}$ presents in comparison with the old pattern set P_W. To do that, jKarma makes available different implementations of dissimilarity measures (such as Jaccard dissimilarity, etc.) defined on several notions of evidence of the patterns (such as relative frequency, frequency ratio, periodicity, etc.). Not all the dissimilarity values are worthwhile of interest, but only those that exceed a desired degree of change, as well as, not all the patterns exhibit a variation in the evidence, but only that exceed a desired degree of evidence. This enables jKarma to provide "explanations" of the changes in the form of patterns that better express the underlying changes (Figure 1, Step 5).

3 Software Framework & Functionalities

jKarma is an open-source highly-modular framework written in Java 8 for defining and executing custom PBCDs. The framework, publicly available under the Apache License 2.0, exposes an API easing the rapid prototyping of custom PBCD strategies, tailored for data coming from transactional data sources, by implementing the general architecture seen in Section 2. Custom PBCDs are in-

https://jkarma.bitbucket.io/

stantiated by composition, meaning that existing modules for the pattern mining, change identification and change explanation steps can be combined to design PBCDs ready to be used. Every PBCD defined with jKarma is completely independent from other data mining and machine learning libraries, and third-parties data sources, thus offering two advantages, *i)* integrability with existing projects using their data sources (such as, relational databases, graph databases, xml documents), and *ii)* interoperability with existing analytics frameworks.

The framework has been developed as a multi-module Maven project in which two modules expose the APIs for defining custom pattern mining strategies (`jkarma-mining`) and custom PBCDs pipelines on top of previously defined pattern mining strategies (`jkarma-pbcd`). In particular, the main functionalities are served by two main factory classes: *i)* `org.jkarma.mining.structures.Strategies` constructs `MiningStrategy` objects implementing the pattern mining algorithm to be used in the *Mining step* of the PBCD architecture,
ii) `org.jkarma.pbcd.detectors.Detectors` constructs `PBCD` objects implementing the details of every step involved in the PBCD architecture.

The expressiveness of the programming interface enables the modular design of custom PBCD strategies. This is done by reusing existing software for the (*mining step* and *identification step*) in the PBCD architecture. In the current version, it is possible to devise PBCDs based on 5 pattern mining algorithms (Eclat, diffEclat, LCM and LCM-Max, and PFPM), 3 pattern languages (itemsets, subgraphs, subtrees), 4 time-window models (blockwise sliding/landmark, cumulative sliding/landmark) and 2 search algorithms (depth-first search and beam search). Furthermore, the API allows the user to implement his modules when necessary.

4 Illustrative Examples

In this section, we report some illustrative examples of how jKarma can be used for building different PBCDs by following a component-based architectural model. Specifically, in the following we will show how the user can specify the details about the *Mining step*, the *Detection step*, and the *Explanation step* in a two-step approach: the first step uses the `Strategies` class to define a `MiningStrategy` object, while the second step injects it into a `PBCD` object via the `Detectors` class. It is evident that the choices are domain-specific and affect the behavior of the PBCDs, thus resulting in different change detection results.

4.1 Definition of mining strategies

The mining strategy is defined by instantiating a generic `MiningStrategy<A,B>` object, hence by specifying the set of items (of type `A`), the pattern language, the pattern evidence criterion (implemented in a class of type `B`), the mining algorithm and the search strategy of patterns. Listing 1.1 shows the definition of a mining strategy, based on the Eclat algorithm, which searches for connected subgraphs. The pattern evidence criterion filters out frequent connected subgraphs

(FCSs) whose frequency is lower than the minimum threshold (`minSupp`). Eclat computes the frequency of a pattern by inspecting its *tidset*, a data structure collecting the identifiers of the transactions in which the pattern occurs.

```
public MiningStrategy<LabeledEdge, TidSet>
defineStrategy(double minSupp) {
    TidsetProvider<LabeledEdge> accessor = new TidsetProvider<>(Windows.blockwiseSliding());
    return Strategies.uponSubgraphs().eclat(minSupp)
        .limitDepth(3).dfs(accessor);
}
```

Listing 1.1: FCS mining strategy based on Eclat.

The strategy, which is an object of type `MiningStrategy <LabeledEdge, TidSet>`, is instantiated by the `uponSubgraphs` method that specifies the FCSs pattern language. The `eclat` method injects the mining algorithm into the mining strategy, while the `limitDepth` method limits the maximum number of edges in every FCS. Then, an instance of type `TidsetProvider <LabeledEdge>` (`accessor`) scans the transactions and build the tidsets. Finally, the `dfs` method finalizes the strategy and forces the Eclat algorithm to run in a DFS fashion.

An interesting aspect is that Eclat is used to mine FCSs, while natively it is a frequent itemset mining algorithm. In fact, in jKarma the pattern language is decoupled from the mining algorithm, so that equivalent strategies on different languages (e.g.: itemsets and subtrees) can be defined. For instance, the Eclat algorithm can be forced to discover frequent subtrees by replacing the `uponSubgraphs` method with the `uponSubtrees` one. However, since both the strategies are based on the Eclat algorithm, they will compute the frequencies of patterns by intersecting `TidSet` objects. Although this is a good choice on sparse datasets, it could be time-consuming for dense datasets [6], for which the diffEclat algorithm is more appropriate, since the frequency is computed using `DiffSet` data structures. In jKarma, mining strategies based on *diffEclat* are easily instantiated by i) invoking the `diffEclat` method instead of the `eclat` method, and ii) replacing the `TidsetProvider` data accessor with a `DiffsetProvider`. However, the main pitfall of the mining strategies discussed so far is their exhaustiveness, which leads to the discovery of complete sets of patterns. The exhaustive search is caused by the `dfs` method, which forces the mining algorithm to work in exhaustive mode. jKarma can be used to define non-exhaustive strategies based on beam-search and heuristics as done in [7].

4.2 Definition of PBCDs

As introduced in Section 2, PBCD relies on the sets of patterns P_W and $P_{W'}$ to i) compute the dissimilarity score $d(P_W, P_{W'})$ and quantify the degree of change and ii) arrange a change explanation. The dissimilarity score is computed on two equally-sized vector encodings F_W and $F_{W'}$, in which the i-th element corresponds to the weight associated with the i-th pattern in the enumeration of $P_W \cup P_{W'}$. This way, the change is quantified through vector measures, instead of set-based ones. Different weighting schemes and vector encodings could determine different change detection results.

In jKarma, a PBCD pipeline is defined by injecting a `MiningStrategy<A,B>` instance into a `PBCD<C,A,B,D>` object via the `Detectors` class. This ensures the type-checking consistency between the patterns discovered in the *mining step* and those used in the *identification step*. The generic type `C` specifies the type of transactions that will be consumed by the PBCD, while the generic type `D` denotes the pattern weighting scheme adopted. Finally, a PBCD is finalized by providing details on the *identification step* and *explanation step*.

In the following example, a `PBCD` is built by passing a `MiningStrategy` to the `upon` method. Then, a binary weighting scheme and the Jaccard dissimilarity measure are specified via the `unweighted` method. The PBCD will use the `isFrequent` predicate when constructing the binary vector encodings, while the `UnweightedJaccard` computes the dissimilarity score. This PBCD explains changes by discovering emerging patterns via the `Descriptors.eps` method. Finally, the PBCD is finalized with the `build` method which i) sets the minimum change threshold to 0.5, and ii) arranges data in blocks of 15 transactions.

```
public PBCD<LabeledGraph, LabeledEdge, TidSet, Boolean>
buildPBCD(MiningStrategy<LabeledEdge,TidSet> strategy) {
    UnweightedJaccard m = new UnweightedJaccard();
    return Detectors.upon(strategy)
        .unweighted((p,t)->Patterns.isFrequent(p, minFreq, t), m)
        .describe(Descriptors.eps(minGr)).build(0.5, 15);
}
```

Listing 1.2: PBCD based on the unweighted jaccard dissimilarity between binary-valued vector encodings of patterns.

4.3 A complete example: the KARMA algorithm

Detecting changes is particularly relevant for dynamic networked data, that is, networks which evolve over time, for which no common notion of change exists. In fact, different methods ascribe changes to variations in the observed nodes, while others focus on edges or subgraphs observed over time, which leads to clearly different results. Moreover, many proposed methods are not part of existing software frameworks, which limits their versatility. Listing 1.3 reports a complete example in which jKarma is used so as implementing the KARMA PBCD algorithm presented in [1], which detects changes in dynamic networks by observing variations in the FCSs discovered over time. The example also shows how users can react to changes, by following the event-listener paradigm: the `changeDetected` method will be be executed in case of detected changes, otherwise, the `changeNotDetected` method will be executed.

```
public PBCD<LabeledGraph, LabeledEdge, TidSet, Boolean>
getKARMA(double minSupp, double minChange, double minGr) {
    //auxiliary components
    TidSetProvider<LabeledEdge> dataAccessor = new
         TidSetProvider<>(Windows.cumulativeLandmark());
    UnweightedJaccard m = new UnweightedJaccard();
    Descriptor descriptor = Descriptors.partialEps(minSupp, minGr);

    //mining strategy definition
    MiningStrategy<LabeledEdge, TidSet> strategy = Strategies.uponSubgraphs().eclat(minSupp)
```

---

https://bitbucket.org/jkarma/demo-karma-pbcd/

```
        .limitDepth(3).dfs(dataAccessor);

    //PBCD definition
    return Detectors.upon(strategy)
        .unweighted((p,t)->Patterns.isFrequent(p, minSupp, t), m)
        .describe(descriptor).build(minChange, 15);
}

public void runKARMA(Stream<LabeledGraph> dataSource) {
    PBCD<LabeledGraph, LabeledEdge, TidSet, Boolean> detector = this.getKarma(0.15, 0.2, 1.2);
    //change detection event listening
    detector.registerListener(new PBCDEventListener<LabeledEdge, TidSet>(){
        public void changeDetected(
        ChangeDetectedEvent<LabeledEdge,TidSet> e){
            //reaction to change detected
        }
        public void changeNotDetected(
        ChangeNotDetectedEvent<LabeledEdge,TidSet> e){
            //reaction to change not detected
        }
    });
    //consume the data source
    dataSource.forEach(detector);
}
```

Listing 1.3: Example of jKarma implementing the KARMA PBCD [1].

Indeed, jKarma enables the users to detect changes in dynamic networks with alternative approaches. The example shows how to instantiate the KARMA algorithm, which is a good choice when the change has to be detected on subgraphs. However, the solution could not be the best one when changes affects only some attributes of nodes. To this end, jKarma can be used to rapid prototyping of new algorithms in Java.

4.4 Comparative evaluation

To show the effectiveness of jKarma in deploying actionable PBCDs, we compare the detection accuracy and running times of four PBCD algorithms (KARMA, PBCD-1, PBCD-2, and StreamKrimp) on three synthetic datasets with same minimum frequency and change thresholds (equal to 0.5). Specifically, KARMA, PBCD-1, and PBCD-2 have been implemented in jKarma. PBCD-1 and PBCD-2 are non-exhaustive variants of the exhaustive KARMA algorithm that make use of the landmark window model and sliding window model, respectively. While StreamKrimp [8] is a non-exhaustive PBCD based on frequent itemsets discovered according to the MDL principle. The results (Table 1) show that non-exhaustive PBCDs (PBCD-1, PBCD-2, and StreamKrimp) are more accurate than those exhaustive (KARMA). Although exhaustive, KARMA is more efficient than StreamKrimp, which is not implemented with jKarma. Finally, PBCD-1 offers the higher accuracy, while PBCD-2 has the lower running times.

5 Conclusions

We have introduced jKarma, an highly-modular framework for defining and executing customized pattern-based change detection approaches for evolving data,

https://bitbucket.org/jkarma/datasets

Table 1: Running times and accuracies on synthetic data.

dataset	Running times (seconds)			
	PBCD-1	PBCD-2	KARMA	S.Krimp
synth-drifts-1	12.913	6.194	60.763	86.130
synth-drifts-2	12.284	6.522	55.982	77.138
synth-drifts-3	12.603	6.463	58.137	76.750

dataset	Accuracy			
	PBCD-1	PBCD-2	KARMA	S.Krimp
synth-drifts-1	0.987	0.918	0.804	0.931
synth-drifts-2	0.991	0.916	0.799	0.911
synth-drifts-3	0.988	0.918	0.796	0.916

in Java. jKarma enables the modular definition of custom PBCDs, with reduced or none implementation efforts, by following a component-based architectural model. The framework comes as a Java software library which is completely independent of other data mining frameworks and existing data sources. As future work, we plan to investigate the periodicity of the changes [9].

Acknowledgments

We acknowledge the support of the MIUR - Ministero dell'Istruzione dell'Università e della Ricerca through the project "TALIsMan - Tecnologie di Assistenza personALizzata per il Miglioramento della quAlità della vitA" (Grant ID: ARS01_01116), funding scheme PON RI 2014-2020

References

1. C. Loglisci, M. Ceci, A. Impedovo, D. Malerba, Mining microscopic and macroscopic changes in network data streams, Knowl. Based Syst. 161 (2018) 294–312. doi:10.1016/j.knosys.2018.07.011.
2. D. Trabold, T. Horváth, Mining strongly closed itemsets from data streams, in: 20th International Conference, DS 2017, Kyoto, 2017, pp. 251–266.
3. A. Bifet, G. Holmes, R. Kirkby, B. Pfahringer, MOA: massive online analysis, J. Mach. Learn. Res. 11 (2010) 1601–1604.
4. P. Fournier-Viger, A. Gomariz, T. Gueniche, A. Soltani, C. Wu, V. S. Tseng, SPMF: a java open-source pattern mining library, J. Mach. Learn. Res. 15 (1) (2014) 3389–3393.
5. A. Impedovo, C. Loglisci, M. Ceci, D. Malerba, jkarma: A highly-modular framework for pattern-based change detection on evolving data, Knowl. Based Syst. 192 (2020) 105303. doi:10.1016/j.knosys.2019.105303.
6. M. J. Zaki, K. Gouda, Fast vertical mining using diffsets, in: Ninth ACM SIGKDD International Conference on Knowledge Discovery and Data Mining, Washington, USA, 2003, pp. 326–335.
7. A. Impedovo, M. Ceci, T. Calders, Efficient and accurate non-exhaustive pattern-based change detection in dynamic networks, in: Discovery Science - 22nd International Conference, DS 2019, Split, Croatia, October 28-30, Proceedings, 2019.
8. M. van Leeuwen, A. Siebes, Streamkrimp: Detecting change in data streams, in: ECML/PKDD 2008, Belgium 2008, Proceedings, Part I, pp. 672–687.
9. C. Loglisci, M. Ceci, A. Impedovo, D. Malerba, Mining spatio-temporal patterns of periodic changes in climate data, in: 5th International Workshop, NFMCP 2016, Held in Conjunction with ECML-PKDD 2016, Italy, 2016, Revised Selected Papers, pp. 198–212. doi:10.1007/978-3-319-61461-8_13.

AUTHOR INDEX

Acciani, Giuseppe 316
Agosti, Maristella 158
Alvares, Luis Otavio 142
Amato, Flora 181
Amato, Giuseppe 264, 284, 308
Anelli, Vito Walter 316
Angiulli, Fabrizio 46
Bagozi, Ada 300
Barracchia, Emanuele Pio 166
Battaglia, Elena 324, 332
Bergamaschi, Sonia 18
Bianchini, Devis 300
Bioglio, Livio 332
Bodria, Francesco 106
Bogorny, Vania 142
Brocco, Amos 122
Budimir, Verica 94
Calautti, Marco 54
Caliò, Antonio 150
Carrara, Fabio 264
Caruccio, Loredana 38
Castano, Silvana 7
Cauteruccio, Francesco 228
Ceci, Michelangelo 166, 349
Ceppi, Patrick 122
Chianese, Angelo 114
Chiorrini, Andrea 240
Ciaccia, Paolo 200
Corradini, Enrico 228
Cozzolino, Giovanni 181
Cuzzocrea, Alfredo 340
D'Elia, Domenica 166
De Antonellis, Valeria 300
De Pasquale, Giuseppe 272
Deldjoo, Yashar 316
Deufemia, Vincenzo 38
Di Noia, Tommaso 316
Di Nunzio, Giorgio Maria 158
Di Sciascio, Eugenio 316
Diamantini, Claudia 240
Dosso, Dennis 74
Ducange, Pietro 272
Fadda, Edoardo 340
Falchi, Fabrizio 264, 284, 308
Falduti, Mattia 7
Fassetti, Fabio 46
Ferrara, Alfio 7
Ferrero, Carlos Andres 142
Ferro, Nicola 216
Fiorentino, Nicola 54
Firmani, Donatella 248
Francia, Matteo 134
Frozza, Angelo Augusto 142
Furfaro, Angelo 292
Gagliardelli, Luca 18
Gallinucci, Enrico 134
Garda, Massimiliano 300
Gennaro, Claudio 264, 284
Golfarelli, Matteo 134
Greco, Sergio 30, 54
Groppe, Sven 62
Groth, Tobias 62
Guzzi, Pietro Hiram 174
Ianni, Michele 30
Impedovo, Angelo 349
Kavalionak, Hanna 284
Koppehel, Martin 62
Lazzeri, Emma 4
Letinic, Svjetlana 94
Loglisci, Corrado 349
Lucchese, Claudio 216
Lupia, Francesco 292
Maistro, Maria 216
Malerba, Donato 349
Manghi, Paolo 4
Marchesin, Stefano 158
Martinenghi, Davide 200
Masciari, Elio 30, 114
Massoli, Fabio Valerio 308
Maurino, Andrea 272
Meghini, Carlo 284
Melchiori, Michele 300
Mello, Ronaldo Dos Santos 142
Merialdo, Paolo 248
Merra, Felice Antonio 316
Milo, Tova 3
Molinaro, Cristian 54
Montanelli, Stefano 7
Morini, Virginia 86
Moscato, Francesco 181
Moscato, Vincenzo 114, 181
Nieddu, Elena 248
Palopoli, Luigi 46
Panisson, André 106
Pensa, Ruggero G. 324, 332
Perciante, Costantino 284

Perego, Raffaele 216
Perotti, Alan 106
Piaggesi, Simone 106
Picariello, Antonio 114, 181
Pilato, Giovanni 340
Pio, Gianvito 166
Pionteck, Thilo 62
Polese, Giuseppe 38
Pollacci, Laura 86
Potena, Domenico 240
Rabitti, Fausto 264, 284
Renso, Chiara 142
Rizzi, Stefano 134
Rossetti, Giulio 86
Rossi, Andrea 224, 248
Rossi, Matteo 208
Sabet, Alireza Javadian 208
Saccà, Domenico 30, 292
Santana, Luiz Henrique Zambom 142
Schreiber, Fabio A. 192, 208
Schreiner, Geomar Andre 142
Serrao, Cristina 46
Silvello, Gianmaria 74
Simonini, Giovanni 18
Sinigaglia, Lorenzo 122
Spahiu, Blerina 272
Sperlì, Giancarlo 114, 181
Storti, Emanuele 240
Tagarelli, Andrea 150
Tanca, Letizia 208
Terracina, Giorgio 228
Torlone, Riccardo 200, 248
Tradigo, Giuseppe 174
Trubitsyna, Irina 30, 54
Ursino, Domenico 228
Vadicamo, Lucia 264
Vairo, Claudio 284
Valcher, Maria Elena 192
Veltri, Pierangelo 174
Virgili, Luca 228
Vizza, Patrizia 174
Vocaturo, Eugenio 256
Weikum, Gerhard 1
Zaniolo, Carlo 2
Zumpano, Ester 256
Zupan, Mario 94

CURRAN ASSOCIATES INC.
proceedings.com

ISBN 978-1-7138-1850-2

9 781713 818502

11th International Conference on Parsing Technologies 2009

(IWPT 09)

Paris, France
7-9 October 2009

ISBN: 978-1-61738-572-8